SKULLS
AND KEYS

SKULLS
AND KEYS

THE HIDDEN HISTORY OF
YALE'S SECRET SOCIETIES

DAVID ALAN RICHARDS

PEGASUS BOOKS

NEW YORK LONDON

SKULLS AND KEYS

Pegasus Books Ltd.
148 W 37th Street, 13th Floor
New York, NY 10018

Copyright © 2017 David Alan Richards

First Pegasus Books edition September 2017

Interior design by Maria Fernandez

Library of Congress Cataloging-in-Publication Data is available.

ISBN: 978-1-68177-517-3

10 9 8 7 6 5 4 3 2 1

Printed in the United States of America
Distributed by W. W. Norton & Company

Dedicated to

Reuben Andrus Holden
Class of 1940
Skull and Bones
Secretary of Yale University, 1953 to 1971
Fellow of Davenport College

and

Maynard Mack
Class of 1932
Scroll and Key
Sterling Professor of English, 1948 to 1978
Fellow of Davenport College

Off the campus, directly at the end of their path, a shape more like a monstrous shadow than a building rose up, solid, ivy-colored, blind, with great, prison-like doors, heavily padlocked. "It is a scary sort of looking old place," said McCarthy. "It stands for democracy, 'Tough. And I guess the mistakes it makes are pretty honest ones."

—Owen Johnson, *Stover at Yale* (1911)

Young men had to find some way to give body to that system of idealism . . . discovered to exist at New Haven. There was not much in the classroom, on the evidence, to excite the mind, train it, bring it into useful support of healthy principle. With considerable ingenuity, therefore, the undergraduates turned elsewhere—to the feelings—to find a possible source of energy. They constructed in the senior societies, with admirable insight, a mechanism to mobilize the emotions of the selected few to their high purposes. Exactly how this was done, how in nine months, in weekly meetings, in secret places, whole lives were changed, is past all discovery. Such special election produces no doubt a sense of large responsibility; the compressions of the secret can generate great energy. At any rate, for most of those engaged, it worked.

—Elting E. Morison, *Turmoil and Tradition: A Study of the Life and Times of Henry L. Stimson* (1960), on Henry Stimson (Yale Class of 1888, Skull and Bones, son of Lewis Atterbury Stimson, Yale Class of 1863, Scroll and Key)

Apropos of Yale and American Colleges generally, could you put me on the track of any book that gives the history of college societies. It's a thing that I am a good deal interested in.

—Letter of Rudyard Kipling to John S. Seymour, October 17, 1898

CONTENTS

INTRODUCTION

This history is about one year in the college curriculum, in one institution, repeated over the course of more than two centuries. The senior year at Yale, this nation's third oldest college, has birthed and nurtured student associations called "senior societies," more familiarly known now as "secret societies." Their fame has gone far beyond that of typical college fraternities. Called by the leading historian of nineteenth-century American college students "perhaps the most unique student institutions in the country,"[1] they have played a seminal role in the history of both Yale and the nation.

Election to a senior society in New Haven occurs annually in the spring, when groups of fifteen seniors choose their successors in the junior class for clubs where the members' names and elections may be public, but their subsequent activity in windowless, fortresslike "tombs" very private. These groups at Yale—Skull and Bones, Scroll and Key, and Berzelius, all founded before the American Civil War, to be followed in succeeding decades by the establishment of Book and Snake, Wolf's Head, Elihu, Manuscript, and numerous "underground" societies of seniors without their own buildings—are for good reason more popularly known, on campus and off, as "secret societies." But so, too, were their forebears, Phi Beta Kappa from 1778 most prominently among them.

Their arcane rituals, particularly the annual day of elections known as "Tap Day," have fascinated the public for over 175 years (the *New York Times* reported the names of those elected beginning in 1886). The first real secret of these organizations is their original purpose: self-education

xi

by and through exercises with their fellow students, when their founders believed their college did not or would not provide that education. This remains true to the present, although what is sought now is as much emotional as intellectual stimulus.

Soon, however, election to their small numbers became the summit of a Yale College career. The societies were compelled to defend their exclusivity and the privilege of their privacy—their secrecy—by making election choices which were seen on campus to be "democratic," rewarding with the prestige of membership in their last year collegians who had excelled in undergraduate endeavors of all kinds. The senior societies became in time more democratic and diverse, incorporating into their numbers over the years talented outsiders (Jews and blacks, other non-Protestant ethnics, scholarship students, and finally women), and easing the passage of previously dismissed castes into the American establishment, decades before their elders and betters followed suit in the higher councils of the university and the nation.

The statistical insignificance of the sample population, and the brevity of the experience, should consign the subject of Yale senior society membership to the dustbin of undergraduate nostalgia. Although a statistical sliver, at 15 percent, of their respective class cohorts, in one college among hundreds in this country, these young men nevertheless went on to become among the most prominent leaders in American politics, diplomacy, law, literature, publishing, journalism, higher education, religion, finance, the ministry, physical and social science, philanthropy, and the counterintelligence services.

To take only the category of national politics, all three of the presidents of the United States who attended Yale College (William Howard Taft and the two Bushes) were members of Skull and Bones, and indeed were the sons of members of that society. More recently on the major parties' presidential tickets were senior society members John Kerry and vice presidential nominees Sargent Shriver and Joe Lieberman for the Democrats, with a near-miss presidential nominee two generations before in Robert A. Taft for the Republicans. Moreover, six of Yale's sons who became secretaries of state, both of her chief justices of the Supreme Court, and three attorneys general were members. So were three secretaries of the treasury (most recently, President Trump's), two secretaries of war, two secretaries of defense, two directors of the Central Intelligence Agency, one secretary of the army, one of three secretaries of the navy, two treasurers of the United States, and Yale's single secretary of commerce and only postmaster general.

Their membership served their alma mater disproportionately as well: of the eight presidents of Yale graduating after the first society was founded and serving between 1886 and 1992, all but two were members of Bones, Keys, or Wolf's Head. University treasurers for all but five years between 1862 and 1910 were members, as were the university secretaries for more than a half century between 1869 and 1921. The faculty was even more inbred, at least into the early twentieth century, with a remarkable 80 percent between 1865 and 1916 being alumni of Skull and Bones. Graduates of Bones and Keys were also prime movers in the mid-nineteenth-century alteration of the Yale Corporation to include elected alumni, and to this day, these graduates absolutely predominate among the ranks of the university's most generous donors, many recalling the valued warmth of their society membership in making their gifts.

Since election on the New Haven campus at age nineteen or twenty became a frequent predictor of some future national prominence, the societies themselves became nationaly famous. They were the subject of the United States' most famous college novel, 1912's *Stover at Yale*, but also figured thereafter in fiction by William Faulkner, Ernest Hemingway, Stephen Vincent Benét, F. Scott Fitzgerald, John O'Hara, and John le Carré. The societies have been featured in motion pictures like *The Good Shepherd*, *Indiana Jones and the Kingdom of the Crystal Skull*, and in the trilogy of thrillers *The Skulls*. Their legends have even been embellished in cartoons, including *Doonesbury*—Garry Trudeau, a member of Scroll and Key, happy to tweak Keys' rival Bones and its two Bushes—and *The Simpsons*, that show's Harvard graduate writers making Homer Simpson's employer C. Montgomery Burns a roommate of Stover and retroactive member of the class of 1914 and Skull and Bones.

The fame of the senior societies of Yale College—or, for their detractors, the notoriety—springs from the confluence of four circumstances of their existence. The first is the large shadow cast by Yale in our country's political history for the nineteenth and twentieth centuries; the second, the sustained prominence, over almost two centuries, of the societies' initiates in all phases of American life; and the third, the proximity of New Haven to New York City, the nation's social, financial, and media capital, resulting in frequent press reports of the elections to the societies and of the controversies surrounding them. The final circumstance is the provoking secrecy maintained by their initiates after being "tapped" for membership, literally disappearing into "tombs" and a culture which has given the American language new meanings, still current, for "tapped," meaning to be chosen, and "spook," meaning spy.

Their general confidentiality has not stopped secrets of all the societies from leaking out over the decades, through methods as customary as gossip from observant roommates and divorced wives, and as crude as thefts from the societies' tombs by rivals and strangers. Related here are verifiable facts about the Yale secret societies that are attributable to credible published works: there will be no "secrets" here that have not already, somehow and somewhere, been revealed at least once in print, and otherwise verified. "The least-studied and most mysterious group in the history of American higher education," one historian has said, "[is] the students, who composed the largest single group on the rosters of colleges and universities, and who were, ostensibly, the primary objects of the institutions' concerns."[2] Through the prism of the Yale senior societies, part of that story may be discerned.

Whatever one's opinion of them, these small student clubs, beginning in the 1830s and '40s during the Romantic movement in the arts and letters, to this day operate on the patently Romantic proposition that the discovery of an inner, authentic self both corresponds with and advances the aim of forming an ideal community. There are now at least forty-seven senior societies at Yale, nine "landed," with tombs or houses, and the rest, nomadic and meeting in rented rooms, known as "undergrounds." With each society electing the canonical fifteen (or a gender-balanced sixteen) members, almost half of the senior class students at Yale are in consequence presently member participants.

Attitudes toward them have usually been influenced by two mystifications. The first sentimentalizes and romanticizes youth and imagination as fields of pure value. The second demonizes such groups, finding them sinister at worst and precious at best. Both views are inadequate, because they are reductionist, failing to take into account the asymmetries and complexities of the past. Talented people are not saints, and even genius is not privileged. Conspiracies are seductive, seemingly dramatic and rational, but as explanations for events are too simple. This book will try to thresh the wheat from the tares, to separate the values from the legends.

Still, the author is in the position of Donald Ogden Stewart, a Bonesman in the class of 1916 and later an Academy Award–winning screenwriter in Hollywood. Publishing a magazine article on Yale in H. L. Mencken's *Smart Set* for December 1921, he detailed the aspirations, tensions, and drama of these clubs, and concluded: "This essay is, furthermore, grossly unfair to the Senior societies in the following respect: I have shown the effect of the more or less false tradition which has grown up in the undergraduates' minds concerning these institutions. I am not able to show the other side of the picture. It is as though a Catholic priest, having described the terrifying effect of an imposing cathedral upon him as a boy, were suddenly to stop before he had testified as to what the Church had come to mean to him after ordination. I do not think, in my own case at least, that the analogy is a bad one."

David Alan Richards
Scarsdale, New York
September 2017

CHRONOLOGY

YALE AND ITS SENIOR SOCIETIES

Parenthetical dates for individuals are each's Yale College class

1701	The Collegiate School is founded by ten Connecticut ministers at a meeting in Branford, near New Haven, Connecticut.
1716	Collegiate School's name changed to Yale College to honor donation of Elihu Yale.
September 12, 1753	Reputed date of founding of **Linonia**, literary and debating society, excluding freshmen until February 1767.
1768	Literary and debating society of **Brothers in Unity** founded, rival to Linonia, open to all classes.
December 5, 1776	**Phi Beta Kappa** founded as a secret society at the College of William and Mary (becomes inactive in 1780 due to the Revolutionary War).
November 13, 1780	Connecticut Alpha chapter of Phi Beta Kappa founded at Yale.
September 5, 1781	Massachusetts Alpha chapter of Phi Beta Kappa founded at Harvard.
July 8, 1819	**Calliope**, literary and debating society, founded by Southerners seceding from Linonia.
1821	Chi Delta Theta founded, second Yale Greek-letter fraternity (dissolves 1844).
September 1827	Society of Alumni formed, first alumni association in nation.
May 1831	Avery Allyn publishes *A Ritual of Freemasonry . . . to which is added a Key to the Phi Beta Kappa*, anti–Masonic agitation follows.

September 1831	Secrecy at Harvard and Yale Phi Beta Kappa chapters ended by votes of members (including graduates, by then outnumbering current students)
October 1832	Opening of Trumbull Gallery, a windowless art gallery.
November 1832	**Scull and Bone** senior society founded (later Skull and Bones).
1836	Alpha Delta Phi college fraternity chapter, known as "A.D.," founded at Yale (originated at Hamilton College in 1832); surrenders charter in 1873.
May 1837	First foreigner, a Brazilian, elected by Bones (with a second in May 1840).
1838	Psi Upsilon college fraternity chapter, known as "Psi U," founded at Yale (originated at Union College in 1833).
November 5, 1841	Publication of first number of the *Yale Banner*, the college annual.
July 6, 1842	**Scroll and Key** senior society founded, after dispute during elections for Bones, for classes of 1842 and 1843
August 15, 1843	Townsend Premiums established for five best English compositions.
1844	**Sword and Crown** and **Star and Dart** senior societies founded, expiring in 1843 and 1851, respectively.
1844	Delta Kappa Epsilon, "DKE," junior society founded (Yale the mother chapter), in schism from Psi Upsilon.
1848	**Berzelius** (Colony Club) founded as final club in Sheffield Scientific School (converted to senior society, 1933).
1852	First award of DeForest Prize, for best senior oration in English.
May 1856	Graduate members of Bones incorporate Russell Trust Association.
1856	Skull and Bones tomb erected on High Street (enlarged 1883, 1903).
1863	**Book and Snake** (originally Cloister–Sigma Delta Chi) founded as final club in Sheffield Scientific School (converted to senior society, 1933).

CHRONOLOGY

1864	Earliest photographic portrait of class year of Keys.
1864	Faculty abolishes sophomore and freshman societies for abuses, for the first time.
May 1864	**Spade and Grave** senior society founded, in dispute with Bones (last delegation in 1871; refounded in 1951).
November 25, 1865	*Yale Courant* weekly newspaper first published.
1865	*Yale Pot-Pourri* first published, Keys-controlled annual publication opposed to Bones and *Yale Lit.*
1866	Graduate members of Keys incorporate Kingsley Trust Association.
1869–70	Scroll and Key tomb erected on College and Wall Streets.
July 6–10, 1871	Yale charter amended to provide for election of six graduates to be (Alumni) Fellows of Yale Corporation, substituted for state senators; alumni at commencement elect Alphonso Taft (1833, Bones), William Maxwell Evarts (1837, Bones), William Barrett Washburn (1844, Bones), Henry Baldwin Harrison (1846, Bones), and William Walter Phelps (1860, Bones), five of six elected; sixth man is replaced in 1873 by Mason Young (1860, Keys).
October 11, 1871	Inauguration of Rev. Dr. Noah Porter (1831, Phi Beta Kappa, and before senior societies), as eleventh Yale president, last non–senior society member college president in nineteenth century.
March 13, 1872	Corporation determines Yale has "attained to the form of a University" (use of name authorized by Connecticut in 1887).
1872	Linonia and Brothers in Unity literary societies disband.
1873	*Yale Literary Chronicle* first published, parody of *Yale Lit.*, opposed to senior societies.
May 21, 1874	Juniors blocked in their rooms by non-society hecklers, harassing the senior electors, and so come down to their dormitory steps for election, necessitating direction, "Go to your room."
May 20, 1875	Election exercises conducted completely outdoors for first time outside, on Old Campus in front of Durfee and Farnam Halls.

1875	First Yale-Harvard football game (October 18); Yale faculty abolishes sophomore and freshman societies for the second time (May 24).
September 29, 1876	Bones tomb broken into by neutrals and its layout mapped and published.
January 28, 1878	*Yale Daily News* publishes first issue as anti-society publication; third issue (January 30) contains first Bones/Keys joke.
March 13, 1878	**Bull and Stones** members vandalize exterior of Bones and Keys tombs.
Spring 1878	Linonia and Brothers in Unity revived, but soon collapse for lack of interest; sophomore fraternities abolished by faculty action.
May 23, 1879	First *Yale Daily News* report of a Tap Day.
1880–1883	Walter Camp (1880, Bones), as Yale student and coach, develops the game of American football.
1881–1906	*The Horoscope* publishes almost annually, with lists of those expected to be tapped.
1883	**Wolf's Head** senior society founded, not to join Tap Day until 1889.
February 1, 1884	Senior class meeting considers abolition of senior societies, but the motion is ultimately defeated.
May 28, 1886	*New York Times* begins annual reports of senior society elections.
June 30, 1886	Inauguration of Timothy Dwight (1849, Bones), twelfth Yale president.
1886	Graduate members of Wolf's Head incorporate as Phelps Trust Association.
1887	Yale College changes name to Yale University.
May 25, 1891	*Yale Alumni Weekly* first published.
May 1892	First published use of phrase "Tap Day" (in 1892 *Horoscope*).
October 18, 1899	Inauguration of Arthur Twining Hadley (1876, Bones), first non-clerical Yale president.
1900	Sophomore societies abolished for the last time by President Hadley.

1901   Book and Snake tomb erected on Grove and High Street corner.

1902   Bartlett Golden Yung, son of first Chinese student in U.S., Yung Wing (1854), tapped by Wolf's Head.

March 1903   **Elihu Club** founded (not a secret senior society for another twenty years).

June 27, 1905   Election of first non-clerical Fellow, Payson Merrill (1856, Bones), among successors to New England ministers as trustees of the Yale Corporation.

1909   Election of first Native American, Henry Roe Cloud, by Elihu.

1910   Berzilius tomb erected on Trumbull Street.

1911–12   Elihu Club acquires 175 Elm Street (built c. 1772) as clubhouse.

Spring 1912   Owen Johnson's *Stover at Yale* published; class of 1915 sophomores organize anti-society protest against Tap Day ostentation, society secrecy.

May 1913   Old Campus closed to visitors, only juniors and seniors admitted for Tap Day by dean's order.

May 1914   Tap Day first moved away from Old Campus, held in Berkeley Oval, where most juniors reside.

May 1915   Juniors comprise own candidate list; Tap Day again held under Durfee Hall oak on Old Campus, only two upper classes admitted, general public barred.

April 19, 1917   Tap Day ceremony held both in New Haven and in Palm Beach, Florida, for naval aviators training there.

May 1918   No Tap Day ceremony, only announcements of those elected in New Haven and in service overseas.

July 5, 1918   Death of John William Sterling (1864, Bones), Yale's greatest financial benefactor, leaves $18 million (equivalent to $275 million) to Yale, $10,000 to Bones.

May 21, 1921   Elihu joins Tap Day ceremony.

June 21, 1921   Inauguration of James Rowland Angell, fourteenth Yale president and first non-graduate (elected out of deadlock between Bones and Keys members on Yale Corporation).

1924–26   Second Wolf's Head tomb erected on York Street.

May 1933	Students stay in their rooms for Tap Day, but both societies and students find this inconvenient.
September 1933	First seven residential colleges open in fulfillment of the House Plan (Branford, Calhoun, Davenport, Jonathan Edwards, Pierson, Saybrook, and Trumbull).
May 1934	Tap Day moved to Branford College main courtyard, and Sheffield Scientific societies Berzelius and Book and Snake compete for first time with academic side societies of Bones, Keys, Wolf's Head, and Elihu.
May 1937	Albert Hessberg (1938, Bones), first Jew tapped by a senior society.
October 8, 1937	Inauguration of Charles Seymour (1908, Bones) as fifteenth Yale president.
May 1941	Tap Day exercises moved from Old Campus to Branford College courtyard.
1945–1947	Tap Day held once more in students' rooms.
May 1948	Tap Day moved back to Branford Court; Levi Jackson (1949), first black football player and captain of Yale team, offered both Bones and Keys, but pre-tapped by and joins Berzelius.
April 1950	"Stay-away-from-Tap Day" movement agitates against Branford courtyard tap.
October 6, 1950	Inauguration of Alfred Whitney Griswold (1929, Wolf's Head) as sixteenth Yale president.
1951	Spade and Grave refounded with involvement of Yale professors.
May 3, 1951	Tap Day in Branford courtyard by Dean DeVane's direction; societies take second floor "stations" to run taps.
1952	**Manuscript** senior society founded as underground.
May 1953	Tap Day exercises removed from Branford College courtyard and elections given again in juniors' rooms.
1957	Senior societies take over the management of Tap Day from Yale administration; Lawrence Bensky, first Jew offered membership in Wolf's Head, its graduate board objects, he joins Berzelius.

CHRONOLOGY

1961	Manuscript comes aboveground; tomb begins construction (completed 1963).
April 11, 1964	Inauguration of Kingman Brewster Jr. (1940, turns down Bones and Keys), as seventeenth Yale president.
1966	Societies agree with Yale Dean's Office not to contact juniors earlier than week before Tap Day.
April 28, 1967	*Yale Daily News* prints results of Tap Day elections for all senior societies for last time.
November 9, 1968	Yale Corporation approves coeducation for Yale College, beginning with freshman class and sophomore and junior transferees entering in September 1969.
April 1970	No Tap Day due to imminence of May Day (Black Panther) weekend; five women elected by Elihu (for 1971 club), the first society to do so.
May 1, 1970	May Day weekend with Black Panthers; Manuscript election nullified, and tomb closed by board; Spade and Grave and Mace and Chain dissolve.
June 1970	Last annual edition of *Yale Banner* to list society memberships.
Fall 1970	Manuscript corporate board elects 1971 delegation, including three women.
April 1971	Berzelius and Book and Snake tap women, the second year of women's election eligibility (leaving only Bones, Keys, and Wolf's Head all male).
1971	First women named to Yale Corporation, Hanna Holborn Gray and Marian Wright Edelman.
1978	A. Bartlett Giamatti (1960, Keys) inaugurated as nineteenth Yale president.
1986	Benno C. Schmidt Jr. (1964, Wolf's Head) inaugurated as twentieth Yale president.
May 1989	Scroll and Key admits women with class of 1990.
April 10, 1991	Bones club of 1991 taps six women; Russell Trust Association changes locks on tomb.
October 24, 1991	Bones' Russell Trust Association votes to admit women.

December 12, 1991	Wolf's Head's Phelps Trust Association votes to admit women, last senior society to do so.
October 4, 1993	Richard C. Levin (Stanford BA 1968, Yale PhD 1974), inaugurated as twenty-second Yale president, only third in twentieth century not to be a senior society alumnus.
2004	Kurt Schmoke (1971, Wolf's Head) becomes first black to be Senior Fellow of Yale Corporation.
2016	Forty-seven senior societies functioning at Yale.

SKULLS
AND KEYS

CHAPTER ONE

BONDING IN SECRET

Secret societies . . . are the consequence of an effort of individuals—
usually and mainly men—to create the social conditions for exercising
their gregarious propensities, the expression of which may be (or may
seem to be) inhibited by their community.

—Lionel Tiger, *Men in Groups* (1969)

"THE TASTE OF YOUTH FOR SECRECY"

Bonding in secret—both the internal process, and the external profile, of Yale's senior "secret" societies—has made them, over the almost two centuries of their existence, objects of fascination, fear, and scorn. Less appreciated is their prehistory of student society predecessors in Europe and more especially England. And almost unknown is how, at their inception in New Haven and in the decades to follow, their members deviated from the common pattern of the new college fraternities being founded on other campuses, and created a particularly American forcing chamber of self-education and prestige, to become nationally renowned over the succeeding decades.

Organized secrecy is a feature of many civilizations. That human beings gather together in social groups is a commonly observed

1

phenomenon, and such groupings are a much examined subject of sociologists and anthropologists. Still, secret societies are not so much studied
unless they are part of exotic native cultures, because such organizations
are more than vaguely suspect in our own culture. The whole subject is
neglected as an area for serious investigation, a noted Oxford historian
has observed, because once "the historian passed by, the charlatan, the
axe-grinder and the paranoaic long had the field to themselves. . . . All
of us have presuppositions which make it difficult for us to appreciate
social purposes when they are expressed in an unfamiliar idiom, and these
constantly ensnare and divert us when dealing with a topic so rich in
irrational elements as this." Unless a secret association is supported by, or
is part of, the political authority of the state, its formation and operation
are always regarded by some outsiders as potentially aggressive. Secrecy
itself is usually perceived as hostile.[1]

These societies have been defined as "any social grouping not based
on blood relationship which possesses some ritualistic element of secrecy,
the knowledge of which is confined to initiated members."[2] Why we
form secret societies, for reasons other than plotting conspiracy, and that
such societies have been primarily male are subjects also examined by
academics, but less understood by the general public. That public does
appreciate one prominent feature: fraternal orders, like churches, are
"expressive" organizations, directed primarily toward meeting the social
and personal needs of their members. In contrast, "instrumental" organizations such as trade unions or professional associations have specific goals
to accomplish, and mediate between members and the outside world.

Secret societies are also an expression of the "play element" in
American culture, which Johan Huizinga has described as a distinct
and fundamental function of life in all societies, where humans create
"temporary worlds within the ordinary world, dedicated to the performance of an act apart." While it cannot be defined exactly, play is "a free
activity standing quite consciously outside 'ordinary' life as being 'not
serious,' but at the same time absorbing the player intensely and utterly.
It is an activity connected with no material interest, and no profit can be

gained by it. It proceeds within its own proper boundaries of time and space according to fixed rules and in an orderly manner. It promotes the formation of social groupings which tend to surround themselves with secrecy and to stress their difference from the common world."[3] These characteristics are shared by the Yale senior societies: a game, most seriously and solemnly played by their members, which necessarily involved those on the outside as well as on the inside of the game.

This play, however, can be offensive or even frightening to the outsider. Fraternal ritual presumes a surrounding network of relations, the community of birth and rearing. Formation of a fraternity, however, is a violation of that community, an acknowledgment of obligations which transcend it, an assertion that the identity conferred by the greater community is lower in the scheme of things. While still *in* the larger society, the initated brothers are never again *of* it. The fact that fraternal ritual surrounded itself in secrecy and mystery suggests as much. "Whether secrecy is a tool for power or a sacred truth not to be uttered before the profane, the secret presumes those from whom the secret is kept. It is based, as are 'rites of passage' in general, on a separation between the included and excluded."[4]

Moreover, a private, self-selected fraternity guarding a secret knowledge seems to many to challenge the value of democratic publicity, causing social tension in the contest between a community's right to knowledge and the individual's right to privacy. Sociologist Georg Simmel's work on secrecy helps to provide a framework for trying to understand this, in noting that the "relation which is mysterious in form regardless of accidental content" is an attractive one: secrecy within a community creates a subgroup that has special reasons for a sense of confidence among the members. Exclusion of outsiders heightens the sense of individual difference, provides a center of unity, and, within the subgroup, "countenances the separatistic factors" that Alexis de Tocqueville had lamented as a consequence of American democracy.

To many, it seems puzzling that fraternity has so often been associated with the secret society. Of course, the secret emphasizes the distinction between insiders and outsiders, and thus strengthens the bonds which unite the former. However, what is critical is the nature and purpose of the secret as viewed by the initiates; that, as Georg Simmel knew, is crucial to an evaluation of a secret society to be a "fraternity." In most instances, the secret is not what is valued most highly by the members. Secrecy is adopted as a means to ends other than the protection of the secret, as is obvious in the case of formal and public "secret" societies. Publicity calls attention to the society and raises the danger that the secret will be discovered. The risk is justifiable only if the members desire the attention which publicity provides, valuing the interest, curiosity, and attention of the community.

A more striking and romantic explanation of the secret society than that of the sociologists and anthropologists, founded on youthful cravings, was offered by Johann Wolfgang von Goethe. In his novel *Wilhelm Meister's Apprenticeship* (1796, translated into English by Thomas Carlyle in 1824), he wrote of a secret university student brotherhood, the Turmergesellschaft, the Tower Society. "The taste of youth for secrecy," he observed, "for ceremonies, for imposing words, is extraordinary; and frequently bespeaks a certain depth of character. In those years, we wish to feel our whole nature seized and moved, even though it be but vaguely and darkly. The youth who happens to have lofty aspirations and forecastings thinks that secrets yield him much, that he must depend on secrets, and effect much by means of them."[5] The college students who founded the first Yale secret societies were possessed of the same belief.

In the twenty-first century, such an attitude seems remote, and even alien. Yet what has been styled "secret fraternalism" represents one of the major patterns of American civilization. In this country's early years, it was of course imported from England. Even before 1700, the English had formulated a new respect for private and informal activity, with the appearance of such meeting places as coffeehouses, clubs, and salons, inventions of men and women making new demands on society and discovering new capacities in themselves which could not be given expression within the historic unities of blood, locality, religion, occupation, and legal subordination. Here, too, were founded the first "secret societies," in the modern sense of that phrase. Sometimes light-hearted, sometimes not, they guarded their secrets jealously and took elaborate precautions against the approach of the profane and uninitiated. Of these societies, immeasurably the most important were those of the Freemasons.[6]

The first grand Masonic lodge was formed in 1717 out of four London lodges that in turn owe their origins to the masons' guild in that city. An early masonic document dating from 1659 contains a mason's oath that a brother "keep all that we or attendees shall be[,] you keep secret, from Man, Woman, or Child, Stock or Stone, and never reveal it but to a Brother or in a Lodge of free masons, and truly observe the Charges in the Constitution." The order included not only "operative" Masons who gathered themselves into "lodges" (the term *Freemason* may have come from the designation of those who worked with freestone, a generic term for any fine-grained stone that could be carved), but also "speculative" Masons, men who were honorary members rather than craftsmen. They came to predominate, and the brotherhood devoted itself to building "spiritual instead of material temples."

The lodge structure was functional, meeting the needs of a craft whose members were often itinerant, assembling sometimes for limited— even if for lengthy—periods on building sites where no urban craft organized. It may have been the craft's itinerant nature that explained the early evolution of a secret system of signs for mutual recognition of its members. The trade secrets of the operative Masons became the esoteric secrets of the speculative Masons. This led to a heightening and dramatizing of the language of initiation: the aspirants' oaths were couched in terrifying terms in order to bring home to them the importance of preserving secrecy about trade practices and signs of recognition in whose defense legendary martyrs were supposed to have died. The order had been introduced into the American colonies by 1730.[7]

In the United States at the dawn of the nineteenth century, there existed only a few thousand members of secret brotherhoods:

approximately three thousand Freemasons, five or six hundred participants in the Tammany societies (the Sons of St. Tamina, born of the
Sons of Liberty), and the handful of members at Yale and Harvard College chapters of the literary society Phi Beta Kappa (not yet the national
scholarly honorary society of today). Growth was explosive thereafter.
By 1825, there were twenty thousand Masons in New York State alone;
in Connecticut, with seventy-five lodges by that date, the organization
served as a vehicle for dissent from Connecticut's religious standing order.
Beyond the eastern seaboard, secret societies, lodges, and fraternities grew
like weeds through the nineteenth century, flourishing in any place with
a concentration of young men, in cities and towns and colleges, offering
social acceptance at a time when other bonds and commitments were
severed for a time, or otherwise in flux.[8]

That such societies formed within America's very first colleges is
not surprising. The honors examinations in the ancient universities from
which those of our nation derived were devised to control youthful
impulses, as well as to impart then-settled knowledge, and to organize
learning for public purposes. In their quest to maintain such control, the
administration and faculty distrusted all undergraduate clubs, suspecting
them of subversion. In the eighteenth century, social clubs and dining
societies had proliferated for various frivolous and ephemeral purposes,
and their rites of passage were boisterous associations of drinking,
gambling, and other dissipations. As student bodies grew larger, new
associations formed to alleviate the anonymity of the larger campuses.
These were devoted to more serious and sober purposes, formulated by
collegians who were themselves more mature than their generational predecessors, with the interests of young adults rather than those of children.[9]

These societies were products of our modern age, the Age of
Enlightenment. Immanuel Kant had declared, "Enlightenment is man's
emergence from his self-incurred immaturity. . . . The motto of Enlightenment is therefore: *Sapere Aude!* Have the courage to use your own
understanding." From Kant's Germany in the Enlightenment, known
there as the *Aufklärung*, came the debating society, with its tendency to

submit all the problems of the world to the test of reason. Knowledge and discussion were exalted above the will and the feelings. The contagion of these new ideas spread to England, and from thence to the fertile soil of its American colonies.[10]

COLLEGE LITERARY SOCIETIES

The doctrines of the Enlightenment, originating in Europe, entered America through the port cities and the great plantations, the "ports of entry" for ideas as well as trade. The new theories, moreover, had appeals which specifically commended them to Americans. The Enlightenment removed the constraints from human imagination and seemed suited to the openness of the continent. Social and political goals became freed from the old country fetters of experience and history and, indeed, from those of reason: what a man could conceive, he might achieve, expecially in America, where the hand of the past fell lightly.[11]

While the first student associations in American colonial colleges were largely religious in nature, like the Moral Society founded at Yale in 1797 by students as a secret society to examine and self-correct their own behavior, the Spy Club at Harvard in 1719 had a different focus. Its constitution stipulated, "That any Difficulty may be propos'd to the Company and when propos'd the Company shall deliver their Thôts upon it," and "That there be a Disputation on Two or more questions at every Meeting, one part of the Company holding the Affirmative, the other the Negative part of ye question." (Each of the Spy Club's six members assumed a nickname by which he would be addressed within the club, a feature that was to be replicated in Yale College's senior societies).[12]

The first effective agency of intellect to make itself felt in the American college was the debating club or "literary society." These appeared first at Yale, founded in 1753 (Linonia) and 1768 (Brothers in Unity), and soon thereafter at Princeton (the American Whig, joined in 1769 by future president James Madison when a student, and the Clio-sophic, founded in 1770), and at Harvard (the Speaking Club, afterward the Institute of 1770, and then Hasty Pudding). John Quincy Adams, Harvard class of 1787, who belonged to both the Speaking Club and Phi Beta Kappa, wrote: "Of these societies friendship is the soul, and literary improvement the object; and consequently neither of them is numerous." Yale also led in establishing the American college tradition of founding not one but two competing societies. Where the writing of compositions drew the student into the interior world of the *vita contemplativa*, the literary society's debates pushed him outward, upon the public stage of the *vita activa*.[13]

"Literary" did not in this era mean "mere" literature—fiction, verse, and drama. In the late eighteenth and early nineteenth centuries, the American college itself was styled a *literary* institution, meaning, roughly, all knowledge (conveying much of the present German word *Wissenschaft*). Students went to college to become men of knowledge, men of literature, men of letters, to become literati. Parents and guardians were clear about their motives in sending their sons to Yale and other colleges, and students too agreed that becoming a member of the literary world was demanding but inspiring.[14]

The earliest American college literary society known to have existed anywhere is Crotonia, founded at Yale in 1738 but disappearing before 1767; it paved the way for both Linonia and Brothers in Unity, which together after 1802 were to include all members of Yale College—the incoming freshmen divided between them alphabetically—up to and beyond the creation of the senior societies. In rivalry, they had not only badges but their own mottoes and colors (red for Linonia, and blue for Brothers), and constitutions permitting membership to all undergraduates who were not a member of the other society.

The waves of political interest produced by Revolutionary War made the new nation's college literary societies for fifty years the strongest force in American student life, with two prominent societies—a strong testimonial to the competitive principle, replicated in the later history of the Yale senior societies—at each of Bowdoin, Dartmouth, Amherst, Williams, Brown, Wesleyan, Columbia, Pennsylvania, and Virginia.

When Yale's Southerners formed Calliope in 1819, the New Haven college was indeed to have three. Futhermore, in their prime on college campuses, these societies were the major, and often the only, student extracurricular activity.[15]

The society members intended themselves for the professions and politics. In the decade of the 1830s, Alexis de Tocqueville pointed to the fact that one-eighth of the members of Congress had been born in Connecticut, a state whose population comprised only one forty-third of the nation's. By 1835, the law rivaled the ministry as a professional choice of graduates of Yale, Bowdoin, Brown, and Dartmouth. At Yale, the ministry slipped from 33 percent as a professional choice of graduates in 1821 to 15 percent in 1861. Those who survived the rigors of university examination, developing the skills of puzzle-solving, mental speed, and verbal agility into tools for self-preservation and representation, knew that eloquence and rhetoric were essential devices for the translation, mediation, and interpretation of their world and work. Clarity of thought, reason and eloquence, and quickness of mind all contributed to their cultural authority to move others, in the legislature and in the courts, from one side of a proposition to another, or one side of a case to another.[16]

This was, in other words, the age of the "self-made man," a term coined by southern Senator Henry Clay in 1832 (the year Skull and Bones was founded) to describe the ability to perfect the self through sustained, concentrated efforts to improve the mind, morals, and body, with an identity that was a voluntarily chosen and consciously constructed. This ideal was not something that had to be achieved by an individual in isolation, nor was it then narrowly identified with entrepreneurship and money-making. In the nineteenth century it applied not to Americans who succeeded in the material world but rather to those who pursued inner self-improvement, forging a balanced character from nature's raw material.[17]

This was to be cogently expressed by Daniel H. Chamberlain, a member of the Yale class of 1861 and Skull and Bones (and later the governor of South Carolina), in an article on the role of American college literary societies written in his senior year. "What is the secret of the success of men whom the world calls *self-made*?," he asked, and answered: "The self-made man . . . is able to marshal his mental forces more readily and precipitate them more effectively than he who has passed through a liberal course of study in the schools, but neglected to use his powers and acquirements, in his progress. To correct this great error and supply this great defect, we think no other agency is so admirably adapted as the Literary Society, since there is scarcely a single faculty of mind which may not here find its appropriate field of activity. . . . Here, in the flash and glow of mental combat, all effeminate softness must be put away, and the strong armor of argument, principle, history, logic, must be put on. But over all this severity and out of all this austerity, shall grow a grander Beauty, a more delicate Grace."[18]

SECRECY AND FRIENDSHIP

In this American student practice of organizing secret societies as preparation for entering the great world, two conditions were essential. Secrecy was the first, a protection against authority (particularly in the consideration of religious questions in a speculative manner), as well as a barrier against the frivolous, the curious, and the idle who would challenge or demean the entire enterprise. The emergence of individuality and cognitive daring was permitted by privacy, and secrecy actually encouraged intellectual dissent. When discussions became more personal, confronting the young men's individual doubts and fears about themselves (and about women), privacy became even more vital; withdrawal behind closed doors was in such circumstances eminently reasonable. Such groups had no public function: their role was to provide an environment within which their members could consider separate, sometimes clashing, and certainly private views without public explanations.[19]

In organizing fraternities in the 1820s and 1830s, which they called and were secret societies, these students were also going against the political temper of their times. The nation had largely embraced the

Jacksonian ideal of this era—everyone equal before God, equal before one another—but the collegians had perhaps known too much equality, with the same class program, the same class subjects, the same professors, the same prayers, the same drab cubicles in uniform dormitories. In the very decades of the Age of Jackson, the students clearly preferred the privileges of secrecy and club life to equality before the Creator, and were inspired and energized by the very exclusiveness which the Jacksonian temper rejected. However paradoxical it may seem, they also came into being during the anti-Freemason fervor in the United States which excoriated secret societies in general and the Masons in particular, a protest and a scandal of which the students cannot have been ignorant, and yet they forged ahead nonetheless.

Even secret societies which hide neither their aims nor their members' names still take extraordinary efforts to forbid disclosure of their rituals. Given this mindset, the most vicious form of disloyalty, according to the principles of the secret society, is disclosure of the ritualistic features of the order to outsiders.[20]

Notably, these manifestations of secrecy were intertwined with the Enlightenment. Language about being enlightened, and at the same time secretive about the commitment to the Enlightenment, was used self-consciously by Freemasons to identify their society with "the highest aspirations of the new secular culture . . . [but this] only reinforced the masonic dedication to secrecy that was as much metaphorical as it was real. The belief that most people were incapable of, or hostile to, the new culture of Enlightenment was widespread both within and without the lodges. Indeed, Kant himself had carefully qualified his description of the age; as he ruefully observed, ours is not an enlightened age."[21] The attitude was one that Phi Beta Kappa in America, founded by newly minted Freemasons who were students at the College of William and Mary, was to pass on in barely diluted form to its successor institutions, the Yale senior societies.

The second essential condition for a secret society was friendship, the foundation of college youth culture. Linonia's first name was the

"Fellowship Club," and its constitution held its first two objects to be "to promote friendship [and] Social Intercourse." Away from things familiar and surrounded by young men of largely similar age and circumstance, university students formed close friendships with their classmates: "A hundred boys entering college together—all strangers to its customs, most of them coming unsophisticated from the family roof—conceive for each other an affection that often lasts for a lifetime, without any better reason than that early community in the charms and against the terrors of a strange life." If liberal learning, after the Enlightenment, was "an intellectual free-trade territory into which those from outside the orthodox and conventional world could now enter," friendship was also an abiding value in a world whose metaphors were drawn from an antique past, fundamental as a political truth in the ancient republics and of first importance to ancient religious feelings as well.[22]

With the Greeks, it involved the love of teachers and their pupils; with the Romans, in Cicero's *De Amicitia*, it involved the love of equals; with the Christians, it called for the feelings described in the Gospel of St. John. C. S. Lewis observed that, for the ancients, friendship "seemed the happiest and most fully human of all loves; the crown of life and the school of virtue." Man must pay homage to the social needs of continuity, nurture, and education, mindful of the hierarchy inherent in human improvement. Only among brothers, however, was a man free to follow up what was best in him at any time, and hence climb the ladder of excellence. The possibility of moving forward in the search for identity requires the support of persons who assure our identity anew, not as authority might, by giving us the conviction of a new, "known" self, but by stimulating us to seek the self which remains unknown.[23]

It was not pretense that caused such student societies (literary societies, then college fraternities) to adopt, as slogans, variations on the idealistic triad of friendship, love, and truth. These very values had been nurtured in the American home and maintained in family life for virtually two centuries past in the growing nation The nineteenth-century families which the young men left for their respective colleges were themselves strong social organizations, often being large, and certainly patriarchal, communal, and socially self-sufficient for the most part. The student society was intended to domesticate the frontier college community.[24]

Yale president Timothy Dwight, an undergraduate member of the Skull and Bones club of 1849, described the centrality of friendship sensitively and eloquently, in the context of the New Haven senior year and secret societies, in his memoirs. "[T]here can be no doubt," he wrote, "as to the positive influence of the smaller bodies [as opposed to the class-wide old literary societies] on the development of friendship among their members. This was especially true of the societies pertaining to the Senior year—and naturally so, in view of the fact that in our College, as contrasted with many others, the active membership in the [underclass] fraternities of the earlier years ceased when those years came to an end. The men who were united in the fraternity fellowship as Seniors came together, accordingly, as a small and selected company, in the latest period of their course, when their minds and characters had developed to the highest point of college life; when the great questions of their future, with the seriousness attendant upon them, were arising before all alike; and when the very approach of the end of the happy period, which they had found so full of blessing, was bringing a sadness of spirit that could not but make the heart open itself with tenderness and sympathy."[25]

More than a construct of literature and sociology, friendship provided the code and social insulation necessary for collegians as they sought vocation. It was the avenue through which they could escape the rigidities of family and religion, and slip away from the confines of the colleges which were otherwise so important to them for their identities. More than companionship, friendship represented a means of social and personal survival in a fraught and antagonistic world, a way they could confront, not alone, the most personal and elemental features of life encountered in their new college community: harsh discipline, financial catastrophe, disease, and death. "Some [in college] fail through indolence," a graduate wrote, "some through want of health; some through poverty, perhaps; some get dishonorable dismissions; some die—too early to be entered with an asterisk in the triennial catalogue" (the usual way in postgraduate publication of noting a society or fraternity member's death).[26] Two of Yale's freshman dormitories on the Old Campus are memorials by their parents to young men who died as juniors or seniors: Lawrance Hall is named for Thomas Garner Lawrance, class of 1884 and Skull and Bones, and Vanderbilt Hall for William H. Vanderbilt, class of 1893 and Scroll and Key.

Life's temptations and devastations, through friendship and fellowship, could be foreseen, better understood, and mastered. Again, friendship was the bridge which the students might cross from self-formation to some vocation in adult life. It allowed young people, secure only with one another, to attack hierarchy, to associate themselves with free-thinking and enlightenment beyond hallowed certainties, to ask and answer, when freed within their secret societies of family restraints and social connections, the fundamental question: what should one believe and in that belief, to what and whom should one be loyal, in a dangerous and risky world? In their quest for learning to be true to themselves, to their duty as they saw it, and to a pure if abstract truth, friendship galvanized and sustained them.

THE CAMBRIDGE APOSTLES

If all this is so, then it is fitting that the motto "only connect" was formulated by the English novelist E. M. Forster,[27] elected in 1901 to the first famous Anglo-American college secret society. This, the Cambridge Conversazione Society, was founded in 1820 in Cambridge, England, in that town's namesake university by George Tomlinson, who would become Bishop of Gibraltar, and eleven other members of St. John's College. Because they were originally twelve in number, and because their evangelical views were somewhat pronounced in the club's first several college generations (of the original twelve, nine took holy orders), they became known as "the Apostles," although they referred to themselves simply as "the Society." Because they believed they were gathered for serious purposes, and not merely convivial gustatory or social pursuits, or for the celebration of athletic victories, they distinguished themselves in tone and membership from other student societies at Oxford or Cambridge. And because these purposes and proceedings were confidential, even to mention membership in the society in memoirs was to break the rules of secrecy.[28]

Although in time the personal and professional distinction of their graduates (including Alfred Lord Tennyson, Lytton Strachey, Rupert Brooke, John Maynard Keynes, Bertrand Russell, Ludwig Wittgenstein, and Forster) would make them famous—and with certain later twentieth-century members, the Cambridge spies Guy Burgess and Anthony Blunt, notorious—there is no evidence that the existence of the Apostles was known in New Haven a dozen years later when Skull and Bones was founded in 1832, or that this English university club provided any pattern for the membership number or traditions of any Yale senior society. Still, the transatlantic parallels in cloaked customs and coded nomenclature are striking. The Cambridge-birthed traditions constitute further evidence that the social and historical forces that converged in the creation of the Yale groups were not unique to America, and in consequence similar institutions flowered at two widely separated locations, alike only in their institutional settings as seminaries of learning for their respective countries' future leaders in church and state.

More than seventy Apostles were elected between 1820 and 1830, but thereafter slightly more than three, on average, were elected each year, their numbers narrowing to members who mostly would attain great marks of success in the Tripos examinations. They did not seek uniformity, but valued individual differences, candor, openness, and intelligence, because only in this way could they learn from one another; they also sought manners, charm, and affection because these qualities were necessary for an environment of intense intimacy. Birth, social position, and wealth counted for virtually nothing in election. They met each Saturday evening after meals in hall during term, with all members obliged to attend and each, at regular intervals, to read an essay.[29]

The Cambridge Conversazione Society, like the Yale senior societies which were to follow in its wake, although not inspired by its example, left an indelible mark upon its members by creating feelings of self-discovery and enlightenment, and giving them feelings of self-confidence, belonging, consequence, and liberation. In his presidential address to the Apostles' annual dinner in 1896, Sir Donald MacAlister of Tarbert, by then the chancellor of the University of Glasgow, said that "The voice that issues from the hearth-rug on Saturday nights has gone through all the earth, its sound to the world's end. It speaks in Senates, though men know it not, it controls principalities and powers, it moulds philosophies, it inspires literatures. To those of us in the world of the unreal who are constrained 'to keep the up-right hat, the mid-way of custom,' the memory of it is a priceless possession."

"We *have* been young," he continued, "we *have* drunk delight of battle with our spiritual peers, we *have* dared to question everything, we *have* sworn at the words of every master. We know that there *are* such things as liberty, equality, fraternity: for we have reveled in free and equal brotherhood."[30] In those words are all of the fierce joy and unbridled arrogance of membership in this Cambridge secret society, sentiments for which the senior societies at Yale were later to be celebrated and damned. But although they still have their Ark, the Cambridge men, unlike those New Haven societies, have never had a permanent home: ironically, these Apostles have never entered a tomb.

THE AMERICAN WAY

It seems doubtful that anyone on the campus in New Haven, Connecticut, in 1832 knew of Goethe's celebration in *Wilhelm Meister* of the *Studentnorden*, the German secret student orders, which were not to have an accessible popular description in America until the publication of Mark Twain's *A Tramp Abroad* in 1880. The Cambridge Apostles, born in one college of several in that university in England in 1820, would have been similarly distant and unfamiliar. The young men in

New Haven were members of, and most familiar with, their own three Yale literary societies, but these were not in any way exclusive, taking in all members of every class, in which they participated throughout their four-year college course. These were secret societies, but the secrets were clearly widely shared, and their internal proceedings remarkably similar.

The Chi Phi Society had been founded in 1824 at the College of New Jersey in Princeton by faculty members for students, but a year after became inactive, and in any event was unknown up in Connecticut; Chi Delta Theta, founded earlier at Yale in 1821 for seniors with recognized literary ability, also at faculty instigation, was thus likewise not a model. Such societies, whether instigated by professors or by students alone, then and thereafter took Greek letters for their names because they were all composed of students who, given their intensive study of the language, knew Greek as well as modern college students know English. It was during the antebellum period that Greece eclipsed Rome as the model for a virtuous citizenry in the American imagination, at colleges particularly. To be Greek was to subscribe to notions of self-improvement through literature and oratory—Demosthenes speaking through the pebbles in his mouth—and more grandly, to hearken back to the ancients, and to their ideals on which Western Civilization was founded.[31]

In November 1825, at Union College in Schenectady, New York, the Kappa Alpha Society was established by six seniors and two juniors. All had been members (two of them its chief officers) of an organized military company at Union that had recently been dissolved by the college's president Eliphalet Nott in summary resolution of an electoral dispute about new officers. These collegians, feeling what was described as "an aching void" left by the company's dissolution, thereupon decided to form a secret society to fill it; by the middle of December, they had initiated another eight members. As for "the most important definite objects of the Association," these were, "as they all thought better, left to the collective wisdom of the active college membership—for the time being—from class to class, as time and experience would suggest."[32]

Kappa Alpha was the product, thus, of the twin desires for friendship and secrecy, but no had special programmatic purpose.

Such fraternities from the start—and Kappa Alpha is agreed by most scholars to be that start in the United States—and the Yale senior societies which paralleled them in measured growth offered fellowship to their members and a way to be distinguished from non-members, perhaps as proof of an elevated status. Smaller and more exclusive than the literary societies, and more strictly secret, they became increasingly more popular as well. That bond, their internal language proclaimed, was thought to last well beyond the time together on campus: calling each other "brother" and cementing ties through a familial model was emotionally comforting, and allowed fraternity/society men to trust one another, believing that this trust would not be betrayed. Brothers would always be brothers, not only in their loyalty, but also in the lack of hierarchical relations between them. Implicit in this construct, however, was exclusivity, which fraternity membership was always understood to be. Competing for new members was naturally acceptable, but membership meant "brotherhood" for life. In offering election, once there were two Yale senior societies after 1842, the candidate for one society was always asked if he had a prior affiliation with the other.

Absent from this shadow family construct were fathers, because young men in nineteenth-century colleges had abundant father figures, charged with trying to control college life. Collegians were adolescents in a particular context: they were a subject people, in a community where they did not make or enforce the rules. Fraternities were begun in no small part to establish an independence from patriarchal eyes, of the real or substitute variety. Their members' dependence was to be upon their peers, not upon someone with the new power to punish them. Mutual dependence was a comforting midway point between the dependence of childhood and the independence of adult manhood.[33]

American fraternities were thus themselves a symbolic form of rebellion against authority, constituted in deliberate disregard or even in repudiation of college administrators. They were initially formed because some student "right" had been curtailed or abolished (the military corps' dissolution for Kappa Alpha, and, as will be seen, the abolition of secrecy in Phi Beta Kappa for Skull and Bones at Yale, and also for Psi Upsilon for the same reason over at Union). The founding of Phi Beta Kappa itself in 1776 has been celebrated as "a revolt against authoritarianism of the college and the assertion by students of their right to assemble, to choose those they wished to associate in their enterprise, to be free to speak their minds, and to make decisions affecting their own welfare." College authorities of this era were accustomed to student outbreaks and did everything in their power to curb them; they logically sought to regulate when, where, and for what purposes students gathered. Yale president Noah Porter, himself an undergraduate member of Philagorian, a secret society which survived only two years, described fraternity life generally in the nineteenth century: "The aggression of constant interference [by the faculty] provokes the resistance of boyish mischief and arouses the wrath of manhood that is half-developed and is therefor intensely jealous of its invaded rights."[34]

And of course, by joining together in secret, their members were often able to engage in forbidden activities, either noble like debating topics in politics or religion which the faculty would not have countenanced in public, or less noble, such as drinking liquor and indulging in profanity or other immoralities illegal under lengthy books of college rules called "laws" on their title pages. *The Laws of Yale College* for 1832, for example, mandated incoming freshmen each to sign an oath "particularly that I will faithfully avoid using profane language, gaming, and all indecent, disorderly behavior, and disrespectful conduct to the Faculty, and *all combinations to resist their authority*"[35] (emphasis supplied).

College officers not only supposed that plots might be hatched, or rules broken, at secret meetings, but objected to the very fact of secrecy. If they were doing nothing wrong, as many society members claimed when queried, why the need to hide? In colleges founded by Protestant denominations that demanded abstinence and self-denial, members could break the official codes among trusted brothers. The professors were not wrong to fear that fraternities institutionalized various escapes—whether drinking, smoking, card playing, or singing—but the student-invented groups did not invent these diversions, which long antedated their founding. Rather, they channeled traditional means of escape into a brotherhood of devoted men, and in time, on many campuses, it became hard to distinguish purpose from manifestation.[36]

"Their secrecy," a nineteenth-century commentator observed, "consists of but two elements: the members hold meetings with closed doors, and do not tell the meaning of the Greek letters by which they are known." Because the constitutions and rituals of many of these fraternities were to be stolen in the early days by members of rival organizations, that general resemblance also existed. *Harper's Weekly* was to report in 1874 that "They 'Mask their business from the common eyes,' but even if their doings were open to public inspection, but little would be revealed not already known or surmised." Their members could still draw a line between those who knew the secrets and those who did not. Fraternal secrecy serves at least two functions: its possessors are elevated by the loyalty engendered when they are first told the mysteries upon initiation, and they are in turn protected when they break the rules of their larger society, in this case, their college.[37]

As evidenced by the existence of at least two literary societies in every American college of note, on-campus competition was another key feature of the fraternities which succeeded them in popular favor. This was more than a natural continuation of childhood games, or a precursor to the competition of the marketplace to be encountered after graduation: a man succeeded by contributing to a group effort, and if that effort failed, he was not alone. Banding together, they could first identify as a select group, and then compete in that group. Loyalty to one's brothers was prized above all else because it was precisely the competition with other individuals that made men so anxious.[38]

This in turn pushed competition *among* such fraternities to the fore, fascinating their members and the greater world. Logically, competition—having archrivals who might be appraised, discussed, and derided—was not necessary for the enjoyment of the camaraderie which was the groups' ostensible first purpose. Nevertheless, such competition became its own focus of activity on the campus, created entirely by the societies' memberships. This competition was self-perpetuating, since the only way for one fraternity or secret society to win a decisive victory was for one of its competitors to dissolve (but there were always others to take up the fight when the vanquished had expired). Even then, there could never be a decisive victory, because the rules were never clearly established, or could be changed by new entrants into the system.[39]

In 1817, some years earlier than the founding of Kappa Alpha, the young men at Union College with the blessing of their faculty had petitioned Yale's Phi Beta Kappa chapter for membership in that fraternity, which with the sister Harvard chapter's concurrence was granted. Kappa Alpha adopted many of Phi Beta Kappa's practices, since most of its founders were members. Its badge, square and silver like PBK's, bore a coffin above a scroll and surmounted by a rising sun, and the letters "C.C.," for Collegium Concordiae (in an uncanny anticipation of the symbols of both Yale's oldest senior societies, Skull and Bones and Scroll and Key). When students at Williams went to the Union campus in 1833 to secure a Phi Beta Kappa chapter, they came back with Kappa Alpha keys, the resemblance of which to his PBK key from Yale in 1790 caused the Williams president to welcome them back.[40]

Still, this first nineteenth-century fraternity's organization was, as an exclusively student group, without faculty instigation or supervision, or further graduate participation or annual dinners as occurred with Phi Beta Kappa, and it doubled as a literary society because that was its only familiar model. The constitutions of successor fraternities almost always included literary pursuits among their stated purposes: that of Alpha Delta Phi, to be founded at Hamilton College in 1832, mandated that each member would "exhibit" three essays per year. Delta Kappa Epsilon, whose mother chapter was to be formed at Yale in 1844, explained that "the objects of the organization are the cultivation of general literature, the advancement and encouragement of intellectual excellence, the promotion of honorable friendships, and the union of stout hearts and kindred interests to secure merit its due reward."[41]

The example of Kappa Alpha sparked the formation of two competitors on the Union College campus, the Sigma Phi Society, formed in March 1827, followed by Delta Phi in November. The three became known as the Union Triad and were followed by three more fraternities on that campus in the next decade. Sigma Phi was the first American fraternity in the classic mold to expand, by opening a second chapter at Hamilton College in Clinton, New York, in 1831; that and an effort by Kappa Alpha to also enter the Hamilton student body led to the formation of Alpha Delta Phi the following year.

None of these fraternities had attempted to expand to Yale by then, although Alpha Delta Phi soon did, as would Psi Upsilon, another fraternity birthed at Union, in 1833. From the several parent chapters at Union and Hamilton, the Greek-letter fraternity by 1840 was introduced into several of the colleges of New England and New York. Most college presidents, before they quite knew what had happened, discovered their undergraduates had ushered into the American college community a social system the administrators had neither invited nor encouraged. None of these fraternities by this time considered Phi Beta Kappa a rival, but in a class by itself, an honor society in which members could accept membership as evidence of scholarly standing.[42]

For the young men who joined them, the first fraternities—or secret societies, as the Union fraternities' members called them—fulfilled a number of needs. From their inception, fraternities "have been middle-class equivalents of the youth gangs, no less likely to make trouble and no less suffused by a spirit of peer loyalty." Primarily, they allowed a form of resistance to the control of an overbearing college faculty. By contemporary standards, these students were neither merely boys nor fully men, and yet they were treated as the former by their instructors, and forming a secret society allowed them to assert, even if only confidentially, an independence and autonomy not otherwise available. Such societies also broke the monotony of college living through bleak winters

SKULLS AND KEYS

and its incessant round of prayer, recitation, and study in dreary student housing. Finally, they provided companionship and a substitute for the families that had been left behind. Later, they would be seen by students bound for the professions, or finance and business, as a way of securing a network of patrons who like them had vowed loyalty and secrecy to the death, as they were launched into an increasingly competitive market economy with daunting competition.[43]

For the administrators charged with confronting this unlooked-for student invention, those same societies were abhorrent. Just as Union saw the birth of the first American fraternity, so too was it the site of the first attempt at extinguishment: on December 3, 1832, President Nott tried to rid his college of the societies' "evil influence" by announcing in chapel before the assembled student body that "The first young man who joins a secret society shall not remain in Coll[ege] one hour, or at least only while we can get him off." About a year later, Nott had relented and given full sanction to such clubs.[44] That set a pattern that was often repeated across American college campuses, with faculty attempts at suppression causing the overground societies to go underground and persist in deeper darkness and defiance.

Fraternities in American colleges were not only founded to push back at an overbearing faculty: some were formed to correct what their members perceived to be abuses, unfairness, and hypocrisy by their fellow students in the conduct of existing societies. This history has been buried because modern fraternities are pilloried as expressions of exclusiveness, snobbery, or other antidemocratic motives, or seen as almost indefensible pits of depravity.[45] Samuel Eells started Alpha Delta Phi in 1832 because of what he deemed to be partisan rivalry between the two literary societies at Hamilton College: "It was a contemplation of these and similar evils that first suggested to me the idea of establishing a society of higher nature and more comprehensive and better principles, providing for every taste and talent."

When Eells moved west and personally sponsored a second chapter of his fraternity at Miami University in Ohio, the resulting dissension

23

impelled John Reily Knox to start Beta Theta Pi, which he hoped, "would embrace the good without the ingredient of evil [and] . . . show how far human friendship can carry us from the shrine of the idol self." Sigma Chi was to emerge on the same campus within a few years, "to exalt justice and to stand for the square deal," when members of Delta Kappa Epsilon were enraged by the refusal of the elder brothers in their chapter to support the election of a well-qualified but unaffiliated candidate for the office of poet in the campus literary society. Rejecting "authoritarianism" and "violations of the fundamental dignity and rights of individuals," they formed a new fraternity "based on no narrow ideal of manhood." In these and other instances which might be cited, those creating new collegian brotherhoods believed themselves to be making an effort to enhance individual liberties and broaden the opportunities for student participation.[46]

These, then, were the common and national foundations of the American way of college fraternities and Yale secret societies. They were provoked by some perceived injustice (administrative action deeply resented by those acted upon, or student political maneuver which offended a minority); were founded on friendship in homelike clubs with lateral and not hierarchical bonds; were formed without prior permission of any authority; and were self-justified in their aims of individual liberty and self-improvement. They were to confront and celebrate competition with other societies in election and renown, insisting on loyalty and exclusivity, and conducting their proceedings in privacy—which was called secrecy by those excluded.

Back in New Haven in 1832, where there were as yet no fraternity chapters imported from other schools, the Connecticut chapter of Phi Beta Kappa was the closest and most obvious model for students seeking to form a new college society there. PBK was a society for seniors, secret as to its proceedings but not its members' names. However, it took in upward of one-third of the class, valued scholarship over good fellowship or other talents, and was a fraternity for life, mounting annual anniversary dinners with public speakers for graduates in attendance, having voting privileges that in numbers trumped the students. The first Yale senior society, Skull and Bones (and thus its successors in that mold), was in all these respects to be very different from any predecessor student organization at Yale or on any American college campus elsewhere.

This new Yale senior society was to be only half the size of the Phi Beta Kappa chapter, and only a tenth of the size of either of the all-class literary societies. It severely limited its annual membership intake, and its yearly drafts silently projected election standards which most candidates could not expect to meet. This society refused to justify its existence, or otherwise engage its critics, or to expand beyond New Haven. Its chosen but confidential name, the "Eulogia Club," was not Greek, like the fraternities founded elsewhere, but Latin, in differentiation from Phi Beta Kappa on campus and the new fraternities on other campuses. In these several ways, the Yale secret society was to be a distinctly new breed of fraternity, compared to those being founded before and after it in other northeastern colleges in the same decade. Furthermore, the men of this new society consciously formulated a specific educational purpose, narrower than that of the ancient literary societies or Phi Beta Kappa, and invented a different and more frequent drill for self-taught speaking skills. In their quest to become "self-made" men, they did not seek administration blessing, and had no faculty connections (until their "high-stand" graduates themselves became Yale College tutors, and then professors, and then university presidents).

Most strikingly, Bones, as it soon came to be known, in its elections was to employ a more autocratic manner and more democratic scope, recognizing, even before popularity or general sociability, proven leadership talents in all fields of college endeavor. These included but were not limited to academic appointment or intellectual achievement certified by the professors whose marking system made Phi Beta Kappa membership possible, or not. Rather, their diverse membership, including some who were strangers to one another before initiation, embraced most forms of student endeavor and all varieties of regional origin.

And that pattern held when those fields of endeavor changed, in the rise at Yale, then the nation's largest college, of the extracurriculum of music, sports, journalism, and religious outreach, followed by the increasing demographic, ethnic, and gender diversity of the student body itself. When, in the classic American fraternity pattern, rival senior societies were self-formed to give opportunity for recognition to more of the growing student body, that notion of membership first for the competitively deserving was to persist, and its very application subject to righteous judgment, printed and otherwise, by their classmates. Over time, the senior, "secret" society system in New Haven became a magnet, and concentrated training ground, for talent and achievement.

It took the ending of secrecy in Phi Beta Kappa to effect the new direction.

CHAPTER TWO

THE SECRETS OF PHI BETA KAPPA
(1781–1831)

Here then you may for a while disengage yourself from scholastic laws and communicate without reserve whatever reflections you have made upon various objects; remembering that everything transacted within this room is transacted sub rosa, and detested is he that discloses it. Here too you are to indulge in matters of speculation, that freedom of inquiry that ever dispels the cloud of falsehood by the radiant sunshine of truth—here you are to look for a sincere friend, and here you are to become the Brother of unalienable Brothers.

—From the Initiation Ritual of Phi Beta Kappa,
College of William and Mary, 1779

The history of the secret societies at Yale College in New Haven, Connecticut, begins not with the founding of Skull and Bones in 1832, but with an earlier student society, founded on December 5, 1776, at the College of William Mary in Williamsburg, Virginia. This the world knows by the Greek initials of the club's motto, Phi Beta Kappa—latinized, *Philosophia Biou Kybernetes*, or "love of wisdom, the guide of life." It was America's first college fraternity and secret society.

Since the name of the Societas Philosophia, the Philosophical Society, was according to the by-laws to be kept completely secret, the group came to be known by its Greek letters, with no public explanation of their meaning.

Phi Beta Kappa was the first college-based society in the United States to have a Greek-letter name (to contrast with an even earlier society at William and Mary, the Latinate "P.D.A.").[1] In the four years of its initial existence, ended when the British redcoats, commanded by the American turncoat Benedict Arnold, compelled the college to close its doors during the Revolutionary War in January 1781, all of the fundamental characteristics of such groups were appropriated or invented. These were election by undergraduates, induction after an elaborate (and blindfolded) initiation ceremony which included an oath of secrecy, and the award of a metallic badge to wear. For those in the fold, there were mottoes in Latin and Greek, a code of laws, a seal, and a special name, "Brothers."

At its regular meetings in the Raleigh Tavern's Apollo Room, the chief activities were literary exercises, especially debating. Four members performed at each meeting, two in "matters of argumentation" and two in "opposite composition," with their worthy compositions to be "carefully preserved." Here they enjoyed a freedom of speech that under their college's "scholastic Laws" they did not enjoy in class; it was this, not merely a taste for the mysterious, which accounted for the emphasis on secrecy. Each initiate was welcomed with the message that "Now then you may for a while disengage yourself from the scholastic Laws and communicate without reserve upon various objects; remembering that everything transacted within this room is transacted *sub rosa*, and detested is he that discloses it."[2]

This formal program was enlivened by social celebrations, especially anniversaries of the founding. High academic scholarship was apparently not a requisite for admission, as it was to become and is today. Its earliest members (fifty over the four years) were distinguished in later life, and included two United States senators, two members of the United States

Supreme Court, and two judges of Virginia's highest court. One member served dual roles as the first clerk of the House of Representatives, and the first librarian of Congress.[3]

In all these features of small numbers, talented members, badges, rituals, and a pronounced fidelity to secrecy, Phi Beta Kappa in its original form set patterns for the senior societies of Yale which commenced fully half a century later, nearly five hundred miles to the north.

Noting their carefully minuted record of "many toasts" in the Raleigh Tavern, a historian in 1888 described the founding group "discouraging to those who would like to consider Phi Beta Kappa as a band of youthful enthusiasts planning a union of the virtuous college youth of this country who were afterward to reform the world."[4] The minutes also speak of the design, "for the better establishment and sanctitude of our unanimity, [of] a square silver medal . . . engraved in the one side with SP, the initials of the Latin Societias Philosophia, and on the other, agreeable to the former, with the Greek initials of Φ . . . B . . . K . . . and an index imparting a philosophical design, extended to the three stars, a part of the planetary orb, distinguished." The three stars on the back side symbolized the aims of the society—friendship, morality, and literature—and the pointing hand in the lower corner symbolized aspiration toward these goals.

The same meeting's record also preserves the text of an "oath of fidelity," which the members considered "the strongest preservative" to their new organization: "I, A.B., do swear on the Holy Evangelists of Almighty God, or otherwise as calling the Supreme Being to attest this my oath, declaring that I will, with all my possible efforts, endeavor to prove true, just, and deeply attached to this our growing Fraternity; in keeping, holding, and preserving all secrets that pertain to my duty, and for the promotion and advancement of its internal welfare." As if this mighty oath were not enough, the meeting of March 1, 1777, further resolved "That a profanation of the preceeding oath of fidelity subjects the Member to the pain of the universal censures of the fraternity as well as the misery of certain expulsion."[5]

The next link in the chain joining Williamsburg and New Haven is Elisha Parmele of Goshen, Connecticut. Parmele completed two years at Yale and then, when college did not open in the fall of 1776 because of an outbreak of camp distemper, transferred to Harvard as a junior. Graduating there in 1778, Parmele went off to Virginia to preserve his fragile health, teaching at a neighborhood school in Surry County, across the James River from Williamsburg.[6] Not long after his arrival in the south, the founders of Phi Beta Kappa on July 31, 1779, elected him to membership in the William and Mary society.[7]

Parmele's election was arranged by chapter president William Short in furtherance of the vision of fraternity brother Samuel Hardy, who proposed to his cofounders a "plan for extending branches of our Society to the different States."[8] Along with eight other members of Williamsburg's Phi Beta Kappa, Short and Hardy also belonged to Williamsburg Lodge No. 6 of the Masons, which had received its own charter from England only in 1773. It seems patent that Hardy's proposal to extend Phi Beta Kappa derived from the Masonic example and influence, even though Phi Beta Kappa was more a student literary society for intellectual self-improvement than a mere social group.[9]

With his connections to both Yale and Harvard (being, with William and Mary, the three oldest colleges in the United States), and his intention to return soon to New England, Parmele was suddenly the perfect agent for Hardy's scheme of issuing charters to new chapters, on "the great advantage that would attend it in binding together the several states."[10] This notion of organization across states would not have seemed as odd in 1779 as it may today, long after the adoption of the Constitution which federated those states a decade later in 1789.

Parmele was eager to undertake the task of expansion across state lines, and at the third anniversary celebration on December 5, 1779, he petitioned his William and Mary brothers to do so. He seems initially to have believed Phi Beta Kappa to be something like Linonia as a literary and debating organization. Despite the fact that Yale College's literary societies were also private membership groups, with meetings closed to the public, led by officers whose names were kept confidential, Parmele was nonetheless dismayed when confronted with Phi Beta Kappa's fierce penchant for secrecy.

Although Parmele's petition for a charter at Harvard had already been approved at the meeting of December 4, 1779, a debate ensued during the meeting the following day on the terms for Yale's charter. Minutes of that foundation anniversary meeting (with the secretary's uncertain grasp on the spelling of Parmele's name) record that it was "Resolved, that so much of Mr. Parmelie's petition as relates to the establishment of a Phi: Society to be conducted in a less mysterious manner than Φ B K be not agreed to, as the design appears to be incompatible with the principles of this meeting." As a grace note, it was "Ordered, however, that Mr. Paremlie be thanked for the proof which he has given of his zeal by openly communicating his sentiments to this Society."

The discussions occurring thereafter seem to have overcome the New Englander's objections to "mystery," and the next week, a momentous resolution was passed by the Williamsburg chapter. "Whereas this Society is desirous that Φ B K should be extended to each of the United States," it was "Resolved, that a second Charter be granted to our Brother, Mr. Elisa Parmele, for establishing a meeting of the same in the College of New Haven in Connecticut, to be of the same Rank, to have the same Power, and to enjoy the same privileges, with that which he is empowered to fix in the University of Cambridge [Harvard]." [11]

President Short then had two copies of the charter transcribed and signed by all nineteen officers and members in Williamsburg; the code of laws and form of initiation were made up in duplicate, and he added to this trove two of the society's medals, for transport to each of the new chapters in New England. [12] Parmele's protest against secrecy had been rebuffed by his new brothers, so the covering letter of greeting which he carried to Connecticut and Massachusetts from the Alpha of William and Mary provided that "the Arcana of this Society be held inviolate." [13]

Parmele then traveled back north, taking ten months to reach Connecticut, carrying the medals, the charters with ribbons of "pink and sky blue" (Yale's being the oldest surviving document of the society), copies of the code of law, and the ritual. Arriving in his hometown of Goshen in November 1780, he initiated his brother Reuben Parmele (class of 1781), Sam Newell and Lynde Lord (1783), and his classmate Ezra Stiles Jr.—who became the first president of Alpha of Connecticut and promptly added the name of his reverend father, Yale's president from 1778 to 1795, as an honorary member.[14] To these initial members were added seven recent graduates and twelve other members of the class of 1781, at a foundation meeting in New Haven on November 13, 1780.[15] Membership in the "Alpha of Connecticut" chapter of Phi Beta Kappa in the classes succeeding 1781 likewise approximated twelve to fourteen members each, chosen from the junior class, after the spring vacation and examinations in July.[16] (Here again, the practice of holding of election in the spring of junior year by members of the outgoing senior class, and restriction of membership to a small number, are antecedent customs for the Yale senior societies of the next century.)

Following Parmele's receipt from Harvard of his second (master of arts) degree in 1781 in Cambridge, Massachusetts, and some ten months after his missionary work in New Haven, he then on July 17 established Phi Beta Kappa's second New England chapter, the "Alpha of Massachusetts." He chose four students from the class of 1782 and presented them with the documents and the model medal for Harvard brought from Williamsburg; they later met to make formal establishment of the chapter on September 6, 1781, and to select additional members from their junior class, replicating what had happened the year earlier in New Haven.[17]

Exactly nine months before the establishment of the Harvard chapter, on January 6, 1781, as the British fleet bearing the forces of Benedict Arnold and Lord Cornwallis had arrived opposite Jamestown, the Williamsburg chapter assembled to close itself down, at a meeting "called for the Purpose of securing the Papers of the Society during the confusion of the Times & present Dissolution which threatens the University." They determined to deliver their records to the college steward, "in the sure and certain Hope that the Fraternity will one Day rise to Life everlasting & Glory immortal."[18] The next rising to life did not occur until 1855, although a few years later, in 1861, the Williamsburg chapter succumbed again to the travails of battle, in the American Civil War, not to be resurrected once more until 1893.

If Elisha Parmele ever notified the Alpha of Virginia of his success in delivering the charters and medals to New Haven and Cambridge, the letters miscarried. On January 15, 1782, William Short inquired of the Yale chapter, "What has become of our very worthy member Mr. E. Parmele? He has been silent as the grave since his return northward. Wherever he is, assure him of our sincere regard for him. He has endeared himself to us here, not only by his personal merit, but by his diligence in spreading the ΦBK. Like the great luminary he carries light with him wherever he goes, vivifies all around him, and exhilarates the spirits of whomsoever he pleases to favor."[19] In fact Parmele, whom his best biographer styled "the St. Paul who carried [Phi Beta Kappa] from the Zion of its birthplace to the far-off Gentiles of Yale and Harvard," had become a minister in Connecticut and then Virginia. He did not long survive the chapter of his brothers: he died of consumption in the upper Shenandoah Valley on August 2, 1784, and was buried on the Abraham Byrd family farm, in a grave that cannot now be located.[20]

Given the the Williamsburg chapter's extinction, if the Yale and Harvard chapters had not been founded, Phi Beta Kappa would probably have been forgotten like its predecessor student societies at William and Mary, the P.D.A. and another, the contemporaneous Flat Hat Club, which boasted Thomas Jefferson as a member.[21] Instead, Parmele's dissemination of its detailed charters established a standard of selection based, however imperfectly, on the scholarship and character of a chosen few, in a fellowship encased in a code of secrecy.

With the extinction of the Alpha of Virginia, the Alphas of New Haven and Cambridge were in charge. These two concurred to found new Alphas in other states: in New Hampshire at Dartmouth College in 1787, in New York at Union College in 1817, in Maine at Bowdoin College in 1825, and in Rhode Island at Brown College in 1830,[22] all with the mandates of secrecy first pronounced in Williamsburg in 1776. Because of the society's secrecy and selectivity, its first half century in Northern institutions aroused not only loyalty, emulation, and curiosity, but jealousy and animosity,[23] all strong emotions which the Yale senior societies, indirectly descended from the Phi Beta Kappa of the late eighteenth century, were themselves to engender.

The exclusiveness of membership and secrecy at weekly or fortnightly meetings, combined with very public celebrations of anniversaries held in connection with college commencements—and perhaps further provoked by condescension or conscious swank—aroused significant opposition to the Alpha of Connecticut, which erupted in successive raids on the Yale chapter's records. The first time, in December 1786, three students "under the united influence of envy, resentment, and curiosity" broke open "the Secretary's door, in his absence, entered his study and feloniously took, stole and carried away the Society's trunk with all its contents." Discovered, the thieves were compelled to restore their booty, including the trunk, paying for the damage done. After confessing in an open meeting, they bound themselves "by a solemn oath, to confine within their own breasts all the knowledge of the secrets of the Society which they had criminally obtained." Six months later, in June 1787, a further theft occurred, and the records were not to be recovered for another fifty years.[24]

Yale's Phi Beta Kappa archives also contain a letter dated August 26, 1789, from Jonathan Nash of the newly founded Dartmouth chapter about a raid there: "We lament that this sad misfortune happened to our young Alpha. . . . Rancorous envy still lies broiling in the breasts of a few, who in that way discover how highly they esteem the ΦBK society."[25] The Harvard chapter took official notice of this outrage in New Hampshire, and voted, for its own conduct of business, "That because several persons not members of the Society have endeavored to discover the manner of salutation peculiar to the ΦBK; this manner to be suspended until the next anniversary."[26] Milder protests had been met with caution: the meeting at the Anniversary Day for the Harvard chapter on September 5, 1788, had voted "that by reason of the dissensions in the Senior Class on account of the election of members, no more than ten members be chosen previous to the anniversary," and a letter to the Yale chapter on September 18 noted that "disagreeable consequences have attended the initiation of persons into the Society, previous to that period."[27]

Secrecy remained a flashpoint. The "oath of fidelity" transmitted by the Alpha of Virginia to the chapters at New Haven and Cambridge contained a stipulation against change, but the mother Alpha was gone, and Yale was then purportedly free to simplify the oath when revising its organizational law in 1787, to read more simply: "You solemnly call the Supreme Being to witness that you will be true and faithful to this Society, that you will obey the Laws and preserve all the secrets of the same, so help you God."

Phi Beta Kappa had drawn support from the example and reputation of the Freemasons, but in the two decades that followed, the Masons suffered from public attacks by those who disapproved of secret societies. The conflict was severely heightened in 1827, when William Morgan, initiated as a Mason in Virginia but not well received by the Masonic lodge in Batavia, New York, wrote and threatened to publish a tell-all book. Titled *Illustrations of Masonry*, it included the organization's first three degrees' oaths of fealty and, for oath-breaking, agreement to blood-curdling penalties of disembowelment, dismemberment, and death. Morgan was arrested in September of that year for petty larceny. Acquitted, he was arrested again in Fort Niagara, and then disappeared, perhaps drowned in the Niagara River or Lake Ontario: a decomposed body was found on the shore not far from the place of Morgan's abduction.

Although no legal case for kidnapping or murder was established (twenty-six Masons were indicted, six came to trial, and four were convicted of conspiracy), the incident was widely publicized and gave new strength to the Anti-masonic movement and political party, the first third party in American history. The outrage turned the office of Freemasonry, in the words of historian Samuel Flagg Bemis, "from that of a handmaiden to Christianity and republican liberty to that of a secret and impious conspiracy against the rights of freemen and the majesty of the law." Thousands of Masons were compelled by public opinion to resign, and about three thousand lodges gave up their chapters; those in Connecticut were decimated. Four years later, this had a direct effect on the Phi Beta Kappa chapters, when one Avery Allyn published *A Ritual of Freemasonry, Illustrated by Numerous Engravings, To which is added a Key to the Phi Beta Kappa.* The book was dedicated to "the Freemen of America," and dated "Boston 1830," with a copyright entry of February 18, 1831.[28]

The Allyn exposé should perhaps have been only another glancing blow at the society, since his book devoted 290 pages to the features of the Masons. Only eight pages described Phi Beta Kappa, but included a plate illustrating the "sign," the "grip," and "both sides of the medal," although he omitted the anapestic knock at the door. The "sign" was given by placing the two forefingers of the right hand so as to cover the left corner of the mouth, and then drawing them across the chin. The "grip" was like the common handshake, only not interlocking the thumbs, and at the same time pressing the wrist. The book's author— whose true identity is still obscure—followed his name on the title page with "K.R.C., K.T., K.M. &c." and claimed membership in Phi Beta Kappa in the text, although his name does not appear in any Phi Beta Kappa catalogue or in the catalogue of any of the six colleges with society chapters on that date. (It was to be said that it was a Harvard man who gave away the secrets.)[29]

Because his book had such adverse consequences for his claimed "respected brethren," it bears extended quotation: "In this day of laudable excitement and anxious investigation into the nature and principles of secret societies, it is my humble opinion, there ought to be no concealment; and that the public good imperiously demands a fair and full disclosure of the nature and principles of all secret societies, and that what is said and done under the cover of darkness, should be openly proclaimed on the housetop. . . ."

"But the reasons I give, which particularly induce me to make these disclosures," he continued, "are principally two: one is the secret nature of the Phi Beta Kappa Society, and the other it its infidel motto. . . . That the Phi Beta Kappa Society is a *secret* association, is well known to the public. It is a species of Freemasonry, and bears a strong affinity to it; and for aught I know, may be a younger branch of the same tenebrous family. . . . Like Freemasonry, the Phi Beta Kappa Society has its secret *obligation, sign, grip, word,* and *jewel,* by which its members are enabled to recognize each other, in any company, in any part of the world; and though it has no bloody code, as I know of, with savage penalties, and consequently none of those crimes which blacken the Institution of Freemasonry; yet, as a *secret* society it is as susceptible of being perverted to unholy and dangerous purposes."[30]

Allyn then repeated his general attack on secret societies as a potential threat to American liberties and as being against religion, detailing the historical myths regarding Phi Beta Kappa as "a branch of the [Bavarian] *Illuminati,* that spurious offspring of the celebrated Weishaupt," while simultaneously, inconsistently, and falsely claiming that "this Institution was imported from France" and planted in this country by "Thomas Jefferson at William and Mary."

Upon the "extinction of that college during the Revolutionary War," he continued, "a charter, technically called an *Alpha,* was obtained by the students of Yale College, where it still flourishes. From thence it was imparted to Harvard and Dartmouth, and since that time, charters have been granted to the students of Union College, in N.Y., and to Bowdoin, in Maine; and very recently, I understand, to Brown University, in Providence, R.I." Yet "all the literary and honorable advantages it affords, might as well be obtained without secrecy as with, and the danger thence resulting, be avoided; and I cannot but wonder why the authorities of our colleges allow of their existence."[31] Those authorities, so challenged, duly took notice.

Despite peddling historical misinformation, Allyn does seem to have described accurately the prevailing manner of election and quality of the initiates of Phi Beta Kappa, which is striking for the parallels it offers to the Yale senior societies, waiting to be born within the next few years. "The way and manner in which this secret institution is perpetuated in our Colleges (and I know of no other places where they exist and meet as societies) is this," he recorded. "Towards the close, or during the last term of the college year, the members of the Senior Class, who belong to the Society, make a selection from the Junior Class of *one third* of its members; and their aim is, however much they may be mistaken, to take those who are reputedly the best scholars, and the most prominent members of the class. They are privately informed of their election; and at the appointed time, are initiated into the Society; not indeed naked, and barefoot, hoodwinked, and cable-towed, but in a more gentlemanly manner, where a promise or oath of secrecy is first exacted of them."[32]

At Yale, Phi Beta Kappa was esteemed over membership in the older literary (debating) societies Linonia and Brothers in Unity. A member of the class of 1821 remembered that "The exercises of Φ. B. K. were generally of a higher order than those of the other societies. They ought at least to be so, since the members, from the higher classes only, are selected for their talents and attainments. The desire to be elected to this society was hardly less than that of appointments at commencement; and for the same reason, namely, that it was regarded as proof of scholarship."[33]

While there had been concern and protest for decades about the secrecy of Phi Beta Kappa, the publication of Allyn's book, in Boston in the spring of 1831, was a breaking point. Edward Everett, president of the Alpha of Massachusetts since 1826 (and fated to speak at length after Lincoln at Gettysburg in 1863), concluded that something must be done before the Harvard chapter anniversary meeting held on September 1. He wrote to Joseph Story, then a justice on the United States Supreme Court, saying he wished to call a meeting to change the constitution: "Several friends, with whom I have conversed, think it expedient wholly to drop the affectation of secrecy and all its incidents."[34]

At the subsequent meeting at the Hall of the American Academy of Arts and Sciences in Boston on July 21, 1831, Everett read an extract of Allyn's work, and John Quincy Adams, then a member of the United States House of Representatives, offered a resolution: "That in the admission of all future members of the Society, no oath shall be administered, and no secret be disclosed to or imposed upon or required of the member admitted." This motion was defeated, but a second moved by Justice Story was adopted, to form a committee to further consider the question; Adams's diaries provide most of the information known about the deliberations of that group, on which he and Story served with eight others. Adams's previously defeated motion was then approved by the committee, and after further electoral skirmishes was adopted on August 11, and again at the anniversary meeting on September 1,[35] in these words: "No oath or form of secrecy shall be required of any member of the Society, and all injunction of secrecy heretofore imposed by this branch of Phi Beta Kappa shall be removed."[36]

Allyn promptly declared victory, writing about Phi Beta Kappa in the second edition of his book, "The members of this Institution have recently removed the injunction of secrecy imposed by its obligations, and have left the world to form a just notion of its moral and social principles. This event has doubtless been hastened by the revelation of its mysteries published in the first edition of this Ritual."[37] However, this action of the Alpha of Massachusetts had been unilateral, in defiance of the fraternal concerns expressed by Harvard members back in 1806 when they had queried the Alpha of Connecticut about changing the oath and stricture of secrecy. Everett may thus have felt compelled to travel to New Haven, because that chapter appears not to have been unduly upset by Allyn's criticism of Phi Beta Kappa's secrecy.

The New Haven chapter's public anniversary was scheduled for September 13, and in attending the business meeting which preceded it, Harvard's emissary insisted that the question of repeal of secrecy be considered. His attendance had also been urged by the notability of the occasion: this was the semi-centennial of the Alpha of Connecticut, and the fiftieth anniversary of the graduation of the orator for the occasion, James Kent, chancellor of the State of New York.[38] Kent's diary describes what happened, at least among the graduate members at Yale, upon hearing of Everett's anti-secrecy initiative. "At 11 A.M. I attended the meeting of the Ph. B. K. in the 3d story of the old Chapel," he recorded. "There I saw Ed. Everett and a crowd of civilians and clergy and Professors. The question was on abolishing the secrets of the Society. Professor Silliman, Doctor Ives, Rev. M. Robbins, the Rev. Mr. Bacon of the 1st Presbyterian Congregation & Judge Daggett spoke. The rule of secrecy was abolished with acclamation."[39]

The contrasting view of the students was only described publicly some forty-two years later, in 1874, in a speech by Charles Tracy of the class of 1832 (a member of Phi Beta Kappa that election year, and president of Linonia). "In those days," he told his audience at the Yale Alumni Association in New York City, "free-masonry and anti-masonry fought their battles; and a grave question of conscience arose about the promise of secrecy exacted on initiation into the Phi Beta Kappa Society. Harvard was for resolving the secrecy and it sent Edward Everett to the private meeting at Yale to advocate the cause. He used a tender tone, stood half-drooping as he spoke, and touchingly set forth, that the students at Harvard had such conscientious scruples, as to keep them from taking the vow of secrecy, and society life was thus endangered. There was stout opposition, but the motion prevailed, and the missionary returned to gladden the tender consciences of the Harvard boys [in truth, the Harvard graduates]. The secret, of course, was out. The world did not stare at the discovery; and when a few years had passed, the society took back its secrecy and revived its grip."[40]

Tracy's sarcasm makes it clear that the Yale students' view was that while their Harvard brothers (and also the Yale graduate members of his own chapter) had lost their collective nerve, flinching from Allyn's exposure, it was all for nothing, as ending the secrecy had the effect of confirming his revelations while spoiling all the fun. The Alpha of Connecticut's minutes subsequent to the General Meeting of September 13, 1831, show that the undergraduate members remained very unhappy with the course of events. The record of that meeting (which concludes with the addendum "Six Weeks Vacation") straightforwardly reports the result: "A motion was made 'That the injunction of secrecy now existing on the members of this society be removed and that it be no more required of those who may be admitted.' After some remarks from Hon. E. Everett explanatory of the course which had been taken by the Cambridge branch with regard to this subject and also from other gentlemen the motion was passed."[41]

Four meetings later at the annual session on December 1, 1831, a small committee was appointed to "examine the constitution of the Soc. in regard to its bearing upon the abolishing of the secrets of the Society." While there is no report of that group's conclusions, the meeting of February 27, 1832, witnessed a broader debate, which probably explains why there was no resolution. "The debate," wrote the recording secretary, "was beyond dispute the most remarkable of all that have been held before any society in any age. The question made—'Ought secret societies to be abolished?'—the arguments were perfectly convincing on both sides and equally clear and as was to have been expected then produced on each side an equal number of votes thus placing the determination of the question 'in equlibro.' Mr. [Seth Collins] Brace then at the request of the meeting gave forth in an extemporaneous motion his sentiments respecting the present agitation of the 'public mind' in regard to secret societies. He touched feelingly upon the dire misfortunes which this agitation had brought upon New England, upon his own state and even upon his native town."

Still nothing was resolved, and the meeting of June 7, 1832, brought into the chapter twenty-six new members, in a class that then had ninety-three members and was to graduate eighty-seven in 1833. These included William Huntington Russell (the first to be elected, ultimately the valedictorian and class orator), Alphonso Taft (to be the "high-stand" man ranking third in his class), John Campbell Beach, and George Ingersoll Wood. Another eight were elected four days later, including Noah Bishop and Robert Robertson (later class poet), bringing the new membership, at thirty-four, to just over one-third of the class limit mandated by the

chapter constitution of 1787 (only eighteen had been elected the year
before). None of these neophytes had witnessed the vote or debates on
secrecy, and none were made to swear the oath of secrecy, but all would
have been aware of the strongly held but evenly divided feelings of their
electors, argued in the debate on the abolition of secret societies held only
seventeen weeks before. The minutes for the meeting of July 5 were the
last for the class of 1832; four days later, the incoming seniors of 1833
began their academic year, electing their new chapter officers, including
Russell as their leader as secretary.[42]

These young men of Yale, deprived of their secrecy in one organization, could easily found another, with the good old ways in place.[43] Of
the thirty-four members of Phi Beta Kappa,[44] six—Beach, Bishop, Robertson, Russell, Taft, and Wood—chose, with eight of their classmates
not in the Alpha of Connecticut (including Asahel Lewis, class orator
to be), to form what came to be called Skull and Bones—the first of the
Yale clubs to be characterized as "the mystic fifteens."[45]

CHAPTER THREE

THE FOUNDING OF
SCULL AND BONE
(1832-1842)

We needed the benefits of a social society which should supplement our College and Society training, by helping us to make the important acquisition of being able to think on our feet without the aids of retirement, pen and paper—and especially to express at the moment whatever opinion we might have on any given topic.

—George Ingersoll Wood (in 1885) about 1832

NEW HAVEN IN 1832

Since the formation of Yale's first "secret society" of seniors followed so soon after the elimination of the oath and rituals of secrecy in the Yale chapter of Phi Beta Kappa, and it seems not to have been the result of sour grapes when friends were not elected,[1] it must be accepted that the attraction of a secret brotherhood was too strong for some undergraduates to give up completely. Let us examine how, in the words of the biographer of Henry Stimson (class of 1888, Skull and Bones), those young men "constructed in the senior societies, with admirable insight, a mechanism to mobilize the emotions of the selected few to their high purposes. . . . Such special election produces no doubt a sense of large responsibility; the compression of the secret can generate great energy."[2]

In 1832, New Haven contained about eleven thousand people, while the state capital Hartford's population was only about eight thousand. Beyond the college, the business of making carriages was the town's leading industry, supported by suppliers of leather and electroplated "coach lace," and the American South was the principal market. For shopping in that market, and less humid weather, Southern families came north and spent the summer in New Haven and other New England towns.[3] Andrew Jackson was president of the United States, visiting the Yale campus in 1833, and John C. Calhoun (Yale 1804, Phi Beta Kappa) was vice president. Twenty-five states made up the Union.

The Reverend Jeremiah Day (class of 1795, Phi Beta Kappa) was in the fifteenth year of his Yale College presidency, not to sign his last diplomas until the graduation of the class of 1846. The class as defined under the college laws—whether freshmen, sophomores, junior sophisters, or senior sophisters—was already named after the normal year of graduation, unlike the English college system at Oxford and Cambridge, where one's particular college identity was paramount. The "friendly sentiment uniting the brotherhood," as Day's successor President Timohty Dwight was to call this class feeling, was already patent. President Noah Porter was to write in 1870: "In college, the class is the charmed circle, within which the individual contracts most of his friendships and finds his fondest and most cherished association. The sentiment of his class is that which influences him most efficiently, and is to him often the only atmosphere of his social life." The applause won by leading members was regarded with peculiar complacency by each member as belonging to the common fund of class credit. After graduation, the glory won by the great men of the class gave a certain prestige to the class itself.[4]

The college population was small: the class of 1833 was to graduate eighty-seven, after losing some twenty-nine original members to early death or to withdrawal for disciplinary, economic, or health reasons. "Socially," Yale historian Clarence Deming observed, "a student life that converged on a single campus and four dormitories was necessarily intense."[5] The enforced intimacy "of the four years' class association resulted in the cultivation of a certain practical judgment of men," another historian of college life has written. "In the old days about three fifths of the talk of the undergraduates was about one another. It began when the sub-freshmen met to be examined for admission, and continued until graduation. The amount of attention which men paid to one another, and the time devoted to estimating one another's social, moral, and intellectual qualities, and discussing details of conduct, were extraordinary. . . . [T]he apparatus for bringing men of the same class together was efficient, and it usually did happen that by the end of the freshman year nearly every man believed he knew, or knew about, every man in his class whose acquaintance it seemed likely to be worth his while to make. Men were misjudged, misunderstood, overestimated, and underestimated, but acquaintance was very general and constantly ripening, and estimates were in a constant state of revision and reconstruction." Indeed, until 1830 or 1831, Yale students voted on the general deportment of their classmates, respecting the relative rank of their fellows as a basis for the action of the faculty in assigning the college honors.[6] These habits were to be integral to the fascination with, and function of, the process of elections to the senior societies.

The boys and men in the class of 1833 ranged in age from fourteen, the youngest age permitted for admission under the college laws, to twenty-eight years, with more than half under eighteen. Forty-one percent hailed from Connecticut (Yale drew heavily from rural Connecticut, and relied upon New Haven to a considerably lesser degree than Harvard did upon Boston, from which half its students hailed). Nineteen percent came from New York, 15 percent from Massachusetts, 7 percent from the South (Virginia, South Carolina, Georgia, and

Louisiana), 3 percent from the West (Ohio and Illinois), and the balance, except for a collegian from St. Croix in the West Indies, hailed from the other New England states.

Yale from 1820 to 1860 was the largest college in the United States, and at this date the nation's most genuinely national educational institution in terms of the origins of its students and the ultimate destinations of its graduates.[7] By 1830, barely 25 percent remained in Connecticut after graduation, most settling in New York, Pennsylvania, Ohio, and other trans-Appalachian states. Yale appears to have become by 1820 an important entrepôt not only for New Englanders seeking greater opportunities, but also for Southerners and Westerners moving toward eastern commercial and cultural centers. Yale's curriculum, with its meritocratic and universalistic emphasis, was ideally suited to socialize this wildly diverse student body.[8]

The student mix was not only geographic. Julian Sturtevant of the class of 1826, hailing from the farm village of Tallmadge, Ohio, and preparing for the ministry, with tuition for that purpose covered by the American Education Society, wrote of his fellow collegians gathered to eat in commons. "That group of students," he remembered, "was a strange medley. The families of merchant princes of New York, Boston, and Philadelphia; of aristocratic cotton planters; of hard-handed New England farmers; of Ohio backwoodsmen, and of the humblest sons of daily toil, sitting at the same tables. Those who wished to be educated at Yale, the Alma Mater of so many distinguished men, were compelled to accept this intermingling of the rich and poor. Yale College . . . was the most democratic portion of American society."[9]

That democracy had been strongly reinforced, from the middle of the eighteenth century onward, by the competition which was explicit in the award of scholarly distinctions by the faculty. At the foundations of both Harvard College (1636) and Yale College (1701), students were ranked in a special order based, in varying degrees at different times, on appraisals of family position, intellectual promise, and parental relationship to the college, and thereafter listed throughout their undergraduate terms, at graduation and in the graduate catalogues, based on that ranking. A man's seat in class, chapel, commons, and all else was fixed by it. "Placing" registered only what a boy's father was—the first-ranked being a son of a governor, or of a president of Yale, then, in descending order, sons of other colonial officials, sons of the college trustees, sons of ministers, sons of alumni, and finally (as said of Harvard) the sons of "farmers, storekeepers, mariners and artisans arranged in an order which cannot be explained by wealth or social position." All classes learned humility from the conclusion of the college prayer: "May we perform faithfully our duties to our superiors, our equals, and inferiors." The Yale Corporation decided to abolish this system, seemingly because of its very complexity, in 1766.[10]

Most students' reaction to this abolition was naturally favorable. A sophomore when the change was effected, David Avery of the class of 1769, wrote Dartmouth President Eleazar Wheelock (Yale class of 1733): "There appears [to be] a laudable ambition to excel in knowledge. It is not he that has got the finest coat or the largest ruffles that is esteemed here at present. And as the class henceforward are to be placed alphabetically, the students may expect marks of distinction to be put upon the best scholars ands speakers."[11] For the first time, intelligence prevailed over family inheritance as a requisite for accomplishment in the society of the college. These "marks of distinction" were to weigh heavily in the formation and member selection of the Yale senior societies, six decades on.

The aim of the college, then employing a faculty of ten professors, was to produce men for the learned professions, for "public employments in church and civil state." (In a typical class of the era, Timothy Dwight's of 1849, thirty-five of his ninety-four classmates became lawyers, twenty-five entered the ministry, seven became doctors, and only nine pursued a career in business.[12]) On the religious front, attendance was still required on Sundays at two services, and prayers on uncushioned pews were held in the chapel every morning at 5:00 A.M. in summer and 6:00 A.M. in winter. Immediately after morning chapel was held the first of the three recitations of the day, often by candlelight. A give-and-take occurred as the student prepared passages from the assigned text for the instructor's in-class examination of him. They studied in three divisions, named for the Old Brick Row building locations in which the recitations were held, the North, Middle, and South Colleges. From 1827 they ate in a common wooden dining hall on High Street, not to be abandoned until 1841. There were twelve weeks of vacation during the year, divided among three terms.

Virtually the only legitimate avenue of escape open to the under-graduate from the monotony of the prescribed existence was the company of his fellow students, and the only fairly comfortable and attractive places were the rented rooms of the literary societies. Societies which featured warm companionship, long and heated orations and debates, dramatic "productions," and comparatively large libraries containing contempo-rary as well as classic literature came into being at most colonial colleges from almost their very beginnings. These grand precursors of the senior societies at Yale demonstrated that the students could build a culture, "a means for self improvement, the 'junto' of the leisured college man," a historian of American campus life has written. "Did the required course of study ignore the basic education desired by collegians aspiring to be men of culture? Then build outside its bounds a fellowship to address contemporary philosophy and politics. Did recitation allow no real cul-tivation of manners and style? Then use the society to improve writing and public speaking. Did the college not provide the necessary books to study the great questions of the day? Then organize a library within the society."[13] Their Wednesday afternoon weekly meetings at Yale College were eagerly anticipated (the administration allowed a half-holiday for them), and their exercises considered to be of much greater importance than regular recitations. The athlete had not yet arisen as a college hero, so the orator and writer represented the ideals of the academic youth.[14]

Physically, the Yale of 1832 was modestly sized: confined to one city block, in expansion from the southeast corner of the present Old Campus—a town square assemblage only finally secured in 1800—with the school buildings faced east to the New Haven Green across the aptly named College Street, between Chapel and Elm Streets. The Old Brick Row, laid out in 1792 by college treasurer James Hillhouse and artist John Trumbull as the country's first planned college campus, was a straight line of seven buildings, four being dormitories with geographical names: South (built in 1793, flanking Chapel Street), the Athenaeum, South Middle (originally, and now, "Connecticut Hall," the first, built in 1750–52), the Lyceum, North Middle, the Chapel, and North (flanking Elm Street), built in 1821, considered the best of the lot at the time, and thus occupied by the seniors.

These buildings served to gather students under one roof where, it was believed, with proper supervision by college authorities, the young men could grow religiously, intellectually, and socially. In the words of Andrew Dickson White, class of 1853, the structures presented a "long line of brick barracks, the cheapest which could be built for money," each four stories high, with two entries, each entry giving access to sixteen rooms, four on a floor. Behind the row of four dormitories and the various religious or academic buildings (of which only Connecticut Hall remains), was the Laboratory, also used as the dining hall. Impecunious students were allowed to live—and cook—in the recitation rooms in exchange for cleaning those rooms and keeping fires in the stoves.[15]

"By no educational criteria derived from any time, place, or philosophy," it has been said, "can the early 19th century American college curriculum as actually taught be made to look attractive. It consisted almost solely of a drill in Latin, Greek, and mathematics, with a cursory view of science and some moral philosophy and belles lettres as the capstone."[16]

A senior year course in moral philosophy was virtually universal among American colleges at the time, although details varied as a function of their respective religious affiliations. This was designed to draw together all the scrambled admonitions and reprimands that had theretofore been lavished on youth, to arrange them in a systematic body, and offer them as a moral legacy of the ages to be studied, cherished, and presumably obeyed throughout life. In the words of the famous and influential Yale Report of 1828—formally, *Reports on Course of Instruction in Yale College by a Committee of the Corporation, and the Academical Faculty*—the bachelor of arts curriculum "emphasized the study of classical languages, science, and mathematics with the aim of building character and promoting distinctive habits of thought."[17]

The Yale Report's embrace of the Enlightenment goal of self-realization could not have been more plain, in a remarkable statement on the subject of how to educate people for autonomy, declaring the the object of college instruction was not to gain information, but to acquire the ability to think independently. "No one feature in a system of intellectual education, is of greater moment than such an arrangement of duties and motives, as will most effectually throw the student upon the *resources of his own mind*. Without this, the whole apparatus of libraries, and instruments, and specimens, and lectures, and teachers, will be insufficient to secure distinguished excellence."

However elevated the goals of the Yale College educational system, as repurposed by the Report's primary author, President Day, their methods of delivery for the "richest treasure of thought" were stilted and the atmosphere arid. (Not that methods up in Cambridge were particularly better: Samuel Eliot Morison observed that "almost every graduate of the period 1825–1860 has left on record his detestation of the system of instruction at Harvard.") "Its power," Julian Sturtevant recalled of Yale in 1826, "lay in its fixed and rigidly prescribed curriculum, and its thorough drill. The tutors were good drillmasters, but often lacked culture and the literary spirit. They did not bring the students into sympathy with classic authors as models of literary excellence. . . . In mental, moral and social science our instruction was far from satisfactory."

Nor was there the student-faculty personal interchange which might have softened the rigors of recitation and learning by rote. "One of the greatest faults of Yale at the time," Julian Sturtevant remembered, "was the absence of any social relations between the instructors of all grades and the students. Professors and tutors held themselves aloof from the students and met them only in an official capacity. For the most part a student could hope for sympathy and help in his moral and religious struggles only from his fellow students."[18]

Because the practices of public speaking and of debate or "disputation," to which allusion was made in the Yale Report, were to be so important to the founding of the Yale senior societies, their role in the curriculum of this era is worth examining. Only in 1776, three-quarters of a century after Yale's founding, was permission given to the senior class for instruction in rhetoric, history, and belles lettres, and then only "provided it may be done with the Approbation of the Parents or Guardians of said Class." By the century's turn, freshmen received training in Cicero's *De Oratore*, and all students, regardless of class, were required in daily rotation to "exhibit" compositions of various kinds, and submit them to the instructor's criticism. Meeting in units of four, they declaimed, publicly and privately, on Tuesdays and Fridays, in English, Latin, Greek, or Hebrew; when required, each had to hand in a copy of his declamation "fairly written."[19]

As for single orators, the professor of rhetoric from 1817 to 1839, Chauncey Allen Goodrich, noted that the program of individual declamations, daily for underclassmen before their respective tutors, was not especially successful. Since the students had no text on elocution, they did not understand "the *technical* terms," and "instruction, however clearly conveyed, must be chiefly unintelligible," Goodrich complained. This training, furthermore, was deferred until senior year, after bad habits had settled in during the underclass declamations, and the class time spent was "hardly equal to that allotted to Geography." Even for those with technical proficiency, the result disappointed. In his journal for 1828, Ralph Waldo Emerson wrote of his brother Charles's Harvard College valedictory address: "[h]e is a *spectacle* instead of being an *engine*: a fine show at which we look, instead of an agent that moves us." By concentrating solely on the technical aspects of his presentation, he was like someone who had "chalked around him a circle on a floor & within that he exhibits these various excellences to all the curious."[20]

The general public noticed these deficiencies: complaints about the poor rendition of orations, debates, and disputations at exhibitions and commencements had been frequent for many years. A contributor to the *New England Magazine* in 1832 voiced his objections to the delivery of preachers and public men, urging that colleges take notice. "It is but recently that they have given much attention to the subject of Eloquence, or elocution, as a science to be taught. . . . A taste for polite literature and the fine arts is becoming too general among the population of the country to allow the colleges to send forth their annual hosts of graduates for the pulpits and the forum, untaught in the most important accomplishment of a public man, without severe rebuke. Yale has already done something for improvement in the art of speaking; and Harvard—good old dull and sleepy matron, is just awaking, and rubbing her eyes, and perceives the necessity of doing a little to stop the public clamor, and shield her alumni from the reproaches of common school-boys."[21]

For training in debate, making its curricular debut as early as 1747, the procedure of "forensic disputation" (which replaced the seventeenth-century style conducted in Latin known as "syllogistic disputation") was practiced, during term time with juniors once a fortnight, and seniors every six weeks, and beginning in 1766 again for seniors at commencement. Here, the tutor or professor appointed the question, assigned the speakers and their respective sides of the question, then gave a determination and decision, usually on the merits of the question, rather than those of the disputants. The number of debaters was no greater than eight, and in the eighteenth century and the early decades of the nineteenth, the forensic disputes held in the classroom were usually written in English and then read aloud.

The written disputations for commencement received a thorough prior examination, in order to protect the trustees and audience from any intellectual and political impropriety. *The Laws of Yale College* for 1829 required the students to submit their pieces to the president and to accept whatever corrections and deletions the officials imposed. To this pattern common throughout the colonial chartered colleges for commencement exercise disputations, Yale, Harvard, and Brown all required a careful rehearsal of the "debate" before its final exhibition at the ceremony, where the forensics, although written in advance, were pronounced *memoriter*, from memory.[22]

Extemporaneous exercises were not completely absent. President Ezra Stiles's diaries for 1781 record a dispute "of the Juniors in Chapel on the Question relating to the proposed Articles of Peace—they disputed orally without writing." Indeed, the Yale Report of 1828 boasted of the "Opportunity . . . given to our classes, for full investigation and discussion of particular subjects, in the written and extemporaneous disputes, which constitute an important part of our course of exercises." Nevertheless, this refreshing change from the drudgery of the more formal and confining forensics was infrequently practiced, and although the forensic disputation lingered on in the Yale curriculum until 1883–84, the practice was already declining appreciably in the second decade of the nineteenth century. Instead of providing for twice-weekly disputes by juniors and seniors, the annual catalogue for 1822 had limited the exercise to "once or twice a week," and in 1827 there occurred the last of the regular forensic debates with two or more participants before a commencement audience.[23]

Collegians hungry for further exercises in disputation and more frequent opportunities to speak extemporaneously on topics they might name themselves were thereafter relying heavily on their three literary societies, Linonia, Brothers in Unity, and Calliope, for more frequent and self-administered debate programs. In the eighteenth century, speaking "extempore" meant well prepared but not memorized constructive speeches. The business sessions of the societies did allow some truly extemporaneous speeches in parliamentary practice, but that was about all.[24] By the 1820s, if not earlier, and not changing through their demise in the 1870s, the ancient literary societies' debates were anything but extemporaneous or even in the modern sense "debates": by then, topics were set far in advance, for the ensuing term, the speeches pro and con were written out, and then memorized for delivery. These carefully planned and written speeches exhibited comparatively little adaptation to immediately preceding arguments, particularly when the participants were less experienced members.

In response to this unsatisfactory situation, nineteen men of the class of 1831 when sophomores in 1828 formed Philagorian, whose constitutionally mandated "primary object" was "improvement in extemporaneous speaking," meeting weekly, but the club did not survive their junior year. It would not be remembered today if one of its members had not been Noah Porter, who was to be elected Yale's president four decades later (and to deplore the secret societies of that era, although he had himself as an undergraduate taken an oath of strict secrecy for the Philagorian). Even the Philagorians did not truly speak extemporaneously, nor were all compelled to speak on the same topic on the same weekly evening: their subjects were given out "two weeks before its exhibition by the disputants," of whom there were only four each meeting, named by the secretary for argument not to exceed twelve minutes each on the day.[25]

The "chambers" in the dormitories of Old Brick Row, chosen by the students in order of class rank with seniors first, were Spartan quarters: these old structures had sagging beams, bare and billowy floors, cracked ceilings, wall panels deep-furrowed by college fire pokers or marred by generations of pocket knives, and a musty odor. The second floor of each dormitory was preferred by privileged underclassmen among the seniors who almost entirely preempted it, because that level avoided the cold and damp (and drainage smell) of the first floor as well as the long walk to the upper stories. The low ceilings could be reached with the hand, the floors were bare, the heat from the coal stoves varied with the fuel supply, and dust and dirt were abundant. Entering the corridor at night was risky, for the stairs were treacherous and unlighted, gas lighting being still over twenty years away.

Bedrooms were dark, small, and unventilated. Few could afford curtains, clocks, rugs, desks, or upholstered furniture, and none could avoid going outside for a relieving visit to the "Joe," or shave or bathe (in a tin tub) other than in cold water available only from the pumps in the college yard. Each man was his own chambermaid, so beds were made once a week, or perhaps once a term. Mildew was perpetual, and drafts blew in through window casings, doors and chimney flues, while cylinder stoves and tallow candles and whale-oil lamps all fouled the air. Professor Benjamin Silliman is reputed to have said that he would not have stabled his favorite horse in such accommodations.[26] There were, of course, no common rooms or other student social facilities within the dormitories. These rude conditions go far to explain why in the early years of the senior societies, even a relative degree of comfort in their society rooms was regarded as one of the chief satisfactions of membership.

Since there were also no athletic sports or facilities (and no gymnasium until 1846, with the students importing their own trainer from New York City), practically the only legitimate avenue of escape from the monotony of the prescribed existence open to the undergraduates was the company of their fellow students and the societies they had formed or were to form. Daniel Chamberlain wrote in his senior year of 1861 that "our two rival public Literary Societies were far more influential thirty . . . years ago" [that is, in 1831], then holding "their true rank in the esteem of Students, as the second great interest of College life" after the curriculum itself. To be "first president" of Brothers or Linonia— i.e., president in the first of the school year's three terms—was to rank in honor with the valedictorian.[27]

More and more students were coming to New Haven from outside Connecticut and even New England, from the South and the Middle and Far West, while fewer and fewer of them were expecting to enter family businesses or otherwise to follow in their fathers' occupations, or to pursue careers in their birthplaces. For collegians so cut off from traditional values and sources of control, finding themselves beyond the support systems of kin and community which supported earlier generations, the process of mutual socialization fostered by the student societies took on extraordinary importance. These societies, furthermore, soon took on a hierarchical form, as those with a broader educational or political focus, beyond the merely social, coming to contain the most talented, influential, and articulate members of the student body. "In time," a modern historian has observed, "possession of a degree and membership in certain student societies came to signify more than the mastery of a body of knowledge; it was a credential of a more general kind of trustworthiness and breadth of purpose which, as the nineteenth-century economy and its political and social activities became more diverse and tumultuous, assumed particular importance, both in the view of the college men themselves and, by the end of the Civil War, in the eyes of society itself."[28]

In his memoir *Annals of Yale College* of 1834, Ebenezer Baldwin emphasized that the opportunities for student recreational association were very limited. The social organization he named "first in rank" was Phi Beta Kappa (although he waspishly notes that "as the proceedings of this society, except are their anniversaries, are not public, it is impossible to ascertain how far they have advanced the cause of learning"). He observed that membership there, of course, "exists during the lives of members," as opposed to only the shared years in college. More important in his view were the "Societies of the Students," the Linonian, Brothers in Unity, and the Calliopean (founded in 1819), into which societies all members of the class were inducted and, meeting weekly for three hours, could debate topics which were not chosen by the faculty.

"Their meetings and ordinary proceedings are private," Baldwin noted, "but strictly confined to literary pursuits, and chiefly to discussions on scientific questions. Whether the Masonic secrecy required of members is a valuable feature in these Societies, may, perhaps, be a matter of doubt: it probably was adopted with a view to inspire confidence in literary exertions, and as a shield for the modesty of young gentlemen, who might act with confidence before their friends, but would shrink under the apprehension of public criticism."[29] Despite his personal dislike of secrecy, whether in the Alpha of Connecticut or in the literary societies, Baldwin's observation of its social utility of privacy provides evidence why the students forming Skull and Bones, and the several senior societies which were founded in its wake, might find secrecy profoundly useful in their intellectual and emotional development.

THE FOUNDING OF SCULL AND BONE

The quality of the young men in the class of 1833 and their immediate successors in the senior class society which came to be known as—in its contemporary spelling—"Scull and Bones" was remarkably high. Founded by the valedictorian and class orator during his senior year, its first membership of fourteen included men who held six places in Phi Beta Kappa, the offices of class orator and class poet, two presidencies of Linonia, and three of the higher appointments in scholarship. In the ten delegations ending with that of 1842, it persisted in electing much of the intellectual and literary talent of each class, achieving in the sum total of its honors twelve presidencies of Linonia and thirteen of Brothers (there were three presidencies a year in each), five class orators and three class poets, fifty-seven places in Phi Beta Kappa, eighteen positions out of thirty on the six *Yale Literary Magazine* boards following the inception of the magazine in 1836, and an average of four of the high-stand scholarship men each year.[30]

How did this aggregation of achievers come to pass? A critic of the senior society system, writing of Skull and Bones in *Collier's* magazine some seven decades later in 1912, observed: "Its tests are democracy, accomplishment, and character. Where it differs completely from the Harvard and Princeton ideal is in the fact that it does not seek social compatibility as a basis of selection. It selects the present leaders of undergraduate activities with a view to future possible achievement, and brings an extraordinar[il]y diverse number of elements under its authority to form a representative strain of what is most vital in Yale life."[31]

Did this first society begin, as it clearly went on, with this passion for excellence? If they wanted something secret, which they could no longer find in Phi Beta Kappa, did they also, from the outset, want some other qualities in their fellow members, which Phi Beta Kappa's informal qualifications for membership did not always seek, or even recognize? Since there was no "club" of 1832 to form the fourteen-member club of 1833, what can be inferred from the biographies of those members themselves, and who did the choosing?

The conception seems to have been that of William Huntington Russell, the class valedictorian, class orator, secretary of Phi Beta Kappa, and a first president of Linonia. ("There is no office or honor in the gift of the students," wrote a Yale senior in 1860, "which is regarded higher than the first presidency of these [literary] societies in each Senior Class.") His singular importance to the new society only begins to be conveyed in a quatrain printed in an early issue of the *Yale News* that touches on his society's famous tomb, called the "T" by its initiates, and the club's identification with the Greek orator Demosthenes:

> *Our good old pater Russell*
> *In the year thirty-two or three*
> *Built a hall for the old Greek*
> *Which suited him to a T.*[32]

His military title was bestowed in 1862, when Russell was named the major general of the Militia of Connecticut. His military career followed his service in the state legislature representing New Haven in 1846–47. The scion of a family with four preceding generations in Yale College, Russell was descended from the Reverend Noadiah Russell, of Middletown (Harvard class of 1681), one of the ten ministers who founded Yale College in 1701. William Russell worked his way through Yale College, frequently walking the twenty-two miles to his hometown of Middletown, Connecticut, to save the cost of transportation. He was one of the older men of the class, being twenty-four at graduation. The lack of consistent age-grading in the college meant that natural leaders emerged from among the older and more experienced students within a class to organize student societies—and occasional rebellions.

After teaching high school in Princeton, New Jersey, for two years, he returned to Yale as a tutor, earning both an MA degree and an MD, before starting his own school in his home in 1836. He was an ardent abolitionist and a personal friend of John Brown (indeed, one of the trustees named in Brown's will). Russell's tombstone in New Haven's Grove Street Cemetery (which does not mention his Yale College class or his senior society), characterizes him successively as "teacher," "patriot," "lover of liberty," and "Christian." It notes under the first title "teacher" that more than three thousand students graduated from the Collegiate and Commercial Institute which he founded and ran in New Haven for decades, many of whose graduates matriculated at Yale. With the addition of military drill exercises, the Institute assumed the characteristics of a military school, its rating second to none except West Point itself, and over three hundred of its graduates became commissioned officers in the Northern armies of the Civil War.[33]

Russell's name was not, in later years, the best known name nationally in his senior society or his class of 1833: that honor belonged to Alphonso Taft, who finished two places behind Russell in the class scholarship rankings and delivered orations at both the Junior Exhibition and his commencement. He is the only American ever to hold the four posts of attorney general, secretary of war, and ambassador to each of Austria and Russia. This Taft was also the progenitor of one of the great Yale and Skull and Bones dynasties. Four of his sons were elected to Bones, including Peter (valedictorian of the class of 1867), William Howard (salutatorian of the class of 1878, later president of the United States), Henry (1880), and Horace (1883, founder of the Taft School). So too were grandsons Robert Alphonso (1910, to be U.S. senator from Ohio and loser of the 1952 Republican nomination for the presidency to Dwight Eisenhower) and Charles Phelps (1918).[34] In a speech given at Yale in 1909, President Taft noted that his father "walked from Vermont to Amherst College, Mass., and then he heard there was a larger college at New Haven, and he walked there."[35] Like Russell, Alphonso was a bit older than the class median, approaching twenty-three at graduation.

However great his later fame and illustrious his family, it was Russell, not Taft, who came up with the concept of the new society—indeed, Taft was among the last invited to join.

The founding of the order of Scull and Bone began with a prank, which mutated into a series of classic college bull sessions, and ended with a high educational purpose. Juniors George Ingersoll Wood and Frederick Mather, who had entered Yale as a second-term sophomore, lived during the 1831–32 school year in 28 North Middle Hall, and their classmate Russell resided on the floor above in 48 North Middle. Some time in the late summer term, according to Wood's memoir of the occasion, Russell came down to their room "draped to personate a ghost with a white sheet closely wrapped around his head and body, to frighten my roommate Mather and myself, making for the moment a decided sensation—though not one of terror." Wood could not recollect which of the three suggested that "we should organize *some kind of a secret society*, in which we should have—among other things of more importance—some *mysterious rites and ceremonies* (suggested by Russell's ghost-like appearance)." A club shrouded in secrecy would certainly have been on their minds if this gathering occurred after Russell and Wood's induction into the newly non-secret Phi Beta Kappa on June 7, 1832. Russell was thereafter elected as meeting chair and secretary for that Phi Beta Kappa election class's first meeting on July 9.

In subsequent discussions, they all "agreed upon one important point, and that was we needed the benefits of a social society which *should supplement our [Yale] College and [Linonia] Society training, by helping us to make the important acquisition of being able to think upon our feet* without the aids of retirement, pen and paper—*and especially to express at the moment whatever opinion we might have on any given topic*. That idea became the nucleus of our Club, and was subsequently embodied in our Constitution or Regulations and reduced to practice in our meetings."[36]

William Wallace Crapo, a member of the Bones club of 1852 and later a member of Congress, was to express the same thought more fully in the *Yale Literary Magazine* in 1886, in an article explaining the demise of the literary societies which the senior societies were to be damned for fatally wounding: "The elaborate written essay, learned by heart and repeated from the platform is a poor substitute for oratory. . . . There is needed the spark which comes only from a collision in the pointed reply, the fallacy exposed as soon as stated, and the argument heard for the first time and answered on the spot."[37]

To Yale students of this time, the personal importance of training in debate and oratory can hardly be overstated. Charles Astor Bristed, grandson of John Jacob Astor II and a graduate of the class of 1839, published in 1852 his two-volume work, *Five Years in an English University*, comparing (to New Haven's general disadvantage) Bristed's experience at Cambridge with his time at Yale. His trenchant observations make clear the implications for their careers of the extemporaneous-debate-seeking student founders of Skull and Bones and the successor senior societies: "[T]o speak and write well, it is said, are the great aims and requisites of the minister, the lawyer, and the political man of any sort. They are the principal means of obtaining fame and power in a free country, and therefore are the highest intellectual ends of man; that is the best education which best prepares the student for them."

Of his time as a student in the decade of Bones' founding, Bristed opined that "all students ambitious of distinction are, by common consent, divided into two classes, called in their own phraseology *scholars* and *writers*." Initially, "The [Yale] Freshman's object of reverence may perhaps be the 'Valedictorian;' but by the time he is well launched into his Sophomore year, his admiration is transferred to the 'First President' of the Brothers' or Linionian Society, the 'First Editor' of the *Yale Literary*, and the 'Class Orator.' Supposing a student to have received the 'appointment' of an Oration from the Faculty, and also to have been elected Editor of the Magazine by the students, he and his fellows would consider the latter a far greater honor than the former—so far above it that the two can hardly be put in comparison. In short," he emphasized in italics, "*the distinctions conferred by the students on one another are more prized than the distinctions conferred by the College authorities on the students.*"[38]

As a former first president of Linonia and class orator to be, Russell—in Bristed's formulation, both a "writer" and a "scholar"—was almost certainly the one who most fervently believed that the forensic disputes in the college's prescribed curriculum were deficient in failing to provide any rigorous training in extemporaneous speaking in debate. Ambitious students were beginning at the wrong end: they were acquiring manner before matter, and a style in advance of thought. Moreover, adequate criticism was lacking. "There are gathered together from thirty to one hundred young fellows," Bristed complained of the Yale literary societies, "whose capacity to criticize is not equal to their disposition, and whose disposition is modified by their interest." Negative opinions of performance seemed like jealousy, and so the loudest and most showy efforts were the most applauded. "The benefit proposed, sometimes without an attempt to disguise it to the pupil, was that [the speaker] should be able to humbug the people and get on in the world (that is the plain Saxon of it), which he was to accomplish by always being ready to talk about anything, and never be at a loss for a plausible argument."[39]

By 1832, some eighty years after the founding of Linonia, the "forensic disputations" were on set questions which were but a small part of the members' program, now including lectures, orations, dialogues, anonymous papers read by a committee, and dramatic exhibitions. The latter had become so frequent and costly that they required the maintenance of large wardrobes for the costumes. Although the exhibitions had ceased about the year 1830, their demise did not revive the debates. Only a small number of the members generally took part, with speeches which were written out (hence Wood's reference to "retirement, pen and paper") and repeated from memory.[40]

That fall, Wood had moved to No. 122 North College with his new but then-suspended roommate, Robert Robertson.[41] Sometime in October or November, the trio of Russell, Wood, and Mather, pipes in hand, held "a long talk and a social fumigation" about their thoughts in the summer term, and determined to proceed with formation of their society (years later, the satirical campus annual *The Yale*

Naughty-Gal All-Man-Ax for 1875 named September 16, 1832, as the founding date). Wood was named secretary and treasurer, and asked to prepare a draft constitution.

At the next meeting of the three, five more men were identified to join: John Campbell Beach, Noah Bishop, Asahel Lewis, Phineas Miller, and Robertson, back from his faculty suspension. Along with Russell and Wood, Beach (who went on to practice law with New York governor William Seward), Bishop, and Robertson (to be elected class poet at graduation) were all members of Phi Beta Kappa. Geographically, of the enlarged group of eight, six men were from Connecticut, one from New York, and one from Virginia. Some were friends from the literary societies, six from Linonia, including presidents Russell and Lewis, and two from Calliope, the Southerner Robertson and the New Yorker Beach. Meeting first on Christmas Eve 1832 and determined to try their powers, they each wrote down debate topics and drew a question. This was argued so vigorously it was said that the tumblers were shaken off the washstand and broken into a thousand pieces.

Another six classmates were invited to join shortly thereafter, hailing, respectively, from Massachusetts (Samuel Bates), Vermont (Alphonso Taft), Connecticut again (John Crump), South Carolina (Benjamin Franklin Davis, who had only just entered the class as a junior), Ohio (Rufus Hart), and Illinois (Samuel Marshall). The number of members, fourteen, seems to have had no special significance; although it became the following year and thereafter a fixed fifteen, the number has never attracted speculation as to its reason. The Apostles at Cambridge University were named by non-members because their founders were twelve in number, but in 1832 that club's membership tally was almost certainly unknown to the New Haveners.[42] All of the subsequent senior societies at Yale were to follow Bones' lead in selecting fifteen members each year—and earning derision on campus when they could not.

Academically then in Yale College, there were already a top fifteen: five high-stand men chosen by the faculty from each of the three divisions of the class at the end of the first term of the junior year. In this sense, the finally settled number of annual membership in Skull and Bones, a number replicated by all the senior societies to follow at Yale, both echoed and mocked the faculty-chosen hierarchy. College men placed a high value on mutuality, on the bonds that united them with each other against the faculty. They insisted that they did not share the social prejudices of their era and boasted of their "democracy." Nevertheless, while their words suggest a degree of egalitarianism, their social structure was "intensely hierarchical," in the words of the leading historian of American undergraduate culture. "What collegiate democracy meant was that college men did not fully accept the status system of the broader society [including college faculty opinion] but created their own," where oratorical and literary achievements, a sense of fair play, social grace, and in time, athletic prowess "weighed significantly." [43]

Seven of these fourteen original Bonesmen were from Connecticut (although none from New Haven), in roughly the same percentage as in the distribution of class population as a whole, and a lesser percentage, with one man from Massachusetts, than those two states' students in the aggregate of the class. The new society included as well the only two members of the class of 1833 from the Western states of Ohio and Illinois, and two of the class's seven members hailing from Southern states, in this case Virginia and South Carolina. In after-college professional or business life, the first club divided itself into five lawyers, two clergymen, one educator, three doctors, two who engaged in miscellaneous literary work, and one farmer.

By way of comparison, the geographical distribution of the class of 1833's thirty-five members of Phi Beta Kappa was markedly different: 57 percent were from Connecticut (when only 41 percent of the class was from Connecticut), and all other members resided in New York, New Jersey, and the balance of New England, excepting only one member from the West (Ohio), and two from the South (Maryland, and Virginia's Robertson). Also, two of the Bones fourteen, Mather and Davis, were transfer students into Yale from other institutions, which was seemingly a disqualification for membership in the older society.

Nor were they the closest of friends. Looking at college housing records, only Mather and Wood roomed together junior year when election was made, though they did not do so as seniors. None of the other Phi Beta Kappa members who also joined the new senior society were roommates at the time of selection. While four pairs of the 1833 Bonesmen did room together in their senior year, none had been roommates before. Finally, except for Russell, with his Yale College founder great-great-great-grandfather, and George Ingersoll Wood, whose mother was the daughter of Oliver Ellsworth, the second chief justice of the United States, none of the original fourteen can be said to be scions of the nascent American aristocracy.[44]

This is all by way of emphasizing that, whether or not Russell was the primary decision maker for the candidates for original membership— which seems unlikely, given how the group expanded over time—the choices made for Bones were much more varied, national, and "democratic" than the choices of Phi Beta Kappa drawn from the same pool of candidates. As such, the composition of the very first senior society contingent set a pattern that was to ripple far into the future, with great consequence for Yale's nationally vaunted "democracy" and great relevance to the arguments over whether the senior societies promoted or retarded that democratic culture.

Moreover, the society's founders were in a position to reinforce this pattern of values in elections to succeeding clubs, because several, ranking in the academical top fifteen, stayed on or came back to be tutors in Yale College, where two lived in each of the dormitories, or continued their studies in the legal, medical, or theological divisions of the college. For example, George Wood attended the divinity school, and after teaching high school in Princeton following his graduation, Russell returned to New Haven as a tutor from May 1835 to September 1836, the second year while studying for a medical degree in the Yale Medical School. Lyman Bagg's memoir of 1871 also tells the story that "the faculty once broke in upon one of its [the Bones] meetings, and from what they saw, determined upon its abolishment, but by the intercessions and explanations of its founder [Russell] then serving as a tutor among them, were inclined to spare it."[45]

Yale president Timothy Dwight, salutatorian of the class and member of the Bones club of 1849, then a tutor from 1851 to 1855, before leaving for further study abroad, found in retrospect that his senior society graduate membership was a positive advantage when tutoring. "With reference to the friendly relations between the younger members of the Faculty and the students," he remembered, "I think that in these years the smaller and secret societies began to exert an influence of a special character. These societies, during the larger portion of my tutorial career, drew into their fraternal fellowship, more fully and frequently than they had done before, their members who were already graduates, and, among them, those who had been appointed to officers of instruction in the College. An opportunity was thus opened for a very free and unrestrained intercourse, from time to time, between the teachers and their pupils. The two parties were easily rendered able to understand each other's thoughts and feelings, and to gain, each from the other, opinions or suggestions which might have the best and happiest influence. . . . [S]uch opportunities . . . gave me the knowledge of the student mind, as well as a familiar and friendly acquaintance with the ideas and sentiments of individual student."[46]

Alphonso Taft was also a tutor, from 1835 to 1837, studying at Yale Law School the second academic year. His students included two men in the famous class of 1837, both to be Bones members, the future chief justice of the United States, Morrison Waite, and the future attorney general and secretary of state, William Maxwell Evarts. When, at the tender age of thirty-three, Alphonso's son William Howard Taft became the solicitor general of the United States, Evarts called upon him on Taft's first morning in his Washington office, inviting the astonished young man to dinner that night, and saying of Alphonso, "he was a tutor there in my time, and I valued his friendship very highly."[47]

Two other Bonesman in the founding class of 1833 also spent time in New Haven after graduation. Frederick Ellsworth Mather studied law at Yale in the 1834–35 academic year, and Phineas T. Miller studied medicine in New Haven immediately after graduating and practiced as a doctor there until 1849, where in the later years he ran the city's General Hospital. While neither was formally a tutor, both probably helped nurture the new society's successive clubs toward a constant standard of rewarding excellence in Yale College achievement (while, more prosaically, Dr. Miller was in a position to contribute a hospital skeleton to the rooms of the fledgling organization).[48]

Still, before the molding of men, there had to be the making of traditions. As Avery Allyn said in his inflammatory book on the Masons, Phi Beta Kappa had "its secret obligation, sign, grip, word, and jewel." He included for emphasis a plate showing the society's "Sign" between members for mutual recognition; the "Grip," which was a handshake variation; and "Both sides of the Medal."[49] The young men in the Yale senior societies which followed were not to be denied their own variations on these themes.

On traditions which must be invented, Professor Noah Porter, who had been in both Phi Beta Kappa and Philagorian when each had all these features of secrecy, noted in his book on American colleges that "This community has its traditions, which are represented to be sacred by age and uniform observance; its customs, which are so ancient that the memory of man runneth not to the contrary, i.e., for one college generation. . . . It is eminently a law unto itself, making and enforcing such laws as no other community would recognize or understand; laws which are often strangely incongruous with the usually received commandments of God and Man. . . . Its social customs, laws, and criteria, are the products of its isolated and peculiar life, and are an unsolved mystery to all other societies."[50] Perhaps there exists no better proof of Porter's observation on a college generation's memory than the testimony of a member of the class of 1844 at Yale, published only a decade after Skull and Bones was founded: "The Skull and Bone Society is of quite an ancient origin. It is one of the most secret associations in the Institution [the college]."[51]

For the new senior society at Yale, the quintet of characteristics making impact on the campus was not the Allyn quintet of "secret obligation, sign, grip, word, and jewel," but rather, the public symbol, badge, catalogue, code, and election method. Both existing Yale societies, Phi Beta Kappa and the short-lived Chi Delta Theta, founded in 1821 and expiring by 1844, and taking in about a quarter of the senior class, had identifying ornaments, and these could be created immediately to make the society's mark in the college community. The other features would take a bit more time to develop and make impressive. At the outset, the new society met in rented rooms. By 1842, it had settled in a commercial building occupied by Linonia numbered 460 Chapel, located just west of the corner of College and Chapel Streets, holding its weekly meetings up the stairs from and to the rear of the larger room used by the literary society. (The famous High Street "tomb" would only be built much later, in 1856.)

The founders of Scull and Bone did not adopt an elaborate statement of principles and rules on the order of Phi Beta Kappa's, with which they were most familiar as officers and members of the Alpha of Connecticut. In the words of Lyman Bagg, "[The society] is believed to have little or no regard for any formal, written constitution, but to be governed chiefly by tradition in its customs and usages." This judgment was echoed in an 1876 pamphlet, titled *The Fall of Skull and Bones*, written by the "Order of the File and Claw," which claimed to have broken into the Bones tomb: "Skull and Bones has no secrets beyond a few that may be handed down annually by word of mouth, and no written constitution beyond a few directions similar to the suggestions appended to the [freshman society] Delta Kappa by-laws."[52] To the creation of their customs and usages they turned.

THE PUBLIC SYMBOL

The young men in No. 122 North College cared more about the raison d'être of their society than its name, and seem not to have selected one when Wood, as secretary, was asked to post a notice of a meeting in the customary place. "When I wrote the first Notice for a meeting of the Club, to be put up on the side of the Chapel door[,]" he recalled with italicized emphasis, "I sketched over the notice a *Skull & Cross-bones*—the thought of the moment—simply to attract attention and make a sensation among outsiders! Which it did very decidedly and excited a great deal of talk among the students. *The Skull & Bones had no real significance whatsoever.* I put this device on every subsequent notice during the year [1832–33], and so it came to be a permanent badge of the Club."[53]

So, Russell's prank with the ghostly white sheet in the summer of 1832, which perhaps subconsciously inspired Wood's invention of the notice's symbol the following winter, impressed upon the new society a name which, for all its lack of forethought, changed the course of society nomenclature at Yale. However unplanned, the Bonesmen's incorporation of the symbol in their formal campus publication printings had a similar effect, in making the new group's name not Greek letters but (as it was to be printed in the *Yale Banner*) the American-sounding "Scull and Bone Society." This formulation was to influence the name of its immediate successor Scroll and Key, and all the Yale senior societies which came after.

The Yale senior societies' imitators to come on other campuses aped the naming style: "Axe and Coffin" at Columbia College, "Owl and Padlock" at the University of Michigan, "Skull and Serpent" and "Owl and Wand" at Wesleyan University, Dartmouth's "Sphinx," and Georgetown's "Second Society of Stewards," but the trend finally went no further. As Bagg was to conclude in 1872: "There is no special difficulty in imitating the peculiar names and mummeries of the Yale senior societies, but the gaining of a similar prestige and influence is quite another matter. It is the high character of their members, not their names and forms and ceremonies, which give the Yale societies their fame."[54] It was decided by its members as early as 1834 that there would be no chapters of the Order of Scull and Bone at other colleges.

The spelling "scull" was neither illiterate nor meant to be provocative. From the first edition of Noah Webster's *An American Dictionary of the English Language* in 1828, through the edition of 1850, the word is spelled "scull," to mean "the brain pan" (although Webster also includes the spelling "skull," with essentially the same definitions). The inclusion of the alternate spellings was not the result of Webster's desire to reform English orthography for Americans, but rather arose from his cut-and-paste method of dictionary making: both spellings are employed in the eighth edition of Samuel Johnson's *A Dictionary of the English Language* (1799), a copy of which Webster marked up for his own dictionary's text.[55]

Linonia, the original Yale College literary society of 1753, was named for the goddess of the flax, λίνον, the pagan divinity most familiar to those days of homespun.[56] Since virtually all other fraternities formed in the 1830s in America were Greek-letter societies, like their progenitor Phi Beta Kappa and including Yale's own Chi Delta Theta of 1821,[57] common English words based on Wood's sketch inadvertently characterized the new club to be a different thing. The spelling of "scull" could not have escaped the influence of the great American lexicographer in any event. Webster was a member of the Yale class of 1778 (graduating two years before the creation of the Alpha of Connecticut, although subsequently made an honorary member of Phi Beta Kappa), living at the time in New Haven on Temple Street, where Silliman College now stands, writing his dictionary when Skull and Bones was founded.

In 1832, there were no Yale undergraduate publications that discussed student current affairs. Although the *Yale Literary Magazine* was to be founded in 1836 by some men who later joined Bones, it did not treat of such subjects, as its name indicated. It is to the yearly *Yale Banner* we must turn for contemporary reporting. A four-page newspaper, the *Banner* began in 1841 as a result of the firemen's riot of that year, then stopped after four numbers, only to reappear in November 1842. That edition contained a catalogue of the members of college and of several senior societies. It appeared annually thereafter, both as a catalogue of the names of the students in all departments and a record of college honors and associations.[58]

The issue of November 3, 1842, listed as the first society at the top of its left-hand column the "Scull and Bone Society." In the issue of 1846, this became the "Skull and Bone Society;" in 1847, the spelling reverted to "Scull;" in 1850, it became "Scull and Bones," and not until the issue of October 1, 1852, did the society's name become the now familiar "Skull and Bones."[59] However spelled, the club's name and its symbols were (at least mildly) frightening, just as Wood confessedly intended in choosing them.

THE BADGE

The Bones "badge" was the analog to Allyn's Phi Beta Kappa "jewel." As noted in the *History of the Class of 1834 of Yale College*, printed in 1875 as part of the fortieth reunion celebrations by the class succeeding Russell's: "The senior society known as 'The Skull and Bones' first took a recognized form in our class by the wearing of a badge by its members, and perpetuated itself by electing members from the next class." (The same narrative records that "the Phi Beta Kappa Society had a nominal existence, but hardly any exercises were held by our class," which suggests not only that the Bones members had decided to become more ostentatious, but that the society's creation had seriously wounded the vitality of Phi Beta Kappa.)[60]

Wearing a badge, in such a small membership group, avoided the need for a secret handshake, or "grip." From Phi Beta Kappa on in the history of American fraternities, the grip allowed fraternity men to verify that a stranger was a brother, as all men in the same fraternity would have the same secret grip. If a man was not wearing his badge, or it was suspected (as was to happen in Yale College history) that the badge was false, all one had to do was shake his hand in order to confirm his membership.[61] The public sporting of senior society badges at Yale, and the lack of chapters at other colleges which would bring unknown members to annual conventions, meant that no tradition of secret grips was to be part of the senior society experience.

The Phi Beta Kappa medal at Yale was closely modeled on the one brought north from Virginia by Elisha Parmele. It was a watch-key, to be worn on a watch chain, silver and square, with "S P" (Societas Philosophia) and the date of December 5, 1776, on one side, and on the reverse, the Greek letters for Phi Beta Kappa, with three stars above, and a hand with a pointing index figure below, topped by a ribbon-like device. Chi Delta Theta (ΧΔΘ), founded in 1821 and expiring in 1844, to which approximately one-quarter to one-third of the senior class was elected, also had an ornament, in the form of a triangular gold pendant.[62] The men of Scull and Bone opted for something simpler.

The society's badge evolved from a flat, square breastpin used through 1848 to the three-dimensional "crab" known since that time. "Its badge of solid gold," Bagg recorded in 1871, "consists of the face of a skull, supported by the crossed thigh bones, with a band, bearing the number '322,' in place of the lower jaw. Its original badge was a rectangular gold plate, about the size and shape of the present Beta Xi pin, whereon the skull-and-bones design and the numeral were simply engraved. Its wood-cut vignette represents the emblems, and is identical with that employed for general purposes in college papers elsewhere. . . . In the cut formally used, the design was smaller than that now in vogue; but there never had been added to the simple emblems anything in the way of ornament or embellishment. The pin is sometimes called a 'crab' from its supposed resemblance to that animal."[63]

The badge was constantly worn by active members, by day upon the shirt bosom or necktie, and by night upon the nightgown. By the third quarter of the nineteenth century, only graduate members wore the badge upon the vest, where for the first few years they displayed it quite regularly; members of the faculty, except the occasional freshman tutors, never displayed a society badge when engaged in their official duties. The *Yale Courant* in 1873 jibed that "the Skull and Bones man worships his death's head and cross bones, as a devout Catholic adores the cross." In her 2006 novel *Secret Society Girl*, Diana Peterfreund captured the paradox of combined display and secrecy: "[O]ur pat little phrases, our *I can't talk about its* and our *I'd tell you but I'd have to kill you*s are a society member's way of bragging without breaking the oath of secrecy."[64]

Rituals, in Skull and Bones and the other senior societies to come, like rituals in in human affairs generally, have a function more likely to be experienced than to be reasoned upon. Romancing couples dining with candlesticks and crystal, suitors on bended knees with rings in hand, or a club's members meeting for regular dinners uniformly dressed in required attire are unlikely to reflect at length on why they are performing these rituals. Nevertheless, they sense that, as lovers, suitors, or just hungry human beings, they perform them not as necessary elements of the romantic dinner, the marriage proposal, or the club gathering, but as essential particulars of human interaction.

Indeed, it has been argued that doctrines exist as much for the sake of rituals as the rituals do for the sake of doctrines. While doctrines can divide, rituals help assimilate doctrines into forms by which they could be experienced, perhaps even better than they can be logically understood. The ritual and symbolic elements of secret societies generally are very important; the wide and long enduring diffusion of a Masonic element seems to go far beyond the point at which any merely utilitarian purpose could be served by borrowing. In the realm of the Yale senior societies, candidates are not queried on their views of the doctrines or tenets of the association, but instead are firmly but tacitly presented with and trained in the means of experiencing what they might learn of those doctrines, through those rituals.[65]

Such rituals soon attached to the display of badges. They were worn in the center of the cravat when photographs of individuals began to be taken for club records in 1856, and they featured in the young men's *carte de visite* engravings from 1852. The *College Courant* for July 3, 1869, noted that, following their initiation the night before, the "newly fledged [senior society members] don their pins at ten this morning." The Bones pin was removed from the shirtfront or necktie and shifted to the waistcoat in the 1887–88 class year, and the annual campus journal *The Horoscope* commended the society for being "the first to notice and to remedy" this sign of "ostentatious bearing" (while the men of Scroll and Key continued to wear their badges on their neckties). The earliest national magazine report is found in *Munsey's* for June 1894, declaring that the Bones badge was then worn "on the lower left side of the waistcoat," and that "even the most bewitching young woman is warned not to make any remark about [a Yale man's] badge (which, by the way, is supposed never to leave his person, even during a bath, when it is carried in his mouth) for the student will feel compelled to receive your question in absolute silence."[66]

The badge fetish had not changed much halfway through the twentieth century. The *Harvard Lampoon* for November 1949 contained George Plimpton's article on Yale's secret societies. Plimpton reported that "the Skull and Bones insists that the member must constantly wear his Society badge or pin. It is said that member will wear it on his pajamas at night, hold it in his hand or pop it in his mouth when taking a shower."[67] In 1913, the *Lampoon* had mocked the Bonesmen's habit of secreting the badge in the mouth to keep the hands free, in a poem published following Harvard's 15–5 victory over Yale in that fall's football game. Explaining the Elis' loss, this chronicled the misfortune of the mythical (but name-rhymable) "Sir Arthur Jones/The mightiest of the knights of Yale/A member—Sh!—of Bones":

> *The pass went high; it struck his lips*
> *And bared his gleaming pin—*
> *A rush of air was heard and then,*
> *The ball lay, punctured in,*
> *A murmur ran around the stands—*
> *"Thus Harvard's warriors win."*

A true and sadder story of a Bonesman and his badge also has a Harvard connection. The great American literary scholar F. O. Matthiessen graduated from Yale in 1923, where he was managing editor of the *Yale Daily News*, editor of the *Yale Literary Magazine*, and vice president of

Dwight Hall; "F.O." won the Alpheus Henry Snow Prize as the out-standing senior, was class orator, and went on to Oxford University as a Rhodes scholar.[68] Having suffered depression before while writing his 1941 masterpiece of literary criticism, *American Renaissance*, he was on leave of absence from his position as a professor of English literature at Harvard in 1950. On April 1 of that year, he leaped to his death from a window on the twelfth floor of Boston's Manger Hotel. Investigators later concluded that he had taken his badge from his shirt and left it on the dresser. "Then suddenly remembering that it should never leave his person, he refastened it to his shirt and content in the knowledge that he who was about to die had saluted, he went to the open window and jumped. The policeman who arrived on the scene not long afterwards found the pin beside the body, glanced at it indifferently, and put it with the rest of the deceased's effects . . ."[69]

The Matthiessen suicide is not, however, the most remarkable story of a Skull and Bones badge at a member's death. That sad distinction belongs to Edward Foster Blake, a New Haven native of the class of 1858, editor of the *Lit.*, an athlete with artistic ability, and winner of the Third English Composition prize. One of thirty-seven students from the North in his class to enlist for the Union, he entered service in October 1861 and was commissioned adjutant of the 5th Connecticut infantry. By early 1862 he was campaigning in the Shenandoah Valley. On June 12 Blake was promoted to major; after a short furlough, he returned to his regiment and was killed in Virginia at the battle of Cedar Mountain on August 9, 1862. His body was never recovered. An imprisoned brother officer later reported that near where he had lain wounded, the corpse of a dead major was rifled by an enemy officer. The Confederate showed him what he had taken, which included a gold skull and crossbones pin.[70]

As so often in the mirrored histories of Yale's two oldest senior soci-eties, there is a Scroll and Key story to match. William H. Vanderbilt of the class of 1893, grandson of Commodore Cornelius Vanderbilt, according to newspaper reports pledged Scroll and Key in his junior year, but died of typhoid fever two days before the afternoon of Tap

Day; his class elected to wear mourning for thirty days. While his name does thus not appear in the society's catalogue for the club of 1893, the young man was buried with a Keys badge on his person. In his memory, William's parents donated Vanderbilt Hall (erected 1894), costing half a million dollars and acclaimed as the "finest and most expensive dormitory in the world."

This ornament of the Gilded Age boasted wainscoted living rooms, modern plumbing, manteled fireplaces, and steam heat, connected to a campus-wide system (by 1899, Yale charged $10 a week to live in Vanderbilt, and 75 cents a week to live in the Old Brick Row dormitories). When women were at last admitted to Yale College in 1969, the administration housed them, not least for security, in Vanderbilt Hall, where the only entrance from the Old Campus to which it turns its back is though a central arch (since the staircase entries fronted on Chapel Street and the street-front driveway gates were always locked).[71] Thus, the line from the old Yale to the new ran through a senior society membership, redeemed in the grave when frustrated in life.

THE CATALOGUE

Another feature of Phi Beta Kappa was its production of membership catalogues. The Alpha of Connecticut published its first printed booklet in 1808, a second in 1818, and another in 1832, with which Russell and his Bones cofounders would have been immediately familiar. The Yale format was fairly plain, simply listing members alphabetically (the deceased's names asterisked), organized into columns headed "Names," "Places of Abode," "Col Title" (senior, junior, or A.B.), and "Time of admission," the latter by month, day, and year. This arrangement was adopted for the Phi Beta Kappa national catalogue in 1811, and then altered in 1839 to order the names by classes and omitting the college titles.[72]

The catalogue for Scull and Bones, the first of which was printed in 1841, and used thereafter annually to check attendance at the annual

conventions, was more intriguingly designed and mysteriously anno-
tated. It was distributed to members in unbound sheets, and the first
page displayed, in Old English capitals in a semi-oval between two
black lines, the letters OTIRUNBCDITF. The members were listed
by the class years, anticipating the change still to come in the Phi Beta
Kappa national catalogues. The pages were printed on one side only,
each six inches by four, sized to be glued on to blank pages added by
the recipient to his bound volume. Each right-hand page, surrounded
by a heavy black border, listed the members of the year, fifteen names
written out alphabetically and in full, with city and state of residence,
all in Old English text.[73]

The title page bore the society cut, with the words "Period 2.
Decade 3." preceding the list of the founders of the club of 1833. In
succeeding issues, there appears a similar set of phrases: for example,
"Period 2. Decade 4." heads the page for the class of 1843, and so on for
each successive decade, the "Period" always being "2," but the integer
for "Decade" increasing each time by one. So, for the class of 1851, the
legend is "P. 249.—D.49," and for the class of 1967, "P.365.—D.165"—the
"D" being always two less than the year of graduation. Put another way,
the "D" of a club is always 1,802 less than the class year. Bagg's memoir
half-translated and half-speculated: "What these 'Periods' and 'Decades'
and 'P.s' and 'D.s' may signify is known only to the initiated; but, as the
catalogue is never shown to outsiders, they are probably not put there
for mystification only. That the founders are put down as belonging to
the 'third decade of the second period' may seem to make in favor of
the German university theory [that Yale's club was a chapter of a European society], in the minds of many; and the blank space in place of the
eleventh man's name in the list of the founders, may perhaps be thought
a straw in the same direction."

Official notices to the graduate members were written upon black-
bordered paper of the catalogue's size, with or without the society cut at
the head, and the Bones notices through the mails were enclosed in black-
edged envelopes, bearing at the end a printed request to the postmaster

to return them to the society's post-office box if not delivered within a certain time, and sealed with a skull and bones and the letters "S.C.B." (Skull and Cross Bones) impressed upon black wax.[74]

THE CODE

Codes and ciphers are techniques for disguising a message so that only the intended recipient can read it. The non-member readers of Bones-generated literature—its catalogues, campus posters, invitations, and other notices to members—were provoked with seeing initials and numbers that are otherwise nowhere defined, as in the "Ps" and "Ds" heading each club's annual list of members.

On its printed ephemera such as invitations to the annual convention held on the evening of commencement and on other communications has always appeared the number "322," deemed by most commentators to mean "the year 322 B.C.," although "B.C." nowhere appears. That supposition, wrote Bagg, "connects it with the names of Alexander or Demosthenes. What these heroes may have in common with the Skull and Bones society, aside from departing this life on or just before the year in question, is not very plain; but it is pretty well established that the Bones' '322' refers to that year B.C., whatever its additional significance." 322 B.C. is indeed the accepted date of Demosthenes's death. Other theories hold that the number signifies the year of the society's founding, "1832;" or that it is "3+2+2" or "7" which is said to be the number of founders of the class of 1833 (actually, the Phi Beta Kappa six), who persuaded the other eight to join them; or that it is the product of "3 × 2 × 2," or "12," the midnight hour of the meetings' breaking up.[75] Even the street number on High Street—64—can be part of this game (32 × 2).

Skull and Bones could not plausibly claim an origin legend, but the appropriation of "322" had something of that effect. Legendary accounts of the antiquity of origins of the orders themselves are common characteristics of secret societies and, as sociologist Noel Gist has written, are "perhaps no more chimerical or grotesque than those sometimes associated with the beginnings of such well-established institutions as the church and the state. In all instances they may be thought of as unifying influences; and whether taken literally or symbolically they represent the collective property of the group and add to its cohesiveness and its permanence."[76]

The society even claimed its own system of time. On the mornings of Yale commencement in the nineteenth century, at the head of the editorial columns of the New Haven daily newspapers appeared public announcements of "The annual convention of the Order," with the date followed by "VI. S.B.T." Bagg insisted that "a current guess—and a wrong one—interprets 'S.B.T.' as 'Skull and Bones Temple.' A more likely reading makes 'T.' stand for 'time,' and so interprets the notice, 'Six minutes before eight,' the hour eight being 'Bones time.' The meetings are held on Thursday evening, commencing exactly at eight o'clock. . . ." (Thursdays may have ultimately been chosen as the weekly meeting night because Wednesday evenings were taken up by the literary society meetings, which all were expected to attend.) In his 1949 article on the Yale secret societies written for the *Harvard Lampoon*, George Plimpton published another speculation. "If at 12:00 A.M. one Bones man asks another the time, he is answered 'It's 12:05 S.B.T.', meaning its 12:05 Skull and Bones time. Whether the Bonesmen consider themselves five minutes ahead of the rest of mankind or the grandfather clock in the Bones tomb has been five minutes fast for over a hundred years is a matter for conjecture."[77]

The society's code words were ways to intrigue and confound outsiders, styled "neutrals" by campus publications, as was its signature number, "322," but there was an adopted language as well, with a different end to achieve within the society. Meeting in a "temple," initiates are "knights," and graduate members are "patriarchs," a term first used in the records of a meeting in 1836: "Several of the Patriarchs visited the Club this evening, and they and ourselves discussed a cold collation with great vigor. We would recommend all succeeding generations to *treat* the Patriarchs when honored with their company." The tone of welcome was more tempered in the records for 1850: "The famished Patriarchs favored us with their presence, drank our coffee, devoured our oysters, and departed as they came."

Among members, the society was known as the "Eulogian Club,"[78] leading to the internal circumlocution sometimes found repeated in their correspondence to Yale newspapers, referring to the society as the "so-called Skull and Bones." Sometimes in campus periodicals its members were styled "Eulogians" ("eulogia" is Greek for "a blessing," and is applied in ecclesiastical usage to the object blessed; in the Benedictine Rule, monks are forbidden to receive "*litteras, eulogias, vel quaelibet munuscula*" without the abbot's leave, with "eulogias" translated as a blessing, but seeming to mean any kind of present[79]). The nomenclature of Skull and Bones has a Greek flavor, as that of Scroll and Key was in contradistinction to be Roman, and Wolf's Head, in its own choice, Egyptian, each group appropriating its special version of antiquity of origin. Outsiders, reflecting the classification made in the ancient Greek language (*barberoi*) and literature the students were compelled to study, were called "barbarians," in contradistinction to the Bonesmen's self-styled Greeks.[80]

In this, too, the young men of Scull and Bone were absorbing what was in the air, as well as in their prepatory education. For this class, *The Laws of Yale College* for 1832 mandated that "no one shall be admitted, unless he shall be able to read, translate, and parse Cicero's Select Orations, Virgil, Sallust, Graeca Minor, and the Greek Testament." Beyond this, the cult of Greece—Philhellenism—was a romantic manifestation of considerable influence at the time, in painting, poetry, and architecture. Beginning in the early years of the nineteenth century, Americans "renounced their tenacious attachment to republican Rome and turned to the art, literature, and landscape of Greece. . . . Greece now emerged as the province of the spiritual and the ideal, the seat of art and learning, representing what was at once unique and universally true." The dichotomy between Greece and Rome that emerged in the antebellum era was summed up in Edgar Allan Poe's poem "To Helen" of 1831, celebrating being "brought . . . home/To the glory that was Greece/

and the grandeur that was Rome." The romantic English poet George Gordon, Lord Byron, had famously gone off to fight in the Greek War for Independence from the Ottomans, dying at Missolonghi in 1824.[81]

The city of New Haven itself participated in the vogue by organizing a fund-raising campaign to establish better schools for Greek children, and the town's litterateur of the 1820s and 1830s, James Gates Percival, wrote poetic pleas in the Byronic manner for the independence of Greece. The students of Yale College contributed $500 to a New York committee raising funds to aid the beleaguered Hellenes against "their barbarous assailant" the Turks. As late as 1834, New Haveners were still interested in "the cause," with crowds attending the lectures of Mr. G. A. Pedicaris on "Modern Greece." Seizing upon Greek civilization as thematic inspiration for coded but inspiring references was a simple matter for a college club initially dedicated to training itself in extemporaneous speech techniques.

As for Demosthenes, in 1805 his work was added to the Yale curriculum's volumes of the best Greek authors, *Graeca Minora* and *Graeca Majora*. For the junior class, until 1875, Demosthenes was included with Homer, Herodotus, Plato, Sophocles, and others in the study of Greek authors—but only Demosthenes was famous for arduous training to make himself a better speaker. By 1829, the course of instruction in Professor Goodrich's class on rhetoric for seniors showcased the "Oration of Demosthenes for the Crown," as "the chef d'oeuvre of ancient eloquence." A life-size statue of Demosthenes, carved in Rome by E. S. Bartholomew, was placed in the corner of Linonia's room in Alumni Hall.[82] The Bonesmen were not always so reverent toward their oratorical hero: a question that is often repeated in their records is, "How did Demosthenes have such numerous progeny when he carried his stones in his mouth?"

Still, the tags abounding on the public notices were in Latin, befitting their intense grounding in that language, usually with puns on the word *bonum*, for "good," such as these legends on invitations to the annual conventions: "*Nisi in bonis amicitia esse not potest*" ("No friendship can exist except in good men," from Cicero, *De Amicitia*, 5, I); "*Grandiaque*

effosis mirabitur ossa sepulchris" ("He will wonder at the huge bones when
[their] tombs have been dug up," from Virgil, Georgics, I. 497); and
"Quid dicam de ossibus?" Cic. N.D.2; 55 *Nil nisi bonum.* Prov." ("What
should I say about the Bones? Nothing except good.")[83] Translation was
not difficult for on-campus readers and graduates: Yale did not abolish
the Latin requirement for applicants and degree awards until 1931.[84]

As an internal code, not Greek-inspired, each member bears a nickname within the tomb, to be used only within the society hall and never
outside its walls, by which he (and now she) is known to his initiated
classmates. Some knights are assigned traditional names by the outgoing
seniors ("Magog," the junior purportedly most experienced with women,
and "Gog," the least likely to have been sexually successful; "Long
Devil," the delegation's tallest member, whose duties after the formation of Scroll and Key included posting his society's notice of meeting
above the Keys notice on the chapel door; "Little Devil," the shortest;
and "Boaz," the varsity football captain). Magogs have included, in their
respective years, William Howard Taft (1878), his son Robert A. Taft
(1910), and Olympic swimming champion Donald Schollander (1968).
Legendary football coach Amos Alonzo Stagg and Harvard professor
Matthiessen were Little Devils.

Others, not so distinguished by physical characteristics or prior leadership positions, choose their own knightly titles. The romantic period
of literature which encompassed the birth of the society produced, particularly in the 1850s and 1860s, a long list of high-flown pseudonyms,
with members named Harold, Sidney, Arthur, Charlemagne, Launfel,
Endymion, and Delores. Rowdier names, such as Caliban, Brombones,
Dingbat, and Suffering Mike then elbowed aside the earlier titles. The
literary taste of the mid–nineteenth century, exemplified by Rob Roy,
Roderick, Waverly, Dombey, Pickwick, Toby Weller, Barkis, and Jingle,
gave way to the underworld in the characters of Moloch, Beelzebub,
Mephistopheles, Moloch, Pluto, Charon, Baal (Henry Luce's name in
1920), and Caliban (his clubmate Briton Hadden's), and to the majesty of
the warring north with Odin, Thor, Tancred, Rollo, and Eric the Red.

Vietnam War historians were thrilled to learn that McGeorge Bundy, Bones 1940 and national security advisor to Presidents Kennedy and Johnson, styled himself "Odin," for the Norse god of war (as well as, the erudite Bundy might have observed, of poetry, wisdom, and the dead). It is said George W. Bush, the second President Bush, whose father George H. W. was "Barebones," chose "Temporary," when he could initially think of nothing else.[85]

THE ELECTION

The most famous of Russell's innovations for his society and ultimately for Yale College was the method, in the words of the class history of 1834 quoted above, of the group's "perpetuat[ing] itself by electing members from the next class." Belden's *Sketches of Yale College* of 1843, published by an undergraduate a decade after the founding of Bones and a year after the creation of Scroll and Key, contains a discussion of the badgeless "College Societies" of the Linonian, the Brothers in Unity, and the Calliopean, but also contains a subsequent section on "Class Societies," naming Phi Beta Kappa, Chi Delta Theta, Skull and Bones, Scroll and Key, and other senior societies (soon vanished) called Sword and Crown, and Dart and Star, with cuts of the badges of each.[86] However, the election process for these senior societies, as opposed to the characteristics of their members, is not described in Belden's book.

Instead we must, and presumably safely can, assume that the election was offered to each of those fifteen of the very first successor club of 1834, from a list developed and then pared down by the seniors, on one or more evenings, who were approached by a representative of the society, or perhaps a substantial delegation of members. In the chapter titled "Forerunners of Tap Day" his *Yale Yesterdays* of 1915, Clarence Deming ruefully noted that "What one seeks of their antique customs must be taken not from the published word but from the lips and memories of old graduates who, some of them, recall the Yale happenings of a half-century or more ago."[87]

Still, there are two published records, predating Deming's book, in the *Yale Alumni Weekly*. The first, in the issue of June 25, 1905, was a letter from "A Graduate of the [Eighteen] Seventies." "When one society was alone in the field [meaning Scull and Bone]," he wrote, "its election was held on a movable day on which each elected Junior was summoned with elaborate privacy to meet a representative of the society at a secret tryst, not earlier than midnight. This had no significance above the rites of other societies and was harmless, if unnecessary, until another society [Scroll and Key] came into the field." The second, "Forerunners of Tap Day," an anonymous article published in May 1910, told of how "[a]fter the Society lists had been made a whole night was spent in the election. And next morning the Societies marched from their halls in a body to Chapel, partly as a bit of impressionism, partly as a kind of theoretical covering of their work by a quasi-religious function."[88]

Since there were no other societies for the senior class graduating in 1834 except Phi Beta Kappa, which still elected its new members in scheduled meetings, and Chi Delta Theta, the "Graduate of the Seventies" may not have been cognizant of how few societies existed in Yale College fully four decades before his own time, and was probably entirely too casual in finding "no significance above the rites of other societies." Surely midnight meetings that resulted in the newly elected sporting their badges the morning after would have attracted keen interest on campus. In any event, elections seem to have been proffered quietly and privately, mostly by word of mouth and without any special etiquette. Notes were distributed by both Skull and Bones and, after 1842, Scroll and Key—"Sir, you are a candidate. By order of our order," or "Sir, you have the honor of being selected," and signed with the name of the respective club secretary—but these were customarily given out on the following day.[89]

The "movable day" did not long stay movable. From at least July 1842 until Bagg's time in the late 1860s, senior society elections were given out in the period from eight to ten P.M. on the Thursday evening in late May or early June which preceded Presentation Day.[90] This was a campus ceremony where the names of candidates recommended by the faculty for the degrees were "presented" to the college president and Yale Corporation, and occurred in June or early July, six weeks before commencement. (It was celebrated in much the same way as its successor at Yale, the modern Class Day, "as a kind of 'domestic commencement,' without the heat and bustle of the Commencement proper.") The seniors left the college at the middle of the third term, being on vacation until commencement, which did not occur for them until August or September.[91]

The election of juniors to Phi Beta Kappa, which most likely provided the timing template for the six members of that Greek-letter fraternity who decided to found Scull and Bone, took place in June. The Junior Exhibition was mounted in April, and juniors who had received high marks and were thus invited to speak used it to demonstrate what they could do in speeches before the president and faculty and friends. The program, which consumed the entire day, featured some thirty-five to forty items, of which a dozen were music (a band played) and the balance were orations, dissertations, and poems in Latin, Greek, or English. An irreverent son of Alphonso Taft was later to say "the first time father ever wore store clothes was at the Junior Ex."[92]

The society's outgoing seniors would want, as they do today, some overlapping time with their newly elected neophytes to teach them customs and traditions. Thus, it seems probable that the day—or rather night—of election, after the working up of a list of candidates in meetings of the senior club, was a function of the Yale College adminstration's forecast date for Presentation Day in June. It also seems probable that such event was occurring on that periodic basis within a few years of 1833, if not that very first year of election by the outgoing club of Scull and Bone. This reasoned reconstruction, if correct, provides a historical basis for the scheduling of Tap Day for late May or early June, as it became more elaborate, involving more societies and more participants. By 1849, the formal notice of election from Bones, sealed with black wax, was on black-bordered stationery (watermarked "Paris"!) enclosing the cut of the skull and crossed femurs, beneath which was the handwritten note of the outgoing club's secretary: "Sir, You are a Candidate. By Order of our Order."

If election for Scull and Bone was some sort of judgment day in the spring of the year, what were the outward and visible signs of intellectual and social distinction? There were then, in a class of fewer than ninety souls, no ongoing campus publications (the *Yale Literary Magazine* was not to be founded until 1836, the *Yale Banner* until 1841, and the *Yale [Daily] News* until 1878); no Greek-letter fraternities other than Phi Beta Kappa and the somewhat smaller Chi Delta Theta; and no faculty-awarded prizes for performance or scholarship named for alumni donors, as were to come later in the nineteenth century with the Townsend Premiums for English Composition (1844) and DeForest Prize for English Oration (1852). There were no heroes of organized sports: crew, in emulation of the eights of Oxford and Cambridge, did not begin until the 1850s, and "base-ball" competitions with the "nines" and football games with the "twenties" until the 1870s.[93]

Instead, in 1833, the first and foremost individual distinction as a basis for society election was a man's "stand" in the junior class, high marks in the grading system which first began in American higher education at Yale in 1813 on the now familiar 4.0 or 400 point scale. President Woolsey is credited with having instituted the "biennial" at Yale in 1830, "a much dreaded period of written examination at the close of the sophomore and senior years in all studies of the two preceding years." A stand of 2.50 or above was required for faculty appointment at the Junior Exhibition. A student not maintaining an average of 2 in all his classes in a term were obliged to leave college, and not permitted reentry until he could pass an examination in all branches of study attended by his class.[94] (Then and later, of course, "high stand" was no certain indicator of success in late life. Chauncey Depew, class of 1856, Bones, and U.S. senator from New York, was to note in his memoirs: "It is a singular commentary on the education of that time that the students who won the highest honors and carried off the college prizes, which could only be done by excelling in Latin, Greek, and mathematics, were far outstripped in after-life by their classmates who fell below their high standards of collegiate scholarship but were distinguished for an all-around interest in subjects not featured in the college curriculum."[95])

From 1833 through 1843, Bonesmen were valedictorians and salutatorians twice for each distinction. In the thirty-six classes after 1844, ending with the class of 1878 (including two of Alphonso Taft's sons, Peter, valedictorian of the class of 1867, with the best record ever achieved to that date, and William Howard, salutatorian in 1878), twenty-one valedictorians and twenty-three salutatorians were members of that society. With Russell (first in his class) and Taft (third "high stand") and four other members of Phi Beta Kappa, Bonesmen began as they meant to go on.[96] It must however be noted, in the spirit of irony, that their meeting debate topic for February 15, 1833, was the question, "Are college honors beneficial to education," and the decision from the evening's chair, Alphonso Taft, was "in the negative." Nevertheless, according to the Yale correspondent of the *New Haven Evening Register* in 1878, in response to a letter from Russell himself, it was said to be "the fact that the valedictorian of each class, in which number [Russell] had the honor to be, received the first election into [the Bones] fraternity."[97]

Another measure was the Townsend Prizes in English Composition, with premiums of $12 each "to the authors in the Senior class of the best original compositions in the English language," first awarded in 1844, with about five men honored each year: through 1876, members of Bones accounted for forty-nine of the 102 prizewinners. Here, competitive zeal may have overcome fair play. It is reported that, in the sprint of 1857, the librarian of Linonia, a Bonesman, locked the literary society's library from inside, slipped out through a back window with help from a clubmate, and then, when Townsend Prize candidates were unable to gain library access for "statistics" and "authority" for their presentations, he claimed that "the key-hole [was] already occupied by somebody inside."

The Yale Review, recounting the affront—"He was made keeper of Linonia keys for a different purpose than to show exclusive favoritism to fourteen of his fellow mortals"—ran a "pome" for the occasion, and recast the narrative as about accomplices "Jack" and "Gill":

> Never was hope forlorner
> For man to skin—for man to skin—
> But "Townsends" must be taken,
> By "Skull and Bones"—by "Skull and Bones,"
> Though archives were forsaken
> And skinned with groans—and skinned with groans—
> And though Gill's face was burning
> With shame 'tis true—with shame 'tis true,
> A "Townsend" he was earning,
> For "three, two, two"—for "three, two, two."
>
> For out the window leaping,
> In S.B.T.—in S.B.T.,
> He to his room was creeping,
> Fast as could be—fast as could be—
> A bag of books he toted,
> With learning's tomes—with learning's tomes,
> To take the "Townsend" noted,
> For "Skull and Bones"—For "Skull and Bones."[98]

This tradition of tapping at least a few men of the highest scholarly achievement, who naturally enough tended to perpetuate themselves in their successors, meant that more frequently than not a small band of Bones members was carrying on postgraduate work in divinity or the law in New Haven, sometimes coupled with service as Yale tutors. As such, they were constantly available both as object lessons of worldly success and, if need be, as recruiters or instruments in pledging. Some of those tutors would later become professors and administrators. Of the fifty-four living Yale professors in all departments and schools which William Kingsley was to commemorate in his 1879 history of Yale College, fifteen were members of Skull and Bones, and one of Scroll and Key; the administrative officers were almost all Bonesmen.[99]

Still, this virtue was to have a defect, which affected as well those who were not the class's top scholars. The society's emphasis on achievement could not fail to attract a large proportion of men, accepting membership, whose postgraduate careers would be distinguished, and successive classes of such men, year in and year out, certainly imbued the organization with discipline and a high seriousness, with both good and ill effects. At its best, such discipline and gravity immeasurably strengthened the society in public opinion on and off the campus, and confirmed its hold upon its members. Yet at their worst, these traits led to attitudes as well as overt acts of arrogance, to obsessive and absurd exactions of respect, and to self-congratulation and self-aggrandizement, for which Bones was to pay dearly in the future.

Second as a qualifier for membership were known oratorical skills exhibited and polished as freshman and sophomores in the large debating societies Linonia, Brothers in Unity, and Calliope, to one of which all members of the class belonged. These experiences led, with appropriate high stand, to being selected by the faculty for the honor of participation in the Junior Exhibition in the latter part of April. Those to be named class poet and class orator, however, were not identified until graduation, nor until 1848 were the twenty or so "oration men" given their appointments by the faculty to speak at commencement exercises (two or three in each class giving "philosophical orations," the Yale nineteenth-century version of summa cum laude). Thus, while adding to the prestige of the society at the close of senior year, these honors could not figure in election at the end of the incoming class's junior year.

However, it is notable that in the twenty classes through 1852, Skull and Bones elected six men in the junior year spring term who were to be class poets the following year, and six who became the class orator (the class orator, who gave the valedictory address at the graduation ceremonies, was an elective position; the valedictorian—a faculty appointment—did not automatically speak to and for the class at commencement). And for the first fifteen years of the DeForest Prize, endowed in 1852 for the best oration from the senior class (with a gold medal worth one hundred dollars, the largest such award then given in any American college), a Bones member won ten times, chosen from among each year's five Townsend finalists.[100]

Of course, not everyone kept up the standard. William C. Whitney, Bones 1863 (later corporation counsel of the New York City, secretary of the navy under President Cleveland, and founder of the Whitney family fortune), was widely acknowledged as a brilliant writer and speaker but shocked his classmates when, delivering his commencement oration, he stopped his recitation, took out his manuscript, and read it through to the end—the first commencement address that had ever been *read* at Yale. When queried later by his clubmate William Graham Sumner (to become the American theorist of Social Darwinism), "Why didn't you say it from memory?," Whitney replied, "It was too much bother to memorize so many words."[101]

President Theodore Woolsey, promoting competitive scholarship, made the intellectual contest clearer, by publishing the names of winners of prizes and scholarships in the college catalogue, commencing in 1848 to list the ranking of seniors in the commencement program: two groups of colloquies (respectable students), three of disputes (better performance), orations (top tier of the class), a very few philosophical orations, and finally the salutatory and valedictory orations. In his *Memories of Yale Life and Men*, college president Timothy Dwight of the class of 1849, among the first to be affected by the change, was to remember: "College standing, as connected with the work of the recitation room—rank in scholarship, as determined by the marks in instructors' books from day to day—was a matter of greater moment to the universal thought. Men had this door of success and distinction open to them. The other doors were not many in number. . . . [T]hose who were moved by ambition, or by higher motives, were constrained to seek their reward either from the records kept by tutors and professors, or in the sphere of writing or debating." Woolsey's scholarly appointments were then made with juniors, and published for all the world to see in the college catalogues for 1856–57 and thereafter.[102]

Third as an election enhancer, as always with any club claiming exclusivity, was social popularity or political prowess. These had been requisite, along with scholarship, for election to Phi Beta Kappa from its founding at Yale over half a century before. These qualities were also manifested by winning officerships in Phi Beta Kappa, like Russell's secretaryship, and the presidencies of the literary societies Linonia and Brothers, where each had three presidents during the school year. Being the "first president," the president for the first term when new members were being proselytized, was the most coveted. The brightest men, as Chauncey Depew noted, are not always the ablest in the larger world outside academia, nor alternatively are they necessarily the sturdiest materials on which to support an institution devoted to sociable relaxation and cooperative effort. The key personal characteristic of such men is their likely value to the group, "a set of men," as a member of Keys in the class of 1845 was to phrase it, "above the ordinary ability who, free from the proximity of cranks, dullards, and the immorally disposed, should be able to think and act together."[103]

Fourth, there were always those men in the election class who did not necessarily meet any of these first three qualification merits (scholarship, debating skills, or team building), but whose personalities were nevertheless attractive to the electors for reasons of singularity or for achieving balance or variety in the incoming delegation—in 1837 and again in 1839, the only South Americans in the student body, scions of Brazilian plantation owners, were elected. (As *Time* magazine was to phrase it a century later, "Quipsters say that Bones always taps thirteen big men, one unknown, and one Armenian,"[104] just before the society actually tapped an Armenian American.) Geographical origin was to become one method of balance: for the classes of 1840, 1850, 1860, and 1870, the membership in Skull and Bones was nearly evenly divided between New England, the Middle Atlantic states, the South, and the

West, in terms of nativity.[105] Still, as these proportions were not those of the student body at large, another pattern is visible.

Although in the index of provinciality, the school drew most of its pupils from Connecticut and the rest of New England, Yale was at this time the college in America which most nearly approximated a national institution, attracting students from all over the then-settled country. In 1788, a graduate reported that throughout the Southeast, Yale was called the "Athens of America," and it was the large number of Southern and Southwestern students in the latter part of the eighteenth century that first marked Yale as having a national character. During the first quarter of the 1800s, Charleston, South Carolina, ranked third in undergraduate enrollments among American cities, exceeded only by New Haven and New York City. As measured by enrollments for 1828 and the years beyond, Yale College was among the most popular colleges in the country, with its student body increasing by more that 60 percent through 1860.

This meant that, unlike its metropolitan rival Harvard, it was attractive to the nation's Southerners. In the class of 1831, fully 29 percent were from the South, the highest proportion ever recorded. In 1830, Yale had sixty-nine Southerners, while Harvard had only sixteen, and Princeton seventeen. For the first quarter century of the society, in consequence, their "unknowns" and "Armenians" for Skull and Bones were classmates from the American South. This was true even though it was no small task for the sons of wealthy planters to find success at Yale. "Southerner to us meant first of all slaveholder," wrote a classmate from Massachusetts. "We liked neither in New England," and they "were slightly haughty in their bearing toward less favored mortals."[106]

The third literary and debating society with members in the first three undergraduate classes, after Linonia and Brothers in Unity, was the "Calliopean Society," named after the muse of epic poetry, daughter of Zeus and Mnemosyne (Memory), and formed in July 1819 by Southerners who took offense at the election of a Northern man to the presidency of Linonia. Because New Englanders did not seek admission "by a long established custom," the Calliopean's catalogue of 1839 was to lament, "which appears now to wear the sanctity of law by prescription," the total membership of the third society necessarily lagged in a college populated predominately by New Englanders. (Such a geographic division was hardly unique to Yale: even before the American Revolution, the literary societies of Whig and Clio at Princeton were similarly riven: a majority of the Southern students entered Whig, while Clio became the usual choice for Northerners.)[107]

Although small throughout its history (never larger than the sixty-nine members of its formation year, and disbanding in February 1853), Calliope retained its Southern character, and in 1851 all Southerners in the two older literary societies withdrew to join it; the *Yale Literary Magazine* observed that "By this change, Calliope . . . has drawn more definitively the sectional differences of the students."[108] This record of successive fissions strongly suggests that, when among the Yankees in New Haven, the Cavalier collegians, for at least a decade before 1832 and for the two decades thereafter, felt a need to bond together protectively with fellow Southerners. Their numbers were proportionately small: students from Maryland, Virginia, North Carolina, South Carolina, Kentucky, Tennessee, Alabama, Mississippi, Georgia, Florida, and Louisiana accounted for less than 10 percent of the student body in the period from 1831 to 1841. By the college generations attending in the 1850s, Southerners for the first time in American history found themselves constantly on the defensive, deeply resenting the implications of evil and immorality attributed to slaveholders.[109]

Planters' sons at Yale were for the first time confronting rules invented in New England and maintained by New England–trained clergy, suggestive to them of the subordination of slavery. These Southern aristocrats disdained the "Mudsills," the poor Northern students who had to earn money for college by waiting on tables or by ringing the bell for morning prayers: it chagrined these men and their Northern allies that the poor rustics took college honors. As a historian of the education of the elite offspring of the Old South has written: "Choosing to be in concert at northern schools and having few northern classmates at southern institutions, southern boys congregated to produce a powerful and regionally distinct peer group. The upbringing of southern gentry boys, the wealth of their families, the intentions of their education, and the legacy of slave-holding combined to produce far more truculence and violence among southern college boys than among their northern counterparts." Enabled by their wealth, they gradually moved out of the primitive college dormitories and into private rooms in New Haven proper; in 1827, fifty-five Southerners lived in college, fifteen in town, while by 1850, only seven took rooms in college, with forty-six in town.[110]

That the Southerners stood out within a Yale class for these and other reasons cannot be doubted. Their attire was picturesque: "Byronic collar, velvet waistcoat, flying scarf, and sumptuous watch chain, all crowned with the glory of locks which Hyperion might have envied—the cynosure of college fashion." (One, later elected to Bones, wrote to his sister that he eschewed the customs of the good scholars, who "never even wear clean shirts . . . are always run down at the heel, and don't comb their hair," while he "set the fashion of my class," paying great regard to my cravat, gloves and cut of my coat.") John Sherwood of the class of 1839 described them thusly in his reminiscences. "They were, of course, the best-dressed men in the class, had more money to spend, and spent it more freely in suppers and other social entertainments than the other students, many of whom, especially from New England, were the beneficiaries of charitable societies, Dorcas societies and other associations who supported them through college with the view of their becoming ministers of the Gospel. . . . The Southern students usually excelled in oratory, but were less successful in competing for prizes in regular studies. . . . Of the twenty-nine Orations, Dissertations and Colloquies given at our Commencement, August 21st, 1839, only a single Dissertation was given by a student from the South."[111]

Their mindset was different: the Southern code of honor was fundamental to this behavior. Southern honor was "a system of belief, in which a person has exactly as much worth as others confer upon him."

The idea of honor meant that, in the words of Wilbur Cash's classic *The Mind of the South*, "everybody, high and low, was rendered more tetchy." This ethic contrasted with the Yankee admiration for character, meant to embody "power, permanence, and fortitude . . . [which for] the person of strong character transcended fickle public opinon and fleeting public repute . . . [C]haracter was a democratic idea limited neither by social class nor by political partisanship."[112]

The Southerners' fiery tempers not infrequently brought them into conflict with classmates and with college rules. Julian Sturtevant of the class of 1826 drily observed: "The atmosphere of a southern plantation was not favorable to the training of youth in the habits of self-government. Southern students often showed that the close relations with the sons of small farmers and mechanics in which they found them-selves was very distasteful to them." John Sherwood of the class of 1839 described how, "one evening in the heat of debate, Henry R. Jackson [Bones 1839, subsequently U.S. minister to Austria and to Mexico and brigadier general in the Confederate Army] sent an inkstand full of ink at the head of his antagonist in debate across the large Hall of the literary society of Brothers in Unity, leaving a black trail of ink behind it and just grazing the head of his opponent." An apology followed.[113]

The seniors of Scull and Bone seem to have found the company of Jackson and his kind desirable: between 1833 and 1842, the class years of the first ten delegations, fully 22 percent of the club membership hailed from ten of the eleven states of the South, excluding only Florida, and twenty-seven of these 149 men, almost a fifth, were members of Calliope. Notably, of those thirty-three Southerners among the society members of that decade, only seven were elected to Phi Beta Kappa, which is another indication of how the Southerners were non-scholarly outliers in the student body. In the same years, nine men were chosen from the Great Lakes states of Michigan, Ohio, Illinois, Michigan, and Wisconsin—6 percent of the successive clubs' membership, when the Yale class percentage was short of 5 percent for those same five states. Eleven of these men had not even spent all four years in New Haven, but entered their respective classes as sophomores or even juniors. That pattern persisted: Richard Taylor of Louisiana and the class of 1845, later to be the highest-ranking Yale graduate in the Confederate Army, transferred from Harvard as a junior and was chosen for Bones, as was William Preston Johnston of Kentucky of the class of 1852, to become aide-de-camp to Jefferson Davis and then president of Tulane. Johnston was the last man to enter his class, in May 1851 (the third term of his junior year), won the Clark premium for English composition and a Townsend prize, and was elected by the society that very term.[114]

A simple reason for the prevalence of Southerners in Skull and Bones, a society founded as a club for extemporaneous debate, would seem to be the remarkable tradition of what all Americans characterized as "Southern oratory." It was an article of faith in the antebellum South that oratory was a key to power. Each crossroads settlement had its debating clubs, and at the University of Virginia there were fully five forensic societies in this period. Patrick Henry was the Southern orator most admired, and his name was revered "on a par with Demosthenes by his Charlottesville votaries," but examples were many: John Randolph of Virginia, Henry Clay of Kentucky, John C. Calhoun (Yale 1804) and Robert Young Hayne of South Carolina, and Jefferson Davis of Mississippi.[115] The Southerners at Yale were themselves aware of the distinction and the intellectual difference: Hart Gibson, class of 1855 and Keys, wrote candidly to his father in his senior year: "While our Yankee brethren are unable to rival us in statesmanship and popular oratory, we are far, too far, behind them in polite literature and science."[116]

Hayne, United States attorney general in the Monroe administration, governor of South Carolina in 1833, best remembered for his eloquence during the Webster-Hayne debates of 1830, was an orator of speed and dash in the romantic manner, "[s]o filled with passion . . . that at times he seemed almost beside himself, and yet he never for a moment lost control of his words." The more famous of the Carolina statesmen was John C. Calhoun, who entered Yale as a junior at age twenty, graduated as a member and treasurer of Phi Beta Kappa, then became successively congressman, secretary of war, vice president, and secretary of state. While equally dedicated to the oratorical cult, Calhoun sought instead to persuade in a logical, concise, even terse manner, directing his efforts on the intellectual plane, whereas Hayne aimed at the feelings of his audience.[117] Russell and his clubmates and their successors, in electing Southerners, seem to have been seeking to capture both skills in their self-administered lessons in extemporaneous debate.

Given the well-attested differences in temperament between New Englanders and Southerners, and the enforced intimacy of the small membership, the cohesion and endurance of the senior society while yoking the two mindsets in a single delegation was remarkable. No doubt, succeeding classes of young men from the same state would have known each other and urged the election of candidates from their native region: in 1843, Ezekiel Belden of the class of 1844 (who would not have known of the Bones classes before 1840) was to claim that "the principal qualification for admission into this society [of Scull and Bone] is a familiar acquaintance with its members."[118] Nevertheless, the result of deliberately joining together in society membership these young men of two sometimes clashing cultural traditions of North and South—"character" and "honor," respectively, differences that were to erupt in civil war in only one more generation—had for some a measurable leavening effect. Hugh White Sheffey of Virginia, in the third Bones delegation (class of 1835), was to write in his class history a half century after arriving in Connecticut: "My associations at Yale prevented me from being a mere Virginian—a mere sectional character, and naturalized and liberalized my views and feelings. I never felt bitter toward a northern man." While he did not here name his senior society—no class member ever did in his essays for the class histories—Sheffey belonged to a Bones club with only one other Southerner, from North Carolina.

For most Southerner collegians, of course, when the Civil War came, love of region overcame all (two members of the Bones club of 1851 fought on opposite sides). Although some 836 Yale students and alumni served in the Union Army—of whom at least one hundred died in service or as a direct result thereof, more than the alumni of any other college in America[119]—eighty served in the Confederate Army (including eighteen, among them Bonesmen William Gustine Conner '45 and Henry Laurens Metcalfe '49, enlisting in Company A of the Jeff Davis Legion of Mississippi), and fifty-five were killed. In the litany of the famous Yale College graduates who were members of Skull and Bones, it is not often noted that these names include the chair of the Louisiana Secession Convention and secretary of the navy of the Confederate States of America (John Perkins, 1840, said to be CSA president Jefferson Davis's "oldest and best friend" considered for his vice president, aided in the drafting of the secession resolution by Lemuel Parker Conner, 1845, whose brother William Gustine Conner, also 1845 and Bones, was killed fighting for the Confederacy at Gettysburg); the chair of the Mississippi Secession Convention and CSA congressman who raised a regiment (William T. S. Barry, 1841); one brigadier general in the CSA Army (Henry Rootes Jackson, of the flying inkstand, 1839); and one lieutenant general, the leader of the Army of the Tennessee, the highest-ranking Southern general officer to attend Yale, and Jefferson Davis's brother-in-law (Richard Taylor, 1845). Also included are three men captured with Davis at war's end: his private secretary, the chief of his personal staff, and a third man, the head of the Bureau of Foreign Supplies, who had been a Yale valedictorian and president of Calliope.[120]

Also to be noted are two Scroll and Key graduates who became Confederate major and brigadier generals: Randall Lee Gibson, 1853, William Johnston's roommate and kinsman, helping him after the war to secure that Tulane presidency, and James Tappan, 1845, recognized at his thirtieth Yale reunion by his classmate, abolitionist and Union brigadier general Henry B. Carrington, as one "who treated surrendered black troops as prisoners of war at a time when such treatment was threatened to be denied."[121] Yale graduates, including the law and graduate schools, accounted for twenty-seven generals (including the surgeon general) for the North, and ten for the South: six of those thirty-three officers were members of Skull and Bones, and five were Scroll and Key men, the two senior societies together accounting together for five of the nine Confederate generals from Yale College.[122]

There was no general amnesty of high-ranking Confederate officials until announced by President Andrew Johnson at the Democratic Party National Convention in New York City in July 1868 (attended by the Gibson brothers and their cousin William Johnston). Nevertheless, the senior societies took the view that the end of the war permitted and encouraged their prewar fellowship, although that often was not reciprocated in the immediate aftermath of the conflict. James N. Brickell, class of 1845, a native of Columbia, South Carolina (and one of five southerners in his year's Bones club), who had served as a first lieutenant in the Confederate Army, returned to the 1866 delegation's secretary his invitation to the annual convention scheduled for July 27, 1865, with this short message: "The events of the last four years having completely severed any connection with the North and every person and thing living in that section, I return the enclosure."

On the other hand, Bonesmen Thomas Bayne and William Johnston, although both having personally served and then been captured and imprisoned with Jeff Davis, returned to a Yale College commencement for their twentieth reunion in 1867 and were the first combatant Confederates to revisit the college at reunion (Johnston had visited his Bones clubmate Daniel Coit Gilman in New Haven in the early spring of 1866); Alexander Porter Root, 1861 and Bones, returned to his sexennial reunion that same year after service as a CSA cavalry major; and Keys member and CSA Major General Randall Gibson, Keys 1853, returned to New Haven for his fifteenth reunion in 1868. "There has never been a moment since I left Yale," he said at the luncheon following commencement, "in which my feelings toward my own classmates and the college were not warm and hearty. I look forward to the day when the old flag will wave in harmony over all the land. (Cheers.) Whatever I, for one, can do to inspire among people hopefulness in the future and a faith in the National Government, will be done."[123]

Long after the creation of Skull and Bones, and long before the creation of the Yale residential college system in the early 1930s, the fictional Dink Stover before his Bones tap in Owen Johnson's *Stover at Yale* (1912) was to say that the point of college should be "to educate ourselves by knowing opposite lives, fellows who see things as we never have seen them, who are going back to life a thousand miles away from what we lead. . . . We ought to get a great vision, when we come up here, as young men, of the business of our country, of the privilege of fighting out its political freedom, of what American manhood means in the towns of Georgia and Texas . . . We ought really to know one another, meet, discuss, respect each other's point of view, independence—odd ways if you wish."[124] Russell and Taft (who later embarked for another clubmate's state of Ohio) and their friends seem to have had this goal consciously in mind in forming their senior society.

A fifth factor which shaped the selection of an incoming club, in addition to the four listed above, whether for Skull and Bones or thereafter Scroll and Key, or for any later senior society, is simply inertia, given that the young men tended to perpetuate themselves in their successors—or as formulated in a negative maxim by an anonymous member of Scroll and Key discussing the election of its crowd for 1844: "The fact is, gentlemen, I have always noticed that if in a Society like this you select one d———d fool, he will be sure to want his representative in the next class, and I am loath to perpetuate the species."[125]

High stand in the class was not, however, incompatible with high spirits, which early on were almost fatal to the club's continued existence. The new senior society was almost immediately offensive to the faculty. On Christmas Eve in 1833 (the regular term was to include that day through 1850), tutor John Radcliffe Davenport, class of 1830 and then studying in the Divinity School, was rudely awakened by the roar of the song and dance at the club's first anniversary celebration, which continued until the early morning hours. He summoned the faculty, and President Day, Davenport, and others in a squad of tutors ascended to the society's hall to break up the merriment. On leaving the room, the president was heard to observe, about the floor, that the group seemed to be "a very litter-ary society."

The faculty then met the next day, Christmas, as its minutes record, to determine punishment for the antics the preceding evening of the "convivial meeting" of the "Society which bears as its insignia the Skull & Bones." Nine members of the Bones club of 1834, including Yale professor's son and future Yale treasurer Henry Kingsley, future speaker of the Connecticut House of Representatives Eleazar Foster, Linonia president and future United States congressman John Houston, future associate justice of the Louisiana Supreme Court James Lea, and future class poet Churchill Coffing, all received warnings, with letters sent to their parents, and two of the club who had not yet "been matriculated" (been formally admitted as members of the senior class) were advised they would not be, with denial of their degrees, although in time the faculty relented and they graduated with their class.[126]

Matters could not have been improved a decade later by the transgression of William Davison Hennan of New Orleans, tapped for Bones in the spring of 1841, "senior and valedictorian of his class," in the words of the faculty minutes, "guilty of immoral and criminal conduct," who was found "guilty of lawlessness" and expelled in August of 1842, for the crime of fornication (in the eyes of Connecticut, and thus of the clerical faculty's).[127]

Faculty hostility remained at a simmer if not a boil, an armistice rather than a peace, and while there were no forced entries into the club after the faculty raid on Christmas Eve in 1833, the club of 1837 determined that a conciliatory gesture needed to be made. They decided to wait upon President Day and the elder Professor Silliman—father of Benjamin Silliman Jr., of the Bones club of 1837, who must have smoothed the way—and ask them to visit their hall as an act of finesse in their outward reformation. The visit went well, and as the years passed and the faculty itself included many graduate members of Skull and Bones, the threat of renewed faculty disfavor faded permanently (at the commencement of 1863, the four new professors named—William

Clarke, class of 1843, Chittenden Professor of Divinity; Daniel Coit Gilman, 1852, professor of Physical and Political Geography; Lewis Packard, 1856, assistant professor of Greek Language and Literature; and Cyrus Northrop, 1857, professor of Rhetoric and English Literature—were all members of the society when undergraduates).

The origins of two more pattern-setting choices of the original senior society, practices adopted by every subsequent senior society in imitation, namely the number of members in a class's club—fifteen—and the weekday night of meeting—Thursday—are not known. Russell and his friends made up, in that fall of 1832, a group of fourteen in the class of 1833 (the black line in place of the name of the eleventh man in the catalogue for that year's club was to cause a frisson in the neutrals who saw it), and "perpetuated itself," in the previously quoted phrase of the later class history, by choosing fifteen successors, a number that has attracted no mysterious explanations whatsoever by neutral classmates or outside commentators. As every successive class made up a new club, that number became fixed and expected, and then replicated by all the societies that came after.

Nevertheless, when James Osborne Putnam of the club of 1839, later the U.S. minister to Belgium and subsequently the chancellor of the University of Buffalo, left college well before the end of the school year, his delegation decided for themselves and their successors not to fill any vacancy for school withdrawal or death, for fear of setting "a dangerous precedent." Moreover, in the club's early years, the fifteen were neither elected nor admitted at the same time, perhaps explained by election needing to be by unanimous vote of the members in town and present at the meeting. It was decided early on that those passed over were not to be identified to the incoming club, although communication to the graduates of potential candidates' names was not forbidden, but such information was still meant to be kept confidential.

As for their weekly meetings, after beginning with Friday night meetings for their gatherings, Thursday evening was substituted, "commencing at exactly eight o'clock," Bagg recorded, "and every acting member is obliged to be in attendance from that time until adjournment, at two or three in the morning. . . . A Bones senior is never seen about New Haven after eight o'clock of a Thursday evening. Nothing but actual sickness ever keeps him from his society, except it be absence from town—and those who have been absent are apt to appear for the first time at Friday morning chapel."[128]

THE FIRST ROOM; THE WEEKLY PROGRAM; REFRESHMENTS

In the first decades of their existence, the halls of all secret societies at Yale were necessarily in the city's commercial buildings since these clubs had no recognition from Yale College, and secrecy as to the place of meeting was considered almost as important as secrecy regarding the club's nature. Fifteen men could not clearly meet in a dormitory residence, and the new society engaged a single room on the southeastern corner of the third story of a building located on the commercial, non-campus side of Chapel Street, near but not at the corner of College Street. Then numbered 460 Chapel, this structure was nearly opposite South College at the southern end of the Old Brick Row, and to the immediate west of a commercial building named Townsend's Block (now numbered 1000–1006 Chapel), where the literary society Calliope met in its upper story. The building in which Skull and Bones met housed Linonia, and their room, leased for ten years, could only be reached up the stairs from the Linonian hall, through an ordinary wooden door with an ordinary lock, easily rifled by the curious.

While that room featured a fireplace, and the members added two small closets in due course, the walls were bare, the two rear windows uncurtained, and the floors uncarpeted. One chair with a leaf served the presiding officer—who, not permanent by custom and constitution, changed with every weekly meeting on Thursday nights—facing fourteen common chairs with wooden seats, and a red-cloth-covered table mounted by a skull and crossed femurs.[129] The uneven light yielded by tallow candles during debates was obscured by clouds of tobacco smoke produced in consuming Connecticut's own tobacco. No great care was taken for amenities: only in 1837 did that year's club appoint a "Spit-Box Committee."

Something is known of their proceedings from the diary of George Sherman, of the class of 1839, who heard about them from a friend of a friend, one Bill Townsend, who lived near the Bones rooms, and could hear and partially see what went on there. "Last Thursday eve when the new members were introduced," this double hearsay records, "great ceremonies were performed. One by one they were introduced into the room, where were seated the members dressed in masks. 'Draw near' says a hoarse unearthly voice. He approaches. They all point him to human skeletons set up in cases on a kind of shelf, each lifting his finger towards one [and] announces his name, & the last says 'And this is Rob Roy Macgregor.' Then with solemn oaths (most horrible, says the young Townsend) the new member swears fidelity to the secrets & to the interest of the society. When the last parts of the ceremony are ended, one person at the close of each utters through a horn 10 or 15 feet in length, a loud unearthly grunt. This instrument he saw as it protruded out of the window, and he has been in the room several times by stealth, before the things were put up, so that he is acquainted with almost everything in it."[130]

At the beginning, for a student organization founded as a club for training in extemporaneous debate, the single room was enough. Each member wrote a debate topic on a slip of paper, and all slips were put into one pile; a second pile contained slips with the name of each knight. The meeting leader drew one slip which established the debate topic for the evening. Rejecting it, in favor of an easier or more familiar topic also in the choices for that evening, was seen as undercutting the discipline of learning to speak extemporaneously on any topic. By the 1860s, a more democratic process was employed, and rejected questions were kicked into the fireplace. The names of the members were then drawn, for discussion of the question in the order of the draw. Of course, the true value of the debate was not from the nature of the topic, but from the clash and interplay of fifteen personalities.

All had to speak, and in this, the membership embraced the discipline of Brothers in Unity, which the Linonians had in derision surnamed the "Cider Mill," because "like such a mill, it moved circle-wise; that is to say, its members were not allowed to debate except in strict rotation, following the order of the catalogue; and in their turn, they must speak, whether they chose to do so or not." (In Linonia, all debates were voluntary, and thus all speakers, volunteers.) Since the first Bones delegation contained six former presidents of Linonia, the choice of the Brothers' pattern of compelled speaking is further evidence of their determination that all should be improved because all must participate. The succeeding delegations of the next decade always contained one, and often two, presidents of Brothers, which would have reinforced this discipline.[131]

The tradition of this senior society's debating was to resonate outside its hall, through the college's history. When William Howard Taft of the class of 1878 returned to Yale after leaving the American presidency in 1913 to teach seniors at Yale College and students in the Yale Law School, he coached the college freshmen's debate team. When the presidential election of 2004 resulted in newspaper reports that candidates George W. Bush and John F. Kerry, two years apart as Bonesmen, had both debated in college, the undergraduates petitioned for the establishment of a course in oratory, which had lapsed with the retirement of Professor Rollin Osterweis, the candidates' and Yale College's longtime debate coach and historian of American oratory.[132]

In due course, the two groups of slips were kept in a skull divided into compartments, known as the "Yorick," after Hamlet's jester.[133] A five-minute sandglass was used to time the remarks of each member, who was bound to speak for that period when his society name was drawn, until all had spoken. In a *Yale Lit.* article in 1886, William Crapo, by then a retired member of Congress, where a five-minute rule on bill amendment debates was enacted only in 1847, reflected obliquely on the discipline of his senior society's sandglass. "The member of Congress who rises in his place and reads from a roll of manuscript," he noted, "although his written speech may be logical in argument, strong in statement, and fruitful with statistics, convinces no one, for his fellow members, as a rule, will not listen to it. But in the debate under the 'five minute rule,' which must of necessity be extemporaneous, and which is direct and earnest, terse and vigorous, aggressive and critical, persuasive and conciliatory, every one listens, for it is in the debate that opinions are formed and changed, votes controlled and legislation perfected."[134] Notes were taken for the club's annual Black Book, the permanent record of its Thursday night meetings for the college year, begun to be kept only after a few meetings, when it was recognized in late January 1833 that "transactions of the club became not infrequent, highly momentous & interesting." The first recorded debate question was, "Is the assassination of a tyrant in any case justifiable?"[135]

As early as the fall term of 1835, the size of the accommodation and the relative lack of security caused the club of that year to consider acquiring a new meeting place, a search accelerated when two attempted entries were made by neutrals, and a new large lock was procured. Further security measures included the addition, by the club of 1838, of a door at the foot of the stairs leading from Linonia's hall, and then replacement of that by an iron door—the first of many iron doors in the history of Yale senior societies—which was installed by the club of 1842. Visible to everyone entering the hall of the Linonian Society below, this was a constant and powerful reminder of the existence of the Order of Skull and Bones, and its members in 1845 began referring merrily to their club's two rooms as "Skeleton Hall."

Another needful addition was a servant, first employed by the club of 1837, one "John Creed, L.L." (lamp-lighter). Creed, a native of the Virgin Islands, arriving in New Haven about 1820, had performed janitorial work for the Calliopean Society and was to organize the society's dinners as the weekly repasts became more elaborate. He attended conventions of Free People of Color in New York City and Philadelphia as a representative from Connecticut, was the New Haven agent of William Lloyd Garrison's anti-slavery newspaper *The Liberator,* and founded a catering and ice cream manufacturing business continued by his younger son; his elder son was the first black graduate of the Medical Department of Yale College, carrying on his practice from his father's home on West Chapel Street. John Creed and his sixteen-year-old son Cortlandt Van Rensselaer Creed, who took over the caretaker's role when his father went to California in 1849, were both made members of the society through initiation. In New Haven's Grove Street Cemetery, the simple obelisk above Creed's gravesite reads: John W. Creed | S.B.T.[136]

In the club's early years, once the debate was finished, the meetings ended at an early hour, but by the 1840s the members had oysters, pies, and waffles delivered to their meeting room, or went to a neighboring restaurant, and liquor was not then forbidden, which led to the club's reputation, as noted by Bagg, of bring a "convivial club."[137] Attempting to reconcile the continuance of refreshments with the intellectual life of the club, a committee appointed in November 1840 recommended that the debate continue for ninety minutes, then "sociality" (oysters and coffee) for a similar period, with debate renewed thereafter until the close of meeting. When the society migrated to its new, permanent hall in 1856, spirituous liquors were forever banned from the tomb.

HUBRIS AND NEMESIS

Nevertheless, the society's run of success was more fragile than it appeared, since it could be changed in the results of one spring's election. When Skull and Bones was founded in 1832, there were no fraternities in the lower classes, but in 1836, Alpha Delta Phi, or "A.D." as it came to be known, originating at Hamilton College in 1832, established a chapter in Yale College. Two years later Psi Upsilon, or "Psi U," founded at Union College in 1833, followed suit by starting a chapter in New Haven, only its third, by a member of the class of 1841, William Erigena Robinson, who was initiated while on a visit to Union during his sophomore year. Few American colleges were left untouched by this movement, which so aptly characterized the enterprise and initiative of the nineteenth-century college undergraduate.[138]

Edwin Griffin Bartlett, a member of the class and Scroll and Key club of 1846 (and before that a cofounder of Delta Kappa Epsilon at Yale in 1844) was to remember the two junior societies as formidable organizations. "Their main object," he wrote, "was to associate groups of students high in college standing, skillful in college politics, who should mutually cooperate to increase the share of honors which should fall to each, while another scarcely secondary aim was in secret meeting to enjoy private drill in oratory and composition—preparatory to the exercises of the open literary societies. Their aims were practical, their methods businesslike. They claimed, too, to make their elections strictly in consideration of the character, as scholars and gentlemen, of the members of the class from which they were made, and that such elections, therefore, were a tribute to the high scholarship and character of the best men in such class. And while others might have differed with them as to their application of their avowed rule, it became to be considered in each Sophomore class that the leaders in scholarship and gentlemanly qualities had a right to, and might expect, an election."[139] That same sense of expectation of election naturally carried over to the next rung in the class hierarchy as the juniors, now elected to A.D. or Psi U, looked forward to the senior society experience.

This also meant that from the junior class to which elections were being offered by Skull and Bones, candidates would have memberships in and loyalties to their classmates in A.D. or Psi U which preceded any immediate concern for the senior society. The great strength of a senior society club is that its core is concentrated horizontally in one class, but since, unlike a fraternity, there are no vertical, lower-class years of membership, that horizontal strength is not created until the year's club is created. In the five years which followed A.D.'s founding in New Haven, Bones recruited thirty-four of its members from this society, and only four from Psi U, perhaps reflecting A.D.'s reputation at Yale and nationally as decidedly literary.[140]

Ironically, Alpha Delta Phi had originally been brought to Yale to spite Bones. Frederick A. Coe had transferred from Union College to Yale and was disappointed in not receiving an offer of membership in the New Haven senior society in the spring of 1836. His response was to initiate the founding of a chapter of A.D. at Yale in which members of the class of 1838 were admitted at the start of their junior year, with the notion that their new fraternity membership would continue through the end of their senior year, thus denying their availability to the older society through pledge or expectation that they would refuse election there. The plan was encouraged by Chauncey Goodrich, professor of Rhetoric and Oratory, a personal foe of Skull and Bones who had previously reported to the faculty his discovery of a "demijohn" of spirituous liquor in the society's clubroom. (If Bones was an early version of *National Lampoon's Animal House* in the motion picture of that name at the mythical Faber College, Goodrich was its Dean Wormer.)

The scheme was thwarted when the ever-resourceful Bones delegation of 1837—the spectacular one boasting William Maxwell Evarts, Benjamin Silliman Jr., and Morrison Waite as members—elected seven members of the class of 1838 who were among the lower class A.D. membership behind Coe's group. These included Tennessean William Fleming (being tutored in mathematics by William Huntington Russell), the Brazilian Carlos Fernando Ribeiro, Joseph Parrish Thompson (later the renowned pastor of the Broadway Tabernacle of New York City), and William Pitt Lynde (thereafter congressman from Wisconsin and mayor of Milwaukee), and they were initiated as early as March 2. When the normal election day for the standard fifteen came round, the A.D. seven were revealed as members of the new Bones club. Alpha Delta Phi, after a little further struggling, retreated back into the junior year.

That initially successful strategy, however, had blowback. Once Psi Upsilon appeared on campus alongside A.D. in 1838, the strains produced by the competition of two junior fraternities not in existence when Bones was begun, each insisting that their "crowd" dominate in the next class year's social pinnacle, became a significant factor in election season, and would almost certainly have eventually fractured the senior society monopoly of Skull and Bones.

That it did so in 1842 was the consequence of the family dynamics of two sets of brothers. The first was John Hunter Robb of the class of 1843 and his younger brother James Madison Robb of the class of 1844, from Philadelphia; the second was the elder Robb's classmate William Kingsley and his older brother Henry of the class of 1834, of New Haven and the first club chosen from the junior class for Bones. A fraternity political squabble born of brotherly love, when later joined to the second brothers' sibling rivalry, had enormous consequences: the founding of a rival senior society, Scroll and Key, and the immediate collapse of the campus prestige of Skull and Bones.

TAPPED FOR SKULL AND BONES, 1833–1842

William Huntington Russell	1833	educator
Alphonso Taft	1833	minister to Austria
		minister to Russia
		U.S. attorney general
		U.S. secretary of war
		Alumni Fellow, Yale Corp.
James Wallace Houston	1834	U.S. Congress (Del.)
Henry C. Kingsley	1834	Yale treasurer
James Lea	1834	assoc. justice, Superior Court (La.)
John H. Tweedy	1834	U.S. Congress (Wisc.)
William M. Washington	1834	U.S. Congress (N.C.)
John Seeley	1835	U.S. Congress (N.Y.)
Thomas Thacher	1835	professor of Latin, Yale
Henry C. Deming	1836	U.S. Congress (Conn.)
		collector, Internal Revenue
William S. Pierson	1836	brigadier general, U.S. Army
Thomas Wills Day	1837	editor, *Hartford Courant*

William Maxwell Evarts	1837	U.S. attorney general
		President Johnson's impeachment defense counsel
		U.S. secretary of state
		Alumni Fellow, Yale Corp.
		second president, Yale Alumni Association of New York (Yale Club)
		U.S. senator (N.Y.)
Chester S. Lyman	1837	Yale professor Physics, Astronomy
Ferdinand Owen	1837	U.S. Congress (Ga.)
		U.S. consul, Havana
Benjamin Silliman Jr.	1837	Yale professor of Chemistry
		author, first college chemistry text
		first oil geologist
Morrison Waite	1837	chief justice, U.S. Supreme Court
Charles J. Lynde	1838	U.S. Congress (Wisc.)
Richard D. Hubbard	1839	U.S. Congress (Conn.)
		governor (Conn.)
Henry Rootes Jackson	1839	U.S. district attorney (Ga.)
		U.S. minister to Austria
		brigadier general, CSA
		U.S. minister to Mexico
James Osborne Putnam	1839	U.S. minister to Belgium
		chancellor, University of Buffalo
Charles Stillé	1839	provost, University of Pennsylvania
Curtis Burnham	1840	U.S. assistant treasurer
William Chauvenet	1840	professor of Mathematics, Annapolis
		chancellor, Washington University

James M. Hoppin	1840	Yale professor of Homiletics, Art
Joseph G. Hoyt	1840	chancellor, Washington University
John Perkins Jr.	1840	U.S. Congress (La.)
		Louisiana Secession Convention chairman
		Confederate secretary of navy
George Richards	1840	trustee, Yale Corp.
William T. S. Barry	1841	U.S. Congress (Miss.)
		Miss. Secession Convention chairman
		Confederate Congress
		colonel, own regiment, CSA
David I. Field	1841	U.S. assistant secretary of treasury
William Law Learned	1841	presiding justice, N.Y. Supreme Court
Donald G. Mitchell	1841	author, humorist
		U.S. consul, Venice
Richard Storrs Willis	1841	compiler, first American college songbook
		Yale professor of Music
Joseph Benton	1842	president, Pacific Theological Seminary
John A. Peters	1842	U.S. Congress (Me.)
		chief justice, Supreme Court (Me.)

CHAPTER FOUR

THE "OPPOSITION" OF SCROLL AND KEY (1843-1855)

Huntington, we must have opposition.

—William L. Kingsley to John M. Huntington,

July 5, 1842

THE FIGHT AND FOUNDING

Yale's whole undergraduate body totaled only 376 students in 1842–43. (Harvard was even smaller, at 254.)[1] While the turbulent details of a college feud of 1842 were not likely to find their way into printed public reports, sufficient records and reminiscences were written down, both then and decades after the fact, to give shape to the story of the creation in that year of a rival to Skull and Bones, named Scroll and Key. The testimony of those documents can be joined with an analysis of facts—who was elected to Skull and Bones that summer, and who chose instead to found and join a new senior society—to allow an approximate reconstruction of this seismic event in the social history of Yale College.

The seniors of Skull and Bones in the class of 1842, choosing their successors, had a candidate pool in the class of 1843 which was riven by a fight between the two junior fraternities, Alpha Delta Phi and Psi Upsilon. Decades later, John Monroe Sibley, a member of the class of 1843 then living in Belmont, California, produced in 1893 a list of what purported to be the Bones club of fifty years before. The fifteen names thereon were John Brandegee (a high-stand scholar performing at the Junior Exhibition), William Burroughs, Gideon Granger (president of Brothers in Unity), Gordon Hall (also Junior Exhibition), Roswell Hart, John Huntington, Alfred Lambert, John Lent, George Meech, John Nourse, George Pierce (First President of Linonia), Lucius Franklin Robinson (class poet to be), Sibley himself, John Skinner (First President of Brothers), and Henry Stevens.[2] Significantly, five of these juniors were brothers of Alpha Delta Phi, and five brothers of Psi Upsilon.

The Sibley list has some anomalies. Missing from it is William Lathrop Kingsley, member of Alpha Delta Phi, son of the Yale professor of Hebrew, Greek, and Latin languages James Luce Kingsley (class of 1799), and younger brother of Henry Kingsley (class of 1834, and member of the first club to be tapped for Bones). Alternatively, Sibley's own appearance has no obvious justification for being selected by Bones: he was never a president of one of the literary societies or a high-stand man, nor was he a member of Phi Beta Kappa, or Alpha Delta Phi, or Psi Upsilon.

TAP DAY FOR CLASS OF 1843

Sibley Pre-Tap List	1843 Skull & Bones Catalogue	1843 Scroll & Key Catalogue
	Julius Baratte	
John Brandegee (Alpha Delta Phi)		John Brandegee (A.D.)
William Burroughs		
	William L. Chambers	
	Benjamin Eames (Psi Upsilon)	

Sibley Pre-Tap List	1843 Skull & Bones Catalogue	1843 Scroll & Key Catalogue
		David Judson Ely (A.D.)
		Isaac Mills Ely (A.D.)
	Charles Gachet	
		Edward W. Gilman
	Christopher Grammer	
Gideon Granger (Psi U)	Gideon Granger (Psi U)	
Gordon Hall (A.D.)		Gordon Hall (A.D.)
Roswell Hart	Roswell Hart	
	Daniel Havens	
John Huntington (A.D.)		John Huntington (A.D.)
		Anthony Keasbey (A.D.)
		William L. Kingsley (A.D.)
Alfred Lambert	Alfred Lambert	
	William Lane	
John Lent (Psi U)	John Lent (Psi U)	
George Meech		
	Thomas Moody	
		Frederick Munson
John Nourse (A.D.)		John Nourse (A.D.)
George Pierce (Psi U)		
	John Robb (A.D.)	
		Edward Robbins
Lucius F. Robinson (Psi U)	Lucius F. Robinson (Psi U)	
		Eli Shorter (A.D.)
John Monroe Sibley		
John Skinner (A.D.)		J. Skinner (A.D.)
Henry Stevens (Psi U)	Henry Stevens (Psi U)	
		Franklin Taylor
		Henry A. Weeks (A.D.)

The Sibley list would seem to be the names of the juniors intended for or pledged to Bones, many (but, with the usual "outsiders," not all) of whose biographies evidenced the hallmarks of Yale success customary for an incoming delegation to that society. The list for the class of 1843 in the Bones catalogue, however, is very different. On it appears no one who spoke at the Junior Exhibition, and only one man with a faculty speaking appointment then or later at commencement. Neither of the First Presidents of Linonia or Brothers are there.

The reason is rivalry among the junior class fraternities which had now appeared at Yale. The fierce pride in their membership is evidenced by a letter to his parents from Vermont's Henry Stevens Jr., later the greatest dealer in rare Americana in the nineteenth century, who had entered Yale as a sophomore and at the end of that class year in 1841 wrote his father about his election to Psi Upsilon. "We have in College a secret literary society consisting of Juniors and Seniors, fifteen out of each class who are annually elected during the last term of the Sophomore year. As it is considered a great honor in the class to be elected into the society there is of course a great deal of strife for it. Fifteen of the best fellows are elected, and no more can be. I have been elected and of course I may draw the inference without vanity that I stand among the fifteen best out of a class of 120 students."

Skull and Bones had taken in thirty-four men from Alpha Delta Phi since its Yale campus founding in 1836, and only four from Psi Upsilon since that fraternity's establishment in New Haven in 1838.[3] The Yale College chapter of "A.D." took an important part in the national fraternity government and the shaping of its policy; the first songbook and, with two exceptions, all the national catalogues until 1860, were likewise issued from Yale.[4] Given these numbers and the significance of the Yale chapter, the virtual absence from the elected Bones delegation for 1843 of anyone from A.D. (a single man), and the presence of fully seven from Psi U (more than all the prior years combined), and the omission of the two Psi U members who were First Presidents of Linonia and of Brothers, as well as of two of the three Psi U members who were editors of the *Yale Literary Magazine*, all suggest a catastrophic upset of initial intentions.

The careful balance shown by Sibley's list, with five candidates from A.D. and an equal number from Psi U, seems to demonstrate that the electing seniors of Bones were trying to overcome the rift between the two junior societies by offering election to the best men of each. When they went for initiation, however, on July 5, 1842 (the evening before Presentation Day and by that year the day of Bones' initiation), peace could not be made by the seniors' offer to join together the leaders of two groups already at each others' throats. John Huntington, the head of the Alpha Delta faction, was asked to withdraw, and two of his friends and brothers in A.D., including William Kingsley, determined to join him in his exile. Keys lore has it that, at a spot now occupied by McClellan Hall in the northwest quadrant of the Old Campus, near the old Laboratory Building, while on the way home from the abortive initiation, Kingsley suddenly addressed his companions with a declaration: "Huntington, we must have an opposition."[5]

For his part, oblivious to the pending birth of his new society's rival, Henry Stevens wrote his mother the following month: "There is a club that has existed in College for many years, made up of only 15 students called the Skull and Bone Society—I have been elected as one of these 15—It is considered one of the greatest compliments that can be paid a student by his fellows to elect him to this honorary society— Two members of the faculty belong to it, and several ministers of all denominations both in New Haven & New York, Washington and all across the country. Nearly every one of its members that has been out of College as long as five years are distinguished men. . . . We meet once a week and after[wards] many of these old members are present and it is very interesting. The night before commencement many from Boston, Hartford, New York, Phil'a & Washington are coming on to attend an annual meeting. It will be a glorious time. One member in Congress will I expect be with us. I will tell you more when I see you."[6]

William Kingsley's own recollection of these events has been pre-served. His older brother Henry in the class of 1834 (later longtime treasurer of Yale, from 1862 to 1886) had been in the very first Bones delegation to be elected, and the younger Kingsley was a member of A.D., the primary junior fraternity feeder to Bones. He thus seemed well situated to be chosen for Bones, "but at this time a great excitement had arisen in the 'Alpha Delta Phi.' A member of our [junior] class was John Robb from Alabama. He had a brother in the Sophomore class and when we [A.D.] came to select from that class, he said that his brother must be the first man elected. The rest of the society were indignant, and no one would vote for Robb's brother. We had many meetings one after another, but in the true spirit of a Southern secessionist, Robb said that nothing should be done until his brother was elected. We would not be intimidated or bull dozed, and matters rose to a high pitch and for weeks the thing was fought over until we expelled Robb from our society."

Robb, Kingsley further reported, "went up to college and collected a crowd of 'Psi Upsilon' and a lot of other men[,] the most of them fiery and hot headed Southerners, and they came down to our society room in the 4th storey of what was known as the Leffingwell building, corner of Chapel and State, with the avowed intention of pitching us out of the window. In some way we learned that they were on the steps coming up. One of our men, John Huntington, had a pistol and we all hurried to the State St. end of the Hall, and in a moment saw a crowd of excited fellows coming up headed by John Robb. They called to us that they would pitch us out of the windows. John Huntington aimed his loaded pistol at them and said, 'If you advance one step I will fire.' I stood close to his side. After blustering a while they thought 'discretion the better part of valor' and retired, leaving us victors for the nonce. We went forward and quickly elected 15 men of the next class [for A.D.] and John Robb's brother was not among them."[7]

Because of Henry Kingsley's prior membership in Bones, William, although not on Sibley's list, thereafter received an invitation to join his brother's senior society. With his proposed clubmates, including Isaac Ely, he was ordered to go to the office in the Old Laboratory (built in 1782) used by Professor Benjamin Silliman the younger, of the Bones delegation of 1837, the class three years behind Henry Kingsley. As the ritual had evolved, candidates were thereafter sent over to the Bones' rented rooms at the corner of Chapel and College Streets.

When the initiates arrived at 9:00 P.M., on July 5, 1842, they found that a large proportion of those present were from Psi Upsilon, including John Robb, Thomas Moody of Georgia, and many of Robb's friends. Kingsley's memoir continues: "They gathered in one corner and whispered together; they were evidently corresponding with men of the [Bones] society. There seemed to be some difficulty, for nothing was done. At last a committee of old graduates of the society, at about 12 [midnight] or 1 o'clock, came down and told us that so large a number of men [of the Psi U group] refused to join if John Huntington [of A.D.] did, that they could not admit him. I said, 'John Huntington is an "Alpha Delta Phi" man and we must stand by him.' [Isaac] Ely said that he would, and so we sent word that we would not enter the society." The Bones graduates tried to calm the waters, according to William's account: John Shelden Beach, a lawyer practicing in New Haven and a member of the club of 1839, argued with young Kingsley "and tried to *make* me join," to no avail, and he and Ely withdrew with their A.D. friends Brandegee, Hall, Huntington, Nourse, and Skinner.[8]

Kingsley then proposed to form another society, and Huntington and Isaac Ely's brother David responded enthusiastically to the proposal for a meeting the next morning, July 6, Presentation Day. Juniors Brandegee, Anthony Keasbey, and others agreed to join if Kingsley would bring in Edward Gilman. The subsequent brief meeting took place at 8 A.M., in senior Isaac E. Hiester's room at 124 North College, where he served as temporary chairman. Committees made up of the juniors and seniors present were formed, to devise a name and a badge, to draft a constitution, and to locate and furnish suitable meeting rooms. That meeting closed with a resolution that thirteen specified juniors be requested to meet two days later. The seniors then gathered in the Old Chapel for the Presentation exercises, and listened to the delivery by the class orator of 1842, Newton Edwards (of Skull and Bones).[9]

William Kingsley's account was prepared, of course, without knowledge of the Sibley list. Only by creating a chart of thirty-three names (see the second page of this chapter), made up from combining the Sibley list with the lists of the members of the respective, final Bones and Keys delegations for 1843, is it possible to discern that six men from that list, the "outsiders" by lack of class distinctions, went to Skull and Bones, and five went to Scroll and Key, leaving the older society to find nine replacement candidates. These included John Robb, the Southerner Thomas Moody mentioned in the Kingsley memoir, two other Southerners—Washington, D.C.'s Christopher Grammer and Georgian Julian Baratte, president and librarian, respectively, of Calliope—and a man from Ohio. To make fourteen, the newly formed Scroll and Key had to gather in nine more, including Kingsley himself and Isaac Ely. Seven of the new Keys members were Phi Beta Kappa—compared to three for Bones—and two, Frederick Munson and Edward Robbins, neither on Sibley's list, were among the five elected editors of the *Yale Lit.*—with none in Bones. In the Keys group, only one was from the South (an Alabaman), and only one from the West, with eight hailing from Connecticut, three from New York, and one each from Massachusetts and New Jersey.

William Kingsley's reminiscences are themselves sometimes problematic, having one major error, and one glaring omission. The major error is the identification of John Robb as an Alabaman, to give flavor to the charge that he had "the true spirit of a Southern secessionist." Robb was born and died in Philadelphia, and practiced law all his life there.[10] The curious omission is any mention of William's brother Henry, of the class of 1834. Only one year separated John Hunter Robb and his younger brother James Madison Robb, for whom John was to fight so hard to get into A.D. that he was expelled as a result. William was eight years younger than his brother Henry, who lived all his life in New Haven, and was almost certainly in that city on election day in 1842. Why is there no mention in William Kingsley's memoir of his elder brother's view on William's repudiation of Bones? Was it perhaps Henry Kingsley, rather than John Beach, who was the Bones elder arguing with

William that day, but whose name could not comfortably be mentioned in these reminiscences of "Societies" dictated in his declining years to his daughter, Henry's niece?[11]

Whatever the explanations for these two anomalies, it is clear that William Kingsley made a choice, a choice for his A.D. fraternity brother, John Huntington—who became the first elected senior leader of Scroll and Key—and against his real brother, Henry Kingsley, in proposing "opposition" to Skull and Bones. All those years later, Kingsley remembered John Robb as having the spirit of a secessionist, but Robb did not "secede" from A.D.: he was on Kingsley's telling expelled. In truth, the roles of Robb and Kingsley were reversed. Despite his memoir's charged and obscuring choice of words, it was instead William who showed, on that election day, what has since been amply demonstrated by sociologists of sibling rivalry: that eldest children like Henry Kingsley identify with parents and authority, and support the status quo, whereas younger children like William are "born to rebel."[12]

THE DUAL DELEGATIONS; THE FIRST TWO HALLS

William Huntington Russell's group of junior class friends proposed to found a senior society in 1832, and so created their own first delegation of 1833. With Scroll and Key, the idea had come from a junior, William Lathrop Kingsley, and in this new society's case, certain outgoing seniors of 1842 simultaneously created with the incoming juniors of 1843 two delegations. Thus, the dozen seniors of the class of 1842— one chosen by student election for class poet, one a former president of Linonia, four Phi Beta Kappans, and four receiving appointments at the Junior Exhibition or commencement or both, one of whom had been elected one of the five editors of the *Yale Literary Magazine* (at that time, along with the offices of class orator and class poet, the highest honor bestowed by the class)[13]—shared only a couple of months together between the society's founding in July and their graduation in August, but their subsequent careers and composition are nevertheless worth examining.

The chair of the founders' meeting held on July 6, 1842, in his room, Isaac Hiester of Pennsylvania, became a lawyer and served in Congress. His career was outshone by his fellow Pennsylvanian and the star of the senior class Keys delegation, John Addison Porter, class poet for 1842, and later professor of chemistry at Brown (1850–1852) and Yale (1852–1864). Named in his honor is Yale University's annual prize for the best work of scholarship in any field, established in 1872 by his senior society. When Porter was serving as professor of Analytical and Agricultural Chemistry in the infant and struggling Yale "Department of Philosophy and the Arts," the first of the series of gifts to the college for a scientific school, eventually amounting to considerably over a million dollars, came from Porter's father-in-law Joseph Sheffield, after the marriage of his daughter to Porter in 1854.[14]

Others of the Scroll and Key founders also led careers of particular distinction. Ohioan Leonard Case Jr. went on to found the Case Institute of Technology in Cleveland in 1881, merged with Western Reserve University to become today's Case Western Reserve. Theodore Runyon of New Jersey progressed from mayor of Newark and chancellor of his home state to United States ambassador to Germany (1893–1896). The other eight members of Scroll and Key of the class of 1842 had more conventional careers in law, the ministry, and the teaching professions, but it is clear that there were promising men in the class that Skull and Bones was not taking in, whom a new senior society could accommodate and honor by election.

At a second meeting on July 8, again in Hiester's room, with six seniors and thirteen juniors present, the decision to proceed was concluded, although only eleven of the thirteen juniors were firmly in favor. During the third meeting, on July 11, with fourteen juniors and four seniors present, the room committee reported that it had located suitable premises next to those of Alpha Delta Phi on the fourth floor of the Street and Leffingwell building, located on the south side of Chapel Street near the intersection with State Street. (The "halls" of the secret societies had to be in city buildings, since the groups had no formal recognition from the Yale College administration despite so many tutors being members, and secrecy as to the meeting place was virtually as important as secrecy regarding the nature of society proceedings.[15])

A subscription of $167 was raised at this meeting to furnish the room, which Kingsley was to remember was "fitted . . . up very expensively." The accoutrements included most prominently a great marble head of Jove, reputed to have comes from the ruins at Agrigento in Sicily, purchased from Ithiel Town, a noted local architect and antiquary; the cost, $57, equaled almost half the annual expenses for a student's college year at the time. Two seniors presented the establishment with an engraving of "lovely nymphs, who wearied in the chase slept on rural banks, while around lay the deer they had taken and above stooped the curious satyrs." Other furnishings included black velvet hangings on the walls, two rented sofas, some mahogany chairs and a rocking chair, a costly carpet, some tables with coverings, a hat stand, and spittoons. These young men intended a retreat more grandly furnished than any of their dormitory rooms, and wanted these decorations to be permanent, befitting what their constitution was to call "the home of friendship, the hall of literature, and the studio of the fine arts." And, as Kingsley's memoir records, "We bought a live eagle which was kept in our room and also used frequently."[16]

Their occupancy here was not a long one: on a Sunday in December of 1842 the upper floors of the Street's Building caught fire, and only "a few papers" were able to be saved by members who went up the firemen's ladders and broke the windows with their fists. The bust of Jove, having fallen three flights, was gathered in smoke-blackened pieces, and the eagle flew away out one of the broken windows.

Oddly, on December 7, 1842, there was also a fire in the Bones club's rooms at 460 Chapel Street in the building shared with Linonia, causing the members to have to relocate their meetings until the following January 19; the records not damaged by the water used to extinguish the flames were saved, and no one except the members entered the rooms before the firemen arrived. The sequence of these calamities (the Bones rooms, then Keys') and the proximity of the two fires (occurring within two consecutive weeks) is highly suspicious, but it is not possible now to know if some neutral turned arsonist to send a message. There was a happy ending for the Bones club of 1843, however: upon moving back in, they broke out the two bottles of Madeira laid down in 1836 by the club of 1837 for the society's centenary celebration and drank them, some ninety years before time.

The Keys members named a new house committee to find a new home. This, a small three-room apartment, comprised of an "ante-room, Temple, and dressing room," was more romantically described as "the Sanctum Sanctorum and the Inner and Outer Courts," but struck an initiate of 1849 as "a stuffy and unventilated nook" which "suggested, as the coffin-shaped table did also, premature entombment." It was located on the fourth floor in Mitchell's Building, on the south side of Chapel Street and somewhat closer to Church Street. Jove's bust was repaired and painted black; self-levies on the classes of 1843 through 1848 gradually replaced the lost furniture and furnishings, and the first gowns were provided before the initiation of their successors by the class of 1843.

A third, more spacious accommodation was engaged by the class of 1850 on the fourth floor of the Leffingwell Building, also known as the Law Building because it housed Yale's law school, on the northeast corner of Court and Church Streets. The society contracted with the builder to arrange the entire "sky parlor" of the top floor to their liking, with a ceiling of black velvet—fifty-seven yards' worth—and a "grand banquet hall." This was to be Scroll and Key's home for the next twenty years. (In an article about the groundbreaking in 1869 for the construction of the present Keys tomb, the *College Courant* reported that these Church Street quarters were "the only college secret society hall, so far as we know, which has never been entered by outsiders; its peculiar location has made it almost inaccessible to the uninitiated.") The rival society was clearly surpassed: Skull and Bones was still using "a small hot room, so far as one could judge," on the third floor of 460 Chapel Street, above the rooms of Linonia, in use since before 1842.[17]

THE NAME, THE BADGE, THE CONSTITUTION

The new fellowship of course required a name. "Bones having set up Demosthenes as its patron saint," writes Lyman Bagg, "Keys seemed determined to 'go one better' and claim the recognition of the great Zeus himself." Two phrases were chosen, *"Collegium Sanctum Pontificum"* ("Sacred Pontifical College") for the society, and *"Collegium Conservat Jupiter"* ("May Jupiter preserve the College") as the trailing motto; the letters "C.S.P." and "C.C.J." were thereafter to be printed with the society symbol or cut, the former phrase above and the latter below it (although the name "Scroll and Key" was sometimes prefixed), in society printings. In campus publications such as the *Yale Banner*, which first began publishing annual issues regularly in 1842, "Scroll and Key" was used from the year of the society's founding through 1849; then until 1859, both the American name and the Latin initials were employed. Thereafter, only "C.S.P." and "C.C.J." appeared in the *Banner* above and below the cut of their symbol, into the late 1860s, when "Keys" understandably came into use as campus shorthand for the group.[18]

Voting on a design by senior Henry Scudder, appointed at the first meeting in Heister's room "to furnish a name and badge," the members established the scroll and key as the society's symbols, and thus its name to the outside world. "The Eagle," the minutes of July 20, 1842, record, "being the bird of Jove, represents the Genius of the society, an emblem of power, superiority and lofty aspiration. Descending from above, he brings to us the Key of Knowledge, by which we are to unlock the arcana of science and art. The Key therefore represents the mysteries connected with the society, the directions to which are contained in the Scroll accompanying. The Hand signifies the receiving of the Key and Scroll, or the initiation into the rights and mysteries of this compact. The Chain which forms the outline of the badge is composed of fifteen Links, representing the fifteen members of the society united together in an indissoluble bond of fellowship. The Chain also indicates that unity of feeling and interest which exists among it members, and the cultivation of the social affections spoken of in our [constitution's] preamble."[19]

The original badge was of the same size and shape as the first Bones pin, a rectangular gold plate engraved with the eagle—perhaps inspired by their mascot, which was Jove's bird borne on Roman army standards—poised above, suspending the scroll, with a right hand below, grasping the key. This form was still worn in the 1860s by a single member at a time, presumably as a mark of office, in place of the then redesigned plain gold pin of a key lying across a scroll, used to this day, Less romantically, it has been said that the scroll depicts the "Declaration of Independence from Scull and Bone," and the key to the Bones temple won by a Keys man in a card game.[20]

Because commencement for the class of 1842 was near, scheduled for August 18, they were quick to find a jeweler to execute the design, even before selecting their fifteenth junior on August 11. At a special Saturday meeting two days later, a resolution was passed that the juniors proclaim the society's existence by appearing with their badges on Monday, August 15, "at the breakfast table" in the common dining hall. The New Haven papers ran accounts of the galvanizing effect on campus of this display.[21] (By 1856, according to a published glossary of national college words, this display had its own name: "The word 'swing' is used for coming out with a secret society badge; 1st, of the society, to *swing out* with new badges; and 2nd, of the men, intransitively, to *swing*, i.e., to appear with the badge of the secret society."[22])

Showing further talents as publicists, they printed a brief notice in the New Haven *Daily Herald* on the eve of commencement, reading below a plain cut of their symbol: "A stated annual meeting Will be held at the Society's Hall, *This Evening*, at 9 ½ o'clock. Aug. 17. By Order." The preceding page featured this news item: "We have had several inquiries with regard to a society which has attracted considerable attention in College. We are not in the secrets of the fraternity, but understand that the members are among the leading students in College. We know not what its name is; it may be nameless, but for a full exposition of its character, design, etc., we refer to a cut of its badge in this day's paper!"

Badges were hardly exclusive to the two Yale senior societies. The New Haven weekly newspaper the *College Courant* in its issue of July 17, 1869, quoting Alexander Pope's line "Pleased with a ribbon, tickled with a badge" observed: "We Americans, to judge from the number of pins and badges of every kind you see in walking through the streets of any city, are growing like [the French], and between temperance societies, masonic orders, college societies, old army corps, and so on, no one can complain of lacking chances to swing out a pin of some kind."

At Yale the badges came to possess a special resonance and were a source of psychological pressure to commit to a society's proffered bid before Tap Day—to be "packed," to ensure the reward. "During Presentation week," reported the *College Courant*, "and the rest of the term, those who have not received elections to the 'Skull and Cross Bones' or 'Scroll and Key' societies, see those who have, sporting their pins and enjoying themselves, and they naturally feel some chagrin. To this no reasonable exception can be taken; but the feeling is so strong that under its influence, when still fresh, a crowd is likely to be packed. Men know the expense, the toil, the worry connected with starting or securely establishing a new society, or with resuscitating an old one; they know they will be thrown in with some whom they would not associate with elsewhere; they know the ridicule, open and secret, that they subject themselves to in college; the risk of failing to get a crowd the next year; the little good the society can do them here, and the little honor it can bring them after leaving college, and yet the ruling passion is still strong after three years of experience, and—they don the pin."[23]

Publicly, with its non-Greek, outwardly American name in three words from Middle English, a symbolic badge, coded language prominently published, and an annual membership of fifteen, Scroll and Key was tracking—and pronouncing its instant equivalence to—Skull and Bones in all these respects. Privately, and in a way Bones was not known to have structured itself with a formal founding document, they strove to explicate their vision and purpose. The preamble of their Constitution provided:

> . . . that the love of beauty is the peculiar distinction of a noble mind; that it is wise therefore to cherish an enthusiasm for perfect forms of grace, whether seen in the works of literature, science, or art . . .
>
> We believe that such studies and pursuits develop the best affections of the heart, and the highest powers of the intellect, and afford a foundation for friendships which are cemented by elevating the character of thoughts, and by giving a decided tone to the finer sentiments of the soul.
>
> In this belief we propose to ourselves the study of those principles of taste which govern in literature and art, of those qualities which excite admiration in the characters of great men, of those features which please or awe in nature; of all things, in short, which are admitted into that portion of the soul, where love and friendship reign.[24]

These sentiments closely echo the robust idealism of Ralph Waldo Emerson's Phi Beta Kappa address to the Alpha of Massachusetts at Cambridge in 1837, "The American Scholar," wherein he proclaimed that "if the single man plant himself indomitably on his instincts, and there abide, the huge world will come round to him. . . . The study of letters shall no longer be a name for pity, for doubt, and for sensual indulgence. The dread of man and the love of man shall be a wall of defense and a wreath of joy around all." In his essay "Nature" of 1836, the sage of Concord had said, "The high and divine beauty which can be loved without effeminacy, is that which is found in combination with the human will." Emerson in 1841 seemed almost to anticipate the next year's founding of Scroll and Key itself and its chosen patron in "The Over-Soul": "And so in groups where debate is earnest, and especially on high questions, the company becomes aware that the thought rises to an equal level in all bosoms. . . . It arches over them like a temple, this unity of thought in which every heart beats with a nobler sense of power and duty, and thinks and acts with unusual solemnity. . . . The action of the soul . . . broods over every society . . . and Jove nods to Jove from behind each of us."[25]

Emerson had become a favorite lecturer on college campuses in the 1840s and 1850s. He visited New Haven to speak six times between 1852 and 1868, writing in a letter "the beautiful town—city—is it not? of New Haven . . . always appears to me eminently attractive." Andrew Dickson White, Yale and Bones 1853, recalled that Emerson's lectures on the college circuit "made the greatest impression on me."[26] Although Emerson did not talk specifically about student societies, "he confronted a young man with the crisis of his individual ambition and his need to make decisions. . . . Emerson laid out an ideology that established young manhood as the critical period of genesis for the maturing mind, a period when the success or failure of a developing life hung in the balance." He justified the dissatisfaction of college youth with the American system of education and its incongruous fit with the modern occupational world.[27]

A speaker who told young men to respect their own private minds, to make the special cast of that mind the basis of an individual life, captivated them. In Emerson's romantic metaphor, "education as a *mirror* no longer reflected the general state of the community. More radical than politics, religion, and the law, education as a *lamp* threw light on the new opportunities of the student as a young man."[28] Every man might be a specialist, every profession was honorable: "One man is born to explain bones and animal architectures; and one, the expression of crooked and casual lines, spots on a turtle, or on the leaves of a plant; and one, machines, and the application of coil springs and steam and water-wheels to the weaving of cloth or paper; and one, morals; and one, a pot of brandy, and poisons."[29] Each man had a social contribution to make, but that demanded the active involvement of the individual in his personal development. The debates and friendships of the senior societies were a part of the path to that end.

The phraseology of Scroll and Key's constitution reflects as well the artistic faiths and political creeds of the age: in politics, Jeffersonian democracy; in the arts, the Romantic movement; in social theory, the perfectionism associated with Brook Farm and the Mormons; even the concept of human progress toward a not-so-distant millennium. At their constitution's close, following the articles of government it established, the Keys delegation of 1843 dedicated themselves to "the study of literature and taste," and their meeting place to be "the home of friendship, the hall of literature, and the studio of fine arts." "The general idealism of their time," writes their official historian, "invited them to set up an organization which would afford a freer scope than the curriculum to expressions of the individual which were not exclusively scholastic."[30]

The named qualifications for admission were "morality, amiableness of disposition and manners, good literary acquirements, a superior order of talents, and a total disconnection with any other rival Society." The constitution gave effect to the society's purposes by stipulation that "at each regular meeting, orations, or an oration and a poem, shall be read by two of the members, who shall have previously volunteered, by those pre-appointed. And it is recommended that the productions of the group embrace a great variety of subjects, of matter, and of style, as is consistent with literary excellence." Following these presentations of oration and poem, a "familiar debate" was to be held "on some literary question, drawn by lot at the time upon which each member shall speak at least once. . . . In general, these exercises should be conducted so as *to combine intellectual improvement with the cultivation of the most intimate friendships*"[31] (emphasis supplied).

In other words, the "program" of Scroll and Key was very like the exercises of the historic literary societies, Phi Beta Kappa, Linonia, Brothers in Unity, and Calliope, only with many fewer members in a more intimate setting, and very likely resembling the first senior society's program as well, given Bonesman Henry Kingsley's conversations with his younger brother William over the years about the doings of Skull and Bones, and William's role as leading founder of Keys.[32]

The most pronounced difference between the old literary societies and the new senior societies is to be found not so much in the practice of debates or the broad variety of topics but, in the language of the Scroll and Key constitution, in "the cultivation of the most intimate friendships." That was the new ingredient in Yale class societies, initially forged by Bones and now annealed by exact replication, in form and membership number, in Keys. A collateral consequence was that, like Bones, Keys was not a "chartered" organization: it was to refuse all applications for charters from other colleges and universities.[33]

CODE, CLASS PHOTOGRAPH, AND CATALOGUE

Like its older rival, Keys paired internal secrecy with public proclamations which could be read by all, but comprehended completely only by initiates. "The posters, which, until within a few years [of 1872] were put up about the college yard and elsewhere at Commencement season, for the benefit of graduates," Bagg recorded, "displayed an eagle poised above the ordinary emblems, with no print—in addition to the inevitable letters—except the day and hour of the meeting—'9 P.M.' perhaps—or the numeral '142.' A small, seal-like wood-cut of the society, displays the clasped hands upon an open scroll, with "Adelphoi" in Greek capitals at the top, '1852' below, and at the bottom two hieroglyphic characters, the one like a Gothic 'T,' the other like an old style Greek 'Γ' while the only trace of the key is its head, which projects from the top of the scroll. Another, steel-engraved seal represents the eagle, looking down from above upon the central scroll and key, upon which the letters are indicated, while an open right hand reaches up from below. The framework of the device is made up of fifteen oblong lengths, and its shape cannot be better described than by saying that if there were sixteen links it would be an eight pointed star."[34]

The posting of placards or notices was another way the two senior societies kept their names and symbols before their classmates, and not just at commencement ceremonies for the guidance of returning graduate members. The diary entry of professor of Greek James Hadley for March 5, 1851, is illustrative: "Difficulty at prayer on Thursday night, when Blackman [not from Keys, but a "neutral"] attempted to take down a Scull and Bone notice, and had been more or less abused by Crampton, Dana, Alexander, and Beman, Seniors of that Society. Admonitions to the offenders. Renew our [faculty] rule of no notices in the Chapel." Another squabble over society posters seems to have occurred in the fall of 1857, when students affixed notices to the "Chapel Elm." The freshman fraternity Kappa Sigma Epsilon punctured the dignity of the Bones in defacing a meeting announcement. The *Yale Review* of March 1857 reported on "the terrible affray of last term between the former institution [unnamed, but having a 'mystic emblem'] and 'Sigma Eps,' relative to 'posters,' in which though no skulls or bones were broken, it would seem that some must have been cracked. If this be the case, we hope the 'Eulogians' will become reconciled to their freshman brethren, and the college world would again be entertained by their caricatures on common sense. We marveled that the 'Troubadours' [Scroll and Key] did not 'roll up their scroll' in sisterly sympathy."[35]

Communications among Keys members, meant of course to be seen by their contemporaries, were equally ornate. "The invitations to the 'Z.S.'—or 'bum' [undergraduate slang for feast] held at the middle of the first and second terms—are printed," reported Bagg, "within a scroll-like design from which the key is absent; or else with the ordinary cut at the head of the note. The company of the 'brother' is simply requested upon the appointed evening, and he is directed to answer the secretary, which officer is designated by the letter 'G.,' and is his 'in truth.' Aside from these initial letters there is no mystery about the affair, which is either printed in gilt or, if in black, has mourning bands about the edges of the page. All society communications are also forwarded in black-edged 'return' envelopes, as in the case of Bones, sealed in black wax with the society emblems and letters. . . . The anniversary of Commencement night used to be announced among the ordinary advertisements of the city papers, in connection with the society cut. More recently, at the head of their editorial columns of Commencement morning, 'C.S.P.—P.V.S. 9.p.m.—C.C.J.,' or something of the sort, appeared, between double rules of black."[36]

Keys also issued catalogues (the first covering the three classes of 1842 through 1844) with printed lists of elections of the new club or "convivium" forwarded each year to every graduate member (the "veteros") in connection with the invitation to the celebration of commencement night.[37] The men of Keys each had two names within the society, one for an office and one personally chosen, as with Bones. The names for their offices did not change: Zanoni was the senior leader, Anselmo the secretary, and Periander in charge of the physical properties of the hall, while the various other functionaries of the year's crowd were assigned the names Chilo, Eumenes, Belus, Arbaces, Nichao, Nolero, Thales, Prasatagus, Mago, Guelph, Pirones, and Glaucus. Their society or "pontifical" names varied, with a classical cast: Charon, Orpheus, Polus, Milo, Margias, Phryius, Clodius, Adonis.[38] From 1864 onward, a card-sized photograph of each new group of fifteen was similarly distributed: in it, the central figure Zanoni held a large gilt model of the society badge (the two sets of three letters inscribed on the scroll) and each of the end men grasped a large key, pointed toward the center of the group. Eight were seated, including the three holding symbols, and the remainder, the "upper court," stood. Enlarged photographs of the same image were framed and hung in the rooms of graduates.[39]

Now that there were two competing senior societies, the election process began to be formalized. After the candidate lists had been made, a whole night was spent in the election. Since no junior in those days was ever pledged or spoken to in advance, the excitement prevailing among the "likely men" was intense. Both societies' senior class delegations marched in a body, Skull and Bones at midnight and Scroll and Key about an hour later, each led by a marshal conveying a bull's-eye lantern marked with the society's symbol. The Bones contingent also traveled with a human skull and femur; their Keys counterparts bore a large gilt scroll and key some two feet in length. They processed from

dormitory entry to entry along the Old Brick Row, offering elections
in the gloomy rooms. With the blinds drawn and the door shut and all
lamps extinguished, the lantern was aimed at the prospect's face, and he
was asked if he was "prejudiced in favor of any society." An affirmative
answer meant that he had pledged Bones, and the Keys crowd decamped.
If he instead said no, election was offered. Those accepting Keys were
then dispatched to report on their acceptance, and on any known decisions for Bones by their classmates. When fifteen candidates had been
secured, both group processions returned to their respective halls. The
next morning the societies marched from their halls in a body to Chapel,
partly as a bit of impressionism, partly a kind of theoretical covering of
their work by a quasi-religious ceremony.[40]

Following the Civil War, the Keys practice was for two members,
one a senior, the other a graduate, each carrying one of the exaggerated
keys, to proceed together to the room of each chosen man. "The Senior
raps sharply with his key upon the door, and, both stepping in, says, 'I
offer you an election to the so-called Scroll and Key. Do you accept?'
If the answer is Yes, both Keys men shake the Junior by the hand, and
tramp back to their hall, where the result of the first election is received
before a party starts out to confer the second, and so on for the others.
On this account the elections progress much more slowly than the case
of Bones, and more opportunities are given to the rabble in the yard to
yell, "Keys! Keys! Keys!" and surge about the bearers of those imple-
ments, whose approach is usually announced, by self-stationed outposts,
in the neighborhood of the State House steps. . . . There seems to be no
very great significance in the order in which the elections are conferred,
except that the one first received is perhaps to be interpreted as especially
honorable; but on the other hand this is sometimes offered to a man, who
is by no means the society's first choice, in order if possible to anticipate
Bones in securing him."[41]

So, the beginning forms and initial traditions were in place, but
before the decade was out, Scroll and Key was struggling: in 1850,
instead of the normal complement of fifteen, it was only able to attract

seven new members for the delegation of 1851. "We are but seven," one of them wrote, "and why? Because in this our class of '51 there seems to be a stampede to that foster-child of Linonia—Skull and Bones; to use a low idiom, the class of '51 flocked to Skull and Bones like Buzzards to a carrion, and to my certain knowledge are as well pleased with what they have found." [42] The reasons for the flocking were more complicated.

CROOKING

Skull and Bones, of course, mounted a determined, year-by-year resurgence in class prestige after the election disaster of 1842. By virtue of its head start of a decade, its members had "crooked" significant items of Yale memorabilia for their society's rooms, with one very recent prize about which they were probably indiscreet: the Bully Club. Riots between gown and town—firemen, or off-duty sailors in New Haven port—had been a feature of the college's history since at least 1799, and by 1806 the office of college bully (a title bestowed by the people of the town, although in use at English universities for a similar student system) came into existence; the students turned the epithet into a title of distinction and, in proper feudal fashion, made it an all-college elective post. The college bully commanded his class in its rushes in fights with the town toughs, but it was his particular honor to lead them in the commencement exercises, and head the line of march at the time of presentation of diplomas. The officeholder was possessed, "by right of physical superiority, of the Bully Club," a black knotty stick, first passed down from powerful hand to powerful hand by bully Isaac Preston (valedictorian of his class of 1812, and later judge of the Supreme Court of Louisiana), although the biblical-minded proclaimed that it came straight from Hiram, King of Tyre, while the classical lot swore that it was the original bludgeon of Hercules. [43]

The post of college bully had been held in the class of 1841 by Bones member Henry Sturges, the largest man in the class at six feet two inches and two hundred fifty pounds. By abolishing the position of this class officer in October 1840, the Yale faculty made him the last college bully. Sturges presented his badge of office to his senior society.[44] Lucius Robinson, class poet of 1843 and Bones, wrote a poem which began:

The "Temple"—now so rich and rare
Was never furnished fully
Until they consecrated there
The Club of the College Bully.
Sweet bully, sin has fled like dew
At the Faculty's parching tones, boys—
Let it rest in peace till the Order anew
Is endowed by the Skull and Bones boys.

Robertson's poem also celebrates his society's possession of "The drum, that whilom used to raise/The calliathump alarum," and "The old card table . . . /Of relics much the oldest/For seventy years handed down/To him who played the boldest."[45] The drum was one of many instruments used on Christmas Eve, the night of the college year's noisiest demonstrations, and on graduation sounded the march of the procession of seniors when they crossed the campus to form a circle in front of the Lyceum, around the college bully who there resigned his office and symbol to his successor in the junior class. The drumheads were inscribed with the signatures of all the class bullies. The faculty ended the disturbances in 1850 by the simple expedient of ending the term before the arrival of Christmas Eve. The drum was retired to the office of President Day, who allowed it to be used at the Junior Exhibition of 1842, "in the service of song" in the chapel, from whence it disappeared. The card table had been owned by a card and chess-playing club established by the class of 1837, used first in rented rooms, and then in North College, where the college authorities took alarmed notice; when the club disbanded in 1845, its furniture was dispersed.

As Bagg wryly noted in 1872, "when anything of the kind disappears, this [the Bones hall] is surmised to be its final destination." Other treasures reputed to have found a home on High Street include the college gong from the treasurer's office (or perhaps from the original "Commons Hall" which ended in 1842); a small college bell from West Haven, crooked from an exhibit by a returned missionary, as a curiosity connected with heathen worship; the banner emblazoned "Yale" created by students from New Haven in Boston who carried it in a procession in the latter city in honor of President William Henry Harrison in 1840, retained and presented by William Tappan Eustis of the club of 1841, and later carried in a public procession in New Haven for President Zachary Taylor (father of Richard Taylor, Bones 1845); the tongue of "the hated College Bell," stolen not from the college but from the sophomores who had removed it "from its high position;" the old college punch bowl and ladle, banished from active use under President Day following temperance reform; the constitutions of defunct societies; and examples of the society badges of all Bones' rivals and juniors.[46]

Not all such "relics" were summarily and secretly appropriated. After the disbanding of Calliope in February 1853, the portrait of the society's patroness was purchased at auction for $18 by Henry White of the Bones club of 1851 as agent for the Bones club of 1853 in July of that year, prevailing against an agent bidding for Keys.[47] As for the college bell cast in England used to summon the collegians to prayers and recitations under President Thomas Clap in the 1740s, it had been relegated to the New Haven alms-house when a larger bell was purchased by Yale to summon a larger, if not sleepier, student body. When New Haven constructed a bigger alms-house in 1852, four members of the Bones club of 1853, namely James Whiton, Andrew Jackson Willard, George Asbury Johnson, and Andrew Dickson White, banded together using their recently won Townsend Prize premiums to make the purchase of the Clap-era bell.[48]

Other relics were acquired by gift from members and alumni. A bust of Demosthenes, copied from the one in the Vatican Museum, was presented to the society at the convention held in July 1858 by Daniel Coit Gilman (1852), on behalf of the society's mythical "German chapter." He also brought back from his three years of study in Europe and left in the tomb a print of an open burial vault in which four human skulls lie, with the legend, from an initiation rite of the Illuminati, *Ob Arm, ob Reich, im Tode gleich* ("Whether poor or rich, all are equal in death"), with his card on which is written, as a joke, "From the German chapter. Presented by Patriarch D. C. Gilman, D.50."[49]

Both the students and the senior societies made collections of memorabilia—abbreviated to "memorabil," a word made popular by the *Lit.*—such as programs, silk badges of societies, examination papers, posters, invitations, or pieces of a sophomore's shirt or hat band.[50] Like all antiquarians, the memorabil hunter valued a thing for its rarity more than its worth, and so the senior societies prized especially objects of historical or other college-wide importance.

This led, in the 1850s and '60s, to the practice of "crooking," inflicted by upperclassmen on lowerclassmen, by individuals on anyone, and by the societies of all classes upon each other and the college. "Almost anything was apt to disappear from anywhere," writes Keys' historian, "and since, regardless of the identity of the original thief, the stolen object was certain to be seen sooner or later by a thief with society affiliations, all such articles tended to accumulate in the society halls. The Senior societies, with their memberships of prominent Juniors holding prominent offices and of men who had belonged to all the lower-class societies, were in an especially favorable position for this sort of thing, and practiced it without shame. 'Thus we hold this property,' said a member of Scroll and Key referring to a 'crooked' boating flag in 1860, 'by a double power, the right of original ownership and C. S. P.'s privilege of "crooking" whatever the members choose; but it should be observed that the *latter* is by far the best title.'"[51] In a letter published in the *Yale News* for June 6, 1878, purporting to be written by a new Bonesman in the class of 1879 following his initiation, the mythical senior writes: "The two base-balls used in the game with Harvard this year, are not yet in the case, as the one which has been stolen from the Captain of the nine has not yet been gilded and inscribed, and the second one the most earnest search has failed to discover, as it is probably on College St., in Keys hall."

Since no official repository existed or had been conceived by college officials for Yale memorabilia of some major historical, social, or athletic interest, the sequential disappearance of this or that college object or treasure—the college gong from the Treasurer's office, the presidential punch bowl, the tongue of the college bell—was apparently accepted for decades without ethical reflections hindering the undergraduates' fun. From this attitude of benign neglect, the societies inferred acquiescence, reasoning that what was so purloined were only mementos of college history in former years and, as such, might as well be preserved in some secure place. What places were more secure than the tombs of the senior societies?

"Crooking" was thus seen as morally different from unlawful plundering. The distinction was not sharp: new Bonesmen upon initiation were told not to steal things, but to look for "relics." In time, however, a sense of general campus ownership of some items did arise, and the theft of the championship prize flags from victories over Harvard in the last half of the 1860s, "crooked" by the president of the Yale Navy for use in the initiation of the crowd of 1873 into Scroll and Key, was to lead to widespread revulsion among the neutrals and considerable damage to that society's reputation, at a time when both senior societies were under severe attack for their "poppy-cock."

ELECTION COMPETITION AND NEW RIVALS

In addition to its reputation for having crooked or otherwise acquired the best memorabilia, from the class of 1844 forward, Bones again sought the best men among their classmates. The club of 1844, the first after the debacle of the spring 1842 elections which chose the club of 1843, with no men from A.D. and four from Psi U, included a president of Linonia, an editor of the *Lit.* (and Townsend Premium winner), the man giving the First Philosophical Oration at commencement (and winner of the Berkeley Premiums for Latin and Greek), and two other commencement orators. Of its other, nonacademically distinguished members, Orris Ferry, was to serve as a congressman and senator from Connecticut, interrupting that service to be a brigadier general in the Union Army; Samuel Fisk was president of the Massachusetts Medical Society; Joseph Cornell was a brigadier general in the Confederate Army; and William Washburn was elected successively congressman, governor of Massachusetts, United States senator, and member of the Yale Corporation.

The Keys crowd for 1844, by way of contrast, included more members of Phi Beta Kappa, six to Bones' four, and six members of A.D. (with one Psi U initiate), but for those with class distinctions, only two editors of the *Lit.*, the president of the smallest literary society Calliope, a commencement orator who had been president of Brothers in Unity, and two other commencement orators. None later served as a high state or federal political official, or head of a professional society, or general officer in the Civil War to come. The older society seemed to attract the stronger candidates that year, and it was later alleged by a member of the Keys crowd of 1844 that "the Skull and Bones being that year quite under a cloud . . . [i]n desperation, at the close of the year, and with the aid of some of the resident graduate members [tutors and others living in New Haven] . . . sought to rescue their lost fame, and succeeded in secretly pledging men, into whose hands we expected to place our own society. We were caught by surprise, and had to take inferior, though good men."[52]

By the next year, with the class of 1845, eleven of Bones' fifteen men were Phi Beta Kappa (to Keys' five), the deficit from Alpha Delta Phi had been reversed—nine, to Keys' four, while Psi U was not neglected, with four to Bones and one to Keys. Class distinctions from both groups seem to have been light: Bones tapped a president of Linonia and editor of the *Lit.*, who became class orator; Keys tapped a commencement orator who won the English Composition prize. The class of 1845 was not, in after life, a distinguished Bones club (it included one United States District Court judge, and four senior Confederate Army officers), and one of those was CSA Lt. General Richard Taylor, son of the eighth president of the United States, Zachary Taylor. The Keys crowd of 1845 all had successful professional careers, but only three (Carter Harrison, member of Congress and assassinated mayor of Chicago; Isaac Peet, principal of the New York Institute for the Deaf; and James Tappan, speaker of the Arkansas House and Confederate brigadier general) attained some national political or educational distinction.[53]

The members of Kappa Sigma Theta, the first of the sophomore societies at Yale, founded in 1838,[54] sensed this weakness, and in October 1845, with the cruelty of the clever young, published the *Yale Banger* (named after the wooden stick the students carried in case of a fracas with the townies), containing burlesques of the symbols of the senior societies. The skull of the Bones symbol had its cranium cut off, to serve as a punch bowl, with the two femurs placed inside as toddy sticks. The caricature of the Scroll and Key cut depicted the scroll inscribed as a "Declaration of Independence and Rejection of the Skull and Bone," signed at the foot by the "great seal," which consisted of the proverbial fox reaching after the equally proverbial sour grapes.[55]

Keys' existence for the first dozen years was a precarious one. In only three classes before 1852 did it obtain the regular number of members (fifteen), which Bones never varied in electing, but ranged from seven— the lowest, in '51—to fourteen.[56] The gaps were filled by "honorary members," inducted as a reward for "their great exertions on behalf of the society" in recruitment of members, and the catalogue lists for the lean years always showed fifteen names.[57]

Furthermore, the lèse-majesté of Keys in challenging Skull and Bones could, once conceived, be repeated, and Keys itself had not one but two new rivals, "Dart and Star" and "Sword and Crown."[58] The latter, complete with elaborate badge, is noted in Belden's book of 1843, along with Dart and Star, and is classed with the contemporaneously born Scroll and Key as "professed rivals of the Skull and Bone." The secret exercises of Sword and Crown, he wrote, "are said to be of a literary character" and the "number of members, the requisite qualifications for membership and the manner of wearing the badge in this and [Dart and Star], are the

141

same as in the others."[59] Edwin Bulkley of the Keys club of 1844 was later to write that ". . . good men—and who had choice of being with us—were carried away by the anti-secret society epidemic of the period, and went into an organization called Star and Dart, in the expectation of breaking all down, by making societies numerous and common."[60]

The badge of Dart and Star—by 1849, when its cut was published in the *Yale Banner* for that year, called "Star and Dart"—was a burlesque upon the badges of both Bones and Keys: the framework was an exact copy of the Bones pin, and the engraved central design showed the eagle of Scroll and Key, matter falling from its beak as it pecks at the shattered skull lying at its taloned claws, represented as having mastery over Bones, while a dart in the upper left corner aimed at the eagle's back shows destruction about to fall on Jove's bird. A star in the upper left corner of the cut, Belden explained (perhaps suggesting his own membership), "demonstrates the prosperity and final success of the [Dart and Star] society over its rivals."[61]

This design as a wood-cut copy surmounted a notice in a local paper: "*Nos in vita frates sumus.* C.2954 a. F ∞ [D on its back to right, L on its back to left]. There will be a general meeting in New Haven on Thursday evening, Aug. 15. 1844. Yale College, Aug. 10." Doubtless posters to the same effect were also displayed about the college buildings at such seasons. There was a hiatus in the new society's existence after 1845: the *Yale Banger* ran a "death notice," reading: "Died during the past year, the Chi Delta Theta, and Star and Dart societies of the Senior Class. '*Nil mortuis, nisi Bone-um,*' which may be translated, 'they would not have died but for the Skull and Bones'" (instead of the proper translation of the motto correctly spelled in Latin, "Of the dead, speak nothing but good.")[62]

The Yale Tomahawk, first published on December 5, 1848, by sophomores in Alpha Sigma Phi, ran a similar deprecatory notice: "The President and Vice President [of Star and Dart] will meet, immediately after ten, at North College, to weep. After the weeping, the third and last member of the Society will expatiate upon the virtues of the deceased;

when the entire corps wilt proceed to the grave-yard. Juniors who have been pledged to the Star and Dart, will attend the funeral without further invitation." The society was revived in the class of 1849, and the *Yale Banner* published the names of fifteen members in the class of 1850 and eleven in the class of 1851, below the society cut and the numeral "2954." Whether it had a hall of its own, or regular weekly meetings and exercises, or had pretensions to equality with Bones and Keys, or "died by choice or necessity," all remain uncertain.

The members of Star and Dart were not of quite the class eminence of those tapped for Bones and Keys, but nor were they nonentities. The Dart club of 1850 included the valedictorian and president of Brothers in Unity (Martin Kellogg, who went on to become the president of the University of California), the class orator, one commencement orator and three other members of Phi Beta Kappa, the president of Linonia, the vice president of Brothers in Unity, four men from A.D., and five from Psi U. Leonard Woolsey Bacon of that club became a well-known preacher and author, receiving a DD from Yale in 1879. The relative lack of distinction of the eleven members of the club of 1851, however, presaged the society's demise. While including an editor of the *Lit.*, the president of Linonia, and a commencement speaker, there were no members of either A.D. or Psi U, and only one member of Phi Beta Kappa, David Page Smith, who became professor of Medical Theory and Practice at Yale. Still, that year Star and Dart found eleven men, when Keys could only find seven.

Sword and Crown quickly disappeared, and Star and Dart finished with the class of 1851,[63] but their mere listing together in Belden's book as equivalent groups, without sharing our after-knowledge that of the three, only Keys would endure, indicates the severity of the challenge Keys immediately faced in attracting members so as not to meet the others' fate. William Atlee of Keys' 1851 delegation later wrote about his delegation's experience (which must have had some precedent in earlier years' elections) to David Trumbull (class of 1876) that "there was considerable skirmishing among the societies, and in some way we did not get our full number. There was a third society then, 'Star and Dart,' and it made some confusion."[64]

This unhappy yield of seven in the spring of 1850 also reflected the third threat to the continued existence of Scroll and Key, the steady decline of the founding members' initial enthusiasm and ambition. The records of the class of 1844 show the drift away from program discipline: November 9, "A few . . . came straggling in . . ."; November 23, "At last . . . a goodly number were present, allowing for the usual toothaches, engagements, and other good excuses . . ."; January 23, "In the absence of all the appointed performers . . ."; January 30, "Only a scanty number were present . . ."; February 19; "After a protracted inter-regnum of some two weeks . . ."; April 2, "Though several of our number were absent . . ." Failure to prepare the exercises, lateness, unauthorized absences, and early departures continued through the succeeding clubs. By 1847, essays and conversations grew more perfunctory, and society record-keeping became intermittent, then ceased altogether. Wine, punch, and cards displaced the orations and play readings, dancing, singing, storytelling, amateur instrumental music, whist, and other merrymaking became the norm rather than the occasional exception.

The records of 1849 are in stark contrast to the sentiments of the Constitution of 1843. "Now Liquor is an Honorary Member of C.S.P. and . . .his virtues are *in the mouths* of his fellow Members . . . And the punch was made; for Lemons, and Pineapple, and Sugar, and Rum, and Water (so little, that it couldn't go down alone) had met together and said, 'Let us be Punch,' and they were Punch. Then the spirit descended like a dove, and made glad the hearts of all." After seven years, Scroll and Key had become, in a member's later expression of distaste, "a convivial club," and by 1848 attracted a sarcastic catchphrase for the society: "Lo, it is still here." (Skull and Bones, at the time, was no less "convivial": one graduate was to remember a Bones supper at which only he and the society servant John Creed were sober.)

Efforts at reform were not lacking: the crowd of 1848 decided that literary exercises were already well provided by Linonia, Brothers, and Calliope, and that they really needed a greater "opportunity for improvement in the elegant art of conversation," in addition to scheduling original essays or poems. Structural change was also effected. In the pure democracy of the founders' constitution, there was no final source of power: the articles could only be amended by a vote of all active members, thus putting reform at the mercy of the weakest man, and the officers were elected three times a year, in every term, so the tenure was impracticably brief. Under the leadership of Cyorian George Webster of the class of 1848, new authority was given to the senior officer, so that each member "shall do whatsoever he commandeth him: he shall say 'Go there' or 'Go here,' and each [member] shall go even as [the officer] has directed."[65]

Still, new practices in a small group whose members only abide together for one year take time to become the new traditions, and considerable damage had apparently been done to the campus reputation of Scroll and Key. With assaults from two sides, from a revived Star and Dart and from a resurgent Skull and Bones, in the spring of 1850 much of the solid element in the class of 1851 went again to Bones: the class salutatorian and Clark Prize winner, the president of Linonia and philosophical orator at commencement, three presidents of Brothers, the president and also the librarian of Calliope, an editor of the *Lit.*, the winner of the Berkelian Latin Premium, the winner of the first prize for Latin Translation—and two men without any class prizes who went on to otherwise undistinguished careers as a merchant and high school teacher, respectively. Of the Bones fifteen, nine were members of Phi Beta Kappa.

In his memoirs published in 1903, former Yale president Timothy Dwight reflected on his senior year of 1848–49 in Bones (without explicitly naming it), making it clear that family wealth was far from requisite for election. "We were a democratic community," he remembered, "with small temptation on the part of any among our number to indulge in aristocratic feeling, so far as that feeling had relation to the sphere of money. During a brief portion of my Senior year—as my family home was closed at the time—I took my meals with a club the members of which, about fifteen in number, were classmates of mine. These classmates, I think, were all of them, with the exception of three or four, men who either received financial aid from benevolent funds or were obliged, for want of sufficient means, to support themselves throughout their course of study, partly or wholly, by their own efforts. They were, however, among the leading men in the class in the different lines of college success and prominence—much more truly so than most of those who were regarded as the richer members of our class brotherhood. They were most influential in every way and most highly esteemed by every one."[66]

Dwight's reminiscence also perhaps makes clear why the Yale faculty, even beyond those professors who had been in delegations of Bones and Keys in their undergraduate days, never seriously moved to ban the senior secret societies in New Haven, as was to occur by administrative edict in 1857 at both Harvard to the north and Princeton to the south. When campus student leaders were elected year in and year out, and their later fame in politics and the professions across the nation brought reflected glory to the college, these societies became settings for display of Yale College's primary product, a good character—for only men of character, "those who were intelligent, honest, poised, and dependable, could attract the attention of the upperclassmen who selected their successors for the societies, and of their classmates, whose opinion was decisive in determining class leadership, to be elevated to the most prestigious societies."[67]

The Bones choices, however, were never exclusively the outstanding scholars and high achievers in the class. James Luce Kingsley, professor of Latin Language and Literature (and father of Henry, 1834 and Bones, and William, 1843 and Keys), asked his nephew and student Daniel Coit Gilman (1852 and Bones, living with his uncle's family while an undergraduate), "How is it that they make up the Skull and Bones Society? There are A and B, who are the leading religious men of the class, and then there is C, who is dissipated and loose, in the highest degree. There is such a one, who is the Valedictorian, and such a one, who is hopelessly out of sight, below a second colloquy. There is X, who has all the refinement of an early education in the midst of wealth and social privileges, and Y, who has never risen above the impolite roughness of his boyhood. There is one, who has commanding influence in the College, as a speaker or writer, while another is without the slightest power in either direction—a man of no prominence in any respect whatever. How can you explain it?" Gilman's answer is not recorded.

The pattern held over the succeeding classes: fourteen years on, the Bones club of 1865 contained the valedictorian, the salutatorian, the DeForest Medal winner, the class poet, the winner of the senior class debate and English composition prizes, three of the five *Lit.* editors, and the Wooden Spoon Man, but also four men lacking faculty or student honors, who later became, respectively, a businessman, a lawyer, a doctor, and an artist.

Even if the Bones choices sometimes seemed quixotic, this did not help Keys. Eleven more classmates moved to Star and Dart, and C.S.P. was left with seven in the class of 1851, a delegation they filled in with four others elected during the senior year, when they held only scattered meetings (the class of 1850 had recorded only one, their initiation). Yet, like the Bones club of 1843, the Keys crowd with their next election snatched victory from the jaws of defeat. They seriously considered whether to revive Star and Dart, or to form a new society, or to make a concerted effort to reverse their fortunes in the next election, for the class of 1852. Choosing the last course, they succeeded in the effort: Keys that year attracted all three first presidents of Linonia, Brothers, and Calliope, the DeForest Prize winner (best oration by a senior in a competition), the class orator, one philosophical orator and three other commencement orators, and the first of the five men to be elected editors of the *Lit.*

The Yale College enrollment in the class year of Bones' founding, 1832–33, was 354; two decades later, the number was 447, a 26 percent increase. The number of talented young men was simply greater, producing in the membership of the two senior societies remarkable constellations. Jacob Cooper, himself professor of Greek at Rutgers, in a memoir of his Bones clubmate and classmate William Preston Johnston prepared for a reunion of their class of 1852, noted it to be "a remarkable fact, that the founders of three great universities of our country, which, like that of Berlin, started out at once as thoroughly equipped teaching powers, were here together at the same time. Two of them, Presidents Gilman [of Johns Hopkins] and Johnston [of Tulane], were members of the same class; and President White [of Cornell], of the next; while all three were brought into the closest companionship by becoming members of the same senior fraternity. We have no other example in our country, nor, in fact, in the world, of three great universities being founded severally, and fully equipped, by the genius respectively of three men, undergraduates and companions at one time and in the same college. Nothing at Oriel College [Oxford] in the palmiest days of Whately, Keble, and Newman, can parallel this. . . . Gilman, Johnston, White, created their corporations *de novo*, and inspired into them the breath of life."[68]

The Bones clubs of 1853 through 1855 included the three men who became salutatorians of their respective class years, two of the three winners of the DeForest Prize, eight of the fourteen Townsend Premium men, and the president of the Yale Navy (a sign of things to come on the Yale sporting scene). In one of those wonderful pairings which the senior year at Yale sometimes threw up, Andrew Dickson White of Bones and the class of 1853 was to become the president of Cornell University, twice ambassador to Germany, and ambassador to Russia. His classmate Randall Lee Gibson, of Keys, was in later life a large slaveholder (and had an unknown great-grandfather who was a "free man of color"). A United States senator from Louisiana at his death, Gibson at Yale had helped overcome resistance to White's election as editor of the *Lit.*, where "a very considerable body of Southern students and their northern adherents declared against" White for his vocal anti-slavery sentiments.[69]

Gibson's prominence in the class and presence in Keys was another echo of the elective strategy of Bones adopted by Scroll and Key: they too were soon tapping Southerners. There had been only one in the first delegation, of 1843, then six in 1844, four in 1845, three in 1846, six in 1847, four in 1848, five in 1849, six in 1850, and (a proportional) three in the deficient, seven-man tap of 1851. Four Southerners joined in 1852, three in 1853 and 1854, and two in 1855.

After its first decade and partly as a result of the Keys initiative, Skull and Bones was electing relatively fewer men from below the Mason-Dixon Line: two in 1844, five in 1845, three in 1846 and 1847, four in 1848 and 1849, none in 1850, three in 1851, one in 1852, two in 1853 and 1854, and only one in 1855 (thirty, to Key's fifty-one). The Bones partiality for the mid-nineteenth-century equivalent of "Armenians" had not ended, of course: that society in 1838 and 1841 tapped two sons of the plantations from Brazil, and in 1855 collegians from Quebec and from Hawaii, then still a Pacific island kingdom ruled by King Kamehameha. Keys tapped a Nova Scotian in 1852, but no other foreigners in the dozen years after its founding.

It should be noted that there were, by 1855, simply fewer Southerners to choose. Seventy-two Southerners were attending Yale in 1850, and by 1860, only thirty-three were (while Harvard and Princeton, at sixty-three and one hundred thirteen that year, respectively, were at virtually their numbers of Southerners of ten years before.) After the abolition of the Missouri Compromise, the general sentiment at Yale "favored almost any concession to save the Union." Against that common grain, wrote Andrew Dickson White in his memoirs, the anti-slavery sentiments of Yale president Theodore Dwight Woolsey and his classmate of the class of 1820, the Rev. Dr. Leonard Bacon, pastor of New Haven's Center Church, "were supposed, at the time, to endanger the interests of Yale by standing against the fugitive slave law [enacted September 18, 1850] and other concessions to slavery and its extension. As a result, Yale fell into disrepute in the South which had, up to that time, sent large bodies of students."[70]

Yale's assistance in sending Sharps rifles to the Northern emigrés in Bloody Kansas at the urging of Professor Benjamin Silliman Jr. and Henry Ward Beecher was publicly resented. A letter to the North

Carolina *Standard* in the fall of 1856 noted that the student catalogues of the Northern universities had only a few Southern names, but "shame upon those few." He specifically alluded to Yale and the so-called Beecher Bibles. "We are proud of such names as Harvard and Yale, and feel that such benefactors of the human race should be held in everlasting remembrance by a grateful country. But their laudable objects are being frustrated by . . . fanatics that have obtained possession of the government of the schools their charity has founded. . . . Southern young men see their professors and fellow students, in the name of the college—nay, of the very *class of which they are members*—buying *religious rifles* to shoot their own brothers that may be seeking honorable and profitable employment in Kansas. These colleges have been turned from their legitimate channels and been perverted into strongholds of fanaticism; and from being links of union between all parts of the country, have become hothouses for the nurture of artificial statesmen of the Garrison school and manufactories of 'bleeding Kansas' tragedies."[71]

Southerners, who had constituted roughly 13 percent of the undergraduate student body in 1845–46, made up less than 9 percent a decade later, a number that was to fall below 4 percent by 1860–61. The class that entered Yale in 1853 contained thirty men from Southern or border states (twelve from the lower South, eight from the upper, and ten from the border); 1860 had fourteen (four upper, two lower, eight border); and the class that entered in 1861 saw only three, all from border states. The nadir was reached on Sunday, January 20, 1861, when Southern students raised a secession flag on the battlements of Alumni Hall, which was stormed by northern students who removed it, as pictured for the nation in dramatic drawings appearing in *Leslie's Illustrated Weekly Review.*[72]

The rough equivalence of the drawing power of the two societies after Keys' first decade only lightly masked the oscillation inherent in the pattern of the annual elections in a senior class still no more than one hundred in number. Keys began, perhaps unconsciously but soon deliberately, to emphasize the "set of men," the group, as against the selection (often, against a competing Bones tap, doomed to defeat) of the individual achiever. Both societies aimed to find and secure for membership men who combined intellectual distinction with the prized qualities of character and amiability, but (in the words of Keys' historian), "since such men are never plentiful and the number of them that a given society can attract still smaller, [a society] will often be faced with the choice of taking achievement without the other virtues or the other virtues without very much achievement."[73]

The next decade was to find Bones and Keys each grasping the opposite horns of this dilemma, with enormous consequences for the development and reputation of each. Bones was also to change the dynamic and up the ante by building a windowless "tomb," an effort which was soon to be replicated—but first by the new junior fraternity Delta Kappa Epsilon, not Scroll and Key. And both senior societies were to be affected by substantial changes in new collegiate social activities. These included the creation of the Yale Navy and its commodore, the first of the Yale teams and the tradition of athletic honors; the revitalization, under a newly prominent office of president, of the music society which had performed at the college religious exercises, now rechristened the Beethoven Society, acquiring (in a break with Puritan tradition) an organ in 1851 and, for better communal singing, publishing a book of Yale songs in 1853, the first songbook of any college; and the metamorphosis of a student lampoon of the Junior Exhibition into the "Society of Cochleaureati," soon recognized as the nine "best fellows" in the class, and that group's best of all, the Wooden Spoon Man.

In the same coming decade, the graduate members of both of the senior societies were also to organize themselves for the first time in corporate form, becoming the Russell Trust Association and the Kingsley Trust Association—in their respective names, appropriately honoring the primary founder of each—thus securing perpetual legal life in the Connecticut state capital. This enabled the ownership of land, and the subsequent construction of the societies' famous "tombs."

151

TAPPED FOR SKULL AND BONES, 1843–1855

Benjamin Tucker Eames	1843	Congress (R.I.)
Henry Stevens	1843	leading American bibliographer and antiquarian bookseller
Orris S. Ferry	1844	Congress (Conn.) U.S. senator, Conn. brigadier general, Union Army
Samuel Fisk	1844	president, Massachusetts Medical Society
William Barrett Washburn	1844	governor, Mass. U.S. senator, Mass. Alumni Fellow, Yale Corporation
Constantine Esty	1845	Congress (Mass.)
Richard Taylor	1845	lieutenant general, CSA leader, Army of the Tennessee
Leonard Wales	1845	U.S. District Court judge, Del.
Joseph Backus	1846	Fellow, Yale Corporation
Henry Baldwin Harrison	1846	governor, Conn. Alumni Fellow, Yale Corporation
Stephen Kellogg	1846	Congress (Conn.)
Rensselaer Nelson	1846	U.S. Distict Court judge, Minn.
Dwight Foster	1848	attorney general, associate justice Second Circuit, Mass.
Henry Hitchcock	1848	dean, St. Louis Law School president, American Bar Assoc.
Augustus Brandegee	1849	U.S. Congress (Conn.)
William Barker Clarke	1849	Yale professor of Divinity

Timothy Dwight	1849	Yale professor of Sacred Literature
		Yale president
Francis Finch	1849	dean, Cornell Law School
		associate judge, Court of Appeals, N.Y.
Franklin Fisk	1849	president, Chicago Theological Seminary
Henry Martin Dechert	1850	president, Commonwealth Title & Trust Company
Ellis Henry Roberts	1850	Congress (N.Y.)
		U.S. treasurer
Rufus Crampton	1851	president, Illinois College
Edward Evans	1851	professor of Mathematics, Cornell
Richard Haldeman	1851	Congress (Pa.)
Robbins Little	1851	superintendent, Astor Library
James Vose	1851	professor of Rhetoric, Amherst
Jacob Cooper	1852	professor of Greek, Logic, Rutgers
William Crapo	1852	Congress (Mass.)
Daniel Coit Gilman	1852	Yale professor of Geology
		Venezuelan Boundary Commission
		first president, Johns Hopkins
		first president, University of California
		first president, Carnegie Institute
		president, American Oriental Society
		president, American Social Science Association
		president, National Civil Service Reform League

William Preston Johnston	1852	chief of staff to CSA president Jefferson Davis
		professor of English, Washington & Lee University
		president, Louisiana State College, later Tulane University
George Griswold Sill	1852	lieutenant governor, Conn.
		U.S. district attorney, Conn.
		Alumni Fellow, Yale Corporation
Thomas Frederick Davies	1853	Episcopal bishop, Mich.
George Johnson	1853	attorney general, Calif.
Albert Emmett Kent	1853	founder, meatpacking industry
		donor, Kent Chemical Laboratory
Andrew Dickson White	1853	first president, Cornell
		Venezuelan Boundary Commission
		ambassador to Germany (twice)
		ambassador to Russia
		president, American delegation to Hague Peace Conference
		first president, American Historical Association
		president, American Social Science Association
James Morris Whiton	1853	originator, American intercollegiate sports, first Yale PhD
Carroll Cutler	1854	president, Western Reserve College
John Worthington Hooker	1854	professor of Hygiene, Amherst

Luton Burrit Morris	1854	governor, Conn.
William DeWitt Alexander	1855	surveyor-general, Hawaii
		president, Oahu College
Charles Johnson	1855	professor of English, Trinity College
Charles Mellon Tyler	1855	professor of Ethics, Cornell
Henry Yardley	1855	professor of Homiletics, Berkeley Divinity School

TAPPED FOR SCROLL AND KEY, 1842–1855

Leonard Case	1842	founder, Case School of Science
John Addison Porter	1842	Brown, Yale professor of Chemistry
Theodore Runyon	1842	chancellor, N.J.
		U.S. ambassador to Germany
William Lathrop Kingsley	1843	editor, *The New Englander*
Charles H. Crane	1844	surgeon general, Union Army
Isaac Atwater	1844	chief justice, Minn.
Carter Harrison	1845	Congress (Conn.)
		mayor of Chicago
Isaac Peet	1845	president, New York Institute for the Deaf
James C. Tappan	1845	speaker of House, Ark.
		brigadier general, CSA
Daniel Bonbright	1850	dean, Northwestern University
John Walker Fearn	1851	professor of Spanish, Tulane
		U.S. minister to Romania, Serbia, and Greece
Jacob Cooper	1852	proefessor of Greek, Rutgers
Homer Baxter Sprague	1852	professor of Rhetoric and English, Cornell
		president, University of North Dakota

Randall Lee Gibson	1853	brigadier general, CSA
		president, trustees, Tulane University
		Congress (La.)
		U.S. Senate (La.)
Charlton Thomas Lewis	1853	Yale professor of Greek
		president, Troy University
		deputy commissioner, Internal Revenue Service
George Shiras Jr.	1853	associate justice, U.S. Second Circuit
Benjamin Cutler	1854	president, Western Reserve College
Charles Goddard Child	1855	U.S. district attorney, Conn.

TAPPED FOR STAR AND DART, 1843–1851

Martin Kellogg	1850	professor of Ancient Languages
		president, University of California

CHAPTER FIVE

THE MAKING OF TOMBS, TEAMS, AND GIFTS (1856–1871)

The society halls are retired and guard their own secrets. Curiosity
stops abruptly at the iron doors.

—Henry Howland, "Undergraduate Life at Yale,"
Scribner's Magazine, July 1897

Through 1855, the delegations of Skull and Bones, like those of
Scroll and Key, held their meetings in rented rooms in commercial
buildings in New Haven. Furthermore, Bones like Keys that year had
no particular legal being or tenure, thus running the risk, in any annual
election gone wrong or during a fractious club year, of simply imploding
and disappearing, like Rose and Crown or Star and Dart. These two
circumstances were not tolerable to the Bones graduate members, many
of whom lived in New Haven and who as the group's elders now had
over two decades of reputation to protect and memorabilia to preserve.
They acted decisively in 1856 to rectify both situations, incorporating the
society in the State of Connecticut as a trust and granting it fee simple

title to a remarkable structure that announced, if any were in doubt, the Skull and Bones was here to stay.[1]

THE FIRST TOMBS

In his *Lives of the Twelve Caesars*, Suetonius wrote of the Divine Augustus and the city of Rome, "He would boast that he inherited brick and left it marble."[2] The same could not be said of the New Haven divine, Jeremiah Day. He inherited Yale's Old Brick Row on his inauguration as president in 1817, to which under his tenure were added North College in 1820 (flanking Elm Street), then the Second Chapel in 1823, the Trumbull Gallery behind the chapel in 1832, and the Divinity College in 1835. All the new buildings, like the old, were made of brick. Not until the construction in 1842 of the Old Library (now Dwight Hall) in Early Victorian Gothic style was there a college building to make pretentions to architectural beauty. It was the very first to be built with stone facing, of roughly dressed Portland brownstone. A second such, Alumni Hall, was completed in 1853.[3]

So, when the block west of the central campus on High Street near the corner of Chapel was mostly occupied by large, single- or two-family houses and stables, a campus sensation was caused by the construction of a windowless, tomb-like structure. Called "Yale's version of the Great Sphinx," this was built in Egypto-Doric style with the same brown Portland sandstone used for the college library. What is now the southern (left-hand) third was the original building, its centered door where there is now a slotted, darkened window. The annual dinner invitation to returning alumni who would behold the new hall proclaimed: "*Quid dicam de ossibus?* (Cic. de Nat. Deorum. II. 55.) *O fortunate, quorum jam moenia surgunt!* (Virgil. Æ. I. 430.)" "*And where shall I begin about the bones? Ah, happy are you whose walls rise today!*"[4]

From its outer facing the new Bones hall seemed large and sumptuous. Its cost was estimated to be about $30,000 (wildly off the mark), but the cost of the Old Library had been less. The society's lot was approximately forty-five feet wide along High Street by one hundred seven feet deep to the west, and was thus only partly covered on the east-west axis by a building rectangular in shape, with a frontage of twenty-nine feet, a height of about thirty feet, and a length of forty-four feet. This made the Bones structure only one story shorter than South Middle (Connecticut) Hall, and almost half the length of that dormitory in its depth facing High Street. The forbidding façade was not yet softened by the covering of Virginia creeper planted eight years later in 1864, and the "tomb"—for that was the name it attracted, to be used for the windowless halls of all the succeeding senior society buildings—stood back a rod or more from High Street, separated from it by a post-and-chain fence.

Its aspect was forbidding: the sandstone blocks, quarried in East Haven, were darker than the surrounding buildings. The hall seemed to be entirely cut off from the light as far as the interior was concerned, since no windows were to be seen. The massive, close-fitting doors were of iron (a common feature of side-hill tombs in New England), twelve feet high and five feet wide, upon which the society emblems were displayed. These were replaced in 1864 by new iron doors of a dark green color, again a dozen feet high, finished off in panels; heavy clasps of brass closed over the keyholes, secured by padlocks, beneath one of which the bell-pull was concealed. The roof, nearly flat, was covered first with plates of tin, replaced in 1867 with half-inch plates of iron. The skylight was similarly protected, with the chimneys and ventilators ranged around the edge of the roof. In the rear, a pair of small, blind windows were barred with iron, and below at the foundation level were scuttle holes, openings into the cellar which were also barred.[5]

From the time the current year's club took up occupancy on March 13, 1856, the tomb became a campus focal point which itself inspired new rituals for the society's members and new habits for outsiders. Its features, such as the beveled sandstone pylons along the street frontage and the padlocks, figured in the edge-burned letters sealed with stamped black wax inviting the neophytes to come to the tomb (invitations that were inevitably seen by roommates and others). "Pass through the sacred pillars of Hercules and approach the Temple," the text read. "Take the right Book in your left hand . . ." Would-be intruders discovered that if the wrong padlock was pulled or the right one twisted the wrong way, a warning bell was set off inside, indicated a non-member's approach on the steps.[6] Members to this day are discouraged from entering or leaving the building before witnesses. If observers are unavoidably present, those same members refrain from making eye contact with them and with each other, and enter in quick single file, silently.[7] Senior society men of all societies, starting with Bones, also refused to speak when passing in front of their halls.[8]

Very soon, casual pedestrians with some knowledge of the tomb's identity would pass it by only along the eastern, far side of High Street, and not in front of the building.[9] The seemingly unrestrained growth of the Virginia creeper plantings over the years made the tomb look neglected (the *College Courant* of July 3, 1869, reported that the "woodbine on Skull and Bones is very luxuriant this year"), and the front yard landscaping between the pillars and the big doors was often unkempt (the *Courant* two weeks later noted that "the grass has recently been mowed in front of the Skull and Bones hall"). "The society halls," a commentator of the 1890s was to observe about them all, "are retired and guard their own secrets. Curiosity stops abruptly at the iron doors."[10]

The Bones tomb today is well over twice the size of that constructed in 1856: a second block was added onto the rear in 1883 (on the balance of the land originally acquired in 1856); then the original block was faithfully duplicated to the north (to the right, when facing the hall) in another expansion in 1903, when a new entrance was placed between the old and new "testaments," or wings. The architect was Alexander Jackson Davis (1803–1892) and not, as has sometimes been speculated, Henry Austin (1804–1891), who was responsible for the somewhat architecturally similar brownstone Egyptian Revival gates erected in 1845 at the Grove Street Cemetery just a few blocks north of the Bones tomb. Davis had in 1853 designed Alumni Hall, financed partly with donations from Linonia, Brothers in Unity, and Calliope for their respective new meeting rooms. Demolished in 1911 to make way for Wright Hall, the stonework of its twin Gothic towers in "an act of filial piety" (arranged through a college administration dominated by Bones members such as President Arthur Hadley and Secretary Anson Phelps Stokes) was moved down and across High Street and reerected behind the Bones tomb, where they now loom over an otherwise hidden garden.[11]

The original Bones hall is among the very last to be constructed of the examples of the Egyptian Revival in American architecture (1808–1858): there are at least eighty such structures in the United States, and almost every major American architect of the period worked in the mode. Ancient Egyptian monuments had received featured article treatment in the *American Quarterly Review* in 1829, which relied on 930 engravings in the twenty-one-volume *Description de l'Egypte* appearing sequentially in Paris from 1809 to 1828, prepared by the Commission on the Arts and Sciences which had accompanied Napoleon's military campaign in Egypt from 1798 to 1801. The second edition was available to Austin in the New Haven library of his fellow architect Ithiel Town, as was Baron Dominique Vivant Denon's illustrated *Voyage dans la Basse et la Haute Égypte* of 1802.[12] After publication of those monumental volumes, Egypt was no longer some vague country vanished, except for biblical references to the Israelite captivity, in the mists of time: Americans revered the history of democratic Greece and republican Rome, but had a new awareness of the older civilization which those ancients themselves thought of as ancient.

Such buildings and monuments (including obelisks, such as the Bunker Hill monument of 1833, echoed in the memorial graves of ten out of the first seventeen United States presidents) were also treated at length in the first complete book on architectural history published in the United States, Mrs. C. Tuthill's *History of Architecture* of 1844, where she writes of their "size and magnificence" and their "grave and sublime [effect]." The style was also hailed as "economical," not only in the sense of simplicity of form, but economical to build as well, "having few and bold details; and consequently, not requiring expensive workmanship or materials." All of this—sublimity, gravity, and economy—would have appealed mightily to Davis's senior society client, rejecting his designs which resemble the Gothic-ornamented Dwight Hall for the simpler, windowless structure erected on High Street. As Emerson had observed in his "American Scholar" of 1835, "Instead of the sublime and beautiful, the near, the low, the common, was explored and poetized."[13]

Davis's design seems to be based on no one structure's image in the *Description* or Denon's *Voyage*, although features of several plates from both are suggestive. Framing the doorway were straight walls, like those in Denon's engraving of the Tombeau Egyptien at Lycopolis. To crown the portico, he imported a classical Greek pediment (the low-pitched triangular gable following the roof slopes, necessarily pitched to weather the rains and snows of New Haven, instead of the flat roof of the torrid Nile Valley), and added Egyptian plain horns at each pediment end and, at its apex, a small conical cap echoing the large one above the door of the Temple of Thebes at Kornou. The society's "portal" in its relative monumentality suggested those at the Temple of Karnac as depicted in the *Description*.[14] The windowless nature of the building provided challenges in designing for ventilation: flues were built within the walls, and drafts were started with Bunsen burners, perhaps suggested by Professor Benjamin Silliman Jr., Bones 1837 and the author of America's first college chemistry text.

The new Bones hall also resonated backward in Yale campus architecture. On October 25, 1832, just weeks before the founding of the first senior society, Colonel John Trumbull had moved his collection of history paintings, chiefly commemorating the events and self-sacrificing heroes of the American Revolution, into the almost windowless but skylit box of the Trumbull Gallery. This "taut little tomb with stucco imitating stone" was erected at the northern end of the Old Brick Row in the northwest corner of the campus, and the artist as arranged in the deed of gift was interred in its basement upon his death in 1843. This was the first art museum connected with an educational institution in America, and one of the oldest in the English-speaking world, its chief chronological rival being the National Gallery in London.

Trumbull had studied some architecture at Edmund Burke's insistence while in prison in London as a reprisal for the arrest of Major André, and designed the gallery himself. He asked the architect Ithiel Town for advice, and Town and his then partner Alexander Davis prepared a watercolor drawing of a small Greek Doric temple with pillars articulating the unbroken, windowless walls. In altering this design, Trumbull retained many of the primary features: vertical columns on the plane of a façade without openings emphasized the fundamental boxlike nature of architecture as enclosure, on a highly reductive level.[15] Given the similarities, it seems almost certain that the first version of the Trumbull Gallery temple proposal was the starting point for Davis's work as architect of the Bones tomb. The floor plates of the two buildings are virtually similar in size and proportion. "Whether or not there is a causal link [between the two buildings]," writes architect Patrick Pinnell, "the similarity of form and purpose is striking: inside a sepulcher, mysterious processes take promising but uninitiated young men through a *Lehrjahre* [an apprenticeship or learning year] of self-discovery and group bonding."[16]

The period from the Bones hall's conception to its opening was a relatively short four years. The club of 1853, under the leadership of Albert Heard and of William Crapo of the just-graduated club of 1852, formed a committee to raise enough money over five years to build the hall—"a stone building devoted entirely to our own use and convenience"—for which they had already considered plans. The proposal was so daring (no society or fraternity at Yale had ever built its own hall) that the possible opposition of the faculty had to be explored first. Crapo approached tutor William Kinne, of the club of 1848, who favored the idea and agreed to speak with Thomas Thacher, Yale professor of Latin since 1842 and a member of the Bones club of 1835, for sounding out the college administration. (Thacher, according to a memoir of a member of the class of 1859, "probably knew the students and their affairs most intimately [of the fourteen professors then on the faculty], and at one time was so popular as to be designated Vir [Man] in a mock catalogue.")

Thacher replied that the faculty could give no recognition to Skull and Bones any more than to any other student society, since it was inappropriate to make any distinctions among them, but if the society's alumni chose to put up a building for their use at commencement meetings "to renew old college associations . . . the faculty nor any other power about the college could not prevent it—that if the graduates after having erected such a building for their own purposes & conveniences see fit to permit students to occupy it, he did not see that the faculty could prevent that!"[17] The message was clear: there would be no formal faculty permission to build a hall, but no assertion of power to forbid such an effort, and no particular will to do so. In conformity with the professor's sinuous counsel, the graduates became the outside movers, and the seniors' club stayed in the background. William Elliott (class of 1844), Henry Harrison Baldwin (1846, three decades later the governor of Connecticut), and Franklin Fisk (1849) took leadership roles in pledges and agreed that Robert Bliss (1851), a New York stockbroker and banker, be engaged to call upon other graduate members and invest the funds so raised.

Religious buildings in Egypt, Greece, and Rome were not planned with interior sizes to accommodate large groups of people, or conceived in terms of complex and varied functions. Rather, they were sacred shrines of a restricted size and form to be visited only by the elect, and the final design for the Bones hall met this standard. Using the $6,000 budget produced by the builder Atwater Treat for lot dimensions of 25 by 45 feet, Bliss was directed by the building committee to approach the New York–based architect Davis, who had worked with the contractor Treat on other projects. In the end, the cost was $7,500, with the last payment made in July 1862.[18] The groundbreaking was on May 17, 1855, and the cornerstone was laid two weeks later on May 31. The builder's proposal for an iron fence was denied for reasons of cost, the notion of a wooden fence was rejected because of probable vandalism, and the idea of a box hedge was eliminated because it would take too long to cultivate it. Instead, six stone posts with two chains running between them were installed, a distinctive feature of the tomb that exists to this day.

The only public record of the interior of the original 1856 hall of Skull and Bones was published in 1876 with floor plans by the "Order of the File and Claw," in a pamphlet titled *The Fall of Skull and Bones*, recording a break-in on the Friday evening of September 29 of that year. The intruders (self-described as "neutrals . . . [having] the vulgar eyes of the uninitiated") went through the one-inch iron bars of the back-cellar windows of the "Eulogian Temple," using files and a "powerful claw" to draw out the long nails that fastened the iron netting to a wooden frame behind the window bars, and a hatchet to dig through the brick damp-wall to loosen the iron plate to which the window bars attached. Breaching all those protective measures to gain entry into the basement, then breaking through the wooden door at the top of the cellar stairs, they opened the two iron shutters which covered the back windows of the main hall, and "proceeded to examine the Temple at our leisure."

Their pamphlet, a narrative of the invaders' discoveries, included floor plans of the cellar, first, and second floors. The cellar included a kitchen, pantry and sink, and furnace. Not mentioned were any improvements on which the *College Courant* of April 9, 1870, had speculated, reporting that "last week Skull and Bones hall underwent several midnight repairs under the direction of Jesse Cudworth Jr., the well-known stove dealer and tinner of New Haven. Our reporter doesn't see the use of having these things done at midnight, for he objects to being up so late at night in order to serve the College world with all news items of interest." Also located there was the "Jo" or toilet, where "a light is always kept burning," and which was "ornamented with a dilapidated human skull and a framed set of 'Directions to Freshmen,' signed Thomas Clap, and dated *Yale College*, 1752." The dishes in the pantry pictured a skull and crossbones, and each spoon and fork was marked "S.B.T." On the first floor, another toilet was situated above the basement Jo, and the main hall, "called by the initiated '324,'" was decorated with colored tiles, while the walls were "gaudily frescoed." The only objects of interest in 324 "were a glass case . . . containing a large number of gilded baseballs, each inscribed with the date, score, etc., of a university game."

The intruders were disappointed, because "thus far we had found little to compensate us for our trouble."

On the second floor they found three parlors, one containing the library, with "the Constitution of the Phi Beta Kappa and a catalogue of Scroll and Key Society through 1868." The middle room, numbered "322," was the *sanctum sanctorum* featuring a "life-size *fac-simile* of the Bones pin, handsomely inlaid in the black marble hearth" of a fireplace, which also bore the marble motto just below the mantel in old English text, "*Rari Quippe Boni*." A collection of French-made pipe bowls with the members' titles and club numbers inscribed thereon and "packs of well-worn cards served to indicate how the society manages to kill five or six hours every Thursday evening," they speculated. Along the hallway walls fronting the three parlor rooms were forty years of photographs, each representing one of the fifteen-member clubs, of "poor" finish and thus probably "taken each year with the apparatus belonging to the society." The society's hallway safe was also rifled, but to the invaders' disappointment, they found nothing but "a bunch of keys and a small gold-mounted flask half-filled with brandy."

Finally, they noted a small closet containing unbound sheets of the society's catalogue, "a set of handsome memorabil books, one for each year," and two general storerooms filled with boating flags and foreign language books. The disappointed authors observed that there were neither billiard tables nor musical instruments, and "a total absence of all the 'machinery' which we had been led to expect . . . [A] thorough examination of every part of the Temple leads us to the conclusion that 'the most powerful of college societies' is nothing more than a convivial club."[19] They could see, in other words, only what they could view, so the society's true secrets remained safe. Nevertheless, reports the pamphlet, after the break-in was discovered the next evening, all five basement openings were duly sealed or resealed.

Subsequent break-ins provided further public reports of the interior. A Denver newspaper in 1886 carried an article in which the writer claimed to have seen the inside of the Bones hall, in "brown stone" and "by a recent addition [occurring in 1883] more commodious than the others . . . It is nicely fitted up, the walls are appropriately frescoed in lavender, maroon and chrome tints with skulls and cross-bones in the panels, and the chandelier globes have their symbols ground in them, but there is not enough difference between this hall and the others [of Scroll and Key and Wolf's Head] to pay for any further description here."[20]

So, befitting its seniority and graduate member financial strength, Skull and Bones became the first "landed" senior society, or indeed fraternity of any sort, to have its own free-standing building at Yale College—today the oldest surviving college society or fraternity hall in the United States. It also established a trend on the campus, and soon nationwide for the next few decades, for fraternity buildings to be windowless (the only Yale senior society building with actual windows one may see through, except that their venetian blinds are drawn, is Elihu's clapboard house facing the New Haven Green).

The second such was not the hall of Bones' rival Scroll and Key, but rather one built by the junior fraternity Delta Kappa Epsilon, founded in 1844, which was then sending more members to Keys than either of its junior class rivals and had been using rented rooms in the Adelphius Hall at the corner of State and Chapel Streets. The door was iron, and there were no windows, save the skylights in the flat tin roof. As described in that fraternity's 1910 official history, "The parent Chapter from the beginning developed architectural aspirations, the earliest temple-like halls of secret societies in this country being those of Skull and Bones and ΔKE at Yale. . . . The old 'Tomb' at Yale with its windowless walls, its forbidding exterior, and its mystic symbols has raised the hopes and desires of many an undergraduate, and its original plan has been copied by . . . a number of other fraternities."[21] It was erected in 1860–61, through a generous loan from Henry Holt, a member of the class of 1862 and in time the founder of his eponymous publishing house.[22] The brothers of DKE were still calling their hall a "tomb" in 1916 ("it was never called a 'frat house'; that collegiate stuff was for places like state universities," author and screenwriter Donald Ogden Stewart of that senior class remembered).[23]

Scroll and Key desired a new hall with the delegation of 1855, just five years after moving to the Leffingwell building on Church Street, and successor clubs were urged to begin saving to that end. A committee was organized by one of the graduate founders of the class of 1842, John Addison Porter, by then a faculty member of the newly formed Yale Scientific School, and money was subscribed. The fund of $555.27 inherited by the club of 1860 was of course inadequate to the goal, and two initiatives were undertaken to pick up the pace: graduates began to be invited back to every possible society meeting, and an application was made to the Connecticut Legislature for a charter, creating the Kingsley Trust Association in order to hold and convey property up to the value of $10,000.00.

Architect Richard Morris Hunt of New York was asked to prepare an elevation in Egyptian or Byzantine style, which was approved by the society in January 1864. Why these devotees of Ruskin—to judge from the language of their constitution—chose Hunt to be their architect is a mystery; perhaps family friendships formed when Hunt's widowed mother brought her young children to reside briefly in New Haven lay behind the commission. A surviving presentation drawing shows that the tomb as built was less than a third of its proposed scheme, which included a low wing to the north, toward what is now Woolsey Hall, penetrated by a central pass through, to join a projected three-story pavilion with eight bedrooms under a pitched roof.[24]

Its high style and elaborate finishes were ruinously expensive, but very pleasing in prospect to the men of Keys: "It would rag the old charnel house in High Street beyond the hope of recovery . . ." A lot was bought on Prospect Street, backing up to Joseph Sheffield's garden, and thereafter sold as inadequate; another lot, on High Street, where the Bones hall was located, near Atwater (later Library) Street—now closed and built over by the walkway between Jonathan Edwards and Branford Colleges—was bought by the Yale Corporation to keep it out of C.S.P.

hands, either as an act of long-range planning policy (it became the site of the Kent Laboratory in 1887), or perhaps as a cat's-paw for Bones to frustrate its rival from building on High Street.

The fits and starts of the building committee and the fundraisers over fourteen years ended when there became available for $5,000 a lot 36 by 110 feet on the corner of Wall and College Streets. This belonged to the Berzelius Trust Association, a fraternity and not yet a secret society, of the renamed Sheffield Scientific School, in a deal which cannot have been a coincidence (given that John Addison Porter was Sheffield's son-in-law). Contracts were executed and delivered, and on November 25, 1869, ground was broken with appropriate festivities before graduate members representing classes as far back as 1843, using a silver spade which had been consecrated in the hands of President Woolsey for the groundbreaking for the divinity school the month before ("this moment," reported the *College Courant*, "was accompanied by a low murmur of the entire circle but the words were indistinguishable").

"Gaily the Troubadour," the society song which accompanied the Keys seniors' return home after meetings, "was then sung as it never has been sung before, and again forming in line, the procession returned to the soon-to-be deserted Hall on Church Street." Perkins & Chatfield were the contractors, the foundation was laid in January 1870, and the completed building was delivered to its new owners in May, with the dedicatory celebration taking place at the commencement meeting on July 13, 1872. Hunt had gone over budget, and many items, like the stone and cast iron fence along the two corner street fronts, were added later. A Bonesman of the club of 1871 who gained surreptitious entry drew a rough floor plan, showing a parlor, dining room and washroom on the first floor; a "lounging room," meeting room, and library on the second; and in the basement, the kitchen, wine cellar, furnaces, and the "joe."[25]

Writing just three years after its construction, Bagg noted that the new structure was "far superior in costliness and architectural beauty, not only to the Bones hall, but to any college-society hall in America."[26] One newspaper report put the cost at $60,000 (the actual costs with architect's fees amount to about $45,000), with "a marble exterior, while the interior is furnished to correspond." After comparing Yale's Old Brick Row to barracks, its chapel to a highly ornate stable, and the divinity school to a French apartment house, the *American Architect and Building News* said of the Keys hall: "The doorway is rich and graceful; the whole building is designed skillfully, and with special skill for its purpose."[27] Nineteenth-century artists' studios commonly had exotic orientalia lying about to suggest that the painter was sophisticated, well traveled, and in touch with mysterious powers: Hunt's Keys hall is one instance in which the trope got turned into a building.[28]

Richard Morris Hunt was the first American to attend the École des Beaux-Arts in Paris, and later cofounded the American Institute of Architects. His many notable later assignments included the Fifth Avenue façade of the Metropolitan Museum of Art; the pedestal of the Statue of Liberty; and various palatial residences for the extended Vanderbilt family, including "Marble House" and "The Breakers" in Newport, Rhode Island, and the Biltmore Estate in Asheville, North Carolina. According to the *Architectural Record*, his final design for Scroll and Key's tomb was "devoted to the celebration of Eleusinian undergraduate mysteries, as one might infer from its architecture. . . . The Moors in Spain devised an architecture of which the exterior was almost exclusively dead-wall, and the Spanish-Moorish naturally provided a precedent for so much, or rather so little, of decorative detail as the exterior shows, only the columns that bear the stilted arches and the enriched band at the impost."[29]

Truly the Xanadu of Yale, the new hall in Moorish Revival style provided a frontage of thirty-six feet on College Street, fifty-five feet long with six feet of ground on each side, and open spaces of about twenty feet before and behind. Set behind a street-front Moorish gate and patterned forecourt, the thirty-five-foot-high building is composed primarily of light yellow Cleveland stone, accented by thin layers of dark blue marble, and four pillars of Aberdeen granite with marble cappings in front supporting three projecting arches, all features extracted from Islamic architecture. The narrow openings they frame, pattern-pierced stone window screens which are only decoration in the wall pattern, are provided with three bull's-eyes, admitting air. Beneath the central arch, at the top of a half-dozen stone steps coming up from either side, are a pair of massive paneled iron doors. Five similar arches ventilate each side of the building, and a corresponding number of barred scuttle-windows gave some light to the cellar. At the top are rows of short pillars, with two stars cut out between every such pair.

Hunt's modern biographer has observed that "The large areas of blank wall seem intended to conceal what may be transpiring within; indeed, the exterior design of the hall proclaims that the activities it houses are to be kept secret, while the weighty, almost impregnable structure implies that they must be of great importance." Soon, quickly growing ampelopsis was imported and trained over the hall, making it look even more hermetically sealed. Its patterned design even figured into coded messages of possible election: Robert Simpson Rodman, tapped for the Bones delegation of 1879, was said in his freshman year to have "received the mysterious warning, 'Beware of the zebra-striped edifice on College street,' which most people construe: 'You may go to Bones.'" The *Yale News* quoted the collegians referring to the hall the same year as "the College Street tea chest."[30]

The sheer expense of the construction of these society halls was occasionally a subject of faculty meetings. Professor of Greek James Hadley (whose son Arthur, the first lay president of Yale, and grandsons were in their respective classes tapped for Bones) is said to have remarked, on hearing a report that when "one of the secret societies was about to bore an artesian well in the celler of their club house . . . [and] [i]t was suggested that such an extraordinary expense should be prohibited . . . [the professor] closed the discussion and laughed out the subject by saying that from what he knew of the society, if it would hold a few sessions over the place where the artesian well was projected, the boring would be accomplished without cost."[31]

TEAMS

In the beginning, American college officials looked unkindly on sports. The prerevolutionary laws of Yale College stated that "If any scholar shall play at Hand-Ball, or Foot-Ball, or Bowls in the College-yard, or throw any Thing against the College, by which Glass may be endangered . . . he shall be punished six pence." By the early nineteeth century the ability to play sports at Yale was a function of the schedule of studies. The rigid scheme of recitations called for three classroom exercises a week, omitting Wednesday and Saturday afternoons, and leaving those weekdays the only half-holidays. Five P.M. recitations four days a week allowed insufficient time for both the afternoon lesson, and getting back and forth to a boathouse or field for practice in a shell or on the diamond. However, the classes were released all at once on the biweekly half-holidays: four hundred fifty men could then find recreation, which this common schedule concentrated.[32] The discovery of the glass case of gilded baseballs in the Bones tomb during the break-in of 1876 is strong indication, twenty years after the hall's construction, that organized sport had become a new and important element of undergraduate life, and that the leaders of those teams had become desirable candidates for the senior societies.

The first manifestation of these twin phenomena was the Yale Navy. New Haven in the nineteenth century was a popular beach and resort area, and the students at Yale swam and sailed in Long Island Sound. In 1843, the year Scroll and Key was founded, junior William Weeks organized classmates into a club—the first rowing club in any American college—to buy a nineteen-foot boat, the *Pioneer*. Within a few weeks, freshman and junior syndicates were formed to purchase similar craft, and "scrub races" or other informal tests of strength and skill occurred. By 1853, no less than fifteen boats were owned by class clubs, most bought secondhand and often passed down to a club in a lower class. The entire college was divided into twelve clubs of twenty men each, on the Oxbridge college model, in 1859, but by 1868 there was a reversion to clubs once more organized by class.[33]

The organization of six- or eight-man crews and coordination of races began to generate team spirit: the *Lit.* of 1851 spoke of these "jovial remigiary expeditions" as producing some of "the strongest bonds of friendship and fellow-feeling."[34] The man who effectively originated intercollegiate athletics in America was the bow oar for the eight-oar barge *Undine*, a just-elected senior society member named James Morris Whiton, second high-stand man in the class of 1853, Junior Exhibition speaker, Phi Beta Kappa, Alpha Delta Phi, Skull and Bones, and the first recipient of a PhD degree in the United States, from his alma mater.

Whiton's grandfather John was an 1805 graduate of Yale; his son James, skipping college, became a wealthy merchant in Boston, enabling our James to attend Boston Latin School and then Yale. In 1852 his Boston Latin classmate Joseph Brown up in Cambridge was captain and coxswain of the eight-oared *Oneida* that had inaugurated Harvard rowing in 1846 and was now owned by the class of 1853. At Whiton's suggestion, the two decided "to test the superiority of the oarsmen at the two colleges" at a regatta at Center Harbor on Lake Winnipesaukee in New Hampshire, which Whiton had first seen while riding a train on the Boston, Concord and Montreal railroad line, of which his father was a director.

The contest on August 3, 1852, over a two-mile course occurred among three Yale boats (including the *Shawmut*, in which Randall Lee Gibson rowed, and Whiton's *Undine*) and one from Harvard, involving thirty oarsmen from New Haven and eleven from Cambridge. Treated in the contemporary press as resort news and thought by Whiton at the time to be "an eight days' junket at the expense of a railroad corporation . . . as unique and irreproducible as the Rhodesian colossus," this regatta was instead later to be justly remembered as the first American intercollegiate contest of any kind, repeated almost annually for the next forty years. The character of the first regatta may be inferred from the fact that the New Haveners' training table consisted of abstaining from pastries, and a remark made by one of the Harvard crew that "they had not rowed much for fear of blistering their hands." Although there were no professional coaches, nor regimented training, nor any abstention from drinking and smoking, here were demonstrated for the first time in American college sport most all the features of athletic rivalry which have since played such an important part in the history of our universities: "the hard training, great popular excitement, the special trains, the cheers and colors of contending colleges, the recriminations and charges of unfairness, the newspaper sensationalism, and the fierce exultation and abandon of victory with which the modern audience is so familiar."[35]

While more than three years were to pass before the next race at the lake, the excitement generated at Lake Winnipesaukee found more immediate expression in the combination of the New Haven fleet as the "Yale Navy."[36] The distinction of holding the commodoreship of the Yale Navy (the presidency, after 1870), and even being an officer or member of the five class boat clubs, began to be noted in the Psi Upsilon fraternity catalogue, along with class prizes and oratorships. The senior societies similarly took note: of the eighteen commodores between 1853 and 1870, the only athletic honor of its era, Keys boasted eight, Bones two, the new senior society Spade and Grave two, and neutrals six. In the election for the class of 1880, five of the university crew and its coxswain were elected to the two senior societies.[37]

The second sport to rise in popularity on the campus was baseball. A letter home to his mother from the Yale College protagonist of John Wood's novel *College Days*, set in the mid-1870s, recites that "In the afternoon we go out and play ball at Hamilton Park or row on the harbor." The game had been played informally at Yale before the Civil War, but not until the troops brought it home did the pastime sweep the country. The first college nine was formed at Princeton in 1858, and Yale class clubs were featured in the *Yale Banner* from 1859. The first regular varsity baseball nine was formed from the best men of the class clubs in 1865, following the formation of the "Yale University Base Ball Club," under the presidency of James Coffin of the class of 1868, and the first intercollegiate game was played against Wesleyan that year.[38]

The growing prominence of sports almost immediately affected the candidate pool for the senior societies. Wood's 1894 novel describes the speculation: "The question was always being asked—will So-and-so go to Spade and Grave [the novelist's code name for Bones]? Where will So-and-so fetch up? To hear a knot of men talking on the sophomore fence one would have imagined that the elections into the senior societies were just then about to be given out. Then [the mid-1870s] as now the senior societies were considered as more or less of a reward of social standing, or merit in the class. There were certain men whose honors always entitled them to membership, such as Yale *Lit.* men, prominent boating and baseball men, popular men, committee men or high-stand men."[39]

Bones at first did not elect the varsity baseball players, and when the intercollegiate series against Harvard began in 1868, with Yale losing to Harvard that year and for the next five, that society was explicitly blamed (although Henry Rutherford Elliot, Bones 1871, had been president of the B.B.C.). The *Iconoclast*, an undergraduate publication attacking the society in October 1873, proclaimed that "Bones prefers to give her elections to the high-stand man and the literary man while she looks coldly on superior ball men and passes them in disdain. If it were understood that the best base ball player in every class was as sure of an election to Bones as he who takes 1st prize compositions, would it not call out a great amount of latent talent? . . . It is evident to all who witnessed the disappointment of '74 when her best ball player—we might add, one of the best players that has ever entered college—failed to receive an election to Bones, and when men of no merit whatever supplanted him, that the society does not make it a point to encourage base ball. *Here, then, lies the evil; all men want to go to Skull and Bones; playing ball will not take them; hence men will not play base ball to get there.*"

Sometimes Skull and Bones, like the United States Supreme Court is said to do, follows the election returns: the captain for 1870, Samuel McCutcheon, and Clarence Deming, the captain for 1871 and 1872, were both made members, and Samuel Clark Bushnell, chosen for the delegation of 1874, was elected B.B.C. president his senior year. The captain of the 1874 and 1875 teams and two of his teammates were elected to the Bones club of 1875, and the captain for the 1876 and 1877 teams was elected for 1877. Charles Francis Carter, tapped for Bones in 1878, is generally credited with introducing the curve ball into college baseball pitching (it had been used in the professional leagues for about a decade), and struck out fifteen Harvard men that year. From 1880, Yale began to win consistently in baseball, and the team captains for 1881, 1882, 1885, and 1886 were chosen for Bones. From 1886 to 1890, largely as the result of pitcher and Bonesman (1888) Amos Alonzo Stagg's run of fifteen victories in twenty-one games against Harvard, the championship remained in New Haven.[40]

Football at Yale took longer to develop. No games were allowed in the college yard, so they were always played on the New Haven Green: as early as 1840, an annual game was played by the freshmen and sophomores. The rules had changed little since the eighteenth century, but there was some evolution, from kicking the ball over the goal line, to allowing the ball to be run laterally out of bounds, and then by 1863, to a rushing game where a ball carrier tried to evade tackles. The roughness of the annual freshman–sophomore game became so dangerous that the faculty banned it in 1857, and then the town banned the student use of the Green, despite the opposition of the college authorities in support of the old prerogatives.[41]

The first ever American intercollegiate football match was played in 1869 between Princeton and Rutgers. Three years later, Yale played its first intercollegiate game, against Columbia, resulting in a victory that was the beginning of what would become the most successful college football program, in terms of victories, in the first century of college football. Representatives of Harvard, Yale, and Columbia met in Springfield, Massachusetts, in November 1876, denominating themselves the Intercollegiate Football Association and formalizing for the first time rules to apply to all future games, fixing the official type of ball (a rugby ball), the dimensions of the playing field (140 by 70 yards), and the duration of play (ninety minutes).

The further reformation of the rules of the game, its national dominance by Yale under Walter Camp (class of 1880, Bones), and the resulting influence on the senior societies were all products of the succeeding decade. By that time, leadership roles in the baseball "nines" and the football "twenties" were positions of prominence: as stated in the *Yale Record* for June 18, 1881, "The presidences of our athletic interests are as important and responsible postions as any in the gift of the college." Elections to Bones were accepted by the captains of every Yale football team in the decade from 1878 through 1887, excepting only those of 1880, 1881, and (when the captain went to Keys) 1882. During the fourteen years between 1875 and 1890, Yale won every game played against Harvard and most of the games against Princeton, the other acknowledged leader of intercollegiate football in America.[42]

What Yale historian Brooks Kelley has styled the "rise of the extra-curriculum" manifested itself in other ways besides organized sports: a chorale society with an orchestra was also something of a team. James Fenimore Cooper, originally a member of the Yale class of 1806 but expelled as a junior for a prank which exploded another student's door, was to point out in his *The American Democrat* of 1838 that not only did American culture lack serious music, but moreover the public did not understand the importance of this shortcoming. A music society had been founded at Yale by undergraduates as early as 1812, and this became the Beethoven (Sacred Music) Society in 1826. This group always formed the college choir until 1855, and provided, in the absence of an organ, orchestral music at religious services; by that date, it numbered about thirty members, two-thirds of whom were singers and the rest composing the "grand orchestra" of strings, wind instruments, and a "big drum."[43]

Even as Cooper wrote, undergraduate Richard Storrs Willis worked in New Haven to further the cause of music in America. He served twice as president of the Beethoven Society, in his junior year, when he was chosen for Bones in 1840, and again as a senior. Before his graduation, he organized Yale's first orchestra, and later studied with Mendelssohn in Europe. He introduced "Gaudeamus" and "Integer Vitae" to the Yale campus in 1848, bringing them from German universities, and with the assistance of James Kittredge Lombard (Bones 1854) published the first collection of college songs, arranged for tenor, baritone, and bass, in 1853—the first songbook of any college, with new editions following every few years. The lyrics of "Gaudeamus," often performed as the opening piece of concerts by the Yale Glee Club, reflect an endorsement of the bacchanalian mayhem of student life, while simultaneously retaining the grim knowledge that one day we all will die. The seventh stanza would particularly have amused the Latin-learned Willis and Lombard, and all their auditors who were society members: in its English translation, "Let sadness perish! Let haters perish! Let the devil perish! And also the opponents of fraternities and their mockers, too!"[44]

Under Willis's leadership, the Beethoven Society pushed toward its objective, the installation of an organ in the Yale Chapel, achieved in 1851—a revolutionary innovation, because of the ancient Puritan prejudice throughout New England against the use in public worship of Bach's chosen instrument. President Woolsey, using the gift of Joseph Battell, in 1845 appointed Gustave Stoeckel to be the organist and choirmaster in the college chapel, commencing formal instruction in music at Yale. With the appearance of an organized choir in chapel, the function of the Beethoven Society had come to an end, and after the Civil War, it gave way to the new University Glee Club.[45] Still, before its demise, the Beethoven Society's president and other officers were recognized as important men in the class: the president for 1851–52, the treasurer for 1852–53, the secretary for 1854–55, and the president for 1868–69 were chosen for Bones, and the presidents for 1861–62 and 1863–64 were elected to Keys.

Singing had also become a feature of the public face of the senior societies and fraternities. The *College Courant* for June 24, 1868, reported that during 1865 and 1866, "each of the three societies [Bones, Keys, and Spade and Grave, founded in 1864] were accustomed to sing a song upon the College Green" upon returning from their Thursday evening meetings. About two or three o'clock Friday morning they were always to be heard, with the Bonesmen singing a familiar Yale song, known as "I Shall Be His Dad," the members of Keys their well-known "Gaily the Troubadour," and Spade and Grave warbling the modern "How Can I Leave Thee." By 1870, a cappella duels between groups crossing paths on their way back to their dormitories drove the college administration to ban all society singing outside of the halls because these informal contests in the middle of the night were interrupting sleep. Bagg wrote in 1872 that "[t]his custom of singing is a comparatively modern one, and the secret societies have the credit of introducing it—several of the college melodies having been originally their private property."[46]

The most famous of all such anthems, Scroll and Keys' "Gaily the Troubadour," was first sung by the delegation of 1856 to accompany its marching home. Initially the society members had not retired in a group, though sometimes, and especially by the club of 1849, serenades were offered to certain ladies of Hillhouse Avenue, "who testified to their pleasure in various unmistakable ways." The usage completely changed by 1855, with a march across the Green at midnight, singing lyrics to the tune of "Juvallera." The next delegation adopted "Troubadour" in its place. A member of that year wrote: "We left the Hall . . . walked two abreast, the fifteenth man leading each in turn. As we entered the Green at Church Street, we started 'Gaily the Troubadour' and continued singing, separated in front of the Lyceum, keeping time to our music, each one ceasing to sing as he entered his hall." By 1860, the line of march was varied, to cross the Green as far as Temple, then shifting left and up Chapel to the Brick Row. There the group passed "the whole line of College buildings in profound silence" to the steps of the Chapel, where the "Troubadour" was sung, the singers thereafter dispersing to their rooms. Because this would occur anywhere from one to four A.M. in the morning, on certain lengthy meeting nights it had become daylight, so the whole club continued into chapel for morning prayers. (Bones, too, had a parting song in the 1850s and '60s titled "Farewell" and sung to the tune of "The Old South Joe," but neutrals so disapproved that it was ultimately abandoned.)[47]

COCHS

Less elevating than the Beethoven Society, but ultimately more significant to the rising classes and the senior societies, was the Wooden Spoon Presentation and Promenade. The Junior Exhibitions, held over an entire day in April, had showcased oratorical presentations in front of the college president, faculty, and friends of the juniors who received high appointments. To this was joined in 1851 the Junior Promenade, held either the day before or the day of the exhibition.

The Spoon presentation began as a burlesque of the "Junior Ex," but in time came to overshadow the older exercise and dance. It was defended as an opportunity for those not chosen for their grades by the faculty for the Junior Exhibition to exhibit their other talents: "This presentation of the Spoon affords an opportunity to them who do not speak upon the College stage (although not to them alone) to appear before an audience and show what are their powers." The Presentation of the Wooden Spoon was also championed as a true tether to the college: "What will make [the early graduates] soonest shout, old Yale *was* a glorious place? Is it the strictness of the College laws, the order of the recitations, the discipline of every exercise, or it is some little piece of fun, some trivial joke, some odd custom, unworthy perhaps of full grown men, and yet which bound them when young to their College home with cords which Time itself is unable to sever?"[48] The wooden spoon was originally presented as an award to the biggest eater in commons, and then, aping a Cambridge University tradition of nicknaming as a "wooden spoon" the person who came last in the mathematical examinations there, it became a booby prize. At Yale, this went not to the poorest scholar in the class but to the lowest on the list of fifty appointed to speak at the Junior Exhibition.

Soon the award metamorphosed into a popularity contest. From 1854, the junior class was electing a Spoon committee, styled the "Society of the Cochleaureati" (from the Latin *cochlear*, for spoon, and *laureatus*, crowned with a laurel). Chosen by the whole class from the men *without* faculty scholarship appointments, it was a classic secret society, with closed meetings, small gold spoons nearly an inch and a half long worn on the vest lapel, and a "midnight doxology" sung after gatherings. The steel plate emblem engraved on the invitations to their annual festivals included in one quadrant a Phi Beta Kappa pin—upside down. Those elected were said to be the nine "best fellows," the "wittiest, most 'popular,' genial, and gentlemanly men of the class." The Wooden Spoon Man, supposed to be the best of the best, was elected from their own number by the "Cochs" (the sole abbreviation, pronounced with a hard "ch" [or "k"], which encouraged visual puns, too). "Thus the position of Spoon Man grew to be the highest elective honor of the college," wrote Bagg in 1872, "and that of Coch [a single member of the committee] but little inferior to it."

The Spoon Exhibition thus became the event of the college social season, drawing the largest and most remarkable audience of any event in New Haven, especially "snab," the college term for fashionable ladies and pretty girls. The Spoon Promenade of the evening before the exhibition was similarly brilliant, with orchestral music, and oversubscribed admissions for a hall with a capacity of over 2,500 persons. The spoon itself—by this time a two-foot wonder of rosewood or black walnut, ornately carved, with an engraved silver label, in a velvet-lined case— became "a prize more craved than the Valedictory or De Forest Medal. . . . Nor at Yale did the fact that the Wooden Spoon Committee was a sure step to Senior society election dull undergraduate ambitions to become 'popular' and win a place among the nine 'Cochs.'"[49]

Ceremonies usually were scheduled for the Monday and Tuesday in July preceding Presentation Day, but in 1871 that event was moved to the Tuesday, a schedule shift coupled with the elimination of the two-week vacation which had always followed. This calendar alteration, along with dismay over both the ever increasing expense for mounting their ceremonies and preelection "spreads," and the political machinations which now surrounded election of the Cochs (at the end, the two leading junior societies divided the Spoon Committee memberships between them, and then annually alternated the Spoon Man's society origin), brought the sudden end of the Wooden Spoon ceremonies, through disgust of the students themselves at what had become an affront to their prized Yale democracy.[50]

Of the relative standing of college honors in this decade, Bagg is instructive: "The position of DeForest Man corresponds in rank to that of Valedictorian in scholarship, of Wooden Spoon Man in popularity, of Navy Commodore in boating matters; it is the very highest of the literary honors, and, as these are thought more of than any others, it may be called the highest honor of the whole college course."[51] The comet of the Wooden Spoon in the twenty-two classes between 1848 and its abrupt demise in 1871 cast a gravitational pull upon the senior society system, and the practices of the Cochs themselves reflected that system. According to the New York *World* of June 26, 1867, the newly elected juniors "are initiated by the cochs of the Senior class into a sort of secret society, hold meetings every Friday in their rooms, in succession, when a supper is served, and the future exhibition promised, and at one of which they choose of their number the *spoon* man."

The Spoon Man in the 1848–1871 span (there were none in 1849 and 1851) came nine times from Bones and six times from Keys, reflecting the elder society's policy of tapping the topmost individual in each field, but this census evidences that seven were neutrals. In the same span, of the 205 individuals on the Spoon Committee, Keys claimed seventy-four, Bones sixty-four, and other societies twelve, while fifty-five were neutrals. The only class in which all of the Cochs belonged to the two senior societies was 1864, with four from Bones and five from Keys. Popularity, however, certainly did trump intelligence: it was a faculty proverb that the Spoon Exhibition always dropped one of the committee from his class, but of the whole number, only a dozen Cochs failed to graduate, two of whom were Spoon Men.[52]

Still, the Bones strategy of tapping the high achievers carried its own significant risks. The older society clearly missed, through mistake or caprice, men in the junior class who, if raw excellence was the main criterion, deserved to be elected, even allowing for the occasional "outsider." That failure, and the society's seeming indifference there-after to those passed over, compounded its reputation for arrogance. Potential could also be misperceived, and promise overlooked. After his twentieth reunion, a Bonesman of the class of 1870 wrote his sister that it was "rather curious to note some surprises in the careers of the men. Some who could hardly keep up in class were now distinguished men, and some whom we had expected to lead armies and govern nations are keeping dry goods stores or making coffins in western country towns."[53]

The senior societies and respect for their elections depended for continued existence on both the tolerance of the Yale administration, and the rough sufferance of the lower classes to shoulder the personal judgments of election day, mostly content that the individuals so chosen were indeed intellectual or social leaders. When both faculty consent and student satisfaction were withdrawn, as happened in 1871 with the Cochs—and as was to be threatened again in later years when men took pledges in groups not to entertain senior society election as juniors—an abrupt end to the entire system was suddenly possible. Whether the members of Bones or Keys were chosen for their intellectual or leadership prowess, or remarkable social gifts, if either group allowed their campus elevation to issue in superior attitudes, silly and obsessive demands for respect, self-aggrandizements, and overt acts of arrogance, the strains could become cumulative and explosive.

Even in this decade, the societies were well aware that the toler-ance of the neutrals for their prominence and ceremonies was seriously strained. In 1853 there appeared the first signs of justifiable and specific resentment, as noted in a brief description of societies in general in the campus publication *Gallinipper*. "Senior societies are noted for little except their exclusiveness and mysterious humbuggery. Their members cut their old acquaintances as much as possible, and monitors who belong to them take off for their own Society men, and leave others to whistle. Treat them with contempt. As they never talk of themselves, never talk about them, but if you have any ambition to get in . . . tear down their notices, and you will get the reputation of men of spirit."[54]

In 1856, the editors of the *Lit.*, three of whom were Bonesmen, permitted an article to run by N. C. Perkins, "Secret Societies among Us," published nine months after the first occupation of the Bones High Street tomb. Perkins, a neutral, wrote that he had not "the least intention of applying the pick ax and crow bar to anybody's 'Marvelous and Portentous Tower,'" as ancient Spanish legend said had been built by the Lybian Hercules near the city of Toledo, with which "he hid a mighty secret, and closed up the entrance by a great iron door, with a lock of steel." Still, Perkins deplored the "five or six enterprising" Yale societies' "political maneuvering, by which they manage to control the action of the Classes, and not unfrequently, of the whole College," their "horribly *mysterious* way of doing everything," their "convivial entertainments" leading to hangovers in chapel, their badge fetish, and their patronization of non-members.[55]

The short-lived *Yale Review*, in its first issue of February 1857, ran its own article under the same title. While seriously apprehending "the most injurious effect of secret societies" to "arise from the necessity of assuming an artificial character, on the part of the members . . . especially true of Senior Societies, where there is little else to do," the essay, in macabre mockery, compared the *Lit.* piece's author to the man murdered by the Masons for publishing their secrets, and also seemingly targeted both Keys and Bones. "While we unhesitatingly pronounce the author of the leader of the Lit. for December, a bold man; yet, with the fate of poor Morgan, at the hands of the sons of Hiram, before his eyes; we must say his courage savors more of rashness than reason. After such 'disclosures,' we need not be surprised, if, at the beginning of next term, like Paddie's pig, he should 'come back missin.'"[56]

This was followed in 1858 by another notice in the *Gallinipper*, which was both more insightful, and more detached in tone. "The members," this journal noted, "never deign to communicate either by look, word, or action about these associations. Their great apparent desire to have their very existence ignored is only equaled by their intense wish to have that existence brought into view. . . . No reflection would strike a deeper pang into the hearts of members than the conviction that no one puzzled his brain at all about them. Of course, with all the care exercised, a secret will occasionally leak out, until now in the whole Senior class, at least, very accurate impressions of these institutions are always formed. They are designed principally to secure the formation of aristocratic cliques for the control of all college politics and the elevation of members to posts of honor. Holding in subjection the three lower classes by hopes of receiving elections, they wield a considerable influence. . . . The Societies are 'codfishey,' aristocratic in their tendencies, and consequently do not deserve sympathy from outsiders."[57]

The charge of political intriguing is probably just, and surely the indiscriminate ragging of society members by neutrals, if it had effect at all, would tend to make the two senior societies even more taciturn and exacting in their external usages, as did, probably, their general consciousness of each other.[58] "I am really very much concerned about this," a recent graduate of Keys wrote the club of 1866. "[It] seems to me as if some of our friends [the Bones members] were endeavoring to establish a divine origin, as if they belonged to a better class of mortals. . . . Behave as your predecessors have done and you will always have the good will and respect of your fellows. There is a difference, you know, between modest dignity and obtrusive snobbishness. Don't make C.S.P. stick out like a sore thumb, but if you do, don't get angry if anybody sticks a knife into this sore thumb—at any rate, if they do, it will heal the sooner."[59]

Counsel like this, or mere reflection on the toxic atmosphere, caused the Bones club of 1857, following an attack by a crowd on neutrals on the club's posted notice of meeting on the college chapel door, to vote to abandon the custom of such notices: none appeared on the Thursday meeting date of October 16, 1856, or thereafter. In three years, the exercise of evening prayers in the college was to be abandoned.[60] The students gathered for that daily occasion would no longer be compelled to see the society notices on their meeting days, but when Bones, before that time, took the lead in retiring what had become a severe provocation, the disappearance of the ritual notice reportedly caused a campus sensation as great as the posting of the first skull and crossbones–marked notice by George Wood back in 1832.

NEW (AND REVISED) ANCIENT TRADITIONS, AND SOME DIVERGENCES

In the fifteen-year span from 1856 to 1871 that straddled the American Civil War, Skull and Bones and Scroll and Key continued to develop traditions which, for the incoming delegations, had the immediate patina of age. One was the custom of singing a society anthem while marching in a group back to the dormitories of the Old Brick Row after weekly meetings. Photographic records of the seniors was another: from 1861, the fifteen members of Bones were ranged standing (except for two who were seated) to the left and right of a small central table with their emblems of skull and crossed femurs atop, in front of a tall case clock with the hands pointed to the hour of eight, and from 1862, specially bound books with head shots of each member were produced.[61] In due course, Keys followed suit.

Honorary and "silent" memberships were two other practices. There was on-campus society precedent: both Linonia and Brothers in Unity provided in their respective constitutions for honorary members. While Bones never engaged in the practice, the Keys constitution permitted their delegations to admit "distinguished artists" as honorary members. Under this rule, George Vandenhoff, a leading actor and elocutionist, was admitted in 1848, and Boston journalist E. P. Whipple was elected in 1853.[62]

The most famous of Keys' honorary members was Samuel Langhorne Clemens, "Mark Twain," elected in 1868 when he was thirty-two. He became an occasional visitor to graduate sessions of C.S.P. thereafter, escorted by his Hartford neighbor and sponsor, the Reverend Joseph Hopkins Twichell of the club of 1859, in his class the president of Brothers in Unity, a Coch, and on the first varsity crew to beat Harvard. Twichell was to serve as president of Keys' corporate parent, the Kingsley

Trust Association, from 1866 to 1872 and was the author's pastor and best friend. Twain wrote to "Mr. President of the Scroll and Key" on November 18, 1869: "Allow me the privilege (in haste) of remembering myself most kindly to my esteemed and honored brethren of the S and K—whom God preserve! Fraternally, Mark Twain."[63]

The famous humorist had, of course, only a partial and fragmentary view of "his" senior society's character and purposes. In an article appearing in the *Yale Courant* for February 21, 1874, Twain publicly alluded to his honorary membership and attendance at several gatherings, "but as its meetings were confined chiefly to eating and drinking, he had not gained much experience except a pleasant time." The custom became an object of campus satire, thus ensuring its demise: the *Yale Literary Chronicle* for 1873 stated that "[New York newspaper publisher Horace] Greeley denies that he is a member of Keys." Such memberships fell out of favor after the era of Twain's election, other than for wives of members, who held the like privilege and kept it until the 1890s.[64]

"Silent" members of Scroll and Key were also honorary, but differently originated: these were classmates elected by members of the current delegation in their senior year whom they simply wished to include but had not made the first fifteen. This had begun in 1845 when that year's set elected before their graduation a senior who had spent his first three years at another college. Over time, such unofficial elections became common: one in 1849, two in 1850, six (one a law student) in 1851, five (one from the scientific school) in 1852, and a total of one or two in five other years, the last in 1861.[65]

Initiation traditions were fluid, to say the least. In Keys' early years, the juniors elected were privately and individually notified to meet on a certain evening at a certain hour and place (never at the hall). Each member-elect was then conducted to the tomb and initiated in turn. Black wax seals were broken, locks were undone and chains noisily withdrawn, and stairs were mounted from a "dismal outer court" to "the brilliant light of the temple." Here the bewildered and bedazzled neophytes were ranged silently around a coffin, to listen "to the history and regulations of the venerable institution," after which "they were shown to the festive board, laden with the luxuries of every clime." The evolutionary steps thereafter became both more precise and more complex, with initiates led from room to room, hearing interrogations with antipodal responses by members of the outgoing club, calling out from behind various shrouded doorways.[66]

In the fevered imagination of the neutrals, the images of initiation were more like those in a panel from the graphic narrative—possibly America's very first comic book, published in 1850—of *The College Experience of Ichabod Academicus*, illustrated by William Thompson Peters and written by "H.F.P. and G.M." (Hugh Florian Peters, member of Alpha Delta Phi and Keys for 1849, and Garrick Mallery), in which the panel captioned "He is initiated into a secret society" shows a grim-faced student atop a charging ram, gripping its horns and pursued by a skeleton thrusting a spear at his back.[67]

Before his initiation into Skull and Bones in spring 1869, William Welch, a member of the class of 1870 and later the founding dean of the Johns Hopkins School of Medicine (in his lifetime hailed as "Dean of American Medicine"), wrote his father that "nearly all the members of the faculty are members of this society and keep up their interest in it. . . . It is understood to be very literary in its character and has in its possession a very fine library. . . . I have spoken thus at length for when I become a duly initiated member I shall have to adopt the strictest secrecy." A letter to Welch from his clubmate, class valedictorian Dwight Whitney Learned, evidences that the management of the college was often a subject of discussion in their tomb: not only the matter of undergraduate offices, although that was important, but also faculty appointments, the nature of the curriculum, and the general policies of Yale.[68]

Over at Keys, the formal program of "familiar debate," coupled with a Shakespearian essay and the oral reading of one of the Bard's plays, was varied with a substitute plan of art study, calling for an appointed member's essay on the Byzantine, Italian, Flemish, or French schools of painting, to be followed by remarks by each member of the crowd on "the prominent characteristics of some painter of the school." To relieve the fatigue of the long play-reading evenings, the club of 1864 introduced a program of literary sessions, with an hour-long debating session at 8:30, followed by the social session ("music, dancing, cards, etc.," which last seems to have included hard liquor), then a second session at 11:00 P.M., with the essay and play reading. The debating sessions were suffering in quality, as the oratorical and parliamentary skills formerly honed preceding senior society elections, in the glory years of Linonia and Brothers in Unity, waned with the fortunes of those ancient literary societies, and alcohol did not improve matters. The crowd of 1853 had abolished the demon from their rooms, but backsliding led to the custom between 1867 and 1869 of "drowning the Philaloo bird," either in the hall or at a nearby local tavern.

Slotted somewhere among the formal exercises of Keys and the social hour was the joyous and ever more elaborate supper. For the dozen years after the founding in 1842, this consisted of an infrequent but treasured "bum" or feast of peanuts or molasses candy, with lemonade on hot summer nights, and perhaps a special treat of oysters when member contributions could fund the expense (society funds could not be so used). By Keys' second decade, the regular valedictory meal started at eleven, at which hour "the drum sounded," and the feast was begun with the raising of a silver goblet accompanied by the leader's cry, "*Quid tempus est?*," to which the group response was "*Tempus est bibendi, et edendi, et ludendi,*" after which all present sat down, "pounded the table for about a minute, then sang the table song, and proceeded with the meal." The basic dish was still oysters, supplemented under a more prosperous membership with beef steak, or cold chicken sandwiches, or sardines "as plentiful as in the Mediterranean," or ice cream, all washed down with "torrents" of "rich dark coffee."[69]

Meanwhile, over on High Street, the installation of a kitchen in the cellar of the new Bones hall obviously gave the elder society a significant advantage in the culinary sweepstakes, allowing for improvements over the cold collations served in rented rooms. This also facilitated the entertainment of returning graduates, who were invited to "the annual convention of the Order" on the evening of commencement (which occurred six weeks after early summer's Presentation Day, in August), and again in the following spring for a supper in connection with the Bones initiation ceremony, which was, "at least the outside part of it . . . conducted by graduates alone."[70]

The "outside part" resulted, from 1856 onward, from the presence of the new Bones tomb. The inherent tension for candidates was increased because the seniors did not speak to those to be initiated (except to deliver the summons to initiation) from the date of their election to the evening of their initiation. "The initiation begins, after the close of the Wooden Spoon Exhibition, at midnight of the following Tuesday, and lasts till about daybreak," Bagg reported. "The candidates for the ceremony are assembled in a room of the college Laboratory, which is guarded by Bones man, and are singly escorted thence, by two of the latter, to the hall. As the grim doors open for each new member, there are sounds as of a fish horn, as of many feet hurrying up an uncarpeted stairway, as of a muffled drum and tolling bell—all mingling in a sort of confused uproar, like that from a freshman initiation a good many miles away."

"Perhaps," he continues, "while being led to a hall, a candidate may pass between rows of neutral Juniors or other college men, some of whom may 'bid him goodbye,' with expressions of congratulation and good will, if they think his election deserved, or insult and revile him, if their belief goes in the contrary direction. There is usually some one to flash a dark lantern upon each approaching candidate, and, if he makes no other personal comments, to at least shout forth his name, for the edification of the rest. To all this the Bones men of course pay no attention. It perhaps takes an hour or more thus to initiate the fifteen candidates; and when the self-constituted leader of the outside hangers on announces that 'the last man's in,' his followers agree that the fun is over, and sullenly disperse. If they stayed longer perhaps they might hear songs sung to strange old tunes, and the applause which follows it, and prolonged cheers for 'the Skull and the Bones.'"[71] The presence at the societies' initiation ceremonies of these neutrals, who could become hostile bystanders, was to result in 1865 to a Yale faculty directive that each society was only to initiate in its own hall and in the presence of members alone.[72]

Of course there was intrusive interest by neutrals as well on election night itself: two bodies of fifteen solemn seniors parading in and out of college dormitories was an irresistible invitation to harassment. For example, in 1867 "there was," according to the *Yale Courant* for June 26, 1867, "considerable disturbance. . . . Doors were fastened, and halls blocked up. One thing praiseworthy may be noted this year—that most [of the elections] were given out early in the evening." By 1874, the *Courant* was reporting "the usual demonstrations, consisting mainly of hooting, laughing, cheering, and similar signs of interest. This, as the neutral blood began to rise a little higher, was followed by the imprisonment of a Bones man in a Durfee entry, from which he effected an escape by means of an underground passage." A crowd followed two other Bonesmen back to the tomb, to block its entrance; when the iron doors opened, "an attempt to enter a pole into the door was frustrated by the muscle of an old-time member of the university crew." Someone summoned a "gentle peeler" [policeman], and then a faculty member, who eventually convinced the crowd to disperse.[73]

To minimize this interference, both societies were compelled to change tapping customs. After 1867, they sent out only one man or two, and at earlier hours. The emissary in the candidate's room asked all others to leave, confirmed by query that the candidate was then alone, inquired whether he was "under any obligations to any other organization," and said, if he was a Keys man: "I have the honor to offer you an election to the so-called Scroll and Key Fraternity. Do you accept?" If the answer were in the affirmative, the society representative was instructed to "shake hands with the member elect, and . . . immediately thereafter leave the room without further remark."[74]

The Bones approach was essentially the same. "[A]t an early hour of the appointed evening, a Bones Senior quietly calls at the room of a Junior, and having been assured that 'we are alone,' says: 'I offer you an election to the so-called Skull and Bones. Do you accept?' If the answer is affirmative the Senior—and perhaps the graduate member who sometimes accompanies him—shakes hands with the neophyte, and bidding him to keep to his room for the present, hurries back to the hall to report the result. If the election is refused, the result is likewise reported to headquarters, and influential members are sometimes sent back to argue the case; but as a rule, few men who refuse elections are offered a chance to repent. Bones will not be dictated to, and when a man says, 'I accept, in case So-and-So is elected with me,' or 'in case Such-a-One is kept out,' he is never allowed to carry his point; Yes or No is the only answer recognized."[75]

With the process thus starting at about seven o'clock, the full complements of fifteen might be made up by nine P.M. in case there were no refusals; if there were refusals, it took longer, and Bones at least was said to choose nominally a half-dozen extra men, in case any of their first fifteen turned them down. This was necessitated by Keys' strategy of preelection pledging, as exemplified in the elections for the class of 1867, where Bones received seven refusals from men who went together to Keys, although urged to reconsider by "certain resolute members of the Faculty, and of one Major-General [Russell] . . . called in to over-persuade the reluctant Juniors," and again for the class of 1870, where, reported the *College Courant*, "some not over-trusty member had quietly let out the whole thing, including the pack, which, it if had duly been regarded by the Bones men, would have saved them some little embarrassment," as of the six named by the paper as declining Bones, five went to its rival.

By going quietly and swiftly about their business, the societies thus managed to largely elude the attentions of the rabble-rousers ranging around the college yard on election night (the same issue of the *Courant* reported that, "as the darkness increased, the crowd of Neutrals also increased both in size and in the amount of its howling capacity, till a very respectable degree of proficiency was attained in this last respect"). The names of the chosen were known very quickly, of course—a member of the class of 1865 was to recollect an announcement of completed elections at midnight on June 16, 1864—and many in each society made lists for circulation at the breakfast table or division classroom for the following morning, where they formed "the sole topic of discussion throughout the college," and saw print in the *Courant* of the Wednesday following, and indeed sometimes appeared in the enterprising New Haven city dailies in the next morning's issue.[76]

For Skull and Bones, the most significant change of this era was the inception of Saturday evening meetings and the new custom of discussion there. The ability to gather informally in their newly secure hall, finding clubmates there more frequently, had increased. The clubs began to meet regularly, in addition to the Thursday debate meetings, on Saturday nights at the end of the school week. These Saturday nights had no rules or regulations other than a requirement not to leave the tomb until midnight: they simply wished to converse, three, ten, or even fifteen together, in the strengthening of bonds of trust and friendship, without the edges of argument or rivalry inherent in the Thursday evening debates.

Thus they elected to relate to one another, in the privacy and confidentiality of the tomb, the stories of their individual lives. Perhaps inevitably, they began to vary the diet of discussion with presentations on that subject of perennial fascination for young men, "woman." At that date "there were no promenades or balls," a member of the class of 1846 was to lament. "Dancing seems to have gone out of Connecticut about 1825, and not to have come in again until after the [Civil] war. . . . The Puritan theology regarded anything that was pleasant with more or less suspicion." What eventually became known in Skull and Bones as "Connubial Bliss" (or "C.B.") was at one and the same time a topic and an exercise on Saturday and then Sunday evenings in the spring where one member delivered his romantic history to his fourteen clubmates in a fireplace-lit room for several hours; ultimately by natural association in later years, "C.B." became a noun describing a member's girlfriend or spouse.

A longer-range perspective of the society's views on marriage is to be found in the memoirs of Mrs. Burton Harrison on her wedding in Richmond, Virginia, in November 1867, just two years after the Civil War, in which her husband (class of 1859) had served as Jefferson Davis's private secretary; she wrote about the "'Bones men' summoned by the bridegroom to stand by their loyal brother on his translation into married life." This is echoed in a letter of William Howard Taft (class of 1878) to his fiancé, Nellie Herron, when planning to construct their home on land in Cincinnati gifted to them by her father: "I shall have the greatest pride in entertaining my classmates, Bonesmen, under our roof where you and they can know each other." Still, secrecy was not sacrified: at the wedding of a senior society member, "the bride was inducted and made to promise that she would never divulge any society secrets her husband might let slip in pillow talk."[77]

The tradition of the members telling their life histories seemingly began as a natural progression from the C.B.s. What might have seemed a small step was instead a major one. The challenges to the individual presenter were twofold: what degrees of self-assessment and personal honesty would be shown, and—as with the Thursday debates—what oral skills could best be employed to convey the results of introspection which the occasion demanded? For the listeners, the intimacy of the environment elicited revelations which compelled them to learn humility and exercise tolerance with classmates with whom they were bound to spend at least two nights a week throughout their senior year. It was all only possible on the mutual understanding that these sessions were completely private, not even to be discussed with alumni (forbidden to disturb the undergraduates then), let alone roommates who were neutrals.

The consequences of this program innovation were profound, both for the individuals participating and for the strength and perdurability of the Yale senior society system. Within the society one could take as natural and confident a place as one might find within his own family. Like family privacy, the institutional secrecy permitted the disclosure of thoughts and feelings without reserve; stormy emotions elsewhere bottled up could find expression. Here was a place where loyalty had claims prior to those of individual success, and a man was recognized not because he won prizes but because he was himself. Against the enemies of time and chance, the members were a phalanx more solid than one could find anywhere. And the strength of the phalanx was trust, extended unqualified one to another. In the Skull and Bones society's first two decades, training in extemporaneous debate had been deemed fundamental to the society experience. By the third quarter of the nineteenth century and going forward, when its members spoke of their essential club life, they meant the experience of sharing the life histories.

For Henry Stimson, class of 1888 and future secretary of war (for Presidents Taft, Franklin Roosevelt, and Truman), governor-general of the Philippines (for President Coolidge), and secretary of state (for President Hoover), it was a great discovery. In later years he made use of it in the formation of policy in many different offices and in the conduct of negotiations with many different peoples. He proposed, in the last recommendation of his public service, that the country should share its knowledge and control of nuclear energy for peaceful purposes with Russia. He made this proposition, he told President Truman, because, "the chief lesson I have learned in a long life is that the only way you can make a man trustworthy is to trust him." He had said the same thing often before, and usually when he said it he added that the had learned this thing first when he committed himself to membership in Skull and Bones.[78]

The emotional risks were patent, because, to vary the rhythm or to break some tension, members would ask questions or demand elaborations; candid analysis of the speaker's account was not uncommon, even if made in a sympathetic spirit. In the early twentieth century, a member about to deliver his "Life History," or "L.H.," as this feature came to be known, received his clubmates' critiques of his conduct and character before his delivery, presumably to allow response in his presentation to what they perceived as his flaws. The irreverent undergraduate paper *Harkness Hoot* was to describe it this way in 1933: "Skull and Bones, which leads the other three [senior societies] in cloying and fraternal fellowship, subjects its members to evenings of mutual character analysis." The discomfort engendered in the process, as it developed, was real, but so too was the value in an enhanced, intensified version of an activity that occurs in everyday life.

It has been said that one reason secret societies endured at Yale during the turbulent 1960s was because they were, as an undergraduate of the era put it, "therapy groups with million-dollar buildings." A late-twentieth-century Bonesman in his thirties explained, "It's a human bonding experience. You can do it on a train with a stranger, you get something out of it. You can do it in a society with strangers, you get something out of it." Today, writes a twenty-first-century observer, virtually all Yale senior societies (although not Keys), "revolve around the 'autos' [autobiographies], in their attempts to model themselves after the Bones."[79] Unforeseen by the founders and not required by any constitution, the tradition of oral delivery of life histories became the greatest invention—and, from its widespread imitation, worst-kept secret—of Skull and Bones.

The less earnest and more gregarious strain in Keys was exhibited in that group's policy toward women. Near female relatives were allowed to enter the hall as early as 1848, and later permitted to enter the rooms on taking an oath of secrecy, "provided they do not reside in the city," presumably a precaution against a suspected tendency to gossip. By 1855, wrote a graduate of that year, "The wives, sisters (and sometimes the sweethearts) of members were considered to have a right to be shown the Hall; this privilege, though rarely occurring, was highly prized by the young ladies and gave social importance and popularity to the [Keys] Society. In those days, when the prestige of Skull and Bones had been so long established, there was more need for winning social support for our society than probably any of the present members can comprehend as ever being desirable."[80]

The criteria of election, as between Bones and Keys, had by this third decade of their parallel existences begun to be perceived as patterns by neutral observers, including the new elements of what became known as "legacies" (for Bones) and "packing" (for Keys). A newspaper article of July 2, 1870, titled "Secret Societies" purported to state those differences. "*Skull and Bones* claims to give elections to the *first* fifteen members of the class. The *first* is defined as excelling in literary ability, scholarship, etc., literary distinction being reckoned the highest. Thus the valedictorian, spoon man, commodore of the Navy, prominent *Lit.* editors and heavy politicians are considered 'sure.' Of late years a new element of fitness has asserted itself and with a high place in the category of essentials, viz.: birth. That is, he who in previous classes has had a near relative in the society, may begin to figure up his initiation fee, but a brother in a recent class is worth more than a father in a forgotten one, for even the name of Gen. Russell was not adequate to procure an election for his son."

"*Scroll and Key*," this article continued, "cultivates the lighter weights. While she is willing to accept any of the scholars, writers, &c., who will refuse 'Bones'—as her rival is sacrilegiously called—she dotes on broadcloth, sunny faces, nice moustaches, good fellowship, and port-monnaies [wallets]. Generally making a bid sufficient to get one or two literary gods as proper candidates for the class-day honors, she fills out her list with the members of the Spoon committee, and such other well-dressed and generally recognized good fellows as the catalogue [of class members] affords. While *Bones* listens submissively to the commands of elder brother, *Scroll and Key* allows herself to be talked to by her own candidates, who often get up a 'Pack,' as it is called—*i.e.*, a certain number of desirable men club together and say, 'Take all or none.' In this way the members of the class of '69 elected themselves."[81]

GIFTS TO THE ALMA MATER

Another tradition began in Keys in this decade which is unexampled and unmatched in the history of any other Yale senior society. On July 13, 1871, at the dedication dinner in the new hall, the first toast offered was to "Yale College and the President." Even though the society had a 45 percent mortgage on its just-constructed hall and was otherwise burdened with debt, Scroll and Key determined to found a university-wide prize, offered for the best essay upon one of a group of prescribed subjects, to be "practical, worth of original research, and of interest to young men." In honor of one of the senior class of 1842 founders of the society, it was named the John Addison Porter Prize. The first winning essay was submitted by a senior in the class of 1872, titled "Essay on the Morality of the Greeks, as Shown in Their Literature, Art and Life." In the award's early years, the society also funded the publication and sale of the winning submissions. Ultimately, the administration of the prize was transferred to the university in 1908.[82]

In the same generous spirit, Scroll and Key, its debts largely retired, established with a $2,000 gift in 1888 the Ten Eyck prizes, founded in memory of Henry James Ten Eyck of the club of 1879 and "given annually in the undergraduate Academical Department, either for scholarship, or for a literary essay, and awarded in such a manner and for such a purpose as shall, after consultation with the President and the Academical Faculty, be deemed most advisable." Even the student body took respectful, if journalistically sarcastic, note: the *Yale Illustrated Horoscope* for May 1889, which favored Keys over Bones, spoke of these gifts as "right loyal acts. The establishment of the John A. Porter and the Henry Ten Eyck prizes, for example, are highly commendable investments out of the surplus of the wine fund, and its older rival, with its poppy-cock and self-sufficiency, would do well to copy."[83]

A Bonesman in this decade, too, was laying down the foundation for generosity to Yale University, but that was not to be known for another half century, in 1918. On July 17 of that year, the *New York Times* ran a long article on the publication of the will of John William Sterling, Bones 1864, and on the date of his death at age seventy-four, the surviving, senior, and still working partner of the renowned New York City law firm of Shearman & Sterling. His pallbearers, most of whom had been his clients, included William Rockefeller (John D.'s brother, with a grandson named John Sterling Rockefeller, to be tapped for Keys in 1928), Yale president Arthur Hadley (twelve years Sterling's junior, Bones 1876), and the chief executives of what were then or were to become Citibank (Sterling oversaw its amalgamation as National City Bank, the nation's largest bank by 1900), the two utility predecessors (gas and electric) of Consolidated Edison of New York, and Anaconda Copper.[84]

Sterling was the valedictorian of the Columbia Law School in 1867, and in Yale College had been a member of Brothers and a respected lightweight boxer, elected to Phi Beta Kappa (with five other members of his Bones club) and to Alpha Delta Phi. He was president of Brothers in Unity, a Coch, a Junior Exhibition oration appointment, and one of the Townsend speakers. Sterling never married, never attended a class reunion after his triennial, accepted an LLD from Yale in 1893 only on condition that it be given *in absentia*, and never while living made any notable gift to any religious, charitable, or educational institution or fraternity. (President Hadley had said wryly that he was chiefly generous with his advice.)[85] So his loyalty to his college, engendered by his strong friendships there, were patently the result of his membership in Skull and Bones in 1863–64, as his last will and testament makes clear.

Article 24 of his will, the first such article to be quoted in the *Times*, reads: "In grateful remembrance of the benefits resulting to me when a student in Yale University, from my connection with the so-called Russell Trust Association, and the advantages which I have since reaped in my professional life from the discipline and experience gained thereby, and as a testimony of such benefits, I hereby direct my said Trustees, out of the residue of the estate vested in them not hereinbefore effectively disposed of, to pay the Trustees of said association and their successors in the trust the sum of $10,000; and it is my wish, although I do not impose it as a condition or trust, that they will invest the said sum and hold it for the purpose of applying the income to defray the annual expenses of the members of the said association while they are in the senior class of the Academical Department of Yale University, or in some way to provide for their comfort."[86] A bequest of $10,000 made in 1918 would today be approximately $150,000. The amount is probably the now-obscured foundation of the persistent legend that Bones members are each to receive a graduation gift of $10,000 (or as the years passed, $15,000, then $20,000).[87]

The more stunning news, however, was contained in the *Times* headline for this article: "$15,000,000 Sterling Bequest to Yale." A year later, it was determined that the lawyer's residuary estate (earned primarily from canny real estate investments) actually amounted to $18,000,000, which was in 2016 equivalent to about $285 million. Sterling's will required Yale to fund with his gift "at least one enduring, useful and architecturally beautiful building, which will constitute a fitting Memorial of my gratitude to and affection for my Alma Mater . . . and to the erection of other fine and enduring buildings for the use of students." The main result was the Sterling Memorial Library, but the bequest also funded the construction of the Sterling Law Quadrangle, the Sterling Hall of Graduate Studies, the Divinity School Quadrangle, the Sterling Hall of Medicine, and Trumbull College. The architect who designed all these structures was James Gamble Rogers, a member of Keys in the club of 1889, having declined a Bones tap. To state it plainly, the major buildings on the modern Yale campus are the product of the financial munificence of a Bones man and the architectural brilliance of a Keys man. It is entirely fitting that their portraits should flank the main desk in the nave of the Sterling Memorial Library.[88]

This Sterling bequest, in all senses, was at the time the largest sum of money ever donated to an institution of higher learning. In 1999, by way of comparison, Paul Mellon, Keys 1929, at his death left $90 million to the university, together with hundreds of artworks now at the Yale Center for British Art, and after having funded the construction of Morse and Stiles residential colleges, while endowing their masterships and then the deanships of all twelve residential colleges. Stephen Adams, Bones 1959, donated $100 million in 2005 to the Yale School of Music, making it tuition-free for the foreseeable future, plus another $10 million in 2013 for the renovation of Hendrie Hall, renamed the Adams Center for Musical Arts; Stephen Schwarzman, Bones 1969, donated $150 million in 2015 for the improvement and conversion of the Bicentennial

Buildings into a university cultural center. When Charles B. Johnson, class of 1954, donated $250 million to Yale in 2013 for the construction of two new residential colleges,[89] it was Yale's largest gift ever, as a sum, but still less than Sterling's when adjusted for inflation.

Gifts from members of Bones or their heirs both preceded and followed the announcement of the Sterling bequest. The first example is Farnam Hall (1869–1870), the first building in what became the quadrangle of the Old Campus, built on the site of the Second President's House and named after a New Haven railroad developer whose three sons, William Whitman Farnam, Charles Henry Farnam, and Henry Wolcott Farnam, were all Bonesmen (1866, 1868, and 1874, respectively) who continued their father's pattern of gifts to Yale, which he had not attended. Lawrance Hall (1885–1886) was donated by his mother as a memorial to Thomas Garner Lawrance (Bones 1884), chairman of the junior prom committee (successors to the Cochs) who died in his senior year. Phelps Hall (1896), the gateway to the Old Campus, was donated by members of that family in memory of William Walter Phelps (Bones 1860). Wright Hall (1912, now Lanham-Wright Hall), the home of Yale's post office built on the site of Alumni Hall, is named after Henry Parks Wright (Bones 1868), first dean of Yale College, and was funded by his society's members and other alumni.[90]

In the history of the two senior societies' gifts to Yale, once definitively established in the seven years beginning in Sterling's senior year in 1864, with the "discipline and experience gained thereby" in the Bones tomb on High Street in the words of his bequest, the Bones way of donations was emphatically personal. Starting with the John Addison Porter Prize foundation in 1871, conceived in the Keys tomb on College Street, later supplemented by the Henry James Ten Eyck prize, the Keys style in philanthropy to the alma mater remained fraternally corporate.

THE BIRTH OF SPADE AND GRAVE

The prestige and power of the two societies within the class, and their consequent control over significant college committees and organizations, allowed them to preen. The second toast at the Senior Dinner of June 18, 1864, after that to the Yale president, was titled in the printed program for the occasion:

The day we celebrate—the Societies of Yale

"You are *bones*, and what of that?
Every face, however full,
Padded round with flesh and fat
Is but modeled on a *skull*."—*Tennyson.*

"He grasped the *Key* of knowledge and wrote his name
Boldly on the *scroll* of fame."—*Richter*

Such self-congratulation was not to go unanswered. Star and Dart, rival to Bones and Keys in the 1840s, was long gone, but a new senior society was formed, called "Spade and Grave." That name was taken from its golden badge, featuring a spade partly thrust into a grave, resting on the grave's footstone, while a crown topped the headstone. At first it was called "Bed and Broom" by irreverent outsiders. As the formally titled "Society of 1864" gained some respect, it became simply "Graves," on the pattern of "Bones" and "Keys," and its members "Graves men," although "Diggers" soon came to be the primary title by which the society and its members were popularly known in Yale College.[91]

It was birthed in a quarrel in the class of 1864, in which year's set of five *Lit.* editors, three were members of Bones and two were neutrals, Samuel Carter Darling and Lewis Gregory. Bones had long dominated the *Lit.*, having elected four of the five founders in 1836, and being represented on every board thereafter through decades of class-wide elections of the "best literary men," understood to be "those who have taken the highest composition prizes and to have succeeded best in prize debate—without regard to those special editorial and business qualifications no less necessary to the proper publication of a magazine." The *Yale Review*, in an article deploring the formation of society coalitions aimed at rigging the class election for editorships, was to contend in February 1857 that the literary magazine "is regarded by the community, in some degree at least, as the exponent of the first talent of our Alma Mater." The *Lit.* has been called "the most successful periodical in American college literature" and also, more archly, the "favorite college vehicle for Yale undergraduates with literary pretensions."[92]

Election to the magazine board was made by each junior class at a meeting called for the purpose. In the thirty-four classes from 1842 to 1871, of the 155 editors, ninety-four belonged to Bones, seventeen to Keys, and the rest were neutrals, excepting the three who were to become Diggers after the brawl of 1864. Each editor had veto power over his own number of the six published in an academic year. In theory, a majority of the board could suppress an article which a particular editor wished to publish in his number, but they could not by custom publish anything in it which he wished to suppress; in practice, each editor had nearly absolute control of his number, the galley proofs of which his associates rarely troubled to review without special request.[93]

There were also three Bonesmen on the editorial board of 1856–57, but there had been no suppression of neutral editor Norman Perkins when he wrote and published "Secret Societies among Us" in the December 1856 issue, the very first critical appraisal of the Yale society system to appear in any campus publication. Perkins was a man of parts (a Coch, a winner of a Townsend Premium, and upon graduation, a commencement orator)[94] and did not stint in his indictment: "So long as the principal object of Secret Societies [never named, but including at this date two sophomore societies, as well as three junior fraternities, Bones, and Keys] is intellectual improvement without the admixture of narrow, clannish feelings or ungenerous rivalry, we apprehend very little [to] be argued against their utility or propriety." Nevertheless, "the leading feature of our Secret Societies is their political maneuvering, by which they manage to control the action of Classes, and not unfrequently, of the whole College. . . . No office 'in the gift of the people,' whether important or trivial, can by any possibility be filled acceptably without a course of dabbling by five or six enterprising Societies."

The self-satisfied celebration of their rituals, he argued, was offensive to class routine and order: "Secret Societies must of necessity have a horribly *mysterious* way of doing everything, so their 'conclaves' become wonderfully 'nocturnal' . . . interspersed with various gastronomic, potatory and fumigatory processes. We have seen a dignified company regularly straggling into Morning Prayers together, directly from their hebdomadal [weekly] gathering, looking dull and sleepy, and, as a matter of course, totally unfitted for the duties of the day." Often, Perkins noted, many of those coming into chapel prayers as a society after intiation night were still not sober. On "one occasion, one of the 'initiated,' instead of giving his Latin exercise to his Tutor at recitation, very innocently handed out a *Bill of Fare* with the Wine List wonderfully underscored."

Perkins ended his article not with a call for the societies' abolition—that was not likely—but with an appeal for conscious improvement by secret society members. "Let not the humbug of mystery, nor the humbug of silence, nor any senseless mummery, take the place of that positive power for good which such organizations ought to possess. . . . If, in short, we are to have Secret Societies among us at all, as it seems destined we shall have, let us make them something more than mere machinery—something loftier than an embodiment of conceits and jealousies—something more real than mystery, and more efficient than dumbness; let us make them a living means of good, and a constant promoter of kindly feeling; let us fashion a system which shall be elevating and ennobling in its entire aim—not a dark index of our College life, but worthy of ourselves and of those who shall come after us."[95]

Seven years after the appearance of Perkins's unsuppressed article, aimed at all of the college's societies, none of that *Lit.* board's three Bonesmen troubled to review galley proofs of the February 1864 number, in which one of the board neutrals published a leading article called "Collegial Ingenuity," by Samuel Darling. It contained subtle references to their society, mocking those who "shall travel over one hundred miles of wet, unmacadamized road for ten rods in a high street." (High Street being the location of the Bones tomb.) The typical Yale College man, the author maintained, was willing to suffer indignities to gain election until "flesh and strength shall gradually fail its possessor, and bring him ultimately through anxious care to a mere skeleton! Gloriously shine the bones through the skin, eloquent witnesses of self-exhaustive toil for democratic work." This article's author was seen by some readers to suggest that men might "worm their way into Bones." In the reminiscence of a member of the class of 1865, published eighty years later, he wrote that the Bonesmen claimed it was "derogatory to one of their members, on the meanness of toadying and bullying."[96] The apparently recognizable member of Bones was Henry Boyden, who allegedly failed to honor a promise to Darling that the contest in a Linonia Prize debate be decided by lot, to which Darling had alluded by an otherwise innocuous reference in his article to a "coin toss."[97]

After voting to suppress the piece, the Bones editors seized all the printed copies from the distributors without explanation and stored them in their rooms, while demanding a replacement article from its author. The other neutral editor refused to be cowed and called on his class to support Darling: after a strong show of college support, the two neutrals insisted that the Bones editors surrender the sequestered copies or be expelled from the *Lit.* office. Since the Bonesmen defied this demand, the class, in a specially convened meeting on February 22, 1864, expelled them from their editorships and elected three other neutrals in their places, who with the two original neutrals duly produced a second issue of the February number, including the now notorious "Collegial Ingenuity."[98] The newly elected board then proceeded to edit and publish a further two numbers, stopping only with the end of the academic year and term limits. In their April issue appeared an article even more critical than Darling's had been, titled "Secret Societies" and beginning, "Would it not be well for us to do away with Secret Societies?"[99]

The Bones rump board members at their personal expense then printed a new February number, substituting with explanation another "leader" for the one they had found so obnoxious; when it was advertised for sale, one of the large-framed boating men of the society strode up and down in front of the Brick Row dormitories to prevent the posters from being torn down from the trees. They duly published their own two remaining numbers, under a masthead bearing the original five names, as though nothing untoward had occurred. Since the Bones-dominated board had the legal right of the matter—the class had no precedent for holding a second election to effect a recall—the three magazines issued by the second board, through the balance of the term, also at the editors' personal expense, are now known as the "second issues."

The grave scene in *Hamlet*, where the cheeky gravedigger tosses up the skull and bones of the jester Yorick with his spade, is said to have been the inspiration for the symbolism of the new society's badge, in an emblem typifying implacable hostility to, and the overthrow of, Skull and Bones. The *Yale Courant* for October 23, 1867, contained intriguing campus news. "Jolly mourning.—Last Saturday afternoon our attention was drawn to a newly erected mound in the rear of the Trumbull Gallery. A head board and foot stone had been appropriately erected at the ends. The handle of a shovel placed in the center of the mound leaned upon the head board, while the grass grew green at the other end. On approaching we reverently raised our hat, but were scandalized at the laughter and shouts of what we took to be the mourners. . . . We hurried away from this sad scene, but chancing to pass that way in an hour or two after, saw that vandal hands had desolated the mound. . . . We were surprised to see that the jolly mourners spoken of were juniors. Will any of them ever be more sedate and less communicative on the subject?"

The Diggers' anthem, sung outside their rooms at the close of meetings, either while marching or on arriving at the college yard, was "How Can I Leave Thee," the English version of a traditional German song of the era, "Ach, Wie Ist's Moglich Dann." The new society's hall was in the Lyon Building, at 769 Chapel Street near the intersection with State Street, on a floor with the freshman fraternity Gamma Nu, and had iron doors at the entrance and a billiard table inside. They treasured their pins as fiercely as their rivals: "I took the badge," remembered one Digger, "and vowed that we should never part, that in sickness and in health, she should always cling either to my vest or to my nightgown or to my bathing trunks when I wore one . . ."

Still, against the established powers of Bones and Keys, Spade and Grave struggled. Well-laid plans of electioneering and "packing" were not sufficient in some years to make up its fifteen, although their elected numbers included Cochs, and men on the varsity crew and baseball nine. Suffering seven refusals for 1866, they pledged fourteen in 1867 and again in 1869, with four refusals for 1868 (the *New York Times* reported in July 1868 that "the Spade and Grave Society is regarded as defunct"). There was no delegation at all in the 1869–70 class year: three men were elected, but when the rest of the 1868–69 delegation could not be secured, those elections were withdrawn. Psi U men used to boast that none of their number were members, until one accepted a Digger tap for 1869, and three classes between the first and the last in 1871 (1864, 1865, and 1867) were comprised exclusively of men from the junior fraternities Alpha Delta Phi and DKE.[100]

To stem the decline, they invented a new name, Crown and Sceptre, and created a new badge, "a crown within which a sword and fire-dog cross one another." The initials "S.L.M." ("*Sceptrum Ligonibus Mors*"— "Death makes the scepter equal to a mattocks," a kind of pickaxe, or more freely translated, "In the dominion of death we are all equal")[101] replaced the old name on the society cut in publications. In the irreverent Yale College fashion to degrade, the abbreviation was quickly characterized by detractors as "Slim" or "Slimey," and was not sufficient to reverse the fall of their reputation: Bagg writes that no man who thought he had a chance for Bones or Keys would accept a Graves offer of election, and by the class of 1870, no one would pledge. In its report on the senior society elections in the spring of 1869, the *College Courant* in its issue of July 3 noted that Space and Grave "for some cause best known to themselves, failed to appear, except 'for consultation.' We certainly hope, without any ill will to the society itself or its members, that they will have the good sense to give the thing up as an impossibility and as an utter waste of money." The society soon gave up its hall.[102]

On November 2, 1870, eight members hailing from the Spade and Grave (now S.L.M.) clubs of 1864 through 1869 printed and signed a two-document appeal for funds to reestablish the society, and seeking to pledge members from the class of 1871.[103] They succeeded in forming a new delegation of fourteen, including the musicians Gustave Stoeckel (son of the first Yale professor of music) and Harry Baldwin, along with the class poet, the class historian, the Yale Navy commodore, and nine other men delivering orations, colloquies, or dissertations at commencement, but this proved to be the last delegation in the nineteenth century. The society had not been formally incorporated and never printed a catalogue. Another contemporary rival had been seen off by Bones and Keys, although Spade and Grave was to be partly reborn in the founding of Wolf's Head in 1883, and then revived under its original name in the mid-twentieth century, finally owning its own hall, with the help of alumni, in the twenty-first.[104]

Not so quickly disposed of was a mock society called "Bowl and Stones," also aiming to denigrate the Bones by its name and antics. Formed in the class of 1861, it included anyone who wanted to annoy the men of High Street returning to their rooms after a Thursday night meeting (although sometimes the Keys members were ridiculed by a burlesque of their singing their home-going anthem "Troubadour," and the college administration laid down a rule against the outside singing of all society songs, in an attempt to curb the Stones men). This collection of marauding neutrals prowled about the campus early in the morning, haranguing those in the tombs with catcalls, singing their own athem to the tune of "Bonnie Blue Flag"—*Haughty Bones is fallen, and we gwine down to occupy the skull*"—and stealing ice cream and other food deliveries outside the Bones tomb in 1870 and again in 1873.

The theft from the grocer Radcliffe's wagon was an expensive loss for the Bones and a memorable occasion for the neutrals. As reported years later in a Denver newspaper, "Once their initiation spread was stolen from the caterer's cart as it stood before the hall. It was a $350 'smear,' the toothsome articles of which were soon scattered in the dormitories among a reveling crowd. In one room a man was doling out ice cream with a tooth-mug from the can, and for lack of spoons, pocket knives, lead pencils and impromptu paper scraps were used. There was an abundance of sherry captured, and the one man who had got happy thereon was festooning a classmate's cropped head with charlotte russe."[105]

The Stones men offered bogus elections to gullible classmates, and even to underclassmen, who were sometimes convinced (the *Yale Naught-ical Almanac for 1872* announced in its page for June that on the 16th "B—l and St—nes elections given out. 'They dreamt they dwelt in marble halls'"). In 1867 they wantonly smashed bottles of ink upon the front of the Bones tomb and tore the chains from the fence posts. An 1866 article in the *Hartford Press* by a member of the class of 1865 reported three break-ins to the Bones hall, "twice through the skylight and once through the barred windows in the cellar"; valuables in the safe could not be got at, but "two or three ink bottles and other trifles were brought away as trophies of the exploit."[106]

This "neutral" group's name changed, in popular parlance, to "Bull and Stones" (corrupted for obvious reasons), and some members of the class of 1870 invented a badge, a small gilt representation of a bull standing upon stones, worn in public and regularly during the first term of their senior year. There were no meetings or program, and its membership was "few or many depending on the state of the weather," to be joined by any ready for an uproar on a Thursday night, although a New Haven newspaper in November 1872 carried an announcement with fifteen names respecting a recent election to Stones.[107] The meeting night presence of a policeman was of some aid to the harassed society. The majesty of the law was no help, however, when the Stones men stretched wires across the known path by which the Keys members returned to their rooms, to make them stumble and fall.[108] The Bones' protest at this treatment of their rivals at Keys earned them only an attack upon their own group's initiation of the club of 1874.

It might indeed have been worse, had not fourteen men in the class of 1869, who had been neutrals since freshman year and were potential

"Stones men," effected a milder satire, appearing on Presentation Day with gilt coffin lids, about an inch long, on their shirt bosoms. These "Coffin men" or "E.T.L.s" (full meaning unknown) were printed in the annuals of the next term, under the senior society column heading beneath a woodcut of the badge, but no name. They seem to have met weekly on Thursday night in a rented room, but gave no election to the class of 1870, and so disappeared from history.[109]

The persistence of the hostility of Bull and Stones was an unveiled warning, in the late 1860s, of the provocation represented by the very existence of the two senior societies. When the new iron doors for the Bones tomb were being erected in the fall of 1864 behind a large canvas sail placed in front of the building, which resembled the screen to the tents of traveling menageries and circuses, a placard was printed and posted throughout the college early one Thursday evening:

S.B.B.

Grand Menagerie!

No. 322 High Street.

The Proprietors of S.B.B. take pleasure in informing
the Public that they will give a Performance
At the above place on Thursday Evening, Nov.10.
This collection of animals is wonderful and rare.

Tickets 25 cents

The proceeds will be applied to defraying the expense of recent
improvements to the building. Don't forget the number, 322.

This was harmless satire (and indeed is said to have come from Keys), but in 1866, even before the Stones defacement of the Bones property, the tomb was, in the words of the *Yale Courant* of November 7, "defaced with some black substance in a scandalous manner."[110]

In a mocking poster posted six years later, just before election day in the early summer of 1869 for the delegations of 1870, Bull and Stones boldly identified itself as the publisher:

SKULLS AND KEYS

SENIOR SOCIETIES
Will give out their Elections in the following order:

BONES
Will issue from their Cave at 12 Midnight, without underclothes, their right wing resting on North College.

KEYS,
Led by the New York Giant, will remain beneath the North steps of the State House until 2 P.M.

DIGGERS
With strings of Billiard Balls around their necks and Cues in their hands, will sit in a pool under South Joseph, scratching their heads, until four o'clock.

BULL AND STONES.
(last, but ye Gods, not least) have kindly promised to furnish escorts to each of the crowds in order. The B. & S. men will be dressed in silks and broadcloth, with horns in their hands and melodies on their lips. The great Digger deacon will offer prayer at the Lyceum door, that heaven may grant them ability to find fifteen men willing to bury themselves in their grave.

KEYS will exhibit the new plan of their future Hall at the hands of the Massachusetts Shoemaker, and will discourse on the honor of the Zenome.

BONES will exhibit the mottoes on their dining room wall— such as AMOR IN OSSIBUS—and prove the difficulty of their being locked in their Hall.

DIGGERS will take up a collection to pay off their back rent.

All relics dropped on the line of march, such as dry bones, wooden keys, rusty spades, etc., will be given to the Orphan Asylum.

Neophytes will be in their rooms by 8 P.M.[111]

The toxic atmosphere of hostility to senior societies, largely directed at the Bones but, as these quotations from the publications of the neutrals show, also at Keys to a lesser extent and even at the relative newcomer Spade and Grave, was to find a spark and explode when Keys perpetrated a crook of the college's boating flags in 1872.

TAPPED FOR SKULL AND BONES, 1856–1871

Stephen Condit	1856	supervisor of U.S. Census
Chauncey Mitchell Depew	1856	president, chairman of the board, New York Central Railroad
		U.S. senator (N.Y.)
		Alumni Fellow, Yale Corp.
Benjamin Drake Magruder	1856	chief justice, Ill.
Lewis Richard Packard	1856	Yale professor of Greek
		president, American Philological Association
Eli Whitney Blake	1857	professor of Physics, Cornell, Brown
John Thomas Croxton	1857	brigadier general, U.S. Army
		U.S. minister, Bolivia
James Payne Green	1857	president of faculty, Jefferson College
Joseph Cooke Jackson	1857	brigadier general, U.S. Army
Cyrus G. Northrop	1857	president, University of Minnesota
Moses Coit Tyler	1857	professor of English, Michigan
		professor of History, Cornell

Samuel Henry Lee	1858	president, American International College
Addison Van Name	1858	librarian, Yale University
Charles Franklin Robertson	1859	Episcopal bishop, Mo.
Burton Norvell Harrison	1859	private secretary to Jefferson Davis
Eugene Schuyler	1859	U.S. minister, Greece, Romania, and Serbia
		American translator of Turgenev
William Walter Phelps	1860	U.S. Congress (N.J.)
		U.S. minister to Austria, Germany
		Alumni Fellow, Yale Corp.
		Phelps Hall his family's gift
William Thayer Smith	1860	professor of Physiology, Dartmouth
		dean of Medical School
Lowndes Henry Davis	1860	U.S. Congress (Mo.)
Simeon E. Baldwin	1861	chief justice, Conn.
		governor, Conn.
		Yale professor of Law
		president, American Social Science Association
		president, American Political Science Association
		president, International Law Association
		president, American Bar Association
Franklin P. Dexter	1861	registrar, secretary, Yale University, Yale professor of History
Anthony Higgins	1861	U.S. congressman (Del.)
		U.S. senator (Del.)

Francis Kernochan	1861	founder of University Club, NYC, first American city university club
Sanford Newell	1861	U.S. minister to the Netherlands
		delegate, Hague Peace Conference
Tracy Peak	1861	Cornell/Yale professor of Latin
Edward Rowland Sill	1861	professor of English, University of California
		poet and literary critic
Daniel Henry Chamberlain	1862	attorney general, governor (S.C.)
Edward Benton Coe	1862	professor of Modern Languages, Yale
Sherburne B. Eaton	1862	president, Edison Electric Light Co.
Henry Phelps Johnston	1862	professor of History, City College of N.Y.
Cornelius L. Kitchell	1862	secretary, bureau of appointments, Yale
Franklin MacVeagh	1862	U.S. secretary of the treasury
William W. Seeley	1862	professor of Opthamology, medical dean, University of Cincinnati
John B. Taylor	1862	professor of Theology, Andover Seminary
Leander T. Chamberlain	1862	president, U.S. Evangelical Alliance
Henry Farnam Dimock	1863	Alumni Fellow, Yale Corp.
Joseph F. Kernochan	1863	president, N.Y. Free Circulating Library
David Brainard Perry	1863	president, Doane College
George C. S. Southworth	1863	professor of English, Case Western

William Graham Sumner	1863	Yale professor of political science
		theorist of Social Darwinism
William Collins Whitney	1863	U.S. secretary of the Navy
Charles Fraser MacLean	1864	Police/Parks/Health Commissioner, New York City
William Henry Palmer	1864	professor of Opthamology, Cleveland Medical College
John William Sterling	1864	founder, Shearman & Sterling
		Yale's greatest single alumni benefactor
Francis Eben Woodruff	1864	imperial commissioner of customs, China
John L. Ewell	1865	professor of Latin, Washington University
		professor of History, Howard University
Payson Merrill	1865	Alumni Fellow, Yale Corp.
		founder and chair, Yale Alumni Fund
Charles E. Smith	1865	Yale professor of American History
Henry A. Stimson	1865	minister, trustee of Mt. Holyoke, Carlton, Drury Colleges
Henry W. Warren	1865	board chair, Alcorn University
		speaker, Miss. House of Representatives
William W. Farnam	1866	Alumni Fellow, Yale Corp.
John Manning Hall	1866	speaker, Conn. Legislature
Edward Hincks	1866	professor of Theology, Harvard
George Holt	1866	U.S. district coourt judge, N.Y.

Frederick Judson	1866	professor of Greek, Nashville University
Henry T. Sloane	1866	donor, Sloane Physics Laboratory
Levi Wade	1866	speaker, Mass. legislature
Thomas Hedge	1867	U.S. Congress (Iowa)
James Merriam	1867	professor of Mathematics, Gallaudet
George Peabody Wetmore	1867	governor, R.I. U.S. Senate (R.I.)
Chauncey Brewster	1868	Episcopal bishop of Conn.
LeBaron Colt	1868	U.S. Senate (R.I.)
Thomas Sloane	1868	donor, Sloane Physics Laboratory
James Kingsley Thacher	1868	Yale professor of Physiology
Henry Parks Wright	1868	Yale professor of Latin, dean of Yale College, Wright Hall donated by clubmates and other alumni
Henry Augustin Beers	1869	Yale professor of English
Wilson Shannon Bissell	1869	postmaster general, U.S. chancellor, University of Buffalo
Henry Varnum Freeman	1869	chief justice, Ill.
Bernadotte Perrin	1869	Yale professor of Greek
Henry Warren Raymond	1869	director, American School of Classical Studies, Athens
John Wallingford Andrews Jr.	1870	U.S. attorney, Mt.
William Carlos Gulliver	1870	professor of Languages, Knox College
Dwight Whitney Learned	1870	professor of Greek, Doshisha College, Kyoto, Japan
James Gore King McClure	1870	president, Lake Forest University

William Henry Welch	1870	professor of Pathology, first dean of Medicine, Johns Hopkins University
		founder, doctors' post-graduate training
		founder first school of public health
		president, American Medical Association
		president, Association of American Physicians
Charles Hopkins Clark	1871	editor, *Hartford Courant*
Howard Mansfield	1871	Whistler etching scholar
		Grolier Club president
Watson Robertson Sperry	1871	U.S. minister to Persia
Thomas Thacher	1871	Yale lecturer on corporate trusts
		founding partner, Simpson, Thacher & Bartlett
		founder, Yale University Alumni Fund
William Kneeland Townsend	1871	Yale professor of Contracts
		U.S. Circuit Court judge (Second Circuit)

TAPPED FOR SCROLL AND KEY, 1856–1871

John Monteith	1856	president, University of Michigan
Sidney Edwards Morse	1856	editor and proprietor, *New York Observer*
David Plunket Richardson	1856	U.S. Congress (N.Y.)
John Wager Swayne	1856	major general, CSA
		military commission, Ala.
		general counsel, Western Union

Ahab George Wilkinson	1856	principal examiner, U.S. patents
Augustus Field Beard	1857	successor trustee, Yale Corp.
George Pierce Andrews	1858	corporation counsel, NYC
David Garrison Brinton	1858	professor of American Archeology and Linguistics, University of Pennsylvania
		president, American Association for the Advancement of Science
Channing Richards	1858	U.S. district attorney, southern district, Ohio
Elisha Thomas Smith	1858	Episcopal bishop of Kansas
Felix Ansart	1859	president, Automobile Club of America
Charles Hodge Boardman	1859	professor Med. Juris., University of Minnesota
Joseph Hopkins Twichell	1859	Alumni Fellow, Yale Corp.
Francis Delafield	1860	professor of Pathology, Columbia
		first president, Association of American Physicians and Pathologists
		founder, first U.S. pathology laboratory
Daniel Cady Eaton	1860	Yale professor of History of Art
Mason Young	1860	Alumni Fellow, Yale Corp.
James Nevins Hyde	1861	professor of Dermatology, Chicago Medical College
		president, American Dermatological Association
James Wood McClane	1861	professor of Obstetrics, Columbia
		president, Roosevelt Hospital

Joseph Lucien Shipley	1861	editor and proprietor, *Springfield Union*
Frederick Irving Knight	1862	professor, Throat Diseases, Harvard
		president, American Laryngologists Association
		president, American Climatology Association
Richard Cary Morse	1862	general secretary, International Commission, YMCA
Buchanan Winthrop	1862	Alumni Fellow, Yale Corp.
Samuel Shorty Hollingsworth	1863	professor of Law, University of Pennsylvania
Edward Lawrence Keyes	1863	professor of Genito-Urinary Surgery, Bellevue Hospital
		founder, president, American Association of Genito-Urinary Surgeons
Lewis Atterbury Stimson	1863	professor of Surgery, Cornell
Frederic Henry Betts	1864	Yale lecturer on patent law
Charles Henry Burnett	1864	professor, Diseases of Ear, Columbia
		president, American Ontological Society
Olof Page	1864	surgeon general, Chilean Army
John Dalzell	1865	U.S. Congress (Penn.)
William Henry Sage	1865	donor, Sage Hall
Maurice Dwight Collier	1866	Yale lecturer on judgments
George Augustus Adee	1867	Adee Boathouse memorial
David James Burrell	1867	professor of Homiletics, Princeton
		pastor, Marble Collegiate Church

William Henry Goodyear	1867	curator, fine arts, Brooklyn Institute
		discoverer, use of curves in Roman and Egyptian architecture
Boyd Vincent	1867	Episcopal Bishop, south Ohio
Charles William Bingham	1868	Bingham Hall family donation
Edwin Gustin Coy	1869	first headmaster, Hotchkiss School
Eli Whitney Jr.	1869	president, New Haven Water Co.
		president, New Haven Hospital
Edward Salisbury Dana	1870	Yale professor of Physics
		editor, *American Journal of Science*
Robert Weeks de Forest	1870	president, Metropolitan Museum of Art
		organizer, Yale Club of N.Y.
Robert Wodrow Archbald	1871	U.S. Circuit Court judge

TAPPED FOR SPADE AND GRAVE, 1864–1871

David Brainerd Lyman	1864	president, Chicago Title & Trust Co.
Charles Greene Rockwood Jr.	1864	professor of Mathematics, Princeton
James Glynn Gregory	1865	surgeon general of Connecticut
Charles Henry Smith	1865	professor of Mathematics, Bowdoin
John Warren Hicks	1865	supreme commander of America, Knights of Malta
Edward Alexis Caswell	1866	founder, American crematoriums
John William Showalter	1867	U.S. Circuit Court judge

Edgar Abel Turrell	1867	dean of Law, Drake University
Edward Spencer Mead	1868	partner, Dodd & Mead publishers
David McGregor Means	1868	professor, Political Science, Middlebury College
Richard Austin Rice	1868	professor of Languages, University of Vermont
Alwin Ethelstan Todd	1871	Professor, Natural Sciences, Berea College

CHAPTER SIX

PROVOCATIONS OF POPPYCOCK,

AND TAP DAY'S INVENTION

(1872–1882)

Our object is to ventilate a few facts concerning "Skull and Bones,"
to dissipate the awe and reverence which has of late years enshrouded
this wall of Poppy Cock . . .

—*The Iconoclast*, October 1873

DENOUNCING SECRET SOCIETIES

John Bascom wanted to attend Yale—through his mother, he was a
descendant of one of its ten clerical founders—but family pressures
directed him to Williams College, the school of his father and uncles,
from which he graduated in 1849. He spent most of his career in higher
education there, serving as professor of Rhetoric before becoming president of the University of Wisconsin.[1]

The position and prominence of secret societies had long been contested at Williams. Beginning with the class of 1850, membership in these

222

fraternities frequently included more than half the class, and after 1866, it was unusual if fewer than that number belonged. A college debate on the subject had been organized in 1855—James A. Garfield of the class of 1856, the future American president, spent his vacation in New York libraries building his case against them—but the debate was aborted when the societies refused all reform. In July 1868, the college's board was in receipt of a student petition that the societies be abolished. That September, Professor Bascom preached a biting sermon, which he later published, titled "Secret Societies in College."[2]

The pamphlet does not mention Yale, let alone its then existing senior societies, but was instead aimed squarely at the secrecy of the Williams fraternities. Nevertheless, it was promptly summarized for the New Haven audience by the *College Courant* for November 7, 1868. The powerful indictment came from a man claiming to "have seen these college societies on the inside and the outside, have enjoyed their advantages and marked their evils." At the time of his sermon, there were six fraternities in Williamstown on Bascom's campus, and they were all secret societies. "My first objection against secret societies," Bascom thundered, "is that they are *necessarily* frivolous. . . . A secret society in college can have no worthy, ostensible end, to which secrecy is a fit, natural, necessary means. Literary ends are sufficiently met by other societies, or, if not, do not require secrecy, [and] are not in the least aided by concealment."

His remaining indictment was a lengthy one: the fetishizing of badges, the rigging of campus elections, the conformity forestalling the "untrammeled action of judgment and feelings," their injury to the "intellectual and moral character of their members," the "society-house or rendezvous" as "places of indolent resort," and the "pernicious" results of "hot-bed intercourse" where physical and spiritual unions might be subject to corruption.[3]

All of Bascom's charges (except perhaps his final, feverish references to moral turpitude and even possible sexual irregularities, which allegations never appeared in any published attacks on the Yale societies) would have echoed there among the critics of Bones and Keys within the student body neutrals and the faculty: the exclusivity, the badges, the "wire-pulling" in elections, the supposedly luxurious clubhouses. But elsewhere, at the College of New Jersey at Princeton, and at Harvard College in Cambridge, Yale's rivals had taken markedly different paths, away from secret societies. The Reverend Bascom's strong "objections" would not have resonated at all on the campuses of Yale's two greatest rivals. As a student once pithily explained the essential distinction between classic fraternities and the clubs at Princeton and Harvard: "You see, the frats eat you and sleep you; the Princeton clubs eat you, but don't sleep you; and the Harvard clubs don't do either."[4]

THE EATING CLUBS AT PRINCETON

The literary societies at Princeton, founded in the 1770s, were named the American Whig and the Cliosophic, and with their extensive society libraries, they became, like Linonia and Brothers at Yale, the main intellectual stimulation for students. Secret and fiercely competitive—as in New Haven, students were recruited for membership before they even came to the college, or were besieged at the railroad station—they complemented the formal curriculum with organized public speaking on political and intellectual issues of the day.

Greek-letter social fraternities appeared at Princeton in 1843, the year Scroll and Key was founded at Yale. Although the chapters were small, ten men or fewer, and met only infrequently in dormitory rooms, faculty opposition grew on the perception of the deleterious political influence which the fraternities had on Whig and Clio, and President John MacLean Jr. banned them from campus. Beginning in 1856–57, Princeton required each student to sign a pledge at matriculation, on pain of expulsion for breach, that he would not be associated with a secret society (meaning a fraternity), while excepting the literary societies: "We, the undersigned, do individually for ourselves promise, without any mental reservation, that we will have no connection whatever with any secret society, nor be present at the meetings of any secret society of this or any other college, so long as we are members of the College of New Jersey; it being understood that this promise has no reference to the American Whig and Cliosophic Societies. We also declare that we regard ourselves bound to keep this promise and on no account to violate it."

MacLean was to claim in 1864 that fraternities no longer existed at Princeton, but even seven years after his successor James McCosh assumed the presidency, several chapters were being maintained with the encouragement of alumni. The expulsion of the culprits who had broken their signed pledge caused an uproar, and an outraged group of alumni submitted a thirty-page report to the college trustees, reprinted in full in the January 15, 1876, issue of the *New-York Tribune* and reported widely elsewhere, denying the organizations' harmful influence and objecting to the coupling of the pledge to admission to the college. In the end, the students apologized and were readmitted, but fraternities were discontinued at Princeton for the next century.[5]

Meanwhile, there were perennial student complaints about inedible institutional fare, and student revulsion by the 1840s was so intense that the trustees no longer required the young men to take their meals in the college facilities. When a fire in 1855 destroyed Nassau Hall's interior, food service was entirely discontinued, and students were compelled, as had occurred in New Haven the decade before, to make their own arrangements to eat in the town's boarding houses. Informal eating clubs of no more than a dozen members began to be formed in consequence, disbanding upon graduation. By 1864, there were twelve of these, growing to twenty-five by 1876. Gastronomical dissatisfaction was not overcome when the college opened a new dining facility that year, and the men in Ivy Hall conceived of renting a stove and employing a cook to prepare their meals.

In the words of Princeton's leading modern historian, "College students have always eaten with gusto, but only Princetonians turned eating into a contact sport. Their competitive juices were stimulated—to a degree unusual in the history of American higher education—not by *what* they ate, but by *where* and *with whom*. In the process, they created a social system that did much to diminish Princeton's vaunted democracy and to retard its growth as a truly meritocratic institution of higher learning. . . . Even with fourteen clubs by 1910, only three-quarters of the upper class could join; the rest were consigned to culinary and social purgatory. Some men were so crushed by rejection that they left college, and many who stayed were dispirited for their last two years, feeling cut off from their privileged classmates and *in* but not *of* the university."[6]

The Ivy Hall Eating Club became the first permanent upper-class eating club at Princeton, inaugurating a stystem which was nurtured by the desire for continuity enjoyed by fraternities at other colleges, by the expanding social significance of affiliations in a growing student body, and by the benefits of attending in a fixed and accommodating location. The students raised money from their parents for their own building in 1881, and prepared a constitution and by-laws, which were submitted to and approved by the faculty and then the college trustees, whose consent was conditioned on the proviso of prohibition against liquor and gambling on club premises. In 1883, the Ivy Club was incorporated, to be followed in due course by the founding and subsequent incorporation of University Cottage Club (begun in 1886), Tiger Inn (1890), Cap and Gown (1890), and Colonial Club (1891).

With the establishment of Cannon and Elm by 1895, there existed seven eating clubs gathering in membership approximately a quarter of the two upper classes, a proportion not yet inviting odium. Princetonian Edmund Wilson, there from 1912 to 1916, complained that "there was little or no serious activity in connection with these eating clubs." The social dynamic was to change dramatically in the twentieth century, when the quest for membership became, as one professor later complained, "a religious frenzy over the choice of a restaurant," and this shift was ultimately to lead to the resignation of Woodrow Wilson as president of Princeton.[7]

THE FINAL CLUBS AT HARVARD

The so-called final clubs at Harvard are limited to seniors, like the Yale senior societies. They take their name from the fact that, as the three lower classes in Cambridge each had their own organizations, these were the last social clubs a collegian might join before graduation. The Hasty Pudding Club, founded in 1795 as a seniors' debating club, was not a final club, and by the middle of the nineteenth century, emphasized belle-lettristic programs, mock trials, and plays, rather than debates on current issues. In 1834, it became a secret organization—every member-elect, its constitution held, *"shall solemnly promise secrecy,"* and according to an article in the *Yale Record*, it was still so in 1874.

The phrase "final club" also means "mutually exclusive": a senior can belong to but one final club, but is not restricted from joining other clubs of other kinds.[8] Their genesis, however, is more complicated than that of the New Haven senior societies or the Princeton eating clubs, which, after the founding of the first on each campus, multiplied through simple replication. After the fraternity Alpha Delta Phi's founding in Cambridge in 1837, followed by chapters of Psi Upsilon in 1850 and Delta Kappa Epsilon in 1852, the Harvard faculty banned secret societies, although A.D. and DKE both continued to exist in secret thereafter. Above the Pudding, the four largely intermediary clubs, called "feeders," had a total membership of about eighty.[9]

The most iconic of Harvard's final clubs, often bracketed with Skull and Bones and Princeton's Ivy Club, is Porcellian (the "Porc" or "P.C."), founded with sixteen members in 1791 as "The Argonauts," and begun anew with a roast pig dinner and a different name in 1794. Making no pretense of cultivating literature or public speaking, and for some years the largest college society in Cambridge, by 1800 it had become "the most aristocratic, and the highest goal of undergraduate social ambition," merging with another club in 1831. (From its founding, many members of Porcellian were also members of Phi Beta Kappa and attended dinners of both clubs, but ceased to do so after 1846, when the Massachusetts Alpha, in response to the persuasive New England temperance movement, banned all alcoholic beverages.) A travel book of 1870 pronounced: "A notice of Harvard would be as incomplete without a reference to the Porcellian Club as a notice in Oxford or Cambridge would be in which the Union Debating Society held no place. . . . The Porcellian is hardly a place of resort for those who cultivate the intellect at the expense of the body. The list of active members is small, owing in part to the largeness of the annual subscription. The great desire of every student is to become a member of it . . . the doings of the club are shrouded in secrecy . . ."

Tom Hughes, the English author of *Tom Brown's School Days*, noted in an Oxford University newspaper in 1871 that the Porcellian membership had "dwindled to five, as the Apostles at Cambridge did to two some twenty years ago." The rule was "rigidly enforced, that no student, not being a member, be allowed to set foot within its exclusive precincts. . . . Prescott, the historian, and Everett, the orator, were Porcellians and signed their names to the club formula: 'I solemnly promise and declare that I will not in any way reveal the acts or constitutions of the Porcellian Club.'" Suspended from a green and white ribbon, its adornment is a silver, eight-pointed star, bearing crossed swords, the two dates 1791 and 1831, and the motto *Dum vivamus vivamus*. Its black steward George Washington Lewis at his death in 1929 had ten Porcellian pallbearers, echoing the Bones' tribute to its lamplighter John Creed (except, unlike Creed, Lewis was not initiated).[10]

The Alpha Delta Phi chapter surrendered its fraternity charter in 1865 (which Harvard men did easily), becoming the A.D. Club and then the Dickey, and by 1871, mirroring the Yale senior societies, was electing fifteen members: "The out-going Seniors elect seven Juniors, who proceed, in their turn, to choose eight of their own classmates and so the ordained number is preserved."[11] The Fly Club also traces its beginning to Alpha Delta Phi, its name combining the "ph" from Alpha, the "l" from Delta, and the "i" from Phi, equaling "Phli," or "Fly."[12] Among the five other final clubs at Harvard today (the Dickey having expired), the Spee began in 1852 as a chapter of the Zeta Phi fraternity, the Owl Club was founded in 1896, the Phoenix-S.K. Club spun off from the sophomore society Theta Nu Epsilon in 1895 and a secret society known as the Sphinx Club of 1897, while Fox Club was founded in 1898 and the Delphic the same year, formed out of the existing fraternity Delta Phi, when J. P. Morgan Jr. did not make the final club of his choice.[13]

Because of the sheer quality of the Harvard student body, each of these final clubs can boast of renowned graduates: in Porcellian, orator Edward Everett (who ended secrecy in Phi Beta Kappa), poet James Russell Lowell, essayist Oliver Wendell Holmes, Senator Charles Sumner, novelist Owen Wister, and President Theodore Roosevelt (but not, to his dismay, Franklin Delano Roosevelt); for A.D., press baron William Randolph Hearst and Supreme Court Justice Oliver Wendell Holmes Jr.; Harvard president Abbott Lawrence Lowell and Franklin Roosevelt in Fly (where the fireplace is said to have inspired FDR's "fireside chats"); historian Samuel Eliot Morison and Facebook cofounder Eduardo Saverin in Phoenix-S.K.; John F. Kennedy and Robert F. Kennedy in Spee (although their father, Joseph Kennedy, was not a final club man); poet T. S. Eliot and Microsoft cofounder Bill Gates in Fox; and Senator Edward M. Kennedy in Owl.[14]

Nevertheless, there was no plan in these elections to gather in the campus achievers sought by Bones or the social skills celebrated by Keys. "The man who comes to Harvard unheralded," wrote a contemporary journalist, "without the proper school connections, may become chairman of the *Crimson* or of the *Lampoon*, or Captain of the Eleven or Crew. He will make the Institute and the Pudding, he may—not necessarily—make one of the new final clubs, but if he succeeds in penetrating into the social sets of A.D. and Porcellian, which are the social prizes—without money, without social connections or extraordinary natural social genius, it will be a miracle and a miracle of such rarity as not to overtax the credulity."

Rather, membership more often reflected a healthy respect for "Harvard's social taboos . . . including over-careful dress, undue athletic exertion, serious literary endeavor [and] grades above C." Education at New England's elite Episcopal Church schools—Groton, St. Mark's, St. Paul's, St. George's, and Middlesex—was also important. Finally, in the late nineteenth and well into the twentieth century, Boston family social standing was paramount, although Porcellian, Delphic, Spee, and

Fly numbered in their annual membership a fair proportion of New Yorkers, with occasional men from Philadelphia and Chicago, and the competition to attract other final clubs' legacies was fierce. The Porc for the better half of its Boston/Harvard history has embraced generations of Adamses and Ameses, Cabots and Cutlers, Lowells and Lymans, Gardners and Gardiners, Halliwells and Hunnewells, Salstonstalls and Searses, Warrens and Welds. This exclusivity is reflected in the legend of the Porcellian stroke of the Harvard crew, of whom it was said: "He's democratic all right—he knows all but the three up front."[15]

Membership in a Harvard final club could engender strong feelings. *The Virginian*'s author, Owen Wister, over a half century following his election to Porc in 1879, told a magazine reporter that even his best-selling novel's national success did not mean as much to him, and that his final club's bond could be "felt but not analyzed." In the same vein, when informing Kaiser Wilhelm of Germany of the engagement of his daughter Alice to Speaker of the House Nicholas Longworth, Theodore Roosevelt volunteered that "Nick and I are both members of the Porc, you know."[16] Yet these sentiments did not issue in any special engagement with Harvard College, which officially ignored the final clubs, as did the undergraduate newspaper the *Crimson*.

Their existence, while largely confined to the Boston social elite and numerically limited to about 15 percent of the student body (the Porc elected three to eighteen from each class), did not provoke attacks on their clubhouses, which were not meant to be architecturally distinguished, and their often unlocked doors were not iron. There were no shiver-inducing initiation rituals, and Porc members' golden pigs on their watch chains did not inspire awe (unfortunately, convicted embezzler and New York Stock Exchange chief Richard Whitney was photographed with his on the way through Grand Central Terminal to Sing Sing prison in 1938).[17] Achievement was not rewarded or to be reinforced by membership. "The small clubs are not conducive to sustained effort in the public service on the part of their members. . . . For superior men who are too active to be pocketed, the clubs are pleasant without being unprofitable," wrote an observer in 1897. "There are usually such leaders among the Harvard clubmen, but they are leaders because it is in them, and rather in spite of the clubs than because of them."[18]

Samuel Eliot Morison in his 1936 tercentennial history of Harvard, making the slightest of references to Yale and the very different ethos of its senior club system, observed: "The [final] clubs are not the best preparation for living in a democratic society; yet many of their graduates have been faithful servants to the University, to the Republic, and to learning. The split between [Harvard] Yard and Gold Coast that the clubs helped to create often resulted in bitterly contested class elections; but this hard feeling vanished at graduation, and anything like fraternity or senior society politics in after life is unknown among Harvard men." In New Haven, it was noted in 1901 by another historian of colleges, "the existence of the lower-class societies facilitates the sifting of men so that the ablest students are well-marked characters by the end of the junior year. Harvard is the only other institution in the country where such [Yale-like senior] societies would have been possible, and Harvard, as we have seen, developed social clubs on the basis of congeniality rather than any society system properly so called."[19]

When Harvard graduate John Morton Blum was in his first year of teaching in New Haven in 1957, lecturing on Theodore Roosevelt, he noted that future president's membership in Porcellian, explaining that "The Porcellian Club is the nearest Harvard equivalent of Skull and Bones." Two days later, at his class's next meeting, he arrived to find at his lectern a small white envelope, stamped with a black wax seal bearing the Yale society's insignia, containing an unsigned note reading: "Professor Blum, May we ask you please not to mention the name of our club in your lectures." Blum read the note aloud to the class, and then never committed that error again.[20]

PROVOCATION: THE PAIN OF REJECTION

In the academic year of 1831–32, the year prior to Bones' founding, Yale College undergraduate enrollment totaled 354. Thirty years later, in 1861–62, in the senior year of Henry Holt, that number had grown to 462, an increase of 30 percent.[21] By the later date, with the creation of Scroll and Key in 1842, there were two senior societies, with room for only thirty men, and proportionately a man's chance of being chosen for one of the two had increased, from one in six in the first Bones year of 1833 (in a graduating class of 91) to better than one in four in 1862 (in a class of 100). Psychologically, however, the reverse was true: in a larger class, when the senior societies had accumulated more than two decades of on-campus prestige, the pain of rejection was both more keen and more public.

Other critics of the system argued that compression was distorting the camaraderie of the two societies themselves. A commentator in the journal *Yale Critic* for June 20, 1882, observed that "Fifteen Bones' men were born of the class of '33 (which numbered 89) and, although the size of the classes has increased 75 per cent. since then, there has been no enlargement of membership. To keep pace with the times necessitates an increase of membership commensurate with the growth of classes, the neglect of which is stultification; and, as the number of struggling applicants becomes larger, the confliction of individual interests more intricate, and the question of election more complicated, the greater will be the admission either of men with more cheek than character, or of a minimum of the most deserving. Even now, as one friend complains, so little attention is paid to congruity in choice that men of the most opposite character, personal enemies, are taken in, men who, though under the 'sacred' mantle of Bones or Keys, will not associate except in such exercises as are necessary for performances in concert."[22]

More troubling was the long shadow which the prospect of so few places cast upon the lower classes. As a recruiter for a freshman society puts it in John Wood's 1894 novel *College Days*, about Yale in the 1870s: "[Y]our one aim in college will be to get into a senior society. That's what we're all here for, and as there are but thirty vacancies, and a hundred and forty odd in your class, why you and your friend want to hustle and make a right start *now* in the freshman year, if you want to reach them, d'ye see?" Bones in particular was further attacked for reducing the odds by taking in legacies: "It is the rule (with exceptions) that a Junior whose father or brother has been a 'Bones' man will go there too. I recall," read a letter to the editor in 1884, "an instance in one class where four of the fifteen 'Bones' men owed their elections to this cause rather than to any merit of their own."[23]

The lengthiest cri de coeur on the pain of rejection in the decade of the Civil War was penned fully sixty years later in 1923 in the memoirs of Henry Holt, author and founder of the publishing house which still bears his name. He was both an editor of the *Lit.* and a Coch—indeed, the Wooden Spoon poet of the class of 1862—and vice president of Brothers in Unity.[24] Holt prepped at General Russell's school from the age of six, and entered Yale at age 18 in 1858 as a sophomore for the class of 1861. His two great college friends were Edward Rowland Sill, *Lit.* editor, Wooden Spoon poet of his year, and class poet to be, and Sextus Shearer, also on the *Lit.* board. In Holt's retrospective view, those two men were themselves "closest of friends" whose "united influence on the whole class was an intellectual and moral stimulus vastly greater than all else that the college provided." Holt was sent down for college rule infractions, and received enough demerits under the system of "matriculation" that he fell back a year in class.

Still, he had been awarded the *Yale Literary* medal, the leading essay prize, "and with Sill, Shearer and my other intimate friends in the leading senior society"—Simeon Baldwin, later the salutatorian; William Fuller, fellow *Lit.* editor; Francis (Frank) Kernochan, a DKE clubmate and president of Brothers in Unity when Holt was vice president; Anthony Higgins, president of Linonia; and Sanford Newell, the Spoon Man, dubbed "Apollo Belvedere" by his classmates—"my election to [Bones] was very generally regarded as a matter of course. The conservative element, however, very justly regarded me askance, and I failed of election."

The Bones club of 1861 which passed over Holt was one of the more remarkable in the society's history for later prominence and gravity of purpose. Baldwin became chief justice and governor of Connecticut, then president of the American Social Science, American Political Science, and American Bar Associations. Higgins was a congressman and then a senator from Delaware. Kernochan was the founder of the University Club in New York City, the first of all university clubs in the country, and Newell was U.S. minister to the Netherlands and later delegate to the 1899 Hague Peace Conference. Unmentioned by Holt in his memoirs, that club also included Franklin B. Dexter, to become Yale University secretary and professor of History, and professor of Latin Tracy Peak.

The hurt for Holt never healed. For fully four pages in his memoirs, he denounces the "sham secrecy of the student societies, even though the experiences reflect a little unfavorably upon some friends who are dead, and giving the experiences [sixty years later] may tend to alienate some of the few who are living; moreover my giving them not only may be set down to personal pique, but my judgment may be regarded as biased by it. On the other hand, however, my experiences could not have been unique; and they bear upon what many unprejudiced judges, including at least one supremely eminent member of the chief senior society [William Maxwell Evarts of the Bones club of 1837], have regarded, however much it may have changed since their opinion was formed, as a great curse to the University."

On election eve, "I waited with pleasant anticipation for Sill and Shearer," he mournfully remembered, "and waited all night without their coming. What was more, they did not come near me for weeks. The absurd secrecy prevented my closest friends from preparing me for the blow, or saying anything about it after it fell. Nor did I go near them: I have seldom suffered as during those weeks . . . [T]he procrustean number of the society [the limitation to fifteen members annually] . . . has prevented the inclusion of many men who have proved themselves more desirable than I, in the organization that, whatever its shortcomings, is very properly the chief of the alumni influences that affect Yale."

Holt went on to warn that such rejection had consequences for Yale long after graduation, and found the final club system at Harvard to be less injurious to alumni loyalty, asserting that the senior society system even hurt New Haven's college in its rivalry with Cambridge. "In universities generally, and especially at Harvard and Yale," he maintained, "the chief bond between the alumni is their senior societies, and the alumni influence in university control largely proceeds from them. Therefore they should be elastic enough to include all who ever prove themselves the best. The leading society at Harvard [Porcellian] takes in a few at a time, and has them participate in selecting the rest from their class. They take those they want without unyielding rigidity regarding number, and they have even elected honorary members. The chief influence at Yale in my time alienated some of the ablest alumni, and so must inevitably have been something of a handicap in the fierce competition which began about then, and which, in the days of modern efficiency, even Yale with her staunch Puritan independence and her traditional leisureness, could not escape."

Holt sent his eldest son to Yale, but the persistent strength of the senior societies' hold in New Haven changed the college destination of his younger sons: "[W]hen, at a class reunion some forty years after graduation, I found a brand new marble 'tomb' conspicuous near the college, I said: 'Well, if they haven't got over this nonsense yet, my wife may have her way, and send the little chaps to Harvard.' The last time I was at Yale, I saw they had got over the nonsense far enough to put some windows in the enlarged Skull-and-Bones tomb, but they were ground glass."[25] Ground glass was what Holt was still chewing, decades after he was passed over for senior society election.

He was not alone. In a letter of March 7, 1874, Yale professor Thomas Thacher, who decades before as both Bones alumnus and professor had guided his society through the unprecedented construction of its tomb without opposition from the faculty, answered a questionnaire being circulated by opponents of secret fraternities in American colleges. He admitted that their existence did "give opportunity for slights in the bestowment of students' honors, which embitter the remainder of college life and, in some cases, of after years."[26]

235

PROVOCATION: CRITIQUES BY SOCIETY ALUMNI

The Reverend John Bascom's strictures against secret (and not necessarily senior) societies were in the decade of the 1870s echoed by new
voices, receiving considerably more attention because they were those
of graduates of these very Yale senior societies.

William Maxwell Evarts, since graduating in 1837, had gone on to
a remarkable career as a lawyer, diplomat, and statesman. He served in
the administrations of three American presidents: as attorney general for
President Andrew Johnson, after acting as his chief counsel in Johnson's
impeachment trial; as counsel for the United States before the tribunal
of arbitration for the *Alabama* claims at Geneva, for President Grant;
and as counsel for president-elect Rutherford B. Hayes on behalf of the
Republican Party in the contested election of 1876 (defeating Evarts's
college classmate Samuel J. Tilden, who had won the popular vote), and
then as Hayes's secretary of state. From 1885 to 1891 he was United States
senator from New York, and he sponsored the Judiciary Act of 1891,
also known as the Evarts Act, which created the United States circuit
courts of appeal. His service to his college was to include presiding "de
jure" at his class reunions, being elected among the six original Alumni
Fellows to the Yale Corporation in 1872, and being chosen as the second
president of the Yale Alumni Association of New York, the present-day
Yale Club there.

Evarts, born in Boston, attended the Boston Latin School, but his
father and grandfather were Yale men, and his grandfather was Roger
Sherman, first mayor of New Haven, treasurer of Yale, and signer of the
Declaration of Independence and the Constitution. The Connecticut
college still stood for the orthodox Congregationalism to which the
Evarts family adhered. His uncle Judge Simeon Baldwin arranged for
young William to live at his New Haven home for attendance at Yale,
so, as he later put it, Evarts traveled "two hundred and forty miles from
Boston to New Haven to avoid going to Harvard University, which
was across the bridge."[27] He joined Linonia, becoming its secretary and

vice president. When his junior year roommate William Bacon initiated the project of launching the monthly *Yale Literary Magazine*, Evarts
presided in December 1835 over the class meeting called to approve that
effort, joined Bacon as one of the five original editors, and proposed
both the magazine's name and motto. They produced twelve issues in
two years from their dormitory room, and in time, the journal became
the nation's oldest extant monthly, subscribed to by, among others, the
British Library.[28]

Evarts was elected to Phi Beta Kappa and to the Bones club of 1837,
along with Bacon. Other clubmates included Morrison Waite, Brothers in
Unity president and later to be chief justice of the United States Supreme
Court; Charles Lyman, president of Linonia and *Lit.* editor, later Yale
professor of Industrial Mechanics; William Coit, another president of
Brothers; William Scarborough and Edwin Carter, also *Lit.* editors; and
Benjamin Silliman Jr., like his father a Yale scientist, who chose the *Lit.*
cover likeness of Elihu Yale. At graduation, Evarts was third "high-stand"
man and, together with Waite and Edwards Pierrepont, later to be the
American minister to Great Britain, was chosen as a commencement
orator. On the class's fiftieth reunion, their memorial book celebrated
these individuals' collective fame with a poem: "*Uncle Sam, when days
were dark, with lantern straight proceeded/At once to Yale and Thirty-Seven,
and found the men he needed.*"[29]

For this noted Bonesman and loyal Yale alumnus, then, to deliver
"one of the ablest and most radical testimonies against the society system"
at the alumni meeting held in conjunction with the Yale commencement
of June 25, 1873, was a remarkable turnabout, clearly disturbing to many
in the audience. Given the senior societies' assumptions of "assessments of
immunity from free speech," Evarts's remarks occasioned "a look of holy
horror, of sublime astonishment, or a silly smile of wonderment at the
temerity of the speaker, [which] spread over many faces not yet free from
the awe inspired by these names."[30] The *Hartford Courant* article reporting
the speech makes it clear that his forceful argument was unanticipated:
"A very agreeable break in the monotony was made by introducing the

Hon. William M. Evarts, of the class of 1837. He always makes a capital speech, no matter what may be the occasion; and he did good work to-day in speaking against the evil effects of secret societies."

"A few years ago," the nation's greatest legal advocate declaimed, "the great societies of Linionia and the Brothers in Unity, which included all classes, and were about equally divided in membership, were the weekly arenas of debate, the school in which men were trained to think on their feet. They made men clear and rapid thinkers and ready debaters. To-day they are dead; killed by the class secret societies, which have a tendency to develop snobbishness and nothing else. They are a curse to the college, interfering not only with good-fellowship among the members of the same class, but with the selection of university crews and ball clubs and thus have much to do with the disgraceful series of defeats which have attended Yale for several years."

Evarts argued that the literary societies had "furnished the field for open and manly debate which could not be found in the small numbers and limited opportunities of the secret societies. They prepared the young man to withstand frowns and hisses as well as applause, and turned out men who could meet an adversary in debate without flinching. All this is wanting now, and cannot be supplied unless the old societies can be resurrected." There were hundreds of old graduates, the newspaper reported, who agreed with the speaker when he advocated the revival of the old societies and the suppression of the "foolish secret clubs which have supplanted them."[31]

Thus the senior societies became the scapegoats for the literary societies' collapse, although the rise of college athletics was also blamed. In truth, Linonia, Brothers, and Calliope succumbed slowly, beginning sometime after 1830, to the faculty banning of the literary society exhibitions, which had become too elaborate and difficult for administrative control, and to the growth of the class size which gradually undermined the intimacy which had once existed among the members. When new societies—the junior fraternities, and the second senior society—emerged in the late 1830s and early 1840s, the undergraduates took a more personal interest in them. By 1860, the average attendance at meetings in each literary society was about thirty, being less than one-eighth of the active college members. "One evening each week," wrote a senior in 1861, "is about as much as Students can well, or ought to, devote to such subjects. No wonder, then, that those who, whether it be the secrecy, the freedom, or the sociality that charms them, will attend the meetings of the small societies, have neither time nor the taste to attend those of the larger ones."[32]

The two ancient literary societies, once fierce rivals, formed a joint committee against common perils in 1866, and when attendance further decreased sharply, finally died in the summer of 1872, just before Evarts's speech. In an earlier decline, Phi Beta Kappa at Yale had suspended debates in 1843 and thereafter held only anniversary meetings. Members stopped wearing their badges with the class of 1867, and ended their elections in 1871. All of the open societies ultimately collapsed with the art they stood for, the art of formal rhetoric (literary prose first composed and then declaimed). As the *College Courant* rightly pointed out, the death of the literary societies was a *post hoc*, not a *propter hoc* phenomenon, with respect to the two senior societies.

That newspaper's correspondent noted: "The age of blow and gas, it is to be hoped, has about ended. . . . Mr. Evarts may deliver dithyrambics over the former status of the two societies and shed tears over their present degeneracy, but I am very much inclined to doubt the fact that he owes 'one jot or tittle' of his eloquence to the agency of these effete institutions." Three years later, when the two literary societies had finally expired, an article in the same journal titled "The Two Oldest College Societies" was to note that "The age of the Lyceum has given way to the age of the newspaper. It is significant that the society halls of both Linonia and Brothers are occupied by printing presses."[33]

Most of Evarts's auditors, of course, were not senior society alumni, but literally all had been members of Linonia or Brothers or Calliope, attending secret meetings on Wednesday evenings. Less than a year after Evarts' controversial speech, Professor Thomas Thacher—in the

Bones club two years before Evarts, and professor of Latin from 1842—
answered a nationally circulated questionnaire about secret societies in
his college, noting that "it should be remembered as a circumstance of
great importance that all secret societies in [Yale] college are year by
year, accumulating a constituency of educated men who, passing into the
various walks of professional life, serve as a substitute to these societies for
that public opinion, which controls men in general. Thus all the secret
doings of these societies, if there are any, are subject to the approbation
or disapprobation of a body of men whose average judgment of wrong or
impropriety would be more severe than that of society at large. Thus the
Brothers' and Linonian Societies, each of which flourished more than a
hundred years here, and which, for a very long period, were more secret
than three-quarters of the secret societies are which exist here now, came
to have such a body of old members that no one believed ill of them, and
their decease is earnestly lamented."[34]

Evarts's memory of good fellowship in Linonia was surely accurate,
and he felt strongly about the society, delivering the address for its centenary two decades before in 1853, which the society then published:
"I speak but the common sentiment of the graduates and friends of Yale
College, and of all others who have had occasion to compare the education here, and its results, with the methods of other universities, when I
attribute no small share of the permanent hold upon the confidence and
respect of the whole country which this university has ever retained,
to the influence of these great literary societies."[35] It must have been a
great disappointment to return to New Haven twenty years later and
find them completely extinct.

Yet he was wrong that his literary society prepared him for the
cut and thrust of courtroom debate and the equipoise of swift but dip-
lomatic response; by this decade the debates in Linonia and Brothers
were written-in-advance and memorized speeches. Still, for the former
attorney general of the United States and the then president of the New
York City Bar Association to call his senior secret society and its ilk a
"curse to the college" was a decidedly heavy blow. Five years before, in

1868, his eldest son, Allen Wardner Evarts, had not been elected to Bones, which may have wounded his father's feelings, but in due course two of his other sons were chosen, Sherman (class of 1881), in whose law office Henry Stimson began the practice of law, and Maxwell (1884). However strong his father's feelings against the system, Allen Evarts was to support the founding of the Wolf's Head senior society in 1883 and was the first president of its alumni association, holding that position for twenty years.

PROVOCATION: CROOKING AS THEFT FROM THE COLLEGE

The senior society habit of "crooking"—appropriating or otherwise sequestering college memorabilia of all kinds—was not seen as unlawful plundering in the first decades of the societies, when many students had a similar passion for collecting and preserving "memorabil." By the decade of the 1870s, this had changed, as is shown by two contrasting tales of boat race trophies.

In the *Yale Alumni Weekly* for February 9, 1912, Harrison Freeman, writing in on the fiftieth anniversary of his graduation, told a remarkable story of crook and counter-crook. Captain Henry L. Johnson of the *Varuna* crew of the class of 1860 went off to Lake Quinsigamond in Worcester, Massachusetts, to stroke a Yale crew in a race with Harvard, leaving hanging in his dormitory "a blue Yale flag which the winning crew was to hold until the next annual regatta." He alleged that in Johnson's absence the flag was stolen by a "too enthusiastic member of the 'so-called Skull and Bones society,'" who had entered Johnson's room, "secured the flag, and carried it away as a trophy and then hid it in his society's hall, where not a Yale man—not even the Captain or any of the crew which had won it, unless he was a member of the Society—had ever been permitted to see it," while the other flags won or sported in the college's name were in the trophy room in the Yale gymnasium.[36] Johnson was not only commodore of the Yale Navy, but a member of the 1860 Keys club, so the "crook" began as an intra–senior society raid.

That flag was the first to fly over a Yale boat, on June 14, 1843, and William Plumb Bacon of the class of 1858 while commodore had presented it to the Yale Navy as a champion flag, to be contested for at an annual regatta.[37] "Prominent Yale oarsmen," Freeman's letter continued, "members of the Senior society known as 'Scroll and Key,' who were indignant that the flag had been taken and that the annual contests were ended [no race for a prize which had disappeared], succeeded in getting into the society hall where it was secreted, but when they had secured the flag they forgot the terms of the gift, their indignation and their desire for future contests, and took it to decorate their own society hall." The men of Bones then broke into the Keys tomb to reclaim the trophy.

In 1906, Commodore Bacon himself had written to the *Yale Alumni Weekly* to plead for its return. A Yale Corporation member asked the Bones club of that year to make return "to the undergraduates of the University," but President Hadley himself, that society's alumnus, demurred from interfering, while expressing his frank opinion that the trophy belonged in the university trophy room; other graduate members at their reunions passed resolutions in agreement, but these were ignored by the undergraduates, presumably on the traditional grounds that a crook was a crook.[38] It would be a happy ending to record that the *Pioneer* flag is now in the trophy room at the Payne Whitney Gymnasium, but its present whereabouts are unknown. The public pressures brought to bear in the next such crooking episode were very different.

The championship prize flags won at the Harvard races in 1864, 1865, and 1867 were deposited for safekeeping after 1870 in the Trumbull Gallery, to which windows had been added in its conversion to Yale's central administration building in 1868, thereafter called the Treasury. "These are college property," opined the *College Courant* of June 25, 1870, "and nothing but a vote of all college can remove them. . . . No one of the crew can lay any just claim to [the flag won from Harvard '70 in 1867]. It is class property. They paid for it." All these flags disappeared in 1872. It was common knowledge that they had been removed from the Treasury to decorate the Regatta Ball of July 1871, and then afterward entrusted to the president of the Yale Navy for 1872, Lewis Parsons, a Keysman in whose dormitory room they remained on exhibition until after his graduation. When they could not be found thereafter, the suspicion arose that they had disappeared into his society's tomb. The new Keys president for 1873 wrote to his predecessor: "There are a good many suspicions all leading to the same conclusion. As they were taken away during your term of office, I thought you ought to know something about it."

Parsons did: petitioned to take the flags to the Keys tomb for the initiation of the crowd of 1873, and intending to remove them immediately afterward, he instead was persuaded to leave them in the hall, where they were forgotten upon his graduation. The incoming club was reluctant to surrender them, feeling they had as good a claim as could be made out under the prevalent philosophy of crooking—and since four of the five members of the winning crews having been members of Keys, the booty of conquest ought to go, as it had historically done, to the victors and thus their senior society. This time, however, the Yale Navy was determined to prevail, and did so under the guidance of recent graduate (1869) Lyman Bagg. Recognizing that "'Scroll and Key' might be cursed and abused till Doomsday without producing any other effect than rendering individual wrong-doers belonging to it doubly tenacious of whatever college property they might have laid their hands upon," Bagg decided that "the only rational way of getting at the matter was to hold the ex-president himself strictly accountable for the property." The public denunciation of a prominent member of Scroll and Key as the betrayer of a newly recognized high official trust in the possession of all-college trophies was "a thing that could not be ignored."

In due course a college resolution was drawn in February 1873, holding that the Yale Navy, "in default of a suitable response within a reasonable period ought to take any measures that may be feasible for the recovery of its property, and to give some public token of its sincere disapprobation of the betrayal of trust, of which its late president will have acknowledged himself guilty." The distribution of this pronouncement to the newspapers did indeed dispose the culprit to persuade his society to restore the banners, which was accomplished during that summer as mysteriously as the theft.

Despite this restoration, the damage to the society had been done. A graduate member of 1872 wrote that "Our popularity with the neutrals [during elections and generally] has been the one thing which has helped us in times past more than anything else, and now when we are hoping that this feeling is becoming real respect and admiration . . . it is very unfortunate to sacrifice or even endanger it for the sake of a few ornaments." But endangered it was: members of the current club were regularly harassed, and the door of the Keys hall was once wired shut, after which two members slept in the building every night to protect it.

The shift in attitude was well caught by a graduate member in writing the seniors at the height of the controversy: "I think they [the neutrals] were really in the right of it, for things of such interest at present are different from the old Spoon and Jubilee relics which concern only our predecessors, especially when the practice of crooking is, to say the least, *questionable*."[39] A *Courant* editorial came down on the side of the neutrals in their animus against Keys. "The evidence is entirely circumstantial, but it is certainly pretty strong. The flags were of no earthly value to anyone except a collector of 'memorabil.' Now it is well known that Scroll and Key boasts the most complete collection of 'memorabil' in the college. . . . These flags would make a very desirable addition to this collection. . . . We suppose there are few in college now doubt that Keys really had the flags all the time."[40]

Going forward, any "crook" of college-wide trophies by a senior society would be viewed on campus with a jaundiced eye.

PROVOCATION: THE RITUALS OF ARROGANCE

For the two senior societies, their secrecy was both a temptation and a handicap. It has been well said that, in their first decades, they were merely "negatively mysterious." Members did not discuss their programs and other activities occurring inside their modest, rented rooms.

While strutting a bit in phalanx and wearing badges, the ostentation was infrequently observed and the badges in those first days, when the societies of all four classes had them, merely symbols of affiliation. The *Yale Banner*'s 1864 issue contained a jeweler's advertisement boasting under the headline "Badge Pins, Badge Pins," that "The subscriber has for the last twenty-three years made BADGE PINS for College and other Societies *THROUGHOUT THE UNION* and his workmanship has been pronounced equal to The Best in the Country." The *Yale Record* for October 16, 1872, contained a letter from an undergraduate who proposed an "alumni badge" so Yale men could recognize one another, although "I am aware that Yale has the reputation of rather rushing badges and society pins; I have seen Sophs with at least four on their vests."

As for the senior societies, their members wore the badge on the shirtfront in the evening, and on the necktie which covered it in the daytime. The theory was that the prominence thus given to the pin served as a warning to all who met them to keep off the subject—a theory that did not comport with reality. Among those who were not familiar with the college and its customs, the ostentatious display of the badge provoked inquiries which the society members were forced to ignore "in grave sacrifice of courtesy," as one uncomfortable member phrased it, "to the exigencies of trivial custom."

Slowly but surely, the negative mystery of the two senior societies became positive, and to the ever increasing numbers of neutrals—630 by 1870–71, in the four classes of both the academic and scientific departments of the college—it seemed the Bones and Keys clubs were in their collective behavior more insistent that they were the elect of the college, and that the literary, social, and athletic officerships were in the members' care and in their societies' gift. They were in general newly demanding regard and deference. As early as 1858 a campus observer wrote that "their great apparent desire to have their very existence ignored is only equalled by their intense desire to have their existence brought into view. . . . No reflection would strike a deeper pang into the hearts of members than the conviction that no one puzzled his head about them."

The *Yale Courant* in a two-part series on secret societies in October 1866 severely criticized their members' affectation that their society's name, or indeed those of the other two (whether Bones, or Keys, or the 1864 newcomer Spade and Grave), were not to be mentioned in any society member's presence, and quoted graduate members from the 1830s who described this behavior as a new custom. The *College Courant* in its issue of June 24, 1868, reported that society members of the class of 1867 had even attempted "to banish from ordinary conversations the words which comprise the names of the societies . . . 'spade,' 'key,' or 'bones.'" Opined the *Yale Courant* a decade later in 1878, "The popular attitude toward the senior societies is either bitterness or idolatry; . . . bitterness if you did not go, idolatry if you did."[41]

The construction of the Bones and Keys tombs gave new occasions for offense, with the mystery that might properly have attended the four walls of the meeting place newly extended to significant distances across and through the campus, while society men now refused to speak when passing in front of their halls. The groups had long stepped out in lockstep after meetings, with society songs ringing through the college night, but now they took public offense if non-members whistled or even hummed those airs. The badges, worn from the first on neckties (while the under classes wore their badges upon their vests), were now constantly displayed, daily on gymnasium or boating or swimming gear, and on night dress visible to neutral roommates. In attacking the system following his graduation in 1881, Edwin Aiken wrote that "one feature helping to create the bitterness which prevails, is the wearing of badges; which is generally a violation both of good taste and good manners. Of good taste, because manhood needs no badge of its nobility, nor friends of their friendship; of good manners, because it is a constant reminder to others of distinction which they have failed to win."[42]

With the intense rivalry that existed between Bones and Keys, the inventive genius of these teenagers in successive delegations must have been always at work. Ritual is a coral growth: new ceremonies are added, but few are ever cut away. Taboos were seemingly invented to emphasize a superiority that may not have been present at the groups' inception almost four decades before. These habits and rituals acquired a collective name on the Yale campus among the neutrals: "poppycock," a word having the same meaning as today, perhaps originating in American colonial Dutch's *poppekak*, doll's excrement, and only in general circulation since 1865.[43] The numbers and attitude of neutrals had also changed over the decades. By senior year, they far outnumbered the thirty society men, had nothing to hope for in the way of election, and were no longer overawed by the presence of an upper class. This all led to a sort of reckless hostility toward those societies.

"If the offence of the generic Keys man was crooking, the offence of the generic Bones man was arrogance."[44] A national periodical in 1871 pronounced: "Some men are ex-officio . . . arrogant, those who have belonged to the Skull and Bones society at Yale College, for instance."[45] The satirical campus pamphlet *Yale Literary Chronicle* of 1873 published a ditty titled "The Bull and Stones Anthem," whose faux society's members sang:

We are not "superior" beings
As the men of the Skull and the Bones,
But merely a crowd of good fellows
Who belong to the Bull and the Stones.

Although we're inferior beings
A high reputation have we,
For we steal not the goods of the college
As they of the Scroll and Key.[46]

Ammunition for the charge of arrogance leveled at the Bones was all too frequently provided by its members. When there was no common dining hall and students had to organize their own class-based eating clubs, the club of 1866 founded their own exclusive eating club for meals outside the tomb. A member of the 1867 club brought a sick colleague back to his dormitory room and sat for an hour beside his bed without speaking to his neutral roommate in the same room.[47] In 1868, upon the appearance of a roast containing bones at a senior class eating club, a Bonesman asked instead for a piece of beef "without any of those *things* in it."[48] Another published a complaint in the *College Courant* in 1873, over the initials "S.B.," that neutrals had annoyed his club on a recent Thursday night, and characterized them as "insignificant, ill-bred and imbecile,"[49] language which could only intensify the resentment the senior of the senior societies was engendering.

Incidents of this sort led to a revival of the Bull and Stones, as the printing of their anthem evidences, and to fifteen neutrals stepping out in imitation Bones badges on the morning following the society elections in 1873.[50] Defacement of the Bones tomb was to follow, with appearances of satirical posters pasted to the hall's iron doors. The first announced a course of medical lectures to be delivered inside "on Mondays, Thursdays, and Fridays with a complete and competent analysis" of several topics, including "The Composition of Bones (including the skull) and their number (15)"; "The time of the formation of Bones (1832) and the softness of them when formed"; "The products of Bones, of which 'our phosphorus of commerce' is most useful, excepting the *Lit.* Editors"; "The hollowness of Bones and . . . their weakness and lack of harmony (as witness the factions of Junior year)." The final lecture, the poster concluded, would see the introduction of "the original skull of Demosthenes."

When the fifteen active members went off to a dinner given by an alumnus in Burlington, New Jersey, that year, the second round of posters was affixed to campus walls, screaming LOST! in a heading of large red letters: "Information wanted in the interests of their WASHER-WOMEN, of fifteen individuals in the class of '73, Yale College. Each of the said individuals wearing a pin or badge of the following description, to wit: death's head with crossbones attached, surmounting the mystic number 322. Said pin apparently of brass. Any information gratefully received by the undersigned. MRS. McGINNIS, MRS. McCARTHY,

MRS. O'FLAHERTY, MRS. O'GALLAGHER."[51] (A nonfictional story involving the Irish women who served the collegians and the members of the senior societies is told in the memoirs of Wilmarth S. Lewis, 1918 and Keys: "Dignified Irish ladies made the beds and cleaned the rooms and followed the careers of the young men. Before the year was over Mrs. Shea, who looked after 655 Wright, confided . . . that on the last Tap Day two of her young men had made Bones, two Keys, and three Wolf's Head. A fine record."[52])

In December 1873, a large black-and-white banner was run to the top of the college chapel, proclaiming "Death to Skull and Bones," and could not be got down before morning prayers were ended. In January 1874, some wag told several "boosy" freshmen that there would be a pantomime at the Bones hall on a Thursday night which they would be permitted to attend; they duly appeared at 8:30 P.M., "and after spending half an hour trying to find the ticket office, departed disgusted."[53] The following spring, on the evening of the initiation supper, the vendors were waylaid and the food stolen, when, according to the satirical pamphlet the *Yale Literary Chronicle*, written in faux-epic language, "the men of Stohns did . . . lay in close ambush . . . and . . . did fall upon the chariot [of the caterer] . . . and the war cry of the the Stohns men went up: 'Hurrah for Bullen, Happy Bullen, Jolly Bullenstohns; None can beat her, None defeat her, How *are* you, Pscullenbohns,' . . . and certain men did seize the food. . . . And there was a great Hub Bubb. . . . And that night the Pscullenbohns men went hungry to bed."[54]

Scroll and Key did not escape its own censures. The *Yale News* deplored "the senseless and puerile 'walk,' that has long been the laughing stock of the college, and effects no end but making Seniors appear like the school boys 'training' . . ." (this was a brisk walk, "attended by a peculiar motion of the heel and toe"). The refusal of its members to mention the society while in conversation with neutrals was called silly by the *Yale Courant* in 1866.[55] Two years later, the same campus journal said that, while they admired "the taste of Scroll and Key in selecting as beautiful an air as that of 'Gaily the Troubador,'" they "deplored the society's attempt to deny other students the pleasure of singing it."[56] Attempting to curb the uproar of the Stones men, the Yale administration banned all outdoors society singing. When the Keysmen of 1872 were able to resume their suspended custom, they decided to make the display less ostentatious by confining its performance to their hall steps, where it has remained ever since.[57] That gesture was soon forgotten, unhappily, in the ensuing scandal over the boating flags crook.

The initiations on the Tuesday following the Thursday of elections gave continued excuse for uproar, although the rituals of both societies were well known. As helpfully outlined for the underclassmen by the *Yale News* on its front page, the incoming members of Bones and of Keys, as well as the men of Bull and Stones, would gather at 6:00 P.M. in front of Bones' High Street hall. The initiates would enter the hall, one by one, from 6:10 to 6:25; graduates were admitted thereafter, while the police would clear out the obstreperous, for whom the main event had concluded. The candidates were held in the cellar, then called up beginning at 9:00 o'clock for individual initiation, concluding by 10:00. After speeches by alumni and the graduating seniors, all retired for a "first-class bum" (supper). Athletes were excused at about 11:30 P.M., so "that the athletic interests of the college may not suffer," and the rear door would be thrown open to permit use of the garden in the warm summer night. If the front door had meanwhile been wired shut by a Stones man, it would be cut open to permit the graduate members to go home. Sitting on the roof until dawn, in accordance with tradition, neophytes who were not sick or athletes stayed the night. After attending morning recitation, they returned to the temple to procure their badges.

The Keys initiation began later, at 8:00 P.M., when the newly elected were directed to go, separate and alone, one to the corner of Temple and Grove Streets, a second to the corner of Temple and Wall Streets, a third on the south side of Grove, near Whitney Avenue, and others on the north and south sides of the Grove Street bridge, at the Church of the Redeemer, and variously scattered along on Orange, Whitney, Wall, and other neighboring streets. Graduate members emerged two by two from the "striped palace," the man on the right gripping in his right hand the foot-long brass key of yore, offering it to his assigned candidate, and the formulaic exchange of offer of membership and acceptance into the order was conducted. Guarded by the two graduates, the candidate was then taken, in the 1870s, to the home of a graduate member on Grove or Temple Streets. Here, the fifteen inductees formed in a line, and arm in arm with fifteen graduates marched rapidly down the south side of Grove, then the west side of College, to their hall. By 9:30 that evening, all were inside. At 4:30 A.M., all attending graduates and the outgoing and incoming crowds came out to their hall steps and sang "Gaily the Troubadour," and then processioned down College to the gate in front of the old chapel, up the path to Battell Chapel, down to South Hall, and back to Durfee at the north end of the campus, where they separated to return to their tomb, to sit, like the Bonesmen, on their roof. They left the hall in the new day, with their badges.

The regularity of these patterns was never completely achieved, being both supported and interrupted by many extra players. The caterer Redcliffe came at 5:30 in the afternoon to set up for the Bones feast, using a double-teamed wagon to bring in "many boxes of strawberries, a huge box of cake, a two gallon can of oysters, two tubs of ice, and various other tempting viands;" a box of cigars was to follow. By 6:15, the fence across from the tomb on the east side of High Street was crowded with representatives of all classes, "the largest delegation, of course, being the 'soured Juniors.'"

The members of the outgoing Bones club then entered their hall, but the tardiness of any latecomer neophytes was attributed to their being locked in their rooms or in the junior society halls. As each eventually arrived, onlookers crowding the sidewalk immediately in front of the tomb cheered or jeered with the enthusiasm of bidding "a last farewell." Some seeking entry were impeded, needing "rushes" from friends, graduates, and the police to get through the iron doors. The "rabble" sang "Pater Russell," "Heigh Skull and Ho Skull," "Awful Skull and Bones," and improvised ditties employing the new members' names. Two officers of the law were retained to deal with the impertinent outsiders, until 2:00 A.M. or later, and then sent off with "a plate of bread, two cigars, and a five dollar bill." Over at Keys, the elaborate and far-flung processions gave those wishing to harass the participants many similar opportunities.[58]

PROVOCATION: SUPPRESSION OF CRITICAL NEWSPRINT

The war between the rival editorial boards of the *Yale Lit.* in 1864, which birthed Spade and Grave, demonstrated that the formal or informal suppression of any criticism in campus journalism was also an increasing point of friction. Yale students published, by 1872, two weekly newspapers (the *Yale Courant* and the *Yale Record*) and a monthly magazine (the *Yale Literary Magazine*); among all other American colleges, only Cornell could then boast producing the two types of periodical.[59] The *Lit.*'s stated mission effectively omitted any treatment of current campus affairs, and its board was often still dominated by members of Bones and Keys. When that reporting role was clearly assumed with the appearance of new campus publications, not controlled by society members, the criticisms could no longer be contained. And when those publications were not critical enough for some readers, they took matters into their own hands and printing presses.

The *Yale Banner*, beginning to appear regularly on an annual basis in 1845, and a single four-page sheet until 1866, was simply a catalogue of the college, of the memberships of the various class societies with their "cuts" (illustrations of their symbols), and of other miscellaneous student organizations. The prizes, honors, and scholarships awarded during the year and other facts of like character were also named, but no editorial matter of any sort was included. According to Bagg, the "good will" of the *Banner* became "the property of the Bones, which probably got possession of it about the year 1850. A resident Bones man—usually a Theologue [a student attending the Divinity College]—who has

graduated the previous summer, issues the paper every year." As there
was no other annual save the official Yale College catalogue, which
omitted the class society details which enthralled the student body, it
was a profitable enterprise, until its monopoly was attacked from both
flanks in 1865.[60]

In the fall of that year the *Banner*'s rival annual first appeared, although
its initial number disclaimed any such character. The *Pot-Pourri*, published
by one or two seniors who were members of Keys, came out a month
or more after the *Banner*, and its contents consisted of a rearrangement
and correction of the *Banner*'s contents, with any updating additions.[61] At
roughly the same time, a true newspaper was born, a weekly which was the
first successful college newspaper anywhere, the *Yale Courant*, "devoted to
college interests, science, and literature." Originated by five members of
the class of 1866, its first issue appeared on Saturday, November 25, 1865
(its publication preceded the *Harvard Advocate*'s founding by a year, and the
Amherst and Dartmouth weeklies by two).

The *Yale Courant* in its October 10, 1866, number criticized
the conduct of the members of Bones, Keys, and Graves for acting
"aggrieved when the bare name of [a member's] society is mentioned,
or even the names of societies with which he has no connection, a
reaction so wrong that it becomes absurd." This chastising must have
stung: when the undergraduate board instituted a policy of allowing any
single editorial board member to forbid the insertion of any article, the
application of which began to prevent the issuance of the paper itself,
the original publication was wound down, reappearing as the *College
Courant* in July 1867.

That publication then birthed a supplement, also called the *Yale
Courant*, an entirely independent publication appearing in the new college year of 1870, and soon selling seven hundred copies a week when
the student population numbered only 657. The originators of the first
weekly in 1865 were all senior neutrals, as were the three successor editorial board members down to the class of 1870. The three editors of 1871,
running the *Yale Courant* as an independent journal, were two Bonesmen

and one neutral, under an arrangement in which membership in a senior society was not to debar a man from election to editorship, but at least one neutral was always to be in place.[62]

So challenged by a rival annual and a weekly news source, the *Banner* transformed itself in 1870, becoming a cased paperback of seventy text pages, tastefully printed on quality tinted paper. Quickly accepted by the college as the best catalogue of the sort which had ever appeared, it seemed well worth its thirty-cent cover price. Since the *Banner* proclaimed its rivalry with the hitherto-ignored *Pot-Pourri*, the collegians were entertained with postings about campus of a rough caricature, showing a pair of pugilists, the first with a Bones badge standing upon a book labeled *Banner*, the second with a Keys pin atop a volume legended *Pot-Pourri*. The competitors continued to publish for years, battling over the same editorial turf, until *Pot-Pourri* (by then, as might have been foreseen, called "the *Pot*" by undergraduates) was absorbed into the *Banner*, with a joint title, in 1908.[63]

One senior society or the other was in control of the *Banner*, the *Pot-Pourri*, and the *Yale Courant*. The last was to run no comment on the societies until May 1874, when board composition had changed, becoming that month the first Yale periodical to report the election results for Bones and Keys promptly following Tap Day. The *Yale Record*, commencing weekly publication in September 1872, followed the *Courant* in printing the names of the elected in May 1875, and was indeed cofounded by a member of Keys, Henry Ward Beecher Howard, who had been active on the *Courant* and the *Pot-Pourri*.

It comes as no surprise that the same undergraduate journalistic energies which started those enterprises could and would be channeled into "unofficial" college-wide publications, aimed directly at the theory and practice of Bones and Keys. In this tide of vitriol, Bones was to be damned for much more than arrogance. Its seniority to Keys caused it to be blamed for virtually everything the critic in question found wrong with Yale. The first example was a pamphlet appearing in October of 1873, the *Iconoclast*, launched to smash the false god of Yale College. The class of 1870s historian was to remember that, in their freshman year, "The *Iconoclast* opened our eyes, and brought down the wrath of the Seniors on the heads of the publishers."

Volume 1, number 1 of the *Iconoclast* had no successor issues, but its aim was plain: "Our object is to ventilate a few facts concerning 'Skull and Bones,' to dissipate the awe and reverence which has of late years enshrouded this wall of Poppy Cock, and to enable its character and influence to be fully and rightly comprehended. . . . We speak through a new publication, because the college press is closed to those who dare to openly mention 'Bones.'"[64] The sins of the society, in this account, were manifold. The anonymous underclass authors maintained that the Bones insulted the senior class and the college both, by manifesting that an election, for marks of distinction which the juniors' class or the college had awarded, was a final, bigger honor. The Bones graduates, it was asserted (but in no way evidenced), favored the society with their donations and not Yale College, although they controlled it, and so impoverished it doubly, because non-members were repelled by the society's "arrogance and self-fancied superiority" and would not themselves contribute.

Moreover, although the faculty had prohibited initiations into the freshman societies because of the attendant uproar, Bones was unfairly permitted to blow fish horns amid stamping feet and howling which could be heard across High Street, "over in the college yard," while the neophytes ran up and down stairs with bladders on their heads. And the society hurt the baseball team by passing over the best baseball player in every class in favor of the "high-stand man and the literary man, as well as the political toady." The *Iconoclast* identified the oppressions as new: "When Skull and Bones was founded, the evil which we . . . unfold did not exist. It is an evil which has grown up—which is growing today. The editors closed with a war cry: *It is Yale College against Skull & Bones!!* We ask all men, as a question of right, which should be allowed to live?"[65]

Privately published pamphlets permitted the release of emotions of the neutrals, stifled in college-wide journals, but now revealed in publications of their own making. The ideas expressed therein crystallized

and perpetuated from one class to another bitter antagonism to the societies and their doings. The next in this irregularly appearing but steady
series was the *Yale Literary Chronicle*, identified in its advertising poster as
"published under the auspices of Bull and Stones." Printed in the guise of
the *Yale Literary Magazine*, this pamphlet was identical in general appearance with the *Lit.*'s green front cover, except that the bewigged head of
Elihu Yale, and his feet, legs, and knee britches, were replaced by the
corresponding head (still bewigged) and back legs of a bull, with cloven
hooves, resting on a floor of cannonball-like stones.

The text featured paragraphs numbered like biblical verses, and told
in like language of "the tribe of Pscullenbohns men, whose fame has
gone abroad into all lands . . . [being] fifteen mightie and strong men
[who] did get themselves up saying, We only are great, and besides us
there is none other." They appropriated private property for their tomb:
"Wherefore when any man of the land of Campus did lose his soap-dish
or other article, he simply folded his hands, and did say, it is well. The
poor Bohns men did have need of it. Now, in all the doings of these men
there was much Poppi Koch . . ."

Keys was equally excoriated in this publication: after building a
"home of finely wrought stone . . . and the pillars of their house were like
polished mirrors . . . these called themselves the clan of the Schroll an Ke
. . . and they made for themselves Pihns which they likewise sported; and
these were exalted even yet more than the highandmightie Pscullenbohns
men." The "Chosenphew" were then triumphantly, dramatically, and
justly dragged down by "The Farfamed Class of the Bullenstohns," setting their tripwires in the paths of the Keysmen returning to their rooms,
wiring shut their hall doors, and stealing food from the Bones' banquet
caterers. "Such were the doings of these three great clans, whereof the
Bullenstohns were by far the most numerous; for in the numbering of
their hosts they did outnumber both of the other clans, and they did
exalt over them, and lifted up their horns many a time against them."[66]

Virtually the same cover image was to be used as the front wrapper
for a pamphlet which appeared in February of the next year, 1874, titled

The Seventh Book of Genesis, Otherwise known as The Gospel According to *Scrohleankee,* written by Robert J. Jessup, a sophomore in the class of 1876—a downward expansion of the student enemies of the societies.[67] Written in the same faux-epic diction and mannered spelling of the *Yale Literary Chronicle,* this pamphlet directed virtually all of its ire toward Keys, showing some knowledge of that society's early history in the classes of 1842 and 1843: "Wherefore do that of Pscullenbohnes [the founders, styled "Sorrheads," were made to say] for a space of nine years set themselves up for us to bow down before and worship? Behold, they are no better than we. Go to now, let us congregate together to make unto ourselves a graven image and a great mysterie. Let it be called Scrohleankee. And let us afterward take unto ourselves from Phortietoo such of them as are to be saved like unto ourselves. Also let Phortietoo dososummore unto Phortiethrie and so on until perchance by doing sosummore we may rival our enemy, even Scullenbohnes."

Keys exaggerated its mystery, *The Seventh Book of Genesis* maintained, choosing "letters of strange portent," C.S.P. and C.C.J. "Nootrahls spoke in derision of Schrolleankee, calling them Keeze and their mysteries Poppie Kock, also C.S.P. cat stew preparation and C.C.J. Chatham stew cheap john, till Keeze was laughed to scorn." The pamphlet then sketched, in an irreverent manner, the progress of "Keeze" down to the year 1872, "when one Noah, surnamed Pohrturr, was King" and the freshman "Klasuv Pseventie Psyx journeyed that way" and, having become sophomores, beheld "the foolishness and thomfoollerrie of the mysterie of the great Poppiekock," and how "very many of the lesser tribes not yet within reach of the gospel of Dososummore . . . cast to the dogs their natural rights and groveled upon their bellies in the dust, that, peradventure, they might be accepted."

The tale ended with a parable of a ram with two horns, attacked by a he-goat with one horn, who smote the ram and broke both horns. The parable was thus interpreted: "The ram with the two horns is Scrohleankee. The horns . . . are the Gospel of Dusosommore, and the doctrine of the Great Poppiekock. . . . The he-goat is . . . Pseventie Psyx

. . . and the rest of the prophecy showeth the hostilitie of Psevventie Psyx to Scrohleankee with its Dusosummore and its Poppiecock, and the manner in which the Psevventies Psyx will destroy Scrohleankee and exterminate it utterly."[68] The class of 1876 was not to bring down Scroll and Key, or the senior society system, but made a mighty noise in the attempt.

Appearing roughly annually, these pamphlet attacks had their sensational effect. It seems that Skull and Bones, by this date, was prepared to let further debate occur. The *Lit.* board of 1873–74 was comprised of three of that society's members, a man from the Sheffield Scientific School, and a neutral, Arthur D. Whittemore, who was allowed to publish in the January 1874 issue an opening article, titled "The Coming Society." Whittemore "purposely refrained from stating, as fully I might, the reasons why our present societies and society system [freshman through senior classes] should in some way be radically changed; feeling that such a statement is not needed by thinking men and might give unnecessary offense."

His article did not envision a return to the ancient literary societies—"Essentially, the same causes that killed Brothers and Linonia are still in active existence. The eloquence which our fathers admired we laugh at."—but he predicted that the students' growing maturity would have an inevitable effect. "As the average age and discipline of our students increase, they will become more and more inclined to put aside the boyishness and foolishness which is so marked a feature of the secrecy of our societies." He foresaw instead a third course, the development and growth of interest group clubs "neither open literary or ultra secret," for which "[s]uitable rooms could be hired, and the present admirable tombs— halls, so-called—could be altered at a slight expense into very fair club houses, by putting in a few windows and making some slight additions." Within six years of his argument, the freshman and sophomore societies were indeed to be ended, by faculty suppression, and the senior societies' continued existence to be put to a class vote, but the interest group clubs he presciently foresaw would take decades to unfold.[69]

Presumably more irritating to the two senior societies in the next few years, if not more corrosive to their reputations, were the pinpricks administered by the *Yale News*, the college's first daily newspaper. Its founders were patently anti–senior society: "We have been asked," they admitted frankly in their seventh week of publication, "what motive we could have for such a relentless persecution of Senior Societies."[70] (Jibes had occasionally occurred earlier, of course: the *College Courant*'s "Yalensulica" column for December 18, 1869 noted that "Dr. Harwood preaches on the POWER of (the) KEYS next Sunday A.M. Fifteen seniors are going to hear him.")

The *Yale News* first appeared on January 28, 1878, without identifying any editors, and the alarmed faculty soon passed a law forbidding publication of any paper by students which did not print the responsible persons' names. According to a memoir of the journal's birth, the first year's strategy of ragging the senior societies was not only persistent, but deliberate. "[F]rom the paucity of other material in those days, which would interest the main body of students, The News naturally turned to the burning question of the hour to, I might say, foment news and sell its copies, and by so doing, I am frank to admit, got everybody by the ears, superinduced all sorts of mischief on the part of the 'Neutrals,' made the lives of the Societies and their members a burden, and finally keep the faculty busy and guessing [or] devising the best ways and means to quell the excitement without too much abridgment of the Constitutional right of free speech &c."

Student politics was the entry point. "Every election of officers for the various College bodies, every College function and issue was in these days rife with contest, and fraught with the contending influences of Senior Societies versus 'Neutrals,' and small wonder then that the only matters of vital interest, namely the attitude of the foregoing counter influences, predominated, and the policy of The News—if policy it can be called—was, to keep before the Collegiate Public eye, those matters which most interested them, namely, the doings and purposes of the Senior Societies political, and otherwise, for there were but two of them—and to influence if not to mould the 'Neutral' opinion." Bones and Keys were chargeable, the *News* maintained, with "all sorts of high crimes and misdemeanors . . . whether defeats at rowing or baseball or deteriorating *menus* in eating clubs."[71]

On March 11, 1878, the daily opened its columns with a full-throated editorial statement, interspersed with candor. "What is the use of 'grinding' [the senior societies] so unceasingly? It does no good. The societies are still in power. The really worthy men in them lose nothing by our ridicule. Why then do we keep it up? We do this not from blind and impatient hatred of the institutions, but from a consciousness of their weak points, and a desire to show them as they are. We cannot deny that Bones, *as a whole*, represents much of the influence of the class; that Keys has many fine fellows, true gentlemen." Nevertheless, "when the Seniors know little or nothing of the under-classmen, and assume the authority of picking out the thirty best men; when these picked men assume that they are the best men and stand aloof from their classmates, and wear pins to draw attention to themselves; when year after year we see the athletic interest of Yale jeopardized by their influence, being used to get and keep men, unfit for their position, on the crew, on the nine, on the glee club, and on anything they can control, we have a right to inquire into the matter."

Five years on, that inquiry was stifled. In a letter to the influential national journal the *Nation*, a member of the class of 1884 laid out the indictment of silent suppression of the freedom of the college press. "We have here a daily paper, two bi-weeklies, and a monthly magazine. Not a sentence which reflects on the societies is permitted to be printed; not a joke, not an item of news, can appear in connection with their names, excepting the solitary case in which once a year the list of new members is published. The *Yale News* was started in 1878 as an anti–secret society paper; the *Courant* about 1876–79 was non–secret society; but the society elections came after the election of editors, and the society men took care to select a sufficient number on all the papers to insure their control. This they have done ever since. The *News*, the *Record*, the *Courant*, the *Literary Magazine* are all in the hands of the societies so completely, that when a person remarked that he regarded a certain one of them as the exponent of Yale College opinion, one of the editors replied: 'Yes, it is the exponent of Yale College opinion, but as modified by the secret societies.' It is easy to see what a tyranny this is when the College is divided on the society question."[72]

This indictment was overbroad: the *Nation* published a letter the following week from a student who said he was not a society member, observing that "There are thirteen secret societies here [counting the underclass fraternities], and more than one hundred other organizations of an athletic, literary, or social character, and not one of them is ever attacked by any Yale publication. It was not many years ago that the College papers were open to such articles, and much ill-feeling and harm to the College was the result."[73] But this counsel of perspective was not widely appreciated.

REACTION: INVOLUNTARY CONFINEMENT, INVASION, ASSAULT, AND POLITICAL EXCLUSION

The satire and mockery of the two senior societies and their members brought on by these various provocations ultimately degenerated into something worse: imprisonment of members within their halls, obstruction of dormitory doors to prevent the entrance or exit of the elective messengers seeking candidates, jostling those messengers outside on the campus and sometimes stealing their society insignia, tying or locking "sure" men within their rooms, followed by the neutrals' attempted or successful invasions of the tombs, and finally the halls' disfigurement.

The Keysmen's entry into the Bones tomb in 1865 to crook the flag of the *Pioneer* and the Bones' penetration into the Keys hall to snatch it back were seen by both societies as border skirmishes, to be deplored and if possible revenged, but still nobody's else's business. An affront of a different order was a second forced entry into the Bones, in the summer of 1865, by three neutrals, two being freshmen and the third a student at the Sheffield Scientific School, resulting in the theft of relics and even the "Bones Bible," Timothy Dwight's manuscript history of the society written for its thirtieth anniversary in 1863. When their names became known, the miscreants were visited by Professor Thomas Thacher, on behalf of the society rather than of the college. The Academical Department thieves reportedly bargained to return the society's property of relics and records against a promise of election when they became juniors; the treasures were restored, but election did not follow.

In 1866, the Bones tomb was "defaced with some black substance in a scandalous manner," according to the *Yale Courant*.[74] The following year, "some neutrals in the Senior class, moved partly by a morbid curiosity, but chiefly a desire to retaliate for the superciliousness of some members of the society, planned and gained a burglarious entrance to the Hall. In fact, the Hall was entered three times."[75] In December 1873, a flag was fastened to the spire of the chapel, proclaiming "Death to Skull & Bones," where to the chagrin of that society it flew all day.[76] Their entrance's padlock was stolen, and a "peeler" was hired for five dollars to guard the tomb the next night until a new lock could be procured. "Dark lanterns" with focused beams were shined upon the open door when members made entry. At the date of the initiation of the club of 1875, in the spring of 1874, an attempt was made to force a beam between the temple's iron doors, "frustrated by the muscle of an old-time member of the university crew"; failing at that, the assailants then pelted the tomb's walls with eggs. The unnamed faculty member who appeared to quell the disturbance, "fixing the responsibility for the disorders of the evening upon the 'puerilities' of the society which was the sufferer, called upon the crowd to disperse."[77]

On September 29, 1876, the building was broken into by those who resented "her mystery and her secrecy," to which the self-styled Order of the File and Claw hoped to put an end with their publication of *The Fall of Skull and Bones*, along with ending "her absurd pretentions and her popiecock." The intruders claimed that, "while robbery was not our errand, on the principle that the second thief is the best owner we helped ourselves to a few pieces of memorabil, which can be put on exhibition, and a few documents which can be printed, should any authoritative denial [of a successful break-in] be made."[78] When the File and Claw pamphlet's text was rewritten and republished in a successor anonymous pamphlet titled *Skull and Bones*, the authors declaimed piously in their (entire) introduction: "Let it be stated in advance that this pamphlet is published solely with a view to clear away the "poppy-cock" which surrounds the greatest society in college. It has no malicious intent. The sole design of the publishers and those who made the investigations, is to cause this Society to stand before the college world free from the profound mystery in which it has hitherto been enshrouded and to lessen, at least in some degree, the arrogant pretensions of superiority."[79]

Hearing of this attack, student newspapers at Princeton and Harvard were sympathetic to Skull and Bones. "A burglarious entrance into a private hall of an honoured society is not exactly a clever or amusing trick," said the journal in New Jersey, and the Massachusetts college editors declared that the invaded society's "mysteries are as much the personal matters of its members as are their domestic secrets, and have a right to the same respect." When the *Yale Courant* printed the story of the File and Claw pamphlet, with its floor plans of the society's hall and exhaustive descriptions of every room and relic, the metropolitan newspapers in New Haven brushed aside such privacy concerns and reprinted that publication's contents at full length, including the diagrams.[80]

Worse was to come, and the tide of the neutrals' resentment did not spare Scroll and Key. Wires were stretched across the sidewalk running in front of the Brick Row dormitories to trip the members on their return to their rooms, which "set off a load of Greek fire [phosphorus], which had the effect of frightening the society men greatly." In January of 1874 the numerals of the class of '76 were discovered painted in black on the doors of the Keys hall, a desecration celebrated in *The Seventh Book of Genesis*; since the doors were iron, the removal was easily managed. Three years later, a second lock-in, mirroring that occurring in 1873, kept the current Keys club imprisoned for hours, necessitating the subsequent purchase of a rope ladder by the next class's club and the installation of a warning bell on the doors.

Harassment at elections and initiations worsened: "From time immemorial the senior society men have been followed at such time by non-society seniors, who badger the former, sometimes shutting them up in the entries or fastening them into rooms from which escape is made by windows." They booed, cat-called, threw old oranges and boots, and once, it is reported, "a large brass cuspidor which struck the head of the last Scroll and Key man in line." Crowds were so great around the societies' halls when the neophytes came there to be taken in for initiation that "[s]ometimes the approaching juniors are lifted bodily and passed over the heads of the crowd to the hall door. Cannon crackers are exploded and a general racket indulged in until the society men get disgusted and send for a 'cop.'"[81]

Some of the harassment was less physical. Three members of the class of 1883, in their sophomore year of 1881, converted a production of *The Pirates of Penzance* in New Haven by the D'Oyly Carte Opera Company into a public affront to the Bones. Visiting the production's pirate king at his hotel before the performance, they told him it would make a local sensation if he would put '322' below the death's head on his hat. The sophomores, sitting in the balcony's front row that evening, were delighted to see that when the hat appeared, several students—Bonesmen all—got up and left the hall, to a "universal grin on the faces of all the other Yale men in the audience."[82]

The Bull and Stones men appropriated the very features of which Bones and Keys were so proud. In 1872, they caused their membership list of fifteen to be printed in the New Haven press, and "swung out" with badges, as they had in 1870 (the *College Courant*'s "Yalensicula" column of November 6, 1869, had reported: "It is rumored that a new society is being formed. The pins have been seen by some one, at Tiffany & Co.'s in New York. The observer says that they are "*bully*.")[83] In the satirical annual the *Yale Naughty-Gal All-Man-Ax for 1875*, a mock one-page history appeared, declaring, with dead aim at the older societies' celebration of their campus antiquity, faculty connections, and glorious stone halls: "Of all college societies now in existence, Bull and Stones is the oldest. Before even Hasty Pudding or Phi Beta Kappa were thought of this fraternity could number its years by the score. Bull and Stones was founded Commencement day 1776, by the Rev. Elisha Williams, Rector of Yale College, Ezra Stiles, Jeremiah Day (both Presidents of the University), the Governor of the State, and other prominent men. With its years, the institution has grown in reputation, the men who have entered it from year to year have added luster to its fame, until there is no society that can show such a record. As is becoming such a high-toned fraternity, its transactions are veiled in secrecy, and its hall is—no one knows where."[84]

On March 13, 1878, the Stones men had attacked the Bones hall, and a Keys representative wrote the *Yale News* to deplore the marauders taking "advantage of [the Bones'] policy of non-resistance, to tear down their fence, injure the padlocks, and deface the iron door with brick bats," which was not "fun" but "vandalism and outrage."[85] Three months later, the Keys hall suffered even worse damage. The legend "522 Scull & Bone 522" (consciously intended to be differentiated from "Skull and Bones 322") was written with black paint on the wall between the entrance staircases at about one o'clock in the morning of June 14, just after the delegation had left its Thursday night meeting. Learning of this outrage an hour or so later, the member rousted out a stone cutter, who succeeded in having all the graffiti removed before the rest of the college awoke.[86]

Nevertheless, witnesses had observed the desecration, and a storm of indignation arose against the unknown culprit or culprits, not only within the society, but within the college community. "All college disapproved the act," reported the *Yale News* for June 17. Two seniors who had been seen watching the progress of the painting, Edmund Terry and Herbert Bowen (a cofounder of the *Yale News* just five months previously, and later U.S. minister to Persia and Venezuela), were arrested on the charge of "defacing the building of the Kingsley Trust Association." This occurred on the testimony of three other students and a tutor, Edmund Salisbury Dana, a Keys man (1870) who was a board member of the Kingsley Trust Association.

Campus suspicions had first fixed on the members of a new anti-Bones society, the "522 men," but it seems unlikely that they would have so implicated themselves with the numbers in black paint, and a newspaper reported that "students who wear the [522] initiation pin say they had nothing to do with the work."[87] The courtroom was filled with current Keys men and graduate members—although, according to the article, "no Bones men were visible." Tutor Dana testified that he had seen Bowen in a group of four or five students who, when they spotted him, started off in a brisk walk, "attended by a peculiar motion of heel and toe, characteristic of the Keys society" (which even Dana characterized in his testimony as "an old, somewhat childish custom"), while singing a Keys anthem. For their parts, while agreeing they were indeed witnesses to a portion of the disfigurement, Bowen testified that he did not recognize the painter, while Terry admitted only to having picked up "a small tube of pigment done up in foil," remarking that the black paint "would make 'first-class memorabil.'"

The prosecutor wanted to ask some questions about senior societies generally, but the Keys men present discouraged that line of inquiry. Keys graduate member John Alling had spoken for the prosecution. The defense lawyer "gave him 'taffy' about his membership in Keys [and] called him the real conspirator, [and] compared him to Cataline"; he further argued that the society "considered its hall not disfigured and disgraced by the paint, but by the emblem of the rival Society." The judge, according to the *News*, "very justly pronounced the work as low and mean and beneath the dignity of any one who pretended to be a gentleman, but said that there being no conclusive proof, he would have to nolle the case," proclaiming, "This is a student's frolic, done in a spirit of fun, and should be settled in college, and not brought to this court."[88]

When the criminal proceedings fell through, Keys had the discretion not to prosecute a civil suit. As a whole, the episode tended to reinstate the society in the good graces of the undergraduate community, serving to obliterate the fading memories of the boat flags crooking scandal. No acts of violence against the Keys clubs or their hall are recorded after 1878. This "522" attack seems to have been a climax of such violence: members of the first three delegations of the senior society Wolf's Head, founded in 1883, canvassed fifty years after the fact, could recollect no "Bull and Stones" activities in the 1879 to 1885 period when they were underclassmen. Scroll and Key changed its behavior, too, altering its post-meeting march home and thus ending the ostentatious parade along the whole Brick Row with the members peeling off to their rooms. (Bones had dropped the march home and the accompanying song with the club of 1867.)[89]

The "522" men were unrepentant. In the May 22, 1878, *Yale News*, someone published a message in bold capitals, the full meaning of which can only be guessed at: "E.E.F. | 522 – 5 – 22 – 78 – 8 -22 | 15 + 10 – BST. | M.T.S." The *Yale Year Book*, appearing on June 19, 1878 (its only issue), edited by the anti-society crusader Frank McDonald of the class of 1879, who had founded the *Yale News*, contained not only the cuts and members' names of Skull and Bones and Scroll and Key for the classes of 1878 and 1879, but listed first, in pride of place, the cut of "Scull and Bone 522," with the canonical fifteen names of the organization's members: Oliver Brown, Charles Dilley, Frederick B. Dubach, John Q. A. Johnson, Edward B. Kellogg, John P. McCune, Frank McDonald, Royal C. Moodie, Samuel M. Moores, James P. Pigott, Clinton Spencer, Edgar H. Stone, William A. Van Buren, George R. Walker, and Reynold C. Wilcox. None of these men were named during the trial over the defacement of the Keys tomb.[90]

Finally, in reaction to the "wire-pulling" that preceded senior society elections, those not so chosen had their own political method of revenge: "The Senior neutrals frequently hold a private caucus before the election of class committees, to exclude every society man from the ticket; a singular proceeding, when it is remembered that the society men are presumably the best and most popular men of the class."[91]

DAVID ALAN RICHARDS

PROVOCATION: THE DISAPPROVAL OF
OMISSIONS—AND THE INVENTION OF TAP DAY

In 1874, the *Yale Courant* began to report the elections and discuss the doings of the senior societies. "It would be an unpardonable oversight to pass without notice," read the May 23 issue, ". . . an event which occupies so much of the attention and interest of the college world as the announcement of elections to the Senior societies. . . . As is always the case, to those inside the results will seem just, while those outside against their will, must mourn the vanity of human affairs, and regret their wasted work which might have been so much more profitably employed elsewhere." The publication reflected the schizophrenia of the student body: anticipating elections and describing election day in detail, while denouncing in a long editorial the evils of the system, especially in creation of a recognizable "tricky politician" type as candidate, and proclaiming: "May the time come soon when Yale shall be delivered of them [such politicians] and of the system which has produced them."[92]

The calculation from inside the societies was more certain. An undergraduate of that time was to write a half century later: "Of the one hundred and thirty Juniors among whom we were to choose, I myself knew all but about a dozen, well enough to have an idea of what they were like and what might probably be made of them. . . . There was less chance than now [1925] that a good man would be overlooked; but there was as much chance, and perhaps more, that he might be misunderstood."[93]

Election day prospects in May 1875 found the *Courant* cautiously hopeful. "The Senior society men of '75 have, as a general thing, conducted themselves in a non-offensive manner, a great deal of the ostentatious 'poppicock' which caused so much trouble with '74 has not been put on; in fact, the way in which they have acted throughout the year has led us to the belief that a wise choice is to be made. However, whether the following year is to be a quiet one or a season of *Iconoclasts*, bogus pins, bum [food] thieving, &c., rests entirely with the society men of the

268

Senior class."[94] With this standard of approval for worthy candidates, the *Yale Courant* launched a new probable cause of annual complaint in Yale College: were the two societies' choices to be found appropriate and fitting by neutral observers, consonant with the standards of literary or social excellence which the societies themselves professed?

On the last Thursday of that month, most of the prominent members of the junior class again went to their rooms soon after six o'clock supper concluded. According to a memoir by Arthur Hadley of the class of 1876, if any candidate had not gone to his dormitory by 6:45 P.M., he was advised to do so by any interested senior who happened to see him. At seven o'clock the senior class representatives of Bones and Keys left their respective tombs at two-minute intervals, heading for the abodes of the candidates assigned to them. Any Bones member could choose to be accompanied by a society alumnus, who was not advised of the destination before arrival. If the candidate happened not to be in his room, the senior would await his return. Hadley recollected that there were thirty or forty juniors in the college yard who thought they had no chance of election, and perhaps an equal number of men from the other classes combined. Those who received elections generally stayed in their rooms until the ceremonial entries into the dormitories were concluded.[95]

After 1875's Tap Day, the *Courant*'s board was still dissatisfied. While the elections "passed off quietly . . . [c]oncerning the choices we have something to say." One man, a "most worthy and desirable candidate, was passed over for Bones "for no earthly reason other than a petty personal dislike," the *Courant* complained. "That is the sentiment not only of this paper, but of the majority of the men of the College." Additionally, three of the Keys taps were found surprising, and they too were guilty of omissions of worthy candidates, "ornaments to the society had they been taken in." A third society was one solution to such miscarriages of college social justice: "There has been some talk about setting Spade and Grave on its legs again, and we think that it would be desirable thing if it could possibly be done. . . . a third society is really needed in Senior year. Of course, it would be difficult to start such a society, but it would surely be a success in the end, provided that it was a respectable organization, and not got together to 'grind' the other two."[96]

Remarkably, a new, third senior society was reported to be founded the next year. The *Yale Courant* for May 27, 1876, said that "the common title of the society is 'Hoe and Fiddle,' with a hall to be erected on the corner of Hillhouse Avenue and Trumbull Street," where "ground was broken last Thursday evening with appropriate ceremonies. Elections were given out the same evening." If this story was not a hoax, as seems likely, Hoe and Fiddle appears to have disappeared as suddenly as it came into existence.[97]

This new mixture of a desire to see social justice done among their peers and the excitement of learning the outcome of an admitted contest had a healthy effect on the conduct of elections in the spring of 1875, according to the *Yale Courant* report. "It has been handed down by tradition that Senior election night is a legitimate time for the non-society men of the Senior and Junior classes to range around Bones' Hall, and make as much disturbance and trouble as possible, and then to howl, in the college yard for the rest of the evening, the praises of Bull and Stones, interfering with the society men as they give out elections, rushing them round the campus, locking them up in the entries and building bonfires. . . . But this year matters have been different. . . . Instead of congregating around Bones' Hall and making the welkin ring there, the crowd thronged the yard between Farnam and Durfee, eagerly comparing notes as the elections were given out, passing a few remarks upon the general make-up of some well-dressed Keys man, and rushing round to congratulate the fortunate or to sympathize with others. As the Bones' men went round they greeted salutations from the crowd with good natured grins, once or twice answering back in a joking way; a thing never before done and which materially assisted in repressing any tendency to rowdyism."[98]

Before the pivotal year which witnessed the elections for the class of 1877, they were offered to juniors who were approached in their rooms. The turning point had come with the elections of spring 1874. Then, as in previous years, members of the lower classes followed the electing seniors from entry to entry, up and down stairs, partly in horse play, partly in their desire to be first to know the results. Disorder naturally resulted from the crowding of the various entries, and ultimately one was barricaded by some of the students not living there, blocking access to the waiting juniors above. The question of whether the visiting seniors would have challenged that barricade in solemn procession was never to be answered, because the juniors residing in that entry chose to come down stairs, sitting on the steps to see what the seniors would do. The latter were almost certainly surprised, but in any event accepted the situation and, singling out their intended new members, tapped each on the shoulder with some early version of the admonition, necessary for the first time and to become famous: "Go to your room!"[99]

Hadley's reminiscence frames the problem which resulted: "In the class which followed us—1877 [and thus, occurring in the spring of 1876]—a large number of the candidates stayed on the street or at the Junior fence after supper, and had to be publicly told to go to their rooms; so that the college could know about a considerable part of the elections half an hour before they were officially given out. To avoid this evil, it became necessary to arrange a system by which the offer of an election could follow immediately upon the public suggestion that it was coming. Hence the institution of tap days which developed rapidly during the next two or three years."[100]

Thereafter, as was to be reported by the annual journal the *Yale Horoscope*, which forecast individuals' chances for election, the anxious juniors "had their new spring suits padded on the right shoulders in anticipation" of being "slapped" or "spanked" on those shoulders, and hearing "hissed into their willing ears" the portentous phrase "Go to your room," ordering the candidate to his room to hear that offer, and accept or reject it, in private, as in former times. It soon came to be called "tapping time" or "slap day," falling on the third Thursday in May, at five in the afternoon.[101]

Some years later a letter to the *Yale Alumni Weekly* maintained that this new situation was the result of a wish by the candidates to prove to the college that they had no knowledge of their chances of election, and that the rumors of combinations and bargains for membership, rife before every election day, were simply not true. This motive was surplus to the simpler explanation of bottleneck breaking. Furthermore, the construction of Farnam Hall (1869–70) and Durfee Hall (1871), joined together at right angles to one another by the hinge of Battle Chapel on the Old Campus's northeast corner, coupled with the erection of the two-rung interior fences fronting the dormitories, inadvertently created an excellent enclosed arena where the election spectacle could easily be viewed from the fence's rails or the rooms above, in buildings which were quickly claimed for prime accommodation by the two upper classes.[102]

Senior society elections as an exercise that could be observed by the whole community, therefore, were not developed by any conscious choice of the electors or by pronouncement of the college authorities, but rather altered organically in spontaneous response to the congestion caused by the curious neutrals. By the spring of 1876, as the language of the report in the *Yale Courant* makes clear, the new way of tapping had become the traditional, immemorial way: "The usual demonstrations took place Thursday evening when the elections were given out to the Junior class. More than half the college assembled in front of Farnam and Durfee to watch the result. The scene was much like that of previous years [in truth, only two prior years]; the same business-like and important air of the Senior as he marched around the campus, followed by the pushing crowd; the touch or word followed by the departure of the happy one to his room; the congratulations of the crowd; and, as the number grew toward fifteen, the nervousness of those who had not yet received the expected notice. There were several surprises, but in most cases, the results were anticipated and satisfactory to the crowd and the class."

The society's delegate came into the crowd and walked through it, without recognizing anyone, until he found the individual for whom he was looking. If a candidate could not be located in the milling crowd, he was pursued with a visit to his dormitory room. After the tap, the senior society man returned to his hall, and the junior, in the quadrangle or coming down from his room, was surrounded by friends offering congratulations. Tutors and professors were in the crowd: "A certain Prof., an old 'Bones' man on the campus last night during elections, seemed to highly enjoy the performance."[103]

This new, underclass-imposed pattern of very public elections gave the two senior societies a new problem. Unless the incoming Bones club or Keys crowd was pre-pledged or "packed" with like-minded friends who had agreed before election day to join, then having an offer rejected—not within the confines of a man's dormitory room, but out in the public square of the Old Campus—was an open humiliation. For Bones, which the *Yale News* said "presents a motley appearance, and it seems to us impossible that certain pillars of rowing and certain *literary* lights could agree"—the risk was greater than that borne by Keys. While one member was sent out from each society's tomb into the courtyard to find and offer election to a particular candidate, the sequence of achieving fifteen acceptances could itself be upended by an unexpected and very public refusal. Not only might the incoming club's membership remain uncertain, but a prospect's interest could be shaken by a prior exclusion of a close friend, or by an election offer to a disliked classmate.

From this social dynamic, it appears, came the phenomenon of "the last man tapped" for a particular society. Over the decades, being tapped last, particularly for Bones, was seen as the ultimate tribute and capstone of a Yale career, and may in some cases have been so (e.g., William Howard Taft in 1877, Yale president Arthur Hadley's son Morris in 1915, or George H. W. Bush in 1947). Nevertheless, the tradition did not start that way.

The twin calculations of society and candidate are best explained by the verbatim report of the *Yale News* in the election for May 1878, for the class of 1879, regarding what the man tapped last for Bones that year. "'Mocassin Cholly,' known to the Faculty as C. L. Spencer, conferred the last election on Mr. O. D. Thompson, Captain of the crew. It is not to be supposed from this that Mr. T. was last choice but as it was expected that he would require as a condition of his acceptance, the exclusion of some enemies or the admission of some friends, with which the Bones men must comply, he was left till the last, in order that the society might plead the fact that all elections were out, as a reason for compelling him to accept the status desired by the '78 men. This supposition is strengthened as it was known last year that Jenks wanted a man in, and was therefore postponed until the last." The following year, when Bones' John Perrin came onto the campus for the fifteenth candidate, it was known he was looking for *Lit.* board chairman Alfred Nichols, and "a line formed between the two and the election was given." By the spring 1888 election, the *Illustrated Horoscope* would write of Bones preserving "its tradition of the past few years of tapping the surest man last."[104]

The *Yale Courant* board of 1875–76 editorialized that the evils of the society system were recognized and endured in all four college classes; the collateral news story concluded that the election results were "anticipated and satisfactory to the crowd [in general] and to the class [in particular]."[105] In 1877 and 1878, only the names of the elected appeared, a list disappearing in 1879, reappearing for 1880 and 1881, and gone once more in 1882. While *Courant* editors had been neutrals before 1880, in the tap of that year some began to be chosen for the two senior societies (one to Bones in 1880 and again in 1882, and one to Keys in 1881). Perhaps, as has been suggested, this was the Machiavellian technique of the societies for the muzzling of the college press, but the frequent election of junior anti-society crusaders to senior societies was to be a repeated phenomenon in the college's history.[106]

PROVOCATION, AND EXAMPLE:
THE SUPPRESSION OF THE UNDERCLASS SOCIETIES

The senior societies were not the only campus fraternity irritant by any means. The two sophomore class societies, Delta Beta Xi, founded in 1864, and Phi Theta Psi, begun the same year, had long been targets of the faculty for their disorder. They were, except for the societies of the senior year, more secret than those of any other class; they gathered on Friday nights to play cards, smoke clay pipes, and sip ale, and seem to have had no literary program or other purpose, although they were known for having stages to accommodate their theatricals.[107] An article in the *Boston Transcript* said that one branded their initiates in four places with a red-hot iron and that the practice had been in vogue for some time.[108] The *Yale Courant* reported in the fall of 1873 that a faculty member had said that "decided action would have been taken against the whole system long since, had not it been deemed impolitic to offend a considerable number of rich and influential graduates, who were members of Skull and Bones and other societies, and who still regard them with affection," and the journal called the sophomore societies so "entirely worthless, that few decent men would mourn their extinction or try to keep them alive."[109]

President James McCosh of Princeton, in an article in the *North American Review* for May–June 1878 titled "Discipline in American Colleges," wittily described the discrimination which the faculty had to apply: "There are some professors who cannot draw the distinction between the immorality of drinking and snowballing. It is true that we have two eyes given us that we may see, but we have also two eyelids to cover them up; and those who have the oversight of young men should know when to open and when to close these organs of observation."[110] With the underclass societies, the Yale faculty found it could no longer close its eyes.

The suppression came on Monday, May 24, 1875, with a notification to freshmen by their academic division officers that they were not to be initiated into sophomore societies until further notice. This was a few days before that peaceful election day celebrated by the *Courant* after the Keys memorabil scandal of the prior year. What the *Courant* described only as "Monday's spree . . . was the last straw that broke the camel's back," and the newly elected senior society members were ordered to remain in their rooms, "probably to prevent any possible repetition of Monday night's scenes." As the later student song was to have it, "*By fell decree / Of Facultee, / They are no more, / Oh, Sophomore.*"[111]

The freshman societies, Delta Kappa and Sigma Epsilon, met a similar fate only five years later, in 1880 (just six years before, William

Howard Taft of the class of 1878 had been Delta Kap's president, a mark of popularity which alarmed his father, fearful for his son's scholarship standing).[112] As had been the case with the sophomore societies, the freshman initiations, peanut bums, and purposeless meetings and politics were founts of continuous disorder. "The initiates," according to one report, "were blindfolded, jostled about, made to walk off the end of a plank into a tub of water, subjected to various tonsorial atrocities with barbers' clippers, carried in a coffin, branded with a 'red-hot iron'—that is to say, a piece of ice, which to a blindfolded man has much the same sensation—stamped upon the foreheads with the Greek letters of the society, in nitrate of silver, which resisted all efforts of scrubbing and remained for days as black as the ace of spades."[113]

This time, the faculty in closing these societies said that it was for the present, adding the hope that upon reopening, they would not be the scene of the historical disturbances between the sophomores and the freshmen. "The clemency of the faculty in giving them another lease of life," reported the *Yale News*, "calls for a suitable return from the societies and it rests with the present members whether to show their appreciation of this clemency by improving the tone of the societies or to accomplish their extermination by persisting in the course adopted in late years."[114] By refusing the faculty invitation to reform themselves into literary societies, they accomplished their extermination.

So over the course of five years from 1875 to 1880, by faculty edict the administration had shut down both the freshman and sophomore societies because of their perceived evil effects on college life. Those suppressions made the extinction of those in the junior and senior classes all the more imaginable, and thus possible. The negative opinion of President Porter (the last nineteenth-century Yale president not to have been a senior society member as an undergraduate), as given over a decade before in his 1870 book *American Colleges and the American Public*, was founded in frustration. "It is not surprising that in American colleges, animated as they must be with the practical and independent spirit of the country, and sympathizing most warmly with every public movement, whether political or literary, these associations have assumed prominence and exercised a powerful educating influence," he wrote. "The social tendencies of young men would naturally lead to associations for other than exclusive literary purposes. The clannish tendencies which result from their warm likings and their violent antagonisms, as well as their newly developed feelings of independence, would tend to make these societies exclusive and secret. We do not propose to discuss the general question of the desirableness or the undesirableness of some associations of this sort. It is scarcely open for discussion. They are so natural to young men, indeed, to men of all ages, as not to need defence or justification."

Nevertheless, "whether it is desirable that they should be secret or guarded by a mysterious reserve, and so involved with a factitious importance, admits of more question. The love of secrecy and reserve is too strong in human nature, and especially in boyish nature, to be easily thwarted. We doubt the expediency [of banning secret societies] because we disbelieve in the possibility of destroying or preventing secret societies. That such societies may be, and sometimes are, attended with very great evils, is confessed by the great majority of graduates. . . . Whatever excesses attend them, of late hours, late suppers, noisy demonstrations and convivial indulgences, should be repressed by the good sense and manly spirit of the college community."[115]

Porter certainly understood that opposition to the societies was clearly unproductive, but it was hard for him and his fellow clerics as college presidents to understand what the student enthusiasm for secret student societies actually involved. In truth, as one historian has summarized the problem, that extracurricular movement proposed "the substitution of worldly powers for spiritual grace as a measure of prestige; the substitution of social status for Christian status; the substitution of attitudes and skills necessary for success in this world, for those considered appropriate for success in the next. . . . In essence, the [society/]fraternity movement was institutionalizing new prestige values, the attributes of a successful man of the world, *this* world, at the expense of those various signs of Christian grace—humility, equality, and morality—which it had long been the purpose of the colleges to foster." As long as Yale remained under the influence of evangelical orthodoxy, as long as a religious orientation was both persistent and sincere, the administration continued its preference for a "brotherhood of professed Christians rather than a multiplicity of Greek brotherhoods. But in no case, regardless of its intentions, could the American college argue very persuasively against the attributes and values of worldly success."[116]

Still, with neutral sentiment building against the two senior societies, because of "poppiecock" and provocation, it would take only the non-appealable action of the faculty, or perhaps the initiative of the senior class itself (as Porter basically called for), to effect a like fate for them. A recent precedent existed for that, too: the extinction of the Wooden Spoon by the students in 1871. When the elderly relatives of the fictional Yale students in the class of 1874 in the 1894 novel *College Days, or Harry's Career at Yale* are urged to revive that celebration among their classmates, "it was 'no go.' 'An institution once dead at Yale never revives;' such indeed has always been the fact in the history of Yale organizations." In such a spirit, Edwin Aiken began the final paragraph of his attack on the senior societies published in the short-lived journal *Yale Critic* in the summer of 1882: "It is to be hoped that the students themselves might act rightly in this matter."[117]

That very prospect—death of the senior societies by class vote—was to arise, on February 1, 1884, when a resolution was introduced at the traditional meeting of the senior class for the election of its class day committees, to kill or cure the malignant society pyramid, by amputating its crown.

TAPPED FOR SKULL AND BONES, 1872–1882

William Lee Cushing	1872	founder, Westminster School
Clarence Deming	1872	editor, *New Haven News*
		Yale memoirist
Frederick Shepard Dennis	1872	professor of Clinical Surgery, Cornell

John Howard Hincks	1872	dean of faculty, Atlanta University
Benjamin Hoppin	1872	polar explorer
Alexander Morrison	1872	professor of Theology, Hartford Theological Seminary
George Fast Moore	1872	president, Andover Theological Seminary
		professor of History of Religion, Harvard
Edward Thomas Owen	1872	professor of French, University of Wisconsin
Theodore Salisbury Woolsey	1872	professor of International Law, Yale
Eben Alexander	1873	professor of Greek, University of North Carolina
		U.S. minister, Greece, Romania, and Serbia
William Beebe	1873	professor of Mathematics, Yale
Herbert McKenzie Denslow	1873	professor of Pastoral Theology, General Theological Seminary
Samuel Oscar Prentice	1873	professor of Pleading, Yale Law School
		chief justice, Conn. Supreme Court
Frank Bigelow Tarbell	1873	professor of Classical Archeology, University of Chicago
Henry Wolcott Farnam	1874	professor of Political Economics, Yale
		general counsel, N.Y., New Haven and Hartford Railroad
Edward Denmore Robbins	1874	professor of Jurisprudence, Yale

James Mulford Townsend	1874	president, New York Law School
John Seymour Wood	1874	author
Carl Thurston Chester	1875	professor of Law, Buffalo
Almet Francis Jenks	1875	presiding justice, N.Y. Supreme Court
John Patton	1875	U.S. senator (Mich)
John Sammis Seymour	1875	U.S. commissioner of Patents
Edward Curtis Smith	1875	governor, Vt.
Otto Tremont Bannard	1876	president, N.Y. Trust Company
Walker Blaine	1876	U.S. ambassador to South America
Robert Johnson Cook	1876	editor, *Philadelphia Press*
Charles Newell Fowler	1876	U.S. Congress (N.J.)
Arthur Twining Hadley	1876	president, Yale University president, American Economic Association
William Waldo Hyde	1876	mayor, Hartford
Rufus Biggs Smith	1876	professor of Law, Cincinnati Law
George Montgomery Tuttle	1877	professor of Gynecology, Columbia
Charles Francis Carter	1878	first college curve ball pitcher
Clarence Kelsey	1878	founder, Title Guarantee & Trust Co. (later Chicago Title)
Charles Langford Spencer	1878	U.S. District Court (Minn.)
William Howard Taft	1878	U.S. solicitor general U.S. Circuit Court judge governor, Philippine Islands U.S. secretary of war U.S. acting secretary of state U.S. president professor of Law, Yale Law School

		president, American Bar Association
		president, National Red Cross
		chief justice, U.S. Supreme Court
		trustee, Yale Corporation
Edward Baldwin Whitney	1878	assistant attorney general, U.S.
Lloyd Wheaton Bowers	1879	solicitor general, U.S.
Lucien Francis Burpee	1879	Supreme Court justice, Conn.
Henry Sherwood Green	1879	professor of Greek, West Virginia University
Walter Belknap James	1879	professor of Clinical Medicine, Columbia
Timothy Lester Woodruff	1879	lieutenant governor, N.Y.
Walter Camp	1880	father of American football Yale football coach
Alfred Nichols	1880	professor of German, Simmons College
Sidney Catlin Partridge	1880	Episcopal bishop, Kyoto, Japan, and Western Mo.
Thomas Burr Osborne	1881	president, American Society of Biological Chemists
Benjamin Brewster	1882	Episcopal bishop, Me.
William Phelps Eno	1882	author, world's first street traffic regulations (NYC, London, Paris)
Asa Palmer French	1882	U.S. district attorney, Mass.

TAPPED FOR SCROLL AND KEY, 1872-1882

Charles Orrin Day	1872	president, Andover Theological Seminary
David Bryson Delevan	1872	professor of Laryngology, N.Y. Polyclinic
Frederick Thomas Dubois	1872	U.S. Congress (Id.) U.S. Senator (Id.)

Edward Stevens Lines	1872	Episcopal bishop, Newark board chair, General Theological Seminary
Frank Davey Allen	1873	U.S. district atorney, Mass.
Edward Anthony Bradford	1873	correspondent, *London Standard*
Atwood Collins	1873	president, Security Co. of Hartford
William Addison Houghton	1873	professor of Latin, New York University, Bowdoin
Hart Lyman	1873	editor in chief, *New York Tribune*
Willis Fisher McCook	1873	president, Pittsburgh Steel Co.
Schuyler Merritt	1873	U.S. Congress (Conn.) Merritt Parkway honors
James Perry Platt	1873	U.S. District Court judge (Conn.)
Thomas Dewitt Cuyler	1874	president, Pennsylvania Railroad chairman, Committee of Twenty-One (planned and built Yale Bowl)
Hollis Burke Frissell	1874	principal, Hampton Institute
William Kelly	1874	president, American Institute of Mining Engineers
John Anson Garver	1875	senior partner, Shearman & Sterling executor of Sterling estate and construction of Sterling buildings
William Nimick Frew	1876	president, Carnegie Institute
Nathan Davis Abbott	1877	dean, Stanford Law School professor of Law, Columbia
Charles Hamot Strong	1877	president, Erie & Pittsburgh Railroad Co.

Howard Clark Hollister	1878	U.S. District Court judge, Ohio
Henry Martyn Hoyt Jr.	1878	U.S. solicitor general
John Addison Porter Jr.	1878	secretary to President McKinley
		proprietor, editor, *Hartford Post*
Alfred Lawrence Ripley	1878	president, Merchants National Bank
Julian Wheeler Curtiss	1879	president, chairman, A. G. Spalding
Henry Herbert Donaldson	1879	professor of Neurology, University of Chicago
John Villiers Farwell	1879	Yale Corp. Fellow, chair, Committee on Architectural Plan
Henry James Ten Eyck	1879	Ten Eyck prizes in his memory
William Montayne Hall	1880	dean, Colorado College
William Forest Hutchinson	1880	pitcher, Chicago National League team
William Montague Hall	1880	dean, Colorado College
William Reynolds Innis	1880	president, Studebaker Bros.
Frank William Keator	1880	Episcopal bishop, Olympia (Wash.)
Norris Galpin Osborn	1880	editor, *New Haven Journal-Courier*
Arthur Elmore Bostwick	1881	president, American Library Association
Morgan Hawley Beach	1882	U.S. District Attorney, Washington, D.C.
		clerk, U.S. Supreme Court
Cyrus Bentley Jr.	1882	general counsel, International Harvester Co.
Stephen Merrill Clement	1882	president, Marine National Bank
John Prescott Kellogg	1882	judge, Supreme Court, Conn.

CHAPTER SEVEN

THE SOLUTION OF WOLF'S HEAD
(1883–1888)

They pledged themselves to become members of a third organization
if a sufficient number could be prevailed upon to join.

—Sidney Wright Hopkins, Class of 1884

THE SENIOR CLASS MEETING TO SUPPRESS

William McMurtrie Speer of the class of 1884 was no member or
admirer of the Yale society system, and did not belong to any
junior fraternity. Clearly the society system was not sacrosanct, because
the faculty had largely done away with the freshman societies in Speer's
freshman year. The sentiments of the anti-society pamphlets the *Iconoclast*,
The Seventh Book of Genesis, and *The Fall of Skull and Bones* were still
current, living on in the *Yale News*, contemporaneously perceived as a
"daily anti-senior society newspaper . . . vigorously conducted so as to
thwart the society men in every way."[1]

The question of the worth of the society system in Yale College had,
indeed, become more vigorously debated during Speer's class's college
tenure, detailed in a wide-ranging attack published in five articles over

three months in the spring and early summer of 1882. These, because they were written by a recent graduate, who then converted his essays into an entire book, received more attention than the criticism delivered by Evarts the decade before. In June of 1882, Edwin Edgerton Aiken of the class of 1881, fresh out of Yale College and Skull and Bones, collected his series which had appeared earlier that year in the aptly titled but short-lived journal *Yale Critic*, and expanded it into a 110-page book, titled *The Senior Society System*.

Aiken was keenly aware of the offense his apparent betrayal would cause. He knew that "When one has enjoyed the advantages of the college course, it is no gracious task to make any public criticism involving the institution to which he owes so much, and which he has honored and loved. . . . Still less gracious is it to utter criticism upon institutions whose honors and privileges one has shared, and whose trusts have been confided to his keeping; and perhaps, in view of the peculiar nature of the institutions in question, it will be simple justice for me to say, at the outset, that the organization, with whose membership I was honored in Senior year, was almost ideally perfect, of its kind. I do not see how any organization of that sort could have been much better."

Nevertheless, he felt compelled to exercise his right of open discussion of public matters "in the name of a free, democratic Yale," and it was "in behalf of a larger and a nobler life within [Yale's] walls that these words are written." Still, such discussion was "limited by the obligation not to use against a party what is confided to me as a member of it, and that obligation I shall always recognize."[2] His criticisms were infused with the robust Christianity which he was to preach as his life's work—the first to propose a building at Yale for the YMCA, he became a missionary in China, and his book's penultimate chapter was titled "Relation to the Church." His arguments on the merits and defects of the secret fraternity system were based on societies at many American colleges, including Amherst, Brown, and New York University.

Those passed over, Aiken maintained, were deeply wounded by an "artificial system"; the desire to belong led to undignified "suping"

(Yale slang for supplicating); membership shielded "men who hold [college] public offices from merited criticism"; the society connections of instructors poisoned "the true relation of pupil and master"; frankness and openness were discouraged in campus relations; affection for their societies sapped their participants' college "patriotism," when money spent for Yale society and fraternity halls might have gone into "the buildings of literary societies [where] . . . they would have done more good"; neutrals were "left out of what they believe the controlling powers of the college"; alumni of the college, because of the dominance of the society system, refused to send their sons and withheld endowments; and, as argued by Evarts and others, they broke up the literary societies.

Furthermore, the supposed merits of the system were either overstated or did not withstand probing examination: the heterogeneity of the membership must overwhelm any literary advantage, while publicity, not secret remarks to a few, was indispensable to true eloquence; secrecy, exclusivity, and badges were the expression of "an aristocratic spirit," not a democratic one; student friendships did not need secret societies to flourish; and the tendency to work at scholarship or athletics, not for the honor of the college but to gain society election, put those strivings on "a false foundation." "Unreality, fascinating mystery, an eager struggle for three years, and silent exclusion with its consequent bitterness," he averred, "make no soil for poetry or eloquence or scholarship or letters."[3]

Aiken's book-length attack was not to be comprehensively answered until May 1884, when John Addison Porter, a graduate of 1878 and son of a founder of Scroll and Key in the summer of 1842, published "The Society System of Yale College," a lengthy rebuttal in the journal the *New Englander,* a publication with a national circulation but traditionally devoted to Yale matters of highest importance. His choice of forum was a recognition of what Aiken's long, New Haven–published argument had effected. The crusade against the senior societies, Porter noted, largely confined until then to campus fracases provoked by Bull and Stones and the presentation of critical views in one-off publications of limited circulation, "was transferred to the columns of prominent metropolitan journals." Alumni groups were aroused: "alumnus and undergraduate emulated each other in striving to point out the enormities commited by the societies." Magazine and newspaper editors across the nation, welcoming the outbreak of public dissension at one of the country's leading universities, found their circulation increased as "the good name of the University was dragged through the mire by her own sons."[4]

William Speer had begun his campaign against the senior societies as a junior, before the elections of May 1883, and so plausibly claimed not to have founded his pronounced hostility to them on being passed over. "[T]here is a movement afoot in the Senior class," he wrote to the *New Haven Courier*, "which, if successful, will do much to force this question to an issue and to induce some action on the part of the college authorities to one side or the other." This letter followed one he published earlier the same week on November 1883 in an influential national journal, the *Nation*: "In the name of '84 I call upon the Yale Alumni, Faculty, and the Corporation to look into this matter and to reform it. . . . For the good of Yale, this system should cease to exist, or be radically changed."[5]

The *Yale News* for February 1, 1884, announced a meeting of the senior class that Friday for "the election of class committees and the transaction of business," and approximately 140 members of the class attended. With the meeting chaired by Selden Spencer, a neutral (non–senior society member) who was equipped with a class catalogue and a blackboard for vote tallies, the attendees voted for John Swift, another neutral, to be class secretary, and for membership in the various committees to conduct the class exercises of Commencement Week: Promenade Committee, Class Supper Committee, Class Day Committee, Class Cup Committee, and Ivy Committee. The elections of Spencer, Swift, and the twenty-five class committee members reflected the observation of Aiken made two years earlier in his book, that before class meetings, neutrals organized in private caucus to exclude every senior society member from the ticket: in a class of 151 men, none of these twenty-seven so elected by the assembled class were among the thirty members of Bones and Keys.

DAVID ALAN RICHARDS

Following these votes, the *Yale News* for the following Monday, February 4, reported, with the diction betraying the drama:

The way was now clear for Mr. Speer to introduce the following resolution, which the meeting had declined to receive before, preferring to postpone its discussion until all other business had been transacted:

WHEREAS, The present senior society system creates a social aristocracy, exercises an undue influence in college politics, fosters a truckling and cowering disposition among the lower classes, alienates the affections of the graduates from the college, and stifles the full expression of college sentiment by its control of the college press.

Resolved, That we believe this system detrimental to the best interest of Yale College and injurious to ourselves. That we request the college press to publish this resolution of the senior class. That the chairman and two others, to be appointed by him, be a committee of three to lay this resolution before the president, faculty, and members of the corporation.

"It was expected," the *New York Times* reported, "that the moment the matter was brought up . . . the 'Bones' and 'Keys' men would rise from their seats and leave the hall. The society men remained . . . although taking little or no part in the discussion." Debate ensued, but in conformity with the general policy of suppressing senior society news, neither the college newspaper nor the *Yale Courant* published any record of the actual arguments. The *Yale News* did, however, make clear the expected result: "The supporters of this motion had made an active canvass of the class in its behalf, and entered the meeting confident of their ability to put it through." The spirited debate that ensued, lasting almost two hours, was recorded in the New Haven dailies and even New York City newspapers.

Edwin Merritt, called by one of the local dailies "that combination of Hercules and Apollo who presides over the [Yale] navy," demanded that the mover "should make known to the meeting his reasons for supporting it"; Speer did so, and Merritt responded at length. While he thought discussion useless, as "every man present had made up his mind how to vote," he argued that the resolution was "a very childish thing," because its adoption could not overthrow the two senior societies, which were "too firmly established" and "favored" by the faculty. Merritt then contended that the action was instigated by "that class of collegians who are known as soreheads—otherwise men who got left out of the spring election," and the class, "pretty thoroughly acquainted with each other . . . knew who those soreheads were." Nevertheless, he invited further opinions on both sides. His opponents then derisively "shouted out their recollections of last spring when Mr. Merritt was one of the most conspicuous in the class to fail on an election and displayed lacerated feelings."

Another neutral then spoke for the resolution, saying it was not an attack upon any society's members, but only on a system which should be abolished. George Judson supported Merritt's stand against the motion, observing with light irony that he had always gotten "a very warm reception from" the societies, having been "thrown down stairs." Another of Speer's party advanced the argument, in remarks that were reportedly "much applauded," that he would not like to come back to class reunions and see the society men "going about the campus with their coats open to show their pins," since he thought he "could open his coat as well as a society man." Robert Lyman, editor of the *Yale News*, then moved to lay the question on the table, seeking to end debate and compel a vote, and his motion passed by a majority—until the chair was forcefully reminded that, in standard parliamentary procedure, a two-thirds vote was required to carry Lyman's motion, after which "much time was spent in deciding how the vote on the resolutions should be taken."

The beleaguered chairman concluded that the motion to table was lost, after which his ruling was again appealed. "Much squabbling"—a New Haven newspaper characterization—finally produced a consensus in favor of a roll call vote (this, as the *New York Times* pointed out, was a victory for the society men, "as many who in secret ballot would have voted for the resolution did not dare to do so openly"). Spencer then ruled again, according to the *Yale News*, that each "voter on his name being called could answer from his seat, could whisper his vote in the ear of the chairman, or could deposit a ballot in the hat at the desk. The vote resulted in the defeat of the resolution by 67 to 50." Said Speer, as he headed for his noontime recitation, "Well, we had a little fun out of it anyway."[6]

The true drama here is belied by the unadorned statement of the tally, and requires an appreciation of the size of the class of 1884, to be 151 men at commencement, of which some 140 attended this class meeting. Yet only 117 votes were tallied. 117 plus 30, the total of the senior society membership, equals 147. One might speculate that either no member of Bones or Keys was at the meeting, or, being present, they were too proud to vote. Contemporary newspaper testimony is to the contrary: "Before going to the meeting a majority of the class had pledged themselves to support it, but when they came to the vote, they weakened, and either went over to the opposition or did not vote at all. The members of Bones or Keys had little or nothing to say in the meeting, with the exception of voting most emphatically against the resolution." Moreover, the members of Bones and Keys were not passive before the vote: one classmate, who joined in the defeat of Speer's resolution, was to record later: "I remember the meeting . . . very well. On this occasion the two societies requested our assistance."[7]

The collective membership of Bones and Keys in the class of 1884 included several men of power and prominence on the campus, in all walks of collegiate life. Even without the contemporary newspaper evidence, it could reasonably be assumed that they were all present at a class meeting so fundamental to their organizations' future existence, and the vaunted Yale democracy meant all should vote. The Bones club that year included the class valedictorian and salutatorian; journalists from the *Lit.* and Amos Parker Wilder (playwright and novelist Thornton Wilder's father), editor of both the *Yale Record* and *Yale Courant*; athletes (the president of the Yale Athletic Association and Ray Tompkins, football captain from 1882 to 1884); a class deacon; and a future dean of Yale College, Frederick Jones. The Keys crowd was equally distinguished, boasting the DeForest Medal winner, the Glee Club president, editors of the *Record* and the *Courant*, the president of the Yale Tennis Club, and the winner of the first Junior Exhibition Premium.

Nevertheless, the outcome of the February 1884 senior class vote, a pleasant surprise and vast relief to the members of Bones and Keys, was not due in the end to either their powers of persuasion or to the merits of their case. Perhaps unknown to Speer and his neutral allies, but if known certainly not sufficiently appreciated, a new element had been introduced into the electoral equation. Back in June of 1883, eight months before this class vote and hidden from Yale College and the world at large, a third senior society was founded, later to be called "Wolf's Head." Among its self-chosen first club were Edwin Merritt, the class meeting's primary challenger of Speer in the debate, as well as three members of the newly elected Promenade Committee of nine, four members of the five-man Class Supper Committee, and all three members of the Class Cup Committee (including Merritt). In other words, over a third of the men elected to class committees that day—apparently popular men on whose "yeas" Speer was counting to take down the two senior societies once and for all—had secretly and previously founded a third senior society, on the model of Bones and Keys. In the words of the New York *Evening Post*, "the members of the third senior society were the principal fighting forces of the opposition."[8]

A shift of fifteen, the number of new members of Wolf's Head, would have reversed the tallies of "yeas" and "nays," making it 65 to 52 in favor of the proponents of the resolution to lay "before the president, faculty and members of the corporation" the senior class's pronounced resolve to end the senior society system. Instead, that vexed system had been saved, in large part, by the quiet, if not completely secret, creation of a new senior society.

THE FOUNDING OF THE "THIRD SOCIETY"

For all his formidable skills as a student politician, William Speer seems to have discounted the existence of a new campus group, which by the time of the February 1884 class meeting was known familiarly as the "Fox and Grapes," for the Aesopian fable of jealousy that was said to have motivated its founding. The *New Haven Daily Palladium* had reported seven months before, on July 31, 1883: "A new secret society is to be formed in Yale College which will be a rival of the far famed Skull and Bones and the Scroll and Key. It is rumored that a building devoted to the new society will be erected on Prospect Street, and the society has been incorporated under the laws of the State. The plan is to elect fifteen men from the junior class and to make the society less secret than heretofore. One young man a member of the class of '84 has contributed $500 for the purpose, and two or three neutrals of recent classes will be elected in order to give prestige to the society."[9]

Edwin Merritt, Speer's primary antagonist, was identified in the city newspaper reports of the February 1884 meeting (although not of course in the *Yale News*) as the founder of "the recently incubated 'Fox and Grapes' society, composed of young men to whose aspirations 'Bones' and 'Keys' had given the cold shoulder." Of these, William Bristow, Charles Phelps, and Henry Walker were by that class meeting elected to the Promenade Committee, James Dawson and Henry Wagner to the Class Supper Committee, and Edwin Merritt and Henry Cromwell to the Class Cup Committee. Whether or not Speer knew these men to be members of a new senior society—and it is hard to believe, given the months-earlier dates of city newspaper stories mentioning them as probable members of this new society, that he did not know at least of the group's existence and size—it is hard to escape the conclusion that he hoped for their votes because of remembrance of their collective affront on the last tap day. "Speer counted on the votes of the Wolf's Head members," Lafayette Gleason was to recall, "as we were supposed to be in opposition to the two societies, but for obvious reasons . . . he did not get those votes."[10] And since, even if there were now forty-five senior society members, they were still only a third of the class, Speer probably also believed he could nevertheless prevail in the class vote, with a solid block of the pledged neutrals. This block, on the day, melted away, and the members of "Fox and Grapes" were not, eight months into their existence, about to dissolve themselves.

Fox and Grapes, of course, was not its self-chosen name (any more than "Skull and Bones" had been for that society). Its first, red leather minute book, containing the history of the society through 1891, is titled simply "Minutes of the Society—Third Senior Society of Yale College." This itself is the recopied version of the original minutes, and contains almost nothing about the weeks between Tap Day of 1883, when Merritt's chagrin at being passed over was transformed into his efforts to found a new society, and the night before commencement day, except a short note reciting for that evening the formalities of "the first regular meeting" to elect officers and honorary members.[11]

The new society was conceived on or about June 5, 1883, when five men from the class of 1884 were sitting in Gus Williams's rooms in 202 Durfee Hall, located on the first floor of the entry next to Battell Chapel. They engaged in discussion which ended in their pledging themselves "to become members of a third [senior society] organization if a sufficient number could be prevailed upon to join" (a caution anticipating the "sour grapes" attack which Merritt was indeed to suffer at the class meeting seven months later). It cannot be determined precisely which of the sixteen collegians later identified as Wolf's Head founders were present, but the original five are hazarded by the society's historian to have been Williams, Hopkins (credited with making the suggestion of founding), Cromwell, Dawson, and Holliday.[12]

Unlike the birthing of Scroll and Key in a similar mood and season four decades before, rivalry between the junior fraternities was not an issue. At this date, Psi Upsilon and Delta Kappa Epsilon took in about a hundred men, or two-thirds of the class. The literary exercises at their weekly Tuesday night meetings were nonexistent, according to one member: "We always had a milk-can full of lemonade and quite frequently would take a keg of beer and sandwiches, and they occupied the entire evening." At initiations, there was "rather too much champagne," wrote another, "each man being given his own pint bottle" at Psi U. Their influence was at a very low ebb, and their vaunted secrecy a farce: "It was not infrequent for DKE men to be smuggled into Psi U and for the Psi U men to be smuggled into DKE."[13] Cromwell, Dawson, and Williams were all members of DKE, while Holliday and Hopkins were brothers in Psi U (and in the final fifteen, ten were DKE and five Psi U).

Rather, it seems to have been membership in the class eating clubs which was the primary bonding agent. (Moriarty's Temple Bar at this date—today's Mory's—served only four eatables: eggs on toast, welsh rarebit, golden buck, and sardines which were grilled and served on toast; its proprietor, the Englishwoman Mrs. Moriarty, served no beer and little else than English ale.) The college commons had been made voluntary in 1839, then closed completely in 1842, and for the next ninety years the students made their own arrangements.[14] In gatherings of eight to a dozen, they moved between establishments, "whenever the soup got too thin at any one place," and formed strong friendships in these small groups (the history of the class of 1883, compiled fifty years later, contains one photograph of a senior society delegation, and four pictures of its eating clubs). Harry Worcester, one of the Wolf's Head founders, was to remember: "The eating clubs of our class of 1884, four in number, controlled, as a rule, the politics, such as there were, of our class."[15]

Worcester's eating club, dining during their junior and senior years at the University Club on Chapel Street for $5 to $6 per week, included in addition to himself Wolf's Head founders Holliday, Hopkins, Pratt, Wagner, and Walker, as well as Bones member Ray Tompkins and future Keys men Julius Doolittle and William Taylor. Frank Bowen and William Bristow met in a dining club formed by Bristow and joined by ten others (including four to become members of Bones, one being William Maxwell Evarts's second son, Maxwell, and a man who joined Keys), which stayed together for four years, ending at Mrs. Alexander's establishment, where they paid "the highest board in town, twelve dollars a week," until graduation.[16] Thus, half of the founders of Wolf's Head, eight men, were members of just two eating clubs.

A second tie binding many of them was thespian ambition: the dramatically talented Cromwell, Dawson, Hopkins, Merritt, Phelps, Pratt, and Williams were all featured in DKE's productions of *Lend Me Five Shillings* and *The Emperor's Diamond*, and Walker played the principal villain in Psi U's productions of *Othello* and *The Grave; The Groan; The Gallows*. "In D.K.E., Jimmy Dawson always took the part of a woman, and a very good looking woman he was."[17] A third bond was rowing: Merritt was president of the Dunham Boat Club as well as of the Yale Navy, while he and Sidney Hopkins rowed in their class crew in freshman year, and Charles Beck rowed with Merritt on the senior class crew.[18]

In the half century since the founding of Skull and Bones in 1832, the senior class's size had increased substantially from the 87 graduating in Bones founder William Huntington Russell's class. In its junior year, the class of 1882 numbered 132, over half again the number in 1832, while the class of 1883 numbered 165 in junior year, and the class of 1884, 164. The college physical plant had been expanded to accommodate the surge, and reimagined as a large, hollow quadrangle with buildings on all sides of what became known as the Old Campus. Farnam Hall was built in 1870 and Durfee Hall in 1871, at the corner of College and Elm Streets, both four-story structures based on the same time-honored entryway system used in Connecticut Hall six generations before.[19] When it opened, Durfee, with room for forty students, was claimed by the college seniors as their own, for it was equipped with fireplaces which Farnam lacked, and the annual ritual of society elections now took place before its jaunty corner collonettes and tourelles and the multiple tall chimneys for those fireplaces. (Another innovation was a mixed blessing: the Old Brick Row had no indoor toilet facilities, but the new toilets in the basement of Durfee, while welcome, were bare vitrified tiles, providing miserable seating in wintertime. The undergraduates then provided their own private and transportable wooden supports, carried by their owners about the campus and even into morning chapel, until the scandal compelled the authorities to supply permanent and official seats.[20])

So, a significantly larger number of talented and popular men were competing for the same thirty senior society openings which had been available for four decades past, and the number of disappointments was proportionally greater. Adding to this building pressure was the appearance of a new campus publication, the *Horoscope.*

Before the publication was founded, there was a palpable sense within the college class that certain of its members were undoubtedly deserving of a senior society election, in reflection of the perceived respective membership standards of Bones and Keys. The *Yale Courant* complained of unjust omissions in the elections for 1874 and 1875, and the editorial board in the spring of 1876 made clear why: "Justly or unjustly, society men are considered the best representatives of each Senior class, leaders in ability or popularity, and the present Junior class is to be congratulated on the election of men, who in most cases represent so fairly the best part of the class. In some cases, mere wealth or 'suping' [supplicating senior society men] may have been the causes of success, but in general, literary or social prominence have been the apparent grounds of selection."[21]

Annual lists in the *Yale News* of prospective members, beginning as early as its sixth issue in 1879, were soon replaced by something much more elaborate. Named for its claimed forecasting qualities for Tap Day results, the *Horoscope* had first appeared on May 23, 1881, announcing itself to be issued annually, featuring no masthead of editors, but adorned with a motto beneath its title: "The particulars of future beings needs be dark." Its self-declared purpose was, at the season "when the magnates of High and College Streets will, in high conclave, choose their successors," to "relieve the dread suspense which convulses the candidates and college at large at this eventful period" by issuing their four-sheet publication, "which gives as nearly as possible a fair statement of the chances of each probable man." The unknown editors claimed to be advised by a faculty committee, "consisting of two eminent Professors, one from each temple," and slyly called them "chargeable [for] all 'gags' and 'grinds' which have been inserted."

The first issue set the pattern for annual appearances that were to follow (with the exception of the years 1882 and 1893–97) through May 1907, briefly describing twenty or so candidates for each of the two senior societies (and, beginning in 1886, for Wolf's Head), coolly evaluating their respective individual merits and defects against the perceived election standards of those societies, and even suggesting names of some alternates who might surprise. It could also be wounding: in Richard Holbrook's novel of 1911 about the class of 1895, *Boys and Men: A Story of Life at Yale*, the "pamphlet called the *Horoscope*," appearing "about the second week in May," consisted "chiefly of a mass of vilification, divided up into brief biographies of all of those who had a chance of elections," and deeply wounded a character in the book by "hinting subtly that Jack's father was a robber baron, and that his mother had been a domestic servant."

The *Horoscope*'s sensitivity to the qualities of leadership and popularity was remarkably sure. Of its nineteen nominations for the Bones delegation of 1882, fourteen were elected, including the president of the Intercollegiate Athletic Association, the chair of the Promenade Committee, two editors of the *Lit.* (including the chairman), the man holding "the 'Bones' editorship of the *Record*," and the "Custos" (Latin for "guard") of DKE. Their list's biggest error, describing a man who was not tapped, speaks volumes about campus perceptions regarding the oldest society's standards: "CHAS. BIGELOW STORRS, New York City. This man has probably more to take him to the mystic temple than any man in his class. He has rowed on the crew two years, played foot-ball two years, has caught on the class nine, and rowed on his class crew. Besides these qualifications, he has taken the first composition prize both times, and has crowned his efforts in this line by dividing the Junior Ex. Prize. His only failing is his unpopularity, which will not, however, be sufficient to disqualify him, and he may be reckoned a sure man."

For the Keys delegation for 1882, the *Horoscope*'s prognostications, this year at least, were wildly off, successfully forecasting only one of the seventeen possible candidates, William Elder Bailey, "a man [who] has the 'Keys' qualifications, being a nice fellow, and possessed of considerable wealth." The others named were passed over, including one whose "strong points are his wit, universal popularity, the *Courant* editorship, and his high stand (philosophical), a point which will make him an especial prize for 'Keys'"; another, the class deacon, who "will probably restrain the somewhat loose morals of the wearers of the Golden Key;" a third who "holds the 'Keys' editorship of the *Record*"; and a fourth, editor-in-chief of the *Yale News*, who "will probably represent 'Keys' on that paper next year." The fifteenth Bones man tapped for the delegation of 1882, Enoch Wilbur McBride, "very popular, [and] a success in New Haven society," was on the *Horoscope*'s list for Keys.

The *Horoscope*'s second annual issue, archly labeled Vol. III, No. 22 (thus, "322," Bones's iconic number), dated May 1883, called itself the "only febrifuge" that could cool the "feverish excitement hovering over the college," and opened with a scene-setting sentence: "One hundred fifty-seven juniors have had their new spring suits padded on the right shoulder in anticipation of the parts they all hope to play in the great moral show; thirty seniors have been rehearsing the keep-your-face-straight, shoulder-tapping act, and the rest of the college listlessly wonders if the usual number of nobodies are to occupy ancestral seats in the conclaves of the great 'poppy-cock' generators of this institution." This annual issue's special value lies in its descriptions of college expectations for the next Tap Day that was to result, from its disappointments, in the founding of Wolf's Head.

Treating "C.S.P." first in succession, the *Horoscope*'s writers identified twenty-four candidates for Keys, of whom twelve were elected, including the incoming president of the Glee Club, the winner of the Junior Exhibition speaking competition, the president of the *News* board and chairman of the DKE convention delegation, a scion of Chicago's meatpacking Armour clan (noting that his "income will make it possible for him to repay in a substantial manner the debt of gratitude he will shoulder for being made celebrated for life"), the financial editor of the

News and captain of the lacrosse team, the financial editor of the *Record*, an editor of the *Courant*, and the "holder of the 'Keys' literary editorship of the *Record*." Passed over on the day, but also on the *Horoscope*'s list for Keys, were Horace Hand, "Budd" Hopkins, Charlie Walker, Oliver McKee, William Bristow, and Henry Cromwell (younger brother of a Keys man of 1883)—all six to be founders of Wolf's Head just a few weeks later.

For "322," the *Horoscope*'s analysis for the class of 1884 held, "'Bones' likes to have a goodly leaven of men in influential standing in its motley, mosaic crowd," elsewhere styled an "oil-and-water mixture," and said of one candidate (unsuccessful in the end) that "it would be his office to teach the *Lit.* men and high-stand men of his society that beef is rewarded by 'Bones' as well as brains." Naming twenty-four, the *Horoscope* was correct about thirteen of these nominees, including the future class valedictorian, a *Courant* editor (later to father the writer Thornton Wilder), the "Custos" of DKE, the class's most prominent athlete (Ray Tompkins, a member of the crew and baseball teams and captain of the football team, "beef through and through"), the chair of the Promenade Committee, the president of the Athletic Association, the son and brother of Bonesmen (Maxwell Evarts), and "the 'Bones' big gun" on the *Lit.* board. Passed over, but on the *Horoscope* list for Bones, were Albert Pratt, "quite a well-liked man, [who] might well be taken in to represent the popular element in 'Bones'"; James Dawson and Henry Worcester, who both had "family claims to the consideration of the devotees of the death emblem"; and Edwin Merritt, president of the Dunham Boat Club and the Yale Navy—four more future founders of Wolf's Head.[22]

So, of the five men thought to have been in Gus Williams's room in Durfee on June 5, 1883, three (Cromwell, Dawson, and Hopkins) had been severely disappointed after being named in the *Horoscope*'s forecast, and the others too no doubt had keen regrets, and thus (in Hopkins's words) "They drifted to the question of starting a new society on a totally different basis from the other two. They pledged themselves to become members of a third organization if a sufficient number could be prevailed upon to join. They had in mind the several abortive attempts made by other classes before them to form an *opposition* society but never before had a proposition to start one on a common sense basis been broached." (emphasis in original).[23]

The "several abortive attempts" to which Hopkins made reference were those of Star and Dart, Sword and Crown, Spade and Grave, and E.T.L., newly remembered for the Yale College generations of the past dozen years by Lyman Bagg's *Four Years at Yale* of 1871, which had become part of the self-conscious senior society literature passed down through the classes. The founders of Wolf's Head were determined to foreswear the hostility evidenced in Bagg's detailed description of the badge of Star and Dart, with the eagle of Keys stabbing its beak at the skull and bones at its feet, while the dart was poised to destroy the eagle.

Members of the class of 1884, reprising the initial experience of Tap Day humiliation suffered by those passed over for 1883, then with "common sense" began to add new members to the core from Williams's room. William Bristow recruited Frank Bowen and Charles Phelps to join the original five, and, through a series of more meetings, more emissaries, and more elections, Harry Worcester, Albert Pratt, and room-mates Charles Walker and Harry Wagner, who agreed on condition of including Ed Merritt, were also asked to join. For some time, exemplifying Hopkins's fear of falling short of the canonical number fifteen, there were only these thirteen, until they took in Oliver McKee and Charles Beck, an '83 man who had been dropped to '84, to complete the fifteen.[24]

The new group's aim of "total elimination of objectional features" of the older senior societies was explicit, as recounted by Franklin Bowen's brother Clarence in the society's "History and Policy": "*First*, [the Founders] believed that the Society should be established because there was room for it and should not be formed as a rival of or in hostility to existing institutions of the same sort. *Second*, the Founders professed a loyalty to and love for Yale College and believed that they could benefit the College if they could succeed in founding a Society that would avoid the evils connected with the older societies."[25] Still, while these principles were clear, the centripetal forces against poppycock which favored an open club were in contention with those centrifugal pressures of tradition and prestige tending toward creating yet another classic senior society.

As the Bones undergraduates had first approached Professor Thomas Thacher in seeking permission to build a tomb, so the Wolf's Head progenitors sought the preliminary blessing of President Noah Porter and the faculty to their formation. Having received that, they then turned literally to their elders, in particular Gus Hopkins to his father, Sidney Wright Hopkins Sr., a businessman in New York City, and Charles Phelps to his father, Edward John Phelps, Kent Professor of Law at Yale. An old-time Vermont Democrat, Phelps had served as the second comptroller of the United States Treasury (under President Fillmore) at the age of twenty-nine, had come to Yale only in 1881, and was already a great favorite with the senior classes, lecturing on constitutional law and international relations. As president of the American Bar Association he brought distinction to the university. When he died in 1909, his pallbearers were eight seniors from Wolf's Head.[26]

Their third mentor was Professor Arthur Wheeler, class of 1857, professor of History from 1865, and supervisor for the college of the construction of Durfee Hall. Professor Phelps drew up the Articles of Association and induced Professor Wheeler—a member of A.D. as a student, then a Yale College tutor before graduate work at the College de France and the Universities of Berlin and Bonn, "the type of teacher who interlarded his history recitations with discussions of the athletic situation in the College and could slyly inform his class that he had sent to Germany for textbooks, to which no cribs are published"—to be the link between the young society and the Yale faculty, on which he served until 1911.[27]

It had been naively hoped that the senior Hopkins would be the boys' financial angel to fund the erection of a proper hall, the second requisite of a senior society (the first being the ability to attract fifteen members). With the stone houses of Bones and Keys prominently situated on High and Prospect Streets, respectively, this construction was seen as vital to the Third Society's survival as an undergraduate institution, and notably something its vanished predecessors had never possessed. When young Hopkins's father's attendance at meetings resulted in nothing substantial for achievement of this goal, the current delegation decided they must create as well, or rather before, an instant graduate membership, "chosen for ability and prominence and, to speak frankly, financial standing." Frank Bowen solicited contributions from his brothers John (class of 1881) and Clarence (class of 1873, and by this date a decade later the business manager and eventual publisher of the New York *Independent*), and Clarence Bowen then persuaded his friend W. E. Stokes (class of 1874) to join the fund-raising effort which was to result in the construction of the first Wolf's Head hall.

Clarence Bowen was thus offered honorary membership in June of 1883 and, enthusiastic about the new society's avowed principles, arranged for the purchase of land on Prospect Street (although not the portion comprised of the corner lot and frontage on Trumbull Street later acquired). The senior Hopkins then contributed $1,500, Cromwell $1,000, and Bristow $500, with the aim of promptly building a hall ready for occupancy when the seniors returned to campus in the fall of 1884.[28] With its initial senior class membership secured and its hall's foundation commenced, the battle for the society's future direction was begun.

The majority of the founders were not sure they wanted a classic secret society. They frowned upon the traditional Tap Day ceremonies, considered "the flaunting of the pin on the neckties . . . something of an affront to other members of the class" and so were resolved not to do it, refused to countenance "secrecy in talking with . . . classmates about Senior societies," and intended to admit general visitors to their new building; only Frank Bowen among the undergraduates was then convinced that a classic senior society was the appropriate goal. Still, on the night before commencement, June 24, the newly gathered club held its first regular meeting in Hopkins's room in Durfee, electing him as president, appointing committees, naming Professor Wheeler and the two older Bowen brothers and a few other graduates as honorary members, and applauding the news that five to six thousand dollars had been pledged in subscriptions. The following day, the Articles of Association were duly executed, and on the next Sunday, in the Bowen family home in Brooklyn Heights, New York, John Bowen composed the words of the Wolf's Head anthem. The new senior society members then departed for their summer break, leaving the organization's affairs in the hands of Professor Wheeler.

Hopkins Senior was acquainted with the prestigious New York architectural firm of McKim, Mead & White, which was engaged to furnish plans. Clarence Bowen and William E. D. Stokes, an honorary member from the class of 1874, purchased a corner lot at the intersection of Trumbull and Prospect Streets, for the improvement of which the architects drew new plans, using stone instead of brick. Here, the battle over whether the new society should be "open" or "secret" came into full flower, with Professor Wheeler favoring the first option, and the property purchasers the second. The matter was settled, at least with respect to the hall's design, after a summer's worth of discussions through meeting and letters, with a compromise on "a building with slits for windows," which of course was indeed a change from the Yale campus's windowless tombs of Psi U, DKE, Skull and Bones, and Scroll and Key. This allowed a groundbreaking, when the members were back for their senior year, on October 26, 1883: Professor Wheeler walked about the lot in the drizzling rain, supervising "a couple of horses and a plow breaking the ground up for the first foundation."

Meanwhile their meetings, regular and special, were held wherever they could arrange or were welcome. The tavern The Quiet House was favored, but they also gathered at 22 Insurance Building, then at the hall of Gamma Nu (paying $2.25 a week for a month), then in Kellogg's room, and finally Pratt's room, 221 Durfee, just across the hall from 202 where the founders' meeting had been held the prior June—a convenience as eight of them resided in Durfee. These meetings were "business meetings," deciding upon the terms of a constitution, and determining that attendance of all members was mandatory, on pain of a $10.00 fine for absence; debates were not then part of the program, but on the validity of excuses for absence.

It was decided by motion on February 7, 1884, that their membership number would be the presently settled fifteen, even though this appeared to be a slavish imitation of the older societies, and thus a policy ostensibly opposed by all the founders. While this policy was never to be repealed, the fear that they might not (as with Spade and Grave, or Scroll and Key in its early years) be able to secure even that number led to the addition of the qualifying constitutional clause "but may be anything under this."[29]

The customary headwinds confronted by new senior societies at Yale—difficulties in raising funds and in gathering new members to an untried, if not completely unknown, society—were now encountered. To hasten the fund-raising, it was voted that "the committee on Graduate and Honorary elections be empowered to solicit and receive subscriptions from Graduate and Honorary members," and that "the committee be empowered to offer an Honorary election to any graduate who would be likely to accept." Eighteen honorary members from the classes of 1869 through 1882 were elected in the first half of December (including Maxwell Evarts's eldest son Allen, not chosen by Bones prior to his father's speech in 1873 which deplored the effects of the senior societies on the ancient literary societies), but petty setbacks soon mounted, following the rebuff from three classmates who turned them down: one week they failed to secure a meeting site, and the letter to the class of 1883 members, reminding them of their subscription obligations, brought in no money. As for the new hall, the foundations at Christmas were at sidewalk level, when work stopped due to lack of funds. In this atmosphere, it was a brave group of "Third Senior Society" members who nevertheless voted at the senior class meeting on February 1 against the motion to abolish the senior society system, signifying continuing hope in their enterprise.

Although the society system (barely) escaped class censure at that meeting, John Addison Porter, one of the founders of Keys, was then working to mount a major public counterattack on the system's critics, responding to Bascom, Aiken, and all who had written articles deploring it, to be published in the *New Englander* in May 1884 as "The Senior Society System in Yale College." Porter contacted the struggling club and offered to insert a description of the "Third Senior Society" in his piece, in order that it should make its first appearance in the national press fully equipped with a name and symbol. It was moved and seconded that "Mr. Wagner be empowered to inform Mr. Porter that in a few weeks the Society would give him some definite instructions concerning the Society."[30]

THE PORTER REBUTTALS

The vote at the senior class meeting on February 1, failing in its call for the abolition of the senior societies, did not end the national debate. *The Critic and Good Literature*, a New York City weekly journal, published an article in March 1884 titled "Senior Societies in College," which was not especially hostile. "Nobody believes that the secrecy hides disgraceful acts, and most liberal persons will agree that the friendships formed by such close and mystic intimacies are warm and useful in after-life. What could be more innocent than two or three clubs of fifteen members selected, as far as can be, from the best men of each class, after the class has undergone the trial of three years' comradeship?" But the societies' demerits, according to the author, were still patent: the exclusivity to the senior class heightened the social struggle which election represented, and they fostered "the wretched little politics among the undergraduates" which was damaging to the college fabric. "Why not open the senior societies to the juniors and sophomores, enlarge them, liberalise them, make them more like clubs and less like leagues of romantic boys?"[31]

Scroll and Key—for so the letter to the editor of the *Critic*, published two weeks later in response, was signed, although the sender noted its origin as Washington, D.C.—begged to differ on certain points. Yale was not, as charged, the college "most infested by secret societies." Yale had only four (counting the unnamed fraternities Psi Upsilon and Delta Kappa Epsilon) with a combined membership of 115 men, whereas many eastern colleges, such as Wesleyan, exemplified institutions where nearly all collegians were members. As for "string-pulling" in college elections, that sort of politicking existed in all colleges, with or without societies, and the cart and horse were also reversed: the "belief that two small societies, of fifteen men each, chosen when almost all of the 'offices' and 'honors' of the course have already been distributed can create 'politics' which shall involve and injure a body of six hundred and fifteen intelligent and frank young American gentlemen one jot beyond their free will, will not be seriously entertained except by pessimists or those who have been misinformed as to the facts in the case."[32]

The correspondent argued that it was impractical to expand the senior societies beyond their present size, if they were to be at all effective and remain attractive—and the first national allusion to the "Third Senior Society" in this letter, as well as its Washington origination, suggest strongly that its author was journalist John Addison Porter, an 1878 graduate, editor of the *Record* and *Pot-Pourri*, and member of Keys, then living in the District of Columbia serving as secretary to his uncle, Congressman William Walter Phelps (Bones 1860), and ultimately to be the first person to hold the position of "secretary to the president," under President McKinley.[33]

Here, he redeemed his promise to the "Third Senior Society" to mention their enterprise and their hall. "In [the] two [junior class] societies it is proved, year after year, that a body of forty or fifty men cannot, by an expenditure of pains or money, be so conducted as to benefit all of its members in a positive way, intellectually, morally and socially, as is easily effected annually by the Senior societies from much the same material, simply because of the smaller number of men associated together. The recent advent of a new Senior society at Yale, choosing exactly the same number of members as the old societies and improving on their history by springing into existence full-armed, like Minerva (i.e., with a commodious club house), would seem to demonstrate both the demand and the supply for more of this species of culture and enjoyment, and that their legitimate attainment lies in this direction rather than a war of words."

Nevertheless, even then Porter was continuing the war of words, finishing up for the May 1884 *New Englander* his lengthy response to Aiken and other critics, "The Senior Society System of Yale College." He briefly recounted the history of the class society system in New Haven, defending their rapid and multiple foundings (nine in all classes begun within fifteen years from 1832) as responses to the barren nature of the curriculum, with no "optional studies" (electives); the decline ("transition" was his word) of the ancient literary societies; the lack of other absorbing college activities; and the discomforts of the dormitories. "The tendency, therefore, for men of congenial tastes and similar habits to form themselves into small groups for wider and more positive culture, than they could otherwise obtain in the Yale College of those days, and, also, for the cementing of innocent friendships, was both natural and altogether praiseworthy," and their development within class lines "altogether in accord with the traditions and character of the College."

Once the institution was invented, the climax of the system in senior year was almost preordained. "The Senior societies became the necessary and logical climax to the others, recognizing friendships which had been formed, perhaps in Freshman year, appreciating the sociability displayed in the Sophomore societies, looking critically though justly at the literary work of Junior years, seeking to mingle in fair proportion in their membership all of these elements without slighting any one of them. So that viewed from the vantage-ground of historical knowledge this same system, which has often been called 'hopelessly confused and purposeless,' is seen to be at once simpler and fairer to all conditions of men, and likely to prove more lasting than those in vogue at any other colleges."

He defended the senior societies against the charge that they somehow muzzled the college press. "Only a half dozen of the two score or more of editors [of the non–*Yale Lit.* college press proper] appointed annually are chosen as society representatives, and then never until they have won their position by fair competition and long apprenticeship as contributors. . . . The society men have never striven to establish an organ of their own. . . . The society men differ among themselves, and to preserve a constant equilibrium between the three or more factions [those competing society members, the society abolitionists, and those interested in more general college news], if general society discussions were allowed to overload the columns of college *news*-papers—as was the case a few years ago, much to everybody's disgust—would be simply an impossibility."

Expense of membership was not an issue: "No men, however bitter, have boasted that they were left out of the societies simply on this score. In both societies [Bones and Keys] almost every year are found students of very little financial means." Nor were they literary society killers, as often averred—"A long list of new attractions claimed the undergraduates' attention and time; enlargement of the curriculum so as to include optional studies; athletics; development of the college press; increased ease in dormitory life, etc."—and in 1878, the revival of Linonia and Brothers had been supported by both the senior and junior societies, but their programs were found to be "useless for present needs," and the scheme failed. Porter cited Bagg's 1871 *Four Years at Yale* to refute the notion that politics were the senior societies' necessary result or object ("The part played by them in politics is simply a negative one."). Indeed, logically, the derided "etiquette" which prevented members from discussing society matters with outsiders was directly opposed to the practice of political wire-pulling, although Porter admitted that when "perverted into rudeness to strangers, or swaggering with under-classmen, it is puerile and snobbish." But comparing the conduct of Yale's college generations, it was also evident "that unnecessary display is on the decline."

The accusations of favoritism or nepotism in elections, he maintained, were actually belied by a review of those passed over, and this was a necessary result, indeed, if the societies were to continue to exist in their present form. "Year after year the nearest relatives, sons, brothers, nephews, the most cordial friends and room-mates, are left out of both Senior Societies simply because they fall below the required standard for membership. Of course the societies are urged strongly to take them, and of course they wish to do so—but their reputation and prosperity are dependent upon their impartiality in bestowing their honors. . . . More than their selectness, their age, their etiquette, or all of these combined, has the independence of the Senior Societies upheld their prestige. Should they lower their requirements but for a few years, they would be left . . . to die simply of neglect."

And if the senior societies were evilly intended or conducted, if their principles proved to new members after election to be hypocritical or mendacious, why was the repudiation of simple resignation not a common one? "How many resignations have there been from Yale Senior societies, with their combined total of ninety-four years and membership of over fourteen hundred men? Just *one* on public record, so far as we have been able to learn" (there is no name of that individual in his article, but perhaps he meant Edward Aiken). And if, as alleged, non-society men tended to avoid coming back to commencements and other reunions after graduation, why did Yale reunions prove in numbers and frequency to be so much more successful than Harvard or Princeton in attracting attendees? "By reason of their class intimacies, which the society system does more than any other one thing to encourage, the Yale non-society men come back to New Haven more regularly and in larger numbers than the alumni of non-society colleges. The Society men as a rule come back oftener still."

It was futile, Porter maintained, for the societies' opponents to think, with the organizations being state-chartered, landed institutions, with many administration and faculty members being graduate members, and no real history of serious abuse of privileges, that the senior societies might be "abolished," the question being one "rather more of an ethical than of a practical character." Even the collection of memorabilia and "crooking," which of course he did not so name, had its merits, in that this society practice "serve[s] the college in a way which nothing else could serve it, by handing down its traditions by word of mouth and by sacredly preserving many of its relics, which, trifles in themselves, though rich in historical significance, would otherwise be consigned to dishonoured dust and decay." And their members were generous: "In proportion to its size the society element has probably contributed more than any other to the financial prosperity of the college," and he noted the creation of the "largest literary prize in the University" (not identified, but the afore-described John Addison Porter Prize, named in honor of his father) as established and sustained by a society, but not naming Scroll and Key as the benefactor, or noting that it was his own senior society.

Porter observed rhetorically that "silence has always been the policy of the societies when assailed, however unjustly, because they have realized that to do justice to their cause they would have to reveal much which, even though highly commendable in itself, rightly concerned no men excepting their members. The Societies have never yet, even with a mob at their doors, been forced to capitulate or offer explanations to their assailants, and it is extremely improbable that they will ever condescend to do so." But his article, in a national journal known for its Yale editorship and affiliations, was in truth a full-throated response to the denigrators of the senior society system. "This bill of particulars," he concluded in his robust defense, "is far more remarkable for what it omits than what it contains, no charges being made against the general morality, scholarship, and good behavior of members of either society for any one year or any series of years. Never have these reform movements at Yale been headed by men who were not candidates for the societies up to the very hour of election!"

Porter's essay's closing envisioned a hopeful future for the system, and found that hope enhanced by the creation of what was to become Wolf's Head. "Whether the system can retain all of its usefulness now that the bottom has been knocked out of it, so to speak, by the abolition of the Freshman and Sophomore societies . . . whether the new Senior society, begun so auspiciously, is not itself the best antidote for quieting all the discontent against the old societies—are problems which time alone can solve. Expansion and improvement rather than abolition seem to be the real order of the day. The sincere hope of every loyal son of Yale, whether a society man or not, will be that the dawning era shall prove one of good feeling."[34] In this, he turned out to be correct.

THE WOLF'S HEAD INTERNAL DEBATE

The low ebb of its financial fortunes, coupled with the emotions stirred by the close vote on the continued existence of senior societies, led inevitably to a vigorous debate by the founders of the Third Society on their ultimate course and identity at their meeting on February 14, 1884. Joseph Holliday urged organizing "a definite policy if you would get any members in the under classes," but Harry Worcester warned against that, while the society's spirits and treasury were both so depressed, and offered a middle ground, "in preserving a moderate amount of secrecy," and avoiding the challenge of humiliation on Tap Day by taking in "our friends . . . provided they are not underclassmen." As Professor Wheeler had insisted on his own plan, that "the Society should be organized on the principle of the Harvard Clubs," as a condition of his support, both Gus Hopkins and Edwin Merritt argued that the minutes of the meeting should be "expanded into a paper to be placed before Prof. Wheeler." Countering, Frank Bowen argued that it "would be a great injury to the graduates who [have] given their money to change the policy from that of a Society to that of a club." Clearly, the opposing camps felt that their respective interpretations of the heralded founding principle of "common sense" and "no hostility" were generally accepted by all, but the devil was in the details.

The cost of the new building was reported at the February 21 meeting to be $14,900, including $3,000 "for steel shutters," which led to a call for the Building Committee to get "an estimate in wood" (the final cost was $18,000). While subscriptions continued to trickle in, some sort of executive action was needed, provided when it was reported at a meeting on March 6 that a graduate member of the society living in New York was offering financial assistance. This was William Stokes, of the class of 1874, who had been one of the two funders of the property purchase and now pledged an advance of $13,000 (inclusive of his $1,500 for the land), provided the society bound itself to repay the principal and interest at 6 percent over three years. All the members signed an agreement to this effect, with Professors Wheeler and Phelps also pledged to sign. In the hope for the hall's completion by June, new attention was paid to its construction, to be described by the *Horoscope* as "the dainty Dutch dwelling on Prospect Street," its Newark sandstone arriving in New Haven harbor in April.

Less immediately fruitful was the search for a name and a badge. Holladay's "Roman Fasces" were not acceptable, nor were several designs submitted by a New York jeweler. John Bowen had written Professor Wheeler back in October, suggesting a name and a pin design, which was firmly on the "secret society" side of the internal debate, but Frank Bowen was not able to advance his brother's proposals while the debate was unresolved. Other indicia of a society were pursued: a book for the constitution was purchased, a catalogue was proposed for the close of the year, and the choice of an "open ballot" for undergraduate elections prevailed over a "secret ballot." In time, Egyptian names were given to new members.

The construction at 77 Prospect Street now had the full attention of Yale College—"[its] building was a College event," wrote Lafayette Gleason of the class of 1885; "I think the whole of the College proceeded there more or less frequently." The architectural reference was to medieval German university life, student solidarity, and *Brüderschaft* (brotherhood). Its crowstep gable, evoking the Hanseatic League, fronted Trumbull Street, and a corner entry made it "face" both Trumbull and Prospect on the intersection's northeast corner.[35] When completed, it measured fify-four by fifty-six feet, with two stories and a basement, The first floor contained a reception hall, a larger reception room, a dining room, and an adjoining pantry, under thirteen-foot ceilings; the second floor housed a "Conversation Room"/library, and the "Society Hall"; the basement held the kitchen, the coal furnace, the only bathroom, a kneipe (German for "tavern"), and a billiard room (the *Horoscope* for spring 1892 mentions the "Wolf's Head pool table"). An article in the *Buffalo Courier* newspaper noted that in the building's design, "more regard was had for architectural beauty and material comfort [than in the other societies' tombs]. There is much more open work, and stained glass windows serve to break the monotony of the walls." Notwithstanding this hall's alteration to accommodate the operations of Yale's Institution for Social and Policy Studies—Wolf's Head moved out in 1924, leaving for larger quarters on York Street and what became Fraternity Row—it was and is the only surviving building in New Haven by the famous New York architects McKim, Mead & White.[36]

The appearance of Porter's article in the May *New Englander* raised to a new white heat the discussion of the merits of the society system, and Tap Day was fast approaching, where tradition demanded that elections needed to be offered in the name a a specific society, with a particular badge with which to "swing out" on Presentation Day. No longer could the differences of opinion on "open society" versus "secret society" be allowed to block action, if the new Third Society was not to be swept away in a backwash of ridicule.

Here, the society's funding made all the difference. Harry Wagner wrote later that if the undergraduates "had been able to finance the Society, there is no doubt that that [a Porcellian type of institution] is exactly what it would have been," but those "who were able to finance it"—those recent graduates who had previously been passed over by Bones and Keys in their day, but now had the chance to be in at the creation of a third but secret society in the classic form, with their retrospective election—"had a different idea," and Frank Bowen's observation that "it would be a great injury to the graduates who had given their money" (on the assurance that it would be a "secret society") beat back the final opposition to that model. This conclusion was quickly reflected, in the May 8 meeting, in the first formal suggestion for a name, which Holliday, seconded by Phelps, proposed be "'Kismet' *pro tempore*." The word, meaning "fortune" or "fate," could only properly attach to an organization grounded on secrecy, but the immediate amendment to the motion was "that we adopt the name with the condition that he [Holliday] hand in a better one if possible at [a] special meeting on Sunday night."

The debates over the name and the badge became secondary battlegrounds for "open" versus "secret." On May 15, the name "Grey Friars" was adopted *pro tempore* on the motion of Harry Worcester, which would seem to indicate a swing back toward transparency in both its style and its proponent, among the firmest of those urging openness from the start. That name was confirmed on May 18, but at the same meeting was also approved the badge design exactly as previously suggested by John Bowen, a snarling wolf's head mounted on the hieroglyph of an inverted Egyptian *tau* (an Egyptian ankh cross). Three further motions passed which were to cement the triumph of the "secret society" proponents. Phelps successfully urged the insertion of a clause in the constitution "that secrecy in regard to the significance of the badge be observed"; Bristow's motion, successfully amended by Williams, was carried, that there must be a vote of at least thirteen members in order to take visitors into the society building; and Merritt prevailed in his motion that "a graduate must be of fifteen years standing before he can be taken in as a visitor."[37]

The members of the Third Senior Society, still nameless to the barbarian world, were not prepared to enter the public lists of election day acted out before Durfee Hall, and the class of 1884 reverted to the old pattern of visiting men of the class of 1885 in their rooms. This drew a mock-reverential bow from the *Horoscope*, which in its annual forecast printed a black parallelogram, where the society's name should normally have appeared, above the newspaper's prognostications about future members: "We speak with reverence. Another mystic sign is sprung on us and the mysteries have added fifteen more disciples to their number. . . . As it is yet undecided as to its name we must be content to use a blank." Still, seventeen prospects were named, and the paper got seven candidates right. (Prognostication for the Third Society's members was difficult: as the May 1885 *Horoscope* noted, Wolf's Head was "of such recent origins and the field from which to select [after eliminating the prospects for Bones and Keys], is of such small compass, that it is difficult to predict with any certainty.") The paper was uncharacteristically milder about the older societies, noting that "they will emerge at the appointed hour and strike joy or regret into the hearts of the chosen and the 'left.'"[38]

While they did not hazard public appearance on election day with its risk of open rebuff, the undergraduates of the Third Society in the class of 1884 were able to assemble fifteen members, ten elected among themselves, and these ten electing five more after meeting over two or three nights. Their names were published in the *Yale News*, under the headline "Elections to the New Senior Society" on May 27, four days after the newspaper's report of those elected to Bones and Keys. On June 25, Class Day of the graduating class, all thirty members of the outgoing and incoming clubs appeared on campus with their new badges, "fully as large as a twenty dollar gold piece," three-quarters of an inch tall and almost that wide, the first "real outward notice of the membership" of this society, wrote an initiate of 1885. Theirs was not an open club, but nor was it a classic senior society, from which "poppycock" was meant to be outlawed. The Constitution provided that "This badge shall never be worn as a scarf pin," as the Bonesmen and Keysmen were wont to do, and in obedience to this rule, the thirty were all wearing their pins on their vests (in time, the eyes of the wolf's head "were often made of two brightly shining diamonds"). The *Horoscope* took notice the following spring, concluding that "This Society . . . has started out well . . . it displays no poppycock and hence demands the respect of the College. The building is all that could be desired, equaling that of Bones for durability and excelling the hedge-enclosed structure on College Street in point of beauty."[39]

The year ended with their first initiation banquet, on May 31, and Professors Phelps and Wheeler were invited. The initial Graduate Committee was elected, including Professor Wheeler and Messrs. Evarts, Hopkins, and Worcester, and plans were made for the inaugural meeting in the at-last-completed new hall. This smooth progression, bringing credit to the entire senior society system, was then rudely interrupted by another Scroll and Key "crook."

The theft on June 18 was reported, among other places, in the *New York World*. "It is the custom for the graduating class to form in a procession before the last examination, and with the tallest man in the class carrying a banner, march about the campus. After the march the '84 flag was placed in a trunk in J. M. Dawson's room, and while the seniors were at examination yesterday, Clifford B. Allen, Henry B. Anderson and Michael Schultz [new Keysmen from the class of 1885], it is said . . . broke open the trunk and carried away the flag. The seniors . . . secured legal advice. A deputy sheriff arrived to arrest the men who belong to the Scroll and Key society, but Prof. [Alfred] Ripley [class of 1878 and assistant professor of German], an old [Keys] society man, interfered and promised that the banner would be returned by noon. . . . The return was postponed until 9 o'clock. At that hour the seniors met H. McDowell, a society man, who returned the flag, swearing on his honor that it was the original one. The seniors then demanded an apology from the kleptomaniac juniors . . . which was at first refused. Under pressure of threatened legal proceedings . . . it was announced that the society would in full session to-night take action upon the proposed apology." The college was indignant and excited: the return of the flag was celebrated with bonfires, many built with dry-goods boxes stolen from Bolton & Neely's store, resulting in one arrest.[40]

The new hall was up and roofed, although not completed within, for the commencement night dinner, following the Senior Promenade. Rain poured outside, candles provided the only illumination among the skeleton partitions, and the windows were covered with pine boards, but songs, supper, toasts, and the big working fireplace made any discomfort remote. A member of the editorial staff of the *New York Tribune*, Ike Bromley, gave a memorable talk. The assembly than transformed itself into the new senior society's first annual meeting, and a subscription paper was passed around to pay off a lien of $5,000. At evening's end, following adjournment, Frank Kellogg and Morrison Young climbed to the building's ridgepole at 4:00 A.M. for a view from astride. The Gray Friars had survived their first year.[41]

Their second year as a society saw substantial further progress. The front part of the grounds were sodded, and the walk paved. House rules were drafted and adopted, among them the forbidding of billiard playing on Sundays and "the billiard balls were to be kept off the table during the business parts of the meeting." New graduate members continued to be elected, sixteen at the October 16 meeting alone. Two constitutions were drafted, to separate the powers and functions properly allocated to the graduate and undergraduate phases of the society's life, in an organization which had created a large graduate class at its inception, unlike its rivals. The "Corporate Constitution" of the "Third Senior Society of Yale College" established a Graduate Committee with three classes of governors, and the "Corporation" was to consist of those persons who were undergraduate members as of a certain date, and those thereafter "elected [by the undergraduates] from graduates and undergraduates of the Academical Department of Yale College." The Graduate Committee transformed itself into a board of governors, and Allen W. Evarts, Maxwell Evarts's eldest son, became the president.

The constitution of the undergraduates proved to be more controversial, and the minutes show five full pages of amendments which the collegians wished to have considered, but after further discussions in New Haven and New York, it was adopted. The end result represented a further victory of the "secret society" proponents over the "open club" faction. While the declaration of the original preamble of 1884 was retained (no hostility, no interference in college politics, and no unnecessary secrecy), as well as the clause forbidding the badge to "be worn as a scarf pin," the general interpretive provisions diluted what remained of the "open club" approach. While the original language mandated that "strict secrecy shall be observed by all members . . . respecting the Constitution, the business and the management and intercourse of the Corporation," the secrecy regarding the hall, initially limited to "the interior . . . devoted to the meetings of the Society," was now expanded to envelop the entire building. The amendment requiring secrecy on the significance of the badge was not repeated but covered by the general mandate on secrecy of the society's fundamental features, while the amendment on guests, permitting any person's admission except undergraduates and members of Bones and Keys, was now changed to read that an *active* member must be the host, not *any* member as in the original.

The biggest undecided question was now decided, following the first meeting of the 1885 delegation in September 1884. "Grey Friars" (or "Greyfriars") had never been satisfactory, although adopted *pro tempore* because of the necessity of a name for Tap Day. But the decision had in effect been taken away from the society, because when they "swung out" on Presentation Day in 1884, they sported, as the only visible symbol of the society, badges featuring a wolf's head, and their classmates quickly dubbed them "Wolf's Head men" or "Wolves." The appearance of the *Yale Banner* in the first part of the college year, meant to contain all the societies' names, members, and cuts, forced the pace, and on September 18 it was moved and seconded "that a cut of the pin be placed in 'the Yale Banner' without any name of Society." Still, there was no further vote to affix a new name to the new society, and the issue hung fire many more months.

In the spring, on March 21, the long-scheduled graduate meeting occurred. Only three days before, on March 19, the appointment of the society's advisor, Professor Edward Phelps, as American minister to the Court of St. James was announced, and the glow of that appointment warmed the meeting, as the appointment was celebrated both in New Haven and across the nation.[42] On March 26, the Wolf's Head men delivered a set of congratulatory resolutions to Phelps, recording that "The Society cannot but feel highly gratified that this honor has been bestowed upon one of its members." The reflected glory was expected to help with the tap of the 1886 delegation, and the society held a gala dinner at Delmonico's in New York City in May as a bon voyage party for the new minister. Fifteen new members accepted offers of election, although not publicly on Tap Day with Bones and Keys, as the founders' disapproval of this ceremony was still being honored. They were offered membership under what became the Third Society's fixed name: the minutes of May 21 contains an entry approving a motion that the election form given out would be "as follows: 'Mr.____, you have received an election to the so-called Wolf's Head Society. Do you accept?"

The name "The Third Senior Society" had quickly been disfavored. After the "Diggers," "E.T.L.," "Star and Dart," "Sword and Crown," all the prior and deceased "third" senior societies, it had an unhappy resonance, so the adoption of its "so-called" name "Wolf's Head" was a good resolution. Like its older brothers, however, it also needed a corporate parent, which had been created, but the laws of Connecticut had evolved further to require that the name of every corporation begin with the word "the" and end with the word "corporation," which additions had caused the corporate name to be the cumbersome "The Third Senior Society of Yale College Corporation."

The considered, deliberate, and periodic election of graduate members from prior classes in the eventual composition of delegations of fourteen or fifteen men for every class year back to the Civil War (with subscriptions for memberbership) distinguished Wolf's Head from Bones and Keys. As this "peculiarity" was described by Louis Welch and Walter Camp in their 1899 book *Yale: Her Campus Class-Rooms and Athletics*, "not only has it filled up its membership list from year to year since its foundation, but has reached back to former classes, where often hindsight has been able to operate better than the foresight of the older societies. It affords an index of the fallibility in the way of omission, by even such carefully operating societies as those of Senior year at Yale, to note how many men of great strength and reputation Wolf's Head has gathered into its graduate list."[43]

Certainly there were examples of this: among them were Edmund Clarence Stedman, 1852, the poet and literary critic; Wayne MacVeagh, 1853, U.S. attorney general and ambassador to Italy; David J. Brewer, associate justice of the Supreme Court; Arthur Williams Wright, 1859, Yale professor of Phyics; William Woolley Johnston, 1862, U.S. Naval Academy professor of Mathematics; George Creighton Webb, 1876, the first president of the Yale Athletic Association and founder of the Intercollegiate Athletic Association, having become an American diplomat to Russia; Frederick Abbot Stocks, 1879, president of the American Publisher's Association, and his classmates Frederick Wells Williams,

professor of history at Yale, and George Dutton Watrous, professor at
Yale Law School; and Frank Frost Abbott, incorrectly predicted for
Bones by the *Horoscope*, salutatorian in 1882, and professor of Classics
at Princeton.[44] The process was elaborate: a proposer and a seconder
were required, followed by a careful investigation by an undergraduate
committee, a detailed report to the Society of the Undergraduates, and
a carefully considered vote. This process—investigation, report, and
vote—was then repeated in the board of governors.

The college did not see this process, and the election of delegations
from the classes of 1865 through 1869 was to include so many men who
were members of Spade and Grave that it was sometimes thought, as
reported in a Buffalo, New York, newspaper in 1890, that the younger
society was the offspring of the older one. With thirty-five of the seventy-
five members of the Spade and Grave delegations of those years becoming
graduate members of Wolf's Head, the confusion was understandable;
but, given the demise of the Diggers, so was the desire of their graduated members to have a society experience. One wrote in, excusing
his absence from an annual meeting: "Just what relation you are to the
old 'Spade and Grave' I can't say—a sort of Phoenix or grand-son or
cousin—except that as you represent progress, you would more properly
be called a 'step-father.'"[45]

THE NEW TRIUMVIRATE

The two older societies continued to suffer by comparison with the
more (relatively) open attitude and demeanor of their new rival. The
New Haven Register in June 1886 reported that "There is none of the
poppy-cock about 'Wolf's Head' that is noticeable in the other societies. A young lady can with impunity converse with the members
about the society, and even remark on the beauty of the badge-pin,
without the wearer assuming that grieved and funereal look which
invariably characterizes 'Bones' and 'Keys,'" men if by chance their
society is mentioned."[46]

Those men were still attempting to run the affairs of the college. *The New Haven Journal and Courier* had reported six months earlier: "Between six and seven hundred undergraduates attended the university meeting last evening, which was to voice the sentiment of the College regarding the proposed change of morning prayers. . . . The usual farce of a deciding vote was held. . . . The effect was that thirty members of the two most prominent societies, taking somewhat the character of ward-workers, succeeding in passing, against the manifest wish of the College at large, the resolutions which will result in having morning chapel at 7:30 A.M. instead of 8:10. Every motion was made by the same group of men, every vote was carried *viva voce* at their instigation. . . . As the matter now stands the real majority are very much dissatisfied with the organized and powerful few."[47]

Here again, Wolf's Head was different. "The antagonism of the third senior society," another city newspaper reported five days later, "was much commented upon. . . . The fifteen members of this club voted against the will of the Keys and Bones men . . . and it is said that they didn't propose to help the other societies to run the College to suit themselves." Readers were reminded that "Wolf's Head is not as far out of the world, in respect to public knowledge of its doings, as are the other two. There is a sufficient veil of secrecy drawn around its mechanism, however, to class it with the secret societies, and this gives it a stability and respectability in Yale College circles that it might not otherwise obtain."[48]

The persistent attacks on the two older societies upset their graduate members, if not the undergraduates. The same issue of the *New Haven Register* which had lauded Wolf's Head also reported "a persistent report that Skull and Bones, because of the attacks upon it, will take no men from the class of '87. A Bones man has declared it quite untrue. 'The source,' he says, 'is as follows: at a recent meeting of the Yale Alumni in New York, Chauncey S. Depew made a speech in which he wrung in the opposition to our society. . . . He said he didn't care if not another man were taken in. The Society would live on just the same until its last surviving member was in his grave. That is what started the rumor.'"

Depew, the president of the New York Central Railroad, had declined nomination for the U.S. Senate in 1885; at the Republican convention in 1888 he was to receive ninety-nine votes for the presidential nomination; and in 1892, he declined an appointment as secretary of state in President Benjamin Harrison's cabinet.[49] For this Bones alumnus to come into the public arena, less than two years after Keys graduate John Addison Porter's robust defense of the Yale senior society system, evidences that the continued criticism stung.

The two *Horoscopes* of 1886, while blatantly profiting from the college's fascination with society elections, did not relent. "[M]ore harm is done every year to Yale College by the senior societies than by all the other deteriorating influences put together." But their successors for 1887, now including the *Yale Illustrated Horoscope*, which included drawings of the candidates (for which they paid $15.00 each to have made up for publication!) divided in opinion—although not about the manners of the Bones. The editors of the illustrated version noted that "Our views on the society system are directly antagonistic to those of our predecessor, for he maintains that it is a direct evil to the University, while we hold it is a real good, partially perverted only to an evil. The ill-mannered customs and haughty mien of the Skull and Bones society are, of course, obnoxious to all outsiders and to these airs and notions can be laid the loss of that prestige. . . . which now rests as a golden crown on the head of Scroll and Key . . . The objections . . . against the system . . . apply almost exclusively to the Skull and Bones organization. No other society has the brazen gall to attempt to crush the will of the majority. No other set of men are so brainlessly puerile and lack the title of gentlemen at times, as the dwellers of 322 High Street. . . . Not another living clan will refuse to salute you on the way to and from the society hall."[50]

Perhaps to further beard the two elder societies, the *Horoscope* was friendly to Wolf's Head, saying in its issue of May 1886, the first Yale periodical to publish the society's wolf's head cut and name, "Wolf's Head does not assume any of the I-own-the-college airs as the others do, and is therefore, titled to very much more respect," and in 1887,

"This conclave of social fellows . . . is growing more and more popular every year. Of all the societies, this comes very near to the ideal of what each should be, although it does not yet secure as prominent fellows as the others."[51]

Despite this measured praise, the various *Horoscopes* and the rest of the outside world could not know that within the Third Society, the "secret society" proponents continued their steady advance in the struggle with the "open club" faction. By 1887, the only provision in its constitution which distinguished Wolf's Head from the two other senior societies in the point of secrecy was the rule relating to the admission of visitors. The privilege was invoked from time to time, and wives and sisters of members were admitted, with a form of oath for them to take. Still, the theory for the grants of permission was based on visits of inspection, not visits for social intercourse. The privilege was too far abused "when one member took his wife to the Hall several times," and so the practice was stopped.[52]

So by 1886, a mere two class years after its birth, Wolf's Head was to all intents and purposes identical to Bones and Keys except in public attitude and the sporting of the badge. The Wolf's Head men were wearing it on their vests instead of their neckties, and when they sat across from their senior society classmates at their eating clubs or met them on campus, they could not but be aware at every moment of the Bones and Keys badges—the golden "crab" of Skull and Bones, or the "Scroll with Key Crossing" of Scroll and Key—confronting them from their classmates' cravats. The fervor of the founders of Wolf's Head not to repeat this offensive poppycock began to waver.

In the delegations of both 1885–86 and 1886–87, it was moved that the constitution be amended to strike "the clause which reads, 'this badge shall never be worn as a scarf pin.'" Recourse was made to Professor Wheeler, who approved a compromise, allowing the pin when worn in New York to be displayed "in a more conspicuous place" such that graduates there might more readily recognize the undergraduate members, but not on the necktie in New Haven during term time. The leader of the restoration faction William Brandegee then proposed a new amendment: "This badge shall always be worn as a scarf pin except during term time. Commencement Week shall not be considered as term time." This was defeated, eight nays to seven yeas. The pattern of proposed amendment and debate and close votes was repeated in the following delegation's senior year.[53]

The controversy did not have to be repeated in the new school year, commencing in the fall of 1887, because the members of Skull and Bones changed their own habit of time immemorial (at least, to collegiate generations). The *New Haven Register* reported for September 23, 1887: "Yale Collegians were all agog yesterday over the biggest sensation of many years. Every Bones man wore his society pin upon his vest. If this is to be a permanent custom, it is one of the most marked innovations in the usages of that very old and very conservative society. From the time whereof the memory of middle-aged graduates runs not to the contrary, every senior member of Skull and Bones has worn his badge upon his necktie, or upon his shirt bosom if exposed white shirt bosoms were the fashion . . . This has been a characteristic that distinguished Skull and Bones and Scroll and Key from all other Yale societies. It has always made their senior members conspicuous objects of awe for freshmen."

Nevertheless, the newspaper reported, "Among the present senior members of Bones there had grown up during junior year a strong feeling that 'poppycock' ought to go. Some of them told their intimate friends during the week before they were initiated into the society that if they could bring it about they would banish poppycock forever. This displacement of the pins from the neckties is looked upon by the collegians generally as the first step in this direction."

The first occurrence of the shift had taken place at the conclusion of the prior college term. A member of the Keys crowd of 1886 was to recollect in 1940 that "In [the class of 18]88's special [railroad] car for the [Harvard-Yale boat] race in June 1887, Henry Stimson, an '88 Bones man . . . came into the car with his pin not on his scarf but on his waistcoat. Then someone else entered with his pin up [on the tie]. The difference in opinion continued even in the fall, but before Thanksgiving all the Bones pins were down [on the waistcoat]."[54] Stimson showed grit, in reversing the society and family customs of his father, Dr. Lewis Atterbury Stimson, a member of the Keys delegation of 1863, and of his uncle, the Rev. Henry Albert Stimson, a member of the Bones club of 1865.

The young Stimson, later to serve as secretary of war for President Taft, governor-general of the Philippines for President Coolidge, secretary of state for President Hoover, and secretary of war for Presidents Roosevelt and Truman, was clearly a leader among his peers even then (and argued contrary positions later in his career, opposing the internment of Japanese-American citizens and then the firebombing of Hamburg, Dresden, and Tokyo, but was overruled). The badge was presumably down on his waistcoat when he won the DeForest Medal for 1888, and locating it more precisely, *Munsey's* magazine for June 1894 was to record that the badge was then "worn on the lower left side of the waistcoat." The retreat continued in the next decade: the *New York Times* reported on December 16, 1909, on "the 'turning down' of the pin, now worn concealed as part of a wise policy of outward society effacement carried out further in association with non-society classmates."

The change was a permanent one. When the *Yale Illustrated Horoscope* next discussed Skull and Bones in the spring of 1888, it found that "as for their secrecy and poppycock, the latter has been practically abandoned. . . . Immediately after the elections of last May and before the initiation night, the '88 Bones men elected pledged themselves to avoid the silly tricks which would serve only to embitter their former friends. In this they have kept their promise. Their conduct has been uniformly straightforward and gentlemanly."[55] While Scroll and Key, to the irritation of classmates, did not change its badge custom in conformity (and was not to do so until 1906),[56] the example of Wolf's Head, and not just the social pressures that birthed the Third Society, must be given credit for the alteration.

Another newspaper report, in the spring of 1888, was probably not off the mark in reporting the elections to Wolf's Head, that "by its freedom from all obnoxious secrecy and so-called poppy cock, has established for itself an enviable and well deserved reputation. . . . The advent of a third senior society has had a most salutary effect on the society system, and many of the most objectionable practices of 'Keys' and 'Bones' have been abandoned in recent years, very largely owing to the force of example." Soon, the Phelps Association, following Keys' example of philanthropy to Yale through the Kingsley Trust Association, in 1890 funded the C. Wyllis Betts Prize of $60, awarded annually for excellence in English composition during sophomore year.[57]

THE REVIVAL OF PHI BETA KAPPA

The class meeting of February 1, 1884, which failed to pass the resolution calling for the abolition of the senior societies, a vote which its proponents expected to win, had a second unanticipated result: the revival of Phi Beta Kappa at Yale. After 1843, the Alpha of Connecticut held only anniversary meetings; its members stopped wearing their badges in 1867 and held no elections after 1871.[58] Lyman Bagg in his *Four Years at Yale*, published that year, noted that after the regular literary meetings had ceased, membership was less highly regarded, and "for a dozen years or more past the sight of a Phi Beta Kappa key would raise a cry of derision," a long fall from the days when '[i]ts key, in fact, seems to have been thought about as desirable as a senior-society pin is now-a-days and to have been as generally recognized in the college world as a badge of exceptional honor and distinction."[59]

The lead story in the *Yale News* of February 21, 1884, just three weeks after the class meeting at the beginning of the month on senior society abolition, was headlined "Revival of Phi Beta Kappa at Yale" and noted that there was "a strong movement at present in the senior class to revive the Yale chapter of the Phi Beta Kappa fraternity. . . .The plans for its revival have not as yet been definitively matured, but the interest of the senior class in the matter at least insures a renewal of its existence here, and possibly a Phi Beta Kappa oration during the next commencement."

On March 8 there was a meeting of graduate members to reorganize the society, and twenty-three seniors were elected (one man declined).[60]

One of them, and the primary undergraduate organizer, who had recognized that the charter had not lapsed since the chapter had not been formally extinguished, was Selden Spencer,[61] the chair of the class meeting on February 1, joined in the revived Alpha by John Souther (who had seconded Speer's motion at that meeting to abolish the senior societies). Also elected in this class were five members of Bones and two from Keys, although none from the self-styled Third Senior Society. Spencer, composer of the statement published in the *News*, "setting forth the aims and prospects of the society," declared, in making clear his opposition to secret organizations was unabated: "Though originally a secret organization, [Phi Beta Kappa] is now to be entirely open and its object is to form and maintain a fraternity, the main requisite of which shall be a high degree of scholarship; and which shall promote in every way 'friendship, morality and science.'"[62] In May, eighteen men from the class of 1885 were elected (four who were to join Bones, three Keys, and one Wolf's Head—but none of whom were Wilbur Cross, later Yale professor of English, dean of the Graduate School, and governor of Connecticut).[63]

The *New-York Evening Post* reported more succinctly and candidly: "The proposition to revive it has proceeded from the anti-society men, who think that its honors will be awarded more impartially than are those of the present [senior society] organizations. The Senior society men, however, have cooperated in the scheme."[64] Even without this newspaper item, the proximity of the vote on the survival of the senior societies and the formal revival of Phi Beta Kappa is too close to doubt a connection, a conclusion reinforced by recounting the names of men from both sides of the debate joined together in a newly restored, class-wide senior distinction. Perhaps it helped effect, as the founding of Wolf's Head itself did, a sort of healing of the rift.

Still, there was no thought that it would, reborn, rival any senior society: it would be, as opined an editorial in the *Lit.*, "limited here . . . to philosophical and high oration men. Anything more of a public appearance than some sort of initiation gathering, perhaps, and an oration or poem at commencement, would be out of the question."[65]

327

TAPPED FOR SKULL & BONES, 1883–1888

Louis Kossuth Hull	1883	U.S. district attorney, N.D.
Edward Tompkins McLaughlin	1883	professor of Rhetoric, Yale
Eliakim Hastings Moore	1883	professor of Math., University of Chicago president, American Mathematical Society
Horace Dutton Taft	1883	founder, Taft School
Sherman Day Thacher	1883	founder, Thacher School
Wilbur Franklin Booth	1884	U.S. Circuit Court judge, Eighth Circuit
Gustav Gruener	1884	professor of German, Yale
Frederick Sheetz Jones	1884	dean of Engineering, University of Minn. dean of Yale, 1909–1926
Henry McMahan Painter	1884	professor of Obstetrics, Columbia
Ray Tompkins	1884	Yale football captain, 1882–1884
Amos Wilder	1884	U.S. consul general, Hong Kong, Shanghai
Samuel Reading Bertram	1885	chief, French War Relief Bureau
Frank Bosworth Brandegee	1885	U.S. Congress, Senate, Conn.
Henry Stanford Brooks	1885	chair, Yale Alumni Fund
Edward Hidden	1885	chairman, U.S. commission on Haiti
Lucius Franklin Robinson	1885	president, Conn. Constitutional Convention
Charlton Minor Lewis	1886	professor of English, Yale
John Christopher Schwab	1886	professor of Political Economy, Yale university librarian
Robert Nelson Corwin	1887	professor of German, Yale
William Kent	1887	U.S. Congress (Calif.)

Samuel Knight	1887	U.S. attorney, Northern District, Calif.
John Norton Pomeroy	1887	professor of Law, University of Illinois
John Rogers	1887	professor of Clinical Surgery, Cornell
Irving Fisher	1888	professor of Political Economy, Yale
		president, Am. Economic Assoc.
Richard Melancthon Hurd	1888	author, *A History of Yale Athletics*
Amos Alonzo Stagg	1888	professor and director of athletics, University of Chicago
Henry Lewis Stimson	1888	U.S. district attorney, Southern District, N.Y.
		U.S. secretary of war (Taft)
		governor-general of Philippines (Coolidge)
		U.S secretary of state (Hoover)
		U.S. secretary of war (Roosevelt and Truman)
Samuel Jameson Walker	1888	professor of Pediatrics, Chicago Polyclinic

TAPPED FOR SCROLL AND KEY, 1883–1888

Gilbert Colgate	1883	president, chairman of the board, Colgate-Palmolive
George Cromwell	1883	U.S. Senate (N.Y.)
Fred Churchill Leonard	1883	U.S. Congress (Pa.)
Edwin McClellan	1884	McClellan Hall honoree
Henry Clay McDowell Jr.	1884	U.S. District Court judge, Va.
Henry Burrall Anderson	1885	president, Auto Club of America
William Scoville Case	1885	associate justice, U.S. Supreme Court

Sidney Morse Colgate	1885	chairman of the board, Colgate-Palmolive
James Richard Joy	1885	editor in chief, *Christian Advocate*
Robert James Pitkin	1885	professor of Law, Denver University
George Edgar Vincent	1885	professor of Sociology, University of Chicago
		president, University of Minnesota
		president, Rockefeller Foundation
William Adams Brown	1886	professor of Theology, Union Theological Seminary
Walter Boughton Chambers	1887	architect, McClellan and Bingham Halls
Charles Henry Ludington	1887	vice president, treasurer, Curtis Publishing Co.
Herbert Farrington Perkins	1887	president, International Harvester Co.
James Rockwell Sheffield	1887	U.S. ambassador to Mexico
Charles Neave	1888	cofounder, Fish, Richardson & Neave
Frank Lincoln Woodard	1888	president, U.S. Golf Association

TAPPED FOR WOLF'S HEAD, 1883–1888

William Irwin Grubb	1883	U.S. District Circuit judge, Northern Calif.
Henry Martyn Hoyt	1883	U.S. attorney, Alaska attorney general, Puerto Rico
Edwin Albert Merritt	1884	U.S. Congress (N.Y.)
Charles Moorehead Walker	1884	chief justice, Cook County Ill.
Alfred Hand Jr.	1888	professor of Pediatrics, University of Pennsylvania

CHAPTER EIGHT

THE THREAT TO
YALE DEMOCRACY
(1889–1911)

The college still preserves the character of twenty years ago in its regard for a purely democratic standard of manliness and worth. The rich man's son still has to fight his own battles, and frequently to overcome a certain democratic prejudice against him. He succeeds, in spite of his income, and his friends like him because he acts and carries himself like a man.

—John Seymour Wood (Bones 1874), *Yale Yarns* (1895)[1]

DEMOCRACY DEFINED

By the 1889–90 school year, Yale College boasted a student body of 1,079 students, a number which trebled the head count in 1832–33, the year before the senior society system began with the founding of Skull and Bones. Then, two-thirds of the student body hailed from New England, with a fifth from the Middle Atlantic states, and a tenth from the South. Fifty-seven years later, New England including Connecticut accounted for less than half of those collegians, the Middle Atlantic almost a third, the Great Lakes a sixth, and the Southern states a bit less than 3 percent. Yale was still admitting more freshmen than Harvard—344 to 324, this year—while becoming less regional and more truly national (and even international: almost 3 percent came from abroad or the U.S. possessions and territories). Among its peers, meaning then Harvard, Princeton, Columbia, and Cornell, "Yale incontestably had the smallest home-state base, but also the smallest state as home."[2]

Not surprisingly, as it aged the college had become more dynastic regarding alumni legacies in admissions: in the class of 1831, 11 percent had Yale graduates for fathers, while by 1891 the figure was 16 percent, a number that was to hold roughly constant for another four decades, through 1921. The collegians were now mostly young men, not boys: the average age of graduates of the class of 1886 was 22 years, seven months.[3] In ethnicity and religion, too, Yale College was homogeneous, and the outside world hardly impinged.

Harvard professor George Santayana, reflecting on a year spent in New Haven, wrote of the New Haven college's "isolation from the outer world and internal homogeneity" for a Cambridge audience in the *Harvard Monthly*. "The first ingredient of the Yale Spirit is of course the raw material of the students. They come, as is well known, from many parts of the country, and this diversity of origin and associations would seem at first sight to be an obstacle to unity. But it is not. . . . The traditions of the place become sacred to him and he vies with his fellow students in proving that he understands them. His family and early friends are far away. The new influences soon control him entirely and imprint upon his mind and manner the unmistakable mark of his college. . . . The college hero is there [in New Haven] more unreservedly admired, and although it is not true that the most coveted societies are open to everyone who gains distinction in scholarship or athletics, other considerations have relatively much less weight than among us [at Harvard]. The relations of one Yale student to another are comparatively simple and direct. They are like passengers in a ship or fellow countrymen abroad; their sense of common interests and common emotions overwhelms all latent antipathies."[4]

It was because of the sameness of their students that spokesmen for Yale and Princeton liked to claim the existence of a near-perfect "democracy" within their student bodies. At Harvard, journalist Edwin Slosson observed, "the word 'democracy' seems to mean 'promiscuity' or else some spiritual condition altogether unaffected by external circumstances." To the ditty respecting Harvard's famous snobbery—*"And this is good old Boston/The home of the bean and the cod,/Where the Lowells talk to the Cabots,/And the Cabots talk only to God"*—Yale had a riposte:

Here's to the town of New Haven,
The home of the truth and the light,
Where God speaks to Jones
In the very same tones
That he uses with Hadley and Dwight.

Of course, this was democracy within institutions that did not reflect all the ethnoreligious, racial, gender, or class heterogeneity of American society, but the self-characterization was strongly believed and nationally debated for all that. Democracy existed in the sense that success in extracurricular activities could offset parental fame or wealth in establishing student prestige. At the same time, as one commentator noted, echoing Santayana's observation on Yale students' conformity, "It is the effect of [such an] organized democracy that it sets sharp, and often quite arbitrary, limits upon individual taste and action." The eminent literary critic and Princetonian Edmund Wilson noted that fear of this social censorship in New Haven caused "the most vigorous and alert intelligences . . . to be coerced into a right-thinking mould, to have their intellectual teeth drawn as the price of their local success."[5]

Yale was indeed "democratic" from one perspective: prejudices "as to birth, or State, or politics" were rare there.[6] Students actively resented the introduction of valets and automobiles as a menace to democracy. A. E. Jenkins while a junior in the class of 1889 declared in *Lippincott's Monthly Magazine* that a "true democratic spirit prevails among the undergraduates. No man is looked down upon because he is poor or of humble birth. Many a student who has 'worked his way through' has attained greater popularity than his wealthier classmates."[7]

In his 1887 Phi Beta Kappa lecture, President Timothy Dwight had celebrated, as an "element in the Yale spirit," "disposition to estimate both men and things according to their true value. There is no place in the world, I am sure, where a man is judged more justly in accordance with what he is, than here. The man who has imbibed the spirit of our University is no respecter of persons, in the bad sense of that phrase. He does not look at family descent or early advantages or wealth, but at mind and character. The externals are only secondary and subordinate—a good, indeed, if the man is worthy of them, but not of the essence of the man. What is internal, what the man is in himself and makes of himself, is the all important thing."[8]

When Dwight's successor, Yale president Arthur T. Hadley, was to reflect on the topic of Yale democracy in a speech in 1914, the emphasis had shifted. "I am sometimes asked whether Yale in all these changes is remaining 'democratic' in the sense that it once was. Democratic it is; but the sense of the word 'democratic' has changed, both in Yale and in America as a whole. Formerly democracy meant equality; to-day it means public spirit, readiness to be governed by public opinion and to take part in making public opinion what it should be." "Nothing," Harvard's Santayana had said, "could be more American—not to say *Amurrcun*—than Yale College. The place is sacred to the national ideal. Here is sound, healthy principle, but no overscrupulousness, love of life, trust in success, a ready jocoseness, a democratic amiability."[9] Once one accepted the traditional values of the community (Hadley's "readiness to be governed by public opinion"), one need never again consider himself an outsider.

College democracy had a social dimension so ubiquitous as to be almost invisible to the earnest competitors within it. The Yale version of "democratic amiability" emphasized an internal struggle for power and position, which was remarkable in its severity. "The spirit of Yale," former Johns Hopkins University president Daniel Coit Gilman declared in 1906, "a mysterious and subtle influence, is the spirit of the hive,—intelligence, industry, order, obedience, community, living for others, not for one's self, the greatest happiness in the utmost service. Virgil's words are on the hive,—*Sic vos non vobis.*"[10] In his book of 1910, *Great American Universities*, Edwin Slosson found something very similar. "I felt on the campus as I do in the dynamo room of a great power house. I knew that I was in the presence of forces obviously powerful but imperceptible to my senses. There is not enough tangible machinery about Yale to account for the work it is doing. The Yale undergraduates seem to train, control, and discipline themselves, leaving little for the official authorities to do in this way."[11]

Not all, of course, could be notable, and if the proof of Yale democracy was only the elevation, in a clean contest, of those who became notable in their first three college years, then otherwise worthy men, quietly building character for future success after their university course, would always be passed over. One aspect of democracy is that someone loses. The class of 1907's Harry S. Lewis, better known as Sinclair Lewis when he became the first American to win the Nobel Prize for Literature in 1930, wrote "on the subject of standard estimation of men" in his *Lit.* essay for June 1906, published the month after senior society elections (in which he was not chosen). "I am confident," he declared, "that in each class there is some seemingly insignificant man, who, by the practice of high ideals, spreading far beyond the reach of his name, has had no small share in our transformation from a narrow, rural school to a great, wise University. . . . Why are these men unknown? Partly because you do not look for them, to your own disadvantage; and partly because they are kept down by lack of money, or racial influences, or interest in some line which is not popular, or from lack of early development, or because they have not seen what there is to be done and that they can do it."[12]

Furthermore, even for the "known" men in the democratic contest, not all could be rewarded with the accolade of senior society membership. When outsiders asked how so exclusive a system might be reconciled with Yale's self-proclaimed "democracy," the answer was that Yale stood for equality of opportunity, not equality of status. As phrased by a correspondent to the *Yale Alumni Weekly*, "The democracy of a college should simply mean that every man have a fair opportunity, and that no unfair or artificial means of preventing a man from rising to his proper level should be permitted. In a word, I believe that democracy means 'Equality of Opportunity,' rather than 'Equality of Position.'" A New Haven newspaper noted candidly when reporting on Tap Day in May 1897, "Some one must always lose when there is aught to gain. The Yale boys understand this, and hence the failure of society life to injure the University." This defense ignored the fact that, when the three senior societies were by election only 15 percent of each class, there were arguably too few places to reward all the collegians of intellectual merit, literary skill, or athletic achievement.

Election of legacies also certainly narrowed the openings, yet as Walter Camp argued in 1896, "Popular belief is that a father or a brother who has been a member makes a strong backing for next of kin, but this has so often proved fallacious grounds for hope, that the opinion is steadily gaining ground that each man must stand or fall on his own merits." In the elections for the class of 1904, Lawrence Mason, whose father's and six brothers' membership in Keys had caused it to be dubbed the "Masonic fraternity," and who according to that year's *Horoscopes* was highly unpopular, was passed over. Still, in the elections for the class of 1908, Keys took in three Auchinclosses, two brothers and their cousin.

In his essay on Yale in *Four American Universities* (1895), Yale president Hadley opined that "On the whole, the Senior society choices are given with conscientious fairness. There are mistakes made, sometimes bad ones, especially mistakes of omission; but they are as a rule *bona fide* mistakes of judgment, and not the results of personal unfriendliness or chicane. There is a good deal of wire-pulling among those who hope to receive the honor, but surprisingly little among those who are to award it." The larger truth was framed in a Sunday feature article by the *New-York Tribune* run just before Tap Day in 1901: "[T]his [choosing the best men] is a harder task each year, as the classes grow and more avenues are opened for men to distinguish themselves in. There are, therefore, more sins of omission scored against the societies each year now than ever before. But this is a natural result, and, while it leaves a good many men unrecognized who have earned society distinction, it makes the competition more worthwhile."[13]

This final conclusion was not universally appreciated. By 1911, there were twice as many senior societies as had existed in 1882, and to an outsider, their relative positions seemed still to follow the order of their respective foundings. The eye of the senior society needle had neither widened nor narrowed: sixty men chosen by the societies, as noted by the class of 1883's twenty-fifth reunion book, formed no greater proportion of the class than did thirty in their year of graduation.[14]

WORKING FOR YALE

The notion that the collegians had a duty to the alma mater had long been a common theme at Yale. In his senior year of 1852, wrote Daniel Coit Gilman to his parents, "I had the pleasure last night of delivering before the three literary societies, Brothers in Unity, Calliope and Linonia, an oration of 'The Claims of Yale College upon its Under-graduate Students.'" Those within the hive which Gilman described over half a century later believed they were "working for" their college if they participated in one or more of a great many activities. "When work is to do," wrote Barrett Wendell of Harvard in 1901, "the Yale spirit knowns no hesitation."

Sidney Brockhurst, who plays the devil's advocate in Owen Johnson's 1911 novel *Stover at Yale*, and who says he is "is not fool enough to believe one Eastern university is different in essentials from another," has the intestinal fortitude to damn that sentiment: "'Work for Yale! Work for Princeton! Work for Harvard! Bah! Sublime poppycock!' exclaimed Brockhurst, in a sort of fury. 'Of all the drivel preached to young Americans, that is the worst. I came to Yale for an education. I pay for it—good pay. I ask, first and last, what is Yale going to do for me? Work for Yale, go out and slave, give up my leisure and my independence—to do what for Yale? To keep turning the wheels of some purely inconsequential machine, or strive like a gladiator. Is that doing anything for Yale, a seat of learning?'"

The effort involved was tremendous, as detailed in a review in the *New York Times* sparked by *Stover*, of the sheer hours taken up by extracurricular activities in New Haven, concluding that these "typical interests whose scope is not as well known outside the university as their importance within it demands . . . [are] one of the greatest, if not the greatest, features of Yale life—the scope of undergraduate interests, their seriousness and earnestness, and the unbelievably large amount of labor which the undergraduate expends in identifying himself with them and keeping them in good running order." The ideal was the man of action, and there were plenty of undergraduates who were sure to make their mark in the economy of the nation in commerce and industry, to become men of colossal energy and ingenuity in practical affairs. Their later success could—or at least would—be traced directly to their exertions in extracurricular activity.[15]

College students claiming they were working for their alma mater were, in point of fact, working for their own betterment, to be achieved through the connections they might make through the activities in which they participated, and the prestige gained among their peers by so doing, but also—and less selfishly—through the reputations they hoped to establish and maintain for their institutions, reputations based on the age and excellence of their publications, the prowess and success of their sports and debating teams, and the quality of their competing glee clubs. The irate Brockhurst was not so much sounding off as an individualist, but showing that he continued to value the education available through the curriculum, and not the extracurriculum which now almost crowded it out in the students' attentions. Some collegians may have been aware of the degree to which their rhetoric of "doing" or "working" some activity for the college was specious or at least self-serving, but the belief was clearly fervently held in any case.

Fueling this effort, of course, was personal ambition: Henry Stimson confessed to his fiancée that "the idea of a struggle for prizes, so to speak, has always been one of the fundamental elements of my mind, and I can hardly conceive of what my feelings would be if I ever was put in a position or situation in life where there were no prizes to struggle for." This emotion fed directly into the society system. In his memoirs, written after serving as secretary of war and of state for four different presidents, Stimson recollected that the "chief fruits of my four years at Yale came from the potent democratic class spirit then existing on the Yale campus; and that experience was most important to my life, both in the character developed and in the friendships formed," because in his view, the "democratic class spirit" found its apotheosis in the senior society system.[16]

The undergraduates were themselves aware of the paradox of extolling Yale democracy as quintessentially American, while competing hard among themselves for preferment and believing that, of all American collegians, they worked the hardest. The *Lit.*'s leading article in June 1902, titled "American Yale," squared the circle in this way: "It has often been asserted that Yale is essentially American. On the other hand, it has been urged that most Yale men spend at least three of their college years in a fierce and soul-destroying pursuit of social and athletic distinction, with the latter always in subservience. . . . The distinction made by calling Yale American is this—that while necessarily only a minority stand in prominence, the great majority of us are availing ourselves of our right to a fairly equal position in the strife for every honor. So that the competition for all things that are worth having here is probably fiercer than in any other university in the world. It is the greatest tribute that Yale can have to say that every many is given a chance to develop himself in the beginning, and that when he has finished, he is held by his class pretty nearly in the honor which is due to his ability and character."[17]

That competition, it was claimed, was not bitter. The *Lit.*'s leading article the month before, in May 1902, was called "The Spirit of Boyishness," finding it to permeate Yale, but nevertheless the foundation of "the boast of Yale that she possesses to an unusual degree the power of sending into the world self-reliant, vigorous men who can and do 'play the game.' . . . If we seek to analyze the point of view of the boy, we find at the bottom the sentiment that life is a game, a contest to be fought to the uttermost but after all a game, not a death-struggle. . . . The full-blooded enjoyment of the passing moment, the democracy that sees its brothers alike in opponent, onlooker and ally; best of all, the self-forgetfulness of excited enthusiasm—these are the characteristics of a healthy boy, and to an even greater extent the characteristics of Yale." An anonymous journalist for *Scribner's Monthly* had said it more concisely in 1876: "Probably no other American college has so distinctive a social life as has been developed at Yale, nor one so rich in humorous or picturesque traits."

The professoriate agreed. In Professor Max Farrand's speech to Phi Beta Kappa in 1910, he declared that "From my own course, that of History, we learn that the American is supposed to go into life as into a game—and he plays the game to win. He picks out something and tries to follow it through—to succeed where others have failed." President Hadley argued that the Christian gentleman was one who manfully engaged in competition, not simply to profit from winning, but more unselfishly to serve society—a patrician formulation that lent moral authority, spiritual legitimacy, and character value to competitive individuality. Through its extracurriculum, Yale College in its entirety cultivated not simply industrious scholars, or responsible Christian gentlemen, but highly competitive managerial individuals. The future captains of industry and finance, wrote university historian George Pierson, "found the informal, romantic, competitive college life incomparably exciting and important—the perfect training ground for success in our confident, acquisitive society."[18]

THE DECLINE IN SCHOLARSHIP

Also recognized on campus was that the enormous effort expended in winning these posts devalued the college's formal purpose of scholarship. "Broadly speaking," another *Lit.* leading article of the time maintained, "there are four college activities, success in any one of which gains for its patron a degree of prominence in his class varying with his individual effort and the relative favor in which the line of his industry is esteemed. These four are Religious, Athletic, Musical, and Literary." These overshadowed "what is a far worthier activity and what certainly has little or no student recognition—Scholarship." Slosson noted in his book that "the professional spirit prevails in Yale athletics, and the amateur spirit prevails in Yale scholarship." The complaint, with regard to society elections, was an old one: in his Yale diary, the earliest known journal of an American Jewish college student, Lewis Ehrich complained regarding elections in his junior year of 1868 that Skull and Bones did not applaud scholarly merit —although perhaps of equal significance was his lack of interest in the secret societies: "As for myself, if an election to Skull & Bones were offered to me in one hand, a set of Waverley novels or any other good books in the other, I should choose the latter ten times."[19]

"A man who comes here to study nowadays," lamented an 1896 *Lit.* editorial, "has found that the societies have trampled him under foot and have passed over; that he, a scholar, is cast aside as a 'freak,' a 'dig', and they of leisure are looked upon as 'representative men' in the classes." In 1903, a Yale faculty Committee on Numbers and Scholarship, chaired by professor of Political Economy Irving Fisher (valedictorian of the class of 1888 and a member of Bones), reported on the widespread disdain for learning, noting that of the nine valedictorians after 1893, none had been elected to a senior society, though in thirty-four prior classes, fully twenty-six valedictorians had been elected. "That is," the Committee lamented, "nine failed of Senior Society election during the last nine years, as against eight in the 34 years between 1860 and 1894." The

Horoscope in 1889 predicted the election of a valedictorian, since "it is an hereditary right of valedictorians for the last few years to get Bones" (but he did not); the *Horoscope* in 1892, sarcastically assessing a prospect for Wolf's Head, noted that "his Phi Beta Kappa stand will be quite an agreeable variation to the list of valedictorians in Wolf's Head," but he too was not elected. The shift back took time: "By certain elections," the *Yale Alumni Weekly* was to opine about the spring 1905 ceremonies, "a distinct impression was made that the College estimate is taking a little more into consideration intellectual attainments and services," because the president of Phi Beta Kappa had been elected to Wolf's Head.

In December 1906, the *Yale Courant* published a table which showed that in the years 1882–1905, 24 percent of the nonsociety men had achieved an Oration "high stand" or better, as against only 13.6 percent of the senior society men, finding that 6.1 percent of these "Honor Men" were members of Wolf's Head, 10.6 percent of Scroll and Key, and 23.1 percent of Skull and Bones. Contemplating these results in his book on American colleges, Slosson noted acidly: "The figures show that only one of the three secret senior societies contained a higher percentage of Honor Men than the college as a whole, and even that society had a less[er] percentage than the student body outside. That is, if a blindfolded man had entered the crowd assembled around the oak tree near Battell Chapel on the third Thursday in May and tapped forty-five men at random, the chances are that he would have obtained men of higher standing than those actually chosen, after the long and anxious deliberations of the secret conclaves." However, Yale's elite club system still compared favorably to Harvard's: the combined membership of Porcellian and A.D. for the classes of 1905–1910 produced only one member of Phi Beta Kappa.

Still and all, Slosson continued, "the faculty estimate of a man's ability based on grades alone is as narrow in its way as the student estimate based on activities which often interfere with the making of high grades." He asked seven Yale graduates of the classes from 1872 to 1896 to mark in the alumni directory the names of their classmates who had achieved distinction since graduation, without further instruction as to the degree of prominence or the proportion of the class to be indicated. His survey participants checked on average 24 percent of the names in their respective class rolls. Slosson compared these classmate-composed lists with the lists of living graduates who were members of the three senior societies and of Phi Beta Kappa (the latter being "Honor Men"), and calculated that 38 percent of the PBK men became prominent, and 37 percent of the senior society men became prominent, while only 19 percent of the men not in Phi Beta Kappa became prominent, and only 18 percent of the men not in senior societies became prominent.

While the poll was informal and narrowly based, Slosson declared that "we should probably be justified in concluding that the senior societies and the Phi Beta Kappa, although their standards of judgment are different, are equally successful in picking out men of superior ability, and that a student belonging to either of these groups has twice the chance of future prominence as one belonging to neither." In naming the high-stand men for Philosophical Oration, High Orations, and Orations, the faculty were largely accurately rewarding the collegians who best performed their "university duties." In electing juniors to the senior societies, the upperclassmen were, largely accurately, rewarding the most successful pursuers of the extracurriculum. Still, President Hadley was to avow "half-humorously" to a gathering of alumni in 1915, "We need to elevate study to the level of an extra-curriculum activity."[20]

For the ambitious student, not participating was not an option. The code of Yale College life exempted no student from some form of extracurricular activity. "The Yale system," opined an editorial by a senior society man in the February 1896 *Lit.*, "is essentially one of work. Incentive to *do* something, vigorous competition—the vital principle of social life—are such integral parts of Yale that idleness and indifference are reduced to the smallest possible factors." In *Stover*, Dink's first days on the Yale campus are consumed with conversations among his freshmen classmates about which among the numerous campus organizations and activities they would choose to pursue. "Stone was out for the glee club, already planning to take singing lessons in the contest for leadership, three years off. Saunders was to start for the *News*. Logan had made drawings during the summer and was out for the *Record*. Hunter was trying for his class team and the crew. Only McNab was defiant,"[21] a defiance that ignited a heated discussion on the advisability, indeed the very possibility, that one might choose *not* to go out for something or other.

That chosen activity, however praiseworthy in itself, could not in this college universe be pursued alone, but had to be a participation for and with others: activity had to be communal, because a student who did all for himself and nothing for his college was a student without the respect of his classmates. To hold oneself off from the group life of the class to preserve time for study or private interests was simple selfishness. Henry Seidel Canby, Yale class of 1899, made this clear in his memoir *Alma Mater*: "To be musical and indulge in music privately was a sure sign of freakishness, as bad as private drinking or the reading of poetry in seclusion. The banjo, the mandolin, and the guitar were respectable, since skillful players could 'make' the instrumental clubs and so gain social recognition; but proficiency on the violin was a sure sign of something wrong, as was skill on the piano not confined to 'beating the box,' and also singing of 'classic' music." (The University Glee Club had gone on its first extensive tour in 1871, and incorporated an orchestra in 1879; in 1885, the Banjo Club participated in the concerts for the first time, and in 1890 the two clubs were united into the Yale Glee and Banjo Club, to make annual trips around the eastern seaboard.[22])

The Fisher Committee found the same logic at work when sounding student opinion on the relationship of scholarship and society honors: "The athlete or manager," it heard, "is 'working for Yale,' unselfishly and self-denyingly; the student is not public-spirited—he is working only for himself." In Ralph Paine's 1909 novel of Yale, *College Years*, a character is a "'greasy grind.' . . . shy and poor . . . toil[ing] incessantly while the varied activities of the college swirled past and left him isolated." Athletic ability, social standing, money, and good looks were each and all highly valued, but there were, Canby noted, "routes upward for men who could write what the college magazine wanted, or make the music that undergraduates like; and a broad path, much trodden in my day, for the energetically pious who could organize religion, and sell God to the right kind of undergraduate. They were sure of a senior society." (Stover in Owen Johnson's novel more cynically styled them "gospel sharks."[23]) The religious student so described was no anomaly, because he was comparable to his athletic or musical peers in his ability to involve others in his work—and make them acknowledge his leadership.

THE PUBLIC LIFE PREFERENCE

Now more than half a century old, the senior societies at Yale, like the fraternity movement in other colleges in the East and then the South and the West, had successfully and irrevocably institutionalized new prestige values. They celebrated the attributes of a successful man of the world, this world, to the detriment of those various attributes of Christian grace—humility, equality, and morality—which it had long been the purposes of the college to foster. The protagonist of Richard Holbrook's novel *Boys and Men: A Story of Life at Yale*, a member of the class of 1895, writes home to his parents: "It is commonly believed here in college that a Senior Society man has much better chances in after life, because he will get fine opportunities in business and be able to go into the swellest society in every big city in the country."

While Yale and other American colleges remained under the influence of evangelical orthodoxy, their religious orientation was both sincere and persistent, in maintenance of their public preference for a brotherhood of professing Christians, rather than a proliferation of Greek brotherhoods. It was hard for their administrators to contemplate that this student invention proposed the substitution of worldly prowess for spiritual grace as a matter of prestige, the preference for social status over Christian status, and the trading of attitudes and skills necessary for success in this world for those which had been considered appropriate for salvation in the next. "The fall from grace," historian of education Frederick Rudolph has written of American fraternities in general in the nineteenth century, "was facilitated by the recognition that the fraternity movement gave to secular values, to good friendship, good looks, good clothes, good family, and good income." *The Yale Illustrated Horoscope* for spring 1891 was indeed to write of Scroll and Key that "good clothes, good cash, good fellowship, and good pull" were "the prime requisites for a bid for membership." The *New-York Tribune*, also celebrating the "peculiar distinction" of Keys, noted that it had "adhered to the principles that scholarship, literary ability, athletic distinction, social aspirations, excellent as they all may be, do not, singly or in combination, constitute a valid claim to membership in the society. The one indispensable qualification is manliness. A gentleman, not conventionally but essentially, is always a possible candidate, and nobody else cherishes a hope of admission."[24]

Yale's students, by virtue of the renown of its graduates as that century came to its close, could claim no little success for their system in terms of national prestige. In 1893, Charles Thwing did a census of the 15,142 persons in *Appleton's Cyclopedia of American Biography*, taking mere inclusion as proof of life success and categorizing those so named by college origin and profession. In the category "statesmen," counting 883 graduates from Harvard and 713 from Yale (a college sixty-five years younger), he found a Yale predominance, 55 to 50, and concluded that "Yale seems to be more American than Harvard. Public life, politics, statesmanship represent a very important part of American life. Therefore a larger number of distinguished men of Yale do we find in statesmanship than of Harvard." He quoted Santayana's article: "No wonder that all America loves Yale, where American conditions are vigorous, American instincts are unchecked, and young men are trained and made eager for the keen struggles of American life." To remind the undergraduates of their distinguished political forbears, the *Yale News* periodically ran articles listing the college's graduates serving in Congress and in the current administration's cabinet. Yalies in this era even appropriated to their number the country's most famous living Harvard graduate: "When in 1902 the Public Orator presented Theodore Roosevelt for an honorary degree [at Yale] he explained that the president 'is a Harvard man by nature, but in his democratic spirit, his breadth of national feeling, and his earnest pursuit of what is true and right, he possesses those qualities which represent the distinctive ideals of Yale.' This was received not with gales of laughter, but with prolonged applause."[25]

In the nineteenth century, the educated middle class widely accepted the impression that Harvard was more the "literary college," and Yale "more of a college fitting one for public life." Slosson found general reasons for such sustained success: "The argument in favor of the truth of the legend of Yale's team play in politics would have as its major premise a list of dignitaries too long for publication in these pages, including, for example, twenty of the fifty-nine governors of Connecticut; and for its minor premise the improbability that such a general recognition of individual excellence by the public was purely spontaneous. There are 15,428 living Yale graduates, probably more closely bound together by common training, a feeling of loyalty toward their Alma Mater, and mutual acquaintance, than any other large body of alumni in America, and inevitably exerting a powerful influence over public affairs."[26]

This characterization was well reported in the national press, and linked specifically to the senior societies. For example, alongside an article on Chief Justice Morrison Waite (Bones, 1837), *Harper's Weekly* ran an article in 1874 titled "Secret Societies at Yale," illustrated with an engraving depicting the halls of Skull and Bones, Scroll and Key, Psi Upsilon, and Delta Kappa Epsilon, and describing Bones and Keys as taking in "each year fifteen new members, who are claimed to be the most prominent in their respective class either as scholars, literary men, or social companions."

The piece identified "prominent members" of Bones, including former U.S. attorney general William Evarts, (Confederate) Lieutenant General Richard Taylor, collector of internal revenue Henry Deming, Connecticut governor Henry Harrison, U.S. Senator Orris Ferry (Conn.), University of California president Daniel Colt Gilman, Cornell's president Andrew Dickson White, New York Central Railroad president Chauncey Depew, and ambassador to Bolivia John Croxton, along with "notable members" of Keys, including *New Englander* editor William Kingsley, ambassador to Germany Theodore Runyon, *New York Observer* proprietor Sidney Morse, and (Confederate) Major General John Swayne. Another article, in *Munsey's Magazine* for June 1894, concluded flatly: "It is noteworthy that the chief arguments against these organizations come from men who have failed in admission to them, and that Yale's greatest alumni have been members of the secret societies."

In 1896 *Frank Leslie's Popular Monthly* published a series titled "American Universities and Colleges," and the first installment, on Yale, devoted fully one-third of its pages to the student society system, proclaiming: "Paramount in importance, and the culmination of Yale's whole society system, are its three senior societies—'Skull and Bones,' 'Scroll and Key' and 'Wolf's Head'—local societies, but the most secret and respected in the country." Contemporary book surveys of American colleges with treatments of Yale, like Slosson's, echoed these sentiments. Mass market magazines such as *Scribner's* published short stories in which Tap Day was a plot point and the ceremony described in minute detail. The *New York Times* began reporting the senior societies' annual election results in May 1886 (mis-naming "Scroll and Keys" and "The Wolf Head"), noting that "there were few surprises, the slates having been pretty accurately calculated by the outsiders."[27]

On campus, the adolescent mentality looked to the future, seeing college as a staging ground for adult life and the larger society the young men were about to enter. Polished manners are necessary for advancement in this world, not the next. There could be no better preparation for success in the second half of the nineteenth century than to have mingled daily with other young men who not only epitomized new patterns of achievement but had institutionalized them in the secret society movement. The college world that they made was, to an important degree, their reading of the present so that they might claim it for their future. To those heading for the combat of American capitalism, the contests and trials of the extracurriculum appeared to offer valuable lessons. (Slosson quoted a Harvard alumnus who sent his son to Yale, because he found that "all the Harvard men are working for the Yale men.") Yale students insisted that their college and social system was "democratic," but the celebration of egalitarianism rested on an intensely hierarchical foundation. What college democracy meant was that the students did not fully accept the status system of the broader society, but created their own where athletic or literary prowess, social grace, and a sense of fair play all weighed significantly—and in which the prizes were allocated on a competitive basis by the students themselves.[28]

New undergraduate interests and passions had arisen since the founding decades of the senior societies, and their membership was soon to reflect those changes. Henry Beers, looking back in his 1895 memoir *The Ways of Yale*, remarked on the "number of clubs and organizations in a modern [Yale annual] *Banner* . . . most of them undreamed of in the simple structure of undergraduate life in the sixties. . . . It sometimes seems to me . . . as if . . . every one was enrolled in some organization or other, was in training for something, and carried on his amusements strenuously and in a corporate way."[29]

MUSCULAR CHRISTIANITY

A new focus of student activity, as indicated by Canby's remark about the "energetically pious who could organize religion," was Dwight Hall. The year following a campaign by evangelist Dwight Moody in New Haven in 1878, a group of undergraduates organized the Christian Social Union, which by 1881 had rewritten its constitution to become the Yale Young Men's Christian Association. In 1886 a benefactor gave funds for a red stone building on the campus's west side to provide the new group a center, containing living quarters for a resident secretary, four small rooms assigned to the four college classes for committee deliberations and class prayer meetings, and an auditorium for larger meetings. The building, a college religious structure but not a chapel, was the first of its kind in New England; called Dwight Hall in honor of the first president Timothy Dwight (his grandson and namesake was inaugurated this same year as Yale's president), the name effectively became that of the Association.

Members of Dwight Hall elected officers, chosen at the end of their junior year, who as seniors directed the affairs of the association and coordinated their activities with the undergraduate deacons of the University Church. The first secretary was Chauncey Goodrich of the class of 1886. Knowing in 1885 that he would become the first graduate secretary of Dwight Hall, he refused an election to a senior society that spring on the grounds that the office required him to be above all campus politics—this was known, but Skull and Bones still offered him an election, at which he "shook his head emphatically before going to his room" and formally refusing there. A tradition was *not* established by Goodrich's self-denial: leadership in Dwight Hall ranked as leadership on campus, and the president customarily became a member of a senior society, as did many of the class deacons, who also served as association governors. Baseball captain and football star Amos Alonzo Stagg, 1888 and Bones, Henry Burt Wright, 1898 and Bones, and James Howard Merriam, 1909 and Bones, all served as YMCA postgraduate secretaries, and in time, it was even charged that there was a "Dwight Hall ring," with an underground tunnel beneath High Street into that society's tomb.[30]

In their book of 1899, *Yale: Her Campus, Class-rooms and Athletics*, Lewis Sheldon Welch and Walter Camp wrote that "the most significant, of all the facts of Yale's religious life, [is] that those of influence and leadership in the college world and those who man the student religious organizations are in very many cases identical." The *Lit.* author of "American Yale" noted "a thing somewhat incomprehensible to most of us in Freshman year . . . that men who devote themselves to religious work, are rightly given a high appreciation by the University as they become Seniors." Slosson noted in 1911 that a "capable religious leader is almost as likely to be elected to one of the Senior Societies as an athletic leader." This aspect of Dwight Hall made it a part of the organized and competitive student life, playing a most conspicuous role from 1897 through World War I, but voluntary religious life in Yale

College flourished overall—nearly two-thirds of the undergraduates were members of the same church—and the religious loyalty was genuine.

Taking up religious activities as a means of social/political advancement was undoubtedly practiced by some, but the sheer volume of such activity made clear, in Slosson's words, "the striking difference between Yale and most other universities in the student estimation of religious work."[31] Even to review the range of Dwight Hall activities is exhausting. Deputations of influential undergraduates went out every winter to preparatory schools to speak about Yale and the Christian soldier character which Yale embodied and instilled. A comprehensive handbook was prepared for all incoming freshmen, describing the college facilities, how athletics and college publications were run, and in general what and when to do, and what not to do (but senior societies were not discussed). Newcomers were invited to Dwight Hall to use it as a place to meet Yale's important upperclassmen and as a center for social services they would help to perform: class prayer meetings every Sunday, Bible classes (seven every Wednesday night), Sunday School classes, city missions, a foreign missions committee, a boy's club, and a band.

"In Dwight Hall," wrote Yale's twentieth-century historian, "Yale's impulses toward piety and social preferment—with the political activity and practical altruism which they encouraged—had found happy communion." The *Horoscope* for spring 1892 was more cynical: "Dwight Hall is the arena in which candidates are often expected to struggle, and how beneficial the results are which are sometimes gained may be seen in the case of several members of Scroll and Key. The Pope without ability, conviviality, or wealth, was enabled not only to gain a place in Keys but also an election to the Lit., by means of his Dwight Hall pull."[32]

ATHLETES AND MANAGERS; MUSICIANS, SINGERS, DEBATERS, AND ACTORS

Still, muscular Christianity was topped by athletic prowess on the absolute campus scale. As the *Illustrated Horoscope* for spring 1891 put it, "when athletics came to be a recognized factor in college life, Bones showed its wisdom by forthwith making athletic ability one of the keys (no pun intended) to its iron-clad lock." The Yale victory against Columbia in its first intercollegiate football match was the beginning of what would become, in terms of victories, the most successful college football program in the first century of that sport. This remarkable success was largely due to Walter Camp, who effectively created the American version of football that first became the dominant college sport and thus shaped the course of all intercollegiate athletics in America. A member of the class of 1880 and Bones, Camp while captain in 1879 pioneered the technique of teammates guarding the ball by running alongside him to interfere with tacklers, and as coach, effectively invented signals (nonsense sentences) for calling plays.

While Yale won at all its major sports, it triumphed in over 95 percent of its football games in the years Camp was associated with the football team in some capacity, officially or unofficially: Yale lost only fourteen games in the span of thirty-four years from 1876 to 1909, incontestably the greatest record in intercollegiate history. From 1872 through 1909 in all games of soccer, rugby, and American football, the fantastic Yale teams ran up a record of 324 victories, 17 losses, and 18 ties. From 1883 to 1898, nine of the Yale football teams were undefeated, and three were not even scored against. "Yale's success against Harvard," writes a Yale historian, "was so great that Cambridge men began to think of Yalies as nothing but muckers, while Yale men had serious doubts about the manliness of the Harvards." William H. Corbin, Bonesman and captain of possibly the greatest all-time Yale team of 1888, which outscored its opponents 698 to nothing, invited Camp to be his official coach that season, and Yale captains for years afterward followed suit. Camp led the way in transforming English rugby into American football, incorporating the notion of "downs," and the need for measured chalk marks on the field, creating a "gridiron" and thus a new name for the American football field.[33]

By the 1880s, Yale had established itself as the dominant college athletic institution in America. The faculty did not much interfere with management, as the university had no athletic committee, and the students were thus not wrong to claim credit for their success. Administrative support was not completely absent. In 1881 the Yale athletic field, some thirty acres of land on a bluff on the west bank of the West River, on Derby Avenue, was purchased, and laid out with a football field, grandstand, two baseball diamonds, a running track, and tennis courts, and from the fall of 1884 the college athletic contests were held there. A Princeton man accepted the fact that "there is probably not another university in the land where students have more direct control of College athletics and are less under Faculty rules and where there is less friction . . . between students and Faculty."[34] Walter Camp observed that "Managers and Captains are absolute in their power, the rest of us bearing ourselves with proper modesty and decorum in offering here and there bits of advice," while pointing out that twenty of twenty-six championships came to Yale in three major sports, and attributing the result to the Yale system of undergraduate control.[35]

Yale won five of six football championships, eight of ten baseball championships, and seven of the ten dual championships over Harvard in crew through the 1880s. In 1887, it won quintuple championships, in crew, baseball, football, track, and tennis. When Yale occasionally lost, as happened in the 1896 game, Harvard was not above twitting the four Bonesmen on the team (excluding the captain, Rhodes, a Keys man): *"We showed 'em that the Harvard men/Care not at all about The Bones/But Rhodes instead has lost his head/and nearly went without the scull/He saw that he would have to be/More cautious far about the scull."*[36]

Camp's listing of managers before captains was not a mistake. The captains of the four university teams (football, baseball, crew, and track) were elected by the members of the previous year's team, but the managers were chosen by the university at an annual mass meeting (a parallel to the election of the *Lit.* editors). The captain and manager of the 1894 eleven, both members of Bones, posed together for a Pach Brothers studio portrait in front of a faux Yale fence, the captain in his uniform and the manager in his suit. In 1911, Bones elected the managers and captains of baseball and track, the captain of the eleven, and the manager of the crew. Canby in his memoir recollected, besides the "Strong Silent Men . . . calming the crowded field by the full-breasted dignity of the white letters on their blue sweaters," other "slighter figures in tiny top coats with upturned collars, who seemed to exercise equal authority. These, I was told, were the Big Men, the managers, the powers behind college life, more important, because brainier, than the athletes. These were the real masters."[37]

Of course, beyond the managers were the most successful athletes, recruited from the ranks of ordinary students, amateurs rather than professionals, destined for a career in the learned professions or business, not sports, with special skills put in the service of the alma mater while becoming campus heroes.[38] Their exploits were recounted, fittingly, in the first history of its kind among American colleges, a 150-page book titled *A History of Yale Athletics 1840–1888*, self-published on May 20, 1888, and sold from his South College room by Richard M. Hurd, class of 1888 and Bones. Divided into five parts under the headings of Rowing, Foot Ball, Base Ball, Track Athletic, and Tennis, the chronological chapters gave a full statistical description of Yale's contests with Harvard, Princeton, and other colleges in each branch of sport for the year, and some indications of the developments or changes undergone by the sport in question.[39]

A review of the teams' leadership in Hurd's *History* makes clear that athletic prominence had long been a signifier for society membership. In the thirty years of crews through 1887, Keysmen had captained for nine of those, and Bonesmen for thirteen. In twenty-three years of university baseball, Keys could claim four captains, and Bones fourteen. In sixteen years of football captains, Keys members constituted four, and Bones members seven; when starting in 1881 the position of quarterback became defined, Bonesmen held that position for the teams from 1881 through 1883, and Keys for the years 1885 through 1887.

For the football teams of 1888 through 1911, this hardly changed. Of those twenty-four elevens, only six were not captained by men who had been tapped for Bones or Keys (and two of those as students in the Scientific School were ineligible for the Academical School senior societies). In the same years, nine who served as managers of the football team were elected. The two elder senior societies claimed six presidents of the Yale University Boat Club (Wolf's Head also counted one) through 1903, and five captains of the crew (again, Wolf's Head elected one, and traditionally tapped the coxswain). In athletics, baseball was a close second, with seven captains and three managers. Other sports fell well behind these totals, but still occasionally counted toward society election: two captains of the "Mott Haven" (track) team, and three managers; after 1899, four captains of the golf team, with three chosen by Wolf's Head; and after 1903, two captains of track, two of hockey, and one of fencing. Not surprisingly, the president of the Yale Athletic Association—a "hereditary Bones office," according to the *Horoscope* for April 1889—was often a member of Bones or Keys, numbering seven through 1903.

Nor was it only captains and managers. In 1905, of the forty-five juniors tapped for the three oldest senior societies, thirty-two were athletes. Electing a man for his athletic prowess was not, however, a binary choice against scholarship: it could not be maintained that the athletes were invariably low-stand men. The *Yale News* surveyed the appointment lists (those having a 2.50 or higher academic average, where 4.0 was perfect) and found that in the classes of 1890, 1891, and 1892, 64 percent of the athletes had received appointments. This compared very favorably with the standing of the editors of the college publications, the *Lit.*, the *Record*, the *Courant*, and the *News*, where 68 percent had won appointments.[40]

Besides the "Athletic," in the 1897 *Lit.* essayist's classification of campus activity, there remained the Literary, the Religious, and the Musical. The chairman of the *Yale Literary Magazine* was chosen eight times from 1888 through 1903, and one or more of his fellow editors were also elected, even in some years where the chairman was not: from 1890 to 1902, thirty-six out of sixty-five editors received elections. The chair of the *Yale News*, a publication a half century younger than the *Lit.* but now itself more than a decade old, was "slapped" even more often—ten times—along with its business managers and other senior editors. In due course, the chairmanship of the humor magazine the *Yale Record* was added to the list of class leadership positions recognized by senior society elections, and after the creation in 1900 of the oldest American college acting club, the Yale Dramatic Association, its president too became a likely candidate: Erastus Corning was elected to Bones in 1902, and Buell Hollister in 1904, while Lawrason Riggs (future Catholic chaplain at Yale) was elected to Keys in 1909, followed there by William Bullitt (future ambassador to Russia) in 1912.

As for "Religious," five presidents of the YMCA in Dwight Hall were chosen between 1888 and 1903, and another was the last man tapped for Bones in 1910. All class deacons between 1890 and 1902 received elections to the junior societies, and thirty out of forty-four to senior societies, all but two to Bones or Keys. For "Musical," twelve presidents and managers of the Glee Club, all but one Keys, and two presidents of the Banjo Club, one with Wolf's Head, were elected by the three senior societies. By 1909, members of the a capella singing group the Whiffenpoofs, founded that year, began to be chosen. The gift of musical talent was somewhat marginal, because a gift: as noted in a 1911 *Scribner's* short story about Tap Day, a candidate whose singing "bubbled up without effort" and "put him in the Glee Club" was "not a thing he had done; boys are critical of such distinctions." Three other leadership positions were apparently equally significant: the chairman of the junior prom was elected eleven times through 1903, or more often than the eight *Lit.* chairmen, as may seem appropriate for this institutional successor to the Cochs, and the Custos of the largest junior fraternity, Delta Kappa Epsilon, four times. Similarly, in this social category, the president of the University Club, almost exclusively a Keys franchise, was tapped ten times.[41]

Given that the senior societies were the offspring of the ancient literary societies in which debate and declamation were the main program features, it is remarkable that the inauguration of intercollegiate debates

between Yale and Harvard in 1892 did not automatically make its prac-
titioners preferred for senior society membership. "The debater, like the
athlete, works for the honor of his college rather than for self, and [prize]
money is out of place," wrote Welch and Camp in 1899, but support for
the enterprise was occasional, and not sustained: the May 1898 *Horoscope*
editor noted that "the thick-headed athlete who is frequently, and often
too frequently, the combination of athlete and society man, presses forward to carry off the victorious debater, there are long cheers, a bonfire,
and all is over. The same is true of a victorious Ten Eyck speaker. The
crowd of society men stand outside the treasury building awaiting the
decision, shout lustily the winner's name, and if they happen to know
him, shake his hand and pass on, perhaps secretly chagrined that not a
man from a recognized Junior society happened to be in the contest."[42]

This episodic enthusiasm was not yet sufficient for election. As a
character exclaims in Richard Holbrook's novel of 1900, *Boys & Men:
A Story of Life at Yale*, "But suppose that a man isn't an athlete—I cal-
culate that there are only ninety-nine connected with the University
teams—what kind of a chance has he then of being known? What does
debating amount to, anyway? In my opinion it's a fake. Did the man
who virtually downed Harvard last year receive any recognition? Not
on your life!" Debaters would never be truly significant on campus,
Welch and Camp opined, without "graduate coaches, that they may be
taught how to debate; and then that the great senior societies, which,
by the conferring of their coveted honors can spur men on to work for
Yale in any field, shall stand as ready to recognize the debater as they
now are the athlete." The Fisher Report noted that only six of thirteen
winners of the DeForest Gold Medal from 1890 to 1903 were tapped
for society honors, and "debaters are but rarely taken,"[43] although Bones
had tapped two in 1900, when the *New-York Evening Post* observed that
"It is only recently that debating at Yale has been regarded as worth of
senior society recognition." Not until spring 1910 was a president of
the Yale Debating Union elected to a senior society, William Archibald
McAfee, to Keys.

The horizontal mix, of course, was more significant in the affected class's and entire campus's estimation of the relative standing of the three societies, and in the commentary on the disparities inherent in a Bones or Keys delegation. The Bones club of 1899 included the football captain, the crew captain, the Dwight Hall president, two deacons, the *Lit.* chairman, the junior prom chairman, the Custos of DKE, the Athletic Association president, and the winner of the *Lit.* medal. For the same class year, the Keys cohort could boast of the baseball captain, the baseball manager, a class deacon, the chair of the *News*, both the president and the manager of the Glee Club, and the president of the Tennis Association. In subsequent classes, the predominance of one society over the other in tapping those in class leadership positions was less balanced, but, as was often observed of Scroll and Key, that society picked class leaders more for their compatibility within a delegation than for leadership alone.

This was because, for most if not all of these individuals "working for Yale" in its myriad undergraduate activities, election to a senior society was the ultimate goal of that effort. For that "fancy necktie pin . . . for that little piece of gold," the *Horoscope* for May 1887 noted, "men will work on the crew in the boiling sun and in the cold storm for three years, they will train in inclement weather on the foot-ball team, they will strive like Hercules to reach some prominent position on the baseball team, which will give them the privilege of the society's stamp; others will dig for high stand to be 'taken in'—men will do anything that their muscle and nerve will stand for the sake of wearing that necktie pin. Men who take a medium course, who will not over-exert their powers, are not wanted." Chances for election were now the seasonal concern of the anonymous editors of the successive annual editions of the *Horoscope*, which appeared annually from 1881 through 1905, excepting only the years 1894–1896. Richard Holbrook's Yale undergraduate characters in his 1900 novel were "wearing their brains out over the coming elections to senior secret societies. . . . Some . . . think of nothing else, and spend their days in small diplomacy or calculating the chances of other men. Every possible candidate is scrutinized a thousand times."[44]

In his mid-twentieth-century memoirs, Yale professor Canby of the class of 1899 remembered that "[i]n that moment of college time, actually they were playing the game because it was strenuous, and successful strenuosity was certain of recognition by your fellows. It was power in themselves and credit for that power which they sought, not power over others—that desire came later." Canby maintained that "in that rough-and-tumble of athletics, social drinking and doing something for the old college," all classes of America "except the socially impossible and the intellectually prim were thoroughly mingled. Veils of glamour in older countries [which] have protected rank and wealth—especially in those college aristocracies nearest to our own, Oxford and Cambridge" were stripped away from the young plutocrats of the United States.

"After the sons and heirs who might have formed an American aristocracy of wealth and privilege had been shuffled in the college competitions with the shrewd children of parvenus and the good baseball players whose fathers were Irish policemen," he continued, "cards were redealt in new social categories." The boys were "not impressed by the Great Names of plutocracy—by Vanderbilts, Astors, Rockefellers as such—since we saw them at first hand. And thus, in the qualified democracy of the colleges died the possibility of adding to the economic privileges of the very rich the respect given elsewhere to rank." They knew, Canby concluded of his own institution, "that this college boasted of its democracy, which actually was no social democracy at all, since class lines (once drawn) were tighter in the outside world. They knew well that it was a democracy of opportunity."

Thus, a young man whose parents had invested in a Yale College education might hope to pass by his own native abilities into the brave world of great cities and the gilded corridors of their privileged sets. If he could place himself in the right college group, his own would take care of him, provided his later career was not a great falling off. "From henceforth," wrote Canby, "he would be not Jones of Columbus, but Jones of 'Bones' or some other tight-ringed fraternity. Thanks to his ability to catch a ball, or to organize, or to be friendly, or to drink like a gentleman, or even to capitalize his charm, he was tapped as of the elect at age twenty or twenty-one, and had precisely that advantage (and no more) which rank and privilege still gave in the Old World. This code of competition in, but also very definitely for, the group brought with it other virtues, such as loyalty, tenacity, generosity, courage, and a willingness to cooperate, which made the college career, so trivial in its immediate objectives, so irrelevant to the purposes of scholarship, nobler, or at least less selfish and sordid, than the power-seeking society for which it was obviously a preparation."[45]

Nevertheless in some years (although very few), adding to the seeming arbitrariness of the election process, the traditional "line" taps did not run true: in the class of 1897, Bones had the football manager and the junior prom chair, and Keys the All-American football captain, but no one from any other of the several leadership roles discussed here was picked by any of the three societies, although all of those passed over probably lived in hope.

But that year's yield was not completely barren. The most significant election in the spring of 1896, for the future history of Yale, was that of Edward S. Harkness, a prep school graduate of St. Paul's whose father had been a silent partner of John D. Rockefeller in the founding of the Standard Oil Company, receiving for his investment 15 percent of the shares of the Standard Oil Company. When Edward's mother died in 1926, her wealth could be measured by the fact that her son had to pay the highest estate tax ever assessed to that date in the United States. Harkness was not a striver in the striving Yale mode: his highest campus recognition was service on the Class Supper Committee and in the St. Paul's Club, of which he was president his senior year. Nonetheless, rooming at the suggestion of the college dean with a future leader (and Bonesman) of his class, Henry Sloane Coffin, Harkness made warm friends and achieved membership in Psi Upsilon, and, on Tap Day, he followed his elder brother into Wolf's Head. He later was to see Yale as the one place where he had felt completely at home.

While he had enjoyed his four undergraduate years, it came to trouble Harkness that some men he knew, liked, and considered "average men" like himself had not been selected for the junior fraternities and senior societies, and were consequently excluded from what he had found to be rewarding and constructive experiences. From the family fortune, he donated in the late 1920s sixteen million dollars to Yale for the development of the residential colleges in New Haven, patterned after those of Oxford and Cambridge, in a deliberate attempt to restore to the large college classes a feeling of community, in breaking down social walls between undergraduates.[46] The magnificent donations of John Sterling and Edward Harkness to Yale, generated in no small measure by their respective senior society experiences in Skull and Bones in 1863–64 and in Wolf's Head in 1896–97, must weigh heavily in the balance against all the criticism, aggravation, and social misery that that the senior society system has generated over its history.

Harkness was not, however, the first to envision a quadrangle for deluxe housing for undergraduates in New Haven. George Douglas Miller, a Bones alumnus of 1870, had by the first decade of the twentieth century managed to acquire most of the northern blockfront on Chapel Street between High and York Steets. Filling up the aggregated parcel's center with a great earthen plateau, he planned an Oxfordesque cloister for his senior society, something close to a replica of Oxford's Magdalen College of 1474, with a truncated version of its Founder's Tower to the west. In 1911, Miller seems to have run out of money: his society ended up with a secret garden over the eastern wall and then over that garden the transported twin Gothic towers of Alumni Hall, first constructed on the Old Campus in 1853 and demolished in 1911 to make way for Wright Hall. Miller's incomplete building, its courtyard, and the rest of the property passed to Yale in 1912. The structure was finished as Weir Hall, as recorded on a bronze plaque set into a central windowsill, describing Miller's vision, and as a memorial to this two-year-old son, who had lived and died on this land. Future Yale building architects Louis Kahn, Eero Saarinen, and Philip Johnson all studied or taught there, and the Schools of Art and Architecture still return to Miller's courtyard for their professional school commencement each spring.[47]

CELEBRATION AND PURIFICATION
OF THE SYSTEM

Judge Henry Howland, a member of neither Bones nor Keys (but an honorary member of Wolf's Head, with a son elected to Bones in 1894), wrote in *Scribner's* in 1897, in language that tied the system back to Yale's notion of college democracy: "Except for the curriculum itself no force in the college is to be compared with the senior societies. Their cardinal principle in the selection of members is the recognition of character and achievement. The various activities of a college career are all recognized—literary ability, scholarship, athletic energy, the liking of many friends are all avenues to the temple of fortune. This is the highest honor which a Yale man can receive from his fellows, and because it comes from them he sets it above scholastic distinction or any titles which the faculty can confer."

All this was the result of a consciously maintained system. "The organization of effort, carried to its highest development at New Haven in athletics, debate, or the different phases of social life, which is the 'Yale Spirit' upon its tangible and mechanical side, is due in large measure to the society influences which concentrate into channels of efficiency all the diffuse and vagrant energies of the college. The system is at once the child and supporter of that vigorous democracy which endures because it recognizes the achievements of worth, and yet acknowledges no claims of birth or station."[48]

The larger Yale social system was, by this decade, an intensely hierarchical one: fraternities for freshmen, societies for sophomores, fraternities for juniors, and then the senior societies. By way of example, when the statistics for the class of 1874 were published under the heading of "Secret Societies," of 123 men, only four had "never joined any secret society; of the four, two had entered the class at the beginning of senior year [and so were ineligible for the senior societies]." "Our system of class societies," Nathan Smyth contended in his Ten Eyck prize–winning oration of 1896, "has exercised an influence hard to overestimate in strengthening and purifying that Yale spirit which we count the most precious influence that enters our college life. It is a system far in advance of that practiced in many other colleges—where the student's social standing, friends and influence are largely dependent upon fraternity elections held during the first few weeks of the college course."

Smyth's objection was instead that it was "manifestly undemocratic" that "the men chosen by the Sophmore societies shortly after Christmas of Freshman year should by that election be practically assured of a position in the much coveted societies of Senior year." It was a widely held opinion that for such elections, a sophomore society man "needs only the recommendation of only mediocre social qualifications, while the outsider must have shown especial ability in literary or athletic lines or gained exceptional popularity among his classmates," because the fifty-one men elected to the sophomore organizations (seventeen each, to Hé Boulé, Eta Phi, and Kappa Psi, respectively) "are by that election immediately raised to a position of social prominence," giving them an edge on becoming two years later among the "forty-five most prominent" in the three senior societies. Abolition was the solution: "Rid of the Sophomore society, our system if rightly managed would be well-nigh perfect."[49] An anonymous *Horoscope* editor argued in May 1898, "Over one-half of the entire number of positions in Senior societies are open only to Sophomore society men who hold offices. Count a fourth for family pulls, which in some classes is exceedingly low, and the places open to real democratic competition can be counted on your fingers, and in some years one could lose an arm and still say the same thing."

In 1900 a petition was circulated among the senior class men, calling for the abolition of the sophomore societies; signed by a majority of the class, it was forwarded to the faculty for action. When that body delayed, those societies gave out their elections at the usual time, though secretly, from the class of 1903, prolonging their influence for another year. The agitation was too widespread to die out, and ultimately the faculty abolished the sophomore societies, establishing a new schedule through which the junior societies were to be extended downward, to include sophomores, taking effect in 1902. The criticism was at last telling: in the spring 1900 elections, it was said that there were "more non-sophomore society men than usual, being taken in by the Senior societies," and in the spring 1901 election, a man reported to have "thrown down all three Sophomore societies—Pretty sandy!" was tapped for Bones.[50]

The class in general and the societies in particular saw no lack of logic in composing small clubs of men of disparate backgrounds and achievement. Yale, it was maintained, "is primarily a place where character is developed by the rubbing up of men against each other in a way that surprises men of other colleges."[51] (The *Horoscope* for May 1890 saw that as a conundrum: "The problem with the Bones men are compelled to confront is, how to unite the athletic, the literary and the studious elements in one harmonious body. The task is certainly a difficult one, for literature and athletics do not often go hand in hand, but usually are at variance.") That mix, as among the three senior societies, varied somewhat with each. The *New York Times* succinctly reported the election results in 1893: "As usual, Bones took the specialists, Keys the general society men, and Wolf's Head the good-fellowship men." Society partisans saw their experience in the tomb as superior to their educational training. Bonesman William Welch of the class of 1870, by then an internationally renowned medical educator, wrote his brother-in-law twenty years after Welch's graduation: "If a boy has no chance of Bones it makes little difference to him comparatively whether he gets to Yale or somewhere else but if he is the right sort of man for Bones then I say Yale over any other college or university in the world."[52]

The *Yale Illustrated Horoscope* for 1888 expanded these descriptions in distilling the campus appraisals. "While Keys always requires in its candidates money, tone or good fellowship, all of which are characteristics of a single class of men, Bones includes other elements in its membership, viz: prominence in athletics, scholarship, and literary ability. Bones has in reality a wider field to choose from and consequently is in a position to enroll the best fifteen in each class."

The policy of Keys, on the other hand, "is to make prominent the social element, and in this respect, as far as 'Bones' is concerned, it occupies an undisputed field. Qualities other than social are accounted of secondary importance as qualifications for membership. Its aim is to secure men of ability, where that is possible, but above all else, to secure a congenial and social crowd and one in which there can be no conflicting elements. This, and the knowledge that the wishes of the most desirable man, or as he is more familiarly know, the 'packer,' will be respected in the selection of members, render Keys more attractive to the 'popular' man and leave less of uncertainty in his mind as to whom he will have to fraternize with."

As for Wolf's Head, that society had "steadily increased its capital, influence and popularity, until now it lacks only age to acquire some of the prestige of its rivals. Its general policy has been to select the solid and as far as possible wealthy men who failed to secure an election to Bones or Keys. . . . Nearly all of [its members] have been candidates for the first two Senior societies and would have entered had there been room enough."[53]

Challenged across the class by changing perceptions of the best men, and now from below by Wolf's Head, Bones and Keys in their selection standards were gravitating toward one another. The *Horoscope*'s view almost a decade later found that the "ideals of the two and the fields of activity which each encourages by its elections show, each year, an increasing similarity. For years Bones was committed to a hard and fast policy which rewarded prominence in any line and for its own sake. In late years, however, she has shown a desire and some ability to grow out of the influence of the past, to insist that the man shall, above all, be a gentleman, capable of commanding respect, first for what he really is, and then for what he does. Keys, on the other hand, once content with men whose only title was that of 'gentleman,' has displayed with her rise in favor, a certain restlessness, new aspirations, a desire to challenge Bones in fields where formerly Bones ruled alone. The change for Bones is a natural development; for Keys it involves more of a departure from her old methods and ambitions. Thus we see both Bones and Keys standing in the same fields, bidding for almost the same men and hence brought in closer contact in the brace of a keener competition."[54]

The change was appraised by the national press as not so much a result of convergence as of overlap: *Frank Leslie's Illustrated Weekly*, in the Yale installment of its series "American Colleges and Universities," observed that "Each year 'Bones' and 'Keys' elect a number of men whom the other society would gladly take, and each chooses men whom the other society would never elect. Thus, despite differences, the two have a common ground, and on this they contend for the best men, who usually combine both requirements, and who prefer sometimes one and sometimes the other society."[55]

If their election goals were becoming more alike, however, their methods of tapping were still asymmetrical. The *Horoscope* announced in May 1887 that Keys no longer used a "packer"—"men no longer go to this society because they are friends of the man who is 'going' and taking all his friends with him"—but the competing *Yale Illustrated Horoscope* the same month identified E. C. Fellowes as the Keys packer (president of the YMCA, class deacon, and business manager of the *Yale News*). This second, competing publication was, it admitted, itself the result of a gambit for election: a small band set on being chosen for Keys "held a meeting and resolved to have their pictures published, think thereby to aid their chances." Each paid $15 for having his likeness inserted in the new annual newspaper assessing his election prospects, and printing was delayed "by our waiting for the pictures of some of the candidates." A dozen engraved portraits were printed within the columns of appraisal, and all but one of those depicted were elected. Not to be outdone, the candidates for Bones next year supplied their own portraits.

Rumors of society preference before Tap Day could apparently be damaging. When Dr. William Welch heard that his nephew Frederic Collin Walcott (later a United States senator from Connecticut for two decades) might prefer Scroll and Key over Skull and Bones in the May 1890 tap, he hurried off a worried letter to his sister, the boy's mother, saying that the rumor must be scotched if it were untrue—and he did hope it was untrue. "I of course cannot judge of the special conditions which may prevail in his class, still I feel very strongly in the matter and shall be disappointed if Fred gives up his chances for Bones. . . . I have known many in his position who have never regretted choosing Bones even when some of their best friends went the other way." He also wrote the boy on the subject: "I am afraid I gave Fred more information as to the chances of his election than I ought to have done, but from all I can learn he is universally regarded as a sure man and I wanted to brace him up all I could, but I have no fear that he will not be prudent as to what I wrote him, and of course it was not as if I were writing to a comparative stranger, but rather as a father might to his son." Fred went Bones.[56]

Keys was now thought by the *Horoscope* editor to be equaling Bones in prestige, or even surpassing it, with the "Marble Palace on College Street . . . a rival of the Granite Mosque on High. It was thought strange when [Chauncey] Goodrich [the Dwight Hall director] refused an election to Bones in 1885, but when [James Gamble] Rogers [manager of baseball and future architect of much of Yale's twentieth-century campus] and [Henry] Mosle [captain and coach of his class crew and Junior Prom committee member] refused their election last year and took Keys instead, the real turning point was reached." New York newspapers reported the Rogers and Mosle refusals. Bones, it was suggested, would have to "follow Keys example in pledging her men beforehand." Goodrich seems to have been the first collegian to be noted in campus publications for turning down an election: beforehand, "a report [was] rife to the effect that he will refuse all societies [which he did]. If true, he is one in a thousand and worthy of admiration."[57]

A Hartford newspaper in 1892 advised its readers that "no one was ever known to lose an election to a senior society because he happened to be ill or absent from New Haven at the time the elections were given out. Members of the societies have traveled to New York and Hartford to carry out the announcement of elections and the cable has been used to send the announcement to a student abroad at the time that men were being 'tapped' at the campus."

The Wolf's Head elections from 1885 through 1888 were given out the week following the traditional Tap Day, but by 1889 all three societies were electing in the same Thursday afternoon in late May, as the *New York Times* noted that year in its annual article on the men elected, and those chosen were listed in the *Lit.* feature in the order of the respective societies' ages. In 1890, the names of four men declining Wolf's Head offers were duly recorded; another in 1892; in 1896, two more; and in 1900, one other. In June 1900, the astute reader, by comparing lists, could learn that two men refusing Bones, a football tackle and a prominent Glee Club man, went instead to Keys, and two of four who declined Wolf's Head joined Bones. Four years later, a Bones choice went to Keys, and a Wolf's Head preference joined Bones instead. In 1905, three men refused election to Keys and were subsequently chosen by Bones; in 1908, three men who turned down Wolf's Head, and the passed-over son of the vice president of the United States, were all elected to the recently founded Elihu Club.[58]

Tap Day for the class of 1902 saw the biggest miscarriage, in the eyes of the college, of this era's elections. Charles Gould, football captain and manager of the track team, was passed over by all three societies (he was the real-life counterpart for the fictional football captain Dudley similarly passed over in *Stover at Yale*). Shocked by this seeming injustice, four hundred men packed around him, twenty deep, and the crowd's sentiment for the slighted athlete was signified by "a number of long cheers," eighteen by count, "with his name at the end, which were given with force and feeling," the *Yale Alumni Weekly* reported. "The demonstration, as far as is recalled, is without precedent." The *New York Herald*, titling its report "Yale Man Slurred by Senior Societies" and noting that Gould's three predecessors as football captain had all been tapped by Keys, attributed the disrespectful action in Gould's not having been a member of any of the sophomore societies. Of the forty-five men elected that year, according to the *Hartford Courant*, fully thirty-four had been members of the sophomore societies.

Four days after the elections an anonymous pamphlet appeared, titled *After Tap Day*, the first such since the flurry of anonymous pamphlets of the early 1870s that began with the *Iconoclast*. This publication reaffirmed the college's expected standards, pronouncing the lesson: "It means that Yale senior societies, which ought and are supposed to be above meanness and pettiness, are unwilling to take men who refuse to toady to them. . . . It means that Bones no longer has taken the best men, that Keys has degenerated even from what it used to be, that Wolf's Head no longer accepts men of literary ability and debaters, but confines itself to hangers on, men who are not quite good enough to make the others. . . . Either the Senior societies should come out openly and admit that they do not take men for what they have done, but rather for what they are in a social way, or they should be compelled to recognize merit." [59]

A happier example of the system at its best was the election by Bones in May 1903 of Frederick Erastus Pierce, who had labored six years on his father's farm before entering Yale, where he worked his way through waiting tables and "shaking down" furnaces. Meanwhile, as a freshman, he won the McLaughlin Prize for the best English essay, the Berkeley Premium for excellence in Latin, the Woolsey Scholarship for the best examination in Latin, and tied with a classmate for first place in mathematics; as a sophomore, the mathematics prize; and as a junior, the *Yale Lit.* medal, followed by election to the magazine's board of editors for his prodigious output, then garnering a tie for the Curtis Prize in literary and rhetorical excellence, and taking third place in the Ten Eyck junior exhibition speech competition (as a senior, he was to win the DeForest Prize). He was slapped by Albert Lamb, the chairman of the *Yale News* and the last man tapped by Bones the previous year. [60]

Unnoted among those passed over whose names were highlighted in the several newspaper reports was William Pickens, the "Yale colored phenomenon" from Little Rock, Arkansas, who had actually triumphed just a few weeks before senior society elections in the Ten Eyck contest where Pierce had finished third; with Pierce, he ranked as one of the thirteen men with the highest stand Philosophical Oration appointments. [61]

Neither Pierce nor Pickens is mentioned as a likely senior society candidate by any of the four competing but identically titled *Horoscopes* which were published in spring 1903. The vaunted Yale democracy in action, which could astonish the college by the election of a poor white scholar and prize-winning orator like Pierce, who could not afford to join any underclass society, was not yet ready to do the same for an outstanding black man who was also a scholar and prize-winning orator.

Another football captain was to be passed over by all the societies in 1905, but that was a moral judgment: Tom Shevlin, with a "Y" in three sports, was also a baseball outfielder and the intercollegiate champion hammer thrower, but was known as well for speeding over Connecticut highways in his roadster, "mainly followed by public prosecutors," and he was finally doomed by his pronounced indifference to public opinion.[62]

After election of the "sure men," public opinion noted anomalies, with elections perceived as biased by a preference for wealth, or biased against wealth to correct the first preference, or biased against a worthy campus activity whose adherents could not gain an election foothold. There were the "so-called surprises, either of inclusion or omission." Although Keys was characterized as a rich man's club, electing Vanderbilts in 1892 and 1894, something Bones did not do until 1899, and which Wolf's Head paralleled in 1902, that society, noted the *Horoscope* for May 1890, "always wants one man to keep up the appearance of Yale democracy and [this candidate] is just the one to collect the weekly dues and be relieved from payment himself."[63]

And Skull and Bones, like Scroll and Key, was accused of tokenism for the perception of balance: "She is now accustomed purely for the sake of tradition to elect one man who is pre-eminent for brains and poverty."[64] Furthermore, Bones was seen as erratic or quixotic in some choices, with their occasional but almost traditional "dark horses": "Bones has a little trick of slapping the surprise. . . . As examples of this, we given Buchanan, '89, Morse, '90, and Kenerson, '91, none of whom were even mentioned for election." These examples nonetheless gave unexceptional collegians some hope. Still, the window was small: as one character remarks to another in Meade Minnigerode's novel *The Big Year*, about his class of 1910: "Barring some extraordinary slip-up, there aren't more than one or two doubtful places in either Bones, Keys, or Wolf's Head." Yet even those surprises seemed to grow in stature with their elections. "It is the consensus of college opinion," reported the *New York Sun*, "that these same unexpectedly elected men have a way of proving their qualifications during their senior year and that they are usually possessed of personality and charm which has not hitherto been generally recognized."[65]

What outside observers could only half know were two features of senior society life which, *after* the strained competition of the annual election, made those tapped into the system, including the "surprises," eternally grateful for their inclusion: the spring day's external confirmation of undergraduate success, and the subsequent year's internal benefits of fellowship.

As had happened two decades before with baseball in the criticism of the *Iconoclast*, Bones, seen as having an inherent duty to reward athletic prowess in all Yale's major sports, was criticized for the sin of omission regarding track. "Bones has also brought such ruin on the Mott Haven team, by not recognizing its prominent members, that today Alec. Coxe's band of winners has degenerated into a howling mob of Freshman, a handful of enthusiastic Sophmores, three or four ordinary Juniors, and one or two Seniors, whose aim is not the glory of their Alma Mater, but one or two trumpery medals and a possible election to the New York Athletic Club." Whether the society heeded this counsel or not, track captain (and DKE Custos) Alfred Henry Jones was elected to Bones the following year. As the *Yale Alumni Weekly* noted, the senior societies had "a responsibility which their own self-preservation forces them to meet. Undergraduate ideals insensibly change from decade to decade regardless of outside efforts to maintain old standards. With this change shifts also the attitude toward possible candidates for social honors of the societies themselves."[66]

In the eyes of some observers, an election was valued above all else in Yale College, as can be teased out from the convoluted observation of the *Illustrated Horoscope* in 1891 that "aside from such trivial considerations as character formed, a latent talent developed, or an education acquired, a Senior Society election has come to be the *summum bonum* of our college course." In the eyes of others, it was a spur to further achievement. Another *Horoscope* editor observed the following year about Bones in particular, "It seems to have a good influence on a man to get into this society, and he, becoming involved with its ambitions and spirit works with renewed energy and eventually adds another name to her roll of honor." "The System," opined a third editor, in the *Horoscope* for May 1897, "gathers from the mysticism that envelopes it, the history that strengthens it and the general uprightness of its policy a grip on Yale life such as no Debating Union, Fraternity Chapter or Y.M.C.A. could ever hope to establish."

The outsider and Princetonian Edmund Wilson noted that "The senior societies, whatever their effect on those who are taken into them, have at least succeeded in collaborating rigorously in an ideal of a certain dignity—for these organizations, through their proceedings, have evidently rather an inspirational and intellectual character and arouse an almost religious veneration on the part of those who are elected to them."

A national newspaper's report in 1893 perceptively noted how the advantages of senior society life could inspire a new member to even greater effort and distinction: "The junior fortunate enough to enter, finds himself in an organization almost perfect of its kind. He is in a building comfortably, even luxuriously, fitted, surrounded by trophies reminding him of great men and great actions; breathing an atmosphere of tradition, the fruit of quaint and noble thought; cultivated in thought and expression, especially in 'Keys' and 'Bones' by a vigorous literary discipline; and stimulated to increased efforts for the college by the example of his predecessors. These possessions and the life among them are cloaked from the outside with a mantle of impenetrable secrecy assured and enforced by practice of harmless poppycock."[67]

THE SETTLED RITUALS—INTO THE UNKNOWN

In some significant respects, "poppycock" had diminished. But it was the "old" (circa 1875) tradition of the open-air tap that continued to stir controversy: it was a system in which "the maximum amount of chagrin is inflicted upon the largest possible number of students," as described in his twenty-year reunion book for the class of 1899 by Chauncey Brewster Tinker, first Sterling Professor of English but never a senior society man.[68]

The problem was wel framed in the *Yale Alumni Weekly* of May 27, 1903: "The one thing desired by the largest number [of society and non-society men] is the elimination of the show feature—the presence of a large 'gallery' of men and women and girls, as well as of students. But to eliminate this feature and still to bring the whole class together at one time and one place, to be taken or left, to accept or to refuse, is considered an impossibility." An unidentified pre-1875 "Graduate" in a letter to the editor printed in the same issue was to point out that changing the much-maligned Tap Day procedure would be, in essence, the reform of a reform. "It seems to be taken for granted, that if elections were given out privately their objectionable features would be removed, but it should be remembered that just this private system was used a generation ago and was repudiated by the college public as undemocratic and promotive of trickery and favoritism."

The elections had historically been manifested in a variety of patterns, the correspondent recounted, being "given out at one time in Chapel after morning prayers; at another time on Campus at midnight, and later down to the seventies, when the present system began, they were given out at twilight at the students' rooms, in a manner to excite the least possible attention." The candidates themselves, he argued, "put an end to this system by persistently herding together at the old fence and forcing the societies to seek them out in the presence of student witnesses. Though their reasons for so doing were never formulated, it seemed to be a wish to proclaim to the College that they had no knowledge of their chances of election, and that the rumors, which in those days were rife before every election of bargains and combinations, by which one society attempted to get the advantage of another, were without foundation." To criticize the senior societies at the beginning of a new century for running a system "not of their own choosing, but forced on them to their considerable inconvenience," was not quite fair. "If publicity is the price of fairness, let us by all means have publicity even at the expense of the feelings of the candidates."[69] To suggest reforms, the Russell Trust Association in the early 1900s named a committee of local Bones alumni, composed of Yale Law School professor Simeon Baldwin, professor of Greek Bernadotte Perrin, professor of Political Economy John Schwab, university secretary Anson Phelps Stokes, and Yale College dean Henry Wright, but these solons could not devise a practical system free from the objections sought to be eliminated.

The senior society elections on a late Thursday afternoon in May (generally, the last Thursday) were the culmination of "society week" at Yale. On the evening of the preceding Monday, the various classes of the college met at the fence, and shouting the songs of the old sophomore societies to recall their extinguishment, marched about the campus and cheered each dormitory in turn. On Tuesday evening, the Old Campus elms were illuminated with the flare of calcium lights, the glare of colored fires, and the flash of Roman candles, and the walls re-echoed with the songs of the junior societies, Psi Upsilon and Delta Kappa Epsilon, while their members, grotesquely garbed as white or black friars, conferred elections upon their successors, whose names were printed in the Wednesday *Yale News*.

On the night before Tap Day, each junior fraternity—Alpha Delta Phi, Psi Upsilon, Delta Kappa Epsilon, Zeta Psi, and Beta Theta Pi—held a farewell dinner to which junior members only were admitted. Under the system prevailing then, twelve men were elected to each junior fraternity in the fall of the sophomore year. Those a week later chose eight more, and in the following spring, those twenty would elect five to eight additional brothers. Then, four or five more were picked up during junior year itself, for a total membership in each of thirty to thirty-five, for a grand total of 150 to 170 in a class which varied from 300 to 325 seniors in this era. The result was that before the end of his penultimate class year at Yale, almost any collegian who had really made good by achievement or personal qualities or could by any means afford it, probably would have "made a frat." At their farewell dinner, knowing that only sixty would be tapped by the seniors the next afternoon, the strain of nerve-racked "possibility" was relieved by conspicuous consumption of alcohol. "The result is a gloriously uproarious party in which Keys possibilities slap Bones prospectives hilariously on the back and roll off to observe the time-honored custom of breaking into the other four fraternity houses."[70]

The student body was thus in a heightened state for the main event on Thursday, after the last afternoon session of class recitations. On that day, there was little mingling between the classes of juniors and seniors most concerned. Juniors stayed by themselves, and indeed kept off the campus as much as possible, while the senior society men, who were not usually seen together, walked to recitations in groups of three or four, or passed the time lounging in front of Vanderbilt Hall, where they were unlikely to meet their friends from the class below. "Everything else in college is given up on this day, in order that nothing may interfere with the solemnity of the occasion" reported the *New York Sun* in an 1894 article cheekily titled "It Is Touch and Go at Yale." "There is no athletic training, no crew or baseball practice, nothing to keep the crowd away from the uneasy juniors." During the very hour of society elections on May 25, 1899, the Yale Corporation was voting on a new president for the university, and the result only became known when trustee Chauncey Depew was seen standing on the edge of the crowd observing the student ceremony; when asked, he said, "Yes, we elected Hadley." This news, which all Yale had been anxiously awaiting, had been lost amid the excitement of election to the senior societies.

That public gathering in the northeast corner of the Old Campus was now a great public ritual, and a settled one: the *Yale News*, while reporting only the names of those elected, always wrote annually that it was done "according to the usual custom." Most of the spectators were juniors, but there were seniors, too, and not a few underclassmen, while the graduate members of the three societies were looking about eagerly, getting ready to help the men who were to tap in locating the desired juniors and making way through the crowd. "It might be called," noted one newspaper reporter, "the annual meeting of the societies, for this is the one day of the year when they appear in a body in public, and in selecting their successors render an account of themselves which the college may either commend or condemn." While still not commonly called "Tap Day"—the first use of "taps" for the action of the "coveted slap" appeared in the *New York Times* in 1887 and on the Yale campus in the *Horoscope* for April 1889, and the capitalized "Tap-Day" first appears in the *Horoscope* for May 1892—the choreography on the third Thursday in May for the "circus in front of Durfee" was fixed, to commence with the ringing of the first chimes of the five o'clock chapel bell, and the *Illustrated Horoscope* for the same election said to all the college, "Don't fail to bring your fair [female] friends, if you have any, and show them a characteristic feature of Yale life."

Spectators looked out from the windows of the nearest dormitories, Durfee and Farnam and North College, or stood on the steps of Dwight and Alumni Halls, or sat in carriages and, in one or two cases by 1905, automobiles whose occupants (in a prefiguring of football game tailgating) followed the election events with teas, while "the gallery had its usual proportion of mothers, sisters, cousins, and other people's sisters." The satirical verse of Brian Hooker of the class of 1902, titled "Dirty Durfee," celebrated that dormitory's vantage point:

> There's a place on the Campus, I weel ken its name,
> And the brawest o' view may be had frae the same—
> Gin there's onything doing ye're wishful to see,
> Why, it's up wi' the windows o' dirty Durfee!
> There's a braw time on Tap-Day, when down by the fence,

A' the Juniors gang buggy, and sweat most immense—
When ilka Keys heeler has jumps like a flea,
Then it's up wi' the windows o' dirty Durfee![71]

James Donnelly, the (only) campus policeman, hired in 1893, advised
fascinated onlookers of the latest campus odds-making. From the spring
of 1902 onward, President Hadley, the first senior society graduate
member to be elevated to the university presidency since the beginning
of publicly viewed elections, and other faculty members and their wives
watched the spectacle from the balcony over the entrance to Dwight
Hall. Mory's filled up with graduates come up from New York City for
the event, and the roadways around the Old Campus were lined with
hacks used by the visitors. An 1895 newspaper report about elections that
spring opined that "It would be impossible in any other community. It
could not be originated, even on the Yale campus, in this day of realism;
but it persists and gains in vigor and importance as the years go by." To
the freshmen seeing it for the first time, it had "the same element of the
inexplicable that a heathen's rite possesses for the traveler."

Welch and Camp (graduate members, respectively, of Keys and
Bones) provided an extended description in their 1899 book on Yale.
Admitting in their chapter titled "Tap Day and the Society System" that
"from the point of view of Yale welfare, the custom is either applauded
as one consistent with the best traditions of the place, or tolerated as the
only known expedient for a peculiar occasion, or condemned as undignified and inhuman," they painted a word picture of "a custom as peculiar
as any in all the life of the campus." Speaking to none, the men of Keys
entered the campus one by one through the western Elm Street gate, the
Wolf's Head members by the Battell Chapel gate between Durfee and
the Chapel (styled by the college the "Pass of Thermopylae," in remembrance of a faculty-banned ceremony where the freshmen had to run a
gauntlet between massed upperclassmen), and the Bones seniors from
High Street by Dwight Hall, going straight toward the quietly waiting
crowd of juniors, who held themselves still near the oak just inside the

fence and opposite the Pass and in front of Durfee, where the juniors now lived, awaiting events and hoping for the slap between the shoulders.

"[B]eginning at five o'clock and at intervals of from two to four minutes," their description continued, "each of those members emerges from his society hall, and proceeds to the campus, walking alone, recognizing no one. With solemn face he invades the densest part of the crowd, where the most likely of the candidates from the Junior Class are gathered; finds the one particular man whose election to that particular society has been delegated to that particular Senior; slaps that particular man on his back; tells him at the same time to go to his room; follows that man through the crowd and across the campus to his room, wherever it may be, preserving still the same unbroken silence and grave countenance; announces within the seclusion of that room, the formal election; leaves the room, the dormitory, and the campus, in the same manner and with the same demeanor, and returns to his society hall, not again to emerge until the formal breaking up of the regular gathering of that Thursday evening. As to the man himself, who has received this election, he usually returns to the campus and to his friends, to receive their congratulations, and to talk it all over, and to compare lists, and to ask whether Jim has gone here or Jack has gone there,—to be happy with this man and sad with that."[72]

Tap Day "slaps" were no mild affairs. "They fall with a sickening thud and with the whole force of a young Hercules behind them." The grim visages of the society representatives bespoke the seriousness of the occasion. Said the *New-York Tribune* in 1896: "He may be the jolliest fellow in college, but now he makes his way toward the crowd with set and melancholy visage, which in hardly any instance relaxes into a smile, even in spite of loudly uttered jests which cause the assembled students to roar with laughter." The societies' seniors came "rapidly, each wandering around in the crowd with apparent inability to find the eager fellow who is pressing himself almost into the searcher's path, as when one plays at hide-and-seek with a child."

It was later said the society electors' attire of black suits and derbies was not putting on "side," and not originally part of the ceremonial, but a convenience, to enable a junior to spot a senior. In 1898, it took the last Wolf's Head elector, searching through the scrum, fifteen minutes to find his man, and in 1915, Archibald MacLeish for Bones could not locate his candidate for ten minutes, to the great amusement of the crowd. Some of the more energetic of the onlookers climbed up into the oak tree's lower branches, where they could look straight down at the crowd, and when the spectators, seeing a distant slap or hearing "Go to your room!," would cry out "Who is it?," somebody, usually one of the men up a tree, would answer. Other high vantage points were the top rail of the fence, and even an electric light pole. In 1911, a small boy fell from a tree branch into the arms of the campus policeman below, to a "subdued cheer" from the crowd.

Skull and Bones, by custom and its rivals' deference, usually slapped the very first man, although in May 1909, the Wolf's Head electors started before the chapel bell struck five and claimed the initial choices. Scroll and Key's persistent habit of pledging candidates before Tap Day sometimes accelerated completion of its choices: in 1908, all of its members were taken in within fifteen minutes, while it took Bones and Wolf's Head both an hour longer. In spring 1906, the pace literally picked up. In a number of cases the candidates were not satisfied with the spirited walk to their rooms, but cantered in that direction. The query was raised on campus as to whether this variation of the old custom was by special request of the elector or whether it was more or less involuntary and reactionary on the part of the elected. In one case the successful candidate was halfway across the campus, then stopped and looked back anxiously, to see if the man giving the election was following, or had changed his mind.

The close massing of the students under the historic oak complicated the tappers' efforts, and refusals added to the confusion (1907 saw seven). In the milling of the crowd and the high tension of the most involved participants, it is remarkable that mistakes did not occur more frequently. In the election of May 1897, Curtenius Gillette of Bones tapped Lewis Williams and started him to his dormitory, but suspecting he had blundered, asked the candidate's name before the two had cleared the crowd's outskirts, and then with an apology retracted the invitation. Distraught but helped by two friends, Williams went off to his room to recover, then returned to the campus and received an election to Wolf's Head.

The *Hartford Courant* used this example to run an editorial attacking the publicity of the election process, calling it a "refined cruelty," and suggesting that the faculty "abolish . . . this whole heartless exhibition." The *Courant* editorial was significant, as the editor of the paper, Charles Clark, was a Bones man of prominence, to be elected in 1910 to the Yale Corporation, who himself had been elected privately in his room in 1870, before Tap Day became a campus spectacle. Equally if not more embarrassing to Bones, basketball captain Walter Logan in May 1910 tapped Meade Robinson, who to Logan's consternation stood still when slapped, because he had previously been struck and then elected by Keys in his room and had returned to the campus to accept the congratulations of his friends.[73]

The tapping of some men chosen early in the sequence and of the last two men was always greeted by loud cheers. Others, passed over, sometimes fainted, or worse: "Men have been known to break down completely and cry like women when the forty-fifth man has been selected and they have been passed." When Walter Hoyt, the president of the Gun Club Team, received a tap from Skull and Bones in 1895, "the tears rolled down his cheeks, and for several minutes he was unable to speak," which one newspaper report attributed to his realizing that, by having made a pledge to Keys, "he saw that he had thrown away his chance to go" to Bones, while another newspaper more charitably attributed his reaction to "how intense the feeling is at such a time." In the following spring's election, Thomas Clarke fainted when he received his slap from a Wolf's Head member, and was taken to his room to be attended by a physician, where the society's delegate again found him, revived, and offered formal election.

There was even, one year, a form of group therapy. A number of men who had failed of election in 1907 formed a little circle and began to sing. "As harmony the performance was not a great success. The singers did not have very steady voices, but the men stuck at it and went off the Campus together singing familiar College Songs." The *Alumni Weekly* noted editorially that, to minimize the humiliation, possibly it was time for a "declaration of independence by the eligible . . . to betake themselves to the privacy of their rooms on the fateful day and there await a possible notice of election." No one was to have the courage for such a recusal. The emotion could flow both ways: a local newspaper reported that several "'lucky men' who had received elections in 1899 met at their boarding house and cried . . . not for themselves . . . but because the dearest friend of several of them had not been chosen."[74]

The men who were first touched by Bones and Keys were those that were regarded as doubtful by the societies. If both of them wanted a man and neither knew which he preferred, the doubtful man was likely to be the first tapped (and "there was always considerable betting attached to the priority"). By 1898, a New Haven newspaper declared that "The last man chosen for each society is considered to be the honor man of the society. The first man taken is the second honor man." The practice was well enough known to inspire the title of a short story appearing in *Gunter's Magazine* for September 1906, "The Last Man Tapped, a Tale of the New Haven Campus." Because on account of refusals Wolf's Head sometimes had trouble in filling its complement of fifteen, it became the custom for Wolf's Head to tap the very last man.

In his 1909 novel *Jack Hall at Yale*, Walter Camp added another, comparative detail: "the man who gives the election wears a dark suit and a black derby hat, while the men who are awaiting election are many of them hatless and none of them dressed in their best." The derbies were said to be "shoved down to their eyes in approved fashion." There was a tradition at one time that if a junior wore black shoes, a stand-up collar, and a derby, he was "heeling" (trying out for) Bones, but if he wore a soft shirt, brown boots, and a derby, he was heeling Keys.[75]

Although refusals were infrequent, they were possible, so keeping a running account of successful offers was vital to the societies seeking to reach the mystic number of fifteen. The first and second entries of Durfee Hall were occupied during the election hour by graduate members. Bones alumni, occupying the first entry, kept to themselves, while the Keys graduates in the second took up positions on the front steps, where the messengers would come up to a man with the ledger, giving him a slip of paper, and then dash back into the crowd.

Some students stood around holding what were styled "dope sheets," based on campus rumors and the traditional tendencies of the different societies, and could be seen checking off the elections as fast as the men were tapped. "Dope," according to a contemporaneous newspaper report, was then recent college slang, meaning information of any kind on activities, or schedules, or things in general, but by early May in New Haven it meant the latest chances for election. "Many a man in the junior class had his 'dope sheet'—carried concealed on his person, to be glanced at surreptitiously during recitations, or slid under the papers in the top drawer of his desk, where he can draw it out a night to compare it with those of his classmates."

"Dope" changed from day to day. "The final lists that appear on Tap Day, copied in ink, from the original manuscripts now illegible from much erasure, usually contain, out of forty-five men, from twenty to forty names correctly placed." A dope sheet from the class of 1912 lists eighteen prospects for Bones (eleven borne out), twenty for Keys (of whom two went to Bones), and ten for Wolf's Head. The "official list" against which the student ones were said to be compared was made up by the suit-pressing "Rosey" of the tailor shop Arthur Rosenberg's who, from knowing not only his affluent customers but their friends, and from many years' intensive study of Tap Day results, had developed an almost uncanny technique in picking winners, and bet on the results. Fittingly, Rosey was to die on the morning of Tap Day in 1951, at age 63.[76]

The second great ritual which thrilled the campus was initiation, on the Tuesday following the Thursday of election, although not much could actually be seen or even divined from outside the halls. These ceremonies of course remained forbidden to all but the initiated, although after a chimney fire at the Bones tomb in 1909, the fire marshal reported to the *New Haven Journal-Courier* that he had now been in every Yale secret society house in the city and might be considered "a 'member' persona non grata." That society's tradition forbade communication with their selected candidates from their being tapped until they became full members of the society. Even on the athletic field they communicated with them, before initiation, by means of a third party, and this, said the *New York Sun*, "is another one of those secret things which are so impressive to Yale men."

On the night of initiation, at the Bones tomb, at intervals of about twelve minutes, a hand and bare forearm reached out slowly through the open iron doors, grabbed the candidate by his left shoulder, and fairly yanked him into the building—"pulling them into Bones," the college called it. "From then until the following day," the *Buffalo Courier* was to report, "he is put through the severest course of sprouts he will ever have to endure, if any reliance can be placed on the many rumors of the treatment received. One thing is certain, that although no wine is drunk, the men appear next day in a more dilapidated condition than the 'Keys' or Wolf's Head men." The most unique Bones initiation was for a member of the class of 1926: he underwent an appendectomy imme-diately after Tap Day, and since he was unable to attend the ceremony in the tomb, his appendix was carried in a bottle through the ritual. At Keys, the initiates passed in one by one, in groups of five. After 1904 at the new Elihu Club in the Heaton House at 245 York Street, not yet occupying the historic "Tory Tavern" which became their permanent home facing the Green on Elm Street, the men went up the steps, one by one, in dinner jackets, rang the bell, and entered.[77]

The third great ritual, or rather set of them, concerned the weekly meetings. These were exactly timed by observers: the Thursday night meeting of Bones lasted from about eight P.M. until one o'clock in the morning, and that of Keys until twenty-five minutes to one. "At this exact moment the Keys men emerge silently from their hall, and after securely locking the door, burst in chorus with the beautiful song, 'Gaily the Troubadour,' which wells out distinctly on the silent night. After singing this they form two by two and march to the campus, slapping the left foot on the pavement at each step. You can always find a crowd of awed under-classmen watching their performance from the opposite side of the street, and it never fails to take place at exactly twenty-five minutes of one." The Keys regulations on meeting hours also became known in the trial of a member charged with assaulting a policeman a little before midnight, a charge defending against by a fellow member's testimony that the accused student was in his society hall at the time, that under the rules all Keys men had to be there from 6:30 P.M. until 12:30 A.M., and that no one could leave the building in the interval unless accompanied by another member.

To sing their anthem, in three stanzas, the men of Keys lined up at the top of the stairs which fronted their building, "biting off the ends of the lines, and then the chorus in harmony, with the tenors high up, thrilling in the night . . . Then usually someone in one of the Scientific School fraternity houses across the street would start an alarm clock going outside his window—but at that it was difficult to spoil the effect of the song." On a still night, the regular stamp, stamp of the procession could be heard a long distance, and as they approached the campus, the march was quickened, the regularity of the stamp was lost, and finally the men broke and ran to their rooms.

Five minutes after the Keys performance began at 12:31 A.M., Wolf's Head would come swinging by on their way back from their Prospect Street hall, although they never tramped or made other demonstration as they marched. On the last Thursday before Tap Day, almost the whole junior class used to go to watch Keys "come out," and then there was time to rush breathlessly up to Wolf's Head and see them lining up outside their big gates. Thereafter, often, the juniors would line up and follow that society's members home, but those men spoke further to no one that evening. On Sunday afternoons, the members of all three societies were seen to wander off in twos and threes, headed for their respective halls.

Another custom was accompanying home members in training for
the athletic teams at ten o'clock on their meeting nights, since "under
no circumstances does a foot-ball, base-ball, or crew man stay up after
ten." Two clubmates attended each athlete to his dormitory room: "the
Bones men take their athletes home, undress them, put them to bed,
and after whispering some mysterious words in their ears, march silently
back to their hall. The Keys men do the same thing except that each of
the two marches on each side of the athlete with a great brass key over
his shoulder."[78] This practice, tending to degenerate into farce, ended
about 1912.

The structure and contents of the societies' meetings remained a
mystery to outsiders. Sometimes, the topics for discussion were prosaic,
albeit with flourished delivery: Cole Porter delivered an essay to his
Keys delegation in January 1913 about the opening of the Taft Hotel,
titled "The New Hotel of America," but it was filled with alliteration,
syncopation, plays on words, puns, and rhymes. The atmosphere inside
the tombs was probably well captured by Phelps Putnam, a member of
the Bones club of 1916, in his poem "To The Memory of Yale College," with its hidden pun on the Bones name for undergraduate members in the third line:

> There underneath the elms were large delights
> Beyond the rotten touch of circumstance,
> And there for us the ribaldry of nights
> When the bright harlot, thought, came out to dance.
> A broken lamp swaying in scarves of smoke
> Toward sprawling bodies in the firelight:
> Fred murmured, "Some would say that God's a joke";
> And Charlie shouted, "Spare my God to-night";
> Bill said, "That bright illusion of the soul";
> And I, "You mean illusion of the flesh"—
> The adolescent words began to roll
> So close that light was taken in their mesh.[79]

Fourthly, the badges, of course, were still sported during the school year, even if more discreetly than formerly. "One of the deep mysteries of the Bones," reported a New York City newspaper in 1896, "is the wearing by one of the fifteen men for a half-year, and by another for the second half-year, of two pins overlapping each other." Society badges, the article continued, might very rarely be seen, "though not in New Haven, adorning a pretty girl; but these trinkets are probably in every case the property of graduates of a few years' standing." They were also worn by the African American janitors of the respective halls; when Robert Parks, the second Bones servant, died in the fall of 1895, many newspapers at the time asserted that he was an initiated member of the Skull and Bones Society, entitled to wear the badge. By 1908, the men of Bones were wearing their badges concealed on their undershirts, which perhaps was not very secret. "One should not," Donald Ogden Stewart of the class of 1916 was to write in his autobiography, "allow one's superiority to show: just as the Bones pin was always worn on the undershirt, instead of flaunting it immodestly; I knew it was there, and took it for granted that others would find out about it and be properly impressed."[80]

The fifth senior society activity to attract, if not court, public notice was the mounting of annual conventions held during the week of Yale graduation festivities, where the notable graduate attendees had their names published in the New Haven and New York newspapers. Scroll and Key created an officer in 1874 to represent his delegation after graduation and "to strengthen in general their connection with the society and with each other," preparing a yearly circular letter and organizing an annual reunion of his class year's members. Keys' fiftieth anniversary celebration, held during commencement week in 1892, is said to have attracted nearly half the living members of the society (including, from 1842, founding members Runyon, Kingsley, and Keasbey).

Featured in the four-day celebration, as permitted by university president and Bones graduate Timothy Dwight, was the Sunday sermon in Battell Chapel preached by Keys graduate and Yale Corporation member Rev. Joseph Twichell, titled "The Value of Social Life at Yale."

This very public celebration of the joys of society membership, called by the *New-York Tribune* "an eloquent and admirable expression which the society exercises upon those who belong to it and upon the college world," expressed Twichell's firm conviction that "a very great many of the students of this college, who have been no idlers here, who have done their work well, have found here and carried away with them, as the distinct fruit of the social conditions and participations of the place—in their general, and in their particular aspects—a qualification, a furnishing, for a successful, serviceable, beneficent career in the world, to be reckoned not inferior to any element of benefit besides which they here received."[81]

As for Skull and Bones, the convention at the time of Yale's bicentennial celebrations in 1901 was the largest in the Russell Trust Association's history, and alumni visited often. The doubling of the area of the Bones tomb was in part to provide small rooms where graduated clubs returning to Russell Trust Association conventions could find comfortable seclusion in which to retire, for gathering up the threads of their life histories since the last separation. Bones alumnus and Cornell president Andrew Dickson White, in the course of refusing a contribution to his fraternity Psi U because of its dissipated ways, causing him an "utter lack of confidence" in his former junior fraternity, further noted that "On visits to Yale I return with the greatest pleasure to my Senior Club, which still retains its records, its proper way of conducting its exercises and a proper sense of what is due itself and its visitors."[82]

Sixthly, there were the speculations and the legends: "a man, an outsider, had gotten into Bones once, and had *never been seen* again," recorded Meade Minnigerode, whose 1921 novel *The Big Year* was dedicated to his class of 1910 (where he was a member of the Elihu Club and a Whiffenpoof who was to help adapt Kipling's poem "Gentlemen-Rankers" into the Whiffenpoof Song). The candid autobiography which Bonesmen told each other was alleged to be given while the member was lying in a coffin. "Again, what did anybody know about the 'sixteenth man in Keys,' the man whose election was never announced! And so on endlessly through the improbabilities of legendary lore."

When an iron-doored vault was being constructed at the rear of the Bones tomb in 1908, a local newspaper reported that "the underground apartment was nothing less than a bombproof cavern for retreat in case of a war with Japan, a sudden cyclone or a bad thunderstorm." A newspaper article by a Harvard man published in 1912 claimed that each member of Bones "has an actual skull-and-crossbones over the entrance-door to his room." More darkly, faint wailings escaping from the sandstone blocks on High Street were said to come from the "Bones whore," needed to make men of its members. After World War II, it was told that Hitler's silverware was in the archives of Wolf's Head or, others said, Scroll and Key.

A satirical story of 1913 titled *Stover in Bones* noted how non-society members would give a small personal article to a society man before his Thursday night meeting to be taken into the tomb, to expose it "to the hallowed atmosphere" before being returned to its owner, "who thereafter counts it among his most precious possessions. The cheerful generosity with which Society men always do this is a comforting proof of the all-pervading character of Yale democracy." In an article on Tap Day in *Time* in 1926, the magazine reported rumors that "fabulous treasures and curiosities are stored within the various cryptic walls, brought there by brethren from high office or daring adventures—the original Declaration of Independence, the very skull of Napoleon, a wolf shot by Buffalo Bill, a key to the main gate of the Vatican." In a 1929 *Harper's Monthly* article were mentioned "fantastic stories of huge endowments funds which can be used, if necessary, to provide fifty-thousand-dollar-a-year incomes to otherwise indigent senior society brothers."[83]

The Yale society system began to receive even more detailed treatment in the national press with the November 1908 election of President William Howard Taft, class of 1878, a Bonesman and son of a Bones society founder. Scroll and Key sent a congratulatory note to their rival society, and cognoscenti were especially excited by the originally reported electoral vote count of 322, the Bones society's mystic number (which count fell back in the end to an official 321). Articles like "Bill Taft of Yale," appearing in the May 1909 *Collier's*, advised the country of the new chief executive's college achievements, and the pride of all Yale men everywhere swelled. His son Robert Alphonso Taft, president of both Phi Beta Kappa and the Yale Debating Society and treasurer of Dwight Hall, was the thirteenth man tapped for Bones in May 1909, which also saw the society' election of the captains of the football, baseball, and hockey teams, and of Stanhope Bayne-Jones, chairman of the *News* and later the dean of the Yale Medical School and master of Pierson College.

Further along in his presidential term, the press was to observe that secret society fellowship only went so far, noting that Taft had fired Gifford Pinchot, Bones '98 and the U.S. chief forester, appointed by Taft's mentor and predecessor President Theodore Roosevelt, and furthermore had declined to receive, when he called at the White House, Congressman Francis Burton Harrison, Bones '95 (and son of Burton Harrison, Bones '59 and Confederate President Jefferson Davis's private secretary). The president, the newspaper noted, "did not hesitate to land heavily on a brother 'Bones,' and in so doing teach a lesson to all youngsters now in college that there is something more in life than being slapped on the back and sent to their rooms before the assembled brains, wealth and beauty of New Haven."[84] Taft's impartiality with regard to Pinchot was more than outweighed by the president's replacing him as chief forester with Henry Solon Graves, Bones '92, and furthermore choosing Henry Stimson, Bones '88, as his secretary of war; Franklin MacVeagh, Bones '62, as secretary of the treasury; Yale's treasurer Lee McClung, Bones '92, as United States treasurer; Lloyd Bowers, valedictorian of the class of 1879 and Bones, as solicitor general, a job once held by Taft; and Amos Wilder, Bones '84 and Thornton Wilder's father, as U.S. consul general in Hong Kong and then Shanghai.

Finally, the publication of first one and then two competing issues of the *Horoscope* in the week preceding Tap Day, produced in the first several years by "some unknown person . . . giving pictures of the most prominent men, and taking the opportunity to make sly hits, sometimes vindictive ones, with his hidden pen," also roiled the campus. A New

Haven newspaper headline from May 1900 said it all: "Yale Men Angry. Stirred Up over Horoscope. May Flog the Author. Reward of $50 Offered for the Publisher." It was reported that every copy was immediately bought up at 25 cents apiece—these publications were, and were intended to be, money-spinners for their anonymous authors.

Even without the *Horoscope*, undergraduates ran their own morning line: in the basement of Lawrance Hall, above the bathtubs, as recorded in *Stover at Yale* in 1911, it "had been the practice from long custom to inscribe on the walls tentative lists of the probable selections from the class for the three senior societies." According to the *New York Sun*, "hundreds of such lists are scrawled on more or less secluded walls, for the awful blight of senior ostracism, according to tradition, falls upon one seen writing up such a list publicly." Perhaps these informal but constantly updated personal appraisals (as happened with the fictional Stover) were actually of use to the seniors, the newspaper suggested: "The societies confronted with the necessity of picking the men who most nearly approach their ideals out of a class of 400 and 500 men seem to have realized that the safest way is to follow the estimate of a student's classmates."

On the day of elections, underclassmen bet freely on the results, "the 'book' running often up into the hundreds." In the May 1912 elections, when it had been rumored that Averell Harriman would go to Keys, "wagers had been laid that if tapped for 'Bones' early he would decline the election, awaiting a possible later chance to enter 'Keys.'" Harriman, that year's most prominent "doubtful man," was, as per the strategy in such situations, the first man tapped for Bones, so those bets were lost.[85]

Skull and Bones also garnered attention with the expansion of its tomb. Ground was broken by William Howard Taft's brother Horace on May 27, 1902, for the addition of a fireproof wing to the north, replicating the original hall in size and design, nearly doubling the building's area, with the installation of a new, double iron door between the old and new wings and addition of both a large library for books and memorabilia and a number of meeting rooms for the graduate club gatherings. And while the Sheffield Scientific School fraternities were not yet part of the Academic College's senior society system, the construction in 1901 of the windowless marble hall of the Sheffield fraternity Book and Snake (and now that society's tomb) at the corner of Grove and High Streets, at the western end of the new Commons building for undergraduate dining, reminded all the undergraduates of the society mysteries conducted therein.

What was perhaps more remarkable was that, while membership was desired so fiercely, when accepting election these young men knew virtually nothing of the societies' activities beyond their external prestige. The *New York Sun* informed its readers, in a long article on the societies in 1894, that, "Of course, no inkling of what passes within this arcane region [of the windowless society halls] ever reaches the outside world." The *Horoscope* for May 1890 commented on one (unsuccessful) candidate: "It is to be hoped that Norman [McClintock] will not make so many breaks about his society as he does about everything else; if he does, Bones secrets will be spread far and wide until even the heathen Zulus are reveling in possession of them."

The *Horoscope*'s annual issues made occasional guesses about the quality of the food within, or how exhausting the initiations must be from the looks of the initiates the following morning, but none of their publications over twenty-seven years ever contained speculation or discussion on the societies' internal programs or goals, other than one aside in May 1886 that Keys "was the best place in college for developing speech and oratory." Over on High Street, Bones continued its weekly debates on Thursdays, where graduates were welcome to join them for dinner, but about 1888 shifted its members' delivery of life histories and other personal discussions to Saturday evenings, when their communion of spirits was not to be disturbed by visits of alumni coming to join the mid-week dinners.

In his barely disguised autobiographical novel of 1921, Stephen Vincent Benét of the class of 1919 was to write that what his protagonist, "said or did or had done to him when he finally passed through the spike-topped *chevaux-de-frise* that guards the mysterious building [the Wolf's Head tomb, then] on Prospect and Trumbull Streets, a veil of perfect secrecy will be drawn." Again, Princetonian Edmund Wilson may have said it best: "In the case of the senior societies you have a moral pressure brought to bear probably unparalleled in any other university. It is a pressure exerted by a small group of men supposed to represent the very best in the senior class and *exercised in an atmosphere of mystery which makes its ideals all the more impressive because it is impossible to tell exactly what they are.*"[86]

The fear of being "sad with that" man who was not tapped was seen by the Fisher Report's committee as an aspect of general Yale conservatism which was having a negative impact on the quantity and quality of Yale College admissions, which in 1902 was for the first time lagged the number at Harvard. "Societies mean so much to the students that parents hesitate to subject them to such chances of disappointment as they must inevitably run in Yale College." The number of men taken into the three senior societies remained at forty-five, although the classes at 300-odd were double the size they were when Wolf's Head was founded in 1884.

Even worse, the passing over might reach the newspapers: the *New Haven Evening Register* recorded that the son of Ambassador John Hay had not been chosen in May 1897, and the *New York Times* reported about the May 1900 tap that "Robert W. Forbes, a prominent football player, was not elected for any society. Walbridge S. Taft, a nephew of Secretary [of War William Howard] Taft, who was regarded as certain of election, also failed."[87] The Fisher Committee hoped that the establishment in March 1903 of a fourth organization, "The Elihu Club," as a non-secret society would improve the situation somewhat, but "men hesitate to enter a college where there is only one chance in six of getting into the social 'swim.'"

Elihu, named of course after the university's most famous patron, Elihu Yale, was not regarded as a protest against the existing senior societies, according to the *New York Times* article announcing its formation, "and as evidence of this fact, three graduates representing the present societies have accepted honorary elections," namely Anson Phelps Stokes '96, secretary of the University and Bones; Lewis Welch '89, editor of the *Yale Alumni* Weekly and Keys; and Frederic Wells Williams '79, assistant professor of Oriental History and an honorary member of Wolf's Head in its graduate membership program. In replication of Wolf's Head strategy for acquiring renown and stability, it was announced by Elihu's organizers that other "graduates of distinction will have elections," from the classes of the prior fifteen or twenty years (they were to elect men from as far back as the class of 1880). Its founders also proposed "to reserve the right to elect men after graduation where their record has shown special claims to such recognition," and to elect as members professors in the Yale faculty who were graduates of other institutions.

Elihu held its first undergraduate elections on June 3, 1903, following Tap Day on May 27, naming eleven from the class of 1904: William Alexander Blount Jr.; Frank Farrell Jr.; Francis Spencer Goodwin; Robert Andrew Grannis Jr.; Rowland Hazard; Charles Arthur Moore Jr.; David Ritchie McKee; Wheeler Hazard Peckham 2d; Zeigler Sargent; Edward Perry Townsend; and Carroll Johnson Waddell. (Of the four versions of the *Horoscope* appearing this year, one had predicted eight original members, but named no names, while another identified ten prospects, but got none of them right.) "Several of the organizers," reported the *New York Herald*, "are members of very wealthy families," naming Grannis, McKee, Peckham, and Townsend. The charter members proposed to elect about eleven more members from their own class, and to select from the succeeding class, "a nucleus, probably ten men, to take up the work of the succeeding year."

Robert Grannis had been in the last group elected to the sophomore societies before their demise and was disappointed at not being tapped for a senior society in the spring of 1902. He spoke just two days later with Keys alumnus Lewis Welch, who agreed with him that Yale College needed another senior society, and spent the following summer in a productive search for support among Yale alumni. Meanwhile, Grannis, Charles Moore (to become the first undergraduate president), and four others enlisted at a University Club dinner in New York drew up a penciled statement committing themselves to the concept of a non-secret organization, a "club," and vowed to erect in time "a suitable house, not to be built on the tomb (or windowless club) plan." The founding club of 1903 eventually grew to twenty-four members, and left a gift of $4,800 to their successors chosen for the delegation of 1904.

Welch gave the new organization a boost in the *Alumni Weekly*. "The number of good men available will be the controlling factor," he wrote, although they might not be members of any other senior society; the membership number would not be fixed, "and it will thus adopt itself to the varying conditions in different classes." Dues would be almost nominal in order not to deter men of limited means. Already, enough funds had been guaranteed to cover expenses for two years for meetings of the undergraduates, convening in rooms at Heublein's restaurant. The club—it consciously did not style itself a society, and the "plan to form a fourth senior society, frequently broached within the last ten years of large classes, was, if ever considered by these men," wrote Welch, "definitely abandoned"—continued to take in a varying number of men each year, sometimes as many as twenty, while the other senior societies invariably elected fifteen.

Characterizing themselves as a nonsecret club devoted to intellectual interaction and development of forensic skills, in study of the world's contemporary political and economic affairs, the members staged debates on particular and general social issues; practiced giving after-dinner extemporaneous talks; wrote, presented, and criticized essays, with the members voting on which essays merited retention in the club library; and invited distinguished faculty at Yale and other colleges to lecture at their meetings. It gave out its elections by mail after Tap Day, with no refusals, and conducted no special manifestations or outward rituals remarked upon by their classmates. They chose to meet on Thursdays and Saturdays like the other senior societies, taking a lease on a narrow brick building at 74 Wall Street, then in a 1905 moving into a second rented house at 245 York Street for five years.[88]

The two of the four competing *Horoscopes* (all anonymously edited) for the elections of the class of 1904 which chose to assess the prospect of the new organization reached diametrically opposed assessments, probably fairly accurately reflecting the two poles of campus opinion. One gauged it almost solely in relation to its older rivals: "The existence of the new club, the Elihu Club, which we think in time will develop into a fourth Senior society, has aided Wolf's Head wonderfully. In such large classes as Yale now has, it is an honor for a man to make even this club which fact raises Wolf's Head to a much higher plane. In fact we think that in time, Wolf's Head will be getting much the same crowd that Keys now has and that that society will be taking more the Bones type of man; Keys policy in the last year or two points to that." The other's appraisal was more succinct: "As for the Elihu Club it is an important innovation and is bound to fill a large place in the system. We do not believe, however, that it will ever become a fourth Senior Society."

In late 1912, the new society took possession of a building, numbered 87 Elm Street, renumbered 175 Elm a decade later. This three-story, colonial-era white clapboard house facing the New Haven Green, built circa 1762–1776, as partly reconstructed and completely repurposed, became in fact the oldest of all Yale's senior society halls. The home had belonged to Nicholas Callahan, a loyalist who had purchased it on the eve of the American Revolutionary War, turning it into the infamous "Tory Tavern," which was then confiscated by the town of New Haven in 1781. Elihu had architect Everett Meeks, longtime head of Yale's first formal program in architecture, remodel the structure the year after the society's acquisition, and over further years expanded it to the rear, making it in time among the largest of the society buildings, belying its modest clapboard façade with shuttered (and interior-blinded) windows. The brick basement, constructed in the seventeenth century, is older than the superstructure and contains a rustic "tap room" in keeping with its Tory Tavern days; above are three bedrooms, the house steward's suite, a large formal meeting room, and library.[89]

The new club's mixed measure of success a decade later is captured in the title of a *New York Times* article in the spring of 1913: "Post-Tap Day Honors. Elihu Club at Yale Gets Prominent Juniors Who Were Passed Over." In an election delayed four days, Elihu had chosen its members from the men not taken by the other societies on Tap Day. These included the chairman of the *Lit.* (and, the newspaper noted, the son of the president of the Associated Press), a member of the *Courant* board, two committeemen of the Junior Promenade, two Phi Beta Kappa members, a class deacon, a "football and track athlete," and three others, for a total of eleven. Like each of Scroll and Key, Spade and Grave, and Wolf's Head at their respective births, the new group struggled for its place in the senior society firmament, having like Wolf's Head declared its distinction from that system in shunning secrecy, while meeting in an historic but conventional clubhouse with windows, yet failing annually to elect a full fifteen members.

One distinction, however, they could claim early in their history: in a college which was not diverse in its student body, where social prejudice was focused on the Catholics and the Jews (there were virtually no blacks except college and student society servants), they admitted to their membership Yale's first Native American, Henry Roe Cloud, of the class of 1910. A full-blooded Winnebago, Cloud had moved from his tribe's reservation to Indian schools and then Mount Hermon preparatory school before entering Yale; just two years after graduation, he headed his tribe's delegation to his classmate Robert Taft's father's White House. He joined the fraternity Beta Theta Pi as a sophomore, and in his senior year, an intrigued *New Haven Journal-Courier* hailed him as the most notable student in his class.

Cloud did not follow up his prep school athletic career by competing on a varsity team, but excelled at oratory, earning one of the five second-place prizes in the Ten Eyck speaking contest (tying the young Taft), with an address titled "Missions to the Indians," by-lined when printed in the *Yale Courant* "By H. Cloud, of the Winnebago Tribe, Nebraska." He roomed with a Mount Hermon classmate who had been elected to

Elihu in his junior year, and became a member of Elihu in November of his senior year. At Elihu's annual banquet at New York City's University Club in 1910, he spoke to the graduates' and his clubmates' great applause about the struggle of American Indians nationally, in the relief of which his auditors might have a part. In due course over his life, after attendance at seminary and earning a Yale MA in anthropology, he served as founder of an Indian preparatory school, head of a federal Indian boarding school, administrator in the Indian Bureau, and manager of a reservation.

The election of a Native American, long before any other senior society elected a Jew or a black man, was all the more remarkable, given that Elihu's members were not generally free of the prejudices of the time. This is evidenced by the record of the club's debates on topics of race, ethnicity, and prejudice, such as whether blacks should be admitted to Yale (a majority "yes" vote in 1905, but "no" in 1907 and 1909, all conducted in ignorance that several blacks had in years past already been admitted); should "the present ostracism of the Jews be tolerated" (affirmatively decided in 1905); should the Chinese Exclusion Act be supported (affirmatively decided in 1906); should Japanese laborers be excluded legally from the United States ("yes" in 1906 and 1908); and should the United States sell the Philippines (no, in 1907).[90]

But just after Roe Cloud's graduation, the three elder senior societies were themselves passing through yet another crisis of reputation and confidence, brought on by the publication in 1911 of Owen Johnson's *Stover at Yale*, perhaps the most famous college novel in American literature.

TAPPED FOR SKULL AND BONES, 1889–1911

Thomas Elliott Donnelley	1889	CEO, R. R. Donnelley & Sons
John Cornelius Griggs	1889	professor of English, Langman University

Gifford Pinchot	1889	chief, U.S. Forest Service
		Yale professor of Forestry
		governor, Penn.
		president. National Conservation Association
		donor, Yale School of Forestry
Harry Lathrop Reed	1889	president, Auburn Theological Seminary
George Washington Woodruff	1889	acting secretary of Interior
		U.S. District Court judge, Hawaii
Thomas Francis Bayard	1890	U.S. Senate (Del.)
Fairfax Harrison	1890	chairman, Railroad War Board
Wallace Delafield Simmons	1890	founder, Simmons Hardware
Percy Hamilton Stewart	1890	U.S. Congress (N.J.)
William Phelps Graves	1891	professor of Gynecology, Harvard
Norman McClintock	1891	professor of Zoology, Rutgers
Henry Hallam Tweedy	1891	professor of Prac. Theology, Yale
Frederic Collin Walcott	1891	U.S. Senate (Conn.)
Clive Day	1892	professor of Political Economy, Yale
Pierce Jay	1892	president, Fiduciary Trust Co.
Henry Solon Graves	1892	chief forester, U.S.
		dean, Yale Forestry School
		provost, Yale University
Pierre Jay	1892	first chair, Federal Reserve Bank of N.Y.
James William Husted	1892	U.S. Congress (N.Y.)

Lee McClung	1892	treasurer, Yale University
		treasurer, United States
Francis Parsons	1893	U.S. attorney (Conn.)
Thomas Cochran	1894	chairman of the board, Bankers Trust
Thomas Frederick Davies	1894	Episcopal bishop, Western Mass.
John Loomer Hall	1894	president, Boston Public Library
John Howland	1894	professor of Pediatrics, Johns Hopkins
Ralph Delahaye Paine	1894	author, war correspondent
Benjamin Stickney Cable	1895	assistant secretary of Commerce
		U.S. Congress (N.J.)
Mortimer Norman Buckner	1895	chairman, N.Y. Trust Co.
Francis Burton Harrison	1895	governor-general of Philippines
Arthur Behn Shepley	1895	professor of Law, Washington U.
William Sloane	1895	president, W. & J. Sloane
William Redmond Cross	1895	president, New York Zoological Society
		keeper of maps, Yale University
Anson Phelps Stokes	1895	secretary, Yale University
Frederick Edward Weyerhaeuser	1896	president, Weyerhauser Timber
Henry Sloane Coffin	1897	president, Union Theological Seminary
Clarence Mann Fincke	1897	chairman, Greenwich Savings Bank
Frederic Kernochan	1898	chief justice, N.Y. Court of Special Sessions
Franklin Atkins Lord	1898	secretary, U.S. Shipping Board

James Wolcott Wadsworth Jr.	1898	U.S. Senate (N.Y.)
Henry Burt Wright	1898	professor of History, Yale
William Sloane Coffin	1900	president, Metropolitan Museum of Art
Joseph Rockwell Swan	1902	chairman of the board, N.Y. Botanical Gardens
Frank Wood Moore	1903	professor Homiletics, Auburn Theological Seminary
Russell Cheney	1904	artist
James Ely Miller	1904	organized first air squadron, World War I.
		first American aviator killed in France
Lansing Reed	1904	chair, Yale Alumni Fund
Thomas Day Thacher	1904	U.S. District Court judge (N.Y.)
		U.S. solicitor general
Murray Sargent	1905	president, chairman, Sargent & Co.
John Sloane	1905	chairman of the board, W. & J. Sloane
Edwin Sheldon Whitehouse	1905	U.S. minister to Guatemala, Colombia
Hugh Robert Wilson	1906	U.S. ambassador to Germany
William McCormick Blair	1907	founder, William Blair & Co.
		president, Art Institute of Chicago
		president, Chicago Historical Society
		Senior Fellow, Yale Corp.
Samuel F. B. Morse	1907	president, Del Monte Properties
George Dahl	1908	professor of Hebrew, Yale
Charles Seymour	1908	professor of History, provost, president, Yale University

Harold Stanley	1908	founder, Morgan Stanley
Harvey Hollister Bundy	1909	chairman, Carnegie Endowment for Peace
		assistant secretary of state
		special assistant to secretary of war
James Morrison Howard	1909	director, Union Theological Seminary
Stanhope Bayne-Jones	1910	dean, Yale Medical School
		brigadier general, World War II
		president, New York Hospital-Cornell Medical Center
Walter Seth Logan	1910	general counsel, Federal Reserve Bank, N.Y.
George Harrison	1910	president, N.Y. Federal Reserve Bank
		president, N.Y. Life Insurance Co.
Carl Albert Lohmann	1910	secretary, Yale University
Robert Alphonso Taft	1910	U.S. Senate (Ohio)
Francis Fitz Randolph	1911	senior partner, J. & W. Seligman

TAPPED FOR SCROLL AND KEY, 1889–1911

Robert W. Huntington Jr.	1889	chairman of the board, Connecticut General Life Insurance
Augustus Henry Mosle	1889	cofounder, Curtis, Mallet-Prevost, Colt & Mosle
Edward Lambe Parsons	1889	Episcopal bishop of Calif.
James Gamble Rogers	1889	architect, Sterling Library and many other Yale buildings

Lewis Sheldon Welch	1889	founder/editor, *Yale Alumni Weekly*
Herbert Parsons	1890	U.S. Congress (N.Y.)
Harvey Williams Cushing	1891	Sterling Professor of Neurology, Yale
		winner, Pulitzer Prize
Irwin Boyle Laughlin	1893	U.S. ambassador to Spain
Moses Taylor	1893	chairman of the board, Lackawanna Steel
Thomas Shaw Arbuthnot	1894	dean, Medical School, University of Pittsburgh
Frank Lyon Polk	1894	cofounder, Davis, Polk & Wardwell (grandson, President James K. Polk)
		president, New York Public Library
		chief, U.S. Peace Commission, 1919
William Adams Delano	1895	acting secretary of state, U.S.
		architect, Sage and Harkness Halls, Yale Divinity Quadrangle
Allen Wardwell	1895	cofounder, Davis, Polk & Wardwell
		president, Assoc. Bar NYC
George Henry Nettleton	1896	dean, Yale College
		president, Vassar College
Fred Towsley Murphy	1897	professor of Surgery, Washington University
Julian Starkweather Mason	1898	editor in chief, *New-York Evening Post*
Edward Clark Streeter	1898	professor of History of Medicine, Yale
William Henry Field	1899	secretary, Yale University Press

Mervin Clark Harvey	1899	general manager, New York *Daily News*
Joseph Medill McCormick	1900	publisher, *Chicago Tribune* U.S. Senate (Ill.)
Hugh Auchincloss	1901	professor of Clinincal Surgery, Columbia
Joseph Medill Patterson	1902	publisher, New York *Daily News*, *Chicago Tribune*
Clive Livingston DuVal	1903	president, Carnegie Institute
Howard Phipps	1907	donor, Phipps Field (polo)
James Coates Auchincloss	1908	U.S. Congress (N.J.)
Lewis Hill Weed	1909	director, School of Medicine, Johns Hopkins
Roger Selden Rose	1910	professor of Modern Languages, Yale
Henry Payne Bingham	1910	donor, Bingham Hall
James Dwight Dana	1911	cofounder, Wiggin and Dana
Allen Skinner Hubbard	1911	cofounder, Hughes Hubbard & Reed

TAPPED FOR WOLF'S HEAD, 1889–1911

John Fuller Appleton Merrill	1889	U.S. attorney (Me.)
James Hall Mason Knox Jr.	1892	president, American Child Hygiene Association
Francis Oswald Dorsey	1893	professor, University of Indianapolis
Alfred Kindred Merritt	1893	registrar, Yale College
Robert Hastings Nichols	1894	professor, Auburn Theological Seminary
William Henry Salmon	1894	president, Carleton College
Benjamin Spock	1895	general counsel, N.Y., N.H. & Hartford Railroad
Alexander Smith Cochran	1896	founder, Elizabethan Club
William Darrach	1897	dean, Columbia College of Physicians and Surgeons

Edward Stephen Harkness	1897	president, Commonwealth Fund
		donor, Yale residential colleges and Harvard houses
		donor, Wolf's Head (second) tomb
Charles Reed Hemenway	1897	attorney general, Hawaii

TAPPED FOR ELIHU, 1904–1911

Clarence W. Mendell	1904	Yale professor Latin and Greek
		Dean of Yale College
James G. Rogers	1905	first master, Timothy Dwight College
Charles Sheldon Judd	1905	Chancellor of Hawaiian Kingdom
Kenneth Latourette	1906	historian
Irving Sands Olds	1907	U.S. Steel board chairman
Frederick A. Godley	1908	Yale professor of Architecture
Philip Rogers Mallory	1908	founder of Duracell
Meade Minnigerode	1910	co-author, Whiffenpoof song
Tappan Gregory	1910	president, American Bar Assoc.
Chenteng Thomas Wang	1910	Chinese minister of foreign affairs
Thomas Beer	1911	biographer
Stanley T. Williams	1911	founder, American literature as academic profession

CHAPTER NINE

THE CONFUSIONS OF STOVER
AND DISRUPTIONS OF WAR
(1912–1919)

When a boy comes here to Yale, or any other American college, and gets the flummery in his system, believes in it—surrenders to it—so that he trembles in the shadow of a tomblike building, doesn't dare look at a pin that stares him in the face, is afraid to pronounce the holy, sacred names; when he's got to that point he has ceased to *think*, and no amount of college life is going to revive him. That's the worst thing about it all, this mental subjection which the average man undergoes here when he comes up against all this rigmarole of the Tap Day, gloomy society halls, marching home at night, et cetera—et ceteray.

—Brockhurst to Stover, *Stover at Yale*, 1912[1]

STOVER AT YALE

Entering Yale College with the class of 1900, Owen Johnson graduated in 1901. He was the founder of the Wigwam Debating Club, chairman of the *Lit.*, and a member of Alpha Delta Phi. At his New Jersey preparatory school, he founded and edited the *Lawrenceville Literary Magazine.* In a series of stories about his prep school known collectively as the "Lawrenceville Stories," serialized in the *Saturday Evening Post,* Johnson developed a character named John Humperdinck Stover, a fifteen-year-old at Lawrenceville nicknamed "Dink."

By 1911, he had published seven novels and a major play, appeared in several leading magazines, and been elected to the National Institute of Arts and Letters.[2] In that year, he published Dink's further adventures, as a college student now, in *Stover at Yale,* serialized in *McClure's Magazine* and described by none other than F. Scott Fitzgerald (Princeton '17) as the "textbook" for his generation.[3] A distinguished Yale graduate, finding a different message, declared it the *Uncle Tom's Cabin* of American universities, and the *Yale Alumni Weekly's* book review pronounced it, "a philippic directed against certain tendencies and facts of life at present-day American universities in general, and Yale in particular, as the author and many other people see them." When the book was reissued in 1969, a modern reviewer said that the novel was, "the one where American higher education is split open like a Delicious apple and then allowed to turn brown and rot under the reader's eye."[4]

The author's real intention in writing *Stover* is described in a letter to Harvard's president Abbott Lawrence Lowell from President Theodore Roosevelt (that proud Porcellian alumnus). "This will introduce to you Mr. Owen Johnson . . . a Yale man . . . who is now writing about Yale a story dealing especially with the club and society problems of which you and I have so often talked, and which have so puzzled us. I really wish you would talk freely with Johnson, who can be entirely trusted, and will not quote you in any way if you do not wish, and who sees us as we do both the evils of the club or society system and the difficulties in the way of doing away with these difficulties. . . . Johnson is taking this matter up from the National point of view, the point of view of all universities and not merely Harvard and Yale."[5]

The novel employs all the standard conventions of the muckraking exposés of political machines, trusts, and commercial corruption which proliferated in *Stover's* era. Johnson hoped that exposing secrecy in high places would eventually lead to social reform—that the society system, which then served in his view as an upper-class sinecure, would be transformed under the press of public scrutiny into a "reward of merit" for Yale's natural aristocrats. *Stover* was conceived as a "novel with a purpose," a kind of secular tract intended to draw a moral for the reader.[6]

At the beginning of *Stover*, the hero, who had overcome a poor start at Lawrenceville to distinguish himself as a class leader and gridiron star, trains up to New Haven as a freshman. Here, among his new classmates, he first hears of the senior society system and the tapping ceremonies. A sophomore, stopping by the dormitory to check on the Andover freshmen, advises them in Dink's hearing what extracurricular activity each should pursue. Stover also meets another sophomore, Le Baron, who takes Stover under his wing and counsels him on the long-range importance of winning election to a senior society. Dink is immediately troubled by the prospect of this social contest ("something snapped, something fragile—the unconscious, simple democracy of boyhood" he had known in prep school), and nothing is resolved when he meets Gimbel, seeking to recruit Stover for his openly proclaimed plan to fight the society system, organizing neutrals for class election victories against the societies' candidates.

Stover had been confident that his four years would be "the happiest I'll ever know," in anticipation of "a free and open fight to be among the leaders," gaining both the football captaincy and senior society membership. His path is rocky: winning early renown in the freshman class wrestling contest with the sophomores, he commences his football career on the scrub team, contesting for the starting end position with a senior, where the victory was built on the "broken hopes" of a comrade. "For the first time, a little appalled, he felt the weight of the seriousness, the deadly seriousness of the American spirit, which seizes on everything that is competitive and transforms it, with the savage fanaticism of its race, for success."

The book's second major character, Tom Regan, a classmate and football teammate much older than Dink, admitted to Yale only after six tries at the entrance examinations, is working his way through college waiting tables in order to go into reform politics in the West. He encourages Dink to think and act with more independence, deploring the exclusiveness and conformity of the sophomore societies, still in existence in the years covered by the novel, Johnson's undergraduate years of 1896–1900. After making further acquaintance with outsiders who question the social stagnation fostered by the society system, and a visit from Le Baron warning of the consequences of cutting loose from the men "in your own crowd," Stover throws down his sophomore society pin, stamps it beneath his foot, and resigns, although warned of that act's possible consequence—"what a defiance would mean to those leaders in the class above, men marked for Skull and Bones, the society to which he aspired." He continues to stray, in his three-year journey to maturity, plagued by bouts of self-doubt, followed by "open defiance" when "he chose to appear at Mory's with the wildest element of the class," spending nights of dissolution and drunkenness "in the company of idlers."

Stover's third significant protagonist is Brockhurst, Johnson's alter ego. The undergraduate Johnson had founded the Wigwam Debating Club, and in the novel, Brockhurst proposes the formation of such a class-wide club as a representative forum to replace the class-dividing sophomore societies. Unlike Johnson, Brockhurst loses the contest for chairman of the *Yale Lit.* (Johnson's own last major essay in the *Lit.* was "For Action," calling for an end to "the discord and discontent" over the sophomore societies, which were abolished in December 1900, and are thus so abolished in the novel. Johnson's friends had begged him to delay his essay's publication until after Tap Day, and preserve his chance, as the *Lit.* chairman, for senior society election, but the leader ran, and he was passed over.[7])

Although Dink uses his stature in the class as an All-American star end (Stover's football exploits were seemingly modeled on those of Frank Hinkey, class of 1895 and Bones) to make the debating club a success, recruiting participants from all factions, Brockhurst continues his assault on Yale's cliques fostered by the society system, condemned as a wasted opportunity in colleges with nationally derived student bodies. "We miss the big chance—to go out, to mingle with every one, to educate ourselves by knowing opposite lives, fellows who see things as we have never seen them, who are going back to a life a thousand miles away from what we will lead. . . . We ought to really know one another, meet, discuss, respect each other's point of view, independence—odd ways if you wish. We don't do it. We did once—we don't now. Princeton doesn't do it, Harvard doesn't do it. We're over-organized away from the vital thing—the knowledge of ourselves."

Stover pushes back: "I say I don't know where the trouble is; whether the whole social system here and elsewhere is the cause or the effect. It may be that it is the whole development of America that has changed our college life." Brockhurst concedes that the question is much larger than a society system in New Haven, with blame to go around.

"Do you wonder," Brockhurst exclaims, "why I repeat that our colleges are splendidly organized institutions for the prevention of learning? No, sir, we are business colleges, and the business of our machines is to stamp out so many business men a year, running at full speed and in competition with the latest devices in Cambridge and Princeton! . . . But of course, the main trouble here is, and there is no blinking the fact, that the colleges have surrendered unconsciously a great deal of their power to the growing influence of the social organization. In a period when we have no society in America, families are sending their sons to colleges to place them socially. Some of them carry it to an extreme, even directly avow their hope that they will make certain clubs at Princeton or Harvard, or a senior society here. It probably is very hard to control, but it's going to turn our colleges more and more, as I say, into social clearing houses."

The novel's suspense builds on whether Stover, or any declared society system opponents or skeptics like Regan, despite some qualifications for senior society elevation, will be tapped (Stover has taken himself out of the running for football captain, so that his anti-society stance does not become an impediment to the leadership of the squad). Now as a junior in the spring semester, he is a communicant without choice in the ritual he had first heard described in his freshman room, and then seen for the first time that academic year, when his upperclass football captain is not elected to Bones—"they've done it just to show they're independent." Three years on, with his anxious New Haven girlfriend and her parents watching from the windows of Durfee, Stover first sees Regan elected and then himself become the last man tapped for Bones, struck by Le Baron, and sincerely cheered by his passed-over friend Joe Hungerford: "It's great, great—they rose to it."

Hungerford, in the book's very last paragraph, demands that Brockhurst "own up that the old college came up to the scratch . . . and the seniors showed today that they could recognize honest criticism." Brockhurst responds: "Well, it's good enough as it is. It takes an awful lot to stir it, but it's the most sensitive of the American colleges, and it will respond. It wants to do the right thing. Some day it'll see. . . . I'm not satisfied with Yale as a magnificent factory on democratic business lines; I dream of something else, something visionary, a great institution not of boys, clean, lovable and honest, but men of brains, of courage, of leadership, a great center of thought, to stir the country and bring it back to the understanding of what man creates with his imagination, and dares with his will. It's visionary—it will come."[8]

Though he ends his novel on an optimistic note, Brockhurst is for the most part an extremist—he calls himself "a crank"—who, by virtue of his intelligence and independence, launches a withering attack on Yale, and by extension America. In contrast, Stover is a moderate who, half-persuaded by Brockhurst, must work out for himself the conflicts he finds at Yale between quality and equality.[9] Although the story ends with the hero being tapped for Skull and Bones, the novel's denouement suggests that the goal may be unworthy—or at least not worth the sacrifice of independence and individuality. Without final resolution (will Dink changes his society from the inside?), Johnson had depicted the contest between an older form of Yale civic individualism, identifiable by character and teamwork, and a more contemporary Yale liberal individualism, characterized by soul searching, psychological non-conformity, and modernity.[10]

Johnson's fictional analysis of the Yale social system, published in book form in April 1912, "must have penetrated to a wider audience than any other ever made."[11] When that month the *McClure's* installment of the novel appeared, containing Brockhurst's most scathing criticism of Yale education as reflecting only American business values, the *New York Times* ran lengthy excerpts of the text in a feature titled "College as a Means of Stifling Thought," noting of *Stover* that "the burden of the criticism is that the social organization of the colleges has so overwhelmed them that the intellectual life has been choked out." In the following Sunday's edition of the *Times,* the newspaper published an extensive interview with Johnson, titled "Danger in the Snobbery of Colleges," illustrated with pictures of the Ivy and Cottage Clubs at Princeton, the Harvard Union, and St. Anthony Hall and the Bones tomb at Yale.

"It is my deep conviction," the novelist told the reporter, "that the successful man is the rebel, the one who analyses and criticizes the social system, and will not let his imagination be dictated by it, the man who rebels openly and stubbornly against the particular form of tyranny it may oppose to his liberty of thought and action." The *Times'* editorial page begged to differ: "Mr. Johnson himself seems to have survived his course at Yale. So did President Taft. A lot of other men were not altogether spoiled by their experience there."[12]

The novel's serialization having ended, Johnson shortly thereafter recounted his criticisms and conclusions plainly, in a five-part magazine series for *Collier's* titled "The Social Usurpation of Our Colleges." The first dealt with snobbery as a general feature of student life, and the following four detailed the agencies of undergraduate exclusiveness: the Harvard final clubs, the Princeton eating clubs, the Yale societies, and the nationwide fraternity system. In his examination of the final clubs, he wrote: "It is not that Harvard is indifferent to the vital fact that democratic association is national education, but that no reform can come until Harvard, as well as Yale, Princeton, and other universities abandon the erroneous theory that the social organization of the university is the property of the undergraduate."[13]

In his succeeding *Collier's* article on Yale, Johnson argued that extracurricular trivialities in New Haven were obscuring the college's true function and efficacy as a leading educational institution. The senior societies, he maintained, "the one vital force," bore the primary responsibility for the growth, maintenance, and flourishing of this encumbrance, which like so much untamed ivy had battened on and overgrown the schoolhouse. "The Society of Skull and Bones is, in fact, Yale Academic. Its tone is the tone of the college, to which it transfers its excellent democracy and its clean, ambitious standards. It is respected and deservedly popular." Switching in mid-paragraph from high praise to the attack, he continued: "Directly and indirectly, it is responsible for the deification of success, the overemphasis on unimportant details, the stultifying and indefensibly childish fetish of secrecy, and the reduction to a pattern of the undergraduate who arrives with forceful and original point of view. . . . Unfortunately, its ideals are so high, and its record so consistent that it is the most difficult to convince that the problem is not one of looking in on the internal housekeeping, but of looking out on the program of the world."

As for Scroll and Key, that society "for a long time existed on the opposite theory of a congenial social set. . . . Lately, however, the Keys' standard has strengthened along the lines of its best traditions until its membership, while never making the same recognition of scholarship, compares favorably with the representative quality of Bones." Wolf's Head had "cast a favoring eye on the representatives of dominant social sets . . . [a] change rather forced on it by the growing democracy of Keys." The new Elihu Club, "with the exception of secrecy the fourth senior society confirming its membership after Tap Day," had experienced a "growth in popular estimation [which] has been rapid, and in recent years . . . has compared favorably with the two younger senior societies." The *Yale News* was complicit in this social and intellectual stultification, a "carefully controlled organ of student sentiment . . .

[which] will discuss anything except the vital and present problems in the social system. Here you have in miniature the same process that goes on in the outer world—the alliance of established institutions with the organs of public criticism."

After this searing indictment, his surprisingly mild remedy was insistence that amelioration should come by evolution of the societies, not revolution. "What is most encouraging," he wrote for his final *Collier's* paragraph on Yale, "is the real desire for democracy among the undergraduates and the increasing open-mindedness of the alumni of these powerful societies, who are increasingly alive to the necessity of eliminating the element of fear as a producer of character; doing way with unimportant absurdities, of safeguarding the development of the individual imagination, and finally, and most important of all, of readjusting conditions in such a way that the final result of four years at Yale shall be an education."

In the end, Johnson's discussion of the senior society system as a whole, in both fiction and journalism, was a mixture of sound values and bad logic. Some observations were so sensible and shrewd that they certainly caused at least some individuals in the senior societies, and the juniors they sought to elect, to engage in serious self-examination. His main thesis, that the Yale campus exemplified, "the most bewildering system of overorganization of inconsequential activities that can be imagined to divert the individual from the development of his own individuality and its sacrifice to the exigencies and tyrannies of the average for merely material success," was a critical but an intelligent observation.

Still, as the colloquy of Brockhurst and Stover suggested, in their references to national social standards and reverence for business success, the real guilt of Bones, if any, did not come from having transformed Yale "from a university into a school of character," but only in having so readily adapted its standards for election to the strident and striving values of the campus, the collegians' parents, and the country. As for Keys, it opposed the existing "democracy" of Yale, Johnson thought, for "money and social position," sanctioning a tyranny of the social set no more inherently worthy than the Bones-enforced tyranny of the average, the phrase Johnson defined as "the democracy of a bourgeois commonplaceness that neither comprehends nor tolerates the men of bold and original individuality."[14] Instead, as has been more correctly adjudged, Keys chose "not any man whom a position on the campus glorified, but any man who himself glorified the position. . . . In short, the Keys principle and the Bones principle are both at their best equally in the Owen-Johnsonian sense of the word. No man because of family, environment, or pocket-book need be excluded by either."[15]

Johnson held the notion that "in its centralized organization, the senior society system affords to Yale University the same instrument for the spread of an idea that the concentrated Roman Empire did for the spread of Christianity," if only the fetish of secrecy ("this extraordinary muffled breathless guarding of an empty can") were eliminated. He thought the system could be converted into, "an honest attempt to reward the best of college life, a sort of academic legion of honor, formed not on social cleavage, but given as a reward of merit."[16] This suggests a mistaken belief that the self-imposed revisions of the sanctions and habits of a secretly elected group of young men would, if they but chose to do so, transform the entrenched Yale social system of prestige and reward, and thus the nation's.

TAP DAY 1912

In the real world of Yale's campus, the novel's mixed message resonated, although a poll of the senior class found that 86 percent to be of the opinion that the novel "grossly exaggerated." The juniors, the night before 1912 elections, held a mock Tap Day in their residence the Berkeley Oval, starting at about 11:00 P.M. "With a well advertised novel of college life fresh in their minds," reported the *New York Herald*, "the men began singing 'Everybody's Throwing It' to the discordant strains of 'Everybody's Doin' It,' and the leaders were being carried about on the shoulders of groups of men. . . . Everybody was slapped on the back and ordered to his room; everybody got an election and half of the juniors went through the part of refusing to move, thus showing that they refused elections."[17] Nothing like that had every happened before or was to again.

Worse was to follow, a riot of the kind not seen on campus since the harassment of the senior societies by Bull and Stones in the 1870s. On May 23, after the elections, the juniors locked the Vanderbilt Hall gates against the members of the three societies returning after midnight from their regular Thursday meetings, forcing them to gain entry to their rooms by clambering over the gates, which had been slathered with glue. A huge bonfire blazed in the courtyard, with the neutrals dancing around the flames in pajamas, bathrobes, and silk hats, awaiting the men of Keys, Wolf's Head, and Bones as they returned from their respective halls. Some tried to open the locked gates with a key from the campus policeman, while the troublemakers swarmed against the fence from the inside, shouting the Keys "Troubadour" song into that society's members' angry faces. Some of the seniors picked up bricks from the street, in order to break windows in a corner entry to climb in, but most had to deal with the glue and climb over the gates.[18]

The *New York Times* ran two articles about the Tap Day following *Stover*'s publication, one on May 12, 1912, titled "Yale Juniors Now in Fix of 'Stover'," and the second, on May 17, following elections, headed "Yale 'Taps' in Rain amid Great Tension," with its subtitles, "Nervousness of the Marshaled Juniors Reflects Owen Johnson's Attack on the System. Yale Grit Puts It Through." The earlier piece noted that "For two reasons the excitement over the elections is higher than normal. There are more prominent men, more representatives of leading American families in the incoming senior class than in years. In the second place, the recent agitation over the senior societies, stirred by Owen Johnson's novel, 'Stover at Yale,' has created widespread interest as well as caustic comment."

Up for election were a grandson of Commodore Vanderbilt, "Van" Webb, editor in chief of the *Yale News*, and the first Vanderbilt scion in a dozen years to be a senior society candidate, along with his Groton prep school classmate Averell Harriman, coach of the freshman crew, manager of the varsity hockey team, and son of the recently deceased railroad financier Edward Harriman, who had left an estate of $70 million, equal to $1 billion today, leaving his seventeen-year-old son (then with $400 in the bank and no bequest in the will) as head of the family. Young Harriman, part of the first substantial class contingent to attend Yale from the Groton School, had been the instigator of the movement to enroll in New Haven, considering that and possible election to Skull and Bones to be a democratic rebellion against the elitist tradition of Grotonians going on to Harvard and assured membership in Porcellian. "It gave me purpose," he said more than seventy years after being tapped. "I scoffed at Harvard's Porcellian Club. It was too smug. But to get into Bones, you had to do something for Yale."[19]

The possible suspicion that Harriman's opinion as a prep schooler was one formulated in adult retrospect is destroyed by a more contemporary memoir by Donald Ogden Stewart, chosen for the Bones club of 1916. After graduation, he was recommended as a humorist to the magazine *Vanity Fair* by F. Scott Fitzgerald and became a moderately successful playwright and then a highly successful screenwriter in Hollywood, winning Academy Awards for *The Phildelphia Story* and *Life with Father,* among other films.

In an article on Yale undergraduate life for H. L. Mencken's journal *The Smart Set* in 1921, Stewart was to insist for his readers on the comprehension of "the peculiar relation of the Eastern preparatory schools to the New Haven institution. The majority of the leaders in each Yale class come from Hotchkiss, Hill, Taft, Andover or Exeter [Stewart's school], and those schools fit their men for Yale in a much broader sense than mere preparation for the passing of the entrance examinations. For many years, the 'big men' in the school have gone down to New Haven and 'made good'; in the course of time, and largely through the perfectly natural influence of hero worship, there has been developed in the prep school a reflection of the college—a reflection which bears at times a curious resemblance to a skull and cross-bones." Thus, he confessed, "I went to Yale, primarily, because I wanted to make Bones. There is nothing particularly reprehensible about that; nothing which reflects discredit upon Exeter, Yale, Bones, or me. But [writing five years after his graduation] it does seem unfortunate that the ambition, under the rather hypocritical guise of 'working for Yale,' found, in the over-organization of 'extra-curriculum' activities there, an outlet which almost completely obscured the real benefits of the college and postponed until Senior year the process of obtaining an education."[20]

"The ceremony," noted the *New York Times* in its first story on the 1912 elections, "has been attacked by the *Hartford Courant* editorially as being cruel and pitiless. The pen picture drawn by Owen Johnson does not dwell on this side of the ceremony, but reflects the sunshine that comes into the life of a winner of the grand prize." This last was not true: Johnson fully described the pain and humiliation of those passed over in both descriptions of the two Tap Days in his novel. The second *Times* article, describing elections "carried out under a pouring rain and with unusual tension," explained why. "Johnson's attack on the social system as offering an unworthy aim for struggle, and his saying right out that the awe and reverence for the senior societies at New Haven was a cramping and binding worship of institutionalism, had evidently not been lost on the college audience. The tension was greater than for any previous year. The societies, whose aloofness had never been questioned, have realized that in a measure they have been on the defensive, and to the justly famed 'Yale grit' was added to-day a firmer determination to see the thing through nobly." Remarkably, the reporter was finding that it was not the candidates but the societies showing courage, conducting their ritual with energy and dignity after their national denunciation.

Three hundred juniors took up their positions around the old tree at the corner of the campus between Battell Chapel and Durfee Hall, with five hundred students of other classes, and visitors in every window of Durfee, including society graduate members, while Yale College Dean Frederick Jones (Bones, 1884) looked on gravely. Newspapers reported that in the downpour, with the mud three inches deep on the soggy ground worn bare by pick-up baseball games, the Bones members "clinging to their ancient custom, came upon this scene without a stitch of waterproof cloth to protect them, dressed in dark suits quite immaculately, and with black derby hats." The Keys representatives were more sensibly dressed in raincoats, while the Wolf's Head men "even condescended to wear rough caps and any sort of mackintosh that they happened to have."

Averell Harriman, said the week before by the newspaper's correspondent to be Keys material, was tapped for Bones; to much murmured commentary. Harriman's close friend Walter Camp Jr., son of the Yale athletic advisor and noted Bonesman, accepted Keys' offer. The last man for Bones was George H. Cortelyou Jr., son of President Theodore Roosevelt's private secretary, and manager of the university crew. The last man for Keys was Vanderbilt Webb. Wolf's Head suffered a disaster, receiving four refusals, from the intercollegiate golf champion, a class deacon, a track miler, and a member of the university crew; "The refusal of election is often one of the most trying moments of 'Tap Day,'" the *Times* article noted. "The man's friends, anxious not to see him get left, often set up a cry of 'Take it!' and even start the unwilling candidate toward his room by violent methods. This did not occur today."

The man who had defeated Harriman for the presidency of the Yale Navy, the son of the speaker of the Massachusetts House of Representatives, was passed over by all three societies, as were an oarsman and football star. "I have gotten in a number of letters of congratulations from Bones graduates," Harriman wrote his mother, evidencing his pleasure and then his ignorance of the interior life of the senior society. "It must be a marvelous institution for these men to take it as seriously and to make as much of it as they do." Tellingly, William Rockefeller, brother of the petroleum magnate John D. Rockefeller, wrote a note of congratulations to the widow Harriman on her son's election, as his son Percy had been elected to Bones in 1899.[21]

The *Times* closed its Tap Day report with a quotation of a spectator described only as a member of one of the societies from a recent class, who admitted that a time might come when the ceremony would no longer exist. "Whatever Owen Johnson may say," he said, "these institutions are here to stay. The manner of election may change. I do not believe that any one outside of Yale knows exactly what they stand for. They are entirely different from fraternities. Johnson is undoubtedly giving a false impression of Yale societies to many persons who do not know the college and what the senior societies really stand for."

In a remarkable coincidence, Tap Day in New Haven in 1912 was the day of the American Booksellers' Association's annual convention in New York City, to which Johnson was invited as a speaker. He stoutly maintained his theme that the colleges "are sublimely indifferent to the fact that their role in a great nation is not a pleasant gymnasium or a fairly democratic social clearing house, but to be the inspiration to public service and the vital crucible of the nation . . . The best thing that can happen to [the colleges] is criticism, to wake them up and make them ask themselves what they should stand for." Johnson told the *Times* that his criticisms were not limited to New Haven, noting that "Some of my characters criticised the senior societies, as such criticism will always exist, but in making Skull and Bones tap Stover at the end I did full justice to what I consider the spirit of justice and fair play in that system when that spirit is properly aroused."[22]

In truth, the changes for which Johnson called a dozen years after his graduation had begun by 1912, in the election of collegians whose prominence was not founded on the athletic field, or service on the boards of student publications, or scholarship (which had improved, with six of the fifteen men tapped for Bones in 1910 being members of Phi Beta Kappa).[23] This is evidenced by the presence of two men, to be found under that Old Campus elm on Tap Day that May afternoon, who did *not* receive individual mention in the newspaper accounts.

The first, electing for Bones that year, was Gerald Murphy '12. Son of the president and owner of the Mark W. Cross Company, the New York purveyors of fine leather goods, he was admitted to Yale, like Stover's friend Tom Regan, only after multiple tries at the admissions test, but he had become a big man on campus by devoting himself to what his class history referred to as the "aesthetic side" of undergraduate life. A closeted bisexual and a dandy, voted the class's "Best Dressed," Murphy was elected manager of both the Apollo Glee Club and university Glee Club, while also serving as chief aide to his future Bones clubmate who the chairman of the junior prom (Murphy's date was his future wife Sara Wiborg, whose dance card included Averell Harriman). Murphy was also a member of the Pundits, a quasi-literary club limited to ten undergraduates, and one of the eighteen charter members of the Elizabethan Club, founded to provide, in the words of the *Yale News*, "a center for the literary life of the university."

Murphy could not have been less like Dink Stover, complaining long after graduation that "You always felt you were expected to make good in some form of extracurricular activity. . . . The athlete was all-important, and the rest of the student body was trained to watch and cheer from the sidelines. There was a general tacit Philistinism. One's studies were seldom discussed. An interest in the arts was suspect. The men in your class with the most interesting minds were submerged and you never got to know them."[24] In later life in the Murphys' home "Villa America" on the French Riviera, they entertained Zelda and F. Scott Fitzgerald, Ernest Hemingway, John Dos Passos, Fernand Léger, Jean Cocteau, Pablo Picasso, Archibald MacLeish, John O'Hara, Dorothy Parker, and Robert Benchley. The couple became the models for Dick and Nicole Diver in Fitzgerald's 1933 novel *Tender Is the Night*, for the main characters in Archibald MacLeish's Pulitzer prize–wining play *J.B.* of 1959, and were recognizable as the couple in Hemingway's *Garden of Eden*, published in 1986.[25]

Archie MacLeish, Yale 1915, although in Bones three years behind Gerald, did not know him in New Haven. When the MacLeishes went to Paris in the twenties, and everyone told them that they must meet the Murphys, Archie got the distinct impression that the Murphys were avoiding them. Afterward, when they had become close friends, he decided that Murphy had simply been reluctant to meet another Bones man. However, once their forty-year friendship began, the subject of the society was never brought up. Gerald had been extremely pleased with the traditional grandfather clock given as a wedding present by his Bones clubmates, and after his June 1915 class reunion he had gone for a few days of camaraderie to Deer Island, the society's island in the St. Lawrence, so he had been quite comfortable in the presence of his peers. Yet by the time of the Murphys' departure for Europe in 1921, he wrote that he had become uncomfortable in any "Association, Society, Company (even Mark Cross), Club (don't belong to one), or . . . Set." In time, he avoided all contact with Yale, refusing to supply any information for his class's reunion books. As for Fitzgerald, when it became clear that he was "studying" Sara and Gerald for his novel, a strain was put on the couples' relationship, not improved when Scott asked Gerald "how I got into Skull and Bones."[26]

The second unusual man among those milling in front of Durfee Hall was Murphy's great friend from Peru, Indiana, Cole Porter of the class of 1913. Encountered when Murphy was vetting sophomore candidates for Delta Kappa Epsilon, Porter had then just submitted the lyrics of "Bulldog" for the football song competition, but the five-foot-six-inch, fifteen-year-old candidate in ludicrous clothes struck Murphy as "a little dark man with his hair parted in the middle and slicked back, wearing a salmon-pink tie and looking just like a westerner all dressed up for the east," who had his nails done. Porter did not change much in his career at Yale, and barely passed his academic courses, but his musical talent—with over three hundred compositions worked out on the piano which traveled through his college rooms, including football songs like "Bingo Eli Yale" and "Bulldog"—and his performances with the banjo, mandolin, and glee clubs together earned him social acclaim. He was elected not only to DKE, but to the Whiffenpoofs, the Owen Johnson–founded Wigwam and Wrangler Debating Club, the Pundits, the Yale Dramatic Association, the University Club, and on Tap Day in

1912 to Scroll and Key. None other than Archie MacLeish, two years behind Porter, recited the prologue to and played the part of a baby in *The Kaleidescope*, a musical written and directed by Porter in his senior year for the Dramatic Association.

Porter was also a football cheerleader and the chairman of the football song selection committee, which in view of Cole's well-documented preference for virile, big-muscled men, might have been a manifestation of the composer's homosexuality, but as a classmate stated, "Cole was so bright and talented, one expected him to be a little different." His graduating class considered him one of their most eccentric members, with his loud dress and extraordinary interest in things theatrical, while voting him the most entertaining of their number. He is said to have written several anthems for Scroll and Key, "but if so," in the words of one biographer, "they have vanished forever behind all that ivy" on the society's tomb. Porter's alma mater, to which he left all his original manuscripts and other memorabilia, conferred an honorary Doctorate of Humane Letters upon him in 1960, in his Waldorf Astoria apartment on the composer's sixty-ninth birthday (the first Yale honorary degree ever conferred in a private ceremony, its award delayed by two trustees who disapproved of the honorand's lifestyle).[27]

With Porter as with Murphy, the senior societies were clearly broadening the range of their tolerance for electing men who were distinctly *not* cogs in the machine that Owen Johnson had described and lamented. But perhaps Johnson had covered even that ground in *Stover*: "I'll bet we get a lot of fruits," a new freshmen traveling on the train with Dink to New Haven says to another. "Oh," comes the reply, "some of them aren't half bad."[28]

THE SOPHOMORE CLASS REVOLT

However strong the nonchalance of the junior class in 1912, shrugging off the *Stover* criticisms and accepting elections in the normal course, the class immediately beneath was not having it. Sophomores of the class of 1915 thought changes in the system must be made. A core group of twenty-five made a compact not to take election until the three senior societies had been materially reformed, and then called several meetings of their class to formulate those reforms, to be instigated before their own Tap Day in May 1914. In time about 160 men (of a class of 291) coalesced into a formidable movement. On 13 April 1913 they met at the Taft Hotel to perfect their formal protest, as reported on the front page of the *New York Times*. The next day a meeting attended by two hundred called for committees to be appointed to meet with the faculty and with representatives of the three senior societies, after the entire sophomore class had been canvassed for pledges to refuse election in their junior year unless reforms were implemented.

This canvass produced a further pledge that the protesters would not accept elections to the senior societies unless Tap Day were altered and the basis of choice reformed to the satisfaction of two-thirds of the signers. The first petitions, signed by over sixty men, were more revolutionary, stating that everyone who signed promised never to accept an election to any senior society by the present method, and then stated that none of the signers would accept an election until the secret character of the organizations was done away with.[29] When the demand for the meetings with the three senior societies was rebuffed, the protesters published an untitled pamphlet of four pages, signed openly by ten of the rebels and then distributed to their own classmates and to the forty-five senior society members, identifying their main points of dissatisfaction: "Excessive Secrecy" and "Inadvisable Choice of Members." Reprinting the text, the *Yale News* broke its decades-long, self-imposed embargo on commentary on the societies (beyond reporting election results), and while not discussing the Sophomore Movement on its merits, gave praise to its temper and terms.

While claiming their movement did "not stand for abolition," these sophomores found that the secrecy of the social system stifled spontaneity, engendered hypocrisy, and strained friendships, while the "sensational display" of Tap Day gave undue advertisement to the societies and overemphasized the distinction between the elected and those passed over. As for those elected, there should be "a recognition of merit, not on the basis of actual accomplishment alone, but to a large degree on the basis of what men have attempted to do, and on the revelation in that attempt of qualities of character and of personality." In light of these concerns, the pamphleteers continued, "we suggest that secrecy be reduced to a reasonable privacy; that Tap Day as it now exists, be abolished; and that the greatest care in the choice of men, as outlined above, be exercised."[30]

The criticisms were clear enough, but in the end the reforms proposed were both mild and imprecise. They received fair mockery in the anonymously published student periodical the *Eavesdropper*, in a "Pre-Tap Day Tragedy" titled "The Last Days of Pompilius." The title character proposes "that forty-five men be chosen (by whom, I cannot say), in a new way (I do not know exactly how), and with a new idea (I cannot say precisely what). Then let their names be drawn from an urn by the youngest of the vestal virgins: the first man to go to *Cranium et Ossa*, the next to *Papyrus et Clava*, the third to *Caput Lupi*, and so on. Thus we may secure social equality in its purest form."[31]

Wolf's Head, the youngest of the three societies and the one most likely to be hardest hit in the event of a shortage of candidates, met on March 8 and tried to decide on some course of action. More remarkably, Skull and Bones responded with its own pamphlet in this war of words, titled "322," and dated April 26, 1913. Noting that their society had decided in the fall of 1912 to drop the old customs of escorting the athletes home and of not speaking after Thursday night meetings, the Bonesmen argued that their "reasons for privacy and silence regarding . . . actions within our building" could hardly be understood by outsiders, nor was it appreciated "that the mutual trusts imposed on our members to guard our confidences has been one of the greatest factors in our growth." The offensive sensationalism of the election ceremony, they noted, was bound to be reduced because in the fall of 1912 Yale College Dean Frederick Jones (Bones 1884, as it happened) had decreed the closing of the campus on the day of elections to all persons not members of the university, and had recently requested that the sophomore and freshman classes *not* be present as well on May 15. The students were instead to play an interclass baseball game that afternoon, while the professors were urged to attend a faculty tea in Forestry Hall, a mile from the main campus.

The Bones club repudiated any notion that their society, at least, chose "inadvisable men," and so "we believe it our duty to live on in a manly and independent manner, undisturbed by rumors and criticism, so long as in our relations to other members of the University we do what we consider fair and just." The gravity of the sophomore attack of 1913 may be measured in part by the extraordinary appearance of this Bones pamphlet, the first and last time in the society's entire history that an undergraduate club, one that included Averell Harriman and Sidney Lovett, later the Yale University chaplain from 1932 to 1958, felt the necessity of making a public response to criticism.[32]

The sophomores remained rebellious under Dean Frederick Jones's strictures, some quoted in New York newspapers as saying that they wanted the ceremony "scourged" from the campus, but if not, they wished to "see what's going on." Jones (a Bones alumnus of 1880) told the same paper that he was acting in an "advisory capacity" and that the faculty had "taken no official cognizance of the discussion" and would not unless it became a disciplinary affair.[33] No annual *Horoscope* was to appear, due to the agitation, being replaced with the *Eavesdropper* as a pallid imitator, jesting about the senior societies but making no attempt to forecast results.

Owen Johnson wrote the *New York Times*, hailing the sophomores' courage, "amazing to those who are familiar with the long tradition of underclass subjection." He called for the preparation of a list of one hundred positions "to be acquired as the result of some ambitious effort" in the college's athletic, dramatic, literary, religious, and scholarly activities, demanding that the senior societies agree to recruit only from this list, which would go far "in weeding out the chaff that is so objectionable." Johnson concluded that "the action of the sophomore class at Yale in deciding *to think for itself* is to me the most amazing manifestation in the whole history of university conflict." His suggestion of a list was indeed ultimately to be taken up in 1914, and after these 1913 elections, one newspaper opined that had one for that year been produced in a timely fashion, most of the men tapped would have been on it.[34]

The freshman class voted unanimously on the Tuesday preceding Tap Day not to attend the Thursday ceremony, and the sophomores passed their own recusal resolution early on election day in a mass meeting, some then going off to play baseball as bidden. For elections the campus gates were closed and temporary fences erected over remaining gaps, with the two campus policemen and some seniors deputized to stand guard against entry by the general public. Newspapermen and photographers were banned. These combined efforts reduced attendance to only about six hundred students. A report circulated that Wolf's Head had pledged to the sophomores to adopt the reforms urged and had already given out its pledges to the juniors it would elect. The Elihu Club, never having participated in Tap Day, piously announced that it would refuse to participate and would accept the proposed reforms. This raised the alarming prospect, for the two oldest senior societies, of the sophomore class agreeing to accept elections the following year only to Wolf's Head and Elihu.[35]

In what the newspapers called the "denatured" Tap Day of 1913, the societies themselves conducted the affair differently. Instead of the traditional black derbies and suits and ties, the seniors wore ordinary clothes and no hats, with the Bonesmen alone making any pretense of solemnity, striding along without looking left or right, or responding to the thirty or forty hecklers in the great oak tree. Despite being warned off, many graduates still chose to attend, passed in by "checkers" at the gates who were all younger graduates of the societies. While the raillery from the non-society seniors in the trees was said to be largely good-natured, the levity itself at Tap Day was a startling first: "Seniors' Gibes End Tap Day's Gravity," headlined the *New York Times*. Most of the sophomores watched the elections from their windows in Durfee and Farnam, while the freshmen piled three deep in the windows of their residence Wright Hall, or jammed its forecourt, each class thus technically fulfilling the requirement that they "keep off the campus." Not one girl's face appeared at a window of Durfee, where in former years there were half a dozen tea parties going, and there were no carriages or automobiles.

Whether or not the sophomores found satisfactory the election of eight athletes by Bones and three by Keys, with their remaining new members "prominent in literary work" and eleven of those thirty belonging to Phi Beta Kappa, Dean Jones as the only faculty member present pronounced these results to be proof that these men had been elected on merit alone. Representatives of the underclassmen who had publicly pledged themselves not to join in the future unless changes were made declared they would take a vote sometime in the future on these 1913 elections, to decide whether those chosen had been so on deserts and achievement.[36]

Although many members of the class of 1915, now rising juniors contemplating their own Tap Day at the end of the academic year, remained as disgruntled as they had been as sophomores, nothing more formal was done until after Christmas 1913. While agreeing that the men elected the prior spring were "chosen absolutely on merit," more was needed, and five alternative "plans" to developed to be voted upon: that the signers should not offer themselves for election under any consideration, or that they should not offer themselves for election from principle; or that they should offer themselves for election providing that Tap Day was moved to the Berkeley Oval, where the majority of juniors now lived, across Elm Street on the land now beneath Berkeley College; or that there be elimination of conflicts in the three senior societies' prospect lists (which were never made public or shared among the societies); or that those societies agree to consider a list of seventy men whom the signers considered worthy of elections; or that they should offer themselves without insisting on any further reform. No alternative received the two-thirds vote established as necessary for adoption.

At a March meeting held to vote on the original resolutions, two-thirds of the signers declared that sufficient changes had not yet been made to warrant abandoning their protest. Among the men regarded as likely for election, however, most had voted to drop the matter, while a majority of those believed to have no chance at all for senior society membership voted to continue the struggle and enforce the agreement of the year before. Thus, those (now) juniors who inaugurated the reform movement were apparently to be deprived of the fruits of their labor, denied the privilege of entering the societies on which they had already forced some reform.

A revised plan was brought up at a subsequent meeting, at which the 157 voters, over half the class, with only four dissenting ballots, agreed to offer themselves for election, provided that the societies would in turn agree to consider the "class list" and to give out their elections in the Berkeley Oval. Dean Jones intervened once more, simply mandating that elections for the class of 1915 be held there (the senior societies had also urged this). A fence was ordered to be erected between the gaps in the Oval to keep out the curious, and entry allowed for the May 1914 Tap Day only to the juniors themselves and members of the senior societies. The event was otherwise closed to women and to the rest of the general public.[37]

The class of 1915 then worked on their second condition, taking up Owen Johnson's suggestion of composing a list, theirs of fifty names—five more than the three societies' membership maximum of forty-five— made up from other lists of forty-five men each made up by individual members of the class (both protest resolution signers and non-signers) about their own fellows, deposited into a ballot box in the Yale Station post. The winnowed final candidates' names, tabulated by a faculty committee, were printed in the *Yale News* in alphabetical order on April 29, 1914. This list, the organizers emphasized, was to apply only to the Class of 1915, since such a requirement, if recurring in future, would lead to more than two years of "wire-pulling, fraternity politics, and toadying" before any scheduled election. While the three societies firmly refused to compare their own lists, for the elimination of conflicts, they promised their readiness to consider the *News* list in their selections. Individual juniors were still worried, because if a society required a unanimous vote, it was perfectly possible for a listed man to be ignored, simply because he had had a run-in with some present member.

It was rumored that Bones would take its full complement from the printed list, while Keys and Wolf's Head would each take about two-thirds of their candidates. Many of the protesters were said to be reserving the right to "throw down" the societies' proffers nonetheless, to evidence their belief that the reforms were insufficient. By threatening to withhold their candidacies, the class of 1915 would go down in Yale history as mounting the most successful protest to date against what their predecessors had styled the "poppycock" of the system. While opinions differed as to whether the atmosphere of rebellion significantly affected elections the year before for the class of 1914, with Dean Jones's interventions, Tap Day itself had been stripped of many of its undesirable features.[38]

On election day, the three societies chose thirty-six of the fifty from the list made up by the juniors: all fifteen tapped by Bones, thirteen of those chosen by Keys, and eight by Wolf's Head, so only nine elected had not been identified for society honors by their own classmates, of whom five represented the excess of the class list number (fifty) over the available slots (forty-five). The societies showed magnanimity: two of the Sophomore Movement manifesto signers of April 1913 were elected by Bones in 1914: Bayne Denègre, captain of the varsity crew, tapped last, and Harold Pumpelley, junior prom chairman and star of the football and baseball teams, tapped fourth; Keys chose a third, William Crocker of the varsity crew and San Francisco banking family. Only one man refused an election, from Bones, and went to Keys. Burch Harrison and the other six signers of the sophomore manifesto for reform were not tapped, but Harrison had publicly stated that he would not accept election due to insufficient reform. One signatory, Chandler Bennitt, stroke oar on the freshman crew and third stand scholar in the class, may have suffered the most public retaliation, as the *New Haven Journal-Courier* identified him as "leader of the reformer movement," but held that his failure of election to any society was a "surprise."

Among those elected that day, not among the protesters but both on the published list of fifty, were Archibald MacLiesh, chairman of the *Lit.* and captain of the water polo team and future Librarian of Congress and winner of three Pulitzer Prizes, for Bones, and Dean Acheson, freshman crew coach and future secretary of state, for Keys. (MacLeish, asked in 1923 to be godfather to Acheson's son David, accepted, noting that the boy "may go Bones if I evangelize hard enough"—which David did.) Scornfully describing the Sophomore Movement's adherents as "the Daughters of Dink," MacLeish predicted that many of those who had pledged themselves against joining a society would be fighting to get themselves released from their commitment—which release the creation of the list, meant to force the hand of the electors, had indirectly facilitated for the elected. As for Acheson, he had been bequeathed the job of coaching the freshman crew by Averell Harriman, and when the latter was sacked as varsity coach, Acheson lost his position too. He said later, "I have been fired since, but never in better company." Many years later, President Truman was to bring Harriman into the White House to help Acheson, who as secretary of state was at the center of the administration's most difficult public trials.[39]

The next spring, in May 1915 for the elections for the class of 1916, the ceremony was moved once again, back to the main campus, but now to an open space in front of Durfee Hall so that enterprising onlookers might not climb into the old oak and shout down disconcerting remarks during the affair. Dean Jones issued instructions early on the day that none but juniors and seniors should be admitted to the central campus, that the other classes were to remain in their rooms, that the gates should again be locked and temporary fences put up to keep out those who did not belong to either class; visitors would not be allowed on the grounds—even faculty members were not encouraged to attend—while ropes were stretched across open spaces, and the campus was "closed as tight as a drum." Still, the oak had its climbers, and the dormitory windows their deriding onlookers, yelling as the society delegates entered the crowd, "Not at home," "You are in the wrong pew," and "You can't find him here today."[40]

The following year's elections of May 1916 saw one final spasm of the Sophomore Movement. The exercises were again held on the main campus, and in many respects, the senior society universe had been restored after the controversy and round trip to the Berkeley Oval for elections. Averell Harriman's younger brother Edward, stroke of the crew, was elected to Bones, as was Henry Sage Fenimore Cooper, a member of the relay team which had recently equaled the world's record, and a grandson of author James Fenimore Cooper (expelled from Yale as a junior in 1805 for a prank). Others then chosen by Bones were Alfred Bellinger, to serve in time as Yale's professor of Latin, and Prescott Bush, first baseman on the varsity nine, later senator from Connecticut and father and grandfather of American presidents, as well as three men who were self-supporting, working their way through college.

However, the baseball pitcher Spencer Pumpelly, considered sure of election, refused to go on the campus; instead, he spent the afternoon riding in his automobile, and a New Haven paper reported that the Bones elections were delayed by their search for him. His brother Harold, the former football and baseball star who had been one of the signers of the sophomore class manifesto, had in the end been elected to Bones. Although no one would have remembered it at the time of the younger Pumpelly's dramatic spurning of the now hallowed ceremony, not since William Kingsley repudiated his brother Henry's senior society of Skull and Bones back in 1842 to found Scroll and Key had there been such a marked repudiation of the existing society system by a younger sibling.[41]

And in the spring of 1916, no one knew or even suspected that this would be the last Tap Day for three years, until 1919, after the end of World War I.

THE CONFUSIONS OF WAR:
NEUTRALITY TO PREPAREDNESS

The First World War began in Europe in August 1914, barely eleven weeks after Tap Day for the class of 1915. While America was not to declare war on Germany until April 1917, the graduates, students, professors, and administrators of Yale were in uniform everywhere by 1915, and the ramp-up thereto began with military training camps that summer. Recent and not-so-recent alumni determinedly prepared there for the coming conflict: in September 1915, Hugh Bayne (class of 1892) and a dozen other Bones alumni from that class through that of 1914 wrote to Morris Hadley and the incoming Bones delegation about the graduates' camp training in Plattsburgh, New York, noting that "out of 324 living Bonesmen who graduated after 1891—that is, out of those whose ages were under 46, over 4 percent attended the Camp. This, we believe, is a larger proportional representation than that of any other single body or organization, and is another evidence of the patriotism of our institution."[42]

The Alumni Advisory Board recommended instituting military training at Yale itself. Seven hundred ten men from Yale, in classes ranging from 1880 to 1919, enrolled in Plattsburgh in the summer of 1916. Yale ROTC officially commenced in February 1917, and two months later war was declared. In a speech in May, Dean Jones announced that there were 1,544 men in active training on the Yale Campus, and the *Yale Alumni Weekly* on October 11, 1918, informed its readers that the campus was not the one they knew, but a "national officers' training camp."

A great mass meeting had been held in October 1914 to raise funds for the Red Cross, and twelve ambulances were furnished, followed by the publication of the first list of Yale participants in the war and a call for volunteer ambulance drivers in France. Archibald MacLeish and three other members of the class of 1915 Bones club—his roommate, and the captains of the baseball and track teams—joined the Yale Mobile Hospital Unit in June 1917. However, after reaching Paris, they found the hospital unit to be moribund, and at Archie's petition, Hugh Bayne (by now a member of General Pershing's staff) got the four men transferred to officers' training in the field artillery as second lieutenants.

President Hadley announced plans for the organization of the Field Artillery Battery in the fall of 1915, for which French 75-millimeter artillery pieces arrived in March 1916 to allow training to begin in earnest, Yale's being the only such college unit. Nearly a thousand undergraduates tried to sign up, with 486 men eventually recruited into four batteries, one of them commanded by the Yale president's son Morris, who was the last man tapped for Bones the prior spring, a *Lit.* editor, Phi Beta Kappa president, and later founding partner of the New York law firm Milbank, Tweed, Hadley & McCloy.[43]

The war record of the Yale Battery at the United States Army's Fort Sill in Oklahoma was to have a discreditable coda. So many Yale men were there that on March 31, 1918, a Yale dinner was held in the mess hall, with several Bonesmen in attendance, all captains in field artillery units: 1917's Prescott Bush of the 322nd Field Artillery, who led the singing at the dinner, Neil Mallon (three decades later to give Prescott's son George Herbert Walker Bush his first job in the Texas oilfields), Ellery James, Kenneth Simpson, Knight Woolley, and, shortly to be initiated into the club of 1919, Charles Haffner Jr. Remembering the campus tradition of crooking now largely discredited in New Haven, possessed of a racial consciousness and a sense of Anglo-Saxon superiority, and learning that the iconic Apache leader Geronimo had died at Fort Sill after internment there, these young men saw a chance to add to the collection of skulls and femurs at their tomb. Sometime in May 1918, they claimed to have forced open a grave with an iron door and shipped some of the contents therein back to Connecticut.

Winter Mead, still a student on campus and a classmate of Haffner's, wrote to a recent graduate member that "The skull of the worthy Geronimo the Terrible, exhumed from its tomb at Fort Sill by your club and the Knight Haffner, is now safe inside the Tomb, together with his well-worn leathers, bit & saddle horn." It seems probable, according to several historians, that it was not Geronimo's grave that was desecrated, since no biography of the Indian leader describes his burial in an iron-doored tomb, and his family is said to have quietly removed the remains to an unmarked site several years earlier. Still, if this was not an instance of a fanciful exploit founded on a purchase in the black market in Indian grave artifacts, it seems incontestable that something happened to another burial site, and as has been said, the Geronimo letter of Mead, "with its matter-of-fact reports of troop units and its boast about a grave robbery, speaks to the complex and contradictory mores of the privileged class in early twentieth century America."[44]

Beyond the practice for the batteries, motivated students, faculty and graduates had been anticipating the federal government's needs by organizing training for other branches of service: by the end of World War I, Yale's record included the only college field artillery school, the first American mobile field hospital, the only school training officers for the Signal Corps, and, most remarkably, the first air units. As early as the summer of 1916, in a very different "sophomore movement," the class of 1918's F. Trubee Davison and some of his classmates had formed a Volunteer Coast Patrol squad, hiring their own seaplane, instructor, and equipment, and begun training in Port Washington on Long Island. In the fall they had taken part in naval maneuvers off Sandy Hook, and their "Aero Club" continued work with donated planes at the submarine base in New London. When the winter weather prevented flying, they busied themselves with the study of wireless and the theory of flying, while taking in more members.

The period from April 1917, when America declared war, to the spring of 1918 saw a deteriorating campus situation, with an uneasy and limited role for college men. The 1917 Selective Service Act established the draft age as twenty-one, and so affected only the older students, but the younger undergraduates, impatient and increasingly doubtful about the utility of peacetime studies, began to seek some quicker way into the services than the four-year ROTC course. Some got their parents' permission, left college, and joined up, while others certainly lied about their ages and enlisted. War was declared during the 1917 spring vacation, and through the *Yale News*, the juniors made known their strong desire that Tap Day be moved up, while the seniors were still on campus and "intact" as clubs to hold elections.

There was no commencement exercise for the senior class, and by June, it was estimated that some seven hundred students had left the campus, the senior society men figuring prominently in the departures. The *Yale Alumni Weekly*, in an early autumn issue, announced that no member of Scroll and Key had returned to campus for their delegation's senior year, and only two from Skull and Bones, one from Wolf's Head, and three from Elihu. In November 1917, another *YAW* article by a professor serving as major in the Yale ROTC pointed out that all the high-stand men were gone—the *Yale News* chairman and fourteen of its board members, the *Lit.* chairman and three of its other four board members—and commented, "The intellectual leaders among the students are just where they ought to be—in France or making ready to go there."[45] Not until December 1918 and demobilization was Yale to begin to return to normal, from an armed camp back to an academic campus.

THE FIRST YALE UNIT AND THE SENIOR SOCIETIES

Among Yale's undergraduates, twenty-eight men would pioneer American military aviation, on their own initiative. Their families' immense private resources made possible the formation of the First Yale Naval Training Unit, which became the originating squadron of the U.S. Naval Reserve, growing out of little more than a military summer camp hosted by one of a group of sophomores. Leading members of the group in the class of 1918 included Frederick Trubee Davison, Robert Lovett, Kenneth MacLeish, Artemus Gates, and Alan Ames. In the poem titled "On a Memorial Stone" by Kenny's older brother Archie first published just two years later, he wrote: "And generations unfulfilled,/The heirs of all we struggled for,/Shall here recall the mythic war/And marvel how we stabbed and killed,/And name us savage, brave, austere—/And none shall think how very young we were."

The boys' energetic, self-appointed leader was Trubee Davison, son of the managing partner of J. P. Morgan & Co. following Morgan's death. Trubee had accompanied his father on a business trip to Europe in 1915 and signed on in Paris with the American Ambulance Field

Service ferrying wounded soldiers from the trains to the American Hospital there. His classmate and friend Bob Lovett was the son of the chairman of the executive committee and president of the "Harriman System" of the Union Pacific and Southern Pacific railroad lines, and had grown up alongside the Harriman sons Averell and Roland; he was to be voted the "hardest working" and "most brilliant" member of the class at graduation. A third classmate, football star Artemus "Di" Gates, was like Davison and Lovett a member of Psi Upsilon, but Gates's oldest and closest friend since preparatory school at Hotchkiss was Kenneth MacLeish. Kenny, three years behind Archie, was sometimes asked if he was the brother of the man voted "most brilliant" by his classmates in the class of 1915, and the younger MacLeish aspired to membership in some senior society, although he simply had not had the time in New Haven to match Archie's spectacular record of campus achievements which had brought a Bones tap.

Davison demonstrated to the Yale community how easy flying was by piloting his own plane from his home at Peacock Point in Locust Valley on Long Island Sound, to appear in New Haven at morning chapel and still attend class on time. Classmates in Psi Upsilon were contacted by his telegram in July 1916, invited to learn to fly under the banner of the Aero Club of America and to train privately that summer while staying at Peacock Point, practicing in flying boats purchased by his father and other donors. By summer's end, Lovett, Davison, and Gates could solo. Others of the young flyers included John Villiers Farwell III, a star high hurdler, and hockey player Erl Clinton Barker Gould.

Yet to begin their Yale undergraduate careers at this date were even younger aspiring airmen: Trubee's brother Harry P. Davison Jr. in the summer of 1916 was just leaving Groton School but joined his brother's friends in the first Aero Club group, as did David "Crock" Ingalls, who would come up the same year from St. Paul's, where he had starred in hockey (his later gift to Yale was the Ingalls Rink). Crock's Yale attendance was encouraged if not ordained by his mother being the daughter of Charles Phelps Taft, half-brother of William Howard Taft. Joining the growing unit in 1917 were Kenny MacLeish, Archibald McIlwaine, George Lawrence, Curtis Read, and Reginald Coombe.

Finally securing his own parents' permission and support, Davison over the next year fought tirelessly to have the unit officially recognized by the U.S. Navy, making frequent trips to Washington to petition Navy Secretary Josephus Daniels (Trubee missed the Junior Prom, being managed by Lovett, for one such meeting). Permission was finally secured in March 1917, and the group of fifteen juniors promptly withdrew from college, enlisting in the Naval Air Corps Reserve. What the newspapers began calling the "Millionaires' Unit" traveled south to West Palm Beach, Florida, for further training.

Some four months later, on July 28, 1917, twenty-eight candidates, including members of a second Yale Aerial Coast Patrol unit, were taking their flying tests in order to obtain their Navy wings. Trubee, who was unwell and had fainted the day before, lost control of his seaplane during his test flight and spiraled into the sea, splitting his craft in two, breaking his back and injuring his spinal cord. When he was put aboard his father's yacht for transport home, Lovett, Gates, and Ingalls raced ahead to New York in a Marmon roadster to locate a surgeon. With a broken back, Trubee never saw combat, but he remained active in the affairs of the First Naval Air Unit for the duration of the war and was awarded the Navy Cross for his services.

Living in pain the rest of his life, Davison following the Armistice returned to Yale to room with Di Gates and finished his undergraduate program as a member of the class of 1919. He was named by President Coolidge to head the National Crime Commission, and thereafter served under President Harding as assistant secretary of war for aviation. Retiring from politics in 1933, he went on to be president of the American Museum of Natural History for almost the next two decades, before joining the army when World War II came and leaving it as a brigadier general. Davison was elected to the Yale Corporation as a successor trustee in 1951 and became the first personnel director of the newly formed Central Intelligence Agency.

His aerial brother-in-arms Robert Lovett, after partnership in Brown Brothers Harriman with Bush, Harriman, and Woolley, became during World War II the assistant secretary of war for air (taking the post Davison had held in World War I). He then chaired the Lovett Committee, to advise the government on the post–World War II organization of American intelligence activities, which led to the creation of the Central Intelligence Agency. Lovett served under President Truman as undersecretary of state, then deputy secretary of defense, and finally secretary of defense. When John F. Kennedy became president, he offered Lovett his choice of three top Cabinet posts, State, Defense, or Treasury; although these were all declined, Lovett suggested the three men who were ultimately named to those positions. A friend of William Faulkner, Lovett told him the story of the World War I flyers and coastal boat patrols, which the author used in one of his finest short stories, "Turn About." The tale was turned into the film *Today We Live* by the noted director Howard Hawks, with Gary Cooper in the Lovett role.[46]

The conflict's irruption into campus life, when war was formally declared by the United States on April 6, 1917, caused the three senior societies to move Tap Day up by nearly a month from what had become its traditional date, the second Tuesday in May. Scroll and Key contacted Dean Frederick Jones with the message to be conveyed through him to Skull and Bones that they wanted to conduct initiation before most of the students left campus. Bones countered with the suggestion that elections—for which they had done no groundwork—be conducted in the week after spring vacation, with an accelerated Tap Day at week's end, which was acceptable to both Keys and Wolf's Head. Furthermore, since fifteen leading members of the junior class were now completing their school year, if not their schooling, in Florida, the societies declared they would send representatives there to offer election, as they had done in the past for candidates out of New Haven for illness or other excused absence.

On April 19 on the campus, Prescott Bush led off for Bones, to reach as his society's first tap Newell Garfield, his baseball teammate, a basketball star, and an American president's grandson. Thirty-two other men were elected that day in New Haven, including *Lit.* chairman John Farrar, later to found and chair the eponymous publishing house of Farrar, Straus & Giroux, and, as the last man chosen for Bones, Charles P. Taft II, former President Taft's son, basketball captain, football standout, and second highest scholar in his class. Keys' elections in New Haven included Wilmarth Sheldon "Lefty" Lewis, to serve in World War II as the chief of the Central Intelligence Division of the Office of Strategic Services, a job secured through his friendship with Archie MacLeish, and thereafter to become a long-serving trustee of the Yale Corporation and the greatest collector of the works of Horace Walpole while editing the multi-volume edition of that Englishman's letters. At his prep school graduation, Lewis had been urged to accept a Bones election by his headmaster, Sherman Day Thacher, founder of the Thacher School in California; another teacher there, related to the Rev. Joseph Twichell, told him that Keys was the better society.

Not tapped that day, to his surprise and humiliation, was a close friend of Farrar's, Philip Barry, who was on the boards of the *News* and the *Lit.* A WASP from the fashionable Thacher School, Lefty Lewis was later to say about Barry, an Irish American public high school boy from Rochester, New York, that he was not "terrifically one of the boys" and that "nobody would have been surprised if he had been [tapped], but nobody was surprised that he hadn't been." Barry was to become one of the most fashionable playwrights of the second quarter of the twentieth century, author of *Holiday* and *The Philadelphia Story*, both comedies of manners later made into films with Katharine Hepburn and Cary Grant. It must have been a sweet redemption that the honorary pallbearers at Barry's death in 1949 included Bonesmen Gerald Murphy, Robert Lovett, and Artemus Gates, and two novelists renowned for examining the same American social class, John O'Hara and John P. Marquand.[47]

Earlier that same afternoon in Florida, just over thirteen weeks before the flying tests that would end in crippling Davison, the First Unit members gathered in the lobby of the Salt Air Hotel in West Palm Beach. Albert Olsen, former football manager and Yale senior, traveled there from New Haven to represent Bones, while unit member Samuel Sloan Walker, a senior, represented Keys; a Wolf's Head elector was also present. Alternating turns, Olson and Walker clapped the backs of the chosen among the fifteen members of the junior class on hand and sent them off to their hotel rooms, each being cheered as he made his way up the stairs.

As widely reported in the following day's newspapers, Bones' Olsen directed crew manager Trubee Davison, Dramatic Association manager and Junior Prom floor manager Bob Lovett, football captain-elect Di Gates, Ten Eyck (and later DeForest) Prize winner and *Record* editor John Vorys, and football quarterback Alan Ames up to their rooms to accept formal election. For Scroll and Key, Walker tapped hockey stars Erl Gould and Chip McIlwaine, varsity crewmen Reg Coombe and George Lawrence, and football manager Curtis Read; not eleven months later, Read was to be killed in a seaplane accident, on February 26, 1918, at Dunkirk. Oliver James and Bill Rockefeller turned down Wolf's Head taps, as did Lovett, and stayed downstairs with the remainder of the unit.

The few seniors on hand were already society members, and the underclassmen would have to wait another year for their opportunity. The society representatives sent a telegram to New Haven listing the Florida election results, confirming them by a telephone call, on a through wire arranged by a Bell Telephone executive who was a Bones graduate, to Trubee's father Henry Davison's office at J. P. Morgan in New York, and then relayed the same message to the societies' respective headquarters in New Haven, all before the on-campus tap was held there in the late afternoon in the usual way.

Kenny MacLeish, swimmer, diver, pole vaulter, and active member of the Yale Home Mission, was the only junior to be completely passed over, an event his disappointed older brother was to call a "brutal business." The younger MacLeish told his fiancée some seven months later "how terribly disappointed I was in not making a senior society"; the pain from the blow "almost kills me. I want to get to France and forget the whole thing and start over again." He was to more than regain his honor, nominated by First Unit squadron commander Bob Lovett to be commander of Unit No. 2, in charge of 428 men and ten aircraft, a promotion he refused because it would bar him from flying. Less than a month before the war's end, he was killed behind enemy lines on October 14, 1918, after destroying a German plane. Almost two weeks before, his best friend Di Gates had been shot down while in aerial combat in a French squadron; he was captured by the Germans, and survived, which Kenny was never to know. In World War II, Gates became assistant secretary of the Navy for Air, succeeding David Ingalls who held that post in 1919.[48]

Dean Jones, having intervened several times since the Sophomore Revolt to preserve the senior society system from its most objectionable excesses, now moved quickly to urge the eleven men tapped in Palm Beach to return for their initiations, and set in motion a series of telephone calls to secure the necessary permissions for all of them for a week's leave. Their absence ultimately authorized by Secretary of the Navy Daniels, they departed Florida by private train for New Haven on the Saturday following their elections, and were thus enabled to be initiated in the usual place and way.[49]

However, despite the difficulty and drama of the election and the initiation for the class of 1918, the existential threat to the continuation of the senior society system was only now to be endured. At the thirtieth anniversary of Skull and Bones, in 1863, when Professor Timothy Dwight addressed the annual convention, the battle of Gettysburg was not a month past, and although two of Dwight's classmates were then in service on the Confederate side, and a member of the Bones club of 1845, CSA Major William Connor, perished in that recent battle, no mention of this was made in his remarks: the Civil War had not forced its immediate presence into the college world. Ward Cheney, of the Bones club of 1896, went off to fight in the Spanish-American War and die in Luzon, leaving his $1,200 in government death benefits to his society, but his history was singular. In the First World War, the undergraduates' response to their country's military needs was dramatically different, draining away from campus the very members whose presence, with the inculcation of traditions in the densely packed senior year, guaranteed continuity.

When he left for Officers' Training Camp in San Francisco, Lefty Lewis remarked to President Hadley that it would be easier to die for Yale than for the country because Yale was so intimate and close-knit, and the country so vast and diversified. The only occasion on which Lewis's Keys delegation of 1918 was in their hall together their junior year was the all-night evening of their initiation. The same was true of the Bones club, and its delegation of 1919 never did manage a meeting of all fifteen. Similarly, over at Elihu, after the election of their 1918 delegation, only three members remained to carry on the club, and Thursday evening meetings were essentially abandoned.[50]

By June, only three Bonesmen remained in college, one of them the son of alumnus William Howard Taft, who heard his father vow with fellow society graduate members to do whatever was necessary to "continue the line." The two undergraduates still on campus in the fall of 1917 met weekly on Thursdays, holding debates with whatever graduate members were on hand; by February 1918, those two were also in France. The uncertainty continued into the next year, after a decision at the society's corporate midwinter meeting to hold elections for the class of 1919, with the directors empowered to choose the next club after conference and in conjunction with such undergraduate members as could be contacted in their overseas postings, and with fifteen being sought for election without reference to their being in the United States.

Inspired by Trubee Davison's example, Ganson Goodyear Depew of the class of 1919, a grandson of Chauncey Depew's brother, decided himself as a sophomore to form Aerial Coast Patrol Unit No. 2. For this effort he recruited Edward deCernea, Alexander McCormick, James Otis, John Jay Schieffelin, and four other members of this class and a man from the class of 1920, who together contributed funds for the purchase of Curtiss seaplanes in Ganson's hometown of Buffalo, New York. They enlisted as second-class seamen at the Brooklyn Navy Yard in April 1917, then trained as mechanics in the Curtiss factory at the Navy's direction.

All of them passed their naval pilot's flying test in the autumn of 1917, and Depew was soon made executive officer of the Pensacola Naval Air Station, but was bitterly disappointed when the excellence of his administrative abilities caused him to be kept stateside.

Five of the Second Unit were sent abroad, in November 1917, to England and France, where Ensign deCernea, before hearing by telegram of his election to Scroll and Key, successfully bombed a German submarine; he received the Croix de guerre and Legion of Honor from the French, before a crash ended his career and nearly his life. McCormick, barely four months after his election to Bones, was killed in a forced landing on September 24, 1918, becoming, as *Yale News* memorialized, the first of its editors to fall in service. In the Tap Day ceremonies for the class of 1920 held on May 15, 1919, when publishing in the *Yale Alumni Weekly* the society's announcement of the tap of Henry Luce, Skull and Bones declared that it had been given by Winter Mead "for the late Alexander Andrew McCormick, Jr."[51]

As early as March 1918, Alfred Bellinger of the class of 1917, serving in France with his air squadron, wrote to his society's alumnus Dean Jones that he had constituted himself "a sort of central office for the French chapter" of Bones, offering to contact both graduate members and, when elected, the new members: "I am sure that all those over here will cooperate with me as far at their duties permit. I have the advantage of being well behind the lines at present and it is very unlikely that I shall be killed before June." The *Yale News* announced in April 1918 that, for the elections to be held on May 16, "members of the Class of 1919 on leave for war service as well as those in residence will be eligible. . . . It is understood that elections of men absent on war service may be offered in time to make possible their announcement on Tap Day."

Bones and Wolf's Head each declared for *News* this article that it would not fill its entire complement of fifteen on Tap Day, but that further elections would be announced from time to time, while Keys expected to fill all its openings and would name its new members either on Tap Day or as soon thereafter as possible. Although more twentieth-century wars were to follow, the non–New Haven mass election ceremony in Palm Beach would never again be replicated, as men training for later wars did so in several locations instead of one. In the event, when Tap Day came that spring, it lasted over a month: with Bones, ten elections were offered on the stated day in May, and five in June. The remainder of the junior class in New Haven were asked to stay in their rooms between five and six P.M., but only three were elected there.

Others of the Bones contingent were given their elections, respectively, in Boston; in Oklahoma at Fort Devens and coming in from artillery practice at Fort Sill; in the lobby of the Hotel Belmont in New York City; on a station platform in New London, Connecticut, during a five-minute troop train stopover; in a Washington, D.C., hotel room at 3:22 A.M.; and four in France, although one of those had to be elected by mail since there was no graduate member nearby, and he was told to tap himself and mail the answer back to New Haven. Such a club required at least seven different initiations, spread over fourteen months (after the last normally should have graduated from college), at home and in France, at Saumur and other stations there, because of the difficulty for soldiers to obtain leave. For one initiate, Alexander McCormick Jr., this was his only attendance at the tomb in New Haven: he was killed near Calais, France, only three months later.

In Pensacola at the naval air station, executive officer Ganson Depew received a telegram on May 2 from George Parmly Day, class of 1897 and now the university treasurer, offering election to Scroll and Key. He got a second telegram the same day from Trubee Davison in New York, with an authorized offer of election to Skull and Bones, perhaps the only election to that society ever given by wire. In receipt of his acceptance, Davison sent a second telegram on May 4, advising Depew that initiation would be held on the eleventh, and urging him to obtain leave to attend in New Haven, as Davison's class had secured in Palm Beach the year before. Joseph Swan, Bones alumnus of 1902 and then assistant director of the Department of Military Affairs in Washington, telegraphed Major Bayne in France on May 8 to inquire what had become of the offers of elections referred through Bayne and young Charley Taft for 1919's Parker Allen and George Walker. Taft shortly thereafter telephoned Bayne about Allen's affirmative, and the 1911 club's Lieutenant Francis Randolph telegraphed him with Walker's acceptance.

On May 10, 1918, before the scheduled day of election, for which there was no physical ceremony and on which day no society was to fulfill its quota of fifteen, Skull and Bones announced the names of the three men elected in New Haven, five in military service stateside, including Depew, and two in France with the American Expeditionary Force from whom no response had been received. These were Allen and Walker, whose acceptances by cablegram were announced in the *News* on May 21. Keys named four in New Haven, and six in service, with deCernea and Schieffelin added later, and Wolf's Head chose four men in New Haven, including the already-published poet Stephen Vincent Benét, and four in service. Elihu joined these announcements with eight names in New Haven. By July, of the thirty men honored by Keys and Bones, twenty-nine were absent from college in the service of the government.[52]

"During the absence from the campus of practically all the members of the senior societies on military service," reported the *New York Times*, "the older alumni were rumored to have carried on the business affairs of the societies, although strict secrecy prevented any of the details from reaching the public ear." Trubee Davison served as a focal point for these efforts to sustain regular activities of his senior society while the members were so scattered. Weekly visits to the tomb for the current delegations were simply not possible, for the normal peacetime program, and initiations were particularly difficult, taking place when and where older members were in the same locale in sufficient numbers. New Haven resident graduates of the societies held meetings on Thursdays in their respective tombs during the American war years, inviting the few seniors then still on campus; one such gathering of Bones alumni in December 1918, without any undergraduates, utilized debate suggestions left from the last meeting of the club in attendance a year and a half before. Regular

meetings of the three societies' current delegations were resumed immediately after the signing of the armistice in November 1918.[53]

As the spring of 1918 advanced and the veterans returned from service to finish their degrees, the incomplete delegations for 1918 and 1919
were meeting on alternative nights in their tombs, using Wednesdays and
Fridays, writing to their absent members about the renewed life of and
in Yale College. For Tap Day on May 15, 1919, for the class of 1920, the
elections were once more conducted exactly as in peacetime, without
supervision from the graduates. With the campus again closed to visitors,
the fifteen members of each of the three societies who were members
of the class of 1919 appeared on the campus between the hours of five
and six in the afternoon to choose from the three hundred members of
the junior class. David Ingalls, captain of the hockey team and the only
American ace in naval aviation—six kills, five in his first six weeks in
combat—received the honor of the last man slapped for Bones, by Ganson
Depew, and was elected alongside Trubee's brother Harry Davison. In
another echo of times past, three men refused Bones and went to Keys,
including the man tapped by Unit 2 aviator John Schieffelin.

In their published election reports, both Bones and Keys noted that
several of their electors were tapping on behalf of named seniors still
on active duty overseas. At the last elections in 1918, for the first time
in more than twenty years, both the editor in chief and the business
manager of the *Yale News* had been passed over by all three societies,
but this year the omission was made up, with the admission of men who
had not served with the war heroes. These were Briton Hadden, tapped
by Charles Haffner, and Henry Robinson Luce, tapped by the stand-in
for the late Alexander McCormick, two men who were to embody the
postwar spirit of the next decade, by founding *Time* magazine. Because
Luce's classmates included Harry Davison and David Ingalls, his magazine was to find his friends' annual reunions of the First Naval Air Unit
highly newsworthy.[54]

The month after this final Tap Day before the Roaring Twenties,
in June 1919, at the time of the signing of the Treaty of Versailles, Yale

began planning for a memorial for the university's dead, the alumni agreeing to provide funds to construct a fitting memorial to express sentiment "rather than to serve any utilitarian purpose." The architects of the Bicentennial Buildings created a massive limestone colonnade, suggested to some extent by the Temple of Jupiter Stator in Rome, placed along the southern façade of the dining hall Commons—at the time the largest World War I memorial in the United States. Names of the principal battles of the Great War were incised on the architrave above, and a terrace extended out from Commons supporting a large central block, comprised of an entablature and cenotaph, a monument erected to the dead but not containing remains. It was to be dedicated in June 1927, with Trubee Davison presenting the memorial on behalf of the alumni, honoring the memory of the 233 Yale comrades who perished of the "some ten thousand" who served.[55]

TAPPED FOR SKULL AND BONES, 1912–1919

Arthur Howe	1912	president, Hampton Institute
Gerald Clery Murphy	1912	artist; president, Mark Cross Co.
Alfred Cowles	1913	Cowles Communications
W. Averell Harriman	1913	ambassador to USSR
		ambassador to Great Britain
		secretary of commerce
		governor (N.Y.)
		undersecretary of state
		U.S. representative to Vietnam Peace Talks
Sidney Lovett	1913	Yale University chaplain
		professor of Biblical Literature, Yale
Thomas Leonard Daniels	1914	board chairman, Archer Daniels Midland

Henry Wise Hobson	1914	Episcopal bishop, Southern Ohio
		president, Phillips Academy
Edwin Burtt	1915	professor of Philosophy, Cornell
Archibald MacLeish	1915	Pulitzer Prizes in poetry, drama
		assistant secretary of state
		librarian of Congress
		Boylston Professor, Harvard
		president, American Academy of Arts & Letters
Morris Hadley	1916	cofounder, Milbank Tweed Hadley & McCloy
		president, New York Public Library
		chairman, Carnegie Corporation
Donald Ogden Stewart	1916	author and screenwriter
Lawrence Tighe	1916	treasurer, Yale
Alfred Bellinger	1917	professor of Latin, Yale
E. Roland Harriman	1917	chairman, Union Pacific Railroad
		chairman, American Red Cross
Kenneth Farrar Simpson	1917	U.S. attorney, Southern District of N.Y.
		U.S. Congress (N.Y.)
Prescott Bush	1917	U.S. Senate (Conn.)
H.S.F. Cooper	1917	professor of Surgery, College of Physicians and Surgeons
Henry Neil Mallon	1917	president, Dresser Industries
Howard Malcolm Baldrige	1918	Congress (Neb.)
John Chipman Farrar	1918	chairman, Farrar Straus & Giroux
Charles Phelps Taft	1918	mayor of Cincinnati, Ohio

Charles Jacob Stewart	1918	board chairman, Manufacturers Hanover Trust
John Martin Vorys	1918	Congress (Ohio)
Frederick Trubee Davison	1918	founder, Yale Naval Air Unit
		U.S. assistant secretary of war (Air)
		president, American Museum of Natural History
		brigadier general, U.S. Air Force, World War II
		director of personnel, Office of Strategic Services
Robert Abercrombie Lovett	1918	U.S. undersecretary of state
		U.S. secretary of defense (Truman)
Artemus Gates	1918	first American air ace, World War I
		president, N.Y. Trust Company
		assistant secretary of the Navy for Air
		U.S. undersecretary of Navy
Edwin McCrady Gaillard	1919	chairman, Union & New Haven Trust Co.
Elmore Macneill McKee	1919	Yale chaplain

TAPPED FOR SCROLL AND KEY, 1912–1919

William Christian Bullitt	1912	first ambassador to USSR
		ambassador to France
Mortimer Robinson Proctor	1912	governor (Vt.)
John Adams Appleton	1913	brigadier general, World War II
Albert Beecher Crawford	1913	author, *Football Y Men, Phi Beta Kappa Men of Yale*
Cole Porter	1913	composer, songwriter

Vanderbilt Webb	1913	founder, Patterson, Belknap & Webb
Arnold Whitridge	1913	professor of History, Arts & Letters, Yale
Samuel Sloan Colt	1914	chairman, Port Authority of N.Y.
Henry Emerson Tuttle	1914	artist, director, Yale Art Gallery
Dean Gooderham Acheson	1915	U.S. secretary of state (Truman)
		architect of Truman Doctrine
John Wesley Haynes	1915	undersecretary of the Treasury
Wayne Chatfield Taylor	1916	undersecretary of Commerce
		president, Export-Import Bank
		assistant secretary of the treasury
Daniel Collier Elkin	1916	professor of Surgery, Emory
Otis Love Guernsey	1916	president, Abercrombie & Fitch
Charles Pratt	1916	president, Pratt Institute
John Henry Vincent	1916	special assistant to secretary of Navy
Lawrence Newbold Murray	1917	president, Mellon Nat'l Bank
Dickinson Woodruff Richards	1917	professor of Medicine, Columbia
Lester Armour	1918	chairman, Chicago National Bank
Wilmarth Sheldon Lewis	1918	author, Walpole scholar
		chief, Central Intelligence Division, OSS
John Franklin Enders	1919	Nobel Prize in Medicine
		professor of Bacteriology, Harvard

SKULLS AND KEYS

| John Jay Schieffelin | 1919 | rear admiral, U.S. Navy |
| Charles Gilbert Stradella | 1919 | president, General Motors Acceptance Corp. |

TAPPED FOR ELIHU, 1912–1919

Arthur Bliss Lane	1916	ambassador to Colombia, Poland
Ellsworth Bunker	1916	ambassador to Argentina, Italy, India, Nepal, and South Vietnam
Richard K. Sutherland	1916	MacArthur's chief of staff
Philip Barry	1918	playwright
Allan V. Heely	1919	Lawrenceville School headmaster

451

CHAPTER TEN

DIVISIONS OF CASTE AND
EXPANSION OF THE SYSTEM
(1920–1939)

The new Yale, in so far as it is the creation of Messrs. Sterling and Harkness, is the expression of the alumni mind. Now the characteristic of the alumnus as such is that he is not so much interested in his university as an educational institution as he is in his university as the scene of his pleasant young manhood and the background of his oldest friendships. . . . The new Yale, that is to say, the new Yale of the $60,000,000 worth of buildings, the new Yale of the Colleges and the Sterling Library and the Payne Whitney Gymnasium, is the supreme, the perfect statement of the alumni point of view.

—Archibald MacLeish, "New-Yale,"

Fortune, March 1934

THE PASSED-OVER: JEWS, BLACKS,
AND PUBLIC HIGH SCHOOL MEN

The "democracy" of election to the senior societies could never be more fair and neutral than the dominant demographics of the Yale

College student body permitted. This meant, in the nineteenth and early twentieth centuries, that those who were not white Anglo-Saxons of the Protestant faith, and did not attend a preparatory school, were at a distinct statistical disadvantage on Tap Day. Only occasionally represented in the senior class pool of about three hundred members, Jews, Catholics, and African Americans in particular were thus unlikely to be chosen. Their continued absence in the ranks of society men was a constant and obvious rebuke to those who argued that all undergraduates in the Yale mix had a fair shot for the college's supreme social honor. The finality and exclusiveness of the choosing created a faint and enduring fault line in the Yale brotherhood.

Beyond this, wealth in America's Gilded Age had altered the character of Yale and other top-tier American educational institutions. It became so concentrated in the hands of so few, wrote E. Digby Baltzell, that "it is no wonder that the production of pig iron rather than poetry, and the quest for status rather than salvation, now took hold of the minds of even the most patrician descendants of the Puritan divines."[1] When wealthy businessmen sent their children to colleges like Yale, the presence of a significant affluent number, bearing a disproportionate influence on their fellow students, became an enduring element of social stratification.

For their offspring, the national upper class sought new modes of identification, such as a common educational experience in an exclusive boarding school, and then in one of a select set of Eastern colleges. The founding of the nation's first country club (1882), the Groton School (1884), and the Social Register (1887) were all benchmarks in construction of a national chain of associations defining America's social elite. Attended by the wealthy and fed by wealth, Yale symbolized the condition: a 1926 report on its thirty million dollars worth of property holdings named the university as the country's wealthiest institution of learning.[2]

Still, admissions remained open, and Yale College was by no means an exclusive playground for the rich. Tuition had long been kept at modest levels, within the reach of many Americans—$39 in 1850, and

$160 in 1914—and generous financial aid policies, both the college administration's and those of sponsoring charities, permitted academically talented poor boys to attend. Fully 25 to 30 percent of the students were of an "underprivileged" status, and about 20 percent received scholarships in the 1930s.

Nevertheless, the aspirations of the newly wealthy for admission of their sons to one of the country's preeminent colleges threatened to end this century-old tradition of social opportunity, and the shortage of student housing in New Haven led to concentrations of these monied offspring in private dormitories, where prep school graduates grouped to improve their chances of election to membership in the sophomore societies and junior fraternities, the gateways to the senior societies. Money had now become a major factor in achieving social success at Yale.[3]

Yale was unabashedly Christian, retaining compulsory daily and Sunday chapel until the mid-1920s. In contrast to Harvard, Yale's admission form did not ask for the applicant's race and religion. The university certified to the Carnegie Fund through President Hadley in 1906 that "no denominational test is imposed in the choice of trustees, officers, or teachers, or in the admission of students, nor are distinctly denominational tenets or doctrines taught to the students of Yale University."[4] Indeed, from the long middle of the nineteenth century, Jews were able to join Christian fraternities if they were interested. The class of 1869's Lewis Ehrich was secretary of the freshman fraternity Kappa Sigma Epsilon, and Christian Yale encouraged his Jewish identity by excusing him from Sunday prayers on the condition that he attend Saturday service at a local synagogue.

Not until the 1870s was there a change in the view of American Jewry held by the general populace. By the end of that decade, Jews began to be publicly excluded from the social circles of the upper classes, and prejudice began to focus on both Jews and Catholics. Buttressing the Jewish stereotype on campus and throughout the nation was the arrival of immigrant Eastern European Jews, the first of whom arrived in New Haven in 1882, increasing forty-fold in number over the next four decades. At Yale in 1890, the Delta Kappa Epsilon fraternity mounted a play called "Shylock: The Sarcastic Sheeny, or the Maneouvering Merchant of Verdant Venice."[5]

Thirty-five years later, in March 1926, the *Yale Daily News* responded to Harvard's new admissions policy in its consideration of "tests of character and personality as well as scholastic standards," including requiring photo identification and background information regarding any change in paternal name, practices leading to easier exclusion of Jews. An editorial argued that "Yale must institute an Ellis Island with immigration laws more prohibitive than those of the United States government." To keep the college open, "Yale would be justified even with her ideal of 'service to the nation' in sloughing off the unkempt at the same time she drops the unlettered." The unkempt were not further described, but the reference was clear enough.

The bias of the Protestant ascendancy on the campus had counterpart biases in the disrespected minority which frustrated Jews' election to the senior societies. Lewis Ehrich's diary entry declaring disappointment in Skull and Bones for not rewarding scholarly merit was evidencing a strong difference in the educational values prevailing between Jewish students and their Christian classmates. Academic effort came to be placed well below the pedestal of an all-absorbing extracurricular life of sport and social competition. By the turn of the century, the campus slogan had become "We toil not, neither do we agitate, but we play football."

By 1922, when the question of a quota on "Hebrew" enrollment at Yale became an administration concern, Jewish scholarly achievement was perceived as a detriment to the cohesion of an entering class in which the education of citizens was prized more than academic achievement: Dean Jones noted privately that "Some men say that they are not disposed to compete with Jews for first honors; they do not care to be a minority in a group of men of high scholarship record, most of whom are Jews." Again, many of the Jews were on scholarships, which required a rank in the top quarter of the class to be renewed, a situation requiring intensive study which only reinforced their marginalization in campus life.[6]

Moreover, it was universally believed that the Jewish students were generally not interested in worshiping the college's deity of team sports that so entranced their classmates, although there were exceptions to the rule, such as Robert Moses, class of 1909 and future New York city planner, who swam and championed other minor sports at Yale. This was itself part of a larger shift in the culture: where success had once been regarded as the culmination of a "race" in which victory went to the fleetest of foot, it was now a "game" in which one's own activities were circumscribed not merely by the members of opposing groups but by members of one's own group as well.[7] Because the Jewish students, unlike many of their Gentile Yale brethren, concentrated as well on scholarship, their self-exclusion from varsity team sports in the pre–First World War era was a double-edged sword, removing them from the larger social scene and generating a handicap that existed away from the playing fields.

In other words, segregation of Jews arose from within as well as without, and rather than quarrel over the inherent evils of a caste system or mount a challenge to Yale society, Jewish students seem to have chosen to acquiesce, taking their assigned places in the hierarchy. Some as local residents may indeed have been off-campus members of the "Knights of Jerusalem," founded by six young "townies" in 1871, which dominated for a few decades the New Haven Jewish young men's world of 17- to 25-year-olds. The Knights were a mirror image of the exciting society world that they observed on the Yale campus, complete with their own motto, initiation ceremony, secret handshake, membership badge, debates and orations for the program, and the stated purpose of the "pursuance of exercise of a high literary character, and for the purpose of perpetuating friendship and brotherly love, as well as adhering to the laws of our forefathers in Jerusalem."[8]

Thus, on account of their devotion to achieving good grades, disdain of team sport, and self-segregation, indifference to Jews existed in the fraternities alongside prejudice. Between 1900 and 1916, the annual fraternity elections at Yale brought into membership over 40 percent (roughly 2,000) of the Christian students, and 5 percent (exactly 9) of the Jews. These proportions were common at other universities nationally, and because young Jewish men wanted the benefits of Greek life that had been denied them because of their Judaism, the very first Jewish fraternity in the nation was founded at Yale in March 1895 by three Jews who identified the fraternity as "non-sectarian," not particularly wanting to identify themselves as Jews. It soon branched out to Columbia, Harvard, Cornell, and MIT, among others, allowing Jewish students at these schools access to the Greek life that they were being denied in Gentile fraternities.[9]

Scions of American Jewry's wealthiest financiers were members of Yale's Christian fraternities, such as Joseph Seligman, class of 1908, in Psi Upsilon, and Robert Lehman, class of 1913, in Delta Kappa Epsilon. Occasionally some served as officers of campus fixtures: L. Richard Gimbel (1920, son of "Gimbel Brother" Ellis Gimbel) was business manager of the Yale Record. All had prep school credentials and were the descendants of German immigrants, but none of them were elected to a senior society, nor were any of their compatriots, although between 1900 and 1930 more than 1,200 Jews entered Yale. It cannot be said how much this exclusion was the product of a generally accepted philosophy, as opposed to a specifically implemented policy. Still, a national survey in 1927 evidenced that Yale was among eighteen American universities where Jewish collegians perceived "pronounced anti-Jewish feeling on the part of their fellow students."

However, Jew and Gentile alike were aware that the Jewish numbers at Yale had steadily increased: the number more than tripled from 1902 to 1921. The Academic class of 1901 was only 2 percent Jewish, and in 1909 was still less than 3 percent, while the class of 1915 had a Jewish enrollment of almost 8 percent, and the class of 1925—freshmen in the year 1921—were over 13 percent Jewish, a percentage not to be surpassed until 1962, when the proportion was 14.2 percent. Many if not the majority of these were "townies" from New Haven or nearby cities (half of the in-state Jewish collegians, and 10 percent of all Yale undergraduates), and those living at home did not feel they belonged to Yale, being third-class citizens of the undergraduate republic.

One of them, Eugene Rostow of the class of 1933, who entered Yale on one of the college's eight scholarships given to New Haven's public high schools (a reason his Ukrainian Jewish parents had relocated to the city from New Jersey). He was later to serve as dean of Yale Law School, the first Jewish master of a Yale residential college, President Lyndon Johnson's undersecretary of state, and President Reagan's head of the Arms Control and Disarmament Agency. Rostow authored "The Jew's Position" for the iconoclastic undergraduate journal *The Harkness Hoot* in November 1931. "The Jew," he declared, "along with the artistic, the intellectual, the 'queer,' and the 'furrin,' has been classified as unsocial and socially impossible in this world of money, conformance, and uniformity." As a junior Phi Beta Kappa, water polo team swimmer, member of Alpha Delta Phi and the Elizabethan Club, *Lit.* writer, and future winner of the Yale faculty's greatest award for senior class citizenship, the Alpheus Henry Snow Prize, he thought in May 1933 that he would be the first Jew tapped by Bones or another senior society, and feared he could not resist the temptation. To put it beyond doubt, he had a good friend of his, opposed to the secret society life, drive him out of town on election day, so as not to be found to be tapped.[10]

Nevertheless, at a time when resorts around the country publicly advertised their racial and religiously biased prohibitions, Yale collegians were not inclined to widen their societies' ranks to those of their college class so publicly identified as social pariahs. The Elihu Club had exhibited notable broad-mindedness in electing a Native American in 1910, but the very next year in a fall 1911 debate, the class of 1912 voted unanimously for the motion "That Jews should be denied recognition at Yale."[11] While not so formally or frankly expressed elsewhere, it seems probable that this attitude was generally shared by the other societies, and it is patent that their annual election results evidenced that sentiment. No formalities of final division were enacted prior to Tap Day, but the preceding lower-class years of undergraduate caste formation clearly created gaps between those social strata, even if the prep school Brahmins had not imported their social exclusivity from home, the patterns of discrimination passed on by inheritance.

As for Catholics, immigrants of this faith were historically less inclined than the Jews to send their children to colleges like Yale. In Robert Moses's freshman class entering in 1905, of 351 members, five were Jews—listed as "Hebrews" in the Freshman Blue Book—and eighteen were Catholics, lumped with the Jews under "Miscellaneous Denominations." American Catholics had lower regard for advanced education, warned by their bishops and priests not to educate their offspring beyond their proper station in life, but the same clergy also warned of the dangers found in non-Catholic institutions, to be avoided when their own centers of learning—especially Georgetown, Holy Cross, Fordham, and the Catholic University of America—were readily available.

While prior to the Second World War more Catholics than Jews attended Yale, the percentage of Catholics in New Haven was just below the national average, while the percentage of Jews was greater than their representation on other campuses. The Yale College class of 1904, for example, was 2.8 percent Jewish and 6.1 percent Catholic at a time when Jews represented less than 2 percent and Catholics about 12 percent of the national population; in 1934–35, the freshman class was 8.7 percent Jewish and 13 percent Catholic, when Jews comprised close to 4 percent and Catholics roughly 16 percent of all Americans. Not many of these Catholics, incidentally, were from New Haven, where the Italian population grew from 7 percent of the inhabitants in 1900 to over 25 percent in 1930, because the number graduating from high school was very small, and the Yale policy of admitting a fair number of New Haven sons did not lead to an "Italian problem."[12]

Still, Yale's official and social conduct did not consistently reflect the anti-Catholic bias prevailing nationally, when the pronouncements of the Ku Klux Klan were as anti-Catholic as they were anti-black. No evidence exists of a quota system ever limiting Catholic enrollment at Yale, and these students enjoyed a greater degree of social success at Yale than any other group of non-Protestants or nonwhites. Many were varsity athletes and belonged to junior fraternities and senior societies: in 1912, there were three known Catholics in the junior fraternities Alpha Delta Phi, nine in Delta Kappa Epsilon, four in Zeta Psi, and two known Catholics that year in each of Bones, Keys, Wolf's Head, and Elihu.

Further evidence that Catholics found welcome and status on campus, such that their religious background did not interfere with full acceptance in Yale social life, is shown by the career of Father T. Lawrason Riggs, B.A. 1910. *Lit.* editor, president of the Dramatic Association, and a Keys man who served as Catholic chaplain at Yale from 1922 to 1943, Riggs maintained close associations each year with the series of Keys delegations. The novelist John O'Hara was late in life to write in a letter to his stepson at Yale, which the novelist did not attend but wished to, where he would have been a member of the class of 1927: "At Yale I probably would have made Bones (and wanted Keys) on literary accomplishment, and with little or no consideration of my being a Catholic, which I was then." [13]

Fewest in number by far of the identifiable religious or ethnic components of the student body were African Americans. Yale encouraged exceptional blacks to attend by awarding them scholarships; some were transfer students from southern Negro colleges such as Talladega and Tuskegee, while a few came from New England private schools, and several were local youths. Still, only six blacks seem to have attended Yale College between 1853 and 1904, the most academically successful being William Pickens, a Talledega transfer who won the Ten Eyck Prize in 1903 (among thirty-five contestants in a class of three hundred) and was, like the class of 1874's Edward Bouchet before him, elected to Phi Beta Kappa.

Pickens, having worked his way through Yale College by washing pots and pans at the YMCA, was so thrilled by his Ten Eyck victory that an entire chapter in his memoirs of 1911 was devoted to his success. The complications of caste at this date are exemplified by his reminiscence: "The appreciation of my classmates was generous. When my name was seen among the ten [finalists], there was a mixture of amused and sympathetic interest. The proportion of amusement was overdone only by one Jew who was an unsuccessful aspirant for the honor and who referred to me as 'the black Demosthenes.' I told him it would have been more Jewlike for him to say black David, or black Jacob." Pickens makes no comment on the senior society system, except perhaps obliquely: "I had been with the class two years, just the time required to merit a Phi Beta Kappa key, if one's scholarship warranted . . . The Phi Beta Kappa Society is based on scholarship, and Yale is a very democratic community."[14]

From 1853 to 1923, about thirty African Americans received their undergraduate degrees from Yale College. There were sufficient black collegians in 1909 to form the Yale chapter of the black student fraternity of Alpha Phi Alpha, founded at Cornell in 1906, limited to "Negro male" students and having ancient Egyptian motifs; Yale's chapter, after struggles, was reactivated in 1913 with twelve brothers, only to disappear again in the war years, although there were five blacks in the class of 1916. Even this modest level of black representation was further reduced after selective admissions began: only seven African Americans graduated from Yale between 1924 and the end of the Second World War despite increases in class size during that period.[15]

W.E.B. Du Bois found no evidence of discrimination against blacks in the Yale admission process in 1910, and again in 1926,[16] and university president James Rowland Angell in 1926 expressed his pride in Yale's having avoided the Princeton tradition of systematically excluding blacks, even though this tolerance might have discouraged racially conscious Southerners from attending Yale. Involved in the debate over limitation of Jewish enrollment, Dean Robert Corwin (class of 1887, 1886 football captain, Bones, and chairman of the Board of Admissions from 1919 to 1933), stated in 1931 that "there has never been any negro question here, nor has the necessity been felt for adopting a policy of determining our acceptance of negroes or our treatment of them." Still, as of 1931, perhaps partly due to the Depression, there was only one African American in the undergraduate school.[17] While an undercurrent of antiblack feeling on campus existed, the failure of African Americans to be chosen for senior societies before the Second World War was as much a function of their extremely few numbers as anything else.[18]

Finally, the public school/private school social barriers at Yale were also fully evident in society elections, where a preparatory school background, because of pre-college networks of friendship, was a tremendous asset to society election, as were family traditions of attendance and society membership down the generations. The Carnegie Foundation survey for 1909 had found that Yale drew a higher percentage of its students from prep schools (65 percent) than any comparable institution except Princeton (78 percent); in 1916, just 26 percent of freshmen were from public schools, and only 12 percent came from west of the Mississippi River. By 1934, with the Great Depression's economic pressures, the proportion of high school graduates in the freshman class had *decreased* to 25 percent, with 68 percent of them from New England, and only 3 percent from west of the Mississippi.[19]

From the early 1900s through the 1940s, between 40 and 60 percent of Yale freshmen were educated in private preparatory schools, with another 10 to 20 percent adding a year or two at a private school to their public education. By way of comparison, about 50 to 60 percent of Harvard freshmen and about 70 to 90 percent of those at Princeton were private school graduates. Of these percentages, however, only about half or less were really part of the so-called prep school crowd of the socially elite. The other half were the sons of middle-class business and professional families, who attended a local or neighboring private school of modest social reputation for a few years before going off to college.

The prep school crowd chose to attend Harvard, Yale, and Princeton because of alumni connections, college reputation, or private school affiliation. They were the graduates of the twenty or so best private schools, mostly located in New England. (In the Depression era, only about 10 to 12 percent of the country's high school graduates were inclined to attempt college; since Greek and Latin were still required, a common route was high school and then a preparatory year or two, hence the name prep school.) At the top of the social hierarchy were the five Episcopal boarding schools known as the "St. Grottlesex" group: St. George's, St. Mark's, St. Paul's, Groton, and Middlesex. Together with about a dozen others, these schools provided the candidates for Harvard's ten final clubs, about 11 or 12 percent of the sophomore, junior and senior classes. This and similar groups of private schools sent to Princeton the candidates for the dozen or so upperclass eating clubs, and of course to Yale. future junior fraternity and senior society men.[20]

Thomas Bergin of the class of 1925, an Italian American townie on a scholarship for New Haven natives and later holder of the Sterling Chair of Romance Languages and master of Timothy Dwight College, was to remember that all of the football players in his class came from the prep schools, which provided better coaching. The same proved true for the *News* board ("High school boys were less likely to have training in that sector, too, and most of them could not afford the time that 'heeling' required"), and only three public high school boys his year were tapped for Bones. "[F]undamentally," he concluded, "it was simply a question of money; we high school boys could not afford to waste time. Many of us spent our extra-curricular hours in gainful employment." Of sixty senior society neophytes elected four years later in 1928, only two had come for college in New Haven from a public high school.[21]

Stephen Vincent Benét, who was a prep school product (although, from Albany Academy, not one of the grand ones) and served as *Lit.* chairman for his class of 1919, prepared a series of satirical poems for a drinking and singing group called the Vorpal Blades. Never published as proposed under the title "The Songs of Dear Old Yale," the verses contained one line that sometimes appeared afterwards in magazine articles on the Yale senior societies, "I have seen that poor, dumb, pleading look, as in pre-butchered steers," and depicted the social terrors of Tap Day:

And they all shook hands together beneath the old elm tree,
In the same old fix when the clock struck six and there they seemed to be,

*When Bones passed by, and Keys gave cry, and Wolf's Head jeered
with glee,*
When Hope went marching on.

Another of that set of verses, "The Uncollegiate Damned," imagined
the jeers of the passed-over, the triumvirate of the public high school
men with the more recognizable castes of Jews and blacks, glorying in
their unworthiness:

We never called Rosenberg 'Rosy'
We never wore Brooks Brothers' clothes,
Our Campaign Committees were rare as red kitties,
We slandered the News heeler's prose.
We were seldom respectable souses,
We often said 'Gracious!' and 'Hell!'
So with Hebrews and niggers we're prominent figgers
When the Bones men burst out from Battell! [22]

In his first novel, *The Beginning of Wisdom*, published only one year
after his graduation, Benét wrote more seriously that "Distinct cleavage
between prep-school and non prep-school exists only in Freshman year to
any extent—and then generally in the mind of the non prep-school man.
For a Yale class, like most real and historic democracies, begins with a
hereditary aristocracy, grows tired of it and knocks out its underpinnings
so that its members slide gently back into the general mass." Nevertheless,
the quasi-preppie Benét was himself tapped for Wolf's Head, and as late
as 1942, public school graduates made up only 6 percent of the senior
society men, compared to 25 percent of the freshmen.

Meanwhile, the number of Yale alumni sons was steadily increasing:
in 1924 they comprised only 13.2 percent of the class, rising to the twentieth percentile in the 1930s. More than 30 percent of the freshmen in the
late 1930s were themselves sons of Yale men, with perhaps half having a
Yale grandfather, uncle, or older brother. Society membership reflected

this trend: in the Bones club of 1938, three of the fifteen had brothers in the society and two had uncles (but of their seven children who attended Yale in the next generation, none were tapped for Skull and Bones).[23]

Ultimately, the social situation at Yale at this time (replicated at Harvard and Princeton) demonstrates that the actualization of democratic principles, such as individual merit and equal opportunity, was severely limited by the structure of existing networks inherited from before World War I, and by the way in which rights and opportunities were seen as the property of individuals. This was exquisitely evidenced by the reversal of the Harvard policy of 1922 which had excluded blacks from freshman dormitories, a reversal accompanied by the Harvard Board of Overseers' ruling simultaneously that "men of the white and colored races cannot be compelled to live and eat in the same dormitory if they object to members of the other race." As in business and society, the justification for maintaining inequalities based on racial and ethnic differences in the colleges—and thus in the Yale senior societies—was the right of private association.[24]

Still, the preeminent historian of Jews at Yale, Dan Oren, has written that "In hindsight, it seems that the vanguard of the profound changes in the Yale of the early 1960s was the undergraduate of the 1920s and 1930s. At the time, the Yale social system—based more on breeding than merit—was as strong as ever. In general, people flocked to be with their own kind: some by choice, some because of no other choice. Yet, beneath the surface, the forces that would later permit Jews, Catholics, blacks, public school graduates, poor students, and all at the bottom of the pyramid to claim Yale, once again, to be as much their own as anyone else's, was almost imperceptibly gathering force. The university spirit was slowly invading the college. . . . Undergraduates were beginning to learn that the hidden meaning of university was diversity."[25]

They were to learn of that diversity primarily through the creative disruption of the College Plan, funded by the munificent gift of Edward S. Harkness, a senior society graduate of 1897 attempting to bring to all collegians the remembered warmth of that particular social experience, in building luxurious dormitories with attendant amenities. These were essentially massive fraternity houses without admission fees beyond normal tuition, and comprised a mandated Yale democratic community within which all undergraduates must reside. While erasing the economic disparity in housing comfort, the creation of Yale's residential college system, weakening through compelled dispersion the old social networks of prep school familiarity, was ironically to help save a pillar and product of that older regime, the senior society system itself.

A NON–SENIOR SOCIETY PRESIDENT

The growth of diversity was to begin, shortly into the decade of the 1920s, with a new president for Yale, who was not even a graduate of the College, let alone a product of the senior society system there.

In June 1921 Arthur Hadley, class of 1876, Bones, and Yale's president since 1899, announced his retirement. His personal candidate for replacement was university secretary Angus Phelps Stokes, 1896 and Bones, who had served as Yale's second most important officer for every year of Hadley's presidency. The Yale Corporation then appointed a committee of five of its own members, chaired by Samuel H. Fisher '89, a lawyer who worked with the Harkness family in management of their philanthropies. The committee's members represented varied interests: Academic and Sheffield Scientific; Bones (Fisher and Nathan Smyth '87) and Keys (John Villiers Farwell '79, the first "westerner" to serve as Alumni Fellow); the cities of New Haven, New York, Pittsburgh, and Chicago; and business and manufacturing in addition to ministry and law.

Within the twenty-two-year span of Hadley's administration, the clerical element on the Corporation had been substantially reduced: among the ten self-perpetuating Successor Trustees, only four were ministers, and of the six Alumni Fellows, elected since 1872 by the university's graduates, not a single one wore the cloth. Now, Yale's governing body was dominated by financiers and industrialists, not Protestant ministers. Furthermore, of the sixteen members of the full board, almost a dozen were graduates of the senior societies: five of Bones, four of Keys, and two from the Sheff fraternities.

Further electoral complications were added by regional rivalries and personal enthusiasms and enmities, on top of the society affiliations of several of the leading candidates. Beyond Stokes' Bones affiliation, the rival contenders were Keys alumni: university treasurer George Parmly Day and George E. Vincent of the Rockefeller Foundation (and former president of the University of Chicago). Fisher's papers declare that the Corporation's members on the whole rose above party consideration, although in the informal balloting, preferences tended to follow the tomb: few Bones votes were counted for any Keys graduate, and there were virtually no Keys votes for Stokes, as the Keysmen were joining with the graduates of the Middle West in favor of Vincent or in organized opposition to Stokes. The latter was hobbled in this race from the start: his effectiveness as Hadley's enforcer had gained him many enemies. Furthermore, Stokes was a clergyman, and Yale University was now too secularized to return to the nineteenth-century practice of minister presidents.

The Fisher Committee came up with eighty names for the Corporation's review, to be considered under three heads, namely officers and members of the Yale faculty, Yale graduates and others servicing at other educational institutions, and non-educator achievers in other walks of life. Nominees considered, among others, included Bones' William Howard Taft, Henry Stimson, Corporation Fellow Henry Sloane Coffin, and Professor Charles Seymour, who became university president next time around; Keys' Frank L. Polk, the head of the American delegation at the Versailles peace conference; four other members of the Corporation, including Fisher; and future U.S. president Herbert Hoover. In the end after a thirteen-month search, a dark horse candidate was elected unanimously: James Rowland Angell, professor of psychology and then dean at the University of Chicago, and at this date president of the Carnegie Corporation. Not since the long-ago days of Harvard-bred rectors had Yale chosen a president who was not a graduate of its college.

In the months after his election, Angell was flooded with correspondence from alumni concerning the senior societies, some begging him to suspend judgment, while others urged their abolition with vehemence. He had brought a knowledgeable recent graduate into the center of his administration, naming as university secretary a member of the class of 1921, Robert Maynard Hutchins, voted by his class most likely to succeed, and a member of Wolf's Head, who would go on to become dean of Yale Law School and then president of the University of Chicago. Angell accepted an honorary membership in the Sheff society Berzelius, a status long offered to administration and faculty members—Angell was indeed the fourth Yale president to be so named—and in time he came to think those societies neither wholly good nor bad, but variable from year to year. The new president made tentative efforts to enlist their help, on outbreaks of cheating, the drinking problem, and women visitors to campus, but found their members either afraid to jeopardize such influence as they still retained lest it be rejected, or hesitant to sit in moral judgment on their classmates.[26]

This university president's major and lasting impact on their continued existence was in changing the college's admissions standards, and thus the raw material for their elections. He spoke of Yale's national mission, and the consequent desirability of such entrance standards as would admit the able high school student from the West. Yale should take high school boys into its confidence, he argued in his inaugural address, and try to bring in the rare outstanding boy, however irregular his previous training, because of the tonic effect his presence would exercise on the undergraduate atmosphere. The president periodically urged Yale's graduates to increase the scholarship funds, so that no deserving candidates need be prevented from applying or later have to resign.

In these several ways, President Angell advocated a search for the ablest and most serious schoolboys, located through canvassing a greater number of regions and schools, attracted through an increase in regional scholarships, and sifted for admission through maintenance of the most rigorous and accurate possible testing with adoption of the new Scholastic

Aptitude Tests. As the quality of the student body improved, he championed higher undergraduate educational standards, challenging the class leaders, whose very high levels of ability and background he respected, by deploring their neglect of scholastic opportunities after arriving at Yale. He repeatedly called attention to the fact that high school graduates, often of poorer background and training, consistently did much better in both their studies, standing higher, earning more honors, and losing fewer men by flunking. Because the senior societies had long ago seized control of the most coveted accolade for success in the Yale democracy, attention had to be paid to Angell's repeated message.[27]

TAP DAY REDIVIVUS

In December 1919, having previously announced its second election results for the class of 1920 (including four collegians just returned from war service), the Elihu Club published an announcement that it would give out its 1920 spring elections at the same time and place as "the other Senior Organizations," while adhering to its customs of offering additional elections in the fall to men chosen by the incoming members from their own class, and of having no stated number of members. Notwithstanding this self-inclusion into the Tap Day tradition for the class of 1921, the 1920 delegation insisted that it would "not become a Senior Secret Society," having abjured secrecy for its seventeen years of existence. Still, Elihu was becoming more like its fellow senior clubs: it created in that year a gold badge, a copy of the seal of its namesake Elihu Yale, with distribution of instructions on its display, "as a pin over the hollow of the shoulder by all undergraduates except with a dress suit or tuxedo, when it is to be worn over the lower left pocket."[28]

The revived ceremony could have had no more enthusiastic publicist than Henry Robinson Luce, a Yale missionary's son hailing from Tengchow, China, and managing editor of the *Yale News* board, to which he had returned in January 1919 from military camp with his Hotchkiss School friend and longtime rival Briton Hadden, now *News* chairman.

The two were later to be voted by their classmates as, respectively, "most brilliant," and "most likely to succeed," although only Luce was to make Phi Beta Kappa and win the DeForest Prize. In the upperclassmen's absence on war duty, they had effectively managed the *News* from their sophomore year onward. Luce had written on to the *Lit.*, and was elected to its chairmanship after losing the *News* election to Hadden, but reconsidered and resigned when he was warned that the *Lit.* post might be a disqualifier for society election, since it was now considered too remote from the "grand old Yale" of the senior societies to impress the Bonesmen, and furthermore, Luce had broken the unwritten rule that senior *News* editors were to steer clear of roles on other publications.[29]

He was plunged into despair when the *New York Times* article on the revival of Tap Day mentioned nine men as Bones prospects, including Hadden, but not Luce. Luce wrote his parents that Hadden took him for a walk to propose getting "ten of the sure Bones men together to make it known that none of them would go Bones without" Henry, but he declined, arguing that "Bones means everything for Yale, and that bucking it did no good for the college which means so much to us." Hadden's letter home after elections on May 15, 1920, expressed quiet satisfaction, commenting that "most of the fellows I think most of went Bones too . . . Luce for example" (along with David Ingalls and Harry Davison, Trubee's brother, to rise to the presidency of J. P. Morgan, and Thayer Hobson, who later ran the publishing company William Morrow & Company).

Harry's letter to his parents the next day was more ebullient: "[Y]our elder son received a terrific smack across the shoulders, delivered him by Winter Mead, 1919, Captain of the Crew and President of Phi Beta Kappa, and a member of the so-called society of Skull and Bones. And you can easily imagine that said son upon being told to go to his room did so go, and did moreover vouch for his being Henry Robinson Luce, and did accept an election to the so-called society! . . . I am sure you can imagine what perfect satisfaction is mine."[30]

The Hadden-Luce relationship even within their society's halls was contested: their club scrapbook contained a drawing of them on horseback, dueling with lances, because each was the greater warrior for facing the other. Still, their fraught partnership, within the network of their club and society alumni, was to have remarkable consequences for the history of American journalism: the invention of the weekly news-magazine. In January of 1921, Hadden and his clubmate John Hincks went to Houston to usher at the wedding of another member of the Bones delegation of 1920. Hadden jumped off the train at least twenty times to buy a local paper and talked incessantly of starting a periodical publication based on newspaper accounts. As he explained it later, "I got an idea to start a magazine which comes out Friday with all the news condensed so . . . rich millionaires commuting home for the weekend can catch up on the news they missed."[31]

Hadden joined Luce as young reporters together at the *Baltimore News* while planning this project, which was to become *Time* magazine, but a stock plan which left the two young men in control discouraged investors. Then their society clubmate Harry Davison bought forty shares and passed the prospectus along to J. P. Morgan senior partner Dwight Morrow, who also purchased forty shares, giving the fledgling publishers the imprimatur to attract further investors, and the enterprise was launched in 1923.[32] Hadden died young, in 1929, and his role in creating the *Time-Life-Fortune* publishing empire was eclipsed, but he is remembered in the *Yale Daily News* headquarters, the Briton Hadden Memorial Building, where Harry Davison spoke for the building committee at the dedication in April 1932.

As managing editor of the *News* board of 1920, Luce had the pleasure of announcing his own Bones club's election in what was to become the traditional location in the right-hand column of the daily's front page for reporting (outside the headline, and with no further commentary) only the names of those tapped, their electors, and refusals. Luce transgressed convention by including sub-headlines—"David Ingalls Last Man Tapped for Skull and Bones; DeForest Van Slyck First"—which had never in *News* history been devoted to exclusive, biased attention to a single society. Luce was compelled to issue an apology, shifting the blame the next day: "The Managing Editor hereby apologizes for his oversight in not correcting the headlines submitted by a reporter, on the Senior Societies' elections, so as to make them conform to the traditional NEWS policy of mentioning no names in the headlines of all articles dealing with society elections."[33]

While their members may have been largely abroad in World War I, the societies still exerted the same gravitational pull on the undergraduates in residence on campus. Stephen Vincent Benét (called his class of 1919's "most distinguished classmate" at their twenty-fifth reunion—in 1929 he had won his first Pulitzer Prize for Poetry, following the publication of *John Brown's Body*, and received his second posthumously in 1944) as an underclassman had thumbed his poetical nose at the august senior societies: "*I haven't the brains to go Bones,/I haven't the looks to go Keys,/I'm too much of a dub/To go Elihu Club/So I'll do as I (very well) please.*"[34] In the growing senior society tradition of electing blasphemers, he was tapped by Wolf's Head.

"I hope to God," he wrote a classmate in July 1918, "you haven't accepted an election to that bastardly Elihu Club. If you have, cancel it! There is nothing in our [Wolf's Head] customs to prevent us taking a man in Elihu Club—but he forfeits his membership in E.C. by so doing—a thing which should not cause you great sorrow." Sending on the gossip of the names elected so far, he concluded: "Well, I can't tell you how damn glad I will be to share all the hush stuff we have so consistently blatted upon . . . At least I can assure you of one thing— there is *one* Senior Society which does *not* believe in Prohibition!"[35] In his first novel, a roman à clef appearing in 1921, he recounted that his protagonist "promptly went to Wolf's Head with [three friends]—thus breaking a tradition as old as the *Lit.* itself, that its chairman went to Skull and Bones or nowhere—and for once in his life felt completely content with one of his own decisions. Keys he never considered, and Keys had repaid the compliment."[36]

The *New York Times* in its preelection article on the imminence of Tap Day in 1919 reminded its readers of the ceremony's hallowed prewar features, now revived: the appearance of the three societies' members on campus between 5:00 and 6:00 P.M. on a Thursday afternoon to offer the favored few elections near the historic fence on the "old quadrangle." No "horoscopes" appeared this year, but "shrewd guesses . . . are made by the undergraduates, based upon the records and inclinations of the prominent members of the junior class." Some of the strictures introduced after the prewar Sophomore Revolt were retained, in the closing of the campus, and the on-ground attendance of only the two upper classes.

Except for one year, custom and circumstance were not to change very much for the next two decades' worth of elections. As promised, Elihu appeared on campus for the first time on Tap Day on May 19, 1921, to choose its next delegation; it proved a rocky start, with ten acceptances and seven refusals. The *New York Post* the following spring opined: "Elihu, which emphasizes no secret aspect and has human windows in its house, seems to be abandoning a highly desirable service by participating in 'Tap Day' at all. Its theory has been to 'tap' about ten, and a week later to elect the remaining five. This enabled Elihu to rectify in a measure the mistakes and omissions of the others . . . and election to Elihu was a rather special honor, because it represented a cool second thought and took in men of solid but perhaps less obvious qualities. The tendency now, however, seems to be for Elihu to join the common ceremony. Many of the best and most judicious men in both student body and faculty reject the change."[37]

Although the *New York Times* had begun reporting the first and last men tapped by Keys, as well as by Bones, the leveling out of the societies' respective reputations can be seen over these decades. The first man tapped for Bones in 1923 refused and joined Wolf's Head, and Elihu rebounded, with eleven acceptances (including future Yale Librarian James Babb) and only one refusal. The next year, Elihu gathered in fourteen against a single turndown, while Bones suffered two rebuffs and Wolf's Head and Keys one apiece. One of Bones' 1924 turndowns was Simon Whitney, who had also refused election to all five junior fraternities. One of Keys' 1924 acceptances was varsity and Olympic champion oarsman Benjamin Spock, who was to write the book *Baby and Child Care,* which guided the upbringing of millions of infant Americans from the late 1940s through the decades that followed. In spring 1925, Elihu managed to elect a full fifteen, enduring only two turndowns to Bones' four, which included John Hay Whitney and another who went to Keys, and two to Wolf's Head.[38]

The *New York Times* pre–Tap Day article for 1926 pointed out to its readers that when a slapped junior refused to budge, he was taking his chances, "because it is an ironclad rule at Yale that no member of the junior class shall be pledged in advance by a senior society. Two or three refusals of [each of] the different societies occur almost every year, almost all based on local reasons." One example of this was the choice of John Hay "Jock" Whitney, son of Bonesman Payne Whitney (1898), who was to leave at his death in 1927 the largest estate, at $178 million, ever appraised to that date in the United States, and grandson of Bonesman William C. Whitney, class of 1863, who was secretary of the Navy for Grover Cleveland, as well as of John Hay, secretary of state for Theodore Roosevelt. Notwithstanding his ancestors' membership, young Whitney believed Bones to be ridiculously secret, but moreover, as a polo player and second university crew stroke (credited with coining the term "crew cut" for that haircut), he was more impressed with Keysmen Louis Stoddard and Watson Webb, constituting half of the first United States polo team ever to beat Great Britain, and the Keys members who numbered five of the eight oarsmen who had won the gold medal in the 1924 Olympics.[39]

Similar personal predilections swayed the son of treasury secretary Andrew Mellon, vice chair of the *News* Paul Mellon, standing in the Branford College courtyard on Tap Day two years later in 1928, when two hands came down on his shoulders as the first man tapped that season by both Bones and Keys. Mellon, who was later to name one of his stable of thoroughbreds "Branford Court," calmly smoked a cigarette while the two society representatives stood behind him for five minutes, waiting for the clock to strike, then "said in a low voice,

'Scroll and Key,'" and walked from the enclosure. He recollected in his memoirs that unlike Bones, which took the "more visible and prominent juniors," Scroll and Key was "likely to tap rather easygoing types and perhaps a more heterogeneous mixture of athletes, humorists, literary aspirants, and socialites . . . I accepted [Keys] since I had a fair idea that several of my closest friends would be going that way, too." Mellon's later service on the Yale Corporation with Jock Whitney gave the university a one-two philanthropic punch the likes of which few other academic institutions have ever matched (Mellon's most notable gifts being the Clare Fellowships to the University of Cambridge, and the Yale Center for British Art).[40]

The ceremony and system continued to attract criticism, both local and national, but the critical themes were old ones: first, the societies did not elect men (or perhaps, enough men) for non-social distinction, and second, the system itself was corrupted by non-scholarly ambition. Even the *Yale Alumni Weekly*, after the 1929 elections, found that while "Elections to the Senior Societies at one time meant 'recognition' of leadership and distinguished performance in the undergraduate world, plus character, and for that reason were 'honors' so recognized by the Campus at large," a change had come. "The great size of the Classes since the War (running to over 500 men), the rise of the Junior Fraternities as social clubs and the mixing of all Classes in class-room work, have been subtly and steadily changing all this, so that the character of the Senior-Society elections—and hence their importance on the Campus—within the last few years has materially altered."[41]

What had been said at the turn of the century about the baleful influence of the banned sophomore societies was now being laid three decades later at the feet of the junior fraternities, but the senior societies cannot have felt, by the examples of college leaders in sports, publications, and social eminence invited to join them, that they were sailing under false colors, as measured by results. Bones continued to seek out anointed leaders of the campus's leading social and athletic organizations, and Keys, at Jock Whitney's election, took in as well the *News* chairman, the student council president, the prom chairman, and the captains of the football, baseball, and hockey teams.[42]

For the outside world, the Owen Johnson of the 1920s was Henry F. Pringle, a Cornell man (and a decade later the author of a two-volume biography of William Howard Taft). He weighed into the debate with a long article in the January 1929 *Harper's* titled "Young Men on the Make." Centering his attention on Yale as exemplary, although not without brief sideswipes at Harvard, Princeton, Dartmouth, and even Cornell, Pringle described a type of modern undergraduate whom he characterized as calmly ambitious, self-seeking, and materialistic; who sought the laurels of extracurricular activity to exchange them for a soft berth after graduation; and who planned his college career with Machiavellian cunning and allowed the fact that some Yale alumni were millionaires to color his attitude throughout his college course.

"The hard-working Freshman, lathering himself to exhaustion in an editorial competition for the *Yale News*, may not be moved in the slightest by his potential debt to Yale," but rather understands that a *News* editor, "makes a Senior Society and that 'Senior Society Men are taken care of when they get out.'" The "young men on the make" mocked here "need little coaching to appreciate the possibilities which all this offers. And at Yale because of the fanatical solemnity with which the senior societies—Skull and Bones, Scroll and Key, and Wolf's Head—are regarded, the opportunities are greater than at any other university in America." The *Yale Alumni Weekly*, whatever its own criticisms of the system, wasn't having it. In reviewing Pringle's article, it declared that "'Heeling' is one thing the Senior Societies will not brook. Two sterling and prominent candidates for one Senior Society were passed up not long ago because the merest zephyr of suspicion found a motive in their achievements . . . No; the man is yet to be who can manoeuvre his way into a Senior Society, or who, when elected, can go to his room with an *arrière pensée*."[43]

This means that, more than ever, offers were duplicated, and some necessarily refused. On Tap Day in 1929, Wolf's Head for the first time had no refusals, while Keys and Bones each experienced one, and Elihu suffered five. In the spring of 1930, ten refused elections, with two men declining Bones who went to Keys, and two rebuffing Keys, to Bones; declining Elihu for Bones was Henry Heinz II, later president and board chairman of the family food company. Of that election, the *New York Times* commented editorially, "more and more of the undergraduates are taking non-election casually instead of tragically."[44]

The atmosphere in the spring of 1931 was much different. Wilder Hobson, former *Lit.* chairman and a Keysman of the recent crowd of 1928, said in a letter to the *Yale Daly News* that Tap Day was an institution as obsolete as "the antimacassar, the wall motto and the works of Sarah Orne Jewett." Even before this, into the growing fray came a new campus journal, the irreverent *Harkness Hoot*. Reflecting that magazine's many Menckenesque crusades, the headline in the *New York Herald Tribune* for May 14, 1931, proclaimed "Yale 'Tap Day' Today Likely to Be Its Last," quoting Dean Clarence Mendell's opinion that, because senior societies "are taken much less seriously today than they were twenty or even ten years ago," a "very substantial group of students and alumni think [Tap Day] is a demoralizing factor in the life of the college, and it is entirely likely that it will soon be a dead tradition, along with freshman fraternities and fence rushes."[45]

THE HARKNESS HOOT

The iconoclastic periodical of the early 1930s at Yale was the *Harkness Hoot*, named after its office location in the Harkness Quadrangle. The new journal pledged "to arouse a healthy skepticism regarding many institutions now taken for granted," a pledge redeemed many times over its four-year run of outrage and inspiration. Its first target was Yale's neo-Gothic building program (the Sterling Memorial Library and law and graduate schools then all under construction) as "girder gothic," sterile, and aesthetically retrograde. An editorial in the *Nation,* headlined "Revolt at Yale," observed: "Harvard has a reputation for indulging at times in rather frank self-criticism, but the extremest out-bursts ever heard at Cambridge seem feeble and timid in comparison with the drastic excoriation of Yale methods and Yale men which has been administered by the *Harkness Hoot*."[46] The editors for the class of 1932 were Richard M. Childs, a *Lit.* editor, and Richard M. Bissell Jr.

Childs authored one of the *Hoot*'s most notorious articles, appearing in the April/May 1931 issue, titled "The Elks in Our Midst." Its long subtitle read: "For Decades Fear and Trembling Have Attended Any Undergraduate Mention of Yale's Senior Societies and Their Shrouded Secrecy. Here a Junior Examines the Evils They Represent, the Impos-ture They Encourage, and Concludes That They Must Go." The first evil Childs discerned was that "judgment is made, and . . . a line of distinction is drawn between individuals," which the societies might not intend, but nonetheless effected. While "it may be impossible for any one to appreciate their actual meaning who has not experienced their inner mysteries," nevertheless, "when the fundamental and spontaneous reasons for the existence of a club or Secret Society are lost sight of, when they grow into a social power beyond themselves—and at Yale that social power is symbolized and maintained by so public a ceremony as Tap Day—then the sincerity of such institutions may be questioned."

Secondly, extracurricular activities, good in themselves as worthy exercises and relief from academic pressures, had become effectively blessed or dismissed by election results: "The Senior Society tradition of what is to be accepted and what is not, has attached a definite standard to every position in the undergraduate world and has made it desirable or not," thus perverting both preference and direction of individuals who otherwise might not make choices which were necessarily influenced by hope of election. To be accepted, Yale men fall into one stamp, one mold, and renounce their individuality because of age-long traditions established by the virtuous 'big men' at a Yale of another day." For this, the senior societies had to go. "These campus Elks, Masons, secret what-you-wills, that undertake to select men on a basis of personality and accomplishment, seem so hideously out-dated, so out of step with the very ideals of university life, that it is hard for us to believe in their existence today."

His solution was draconian. "If the members of [the class] of 1932 recognize the issue, and decide that the day of the Societies is past, they can kill those Societies by a moment's action. No more is needed than the juniors refrain from appearing, like slaves for sale, upon the Campus on Tap Day. If the Class simply stays in its rooms for that one hour, the Senior Societies automatically fall. And out of that change of mind, some newer and more fitting social system may arise."[47]

Despite this jeremiad, Tap Day on May 14, 1931, held only weeks after the *Hoot*'s appearance, was not much different than the immediately preceding years' ceremonies, and indeed was witnessed by an unusually large crowd of students, faculty members, and graduates, "possibly," the *New York Times* plausibly ventured, "because of the recent agitation against 'tap day' and the feeling that today's ceremony might be the last." Most of the 585 juniors gathered in the Branford Court of the Memorial Quadrangle, and at 5:45 P.M. marched in a body across the street to the campus and waited in the rain for the ceremony to begin at 6:00. Frederick Baldwin Adams Jr., secretary of his class and later director of the Morgan Library, was the first man tapped by Bones, joining playwright Eugene O'Neill's son there. Three men rebuffed Bones for Keys—a "surprise" was a fourth turndown of Bones for Wolf's Head by Glee Club president Basil Henning, later a Yale professor of History and long-time master of Saybrook residential college—and three men offered Keys chose Bones instead.

The most remarkable result was that one of the new Keysmen was Richard Childs himself, the author of "The Elks in Our Midst." He did not appear on campus (his Keys tapper went directly to his dormitory room to offer election), but he accepted. A Bones representative visited the same room to offer election to Childs's roommate and *Hoot* co-editor Richard Bissell—later, the first member of the Yale faculty to introduce Keynesian approaches and techniques to the study of economics there, and still later for the CIA, overseer of the U-2 spy plane program and author of the disastrous invasion at the Bay of Pigs in Cuba in 1961. Bissell, whose older brother had been in Bones—but never discussed the society with him—refused the invitation.

He was to write decades later that he regretted not having the presence of mind, when told, "Go to your room," to say "I'm *in* my room," but he disapproved of the selection standard of worldly success, as "counterproductive to true education," and "most of the people I knew were happy that I turned them down," although, "I felt a little depressed for a while. It meant I was out of a lot of things I wanted to be in." The *New York Times* later interviewed Childs, who said that he had not changed his view about the societies and still believed that they would eventually be abolished.[48]

The following spring's Tap Day in 1932 had about two thousand spectators, but the next year the class of 1934's student council took up Childs's suggestion, asking all members of the junior class to remain in their rooms from 5:00 to 7: 00 P.M. Many indeed signed an agreement to refuse to go on the campus during election hours. No editorial reason for the directive was given by the council; the *New York Times* reported that some juniors had been known for some time to favor remaining in their rooms during the tapping ceremony, but "whether this change now is a protest against [the traditional method], or an outcome of the present uncertain condition of fraternity life, is not clear."

On 1933's election day the juniors honored their pact: in the sneering words of a *Hoot* editorial which followed, they "trembled this year in their rooms, instead of standing on the campus for an hour in a self-conscious herd to wait the touch and the words without which a Yale career is empty and comfortless." While two lone freshmen were playing catch beneath the old oak where the choosing had been held previously, the seniors walked from the society halls, going directly, as they had not since the 1870s, to the juniors' rooms, quietly notifying them of their offers, then returning to their tombs with the results. "Many sat in their rooms from 5 o'clock, when the elections began, until after 7 P.M., when they were completed," the *New York Herald Tribune* noted, "without hearing such a knock." It was hard on the choosers, too: unable to check a man off their list when he left the campus at the behest of another organization, they had to go to his room and offer an election anyway, sprinting from their headquarters to the widely separated rooms of the different juniors each time, and then reporting back on how they fared. "It could not have been run off in an hour," reported the *Yale Alumni Weekly*, "for there was a great deal of negotiating to be done."

While all four societies elected their full quota of fifteen men, the turndowns this year were almost certainly multiplied by the self-inflicted isolation of the offerees, who, removed from the campus ground and perhaps, "watching furtively out [their] windows," could hardly see or otherwise know to whom offers were made: Bones suffered four refusals, Wolf's Head two, Elihu five, and Keys an astounding ten.[49] A contemporaneous review in the *New York Times Magazine* on "College Ways in America" reminded readers that "The new procedure of having the whole matter handled privately is the original procedure. The public arrest and order to 'go to your room' is a mere interpolated interlude. Yet it is precisely this interpolation which has become Yale's peculiar institution and has invested Yale's senior societies with a glamour for the country at large which does not clothe the proud clubs of Princeton or Harvard, famous among Harvard men as are Porcellian and Signet and such like and illustrious as is Ivy among the Princetonians."[50]

The following year's election was accompanied by renewed condemnation and ridicule of the system. The *Yale Daily News* published a blistering editorial, slamming the societies ("Their method of choice, their breaking apart of old friendships, their demand on student time, their constant secrecy, their political influence at Yale have been criticized with such telling regularity that they need no repetition"), with many echoes of Owen Johnson: "Deplorable in any form is the cult of success . . . This attitude which exists at Yale is not restricted to New Haven but is to be found in most colleges and universities to a varying degree."

The *Yale Record*, the college's humor magazine, in its May 1934 issue featured cartoons, photographs, and short articles mocking the spirit of mystery surrounding the societies, lampooning individual juniors regarded as logical candidates for membership, and ridiculing the institution of Tap Day itself. The barbs included a photograph of a herd of grazing sheep, with the label, "A few prominent members of the Junior class confidently awaiting the climax of their undergraduate careers." A playscript rendering of a society election caucus ended with the direction: "Please remember that if the candidate is found in possession of a copy of the *Hoot*, he is automatically excluded from membership."[51]

The reform did not stick: the class of 1935 was not bound by a student council resolution of the class of 1934, and as reported by the *Alumni Weekly*, the "innovation takes too long a time and leaves both Classes in doubt as to just who has been elected and to what." Meanwhile, there would be further complications the next year from the fact that "the juniors will be scattered throughout the seven new residential colleges." Thus, Tap Day reverted to its old ceremony of public slapping, but in a new venue, Branford College main court in the Memorial Quadrangle, and in relative privacy, with no alumni or relatives present.

The gates of Branford were locked, except for the two used by the participants, and spruce boughs were leaned against the gates to block the curious public's view. The junior class stood at one end of the courtyard, near Harkness Tower, under a spreading elm, and were then approached by the tappers of the six senior societies (the former Sheff fraternities Berzelius and Book and Snake now making their first appearance as senior societies on the traditional election day). John Pillsbury Snyder Jr. of Minneapolis, captain of the hockey team, astonished his classmates by refusing successive offers from to Keys, Elihu, Berzelius, and Book and Snake, and received no more taps, leading to the conclusion that he had decided to accept election to Bones or to none.

Each society had requisitioned headquarters space in Branford students' rooms, where successful taps, or unfortunate refusals, might be reported. The increased number of electing societies multiplied the number of refusals, and the general confusion. One senior tapped the same junior twice at a ten minute interval, the junior refusing to budge both times. More remarkably, two men standing together were tapped one after another by the same society, but this resulted in one refusal and one acceptance. The refuser then changed his mind and proceeded to run off the court after his friend and the electing senior, and the elector who had been rebuffed, seeing the evident change of mind, sped back toward his first choice. As for the torrent of criticism from Yale campus publication, the *New York Times* headline for its elections article said it all: "Societies at Yale Going Blithely On. Blasts from Campus Press for Tap Day Seem to Have Left Targets Unscathed."[52]

In the publication's final year before discontinuance by its student sponsors (it was a private enterprise and had never been censored by the authorities), the May 1934 *Hoot* chose, with its "newly acquired mantle of respectability weighing heavily," to return to campus, "one of Yale's oldest traditional amusements, Senior Society baiting." The issue's introductory piece was a poem, "A Freshman's Prayer on Thursday Night," reminding the lowly underclassmen of the *Hoot*'s opinion of their irrational longing:

> *Hear the clumping of their feet*
> *As they go marching down the street!*
> *Perhaps, some day, if I am good,*
> *I may be of that brotherhood.*
> *There's something fine about a mask,*
> *It saves the mind full half its task;*
> *There's something grand about a club,*
> *So few can join it, there's the rub,*
> *And those outside are filled with awe.*
> *What prompts such awe can have no flaw.*
> *O Lord I pray thee let me be*
> *A god, in such society,*
> *For, tho I know not what they do,*
> *I greatly want to do it, too!*[53]

THE COMING OF THE COLLEGE PLAN

Edward S. Harkness of the class of 1897 had formalized his interest in charity when in 1918, together with his mother, he founded the Commonwealth Fund with the family's Standard Oil investment millions. To organize this institution, "to do something for the welfare of mankind," he called on his longtime friend and financial advisor, New Haven lawyer Samuel Fisher, who shared Harkness's interest in the activities of the YMCA, of which Fisher had been president his senior year, 1888–89. A member of Bones as an undergraduate, and Successor Trustee on the Yale Corporation from 1920 through 1935, Fisher was classmates with James Gamble Rogers, a member of that year's Keys delegation, and the three men became close friends, taking frequent trips together.

For Gamble, as he was known at Yale, the college was the place where this Chicago high school graduate, who knew few if any of his classmates, was introduced to a special culture, a world made up of sports (he was baseball manager), shared amusements, and traditions acquired and constantly renewed in the collective, ritualized activities of a selected group of young men just starting to define their lives. "Nothing," his grandson was to write, "was more important than class spirit while he was at college, nor would anything evoke fonder memories in his days after graduation."

Rogers had designed Harkness's Fifth Avenue home in 1907–08, a great opportunity for an out-of-town architect from Chicago, and a commission probably obtained for Rogers by his Keys clubmate, Dr. William Armstrong. The architect found resonance in his client's desire, generated by Harkness's remembered happiness in Wolf's Head, to do something for the "average men" at Yale who, not being members of the junior fraternities or senior societies, had been left out of the college's most rewarding social experiences. Rogers designed the Harkness Memorial Quadrangle, the family's tribute to Edward's deceased older brother Charles, of the Wolf's Head delegation of 1883. Those linked dormitories were completed in 1921 to provide housing and meals for over six hundred students.

That year Rogers was appointed consulting architect to Yale University, specifically charged with guiding the physical growth of the campus. When he appeared at the Yale Corporation meeting for his first presentation, he arrived with only one detailed drawing, showing the floor plans of one single and one double room: the latter proved to be the plan replicated in virtually every staircase of Rogers's eight residential colleges a decade later, and familiar to generations of Yalies who occupied them, first as doubles, then from the onset of the overcrowding of World War II as quads.

He found himself working closely with an old Chicago friend, the chair of the Corporation's Committee on the Architectural Plan, John Farwell, the first "Western" member of Yale's governing body, elected in 1911, and a key player in the selection of President Angell. Farwell, of the class of 1879, was also a Keys alumnus, as were his brothers in the classes of 1882 and 1884, respectively, and coincidentally related by marriage to Rogers. Through Keys, they were all members of a community which, after graduation at least, depended little on one's class year.

Two other university officers were among the College Plan's dramatis personae: George Parmly Day, class of 1897 with Harkness and Keysman, founder of Yale University Press and university treasurer from 1910; and Charles Seymour, class of 1908 and Bones, professor of History and, from 1927, provost. Seymour had graduated from King's College, Cambridge, before matriculating at Yale, and returned to Cambridge for an MA after graduating in New Haven. Harkness himself was assisted in his office by Malcolm Aldrich, class of 1922, football captain and Bones, who was to succeed Fisher as managing director of the Harkness philanthropies, and became second president of the Commonwealth Fund.

The intertwining of personal and professional motives and relationships, under the benign shadow of Edward Harkness, helped define the roles all were to play in the justification, formulation, and execution of the College Plan. Farwell's insistence that it was "the desire of the Architectural Plan Committee to recommend to the Corporation architects who are Yale graduates" led to the displacement of Bertram Grosvenor Goodhue as the previously appointed architect of the Sterling bequest executors for the Yale Library and other Sterling-named structures. This tight network of Yale graduates which resulted, coalescing around the two principal donors to the university—Sterling and Harkness themselves connected by derivation of their respective families' assets from the Rockefeller fortune—was a small group of men related by marriage, intellectual outlook, and common membership in Yale's three oldest senior societies.

During the summer of 1927, Rogers, Fisher, and Harkness himself accompanied President Angell on a secret mission, traveling to Oxford, Cambridge, and several other institutions to discover what made the "Oxbridge" tradition so attractive and effective. Yale's entering class had grown, between 1910 and 1923, from 302 students to 886. The university as a whole desperately needed to add new dormitory space, and to create smaller, more congenial residential units in the process, while maintaining the atmosphere of the older Yale which they all so admired. The social system, which had functioned beautifully with classes that graduated three hundred at Yale, now was failing. In the middle 1920s Professor Chauncey Tinker was obliged to introduce two seniors to each other, in order that the first might ask the second to move over and vacate his seat!

Harkness wished to create places where rich and poor collegians alike could be educated into high moral thinking and action, in congenial, small-scale surroundings, while isolated from the pressures of the modern world—but enjoying that world's physical amenities. These quadrangles were to become the cloistered settings for social bonding and a place of origin to be remembered by alumni as the common and culturally significant sources of their positions (as were their tombs for senior society members).

This would have been in the forefront of the philanthropist's consciousness, as in 1923–24 he had commissioned Bertram Grosvenor

Goodhue to design a new hall for Wolf's Head, on York Street, to replace the original tomb at the corner of Prospect and Trumbull Streets, a design which Goodhue had completed at the time of his sudden death in April 1924. Its pickled stone façade of blind windows and blind dovecotes in the gables was shielded by a tall, solid wall and lots of shrubbery; modern Gothic and yet remote, the new hall was an across-the-street reflection of the official Yale Gothic of James Gamble Rogers's Memorial Quadrangle, and the first tomb to have a front walled courtyard. It was a commission which Rogers had desired, but loyal Wolf's Head alumnus Harkness could not stand the notion that a Keys man should be the architect for the new Wolf's Head tomb.

Rogers, in a memorandum titled "The Future of Yale College," fashioned an argument for recalling and making real his memories of late-nineteenth-century Yale in a new construct, to soften "the penalty that we have to pay for the great expansion in the sizes of our classes" in the intervening decades. "In our minds," he wrote, "Yale College represented not merely a gracious association but a great spirit, a spirit of fellowship, forbearance, sympathy, and *that highest of education, the culture that comes from close friction of those students who are not of one kind by the usual selection*" (emphasis supplied). This gentleman of Keys, the first junior ever to turn down Bones his election year, here celebrated the glorious diversity of association which all these godfathers of the College Plan—all senior society graduate members—surely foresaw. The project for the subdivision of Yale College was thus an explicitly social one, seeking to establish the small and sheltered academy where men were educated by intimate association into shared social and moral values, so that they might eventually give leadership to the outside world.

The leveling clarity of this program created some opposition, particularly among the Yale fraternities, but the reaction to the plan was considerably more muted in New Haven than it was up at Harvard. When Yale took too long to respond to his gift proposal, Harkness (thinking he had been rebuffed) traveled to Massachusetts to offer his plan to Harvard president Abbot Lawrence Lowell. Lowell agreed immediately, even before consultation with his own faculty, and soon announced a major anonymous gift to start what became Harvard's house system. This declaration provoked the more conservative students in Cambridge to resist the plan's equalizing tendencies, afraid that they might lose the self-selecting intimacy of their eating and final clubs and be forced to room with Jews, Italians, or other groups of social undesirables.

Yale quickly cleared up the misunderstanding with its donor. In the residential college system approved by the Yale Corporation in October 1929, the assumption was at last explicitly made that "at Yale social elements play a significant role in education." In each of the ten planned residential colleges, upperclassmen of all three classes, about 65 in each, would live together, without exception for off-campus housing choice, in deconstruction of the traditional, horizontal class allegiances of old Yale, while absorbing the values and wisdom of those about to graduate. The residential college populations were to be cross sections of the student body, mixing pupils of different economic backgrounds, academic interests, and religious affiliations. Those "average" or in Hadley's formulation "overlooked" men without previous connections, meaning membership in prep school or big city social cliques, would more naturally be considered for and participate in the extracurricular activities that often formed the more memorable part of an education in New Haven.

The Yale Corporation thus adopted Rogers's proposal for creating new quadrangle dormitories, styled "colleges" on the Oxbridge model, each housing between 150 and 250 students, while housing all freshmen on the Old Campus. These were to be administered by a master and a dean, and equipped with a dining hall, a library, common room lounges, and a luxurious master's house, with some three hundred scholarship students working at Harkness's insistence as researchers, library assistants, or organizers of special events in a "work-study" program, rather than serving their rich friends in the dining hall. As a *Yale Daily News* article subheader highlighted: "Jobs for Self-Supporting Students Permit All to Enroll in Colleges in Spite of Meal Minimum." For all this, Edward

Harkness was prepared to spend $15,725,884.96, Yale's largest gift since the Sterling bequest of 1918.[54]

One of the architectural features shared by the Collegiate Gothic residential college façades at Yale are carved ornamental details on chimney ends and entryways, eclectic images of all the extracurricular and academic activities that had one time or another taken place on campus. Although these figures were Rogers's conception, he left no known documentation in his papers regarding their meaning. It has been said that the series of scenes at the end of the west interior courtyard of Trumbull College, above a wooden entryway door, showing horned devils, wolves, magicians, kings wearing crowns, clowns, Indians, and Puritans with broad-brimmed hats, some of them tossing a tail-coated man in a blanket, depict a Skull and Bones initiation. Still, there are no skulls or femurs in the scene, which seems to have been inspired instead by figures in E. Crisand's 1862 engraving *Initiation of Yale Freshman— Secret Societies.*

The College Plan, explained an article in *Town & Country* magazine about both the fraternities and the societies at Yale, archly titled "One Foot in the Grave and One in the Tomb," meant "dividing the University into small independent units, each with a dining hall, a library, and every comfort the fraternity houses could offer, except a dark shrine, suitable for mumbo-jumbo, under the eaves. Moreover, the facilities would be better and cheaper." The senior societies, with "one foot in the tomb," were not existentially threatened by the College Plan, but some Yale fraternities were to go under, having "one foot in the grave," burdened by expensive mortgages on lavish houses (although most would survive).[55]

In the Sheffield Scientific School, by contrast, there were eight clubs, all operating dormitories in which their members slept as well as ate after the sophomore year. For the Sheffield fraternities with both tombs *and* separate members' dormitories, namely Berzelius and Book and Snake, their proffered benefit of undergraduate housing was now a useless burden, and decisions had to be taken urgently about their future.

THE FOUNDING (1848) AND INCLUSION (1934)
OF BERZELIUS

During the nineteenth century's second half, Yale College (also known as the "Academic" division or "Ac") and the Sheffield Scientific School, separated only by a few streets in the city, "were two separate countries on the same planet." Sheffield was a technical science school that stood separate from, and in a second-class relation to, Yale College from 1862 to 1945. It was the fruit of the Land-Grant Act of 1862 that Yale successfully snatched for itself away from the public sector. In 1862, it had graduated six men, and by 1893's class, 110. Academically, President Hadley wrote in 1895, "Sheff," as it was familiarly known, "offers the student a choice of seven courses, according to the line of work for which the student would prepare himself—one for the chemist, one for the biologist, one for the civil engineer, one for the mechanical engineer, one for the mining engineer, one for the agriculturalist, and one for the general businessman."

Nevertheless, in his 713-page magnum opus of 1871, *Four Years at Yale*, Lyman Bagg devotes only four pages to Sheff, then a quarter century old, and mentions its student societies not at all. The gap is further illustrated by journalist Edwin Slosson's simile in his *Great American Universities* of 1911: "President Hadley occupies a position like that of Francis Joseph, Emperor of Austria-Hungary. Yale is a dual monarchy; the person of the sovereign being the bond between College and Sheffield." The social divide was suggested by a character in F. Scott Fitzgerald's short story of 1920, "May Day," attending a fraternity dance in the Yale Club and speaking to disheveled soldiers hiding in a broom closet: "I thought perhaps you might be members of the lovely section of the university known as the Sheffield Scientific School."[56]

While the Old Brick Row on the spacious Old Campus quadrangle nourished Yale College men and their traditions over four years, "Sheff" had but one building, at the head of College Street, and no campus where its students on their three-year PhB course could gather for recreation;

no official dormitory where they could enjoy undergraduate life rooming together; no common dining hall; and no rules and regulations, or compulsory chapel. Comprising so low a percentage of the student body—in 1870, Ac had 522 students, and Sheff had only 125—they made no noticeable impression on the larger college community: few acquaintanceships were formed with Ac men in occasional interactions at the boathouse and gymnasium. When a secret fraternity or society system ultimately formed in Sheff, its seven components were recruited each year by the admission of freshmen, and about one-third of Sheff students were members.[57]

Although the University had by the 1930s effectively integrated the Academical side with the Sheffield Scientific School, the undergraduates' still separate social systems had lagged far behind. In the spring of 1933, the Sheff's two scholarly honorary societies, Torch and Aurelian, announced that they would for the first time elect their numbers from the entire class of 1934, although, as in the past, these societies would be neither secret nor "final." Accepting membership therein, it was made known, would not preclude the Ac men from accepting membership in the classic senior societies if offered later in the month. Whether there would be reciprocity, with the Ac side's senior societies enlarging their own candidate pool to include Sheff men, was then unknown.

Still, a break in the old forms had earlier that spring already been initiated by the Sheffield fraternity the Cloister Club, more familiarly known as Book and Snake, possessors of a formidable windowless tomb just west of the Commons and across from the Law School at the intersection of Grove and York Streets, erected opposite the Grove Street Cemetery gate in 1902. Book and Snake had already decided to become a regular university senior society and to choose its members from the junior class at large.

This had truly scrambled the society egg, making for a total of five senior societies, four (Bones, Keys, Wolf's Head, and Elihu) electing from the Ac class only, and one electing from the entire class, and two non-secret organizations (Aurelian and Torch) choosing from the 800-member class at large. This could leave a sizable number of college juniors, the men in 1934, out on a limb, losing to "prominent young men from the Harkness side of Elm Street," berths formerly allotted to them. That cloud of confusion quickly began to dissipate when Colony, the second surviving Sheff fraternity, made a posting in the *Alumni Weekly* on May 12, 1933: "The Berzilius Society, in keeping with the spirit and purpose of the Residential College Plan, announces that it will become a Senior Society electing its members from the Junior Class of the University."[58]

The rush to a college-wide democracy was ringed with caveats. The end of what little class solidarity still remained at Yale was foreseen, with the creation and construction of ten new residential colleges, seven in number to start, and three delayed by the economic repercussions of the Great Depression. Their occupants would be comprised of the student body of three schools—Academic, Scientific, and Engineering—all for the first time compelled to live together, which to the *Alumni Weekly* strongly suggested that the "Senior Society set-up at Yale may be obliged to undergo drastic reorganization if it is permitted by the changed conditions to survive at all."[59]

Sheffield Scientific School began with the foundation of a laboratory for teaching Agricultural Chemistry in 1846, the nation's first graduate program in chemistry, but without benefit of a Yale degree for its students or salaries for its few professors. The C.T.I. Society, later the Berzelius Chemical Society and then just the Berzelius Society, was founded in the fall of 1848 to satisfy the desire of its members for a more diverse study of the sciences than the school then offered (very like the Ac side's Eulogia Club's members' dissatisfaction in 1832 with their speech training). Its Constitution named for "its objects the discussions of such literary and scientific questions as may be deemed of interest and importance," and it was otherwise dedicated, in a new Constitution of 1857, to the "social and intellectual improvement of members" and the inclusion of all those interested in scientific inquiry.

Berzelius was formed as a secret organization, at a time when the faculty had disbanded open societies and disdained the secret societies, meaning not only Skull and Bones, but the Yale chapters of the first fraternities which were also secret societies. Its own proceedings were only deemed confidential, as described in a club resolution: "The old and discredited science of alchemy was dark, mysterious, and esoteric: the new science of chemistry seeks light and truth and is open to all." The first president was Joseph Willett, a 23-year-old professor of Chemistry at Mercer College in Georgia who came to New Haven to improve his job qualifications, and it was he who founded the society with eight fellow students and suggested the Latin motto, echoing Phi Beta Kappa, which gave the student organization its original name of C.T.I. That changed when in the winter of 1849 news reached America of the death of Jöns Jakob Berzelius, the preeminent Swedish chemist, whom the young men chose to honor by renaming their society.

High-stand students were soon being chosen as members, and its prestige grew in the eyes of the Sheff faculty. By 1852, its fourth anniversary, Berzelius could boast six founding members. William Blake, William H. Brewer, George J. Brush, William J. Craw, Mason C. Weld, and George C. Weyman, some destined to become famous as teachers and scientists, were granted the degree of PhB by the Yale Corporation, thus becoming the scientific school's first graduates. Brewer assumed the role of the society's faculty advisor upon his return to Yale as professor of Agricultural Chemistry in 1864.

In his history of the society, Brewer described the adoption of its pyramidal badge, originally flat, a re-creation of a then familiar chemical apparatus known as Liebig's potash bulbs, in black enamel with the letters "C.T.I." in gold; later, a New Haven jeweler was able to create rounded bulbs. Justus von Liebig was, in 1848, second only to Berzelius in renown as a great man of chemistry, and was made an honorary member of the society. While he never came to the United States, he proudly wore his Berzelius pin on ceremonial occasions in Europe. The Berzelius shield in the 1865–66 *Yale Pot-Pourri* showed fifteen linking rings, symbolizing the number of delegation members, surrounding the C.T.I. initials of the society's motto. Later in that decade, a new shield replaced the old, with the letter "B" surrounded by the potash bulbs in gold, and the letters C.T.I. below.

Meeting first in the laboratory, but frequently interrupted by raids from other societies, and then in each others' rooms, members continued their functions aimed toward the stimulation of interest not only in science, but in debating and literature, and sometimes purely social meetings were mounted. In 1862, eight years after the construction of the Bones tomb and shortly after Keys had built its hall, the society moved to the second-story rear of a house at 744 Chapel Street at the southwest corner of State Street, the ground floor of which was occupied by Whittlesey's Drug Store, securing its first room furnished to the members' own taste. Occupying the whole floor allowed the growth of new customs, such as billiards competitions in their own billiard room and the formation of the "Shelf Committee," charged with procuring "a large pitcher of foaming beer and a bag of crackers"; any repast of the society is still called a "Shelf."

The group's loftier purpose remained central: each week, a student would be responsible for framing that meeting's talking points by introducing an original essay, chairing a debate, or delivering an oration, practices which came to be known as "Literary Exercises," with faculty in attendance to enhance the quality of discussions. The Berzelius Trust Association was incorporated in the State of Connecticut in May 1864, and the society began in 1868 to offer a prize of $10 in gold for excellence in English composition, with its sponsorship accepted by the faculty and the prize awarded among the other competitive college prizes.

Inwardly, however, some focus had been lost, with the Shelf Committee's endeavors sapping strength from the Literary Committee and its programs. Berzelius men had changed, perhaps inevitably, from graduate students in search of a forum to examine scientific research, into undergraduates in search of social fellowship. William M. Scaife, president of the delegation of 1873, wrote a report lamenting the levity with which the members were approaching the Literary Exercises. In response, members voted to modify them, "so as to remove every cause of ill-feeling," without abandoning the underlying commitment to scientific progress that these exercises were meant to foster. A Scientific Subcommittee was created to deliver a synopsis each week of the most important scientific periodicals, to complement the students' coursework and enliven the debates which the Literary Exercises were designed to frame. This "Compromise of 1873" nonetheless marked a departure from the society's original academic mission, by releasing its members from "compulsory" literary contributions—and thus freeing them to pursue the more pressing objective of becoming the leading Sheffield social fraternity.

Having moved quarters from above the drugstore to rooms over the Yale National Bank in a building at Chapel and State, Berzelius advanced plans for a hall of its own, purchasing a lot for $3,200 at the corner of Prospect and Sachem Streets, and expended another $7,325 in construction costs. This building initiative was initially balked by the Sheff freshmen who in 1873 tried to force Berzelius and its rival Sigma Delta Chi (later Book and Snake) to become senior societies, but this revolt was defeated in October 1875, and on June 14, 1877, the first meeting in the new hall was celebrated.

Then, a group of nine members formed a club of their own and, with the consent of the Sheff faculty, rented 88 Wall Street as a dormitory for the following year, an effort deemed so successful in its intellectual and social advantages that plans were soon started for the erection of a society dormitory. Once the necessary funds were raised and plans were designed, in 1897, on the fiftieth anniversary of the Sheffield Scientific School, the cornerstone of the Colony, the society's first and last residential hall, was laid in the presence of over a hundred graduate and undergraduate members. By the fall of 1898, construction was complete, and Berzelius members—sophomores through seniors—moved into their new home at 17 Hillhouse Avenue. Boasting a residential hall, Berzelius in all but name became a college fraternity, housing twenty-five members.

In January 1908 a fire broke out in the Prospect Street hall, gutting most of the structure before the fire department could locate a member of the society to let them in to fight the blaze. To maintain its social leadership, the society recognized that it "ought to have a site and building second to none" and began fund-raising for their next and present tomb. This was erected three years later at the intersection of Whitney Avenue with Trumbull and Temple Streets. This, the only Yale senior society tomb facing on *three* streets, was an adaptation of the Petit Trianon, of which New Haven version it was said "the windows do not appear false or purely decorative; they seem to have been closed following the death of an ancient inhabitant." President Hadley was in attendance at the laying of its cornerstone in a midnight ceremony which saw a copper box containing the society's records placed in the foundation.

In 1933, Sheff was absorbed completely into Yale College, and the Colony itself was sold to Yale because the new residential college system was destroying the demand for independent dormitories (four of seven other Sheff fraternities, all of which operated dormitories, were not to survive). However, the university was of course not also in the market for mausoleums, so the future of the tombs controlled by those societies was in doubt. The Berzelius membership, past and present, voted by referendum to become a true senior society in competition with the others on Tap Day. Yale's president James Rowland Angell, not a Yale graduate and thus never a member of a senior society, had been made an honorary member of Berzelius in 1923 and was approached for his advice and blessing. He responded that "[i]f you [become a senior society] with the high purpose of helping your members and basing your elections entirely on character and achievement, there is a place for you. But if you intend electing only those who are congenial and you are to be only another social body, there is no place for you as a Senior Society."

Recognizing that the objective selection of the best possible candidates from a wide range of campus activities was critical to establishing a sustainable niche within the competition, the society defined its election approach as the "cross-section principle," as opposed to what it deemed the "high-pressure salesmanship or social alignment" of the other societies. The Berzelius Trust Association from 1934 on forwarded to its graduate membership lists of junior class prospects, asking for information on the named candidates, and the names of any other juniors related to graduates; the lists were composed after its Undergraduate Campaign Committee compiled small cumulative record cards for the two or three hundred prospective junior candidates, each with a picture of the candidate, his home address, his father's educational and professional background, the student's scholastic average, and his literary, athletic, social, and other extracurricular interests.

While Berzelius suffered six refusals on Tap Day in 1934, which was not surprising for its first outing (Keys had five that year, and Elihu seven), all of its fifteen acceptances that year were from the Academic Department. This remained true for the next five years running, because the remaining Sheff fraternities—St. Anthony, St. Elmo, Vernon (Phi Gamma Delta), and York Hall (Chi Phi)—did not yet permit any of their members to accept senior society elections. Berzelius told its members that they would continue to give careful consideration to all Sheff men available, and announced a belief that "with the growth of the residential colleges and concurrent decline in residential fraternities, Sheff men will be available for election in the future."

The society was further thrilled, in announcing these 1934 results to its membership, to note that both the *Yale News* and the *Yale Alumni Weekly*, in reporting the final election lists, had placed the senior societies in order of age, which meant Berzelius (1848) came after Scroll and Key (1842), but before Book and Snake (1863), Wolf's Head (1888), and Elihu (1903). After Tap Day in 1936, the Undergraduate Information Committee was able to report that it had only one refusal, matching the results of Keys and Wolf's Head, and bettering the offering fortunes of Bones, Elihu, and Book and Snake. Furthermore, "[i]t will be seen from [that biographical] list of men that Berzelius is following its adopted definite policy of choosing its members on the basis of character and achievement and of selecting men of different types rather than of one type and those representing a cross-section of the various extra curricular activities in the University."

In self-electing to survive as a senior society, Berzelius also simultaneously transformed its program. The Literary Exercises were replaced in 1934 with both a "personal audit," which matched the "life history" evenings of Skull and Bones, but enlivened the presentation with the subjective give-and-take of questions and comments from the member's auditors, to occur on Thursday evenings. This was supplemented by a Sunday night speakers program, hosting successful graduates, Yale administrators and professors, honorary members, and others to share their own life experiences and wisdom. Other traditions, paralleling the maturation of the other Yale senior societies, followed: the Berzelius answer to Keys' "Gaily the Troubadour" was the "C.T.I. Parting Song," written by Fenno Heath, of the 1950 delegation, and Yale Glee Club Director from 1953 to 1992.[60]

THE FOUNDING (1863) AND INCLUSION (1934) OF BOOK AND SNAKE

Berzelius's fifteen-year monopoly of Sheff student society organization from its founding in 1848 lasted only five years longer than Skull and Bones' monopoly of Ac's senior society system. The supply of interested students was outstripping the membership limitation, and Berzelius's solution in 1863 was to create a "brother" society, called the Literature and Science Society, to meet weekly in South Sheffield Hall for literary exercises and debate. Book and Snake's historian has claimed that Berzelius's true aim here was to stop the formation of any other society that might oppose their social hegemony, by appointing to "L. and S." any students who appeared to be restive or on the verge of founding a new group.

This farm-league system collapsed after less than a season, as a band of disgruntled junior class members of this class of 1865 broke away to form Cloister, first known as Sigma Delta Chi and later as the Book and Snake society. The new club did not take long to ape the bad manners of the Ac side societies Bones and Keys. French windows opened from the Berzelius hall onto a flat roof, where on pleasant evenings the members adjourned with their chairs. Professor Benjamin Silliman Jr., the society's first honorary member, attended a meeting where a "spread" from the Shelf Committee had been placed on the roof to keep cool. When the Berzelius delegation went up to eat, the comestibles had disappeared, the first recorded act of "crooking" against the older society, for which its new rival was suspected.[61]

The founders of Cloister, on November 17, 1863, were James Bishop Ford, William James Mitchell, Sanford Robinson, Harry Rogers, William Wheelwright Skiddy, and John Whitman, together with a freshman, Joseph Thompson Whittlesey. Like Berzelius, it was a secret society, and rented a small hall-end room on the top floor of 851 Chapel Street, furnished with plain wooden chairs and a small table for meeting purposes. In 1876 its members chose to set up a residential home of their own, taking a brick structure at 36 Elm Street adjoining St. Thomas Church for living quarters, while ultimately expanding into the full top floor on Chapel Street for their society functions.

The name they chose was the Sigma Delta Chi Society, for a purely Scientific School organization without other college affiliations. When the new group's existence became known within Sheff and its founders identified by anxious members of Berzelius, the rebels were approached and offered immediate membership in Berzelius if they would abandon their plans. The offer was promptly rebuffed and soon Sigma Delta Chi openly solicited new members, electing from all three Sheff classes. After the pledges' initiation in their first rooms, all members the following day appeared wearing pins on their cravats, diamond-shaped with their three Greek letters, in gold on a black enameled ground. Rules of secrecy were laid down: no discussion of the society with outsiders, and no notice to be taken of their remarks about it. By 1868, a sinking fund was started to enable a proper tomb to be constructed.

When the delegation of 1876 rented 36 Elm Street for a members' dormitory, with one toilet and one tin bathtub, that became the first of the Sheff society dormitories, named the "Cloister" by John Hays Hammond of that class (later to become Cecil Rhodes's chief mining engineer in South Africa, a professor of mining at Yale, and a Taft-appointed special ambassador to Great Britain). The same year, the society's name was changed to Book and Snake from Sigma Delta Chi, in determination that there should be no confusion with any national Greek-letter fraternity. The Stone Trust Corporation, named after early member Lewis Bridge Stone, was incorporated in Connecticut to hold the society's property and funds, and, echoing the corporate charters of Bones and Keys, "for the purposes of the social, intellectual and moral improvement of its members."

The Trust secured an option on land at the southeast corner of Grove and High Streets, ultimately purchased for $10,000, but not until 1901 were the funds raised to build a tomb of Vermont marble in the Greek Ionic style, at a total cost of $81,000 for land and building. The architect was a Book and Snake member, Louis Metcalfe '95-S, and upon its completion the two-story structure, forty feet tall, sixty feet long and forty-two feet wide, with four marble ionic pillars framing its doors, was deemed by some "the most perfect example of Greek architecture in America." The steel used in the construction of its alcove was that material's first use in a domestic building in the United States. It has been said that this archeologically correct temple stands as a "solid classisistic answer" to the Egyptian-gated cemetery across the street. "It is the perpetual attempt of establishing an official perfect order on earth, a sort of platonic reflection of heavenly secret societies."[62]

Its front door is a replica of the north door of the Erechtheion building on the Acropolis in Athens. Without a single slit or window in the solid marble walls (and more remarkably, a roof of huge marble tiles), it is surrounded by an iron fence, and the original wooden doors were in time replaced by bronze ones. Smoke from the furnace was carried by pipes to the chimney in the neighboring Commons building. A New Haven newspaper article reported that visiting strangers were told the building was a crematory, and that the snakes or "caduceuses" entwined around the iron pickets (the society's symbol is a book surrounded by the ouroboros, a snake eating its own tail) represented that "all Yale men were bachelors, and the snake was put there to remind all the students of Eve so they would remain bachelors."

When the Yale residential college plan was announced, immediate speculation followed that private dormitories, such as the Cloister and the Colony, would not be permitted to intrude on the university's plans that all undergraduates were to live together. W. W. Skiddy, one of the founders of Book and Snake, had long wanted to dispose of the Cloister and convert Book and Snake into a senior society along the lines of those in Ac, and offered a considerable sum to support that conversion, but found no majority in favor after a substantial and seemingly final discussion of the possibility at the graduate reunion in 1920.

The announcement of the Harkness college plan gift, with residency commencing in fall 1933 and the last distinction between Sheff and Ac disappearing, compelled the Stone Trust to poll its members in May 1932. The votes in June were 189 to become a senior society, 2 to become a junior society, and 32 to await further developments. In spite of the protests of many graduates and undergraduates, the Trust voted in February 1933 to dispose of the Cloister at 1 Hillhouse—the property is now the university provost's office, with a memorial plaque on the first floor—and to make Book and Snake a senior society. The conveyance of the Cloister was announced as a gift, but in truth Yale paid $25,000 for the building, said to then be the oldest society dormitory still standing in the country, and $5,000 for the furniture, with the income used by the society for a complete interior renovation of the Grove Street tomb.

Although the graduate members had pressed for conversion to a senior society, the truth was they could give the undergraduates no help in establishing a new *raison d'etre,* and in shaping traditions that had to be made into the pattern established by others. In May 1934, Book and Snake went onto the campus for elections. They had taken in seven Yale College seniors as members in March, who now worked with the twenty Sheff side seniors and juniors to plan their selections—knowing that taking in a regular complement of fifteen on Tap Day, or as close as may be, was crucial to the new senior society's future. They decided not to pledge any juniors beforehand, as some of the Ac side societies were still said to do, although, without extracting a pledge of acceptance, they told several juniors that their names were under serious consideration, a policy that was to continue. They also decided (as did Berzelius) that they would take in men not only from Yale College but from Sheff and the Engineering School, an ecumenism not at first shared by the original senior societies. In May 1934, Book and Snake received eleven acceptances from candidates they felt to be worthy, and had no trouble filling their full complement in the years thereafter.[63]

Interestingly, undergraduates at the Sheff fraternity St. Anthony's Hall at this time also wanted to become a senior society, but their graduate members forbade it, determining to stay a "final" organization and not allowing their members to accept election in any of the senior societies. Of the remaining Sheff societies, the St. Elmo Club, Vernon Hall (Phi Gamma Delta), and York Hall similarly survived the advent of the College Plan, but the Sachem Club (Phi Kappa Sigma) and Franklin Hall (Theta Xi) expired; all six sold their dormitories to the university as well, although for a while their members continued to live in them.[64]

THE DECADE ENDS, THE SOCIETIES SAVED, AND ONE CASTE BROKEN

In "Senior Societies and the Lord Jehovah," an article appearing in the *Harkness Hoot* issue for the month of 1933's Tap Day, an anonymous society member celebrated the irony that the accession of Berzelius and Book and Snake to the old Ac system of such organizations was that system's very salvation. The recurrent challenges to the senior society social regime since 1928 had set their constituents back on their heels, beginning with the numerous Bones turndowns of that year and continuing through the *Hoot* editors' call for juniors to stay in their rooms. Now, old snobberies were to be eliminated by the College Plan: "Every undergraduate would be just as good as everyone else. No more of the old system that had crystallized while Yale was half as big as it is now," and "a new social order . . . [brings] chiefly new benefits for Yale College's recurringly remembered Forgotten Man. For him, left out of the fraternities and Senior Societies alike, are social reforms such as the House Plan created."

The senior societies, the author reflected, had two possible courses of action to "serve the forgotten undergraduate better (and regain prestige), by taking in a larger percentage of each class," effected by electing more than fifteen men or by founding new societies. The first alternative was unsatisfactory: fifteen men per class had been found to be the optimally sized unit for their purposes. And as the rough births of Spade and Grave, Wolf's Head, and Elihu had shown, "it takes an unusual set of circumstances, combining nerve, luck, good men 'overloked,' a new philosophy, and some financial backing, for the second alternative to succeed. And right here, in walks the College Plan and plunks down in the lap of the undergraduates two new Societies with history, buildings, and famous members equal to any,—Berzelius and Book and Snake."[65]

Edward Harkness had aimed by his gift to induce Yale College to offer its students a satisfactory form of fellowship and social companionship on a common basis, not subject to man-made distinction. Not at all anticipated was the further consequence of the buttressing of the very system which celebrated those distinctions, through the subsequent choices of Berzelius and of Book and Snake to join the other societies in chancing their fortunes on the Tap Day field. Similarly unforeseen by the four senior societies which had preceded their joinder in the May contest were the electoral successes of the two Sheff societies, which were strong from the outset.

The corporate parent of Wolf's Head, the Phelps Association, noted in surprised consternation to its membership in December 1936: "Lacking in prestige, as perforce they must, the two new societies are looked upon by many as being 'as important as any of the others.' As new College generations make their appearance, these new societies will appear always to have existed. This is true not because they have unearthed any newer or more important formulae for the advancement of senior societies at Yale, but because the majority of opinion feels that these societies are 'still a most important phase of Yale life.' It is only natural, then, in view of this feeling, that men will choose from among our newer rivals should they feel that their chances with the others are poor." Wolf's Head could not—nor could any other senior society on the Academic side—"either individually or as an organization dismiss our present status with a cursory pat on the back," but must instead maintain "decent contact with undergraduate opinion in its ever-changing attitudes."[66] In May 1935, Wolf's Head had suffered sixteen refusals on Tap Day, unhappily noted by the New York papers as a Yale record, and did not fulfill its quota until 10:45 P.M. that evening: the wound was hurtful, and better organization the following year yielded only one rebuff.[67]

The annual election ceremony settled into relative equilibrium for the balance of the decade, ninety men being tapped within the established hour for the six societies, about one in five men being chosen from the pre–World War II classes averaging about 450 senior class members. Light relief was provided in the elections for May 1937, with the appearance of six solemn members of the new mystic order, "The Donkey's Ear," who lock-stepped in single file through the York Street gate, their heads hooded in black cotton stockings, followed by two unhooded men bearing a stretcher. Seemingly finding his man, the chief Donkey gave a worried and bespectacled undergraduate a resounding tap, whereupon he fainted, to be carried away by the stretcher-bearers, followed by the hooded band, lock-stepping out of the courtyard before the clock chimed five.[68]

That year, the New York Times was to report, Scroll and Key elected as its last man Willard Brown '38, chairman of the charitable Yale Budget Committee and the first man to be elected secretary of his class as the leader not only in Yale College but in the Sheffield Scientific School and the School of Engineering as well. A wave of rebellion again stirred the junior class in 1938, and hundreds of signatures were obtained on a petition whose adherents pledged not to appear on campus on Tap Day, but virtually all did so, and the leader of the insurgents accepted the supreme accolade, that of being the last man tapped for Bones. That year, the Yale News noted that at least five of the Bones taps were working their way through college, and in 1939, that *Lit.* chair Richard Wilcox '40 refused both Bones and Keys for Berzelius.[69]

Thus, despite persistent attack, the senior societies retained their degree of eminence through the 1930s. This was not attributable to their secrecy, according to an informed contemporary journalist, "which is more and more regarded by non-members as a joke, but to the simple fact that, despite the obvious injustice of some of their elections and omissions, they have always managed to collar most of the outstanding men in every class. Just as the legendary American boy keeps a corner of his eye everlastingly fixed on the White House, the Yale undergraduate still doesn't lose hope of seeing the inside of one of those sinister windowless crypts until the heavy bronze doors have clanged shut without him."[70]

Several of those elected in the five years before World War II began were to become well known in the decades after that war: to Bones, went Lyman Spitzer '35, to become Princeton astronomer and astrophysicist; Jonathan Bingham '36, ambassador and congressman; Brendan Gill '36, *New Yorker* writer; John Hersey '36, journalist and novelist; Potter Stewart '37, U.S. Supreme Court justice; J. Richardson Dilworth '38, financier; William Bundy '39, assistant secretary of state and editor of *Foreign Affairs*; his brother McGeorge Bundy '40, Harvard dean of faculty and national security advisor to Presidents Kennedy and Johnson; Reuben Holden IV '40, secretary of Yale University; and Harold Howe II '40, U.S. commissioner of education. To Keys went Robert Sargent Shriver '38, first director of the Peace Corps and ambassador to France; Stanley Resor '39, secretary of the Army; and Cyrus Roberts Vance '39, secretary of Defense.

Elected to Berzelius were William Proxmire '38, U.S. senator from Wisconsin, and William Scranton '39, governor of Pennsylvania and U.S. ambassador to the United Nations; and to Book and Snake, David Dellinger '36, antiwar leader in the '70s, and Henry Ford II '39, leader of the family automobile company (who gave each of the ushers at his first wedding, including Mac Bundy, a Ford car). The class of 1936 has often been called "Yale's greatest class," but several of its later luminaries were not elected to any of the six senior societies in May 1935, including William Beinecke, donor with his brothers of Yale's rare book library; August Heckscher, author and President Kennedy's special consultant on the arts; and Walt Rostow, a Rhodes scholar and senior counselor to President Lyndon Johnson.

The most remarkable tap, that of football halfback Albert Hessburg II by Skull and Bones, was ignored in the newspaper reports, despite its lack of precedent: Hessburg was Jewish, and thus the first Jew ever to be elected to a senior society. Co-captain of the freshman football squad, and later outstanding in track, he was best known as a swift-footed star halfback on the legendary Yale teams of the 1935–1937 seasons, playing with Larry Kelley and Clint Frank, both football team captains and back-to-back Heisman Trophy winners, and both in their respective years Bonesmen. It is said that Hessburg's tap in 1937 sent shock waves through the Yale community, not of anger, but amazement. For the Bones delegation that chose him, his faith was irrelevant, since Hessburg's achievements in their eyes merited election, and when interviewed years later about this seeming anomaly, Hessburg said he was treated just like everyone else. But a significant social barrier had at last been breached in the undergraduate body. Almost three more decades were to pass before there was a Jew sitting at the Yale Corporation table in Woodbridge Hall.[71]

FAULKNER, FITZGERALD, HEMINGWAY, AND O'HARA

In the late nineteenth century, Yale's senior society system and Tap Day had figured as plot points in the occasional popular periodical, reflecting the sophistication of magazine readers in New York City and other metropolitan centers, mostly in the nation's eastern half, who were aware of the details of Yale College life. The *New Yorker* ran cartoons for its knowledgeable metropolitan subscribers, one published during Tap Day week showing a dowager at a tea party informing a companion, "Oh, yes, Harold is doing very well at Yale. He's been tapped for Skin and Bones."[72]

In these two twentieth-century decades between the world wars, four major American authors—William Faulkner, F. Scott Fitzgerald, Ernest Hemingway, and John O'Hara—reached a much larger public in frequent mention of these organizations, drawing on the societies' national and even international notoriety, and often on close acquaintance with their prominent graduate members. By way of contrast, Harvard's final clubs were to figure in only one well-known novel of the era, John P. Marquand's *The Late George Apley*, the Pulitzer Prize winner for 1938, concerning a family whose legacy membership is maintained—"It is the fondest hope of your mother and me that you will be taken into the Club [Porcellian] which has had an Apley for a member for many generations"—but the name of "the Club" is never actually found in the book.[73]

Although from the upper middle class, the Irish-Americans Fitzgerald and O'Hara felt they were outsiders and sought the perquisites, both outward and inward, of their Protestant betters, with their country clubs and their cars and, above all, their assurance. In the words of an O'Hara biographer: "In those days Yale as a concept permeated the national mind, with various degrees of meaning related to wealth, social position, natural leadership, and the achievement of worldly success. The big block 'Y' had the effect of a Chinese ideogram, signifying all those things, wrapped in a romantic aura of ivy-covered walls, secret societies that met in windowless stone buildings, the music of close harmonizers, and the longest list of football victories in America. . . . The complicated Yale social system of clubs and fraternities also gave the outside something to marvel at, for it appeared to provide enough paneled barrooms, hung with portraits, team photographs, and sporting prints, to accommodate hundreds of well-dressed young men. The world outside believed that most of these youths, for all their genial manners, were engaged in hard and bitter competition within the system of undergraduate Yale. Popular belief had it that the offices and the societies the young men achieved by senior year indicated the leaders not only of Yale College at the time, but of the entire country, a few years in the future."[74]

Yale as such a trope is easily seen in the short stories of William Faulkner. Unlike his fellow authors of these decades who wrote about Yale but had not attended it, Faulkner actually lived in New Haven for a while, working as a clerk in the Winchester Repeating Arms Company in the spring of 1918. He was visiting his Oxford, Mississippi, hometown friend, Phil Stone, a member of the Yale class of 1914, who entered as a senior after graduation from the University of Mississippi and so was not a senior society member, but lived on High Street up from the Bones tomb. Yale, New Haven, and the North were an abrupt shift for the twenty-year-old Faulkner, with considerable exposure through Stone to the college's high culture and social sophistication.

Faulkner's short story characters include Oklahoman Hubert Jarrod of "Dr. Martino" (1931), "with his aura of oil wells and Yale . . . three years now in New Haven, belonging to the right clubs and all and with money to spend"; Allen of "Fox Hunt" (1930), another "Yale boy" whose "poppa had found an oil well;" and "shanty Irish" Monaghan, in "Ad Astra" (1930), a pilot in a Camel squadron whose father's wealth "from digging sewers in the ground" enabled his son's attendance at Yale, and whose own bravery had earned him a Military Cross from Great Britain and friendship with the southerner Gerald Bland, an American "Rhodes Scholar transferred out of an Oxford battalion." In "Turnabout" (1932, and to be included in Hemingway's anthology *Men at War*), worked up from the war stories told to him by Robert Lovett, Faulkner combined the enlarging attributes of education at Yale and Oxford, describing his protagonist Bogard, modeled loosely on Bonesman Lovett, as "not Phi Beta Kappa, exactly, but Skull and Bones perhaps, or possibly a Rhodes Scholarship."[75]

Stover at Yale's fascination for Princetonian F. Scott Fitzgerald (class of 1918) has already been described. When he and his wife moved to Paris in 1924, that fire was further fueled by his friendships with aesthete and painter Gerald Murphy (Yale class of 1912), poet Archibald MacLeish

(1915), and author and screenwriter Donald Ogden Stewart (1916), all Bonesmen living in France in the American expatriate community of authors and artists in the 1920s. Gertrude Stein was to tell Ernest Hemingway that they were "all a *génération perdue*," a lost generation.

Fitzgerald had sent Don Stewart to the magazine *Vanity Fair* to help start the Yalie's writing career and would have known Stewart's 1921 article in H. L. Mencken's *Smart Set* which celebrated the system and his own senior society; the two writers were later paired in Hollywood for the screenplay for Clare Boothe Luce's *The Women*. Stewart may well have introduced the Fitzgeralds to Sara and Gerald Murphy, and Gerald and Archie MacLeish were both appropriated as models for characters in Fitzgerald's *Tender Is the Night*—to the fury of another Murphy family friend, Ernest Hemingway.[76] Beyond occasional mention in his short stories, the Princetonian was to reference the Yale senior societies in all four of his completed novels.

In Fitzgerald's autobiographical first novel of 1920, *This Side of Paradise*, his protagonist Amory Blaine describes the high point in a traveling student production of Princeton's Triangle Club, "a brilliant place in 'Ha-Ha Hortense!'" "It is a Princeton tradition," Fitzgerald wrote, "that whenever a Yale man who is a member of the widely advertised 'Skull and Bones' hears the sacred name mentioned, he must leave the room. It is also a tradition that the members are invariably successful in later life, amassing fortunes or votes or coupons or whatever they choose to amass. Therefore, at each performance of 'Ha-Ha Hortense!' half-a-dozen seats were kept from sale and occupied by six of the worst-looking vagabonds that could be hired from the streets, further touched up by the Triangle make-up man. At the moment in the show where *Firebrand, the Pirate Chief*, pointed at his black flag and said, 'I am a Yale graduate—note my Skull and Bones!'—at this very moment the six vagabonds were instructed to rise *conspicuously* and leave the theatre with looks of deep melancholy and an injured dignity. It was claimed though never proved that on one occasion the hired Elis were swelled by one of the real thing."[77]

Fiztgerald's heroine's father in "The Popular Girl," published in the
Saturday Evening Post in February 1922, "had never quite lost the air of
having been a popular Bonesman at Yale." In the last of eight Basil Duke
Lee stories, "Basil and Cleopatra," also published in the *Saturday Evening
Post* and taking Basil from boyhood in the Midwest through eastern prep
school to Yale, Basil muses: "'I want to be chairman of the News or the
Record,' thought his old self one October morning, 'and I want to get
my letter in football, and I want to be in Skull and Bones.'" Scroll and
Key was not overlooked: *The Beautiful and the Damned*, Fitzgerald's 1922
novel of café society in New York during the Jazz Age, finds the heroine
Gloria Patch having a brief fling with "Tudor Baird, an ancient flame"
who "came by way of the Aviation Corps." "A Scroll and Keys [*sic*] man
at Yale, he possessed the correct reticences of a 'good egg,' the correct
notions of chivalry and noblesse oblige."[78]

In his 1925 masterpiece *The Great Gatsby*, Fitzgerald reimagined himself, or at least that novel's first person narrator Nick Carraway, as a Yale
graduate of 1915, chairman of the *Yale News*, and a senior society clubmate of star football end Tom Buchanan, the brutish and philandering
husband of Jay Gatsby's lost love Daisy. Although no specific society is
named, it is telling that a few months after *The Great Gatsby* appeared,
the *New Yorker* published a "suggested bookplate" for the library of F.
Scott Fitzgerald, featuring a skull-topped figure in a tuxedo and waistcoat
reveling at a party. While the book's sales initially languished, in 1998
the Modern Library editorial board voted it the twentieth century's best
American novel.[79]

Dick Diver, the protagonist of *Tender Is the Night* (1933) and a Rhodes
scholar from Connecticut in 1914, hears "about fraternity politics in New
Haven" from a classmate: "'Bones got a wonderful crowd,' he said. 'We
all did, as a matter of fact. New Haven's so big now the sad thing is the
men we have to leave out.'" Diver's internal monologue shows a great
familiarity with the tensions of Tap Day and the Yale collegians' customs. "Could I help it that Pete Livingstone sat in the locker-room Tap
Day when everybody looked all over hell for him? And I got an election

when otherwise I wouldn't have gotten Elihu, knowing so few men. He was good and right and I ought to have sat in the locker-room instead. Maybe I would, if I'd thought I had a chance at an election. But Mercer kept coming to my room all those weeks. I guess I knew I had a chance all right. But it would have served me right if I'd swallowed my pin in the shower and set up a conflict." [80]

Ernest Hemingway, friend of Fitzgerald and another intimate of the Murphys' circle on the Riviera, also used the Yale society system in his work, but his attitude was distinctly not that of a worshipper. Satire counterbalanced his regret at having had no share in the cultural rituals common to his new friends. Fitzgerald and Edmund Wilson and Harold Loeb (Hemingway's model for the ridiculed Robert Cohn in *The Sun Also Rises*) had attended Princeton; John Dos Passos had gone to Harvard; and MacLeish, Stewart, and Murphy all went to Yale. Hemingway had declined to apply to college, and feelings of inferiority showed in his aggressiveness.

Ironically, his remote ancestor Jacob Hemingway, born in East Haven in 1683, was the first—and for his first half year, the only—student to receive instruction at Yale College, to which Connecticut had granted a charter in 1701; Ernest's grandfather retailed the story to him as a "family legend." [81] While the fledgling author formed friendships with writers in Paris, including MacLeish and Stewart, by 1937 he had quarreled with virtually every one. In his posthumously published memoir about the Parisian years, *A Moveable Feast*, he omitted Stewart entirely and mentioned the Murphys and the MacLeishes in only one sentence. While in 1930 he had written MacLeish that he was "the best living writing poet," by 1945 he told another correspondent, disparaging Archie's "'Patriotic' verse": "You know his bro[ther] Kenny was killed in the last war and I always felt Archie felt that sort of gave him a controlling interest in all deads." [82]

Unlike the references of his fellow authors to the Yale society system, Hemingway's were aimed to provoke or wound. He began cautiously: in 1932, he had inserted into *Death in the Afternoon*, his nonfiction treatment of bullfighting in Spain, the phrase "Bones face," the designation for the hard stare assumed by a member of that society when suddenly challenged in conversation by casual mention of his club.

Not many years later, he was unrestrained, crafting a novel enlarged from his two published stories about Harry Morgan and set in a shabby, corrupt Key West. The protagonist is a rugged individualist betrayed by the forces of wealth and privilege, in a story full of rich and poor people, many of them versions of individuals Hemingway knew, or with whom he wanted to settle scores. When published, winning the author a cover story in *Time* in October 1937, the novel's multi-page passage at the end described the occupant-owners of the yachts lying at night at the Key West fringe piers, and said of one millionaire's daughter: "The fiancé is a Skull and Bones man, voted most likely to succeed, voted most popular, who still thinks more of others than of himself and would be too good for any one except a lovely girl like Frances. He is probably a little too good for Frances too, but it will be years before Frances realizes this, perhaps; and she may never realize it, with luck. The type of man who is tapped for Bones is rarely also tapped for bed; but with a lovely girl like Frances intention counts as much as performance."[83]

The longest reference is found in his play of 1938, *The Fifth Column*, where Philip and Dorothy, the author's stand-ins for himself and Martha Gellhorn in Madrid, are reporting on the Spanish Civil War. Dorothy claims not to understand his plans for the future, provoking the following colloquy:

PHILIP: And because you don't understand, and you never could understand, is the reason we're not going to go on and live together and have a lovely time and etcetera.

DOROTHY: Oh, it's worse than Skull and Bones.

PHILIP: What in God's name is Skull and Bones?

DOROTHY: It's a secret society a man belonged to one time that I had just enough sense not to marry. It's very superior and awfully good and worthy, and they take you in and tell you all about it, just before the wedding, and when they told me about it, I called the wedding off.

PHILIP: That's an excellent precedent.[84]

Perhaps Hemingway thought any Bonesmen in this play's audience would be forced to leave the theater, like those in the Triangle Club production described by Fitzgerald. Since Gellhorn, Dorothy's model, is not known to have aborted a wedding with a Bonesman, the play's otherwise incongruous swipe in this script at the senior society of Murphy, Stewart, and MacLeish seems to have been in general derision for the club of his college-educated friends.[85]

Stewart, who had run with the bulls alongside Hemingway in Pamplona, was instrumental in getting his *In Our Time* published in New York, and gave him large checks to tide him over, said of him: "He was charismatic; and it was for this very reason that the mean streak startled you so much when it came to the surface." Five years later Hemingway attempted to repair the breach of several quarrels with MacLeish by inviting him to Cuba and promising not to be "self-righteous, no-good, and bastardly" as during his "great 37–38 epoch when [I] alienated all of my friends (who I miss like hell)." But what had been committed to paper in abusive letters as well as sarcastic fiction does not come so easily unsaid, and it does not seem possible that either Stewart, who had promoted his early publications, or MacLeish, who had funded Hemingway's skiing vacations, or Murphy, who had loaned the author his artist's studio in which to write, was ever able to feel, after 1938, the same sort of affection for Ernest Hemingway that they had once felt.[86]

The fourth major writer of these decades whose work often referenced Yale and its senior societies was the Irish American John O'Hara. He seems to have been a confirmed Yale man by the time he started prep school. What one individual or event triggered his Yalephilia is obscure: as a boy, he read Yale professor William Lyon Phelps's newspaper columns, which made him impatient with the parochial views of his schoolteachers, and he later claimed *Stover at Yale*'s author Owen Johnson as an influence on his writing.

Still, he seems to have selected the college in New Haven, in the words of one biographer, "because in his youth it was the objective correlative for all the things he admired, which may be summed up in the word *class*. Harvard was effete or intellectual; Princeton was agreeably social; but Yale represented power and an automatic assumption of privilege and style." While it is not clear whether he passed the Yale entrance exams and been accepted, the valedictorian-designate of Lewiston, New York's Niagara Prep went on a drunken bender the night before his commencement and was not allowed to graduate, with his furious father insisting on the reprobate son's working to prove his seriousness ("I'll be damned if I'll send a drunk to Yale!").[87]

When his father died the following year, the consequent alteration in family finances put an end to his ambitions for entering Yale in the fall of 1925—or at least his chances of being a gentleman who browsed at the clothier J. Press and danced at the Fence Club, instead of a bursary boy who waited on tables.[88] Like Hemingway, he never did attend college. After a stint as a reporter, he got a job through the New York Yale Club's placement office at Briton Hadden and Henry Luce's *Time*, then three years old, where he became friends with Wilder Hobson, the wittiest member of the Yale class of 1923, "Most Likely to Succeed," and a member of Scroll and Key, but O'Hara was shortly fired. Meanwhile, he patronized the famous gin joint "21," where he once saw a group of undergraduates from New Haven and invited them to join him, to question them closely about Yale, as he was eager to have up-to-the-minute information about social customs and college slang. He was also dating Margaretta Archbald, a Bryn Mawr graduate who roomed with her cousin Mary Brooks, then being successfully courted by Wolf's Head graduate A. Whitney Griswold. In later years, O'Hara would claim that he always knew Whit Griswold would become president of Yale.[89]

So O'Hara had always wanted to go to Yale. Years later, when he was thirty-seven years old and a famous, established author, an anecdote circulated that when Hemingway, James Lardner, and Vincent Sheean were soliciting funds during the Spanish Civil War and trying to figure out what to do with an unexpected payment, Hemingway said, "Let's take the bloody money and start a bloody fund to send John O'Hara to Yale." Now, spending time with graduates of Yale and other prominent universities, he imagined that he had missed something important, and that if he had gone to New Haven, his career problems would be over (more likely, he would have rebelled against the system and sneered at those who strove for a place within it).

To compensate, he made himself a close student of the customs and benefits he thought accrued, devouring in his study the *Social Register, Who's Who,* Baird's *Manual of American College Fraternities,* and the Yale yearbook for 1924, his never-realized freshman year. He shared with Colonel James Archbald, Margaretta's father and a Yale graduate (some Archbalds were in Scroll and Key), a passionate interest in the arcana of university fraternities and clubs and secret societies.[90]

He put this knowledge to use in his life's literary work of fourteen novels, beginning with the bestseller *Appointment in Samarra* in 1934, and 402 short stories—he virtually invented what the world came to call the "*New Yorker* short story." *BUtterfield 8,* the sexually frank (for 1935) cautionary tale of Winston Liggett, "a yacht racer . . . a big Yale athlete," and the married paramour of Gloria Wandrous, played by Elizabeth Taylor in the 1960 movie version, a woman well known in the smarter speakeasies, and willing to go home with a casual acquaintance. O'Hara—a self-described "Mick" in this novel as James Malloy, "is often taken for a Yale man, by Yale men. That pleases me a little, because I like Yale best of all the colleges"—showed a keen appreciation in this novel of the caste-ridden Yale senior society system, and the place in it of Jews, likely to hail from Connecticut.

In the book, the architect Paul Farley, Irish Catholic product of Lawrenceville and Princeton, and his client Percy Kahan, a Jewish businessman, run into Liggett; after prompting that they were classmates, Liggett pretends to remember Kahan from New Haven, before breaking away. "'I didn't know you went to Yale,' said Farley. 'I know. I never talk about it,' said Kahan. 'Then once in a while I see somebody like Liggett, one of the big Skull and Bones fellows he was, and one day I met old [former Yale president] Dr. Hadley on the street and I introduced myself to him. I can't help it. I think what a waste of time, four years at that place, me a little Heeb from Hartford, but last November I had to be in Hollywood when the Yale-Harvard game was played, and God damn it if I don't have a special wire with the play by play. The radio wasn't good enough for me. I had to have the play by play. Yes, I'm a Yale man.'"[91]

In his 1949 bestseller, *A Rage to Live*, O'Hara revealed to his many thousands of readers more of his knowledge of the inner workings of the senior society he most admired, in describing the program of "Death's Head," an amalgam of Skull and Bones and Wolf's Head, with the added suggestion of inherent scandal. The novel's protagonist Sidney Tate seeks advice on buying a farm from Paul Reichelderfer. "He had also been tapped for Death's Head, the Yale senior society to which Sidney belonged."

The passage that follows shows a deep familiarity with the interior life of the senior societies at Yale. "As part of his initiation into Death's Head a neophyte was required under oath to reveal any and all facts concerning his L.H., or Life History, and C.B., or Connubial Bliss. The life history part was not so embarrassing as details of connubial bliss. 'C.B.' was so called because in spite of the fact that most of the members of Death's Head were bachelors, now and then it would turn out that a neophyte was secretly married and it became necessary to hold a ceremony in which his wife was made a Death's Head wife. But married or not, the neophyte was compelled to tell the members of the society all they wanted to hear about his relations with women, and more than once it had happened that a man had to admit to maximum intimacies with a girl whose brother or fiancé was present. The theory was that one Death's

Head Man could have no secret from another, and that the brotherhood existing among the members transcended all outside considerations." At Tate's wedding, his wife "was initiated with the brief ceremony reserved for all brides of Death's Head men," and his funeral is attended by "four out-of-town members" of his senior society.[92]

O'Hara was haunted by the mystery of the real "Death's Head," accepting it as a fact of life that the men elected every year became a part of the tiny power structure that ran the country. He spoke with reverence the names of the great men who had been tapped for Skull and Bones, the innumerable Tafts, Binghams, and Bundys, and took pride in mentioning as well the names of his several personal friends in the society. Over the years, the writer contrived to accumulate a startling amount of Bones lore, which he would reveal only to Bonesmen: sharing with them his samples of their secrets made him, in a fashion and for the time being, one of them. It was, according to Brendan Gill, the most cherished of his daydreams that if he had attended Yale, he would have been tapped by the oldest senior society.[93]

In his vain quest for an honorary degree, O'Hara presented the manuscript of *BUtterfield 8* and the proofs of *Appointment at Samarra* to the Yale Library. He was invited in March 1948 to speak at the Elizabethan Club, Yale's undergraduate literary society, with remarks titled "Writing, What's in It for Me?" Divulging that he had not gone to Yale, he referred to his friends Fitzgerald, Hemingway, Steinbeck, and Faulkner. Completely off the mark both times, he alluded to Cole Porter as "one of the founders of the Elizabethan Club" and "the only man ever" to "display a special kind of independence: he resigned from Skull and Bones." The event was not a success. O'Hara with universities was the same as O'Hara with clubs: he did not know how to be a diffident gentleman.[94]

In 1959, O'Hara wrote New York city planner Robert Moses, who had graduated from Yale in 1909, that "Yale has no one, and since Red [Sinclair] Lewis has had no one who went to Yale and from there to the typewriter to comment on 20th Century America and 20th Century Yale. For that combination you have to come to me, Niagara Prep '24."[95]

TAPPED FOR SKULL AND BONES, 1920–1939

Henry P. Davison Jr.	1920	president, J. P. Morgan
Briton Hadden	1920	founder, *Time* magazine
Francis Thayer Hobson	1920	chairman, William Morrow & Co.
David Ingalls	1920	assistant secretary of the Navy
		donor, Ingalls Rink
Henry Robinson Luce	1920	cofounder, *Time*, founder *Life, Fortune, Sports Illustrated*
Stover Boardman Lunt	1921	chairman, W. W. Norton, Inc.
Langdon Parsons	1921	professor of Obstetrics, Harvard
Malcolm Pratt Aldrich	1921	chairman, Commonwealth Fund
Frederick Whiley Hilles	1922	professor of English, Yale
Robert Guthrie Page	1922	chairman, Phelps Dodge Corp.
John Sherman Cooper	1923	U.S. Senate (Ky.)
		ambassador, India, Nepal, German Democratic Republic
Russell Davenport	1923	creator, Fortune 500 list
Francis Otto Matthiessen	1923	professor of Literature, Harvard
Henry Elisha Allen	1924	professor of Humanities, University of Minn.
Edwin Foster Blair	1924	partner, Hughes Hubbard Blair
Walter Edwards Houghton	1924	professor of English, Wellesley
William Thompson Lusk	1924	president, Tiffany & Co.
Charles Merville Spofford	1924	president, Metropolitan Opera
		brigadier general
Charles Stafford Gage	1925	treasurer, Yale

William Bunnell Norton	1925	professor of History, Boston University
Benjamin Crawford Cutler	1926	orchestra leader
Charles Graydon Poore	1926	book critic
Frank Ford Russell	1926	chairman, National Aviation Corp.
Wallace Parks Ritchie	1927	professor of Neurosurgery, University of Minn.
Frederic Flavor Robinson	1927	president, National Aviation Corp.
Anson Phelps Stokes Jr.	1927	Episcopal bishop, Mass.
George Herbert Walker Jr.	1927	director, White Weld & Co.
Edward Rogers Wardwell	1927	partner, Davis, Polk & Wardwell
Lancelot ("Lanny") Ross	1928	singer and movie actor
Charles Alderson Janeway	1930	professor of Pediatrics, Harvard
Gaylord Donnelley	1931	chairman, R. R. Donnelley & Sons
		chairman, trustee, University of Chicago
Henry John Heinz II	1931	chairman, H. J. Heinz Co.
Lewis Abbot Lapham	1931	president, Grace Lines
		president, Bankers Trust
William Learned Peltz	1931	professor Clinical Psychology, University of Pennsylvania
John Mercer Walker	1931	CEO, Memorial Sloan Kettering
Frederick Baldwin Adams Jr.	1932	director, Morgan Library
Robert Frank Fulton	1931	professor of Religion, Union College
Samuel Hazard Gillespie	1932	U.S. attorney, Southern District of N.Y.
John Reagan "Tex" McCrary	1933	inventor, radio/TV talk shows

James Quigg Newton Jr.	1933	president, University of Colorado
		mayor of Denver, Colo.
Amory Howe Bradford	1934	vice president, business manager, *New York Times*
Hugh Terry Cunningham	1934	director of training, CIA
Harry Halstead Harper Jr.	1934	executive editor, *Reader's Digest*
Frederick Peter Haas	1935	general counsel, Liggett Group
John Sargent Pillsbury Jr.	1935	chairman, Northwestern National Life Insurance
Charles Seymour Jr.	1935	professor of Art History, Yale
Lyman Spitzer Jr.	1935	professor of Astronomy, Princeton
		conceived Hubble Space Telescope
George Schley Stillman	1935	secretary, Museum of Modern Art
Charlton "Sunny" Tufts	1935	entertainer
Jonathan Brewster Bingham	1936	U.S. ambassador to UN
		U.S. Congress (Conn.)
Brendan Gill	1936	writer, *The New Yorker*
John Richard Hersey	1936	journalist and novelist
John Merrill Knapp	1936	dean, Princeton University
Richard Anthony Moore	1936	president, Times Mirror Broadcasting
		U.S. ambassador to Ireland
Louis Walker	1936	managing partner, G. H. Walker Co.
Richard James Cross	1937	professor of Medicine, Rutgers
John Warner Field	1937	chairman, Warnaco, Inc.
William Horsley Orrick Jr.	1937	U.S. Cistrict Court judge (Northern Calif.)

Potter Stewart	1937	justice, U.S. Supreme Court
James Howard Dempsey Jr.	1938	founder, Squire Sanders & Dempsey
Joseph Richardson Dilworth	1938	chairman, Rockefeller Center
		chairman, Metropolitan Museum of Art
		chairman, Institute for Advanced Study
Lawrence Dunham Jr.	1938	director, Yale Office of Development
John Edwin Ecklund	1938	treasurer, Yale University
Joseph Carrière Fox	1938	founder, Fox International Fellowships
Gaspard D'Andelot Belin	1939	general counsel, U.S. Treasury
William Putnam Bundy	1939	U.S. assistant secretary of state
		editor, *Foreign Affairs*

TAPPED FOR SCROLL AND KEY, 1920–1939

Elisha Boudinot Fisher	1920	chairman, U.S. Radium Corp.
Benjamin Brewster Jennings	1920	chairman, Socony Mobil Oil Co.
Seymour Horace Knox	1920	chairman, Marine Midland Bank
Richardson Dilworth	1921	mayor of Philadelphia
Charles Shipman Payson	1921	principal owner, New York Mets
John Archer Gifford	1922	undersecretary of Navy
Charles Albert Wight	1922	president, Freeport Sulphur Co.
Wayland Farries Vaughan	1923	professor of Psychology, Boston University

Name	Year	Description
James Stillman Rockefeller	1924	chairman, First National City Bank of New York
Frederick Sheffield	1924	founder, Webster, Sheffield law firm
Ostrom Enders	1925	chairman, Hartford National Bank
Augustus Newbold Morris	1925	president, New York City Council
Dr. Benjamin McLane Spock	1925	author, *Baby and Child Care*
Frederick Augustus Potts Jr.	1926	chairman, Philadelphia National Bank
Joseph Warren Simpson Jr	1926	chairman, First Wisconsin National Bank
Carlos French Stoddard Jr.	1926	executive secretary, Yale University Council
Andrew Varick Stout Jr.	1926	chairman, Dominick & Dominick
John Hay Whitney	1926	publisher, *New York Herald Tribune*
		U.S. ambassador to the United Kingdom
		president, Museum of Modern Art
		founder, J. H. Whitney & Co.
William McFarlane Hinkle	1927	professor, Art History, Columbia University
Henry Barnes Potts	1927	chairman, Philadelphia National Bank
Robert Hawthorn Wylie Jr.	1927	professor, Clinical Surgery, Columbia University
Robert Chesney Osborn	1928	artist/cartoonist
James Cox Brady Jr.	1929	chairman, Purolator
Winthrop Gilman Brown	1929	U.S. ambassador to Korea, Laos

Paul Mellon	1929	donor, Yale Center for British Art, Morse and Stiles Colleges president, National Gallery of Art
Horace Reynolds Moorhead	1929	treasurer, Gulf Oil Corp.
Ernest Brooks Jr.	1930	president, Old Dominion Foundation
Thatchere Magoun Brown Jr.	1930	managing partner, G. H. Walker & Co.
Robert Ward	1930	professor of Pediatrics, University of Southern California
Dale Hale Clement	1931	professor of Pediatrics, Yale
Raymond Richard Guest	1931	U.S. ambassador to Ireland
Robert Manueal Heurtematte	1931	Panamanian ambassador to U.S. undersecretary, United Nations
Ethan Allen Hitchcock	1931	board chairman, Educational Broadcasting Corp., Olivetti Underwood Corp.
John Holbrook	1931	president, New York Philharmonic Orchestra
Donald Roderick McLennan Jr.	1931	chairman., Marsh & McLennan
Maynard Herbert Mack	1932	Sterling Professor of English, Yale director, National Institute for Humanities
William Marvel	1932	chancellor, Delaware Court of Chancery
Chales Henry Tenney	1933	U.S. District judge, Southern District of New York
Robert Ferdinand Wagner Jr.	1933	mayor, City of New York U.S. ambassador to Spain
Sidney Norwood Towle Jr.	1934	headmaster, Kent School

Joseph Peter Grace Jr.	1936	president, CEO, W. R. Grace & Co.
Horace Havemeyer Jr.	1936	president, National Sugar Refining Co.
Bayard Dominick 2d	1937	chairman, Dominick & Dominick
Waldo Cory Melrose Johnston	1937	director, Mystic Seaport Museum
Henry Emerson Butler Jr.	1938	professor, University of Arizona
Francis Cowles Cady	1938	professor, University of Connecticut Law School
Gordon Grand Jr.	1938	president, Olin Mathieson Chemical Corp.
		U.S. Congress (Conn.)
Burton Allen McLean	1938	president, Educational Management Services, Inc.
Robert Sargent Shriver	1938	first director, U.S. Peace Corps
		director, Office of Economic Opportunity
		U.S. ambassador to France
Thaddeus Reynolds Beal	1939	president, Harvard Trust Co.
Andrew Nicholas Brady Garvan	1939	professor of History, University of Pennsylvania
Stuart Clayton Hemingway Jr.	1939	president, Towle Manufacturing Co.
Gilbert Watts Humphrey	1939	chairman, CEO, Hanna Mining Co.
Malcolm Muir Jr.	1939	executive editor, *Newsweek*
Stanley Resor	1939	secretary of the Army
		U.S. ambassador for force reductions
		undersecretary of defense for policy

Cyrus Roberts Vance	1939	secretary of the Army
		deputy secretary of defense
		secretary of state
		chairman, Federal Reserve Bank of New York
		chairman, Rockefeller Foundation

TAPPED FOR WOLF'S HEAD, 1920–1939

Walter Millis	1920	journalist and historian
Robert Maynard Hutchins	1921	president, University of Chicago
Philip Pillsbury	1924	chairman, Pillsbury Corp.
Clark Millikan	1924	professor of aeronautics, California Institute of Technology
Douglas MacArthur II	1932	ambassador to Japan
Rogers C. B. Morton	1937	chairman, Republican National Committee, secretary of Interior, secretary of Commerce

TAPPED FOR ELIHU, 1920–1939

Jake Anthony Danaher	1920	U.S. Senator (CT), federal judge
Eli Whitney Debevoise	1921	co-founder, Debevoise Plimpton
William S. Symington	1923	first sec'y of Air Force, U.S. Senator (Mo.)
James T. Babb	1924	Yale librarian
John Collins Pope	1925	professor of English, Yale
Winston F.C. Guest	1927	international polo player

Edward H. Dodd Jr	1928	president, Dodd, Mead publishers
William McChesney Martin Jr.	1928	chairman, Federal Reserve
William Horowitz	1929	first Jewish Yale Corporation member
George B. Young	1934	chairman, Field Enterprises
John Marks Templeton	1934	founder, Templeton Investments
Alexis W. Thompson	1936	owner, Pittsburgh Steelers, Philadelphia Eagles
Ray D. Chapin Jr.	1937	chairman, American Motors

TAPPED FOR BERZELIUS, 1920–1939

David Dellinger	1936	peace activist
William Proxmire	1938	U.S. Senator (Wis.)
William Scranton	1939	governor of Pennsylvania

TAPPED FOR BOOK AND SNAKE, 1920–1939

| Whitelaw Reid | 1936 | chairman, *New York Herald Tribune* |
| Henry Ford II | 1939 | chairman, Ford Motor Co. |

CHAPTER ELEVEN

WORLD WAR AGAIN, AND
OTHER CASTES BROKEN
(1940–1949)

After 1942 nothing at Yale was the same as it had been before and . . .
whatever the so-called "normality" of the fifties, certain radical changes,
in American education and in those who would pursue it, had
occurred . . . [N]othing that had *seemed* stable and enduring in, say,
1940, and *was* clearly a verity in, say, 1914, remained as it had been. . . .
[T]here sets in an extraordinary series of changes in Yale, and therefore
in the Hall: changes in who came to Yale, in where they came from,
in what they chose to do here, in what they were compelled to do,
and in what they did afterward.

—A. Barlett Giamatti, *History of*
Scroll and Key, 1942–1972 (1978)

THE NEW UNIVERSITY COLLEGE—
AND THE OLD DEMOGRAPHICS

Yale had been largely rebuilt under Angell, who found it in brownstone and left it in granite. The college also changed socially and

intellectually during his presidency. By 1941, a fellow Harvard alumnus in John Marquand's novel *H. M. Pulham, Esq.* is described complaining: "That's one of the things that gripes me about Yale. The Elis are always wheeling out the Yale poets and the Yale literary group. Why, hell, we have a lot of the same thing in the Class, except we don't shout about them."[1] A more mature and sophisticated curriculum had emerged with the conversion of Yale into a university college, where the existence of art, music, graduate and other schools added immensely to the under-graduate experience.

In the educational sphere, over that time, the first definite distribu-tional requirements for the freshman and sophomore years were estab-lished, and the Latin requirement for Academic and the PhB degree of Sheffield extinguished. Majors were slowly enlarged under the aegis of the academic departments, reading periods were created, comprehensive examinations (beginning with the class of 1937) were established, and, by 1940, a senior essay was required. It has been estimated that, between the era of Noah Porter and the end of Angell's term in 1937, "the education of Yale undergraduates had gained almost three years in general maturity."[2]

Socially, too, in college life, there had been major milestones of change. The attitudinal transformations of the 1920s, taken together with the growth in numbers of the college, finally killed daily chapel— a tradition over two hundred years old, brought to an end by faculty recommendation and Corporation vote in May 1926. Then, the presence of the residential colleges, the first seven of which opened officially on September 25, 1933, began the demolition of the ancient walls between professors and students (unlike the new Harvard houses, no Oxbridge high tables on raised daises for faculty alone had found their way to New Haven), while the forced admixture of the students from Ac, Sheff, and Engineering removed the old structural divisions, bridging the social chasms among their respective undergraduates. More students were enabled to participate in a wide variety of sports, organized by residential colleges playing one another and, in due course, championship matches against the best Harvard houses on the weekend of the Yale-Harvard football game. Singing and drama groups, individual college newspapers, and special interest clubs sprung up, populated by the three upper classes now housed together in their distinctive quadrangles, fabulous palaces compared to the tradition-wrapped, Spartan community of the 1890s.

Self-help students enjoyed new dignity in the contemporaneous bursary plan which had been envisioned by Harkness. The development of in-college and out-college employment made it possible to eliminate the invidious board jobs of waiter or busboy which had hitherto carried at least a third of the financial load. These were exchanged for posts as advisors and tutors to freshmen, nonworking fellowships for the best scholars, and appointments to help run the colleges themselves, and for outside jobs in other university departments as research and project assistants. A number of bursary men were set to managing the teams, attending the college library, preparing for entertainments, and running errands for the college master's office, gaining in the process considerable experience in dealing with their class- and college-mates, and competing against each other for the top posts. The residential college senior aide became a man of note, in his own community and beyond. Marks of consideration came his way, including recommendtions for professional or business school, and election to a senior society (Harold Howe of the class of 1940, self-supporting in college and later President John Kennedy's commissioner of education, was appointed senior aide of Davenport College, and elected to Bones). Soon men who did not need the money sought entrance into the bursary system, and one father even complained that Yale was discriminating against the rich.

Members of the class of 1936, who entered the residential colleges from their Old Campus dormitories as sophomores, gave the new system their wholehearted loyalty and devotion. With the addition of Berkeley College to the original seven in 1934, Timothy Dwight the following year, and finally Silliman in 1940, all finally found places in the new residential regime. Yet, while this elaborately organized intimacy permitted recapture of some of the smaller Yale College of yore, newly to be shared with the privileges of a great university, the demographic composition of the student body had not altered very dramatically.[3]

The physical Yale College had changed considerably more than had its collegians. Remarkably, the pre–World War II class of 1941 was not that different, even in size, from the pre–World War I class of 1916. The percentage of high school students in the class of 1916 was actually higher than in the class of 1941—29 percent to 26 percent. While most of 1916's high schoolers were from Connecticut, its number of them from outside Yale's top six states, comprising twenty-five from sixteen states plus Hawaii, compares favorably with 1941's count of thirty-two high school graduates from thirteen states and Washington, D.C. The 860 members of the class of 1941 boasted little diversity, including no blacks, one Filipino, and two Armenians. Of the 780 students in the class of 1916, a quarter century before, five were African Americans, three Chinese, two Armenians, two Turks, a German (leaving Yale halfway through sophomore year to fight for his fatherland), and a Brazilian.

Furthermore, after the limitation of numbers policy was put in place in 1923, the percentage of students who were sons of Yale graduates soared upward: 1916's class had 85 legacies, a bit less than 11 percent of the class, while the class of 1941 had 262 members whose fathers had attended Yale, or 30.5 percent, almost triple that of a quarter century before. Moreover, it appears that over half the 1941 class's undergraduates had a male relative who preceded them in New Haven (the 1916 figure is about 23 percent). Adding the curious fact that almost one third of the '41ers came with a "Jr." or Roman numeral after their names, it might be maintained that there was more inherited privilege at Yale on the eve of the Second World War than perhaps at any time since the American Revolution.

For 1941's graduating class, there was about a 10 percent Jewish enrollment, and a 5 percent Catholic enrollment. One-quarter of these young men came from five prep schools (Andover, Hotchkiss, Exeter, Taft, and Choate), and if St. Paul's, Kent, and Hill were added in, a third of the class was included in their collective rosters. The 226 high schoolers in the class were fewer than the intake from the top six prep schools. A letter to the *Yale Daily News* in March 1940 pointed out that "Yale students, as a whole, are rich," and that at their preparatory schools, "the annual tuition due is around $1400, which is only about $1000 less than the annual income of 71% of the families of this country."[4]

The arguments about the merits and horrors of the senior society system remained familiar ones. Sophomores in the class of 1940 were readers of a *News* editorial published shortly before Tap Day in 1938, holding that "There is little to be gained by taking issue with the Senior Societies, or even, it seems, by discussing them: every year they recruit groups of worried and often skeptical juniors and convert them into bands of devoted and sincerely inspired Seniors. This fact has always loomed large enough in all considerations of the societies to silence questioning on their value to Yale." The editor claimed that "nearly all of the Societies are packed," and hoped that, since the days of Dink Stover were over, "Juniors will manage to keep their sense of proportion on Tap Day."[5]

Sophomore McGeorge "Mac" Bundy was the son of a Bonesman (Henry Hollister Bundy 1910, Supreme Court clerk for Oliver Wendell Holmes Jr., and during World War II, Secretary of War Henry Stimson's top deputy on the development of the atomic bomb), and his older brother Bill was a prominent candidate in the immediately upcoming society selection for the class of 1939. Nonetheless, Mac used the column—which his *News* vice chairman brother had specially arranged for him—to attack the societies, while calling for higher standards. He pointed out in his weekly "Visions & Revisions," shared on alternative days with junior Richard Morris Jr., that, unlike the old days of discussion only by anonymous writers of tipsheets, the *News* had printed sober and carefully considered editorials in four of the last five years, analyzing and criticizing the societies.

"One of them," Bundy noted, "has stressed the fact that the Societies enforce a dubious Success Standard; another has excoriated the unnecessary brutality of Tap Day; a third has described mumbo-jumbo and secrecy; a fourth, the most recent, has pointed to the dangers of packing and has deplored the new eminence, in the Societies, of the Social Type." But, he continued, "It should be noted that thus far all of the Chairmen whose comments we mentioned have joined a Society and conformed to its traditions. And this is no blind betrayal of their views. . . . [W]hatever they may fail to do today, the Societies represent a noble tradition of the frank and intimate association of admirable men. Their meetings are not wasted; many of their rewards are life-long in duration. No man can surely analyze the source of their values; no man can deny that it exists."[6] The senior societies, in other words, continued to succeed, because they had succeeded in Yale's past.

His co-columnist, brother Bill Bundy's classmate Richard L. Morris Jr., denied in the succeeding opinion piece that good ends are necessarily compatible with bad means, and deplored the "present morass of subterranean dickering and jockeying for post positions in Yale's most portentous Derby." He maintained that "as a result of secrecy, least important of the considerations surrounding the million-dollar corporations erected in honor of the successful undergraduate, many an avoidable tragedy and many a regrettable corruption is made possible."[7]

In the third column completing the series, the sophomore Bundy agreed that the "monkey business" of "hush hush" went along with "the other besetting dangers of the Senior Societies—packing, family bias, selections based on mere Reputation or physical prowess, and the social emphasis generally"—what he styled "False Gods." Still, he saw another attitude "on its way" which "recognizes the gradual decline of bulldogism; it refuses to have anything to do with the boys; it elects eminent men only when they are justly eminent; it gives honor to the man and not to his position. The partisans of this new attitude will seek quality, knowing that they cannot judge it by the standards of the past."[8] On the date this column appeared, the junior Morris gathered with his classmates in the main court of Branford College at 4:45 P.M. for Tap Day, to be chosen by Scroll and Key (which classmate Bill Bundy turned down for Bones). After Pearl Harbor, Morris was to enter the

Signal Corps in 1941 and perish in Kunming, China, in October 1944. His fellow columnist and iconoclast Mac Bundy, more of a reformer in intent, and later to become dean of the faculty at Harvard, special assistant for national security affairs to Presidents Kennedy and Johnson, and president of the Ford Foundation, was the last man tapped by Bones the following year, in May 1939.[9]

Four months before that, Bundy had penned a leader for the February 1939 *Yale Lit.*, "For the Defense." "[T]he senior societies," he wrote, "whatever their minor imperfections, have contributed notably to a high ideal of friendship and have held up standards of human character that were not perfect but certainly good enough to keep most of those interested pushing up. . . . It may be bad that we have a system that attracts a blind desire and rewards on arbitrary and half-true bases. It would be worse if the ordinary aspiring freshman were drawn by nothing more compelling than the double-feature at Loew's Poli or the dubious glories of the Knickerbocker."[10]

Nevertheless, not two months later he and two classmates, Harold Howe and Charles Glover III, circulated a pledge agreement under which upward of two hundred juniors swore to stay in their rooms, by way of protest against the traditional election method of Tap Day, deemed "needlessly unkind and undignified." Then older heads recollected the chaos of the 1933 election, when a similar protest had been mounted, resulting only in confusion, some double-dealing, and a process protracted over several hours. The senior society mandarins advised the pledge organizers that similar disasters were likely to occur this time around and, against an inferred promise that things might change next year when the junior class protesters were themselves seniors, these rebel leaders told their classmates in an open letter that the election would be held in Branford Court, in the usual manner, and no junior was now bound by any commitment to stay in his room.

On the day, Howe, Glover, and Bundy (reportedly also pressured by his mother, who traveled to New Haven to do so) all accepted offers from Bones. Still, Mac Bundy said later that he followed his brother Bill into Bones only because "it became clear to me that it would be a blow to my father if I didn't join. He believed then in the institution as I do now. But at the time a big part of me was ambivalent. If my father hadn't been a member of Skull and Bones, I am sure I would not have joined."[11] (Senior society legacies, it must be admitted, were not always pleased at first with the opportunity.) As an adult, Bundy kept a ceramic skull and bones propped on his desk in his study, and received correspondence more than fifty years after his initiation addressed with his society name "Odin," the Norse god of war, poetry, wisdom, and the dead.[12]

Several incremental changes were indeed apparent the following year, in the spring of 1940. In April, two weeks before Tap Day, the Yale Political Union held a public debate, unprecedented in the twentieth century and like nothing so much as the senior class debate and vote back in February 1884, the replay resolving 38 to 17 that "the influence of the senior societies is not in the best interests of Yale." An outvoted supporter of the societies had argued: "As for their Democracy. I invite you to show our American Government a more just democracy than the Yale system in which the poorest boy can rise by pure achievement to the highest honor. Playthings for the idle rich perhaps, but there are no less than five bursary [scholarship] students out of the present fourteen members of the most representative of the societies."[13]

Prior to Tap Day this year, all the senior class members of Bones, Keys, Wolf's Head, Berzelius, Book & Snake, and Elihu were scheduled to meet to discuss changing the election procedure to employ a private event in juniors' rooms, instead of a public event at the campus's center. Yale administrators who were Skull and Bones alumni asked that their society's seniors not attend, and without the participation of the eldest senior society, the matter was dropped.[14]

The *News* ran a front-page article on Tap Day, May 9, which went beyond the customary simple announcement of when and where the juniors were to gather for election. Titled "Annual Tap Day Ceremonies Attract Juniors to Branford Where Six Senior Societies Will Seek 1941 Delegations," it included a potted history of the system drawn from

Bagg's (uncited) *Four Years at Yale*. *News* columnist W. Liscum Borden
reported in his "Society Sweepstakes" in the same issue that "*Time* and
Life plan to be on hand to cover one of the greatest shows on earth
. . . while down at the Yale Club in New York, dignified alumni (so
'tis said) will slip into mint juleps as they watch the election returns
coming in by ticker tape directly from Branford Court." Borden ran a
morning line on prospects for Bones (naming seven of the final fifteen,
none of the remaining going to Keys) and Keys (ten correct picks, and
none of the remaining five accepting Bones). But—forecasting his own
fallibility—he noted that "the societies are so on the defensive this year
that they are likely to pass over some of the more obvious B.M.O.C.s
in favor of lesser known entries with sterling character, and hence, lots
of long shots may gallop home with the bacon."[15]

One of those correctly predicted for Bones by Borden, William
Jackson ("because he looks so spooky in a dark suit"), had been a main
organizer of the Political Union debate and wrote his own unprec-
edentedly public post-election reflections in his newspaper column the
following week, "Now It Can Be Told." Although tapped himself (and
not actually in Branford Court that day), Jackson wrote in the voice of
one passed over in the arena. "How bestial the watchers looked, lined
up on the walks, hanging out of windows, morbid curiosity staring from
their bulging eyes—a sort of collective Madame Defarge, *sans* knitting,
assembled at the *place de guillotine*, waiting for the kill." Overcome by "a
feeling of unutterable loathing and revulsion," he concluded that "just
because the ends are good doesn't justify *any* means. Rather, the means
should be consistent and of equal dignity with the ends."[16]

Time magazine indeed ran the article which Borden's column had
predicted, titled "Skull and Bones." *Time* chairman Henry Luce was in
Paris that week, or a tell-all article on his beloved society might not have
run that reported that "Not strictly accurate is the legend that a Bones
man is never without a job, but a Bones man on his uppers often gets
handouts from his fellow Bonesmen," and "The [Bones] ritual is said to
include wrestling matches (from which they often emerge in tatters) and

critical bull sessions in which members tell each other their faults, prod each other to strive for Success."

Also quoted was an editorial from *Yale Daily* News chairman Kingman Brewster Jr.: "Six o'clock will bring a general sigh of relief and a sudden realization that after all the day of judgment is still a matter for the Gods and not 90 Yale men." The piece concluded with the news that nine men turned down Bones, "including Kingman Brewster whom a Bones man found [Harold Howe] in the *News* office. . . . Absent from the Branford Court but eventually bagged by Bones in his room was another critic of the societies, Kingman Brewster's roommate, William Eldred Jackson, son of U.S. Attorney General Robert H. Jackson." In a way that would be difficult for non-Yale people to appreciate fully, Brewster's refusal was seen as a magnificent act of heroism that resonated through the decades and was still a leading signifier of Brewster's reputation at the time of his selection as president of the university a quarter century later.[17]

In a 1968 reissue of *Stover at Yale*, President Brewster reflected once more on the system. "[In Stover's time] it was a pyramid, with Skull and Bones sitting aperch the top. But it was a pyramid of merit to a remarkable extent and reward did not exclude the rebel nor guarantee the legacy." He did not reflect on, let alone mention, his own rejection of election.[18] Although this was viewed by his peers as a rebellion against the system, his actual reasons for refusal were more varied. "I have no scunner [state of disgusted irritation] against the Senior Societies," he later protested. "I didn't join one as an undergraduate for the publicly expressed reasons that they were taking themselves too seriously and flaunting their secrecy as an ornament of exclusiveness: and for the more important private reason that I didn't want to give up my Saturday commute to Northampton [home of the women's college, Smith, where he was dating his roommate Jackson's sister]."[19] Jackson was later to say that Brewster believed a secret society membership would be a political liability in the approaching democratic age. On Tap Day in 1940, Brewster bicycled out to Whit Griswold's house, no doubt expecting that his mentor, then an assistant professor of Government and International Relations (and to be Brewster's predecessor as Yale president), would be pleased by his youthful independence and iconoclasm. Instead, he learned from Mary Griswold that her husband was back downtown participating in the Wolf's Head tapping effort.[20]

The class of 1941's election was again held in Branford Court, to which admission could be gained only by a card to be procured from the juniors' college masters; those unable to attend by reason of illness or otherwise were requested to inform the dean's office. The societies were provided with a list of the attending juniors, and each society was given twenty-five admission cards for their respective guests. Tapped juniors were instructed to go to a corner of the main court or other spot in Branford College designated by the tapping senior, to conclude the election, all to be done before six o'clock. A *News* editorial remarked that the new system would "certainly be an improvement over the former Roman holiday technique," and that "the Societies have shown a willingness to try something new, for which even their severest critics must give them some credit." Liscum Borden's cheeky column on the prospects for Bones and Keys did not prevent an offer from Bones, which he rejected, and no other society tapped him.[21]

The Yale College dean's office was watching too, and promptly prepared a graph which recorded the average grades of the new men in the six societies (Berzelius with the highest marks, followed in order by Keys, Bones, Wolf's Head, Elihu, and Book and Snake), their fraternities, and their residential colleges. Once more a world war, commencing for the U.S. the previous December, was not permitted to interfere with their initiation. High army and navy officials, with the approval of secretary of war Stimson, authorized home leaves and furloughs to the new members of the six societies, elected offsite because of having left school in February, to return in May to their alma mater from their aviation training in Pennsylvania and upstate New York.

Before that election, in the December 1940 bulletin of the Wolf's Head corporate body, the Phelps Association, members were reminded that in their official history, published in 1934 at the advent of the residential college system, author John Williams Andrews, noting the new peril in which the fraternities were placed, had argued that "The senior society groups, too, are unhappily aware of the Sword of Damocles. 'Whether or not they are to survive,' said a high official of the University, whose guess should be better than average, 'will be settled in the next seven years.'" Andrews asked, "Will the segregation of life in the Colleges eliminate or intensify the demand for University-wide contacts which the societies can so naturally supply? Do the societies now offer, or can they be shaped to offer, an additional something which the Colleges will always be impotent to meet in spite of their superb equipment for social intercourse?"[22]

The seven years had now passed, and there was no dangerous prospect of the societies' demise. For the Yale undergraduate, according to the Wolf's Head bulletin, "his college, rather than the university, had become the hub of his college existence." Eating together regularly, as required by the system, "day after day and month after month, goes a very long way to cementing friendships, as well as a long way toward making acquaintanceships that may ripen into friendships. Only lodging in the same entry of the same building, playing on the same team, taking the same trips with the same organization, can compare with the magic of food shared," and now there were "special college entertainments, special college traditions, special college jokes, literary magazines, crafts (such as printing, photography, wood and metal working and so forth)."

Nevertheless, this message concluded, segregation in the colleges had not only not eliminated the Andrews-identified "demand for the University-wide contracts which the societies can so naturally supply," but this demand had been "enormously *intensified*—and not only are the societies meeting this demand, but they must go on meeting it with ever increasing intensity year by year, if the University idea is not to be wholly submerged in the college idea, with Yale [College] becoming no more than a fiction as is the University of Oxford or the University of Cambridge." Wolf's Head celebrated the fact that in their 1936–37 delegation, there were men from six residential colleges out of seven, and in 1939–40 from five, but over the four years past, *all* the nine colleges as their number was expanded had representation in their tomb.[23]

WAR COMES AGAIN

When the radio reported the Japanese attack on Pearl Harbor on the afternoon of December 7, 1941, Yale students poured out of their rooms and began spontaneous demonstrations on the Old Campus, singing "Over There" from the last world war and chanting "Let's go to Tokyo!" By January 1942, thirty undergraduates had departed New Haven to enlist (one-half of one percent of the student body, as opposed to 700 in World War I's first month, when the duration and brutality of that conflict were not fully appreciated). Yale officials had been expecting this day for at least the two prior years, and the ROTC and Engineering School had begun shaping courses to meet such an emergency.

Yale was the first university in the country to make a definite statement of a progressive policy to prepare its students for war and war work. The "Yale Plan" announced on February 25, 1942, structured a course of studies to prepare a man mentally and morally for his duties as an officer in the armed forces, and created liaison plans attempting to accommodate the needs of the army, navy, and industry with the capacity of the facilities of the college. Men were divided into the Navy V-1 class ("V" for volunteer) and the Army Enlisted Reserve Corps plan, and before month's end, almost 30 percent of the student body—nearly nine hundred students—had enlisted in military and naval programs, which kept them temporarily in college. Army, navy, and marines enlisted reserve units were established in the summer of 1942. Put in charge of the marine corps enlisting unit was graduate Lt. Elliott R. Detchon Jr., '41, a star football player and Keys alumnus. Put in charge of Yale recruiting for the Navy's preflight training group was the current football team's captain and All-American center, Spencer Moseley '43, who was then a member of Bones.

There was no longer any place for the usual three months' summer vacation: an accelerated academic program was laid out whereby the university would operate on a year-round basis, dividing its work into three school-year terms instead of the former two. Each term would run approximately sixteen weeks with a brief week's breathing space between. Attending through the summer, students in all departments might graduate ahead of schedule, reducing the time for a full college course from four years to less than three—to two years and eight months, in fact. Except for the week between terms, classes were held every day except Christmas, and this included Thanksgiving and New Year's Day. Thus men under twenty-one would complete their college training before entering into active national service.

The six hundred seniors of the class of 1942 enjoyed the last normal graduation, advanced only a week from the customary date, with the ROTC seniors in uniform and the rest in mufti, as only the faculty wore academic gowns. The first summer session of the accelerated program began in July 1942, and 98 percent of Yale's undergraduates returned for it (the comparable numbers were 75 percent at Princeton, and 60 percent at Harvard). That same month, 1059 new freshmen of the class of 1945W—W meaning "War"—entered Yale, and were addressed by Harvey Bundy '09, special assistant to the secretary of war, and his fellow Bonesman Henry Stimson '88.

The election calendar for the senior societies was necessarily distorted by these events. The class of 1945, 981 of them, had arrived at the normal time in September 1941, just three months before Pearl Harbor, and their class's Tap Day was April 29, 1943, following by only five months the senior society elections for the class of 1944, held in December 1942. For 1945W, the expectation of their total term at Yale was two years and seven months, with a Tap Day of January 1, 1944, in the Timothy Dwight courtyard attended only by juniors and society members (when Bones tapped only a mere ten men, and Keys fourteen), but even those who stayed the longest had less time than that. Men were constantly lost to different branches of the service, and before their graduation in February 1944 the 1,059 freshmen who had entered had suffered on-campus attrition of 86 percent, to fewer than 150 men.

The crowding-in began, as Yale lost control of much of its own campus to the services: the U.S. Army Air Force rented Silliman College, the Freshman Commons, parts of the Law and Graduate Schools, laboratory facilities, and almost the entire Old Campus—where no Yale student was now allowed to step—for the duration. Six of the Yale College fraternities became officers' eating clubs. An advance guard of the Air Corps, coming around to see the possibilities, had stopped in delight before the Skull and Bones tomb, seeing it as "The very thing for the Guard House!" University treasurer Lawrence Tighe, who was handling the renting of the campus buildings, as a good Bonesman not suprisingly refused (and it was not Yale's property anyway). Yale College now resembled an armed camp, housing a student population by the summer of 1943 of 8,000, up from 5,000 before the war.

President Charles Seymour's message in the classbook for 1943 foretold the end of extracurricular activities: "During the years before us, perhaps most of that which characterized the old Yale life will of necessity be sacrificed. . . . Traditional student activities are bound to be strictly curtailed, the pleasant frivolities of leisure hours will rapidly disappear." Shrink in size they did, ultimately to vanish, although through 1942 they struggled to endure. On March 26, 1943, the Whiffenpoofs announced their discontinuance, with the *Yale Daily News*, the only Ivy League college newspaper which was continuing as a daily, reporting the "Temporary demobilization of the little black sheep." The *News* had announced that it intended to keep on publishing for the war's duration if possible, but the self-styled Oldest College Daily succumbed with a last issue on May 8, 1943, one of its final editorials commenting that "Yale is writing 'the end' temporarily to a chapter which has often spelt the neglect of proper study, and which has often created a goddess out of success after the fashion of America."[24]

THE SENIOR SOCIETIES IN WARTIME

The life of the senior societies was naturally impacted deeply by the enforced disciplines of military training and the severe reduction in optional leisure time. Members of the army, navy, and marines awoke at 6:00 A.M. and attended classes or the gymnasium all day until 6:00 P.M., six days a week; after mess, ninety minutes' free time was followed by a study period, with lights out at 11:30 P.M. Society members could now only squeeze in meetings on Wednesday nights, when at least the Navy men had the evening off, and before the end of the war some of the societies temporarily ceased to function. The Navy laid no ban on extracurricular activities, "insofar as it does not interfere with prescribed hours or courses of study"—which was exactly backward, as it was the prescribed hours and courses which interfered with extracurricular activities.

Still, enlisted naval students could join all previously established fraternities on campus available to all students, but were forbidden "to join in any activity or organization not available to membership to all students either civilian or enlisted on the campus," which eliminated the senior societies. With accelerated graduations coming every four months instead of annually, the cascade of blows fell quickly on the societies' seemingly immemorial rhythms, first limiting meetings, then scattering junior class candidates and senior class electors to far corners of the country or to overseas battlegrounds, then making even fifteen members hard to find, and finally forcing the complete cancellation of elections.

The centennial of Scroll and Key arrived in May 1942, and the invitation to their graduates hoped that every one "will make the necessary effort to return to the Hall on these occasions in spite of the obvious difficulty of the times." Attendees were advised that, in recognition of the society's one hundredth anniversary, Wolf's Head had sent over one hundred American Beauty roses ("thornless!") with an autographed poem by Stephen Vincent Benét, read in the Keys tomb on June 9, 1942, by George Parmly Day, the university treasurer and presiding officer for the centennial ceremonies.

The Benét verses recollected that, years before on the fiftieth anniversary of the third oldest College society, Keys had sent "thornless flowers" to Wolf's Head, and reflected the wartime threat to civilization:

For, as in Rome, Briton and Gaul
Alike could man the Roman Wall
And citizens from near and far
Though born beneath a different star
Remarked, with zeal, "S.P.Q.R.,
Civis Romanus sum."—so we,
Whatever else we chance to be,
Remain "cives Yalenses" still
And hail our city with a will.

So, though the Wolf our totem be,
Tonight we honor Scroll and Key
And in our mildly vulpine way
Extol your glad centennial day,
The years as honorably worn,
The honors still so lightly bourne,
The gaiety through years maintained,
The courtesy that is not feigned,
And gaily may your troubadour
Greet the next hundred years, and more![25]

Tap Day, seemingly forever a fixture of late May afternoons, was for the first time since the original election of 1833 seriously accelerated, to December 3, 1942, for the elections for the class of 1944, to graduate on December 19. Because of the shortened winter day and evening blackout rules on campus, juniors were asked to report to Branford Court at 4:15 P.M., with the ceremony to begin at 4:30 (or, predicted a *News* columnist, "perhaps earlier unless the societies want to look for the last few men with kerosene lamps.") Admittees held tickets mailed in individual envelopes to all juniors in the College, and obtained by Sheff and Engineering juniors from the Sheff dean's office.

The traditional *News* election day editorial observed that, unlike in recent years past, "no opinions have been expressed to the public either in condemnation or in affirmation of the senior society system," but also noted that "each junior must enter Branford Courtyard this afternoon with some basis for either refusing or accepting election to one of the six senior societies. A real basis, and perhaps the only fool-proof one, which alone does not involve penetrating the societies' perfectly valid secrecy and mystery, is whether one wants the rare privileges and benefits, together with some of the burdens, of fourteen intimate, life long friends." Men taken in as members were fine men, opined the editorial, but probably would have been fine men without such membership. "In the last analysis," the *News* chair wrote, "the best basis for deciding for or against the senior society system is the friendship tradition, which is its unique gift to Yale life."

That *News* columnist had asserted that about sixty men of the ninety knew they would be tapped. To Bones that day went Dean Witter Jr., son of the founder of the eponymous stock brokerage house, tapped by Spencer Moseley; James Lane Buckley, later United States senator from New York and thereafter senior judge on the U.S. Court of Appeals for the D.C. Circuit; James Whitmore, future Hollywood actor, slapped by Zeph Stewart, future Harvard professor of Classics and Lowell House master; and Townsend Hoopes, to be undersecretary of the air force during the Vietnam War and then president of the Association of American Publishers. Joining Keys that day was John Vliet Lindsay, future mayor of New York City, tapped by Cord Meyer Jr., future president of the United World Federalists, joined in the courtyard by his clubmate George Roy Hill, future Academy Award–winning director of *Butch Cassidy and the Sundance Kid* and *The Sting*. In 1965, when all three mayoral candidates—Lindsay, William F. Buckley Jr., and Robert F. Wagner Jr.—were Yale graduates, a newspaper columnist facetiously observed that while Buckley was in Skull and Bones, Lindsay and Wagner were only in Scroll and Key, and "[T]hat makes them sensitive to the aspirations of minority groups."

To Wolf's Head that day went Sam Wagstaff, who after surviving Omaha Beach on D-Day became a renowned American art curator and collector (his photography collection purchased by the Getty Museum) as well as the artistic mentor, benefactor, and companion of photographer Robert Mapplethorpe and poet–punk rocker Patti Smith. Tapping for Berzelius in Branford Court was Elias Clark, later Yale law professor and longtime master of Silliman College. The tally of refusals, eleven in all, showed that the mismatch of society intents and candidate desires continued in a democratic mix: three turndowns each for Bones, Keys, and Book and Snake, and one for Elihu, with only Berzelius completely successful in choosing its first fifteen without rebuff.[26]

As for meetings in 1942, the Bones clubs of the graduating classes of 1944 (with only four men on campus) and 1945 were sharing Skeleton Hall on Wednesday evenings, eating together, then switching off debate sessions while the non-debating club bided its time, before all rushing back to barracks at ten o'clock; on Saturdays, 1945's contingent had the hall to itself while the older club went to New York City or to a summer beach house in Madison, Connecticut, loaned by an alumnus. Elections were successfully mounted for the class of 1945W on New Year's Day in 1944, a Saturday, although only ten men were elected, the fewest in the society's history (Keys managed to elect fourteen).

By the spring of 1945 with the current members expected to leave for war service in June—since the atomic bomb's existence was unknown and its dramatic impact unforeseen, not being mentioned in occasional talks given in New Haven by those working in Washington with Secretary of War Henry Stimson—it was determined that, for the first and last time in the society's storied history, no elections would be conducted for the class of 1946. The *Yale News Digest* simply if grimly announced: "The Skull and Bones Society will offer no elections this spring."

Fulfilling the prediction made in the *Nineteen Forty Four Class Book*, which had postulated in the spring of 1943 that "should the [extracurricular organization] groups be forced out of existence, some provision will be made for handing over the organization to the trusteeship of faculty members for the duration," a group of local Bones alumni, including Yale faculty and administrators and recently graduated members, formed an ad hoc club, which they styled the "Committee of Fifteen," to continue the life of the society, meeting on Thursday nights from the remainder of 1945 and into 1946, and this group after V-J Day in August 1945 planned for the coming spring of 1946, when normal campus life was expected to resume. Not until May 16, 1946, for the class of 1947, was there to be an incoming club for Skull and Bones chosen at the customary time in the customary way (although men selected for the societies were informed in their rooms), with the full complement of fifteen, after three refusals. Eleven members of the classes of 1944, 1945, and 1945W were on that date still in attendance at Yale as undergraduates, rescheduled after their respective enlistments to graduate in 1946, 1947, and 1948.

As for Keys, its group photographs for the classes of 1942, 1943, and 1944 each show fifteen men, but for 1945, there are twenty-seven faces: an amalgamation of the classes of 1945, with fifteen, and 1945W, with twelve, and at least six military uniforms. For the class of 1946, eight men were photographed, six again in uniform, with four not shown, constituting the second delegation in Keys' modern history with less than a full complement of fifteen. For 1947, ten members are pictured, none in uniform, so over two years in three classes, the canonical number was not achieved. And while the portraits for the classes of 1948 and 1949 once more reflect the prewar pattern, fifteen young men in dark suits, nine of that 1948 crowd were World War II veterans and three would go to Korea, while in 1949 all but two were veterans.[27]

The *1945W Class Book*, published in conjunction with the *1947 Yale Banner*, evidences the confusion and attrition in annual intake of fifteen, in printing the standard page listings beneath their symbols of the various societies' members. The Bones page lists thirty-eight names, and the Keys page thirty-three, hailing from the classes of 1944, 1945, 1945W, 1946, and 1947, while Berzelius and Book and Snake each lists twenty-five, and Wolf's Head twenty.

These Bones and Keys groups of 1949—the former club, similarly all veterans, including two legacies, Henry Sloane Coffin '97's nephew William Sloane Coffin, who had worked in the army's intelligence service as a liaison with the French and Russian armies, before becoming famous two decades later as Yale's chaplain and civil rights crusader, and Trubee Davison '17's son Daniel Pomeroy Davison, a lieutenant in the USAF from 1943 to 1945—would, after some debate, offer election to a man who would have been the first black member in either society's history.[28]

WHEN THE SHOOTING STOPPED

Although the Japanese surrender in August 1945 relieved the tension in the battlefields, Yale did not immediately resume its former peace-time status, having officially opened its 245th academic year with the summer term on July 2. At the special graduation held on October 23 for 53 members of the class that had entered in February 1943, President Charles Seymour gratefully noted that "For the first time in four years and five months a class goes forth from the halls of Yale into a world that will concentrate its power on something other than the annihilation of human possessions and the destruction of human lives." The last navy men did not leave until June 1946, and the boys in uniform could not immediately come home, since demobilization took time. The university resumed its prewar two-term schedule in September.[29]

The pamphlet "Studies for the Returning Service Men" was prepared for eager inquirers: the government was lending a financial hand with the GI Bill, and many men who had no previous college experience were planning to give it a try. At the beginning of the 1945 summer term, 580 freshmen had entered Yale as the class of '48. On November 1 another 250 came, and these together with the 228 who arrived with the beginning of the spring term of March, 1946, constituted the class of 1949. These entering freshmen and their counselors were put directly into those colleges which by now had been turned back to Yale by the navy.

A quota of 650 applications had been set for the fall term of 1946, and more than twice as many applications were received. Furthermore, six thousand former undergraduates wanted to return to qualify for a degree, and Yale received 5,175 formal applications from veterans who had either never attended a college or wanted to switch to Yale. In its inaugural issue for 1946, the war-suspended *Yale Daily News* reported that 5,000 veterans were included in the total registering, with the undergraduate body jumping in number from the normal limit of 3,100 to a total of about 5,600. Over a quarter of the returning veterans, some 1,300 of them, had brought new wives along. Some of them in due course had children, including among those newborns George Walker Bush, to be the 43rd president of the United States, born in New Haven on July 6, 1946.

On Commencement Sunday in 1946, a service of commemoration for the war dead was held in Battell Chapel, a long list, 514 names. The following day saw once again the normal commencement exercises with nearly seven hundred student degrees and the conferring of honorary degrees for the first time since 1942. By the fall of 1946, the physical conversion of the entire University to peacetime status was complete, with the Old Campus available again to entering freshmen.[30] What have been called "the veteran years" which followed, between 1946 and, roughly, 1949, were to change the senior societies, as the veterans elevated and dignified Yale in many ways. It was their battle-worn skepticism which first permitted the intensification of the organized mockery of the societies, forcing them to reassess their standards.[31]

RESUMPTION OF (MOST) TRADITIONS

Tap Day on May 15 in the spring of 1947 for the class of 1948 still did not allow revival of the prewar tradition of elections held in the Branford College courtyard. Elections were offered between 4:00 and 6:00 P.M. to the collegians in their rooms, and those not living in the residential colleges were told to say in their places of residence, whether in or out of New Haven. The campus radio station, WYBC, announced the completion of elections to the several societies as soon as might be done after each society closed its list.

The last man tapped for Bones was George H. W. Bush, whose Yale blue veins and senior society antecedents came from several ancestors and from both sides of the families reflected in his full name. The first Bush to attend Yale was the forty-first American president's great-grandfather, James Smith Bush, class of 1844. His other great-grandfather, David Walker, had built the largest dry goods import firm west of the Mississippi, and the investment firm of his son, George H. Walker and Company, founded in 1900, had become one of the more important in the Mississippi Valley. Walker became president of the W. A. Harriman & Co. investment firm, where Prescott Bush, Yale 1917 and Bones, became vice president in 1924, having first become Walker's son-in-law in 1921.

Prescott's first job after his 1919 discharge from his World War I service as an army captain of field artillery had been at the Simmons Hardware Company, owned by Walter Simmons, Yale 1890 and Bones, in St. Louis, Missouri, where he met George Walker's daughter Dorothy. In 1931, Prescott became a partner of the newly merged Brown Brothers Harriman, where Averell Harriman was chairman of the board and his younger brother Roland, Prescott's Bones clubmate, also worked. In 1952 Prescott Bush was named to fill a vacancy in the United States Senate, serving until 1962. He had lost his first race, in 1950, his ties with Planned Parenthood hurting him in heavily Catholic Connecticut, where he also served as chairman of that state's branch of the United Negro College Fund.[32]

Within the family, his son George H. W. Bush became "Poppy" (a nickname which persisted at Yale), because he had been named by family agreement after his maternal grandfather Walker, known as "Pop" to his sons. He attended Phillips Andover, which many said was modeled after Yale, in terms of social—even secret—clubs and fraternities and Yale-educated leadership. Bush became captain of both the soccer and baseball teams, playing manager of the basketball team, president of the senior class, and (before such societies were abolished after the Second World War) a member of Andover's own secret society AUV (Auctoritas, Unitas, Veritas—Authority, Unity, Truth).

At his graduation in 1942, where Secretary of War Stimson, the commencement speaker and chairman of the Andover Trustees, had warned against early enlistment in the new war, George overrode Prescott's intent that he go directly from Andover to Yale and enlisted on his eighteenth birthday as a naval aviator, the youngest in the service to that date. He was shot down on September 2, 1944, near the Bonin Islands, and later rescued from an inflated raft by a submarine. Dying in that crash was a Bush family friend, Lt. (jg) Ted White, a squadron ordnance officer, Bonesman of the class of 1942 and son of a classmate of Prescott's who had begged a ride on a combat mission in the turret gunner's seat to observe the plane's weapons system. For his 58 combat missions and 126 carrier landings, George Bush received the Distinguished Flying Cross, three Air Medals, and the Presidential Unit Citation awarded his ship the USS *San Jacinto*.[33]

While the GI Bill helped not only Bush but others who ordinarily would have attended Yale, funding $500 of the $600-per-year tuition and $105 for a married couple's monthly subsistence, it also helped thousands more who would not have even thought of Yale, and the social complexion of the campus changed considerably. (Specific scholarships for black students, paid for the by college's "Budget" charity drive for which Bush was an officer, evidenced that the diversification of the student body had solid support within the college.) The veterans were as a group older than the usual undergraduate body, certainly more seasoned, by virtue of their war service, involving 60 percent of the class of 1948. Their ethnicity was radically more diverse: the 1947 Yale football team for the Harvard game included players named Prchlik, Nadherny, Dluzniewski, Tataranowicz, Setear, Pivcevich, Loh, and Booe. They sat in classrooms attentively and struggled with examinations which represented not the pleasure of a gentlemanly collegiate style, but the doorway to a postwar world.

The outward display of collegiate customs and traditions, such as the Whiffenpoofs, Mory's, and yes, the senior societies, had less central a place than before the war. "It is undeniably true that these social organizations were not easily going to regain their previous importance and prestige positions in the history of the new Yale," opined the editors of the 1948 classbook. Still, it was college, not a battlefield, and the yearbook noted that "Yale at war had seen many difficulties" and "studies came first," meaning that "values tended to be somewhat distorted, with studies actually being overemphasized." Yet, "Eli was peeling off the vestiges of militarism. The return of the sports jacket and gray flannels gave rise to the feeling that Yale was, once again, her old self."

That was not quite true for the senior societies, to go by the opinion expressed by Horace D. Taft, Senator Robert Taft's son (and future dean of Yale College), in his social history of the class of 1949: "Tap Day came around for our class and was held in Branford Court once more. Being a new and extraordinary process for most of us, it evinced a great deal of curiosity, but for the great majority it was too incongruous a procedure to be very impressive. These societies, as well as fraternities and other groups, have not recaptured the position of importance they held before the war. There is too much else offered by the University."[34]

Only weeks after his return from the Pacific, on January 6, 1945, Bush married Barbara Pierce. In overcrowded New Haven, the young married couple lived, over the two and one-half years of his college education in the still-accelerated course, in three apartments, losing the first because of Barbara's pregnancy with their first son. The last residence was at 37 Hillhouse, formerly a single-family dwelling next to the one inhabited by President Seymour, now divided into thirteen separate apartments for nine families including eleven children, where the kitchen and bathroom had to be shared with others. Despite having a young family, Bush entered fully into the college's frenetic social and athletic life, joining and then serving as president of the junior fraternity Delta Kappa Epsilon; captaining the Yale baseball team and playing in the first two College World Series (the pregnant Barbara Bush sat in the extra-wide seat in the Yale stadium which had been designed for William Howard Taft to use while teaching at the law school); and being elected to Phi Beta Kappa, an achievement perplexing those who had known him at Andover.

Barbara's father wrote to a childhood friend, updating him on the Pierce family after his son-in-law's graduation, that his daughter's husband was "by all odds the biggest man on the campus, having been the last man tapped for Skull and Bones and having been awarded a faculty prize [the George Gordon Brown Prize for "all around student leadership"] for having done the most for Yale." The 1947 club tapping him included another political scion, John Chafee, great-grandson of a governor and grand-nephew of another governor and of a U.S. senator, but blooded differently as a marine at Guadalcanal and Okinawa, and later to serve as governor of Rhode Island, secretary of the navy under President Nixon, and then four-term United States senator.[35]

In his senior society life, too, Bush participated fully, albeit married, and his clubmates, all war veterans themselves and seven of them pilots, included Thomas William Ludlow ("Lud") Ashley, subsequently thirteen-term Democratic congressman from Ohio; Howard Sayre Weaver, future dean of the Yale School of Art and Architecture; and David Grimes, to chair the founding board of the Association of Yale Alumni. This club discussed admitting both blacks and Jews to their institution.[36]

George Herbert Walker Bush, of course, had the most remarkable political career of all these veterans, and one of the most remarkable of all American politicians, serving one term as congressman from Texas's 7th District, then ambassador to the United Nations for twenty-two months. Thereafter he served as chair of the Republican National Committee for twenty months, then chief of the China liaison office—functionally, ambassador—in Beijing for sixteen months, then director of the Central Intelligence Agency for a year, then vice president of the United States (sworn in by Supreme Court Justice Potter Stewart, Bones 1937) under Ronald Reagan for eight years. Finally, when no sitting vice president had been elected to the presidency since Martin Van Buren one hundred fifty years before, he became the forty-first president of the United States for a single term.

His clubmates and graduate members of his senior society were instrumental over the years in funding this rise and in allowing him to unburden himself at reunions and dinners: a *Washington Post* article in the run-up to the 1988 presidential election was titled "Bush Opened Up to Secret Yale Society" and detailed the group's programs of C.B.s and L.H.s, even describing Bush's anguished retelling of the wartime death of his *San Jacinto* shipmate Ted White.[37] These intersections of intimacy and political power, noted by the media, only served to fuel the conspiracy theories which swirled around Skull and Bones.

While it would have been easy for Bush to go down to New York and be an early success on Wall Street—his 1948 class yearbook lists twenty-five separate affiliations and achievements during his scant twenty-seven months in New Haven—young men of his background had begun looking southwest and west for different opportunities in the bursting economy. But even here, his senior society connections helped. He was taken on as the only trainee, an equipment clerk, for Dresser Industries, an oil services company later known as Halliburton, by its president, Neil Mallon, who had been an intercollegiate All-American basketball player and a member of the 1917 Bones club with Prescott. As George H. W. Bush had been the navy's youngest pilot in World War II, Mallon, at twenty-three, had been the army's youngest major in World War I.[38]

OTHER CASTES BROKEN

The junior class in 1949 was the largest in Yale's history, and in March the Scroll and Key delegation wrote their alumni, inviting suggestions regarding eligible candidates and reminding them that, in accordance with policy, no notice of election intention would be communicated before Tap Day, and so any inquiring should know that the lack of prior contact did not mean a lack of interest. The event itself was once more held in Branford Court, on May 12, with admission only by cards being sent to the juniors. *News* chairman William F. Buckley '50, in an editorial titled "Tap Day Procedure," deplored "the extraordinary callousness which tolerates a mass spectacle wherein scores of students are unnecessarily embarrassed for the sake of convenience, color and tradition." The reforms suggested were that society elections should be delivered to juniors in their rooms, and bids should include a list of all societies tendering invitations to the individual. "The change may seem a small thing, but it can loom large to the junior who leaves Branford gate untapped, lungs full of tobacco, a stiff upper lip, and the necessity of having to make small talk until he reaches the privacy of his room."[39] Both suggestions were disregarded, making what happened in public on that day all the more visible.

The African American Levi Jackson, son of the longtime steward at the Yale Faculty Club, was a graduate of New Haven's Hillhouse High, employed while a highschooler as a turf man in the Yale Bowl. He was elected the captain of the Yale football team in November 1948, the first black both to play on and to head a university team, and the first "townie" to play on the varsity since Albie Booth of the 1931 team. New York newspaper sportswriters promptly predicted a future election to Skull and Bones. For weeks before the election the college was abuzz with the possibility, and notions of demonstrated merit and democratic fairness were reported as figuring heavily in campus discussions.

"Bones' main criterion for election," wrote Joe Williams for the *World-Telegram* on the eve of Tap Day, "is success and leadership in college. This being so Jackson is obviously a natural." He continued: "The Yale crowd have been outspoken in their insistence that if Bones is to justify itself and its lofty conception of brotherhood it must tap Jackson for membership. . . . Unaccompanied by the noisy preaching of liberals and the hamfat posturings of heavy thinkers, Yale struck a telling blow for human decency by naming Jackson captain of the football team, and apparently it is all set to deliver another one of equal force by accepting the Negro half back into is most exclusive society." Jackson, the sportswriter hazarded, could absent himself from campus and avoid the issue, but he "owes it to himself and the democracy of this great university to take a stand on the Yale campus tomorrow, come what may."[40]

Jackson himself had allowed as how he was in doubt whether to accept any society's bid, even until just before the ceremony. "This racial question has been brought up so much," he said. "Even at Ebbets Field last Saturday people came up and asked me if I was going out on Tap

Day." He was an elected class deacon, and a member of the Aurelian Honor Society, but had turned down bids from the junior fraternities. The *1949 Yale Class Book* was to observe that "Yale's fraternities have not been caught as vigorously as chapters on other campuses in the fight over discrimination raised by the expulsion of an Amherst chapter from its national fraternity because of the admission of a Negro. . . . Levi Jackson could have presented the problem in a more vigorous form if he had ever signed up for rushing."[41]

On that day, as reported on the front pages of both the *New York Times* and the *New York Herald Tribune*, Jackson stood with about 1,400 juniors outside the Branford College courtyard, where campus policemen barred entry to reporters, other students, and would-be spectators. With all eyes on him, Jackson was at 5:00 P.M. the first to be tapped, almost simultaneously, first by Bones, then by Keys, but he declined to move, in accordance with tradition for rejecting the offers. He then received a slap from Rick Mapes, a New Haven senior in Berzelius—described prominently and correctly by the *Times* as the "third oldest society"—to whom Jackson nodded and then went to his room.

Contacted later by reporters, Jackson declined to discuss the reasons, although his classmates attributed his choice to the fact that, as he himself was said to have indicated with a grin, three of his friends on the football team were also joining Berzelius, and other sources declare that, as was the pre-tap custom with some societies, he had pledged himself to that society before the tap. To one newspaper, he said merely "I had to make one choice. I just chose Berzelius. I'm sorry, but that's all I have to say. No, I do not know what Berzelius means or what it might have come from." To another reporter, he said he was "quite pleased" at his election but, as among the three societies seeking him, he "actually had no preference." He was later to say, "Being in a society gave me the feeling that I belonged. I felt I was finally getting the real Yale experience."[42] Jackson's election was not without cost to Berzelius: some alumni reportedly severed their connection with the society, as was to happen in a parallel situation when Bones tapped women in 1991.

Both small and large factors were at play behind Jackson's choice, and the choice of Jackson. Bones was no stranger to refusals in the preceding decades, and six others declined the oldest senior society that election day, including Milton DeVane, the son of the dean of Yale College, and James Symington, the son of the United States secretary for air, who accepted Berzelius, as did Payne Whitney's grandson Harry Payne Whitney II, while four men besides Jackson turned down Keys' offers. But there was a larger shift as well, effected by World War II and the tidal wave of veterans returning to New Haven to finish their college careers. Charles Fenton, class of 1948 and subsequently professor of English at Yale, recollected that in the "era between 1946 and, roughly, 1949, which we might call the veteran years . . . the veterans elevated and dignified Yale in many ways. It was the skepticism of the veterans which first permitted the early, organized mockery of the senior societies and caused the societies to reassess themselves."[43]

Jackson served two years in the army as a staff sergeant at Fort Lee, Virginia, before enrolling in Yale in 1946 and won a place on the varsity football team in his first year under a revised rule that made freshmen eligible when they had been in the armed forces. He had served his country and his college honorably, and his fellow veterans were prepared, unlike prior generations, to celebrate that service in spite of Jackson's race. Yale's next black football captain was Rudolph Green, class of 1975, who was tapped for Bones and, unlike Jackson, accepted.[44] Not until 1989, forty years later, was there to be an African American on the Yale Corporation, Kurt Schmoke of the class of 1971, who became Senior Fellow in 1999. And at "The Game" in 2014, sixty-five years after Jackson Levi's senior society election, the captains of both the Yale and Harvard teams were black.

It has been said that, years later, Jackson would joke that "if my name had been reversed [Jackson Levi], I never would have made it."[45] Given Jackson's innate modesty, not only does this remark seem out of character, but it was not true (the Jewish football star Al Hessberg had been tapped by Bones years before, in 1937). More to the point, it was not true again in Jackson's own election year, when Bones tapped and was accepted by Thomas H. Guinzberg, Hotchkiss graduate, winner of a Purple Heart at Iwo Jima, and managing editor of the *Yale Daily News*, chaired by his classmate and new society clubmate, William F. Buckley (a Catholic, Bones' last man, tapped by the outgoing basketball captain, future Boston Celtics star, and Catholic Tony Lavelli). Hessberg and Jackson were both football heroes, so Guinzberg's election represented a further sociological shift, a *Jewish* scholar-striver finally achieving senior society recognition.

Anti-Semitism was still a force: the Fence Club, Yale's most exclusive fraternity, rejected Guinzburg because he was Jewish, until his close friend Bill Buckley advised the fraternity that he would not join if Guinzburg was blackballed.[46] Guinzberg's senior society election, however, did not attract any special newspaper notice, in New Haven or elsewhere. He was to join with his Yale roommate Peter Matthiessen (not a senior society member, having spent his junior year at the Sorbonne), George Plimpton, and others in Paris to establish *The Paris Review* in 1953, and eventually followed his father as president of Viking Press and its successor by merger, Viking/Penguin.[47]

Election prospects were slowly changing for public high school graduates, too. In 1942, when 25 percent of the Yale freshmen were public school products, only 6 percent of the society men were; the number was still 6 percent in 1949, but jumped to 17 percent in 1950. In one decade, that gap would narrow such that when 35 percent of the freshmen were public high school graduates, fully 25 percent of the senior societies' members were among them.[48]

HIDING THE *HARVARD LAMPOON*

After the high drama of the Jackson tap in the spring came the farce of the *Harvard Lampoon* in the fall, on the weekend of the annual Yale-Harvard football game, this year in New Haven. At 1:15 A.M. on Friday, November 18, campus policemen found two Harvard students placing placards on fences and telephone poles, advertising the sale of a special issue of their humor magazine featuring the senior societies. The Harvards were F. Ellsworth Baker, business manager of the *Lampoon,* and a member of the class of 1951, Ernest Monrad, a candidate for the magazine's staff. The campus police advised them that all such placards—featuring a big picture of the magazine cover and the large-lettered legend AN EXPOSÉ—THE YALE SECRET SOCIETIES—could only be put on bulletin boards.

Alerted to the impending insult, five Yale students found Monrad in Timothy Dwight College, where he was staying as a guest, and they demanded, confiscated, and left with his car keys, returning in fifteen minutes with the keys and a warning to "go to bed or else." When Monrad went to his car, he found the Yalies had taken three thousand copies of the *Lampoon* and the remaining posters. Monrad called Baker and advised him of the theft, which was reported to the Yale campus police at 5:00 A.M. Using the 1950 class book, Monrad identified the man who had taken his keys, Evan Galbraith, a member of Skull and Bones (later to be President Reagan's ambassador to France and then the secretary of defense's representative to Europe and NATO for President George W. Bush).

Faced with the law, which had come to his room in Calhoun College, Galbraith advised the policeman that the offending magazine issues were secreted in the Bones tomb garden, and a police cruiser went to High Street with Galbraith to retrieve and return them to Monrad back at the campus police office. Monrad had telegrammed the Lampoon offices in Cambridge to order another five thousand copies, but said he would cancel that order now that the original copies were back in hand. According to the campus police report to Dean Richard Carroll, the Harvards said they did not want to press charges or to get Galbraith into any trouble over the matter; they did not ask, nor were they told, where the copies had been found. The *Lampoon* went on sale the next morning and sold out almost before the majority of Harvard supporters arrived in New Haven, the Yalies apparently being as curious about the cover story subject as those from Cambridge.[49]

Whatever the blow to the amour propre of the Yale senior societies, the insult was no impediment that afternoon to Jackson, with two touchdowns of his own, leading the varsity football team to a resounding 29 to 6 victory over the Crimson. Recalling that weekend, the historian of the class of 1950 remarked of Tap Day that "Most of us watch Levi Jackson out of the corners of our eyes, and when he was tapped we were heartened—more for him than for the ostensible humanity in the gesture. The accolade was rightly his; they could not withhold it. Since Tap Day we have heard nothing except an occasional stealthy tread on Thursday nights. We know only what we read in the *Harvard Lampoon*, and, after all, that's not much."[50]

CHAPTER TWELVE

REFORMS, REVELATIONS, AND RIVALS UNDERGROUND (1950–1962)

The hierarchic structure of Yale undergraduate organization, culminating in the senior societies, was severely questioned as out-of-date and anti-democratic. Many questioned, not only the ideals, but the whole machinery of the system. They insisted that a training for life in a democratic community must take place in a democratically-organized university.

—Prosser Gifford, 1951, in *Seventy-Five: A Study of a Generation in Transition, Yale Daily News,* 1953

LOCAL AND NATIONAL ECHOES

Perhaps the two fires which started a few days apart in December 1842, charring the rented rooms of each of Bones and Keys, were coincidental examples of spontaneous combustion, but the bomb that exploded in front of the Bones tomb on May 9, 1950, forty-eight hours before Tap Day, was certainly an expression of opinion.¹ No individual or group claimed responsibility (and no damage to person or property was sustained), but the decade of the long 1950s so commenced was to be as tumultuous for the senior societies, in its own ways, as the war decade of the 1940s and the student rebellion decade of the 1960s.

Articles on the society system continued to be published by outsiders, and by graduates. The *Harvard Crimson* in its weekend edition for "The Game" in 1950, under the headline "Yale: For God, Country, and Success," found the collegians visiting from New Haven to be alien to their own social experience. Noting that "year-book polls show that 70 percent of the Yalies 'admire students who occupy important extra-curricular positions,' and 69 percent 'would like to be prominent in extra-curricular activities,'" the Harvard authors found that "almost as many varsity athletes want to be chairman of the Yale News as captain of the football team. . . . This would surprise a Harvard man, who usually accepts people on personal worth, and would be hard put to remember the name of the president of the Student Council" (something Yale did not then have). "Since the six [Senior] Societies, blatantly and confessedly, elect members on the strength of their extra-curricular success, an induction into their secrecy is something more for the climbing Yalie to aspire to. . . . For the spooks' philosophy is that the world can best be run by themselves, the outstanding men of Yale."²

This *Crimson* piece explained that "spooks"—perhaps the first published use of the epithet—was what "sour-grapes outsiders" called the senior society members. In their weekly *Current* newspaper's special issue of December 1951, "Current Goes to Yale," the women of all-female Smith College, after admitting that their knowledge of society customs was dependent on their study of the *Harvard Lampoon* of November 1949, brushed off the strangeness of the system and saw a collateral opportunity for themselves. "Smith girls should be pleased to know that despite the deficiency of such societies on campus (the Hibernians, our only claim to clandestine fraternization, is more a social giggle and a bottle of scotch than a coherent organization), they too can become a secret. Marry a Bonesman, and she will remember her wedding as a glorious acceptance into the clique, initiated by the 'Society' ushers who presumably adorn the occasion. A grandfather clock—the normal wedding gift for members—is thrown in, to boot."[3]

For the 1952 Yale-Harvard football game weekend, the *Crimson* waxed sociological again. Even in an article mocking the Cantabs' southern rival (the title was "Yale: High Society | Yale Dances to Senior Society Tune"), the democracy of the Yale system was acknowledged to be in stark contrast to the Harvard social scene. "Unlike Harvard, where there are social, intellectual, and athletic cliques, each with its own separate value system, the Yale ideal is broad enough to contain the athlete and the 'brain' within its all-pervading grasp. When a Yale man has shown the necessary qualifications he is judged successful by a jury of his peers—tapped for membership in one of the six secret societies."

Parsing the differences, this story continued, "It is the societies above all which, by setting the qualifications for success, distinguish Yale from Harvard. As opposed to the [Harvard] clubs, they do not limit themselves to men from the right schools and right families (although wealth and social background help). Their standard of election is, supposedly, campus achievement, and therefore Tap Day exaltation is open to every student who comes to Yale, rich or poor, prep or public school, Jew or Gentile."[4] The last phrase is particularly significant, as the article's Harvard student authors were surnamed Abrams, Halberstam, and Kriss.

The national magazine audience also continued to be reminded of this exotic Yale tradition. The writer John Knowles of the class of 1949, not yet known for *A Separate Peace*, his 1959 bestselling novel about Phillips Exeter and a student secret society there, described the societies' tombs as "enormous icebergs glimpsed through the fog, and pondered over because of the immense Unknowable." He narrated for the readers of *Holiday* in 1953 the story of his own Tap Day, "one of the most singular social rites in our culture." In Branford Court, he remembered, "perhaps five hundred students were milling about, like skittish cattle at branding time . . . In the Gothic windows overlooking us were stationed the members of the six societies, severely clad in dark suits, black ties, with their society pins just below the knot. They looked like pallbearers." He "tensed," thinking he was about to be tapped, but it was the man alongside, his future senior year roommate, who was struck by Bones. Afterward, societies whose first choices had accepted another election "began a rapid shuffling of lists" for second choices. "But then the societies began ostentatiously slamming shut their [college headquarters] windows, a notification that their elections were complete. Our hilarity subsided and we stood like uninvited guests while the members marched solemnly past us and away."[5]

A much more revelatory article appeared in the men's magazine *Esquire* for September 1955, the first of a type and scope that was to be published every following decade or so with a spicy mix of facts and legends. "Yale's Secret Societies" was written by a *Boston Globe* newspaper columnist, George Frazier. Begining with the poignant story of Harvard professor F. O. Matthiessen committing suicide in 1950 by leaping from his Boston hotel window, falling to his death with his Bones badge fastened to his shirt, Frazier then described the traditional Tap Day exercises and named all six societies with their years of founding, recounting their reputations and special rites, their literary mentions (Benét, Hemingway, O'Hara and his quarrel with Brendan Gill), and their famous graduates.

The protagonists of Owen Johnson's *Stover at Yale* were quoted liberally on the merits and excesses of the society system, and Frazier recited the brawls with Bull and Stones, the pamphlet attacks of 1873 in the *Iconoclast* and *The Seventh Book of Genesis*, and the more recent sarcasm of the *Harkness Hoot*. Not surprisingly, he concentrated on the lore of Skull and Bones, detailing the members' communal confessions, special wedding ceremonies, grandfather clocks, Deer Island, and code names—all information gleaned over drinks from divorced former wives of Bonesmen. The piece concluded with the tale of the *Harvard Lampoon* issues' theft and restoration. Overall, it was the most complete and authoritative description of the society system since Lyman Bagg's *Four Years at Yale* of 1871.[6]

A NEW UNIVERSITY PRESIDENT

Yale University itself was in the national news. The year 1951 marked the 250th anniversary of what had been chartered in 1701 as the Collegiate School, and its new leader, A. Whitney Griswold of the class of 1929, having just completed his own presidency's inaugural year, graced the front covers of both *Time* and *Newsweek* magazines for June 11, 1951. His 1933 Yale PhD dissertation, the nation's first in the new field of American Studies, was on the American cult of success. Harvard would not have been surprised.

When university president Charles Seymour decided in 1950 to emulate his predecessor and fellow Bonesman Arthur Hadley '76's retirement from leadership at age sixty-five, Griswold at age forty-three was a full professor concluding two decades of teaching, first freshman English and then history. As an undergraduate, he had cofounded the Yale Political Union. As an administrator, in the words of the *New York Times* piece heralding his selection, he had "turned out military governors for the Army in biscuit batches" during the war, but now "the Hamiltonian era of Seymour is ending and the Jeffersonian age of Griswold" was about to begin.[7]

Despite this postelection acclaim, he was the darkest of horses as a candidate for the post, not even in *Who's Who*, and the maneuvering over ten months to elect him involved significant jostling among members of the Yale Corporation, in which at the start he had only four supporters in a group of seventeen. Politics—senior society and national—played a part, as they had in choosing outsider James Rowland Angell in 1922 as Hadley's successor. Although Griswold was a Wolf's Head alumnus, his champion here and longtime friend was Dean Acheson, a Keysman of 1915, elected to Yale's governing body as a Successor Trustee in 1936, and currently secretary of state for President Harry Truman, Democrat.

The opponent was Senator Robert A. Taft of Ohio, a Bonesman of 1910, elected to the Corporation as an Alumni Fellow in the same year as Acheson's appointment by his fellow successor trustees, and then the most probable Republican Party nominee for president in 1952. Acheson believed Seymour's conservatism had too long perpetuated the composition of a traditional Yale undergraduate body, which was not as intellectually gifted or oriented as it should be (Acheson's commitment to excellence at Yale was said by his biographer to be in part "a reproach to his own extravagant undergraduate days," which of course had helped elect him to Scroll and Key).

Taft saw in Griswold a potential ally of Acheson, and is thought to have distrusted the candidate's lack of reverence for established ways of doing things. Acheson then recruited his fellow Keysman and corporation member Wilmarth Lewis, a full-time rare book and manuscript collector, to play the role of impractical armchair intellectual in nominating Robert M. Hutchins. A member of Wolf's Head in 1921 and a former dean of Yale Law School, Hutchins was then president of the University of Chicago, championing the "Great Books" program of education. Taft, as expected by the coconspirators, was horrified at the prospect, and listened carefully when Acheson in a trustees' meeting indicated qualified support for Hutchins while—seemingly still on the fence—making a speech urging a more mainstream educator, someone like Whit Griswold. Acheson then privately indicated to Taft that if Griswold were not accepted by the Corporation, Acheson would see merit in Lewis's advocacy of Hutchins. The senator, his fear winning out over his distaste, duly joined in the election of the young Yale professor. Discomfited at having advocated a straw man, Lewis reminded Acheson for years after that the political debt would not be easily expunged. Acheson came to love Griswold, and on the afternoon the president died of cancer in 1963, the older man sat at his bedside and, when talk tired him, held his hand.[8]

The *Time* cover article on Griswold noted that "Campus anthropologists like to divide Yale men into 'White Shoes,' 'Brown Shoes,' and 'Black Shoes.'" The "white shoe," made of costly buckskin, had been developed by the Isaacs family of New Haven who owned the campus shoe emporium, Barrie, Ltd., and the phrase came to mean generally "stylishly Ivy League." *Time* explained: "The White Shoes come from the proper families and the proper prep schools; their weekend dress, almost like a uniform, is a button-down shirt, striped tie and Brooks Bros. suit. The Black Shoes are apt to be on scholarship (one-third of all Yale students are), working their way through college. The Brown Shoes are somewhere in between." Their markers of success were membership in "such 'Row Fraternities' as Zeta Psi, the Fence Club, or Delta Kappa Epsilon," and then, "far above these" the six senior societies. As an undergraduate, the magazine reported, Griswold "happily turned down Bones in favor of Wolf's Head." Even as a graduate student, as noted by a leading historian of modern Yale, Griswold continued to lead "the conventional and convivial life of the old boy, singing and drinking with other congenial preppies—many of them, like Griswold, members of Wolf's Head."[9]

Still, Griswold recalled for *Newsweek* that, graduating just five months before the October 1929 stock market crash, "Ours was probably the last class in history to leave New Haven on a magic carpet. Everyone since 1929 has taken the day coach." Even before becoming president, as his champions who helped him to that post knew, he campaigned with his allies on the Yale Corporation and in the faculty to emphasize scholarship over the non-academic, extracurricular activities for which Yale was better known, and which Griswold often privately deprecated as "that Dink Stover crap" and "Bonesy bullshit."

He was said to envy the more academic culture and respect for intellectual achievement which characterized Harvard after World War II, and frankly sought to emulate it.[10] This was not related to the quality of the Yale faculty, which in 1946 under Seymour ranked first in the land, according to the American Association of Universities. In his report to the alumni for the 1954–55 academic year, Griswold argued that "Yale College is not confronted, and never has been, with a categorical choice between curricular and extracurricular activities . . . [T]he extracurricular contributes both life and meaning to the curricular. What is at issue is a sense of proportion, which is always at issue in institutional as well as in private life and is next to impossible to define in rules and regulations."[11]

TAP DAY REFORMS

The annual distress caused by holding elections in an open college courtyard where spectators could see not only the winners in the process, but the losers at their moment of disappointment and humiliation, was finally to be halted in this decade.

As far back as 1947, Yale College Dean William Clyde DeVane, a man of persistence, careful planning, and compromise (but not a society member in his class of 1920, into which he had transferred from Furman University in the midst of World War I), had written out and distributed "Suggestions to the Senior Societies upon the conduct of elections." He advocated that the electors "wear ordinary street clothes and not the customary suits of black," and that offers of election be accompanied by speaking the name of the tapper's society. He suggested that the "resounding thump on the back" be discontinued in favor of a touch on the arm. To stop the running through the streets back to the respective tombs, those so chosen were to be invited back from the courtyard to a suite in Branford College, an election headquarters for the society in question, to conclude negotiations. The desired ends were privacy for the junior class members and the societies, and orderly and expeditious elections. The societies accepted the offer of election headquarters suites, maps for which were thereafter printed in the *Yale Daily News* on Tap Day, but most of the rest of the DeVane calls for reform fell on deaf ears.

Bill Buckley's *News* editorial page before Tap Day in 1949 had advocated elections being delivered in the juniors' rooms, together with a list of all societies tendering invitations to the individual. An "Open Letter" to the newspaper the following spring, "endorsed by 25 members of the class of 1951," cited Buckley's editorial and his apparent conversion, after his own election to Bones, to tolerating the continuation of what his editorial had styled "a fantastic crudity in the system," which the writers accused Skull and Bones in particular of perpetuating.

"In so far as the 'golden twenties' are passed," Buckley had argued, "and undergraduates have become more critical (or at least more cynical) about such institutions," the societies were only hurting themselves, "as well as the 'out-group,' by pursuing a brutish policy which—before a gaping crowd—submerges the individual to an institution about which he is almost completely ignorant. Why, we ask, aren't elections offered in the rooms?" A contemporaneous editorial, remarking that "this is the season of the Annual Howl Against Tap Day in Branford Court," supplied a flip answer: "if the Howlers can figure out a way to squelch everyone's natural desire to see who goes where, they may have a leg on establishing the room Tap. . . . The whole affair is pretty much like a theatrical performance. If you don't like it, you don't have to attend; but the producer may reserve the right to run it his own way."[12]

The May 1950 election went forward in the usual manner, but unusually heralded by a *News* cartoon showing a tweed-coated junior pondering a pyramid with men scrambling up its side, labeled "Athletics" and "Fraternities" and "Comps" (competitions), toward the word "Heaven" above, overarching the badges of Keys, Bones, and Wolf's Head. The same issue featured the "Tap Day Stations" map, locating them around Branford Court, with Keys and Book and Snake on the second floor of the Jonathan Edwards side of the Branford College main courtyard, Bones on the second floor of the Saybrook side, Wolf's Head on the first floor in the range next to Harkness Tower, and Elihu on the third floor and Berzelius on the second floor of the High Street wing. That day's *News* editorial, lamenting that "no positive, early drive moved elections to the rooms," urged juniors elected that day to "enter these sacrosanct organizations with the unshakeable purpose of liberalizing them."

The following day the *News* broke its own seven-decade tradition of never reporting more than the names of those elected, running a detailed article on the colorful events and atmosphere of the ceremony, titled "Senior Societies Tap 90 in Tense Ceremony; Grey-Flanneled Members Finish Annual Elections in 28-Minute Procedure" (DeVane's objection to black suits had prevailed). Approximately three hundred juniors entered the Branford College courtyard en masse, some eating Good Humor ice cream bars. Before that, both Elihu and Scroll and Key marched in, two abreast, and they and all other non-tapping society members took up their observation posts in the open-windowed rooms above surrounding the courtyard; Bonesmen were seen using opera glasses.

The chimes ringing at 5:00 P.M. were followed by the heavy strikes on the shoulders disfavored by Dean DeVane—although, as he had bidden, the electing seniors were now pronouncing their societies' names with their offers. One man, who received two taps simultaneously, fell over backward. Applause accompanied some choices, and the juniors who accepted bids followed the seniors on the run to the upstairs election headquarters. At 5:09 P.M., Berzelius slammed its college headquarters windows shut, signifying its final tap, followed by Keys and then Elihu. The only humorous relief to the day was when someone slammed a window situated *between* the room suite stations of Keys and Book and Snake.[13]

The 1951 *News* editorial pushed back a bit on those who clamored for the elections to be held in the students' rooms, noting that the in-the-rooms system had been tried twice before, and that traditional Tap Day had been restored thereafter. Electing in rooms took too long, two or three hours, and juniors waiting alone there experienced a different form of misery than the misery which loved company in the courtyard. The process was inefficient, requiring "immensely complex" book-keeping. "Exhibitionalism" was if anything increased, with ninety seniors racing from college to college in the late afternoon, and competition between societies "developed into a question of who could run fastest from Timothy Dwight to Pierson," the two residential colleges farthest apart, at the eastern and western borders of the college. Still, the editorial called for "the presentation of all bids at the same time, as the fraternities and Honor societies do now so successfully." The May 1951 election in Branford Court, although marred by a stink bomb ("the only comic relief of the afternoon") was finished in twenty-eight minutes—one man received five slaps at once—with the final spectators to leave lingering to see who was going to be the last man tapped for Bones.[14]

The reformers would not be silenced, and Dean DeVane remained persistent in pressing the societies for further change, although his son had been tapped the old way, in Branford Court in 1949, turning down Bones for Berzelius. As Tap Day for 1952 approached, the *News* published a number of hostile columns and letters, beginning with a long letter published in two parts titled "The Case against the Senior Societies" from the class of 1953's Robert Weinberg. He found the societies' claims of self-improvement to be unverifiable and their role in rewarding "Success" to pervert the university's educational role; he deplored the fact that much of the Yale administration and almost the entire Yale Corporation were alumni, "likely, in all sincerity, to guide University life, faculty promotions, admissions policy, etc., according to the basically anti-democratic Society principles."

Relying on a statistical analysis of society membership published in the *News* the year before, Weinberg argued that the ninety men tapped fell into two broad categories, "those generally recognized as leaders in extracurricular (or, occasionally, curricular) life; and those who have 'social suction,'" which was the "special province" of Book and Snake and Wolf's Head, "not open to non-fraternity men or high school graduates" and with a strong preference for "men who rank scholastically around the lower third of the class. The other four (particularly Bones) are more willing to overlook 'proletarian' social backgrounds and choose recognized 'campus successes.'" Seventy-five of the ninety were fraternity members, and eighty from prep schools, thirty-five of those from Andover, Hotchkiss, or St. Paul's. The residential college residencies were also measurable: Branford, Calhoun, and Davenport had large pluralities of society men, 62 percent of the entire society membership. "In short (and recognizing of course many individual exceptions)," he concluded, "the *Society* ideal approximates the pattern: Greenwich-born, Andover-nourished, and Bones-tapped."

Since those who were often initially critical of the societies, such as the last three *News* chairmen, were following their elections unwilling or unable to effect reform from within, Weinberg argued, the "Program for Revolt" had to come from without. He advocated that the present and future junior classes "1. Show up at Tap Day and raise hell; 2. Demand that the University cease to sponsor Tap Day and to issue the invitations to it; 3. Give no publicity whatsoever to those who join," and finally, sign an advance pledge refusing to join a society if tapped, providing a majority of classmates will pledge likewise. Weinberg, a fellow junior, and two seniors then held a forum on the society system over WYBC, the campus radio station.[15]

At the administration level, Dean Devane delayed his customary announcement of Tap Day in the hope that some alternative method of election could be agreed upon; this was in response to a proposal from fifteen juniors, demanding Tap Day's abolition and requiring interested class members and the six societies each to submit preferential lists to the dean, on the basis of which elections to societies would be determined. When no reforms could be agreed upon, DeVane posted the customary election date notice in the *News*, but announcing that he would study alternative plans over the summer to devise something new for 1953. The barrage of general criticism seems, on Tap Day in 1952, to have resulted in the largest number of rebuffs to date: three for Bones, ten for Keys, eleven for Berzelius, two for Book and Snake, nine for Wolf's Head, and five for Elihu, although many of these refusers joined other societies.[16]

In October 1952, DeVane wrote to the societies enclosing a revised plan for elections, based on one suggested to the societies many years before by Yale Corporation member Irwin S. Olds, an Elihu alumnus from 1907. (This was not printed in the *Yale Daily News* for general perusal until after it had been rejected by the senior societies and the elections for spring 1953 had occurred). The committee formed by the societies to respond noted that historically the procedure (election in the Old Campus courtyard) was started by the juniors for their own convenience. Moreover, it was open and rapid, concealed the identity of substitutes, and provided flexibility of choice for both the elected class and the electors, so the former knew immediately who had been elected and what places were left, with freedom to choose until the last moment. The Tap Day procedure, the societies noted, although hedged round by Branford Court, had been "built up by the non–society public, and is certainly repugnant to the societies, while allowing opportunity for public, pre-meditated demonstrations and disorder."

The "Olds Plan" envisioned an elaborate system of cards or lists submitted to the college dean's office, one from every junior ranking the senior societies in which membership was sought, and a second set from the societies setting forth their first fifteen choices and the names of alternates. The dean was to treat the lists confidentially, but to make matches of junior applicants with society preferences. An inter-society graduate council would preside, in the case of conflicts, over the final allocation of juniors. The *News* in an editorial added more notions to the proposal, asking that the six societies issue a common statement of purpose and concern, justifying the reasons for their existence, to be published in the newspaper or separately, and said that the statement should contain the names of respected faculty, society members in their senior years, who had been counseling candidates in the past but should now be made known to the student body in general. A contemporaneous interview with President Griswold made it clear that he believed any reform of Tap Day had to come from the undergraduates—"The administration has no policy"—and noted wryly that abolition of the societies was impossible: "You just can't get rid of yucca plants and senior societies."[17]

To this DeVane-revived scheme, the societies' committee's objections were manifold: no assurance that all juniors would submit lists, no flexibility after list submission, no certainty that a junior assigned to a society would then accept its offer, revelation (albeit to a restricted group) of alternates, and the general risk of mechanical failures within a complicated system. Meanwhile, the formalized inter-society organization required by the Olds Plan "would by its very existence give the impression of a sanctified group formally drawing the caste line of distinction between the chosen and the rejected." Furthermore, formal inter-society cooperation invited the danger of inter-society recrimination, from which the Yale senior societies—unlike fraternities at Yale and in other American universities—were historically "remarkably free." The letter's enumerated virtues of the historical system would not be met by the Olds

Plan. Still, the opportunity to discuss with the dean "those externals of Tap Day which may be looked upon as offensive" was welcomed by the committee, although they rejected his second alternative as well, which called for election in the rooms in "shifts," with first round choices given to juniors desired by more than one society.[18]

Presumably not coordinated in advance with the six tomb-housed "aboveground" societies was a charm offensive by their truly secret, not-recognized-by-the-university society brethren, known as "undergrounds": an open letter to the class of 1954, produced by underground society members Hamilton Harper and Philip Grover of the class of 1953, to "aid the individual in making a rational judgment on the Senior Society system." "Senior Societies," they wrote, "are groups of men elected to membership in organizations which primarily seek the broadening of the individual member's character through intimate personal contact and group criticism," and the university "openly recognizes six." These authors had not been elected to any of any of the six "aboveground" senior societies with tombs, but were members of what a *News* editorial had recently styled "at least five other units operating sub rosa" which "every junior should know."

Messrs. Harper and Grover wrote candidly of "a number of underground societies of a similar nature [to the tomb-owning six] which meet in owned or rented buildings or rooms also near the campus. These societies vary widely in ultimate purpose, some existing as an alternative to recognized groups, some seeking to gain official recognition and equal footing with the recognized six, and some paying no attention to the Yale society system, but rather pursuing their own intellectual and personal ends." They argued that any of such societies would "provide the fraternal spirit lacking elsewhere at Yale," obtaining its "close bond between members by intimate personal contact through meetings and social activities." Besides what the societies offered members, they also described the loyalty and time commitment that was demanded in return, with requirement for biweekly meeting attendance, and the function of Tap Day for the recognized societies: "the other societies select their members by personal contact at another time."[19]

The six recognized societies then met in the house of Saybrook College Master Basil Henning (class of 1932, a member of Wolf's Head); thereafter Carlos Stoddard, executive secretary of the University Council (class of 1926, a member of Keys) wrote for Keys to the representatives of the other five. He noted that agitation on campus and in the pages of the *News* against Tap Day in its historical form continued to increase, as evidenced by the Undergraduate Affairs Committee's determination that the societies undertake reform, and the presentation of another reform plan presented to the dean by one of the "sub rosa" groups, part of whose appeal was that they did *not* participate in the Branford Court ritual. "In the minds of most undergraduates—perhaps it is in keeping with the times in which we live—there is less and less blind faith in antiquity," wrote Stoddard, "and there is more and more demand for consideration as rational, 'old-young' men upon whose shoulders life has descended pretty squarely and heavily." The current system left "too little room for the expression of their own wishes," and so he urged the adoption of the Olds Plan for the current year.[20]

Further negotiations among the six produced a much reduced version of the Olds Plan, which featured notification to the juniors that those interested in being elected should plan to be in their rooms between 8:00 and 11:00 P.M. on the scheduled day, to be announced in the *News*, or leave word where they would be. No exchange of lists, declaring the candidates' ranked desires and, from the societies, setting forth their preferred juniors, featured in this plan. Each society would offer elections in the manner they respectively saw fit, in person or by written message. The names and addresses of those accepting elections would be published in the campus newspaper on the following day, based on lists submitted by the societies.

Coordination was to come through telephones on the university exchange, in or near the office of University Development in Vanderbilt Hall, where graduate representatives would receive word of completed elections and refusals, and then communicate that information back to the undergraduate groups in their tombs running the elections. It was suggested that no elections be offered between 8:10 and 8:45 P.M., so that information on the initial choices could be accurately and completely exchanged, and society members were urged to avoid ostentation in dress or manner when seeking out their candidates. This agreement was to apply only to the 1953 elections, in a compromise of conflicting opinions, and none were deemed waived as to the coming years.[21]

Dean DeVane grasped the stunted olive branch that had at last been offered (only two societies had supported his plan, two refused it in its entirety, and two said they would abide by a majority decision that never occurred). The societies had finally agreed that there would be no public event, but nothing else had been settled with the administration, other than that Tap Day should be succeeded by "a more civilized form of election," as the dean said. Reporting the stalemate and rather misreading the situation, the *New York Times* noted portentously that "unless a solution is reached by the end of the school year, the societies will be without members next year and societies' buildings will be without occupants."[22]

Forcing the pace, DeVane set Tuesday, May 5, for the offering of elections in students' rooms that evening between 8:00 and 10:30 P.M. The *News* predicted "with almost absolute certainty that this year's tapping in rooms will be unsuccessful." The nation's newspapers and weekly magazines ran articles, many mentioning Dink Stover, on the "death" of Tap Day, *Time* magazine's beginning: "In every Yale man's life, there has been one traumatic experience that other people do not have."[23] The day before the elections, the college newspaper published an analysis of the elected in the class of 1953, finding, unsurprisingly, that "Societies Favor Fraternity Men, Athletes, Organization Leaders," while noting that about 75 percent of all members came from prep schools, and 31 percent hailed from within a 50-mile radius of New York City.[24]

On the day, the candidates as instructed stayed in their residential college rooms, and a central clearing committee composed of two or three graduate members of each of the six societies, hearing from their respective undergraduate delegations searching out their candidates, notified the campus radio station WYBC of the final results. Denying two forms of information always published with the lists in the past, the societies did not make available to the campus radio station or newspaper the names of either their refusals or their electors. As predicted, some confusion on both sides did result (Berzelius was said to have made sixteen accepted offers, and another society was reported to have suffered seventeen refusals), with elections not completed until 9:12 P.M. Not predicted, only one society wore the gray flannels and black tie characteristic of Tap Day in previous years, the others finally acceding to the dean's suggestion of "street clothes" for tapping attire.[25]

REVELATIONS

A class historian in this decade wrote in his yearbook that "People in houses without any windows don't give a damn about stones," but the societies were being knocked back on their collective heels, not only about their election methods, but about the more fundamental question of their value and function. The now annual springtime attacks in the *Yale Daily News*—which in 1954 announced that it would no longer publish the names of those tapped[26]—required some reaction beyond stubborn silence. By the mid-fifties, that response began to be made in an unprecedented way, using the student newspaper as a platform, by guarded but candid revelations about what went on behind the iron doors, to the extent that such information was not already known (if not openly discussed). The *News* had flatly stated in a May 1950 editorial "That some are dedicated to the proposition of the congenial group and some to the concept of heterogeneous benefit, that some are mainly social and others attempt to build character should be common knowledge for the consumption of anybody who cares."

The open letter to the class of 1954 by Messrs. Harper and Grover was quoted extensively in the *News* by its editors in April 1955, in a piece titled, "Senior Societies: A Critical Evaluation." Beyond those excerpts, this analysis was "based upon several months of discussions with faculty and members, past and present, of Yale societies," and was intended "to enlighten juniors who may be tapped this May 5, to dispel many of the myths that have grown up around the societies, and to suggest areas in which the societies themselves might improve their relationship to the Yale community." Skull and Bones, it reported, "does not guarantee its members a $10,000 a year salary, nor do students benefit financially from the societies (except for dues which are granted to bursary students on the same basis as the fraternities)." Being "shoe" was not the essential qualification for admission," because "with possibly one exception [meaning Bones], societies choose their members primarily on the basis of diversity rather than the criterion—'outstanding.'"

And because of personal choice and the "rather anarchic system of election," many outstanding members of each class did not enter the societies, so they were no longer the criterion for success that they had been until the 1930s. Their main purpose was to develop their individual members, through requiring the "presentation of individual biographies, one per week during the first 15 weeks of the fall, for comment and criticism by their fellow members . . . During this psychoanalytic experience the member often enjoys an emotional and intellectual rebirth which is recognized by most psychologists as a normal stage in the development of the individual from adolescence to maturity (or selfhood)." Most of the societies, the report continued, also offered some sort of intellectual program that in some cases involved faculty participation, and "in all," the presentation of reports by individual society members "on topics of an intellectual nature or pertaining to the Yale scene."

Following this description, the editors made recommendations to the senior societies themselves. They should make more clear that intellect and character were membership determinants, by individual discussions or outreach programs; the "pretapping," which included a brief discussion of a particular group's program and ideals, "should be made a universal practice. (It probably will be anyway as soon as the alumni of what used to be Yale's top society awaken to the fact that is has become 'second rate' through its strict adherence to outworn procedures and ideals.)" Bones was being damned here for no longer leading, in preferring demonstrated achievement to diversity. Furthermore, the article maintained, the societies should lessen their insistence on demanding "priority over all other interests and obligations of the member," because that hurt "the maturity and leadership of the campus as a whole." An addendum for the juniors followed the next day, noting that all of the recognized societies and most of the more secretive underground societies required a minimum attendance of at least two nights a week, on Thursdays and Sundays, from 7:00 to midnight"; that at least one of the abovegrounds and several of the undergrounds no longer practiced the "psychoanalytic sessions"; and at least one of the undergrounds required a biography but only for purposes of getting acquainted.

Still another editorial ran the following day, suggesting to the juniors not tapped that week that they should not "head for either the nearest window or bar," in recognition that there were other opportunities and values in Yale's rich extracurricular life which did not require society membership, and that "the tombs have no priority on friendship." This point was remade in an editorial after Tap Day, saying that "the 105 juniors who entered recognized senior societies and countless others who joined underground societies have at long last discovered the big secret . . . that there just aren't any real secrets at all," and that they might have gained little more by entry therein than might, "have been accomplished by a little honesty and the sincere attempt to make friends and participate actively in University life." The 1955 *News* board claimed that its editorials had met with "sudden and unanimous agreement of the public," and called on "Skull and Bones, the Commons Icehouse [Book & Snake], the Woodbridge Hall Outhouse [Scroll & Key], etc., to drop their sinister activities and abnormal practices and start doing Good."[27]

The subsequent year's *News* board took a different tack, announcing in spring 1956 that there would be no campaign against the societies, "either by angry editorials or completely ignoring the elections," and it would not consider them as "an issue" but simply publish results "in the same form as any other elections." Still, the editors could not help themselves on the subject and ran, for the new juniors' benefit, "three or four articles which we consider representative and well-informed sources," beginning with an evaluation by Dean DeVane. He found that "our whole American society seems to be in collusion to place its final accent on the preparation of the student to meet the external trials and challenges of American life," and that there was no doubt that "the individual profits by membership in such a group." (As a student after World War I, DeVane had shared a writing course with Stephen Vincent Benét, Archibald MacLeish, Henry Luce, Briton Hadden, and Wilmarth Lewis, senior society members all.) Still, the societies needed, more than ever before, "to justify their existence in the community which harbors them—not to their members, nor in terms of exclusiveness, but rather in terms of the wholesome and corrective effect which they might have on the climate of opinion of the student body."

The succeeding piece, "A Member's Description," was by Edward Kent, a current member of Scroll and Key delegation, who claimed openly that there were "no great society mysteries," no financial benefits, and no society was boasting that it was electing a "supposed Yale elite." "A student is elected to membership in a society," he wrote, "on two main criteria: 1) some one from the previous year's membership must be acquainted with him, and 2) he is adjudged to be especially qualified by his predecessors in some area of knowledge or activity from which he can contribute to his fellow members." Kent confirmed that debating, public speaking, and writing were activities common to all societies, and in some an autobiography for group analysis. "Potential antagonisms (e.g., shoe vs. non-shoe, scholar vs. athlete) tend to be broken down as the members find grounds for communication." For that reason, all societies needed to retain their privacy, because only within small, private groups could such "forthright discussion" take place. Here at last was stated plainly, for the first time in a Yale student publication, what many had known and others might have discerned.[28]

The *News* board did not remain uniformly high-minded, under the leadership of Calvin Trillin '57, later the noted humorist for the satirical periodical *Monocle* and then the *New Yorker* magazine. In the issue of

April 29, a sort of April Fool's issue printed in red ink, the entire last page was a mock advertisement, picturing the Bones tomb, with the running head "Central Real Estate for Sale." Interested parties were invited to contact "S Pook 322" for an appointment, to see something "attractively furnished in traditional early Gothic style, bedrooms, living rooms, study and children's athletic facilities." The following Thursday, Trillin, a public high school graduate from Kansas City, having become the first Jew to be chairman of the *Yale Daily News*, was elected to Scroll and Key.[29]

The Jewish managing editor of the *News* the next year, Larry Bensky, had a rougher passage to senior society membership. The fifteen seniors in Wolf's Head voted unanimously to tap him, but that society's election system required review of prospective members by an alumni committee, and Bensky's nomination was rejected on the grounds of precedent: Wolf's Head had never previously admitted a Jew. The undergraduates, including future dean of admissions and university secretary Henry Chauncey Jr., pushed back, saying Bensky's faith was not a factor in their decision to elect and should be irrelevant to the alumni; if he was not admitted, their delegation would resign in a bloc. Faced with this ultimatum, the graduate body reversed course, and Bensky was elected. He had another offer, however, from Berzelius, and chose to accept it. Two years later, Lewis Lehrman '60, the New York Republican gubernatorial candidate twenty-two years later, became the first Jewish member of Wolf's Head, to be followed by the class of 1962's Eli Newberger, the undergraduate president of Hillel.[30]

Trillin, before graduating himself in 1957, wrote a *News* column for the rising juniors, "with the assistance of individual members of several societies," quoting a one-off publication that had appeared the prior autumn, *Inside Eli*, written by two members of the class of 1955, Henry S. F. Cooper and David Calleo. This pamphlet repeated what was no longer a revelation: "All societies are essentially a group of fifteen seniors brought together for several hours a week. Each has a different program. Some are particularly concerned with autobiography, self-analysis, self-improvement, and other forms of psychic plumbing. Others place greater emphasis on the less earnest joys of fraternal conviviality, while some are interested in intellectual stimulation." Trillin's column warned: "ANY JUNIOR WHO GOES INTO TAP DAY ARMED ONLY WITH A HURRIED READING OF DINK STOVER OR THE PROPAGANDA OF ONE SOCIETY IS CONSIDERABLY LACKING IN COMMON SENSE." He was to write much later that he had applied to Yale at the urging of his father, because the old man had read *Stover at Yale* and thought his son thereby "would have an even start with the sons of the country's most powerful industrialists . . . and after that it was up to me."[31]

The helpful or humorous tone displayed in these publications was not echoed in other forums. The campus radio station WYBC held a tape-recorded symposium, where the societies were derided by André Schiffrin '57, the president of the Aurelian Honor Society, who dismissed them as unimportant, with ridiculous trappings, as he had done in his *News* column, and philosophy professor Paul Weiss, who found them "the haven of men who are somewhat maladjusted, who huddle together for mutual protection, and who devote themselves to activities . . . which in principle are opposed to the whole idea of the college plan, which is that every man admitted to Yale is qualified to meet with everyone else coming from a wide variety of backgrounds." Both critics were transplanted Europeans in New Haven with little patience for this Yale tradition, which Weiss called on the administration to ban.

Dean DeVane in rebuttal noted that the university had no right to interfere with the "inalienable" right of students to form groups or societies of friends, and while he could wish that Yale men formed "more natural groups," the secret societies were "of long standing, of great weight, of a good deal of power." His side was supported by Richard Arnold, a senior and member of Elihu, who declared circumspectly that "the simple fact is that through the mere having of a place where no one else can come and through the doing of certain things which may appear pointless to people on the outside . . . a loyalty and cohesion is produced among the members of the group."[32]

On Tap Day, Schiffrin and like-minded juniors pretended that the day was meant to center on an annual tiddlywinks tournament, which they ostentatiously mounted on the steps of the University Library, calmly playing while seniors crossed the campus seeking the rooms of the juniors whom they wished to elect. The *News* ran a front-page photograph of the mock tournament, under a headline jokingly asking Schiffrin if he had gone mad. As it happened, he was to recall in his memoirs, Skull and Bones, "the most prestigious and notorious of the groups," offered the dissenter an election, which the society had historically done for many of its harshest critics, but since his "campaign against the societies had not been meant as a subtle way of asking to join . . . I refused the invitation."[33]

UNDERGROUNDS

The *Inside Eli* pamphlet to which Trillin referred devoted a short but entire chapter to "The Societies." Its authors were members of the newest of the "above-grounds," called Manuscript. Its members had written a letter published in the *News* just before elections back in 1955, saying that they would make public the names of those members of the junior class whom it then elected to membership. "The society was founded several years ago, in recognition of a need for an organization devoted to the furtherance of creative activities in the humanities at Yale." Until the Society was firmly established, "it was felt that its 'secret' status should be maintained," but the group's enthusiastic reception now indicated that "the *sub rosa* status" was not only unnecessary but undesirable, because Manuscript was providing "a singular opportunity for the presentation and discussion of creative work and critical points of view in many fields." An editorial in the *News* had used that very status characterization, holding that "the Societies' greatest misdemeanor springs ironically from the attitude of the 'outgroup' in holding the tombs as a sacred, secret sine qua non. That attitude reflects in the upspringing of the *societus spurius*, or sub rosa society—spawned out of some anxiety that nothing healthy can be conducted at Yale where the windows aren't cemented in."[34]

The *Inside Eli* writers confirmed the continuing importance of the system on campus: "election to a senior society confirms the successful undergraduate career." Practically all societies, they reported, "pre-tapped," a process which varied from "an inexplicable invitation to cocktails to a full scale brainwashing by earnest alumni," a strategy compelled because many men were sought by more than one society. An approach on Tap Day could occur without being pre-tapped, not a matter of disgrace, but rather an honor, "since only dull and obvious types are generally among the first fifteen." Commitments before election could be troublesome to freedom of choice on the day. "Above all, don't get excited. Gamesmanship is a great weapon."

Befitting their editorial salute to the *Harkness Hoot*—the pamphlet is claimed to be published by "The Yale Society for the Occasional Resuscitation of the *Harkness Hoot*"—they roughly teased all the abovegrounds in their serial descriptions. Skull and Bones was like the Harkness Tower: "Though it is absurd, we love it." Still the "stamp of greatness seems lost," and it was said that "in certain quarters it is no longer *shoe* to belong . . . especially if your father was a member." Wolf's Head was said to be "the home of all those jocks who are still capable of going in training," while Book and Snake was for those who "have received most of your education from a fraternity bar."

While Berzelius and Elihu were "respectable organizations," the former was "somewhat addicted to moral earnestness and has a strong low-church smell to it," while "Elihu is somewhat more intellectually oriented . . . if not violently exciting." Both "conduct an extremely energetic pre-tapping campaign," thus seeming overeager. Scroll and Key "is probably the leading society in the eyes of the average Yale man," although "a little like an exclusive yacht-club." As for the newly fledged Manuscript (their own membership was not disclosed), it "is the most frankly intellectual of all societies . . . a formidable collection of snobbishly shoe intellectuals, bright good guys, and an occasional grubby guy who writes good poetry (or at least tries to)."

And then, they reported, "there is a varying number of SECRET-SECRET or UNDERGROUND SOCIETIES," groups of fifteen whose existence was known (supposedly) only to themselves. Some had been going for several years, and others sprang into being and disappeared after two or three classes; none of them possessed extensive physical facilities. While not named in the pamphlet, these included a revived Spade and Grave, and others named Sword and Gate, Mace and Chain, Ring and Candle, and Demos. "The value of membership depends mostly on the other people who happen to be in the group your years."[35] As a *News* columnist had said in 1955, the year of this pamphlet's authors' graduation, "the undergrounds had, of necessity, to copy much of the system which they were designed to moderate."[36]

What seems to have been the first, Sword and Gate, was founded by fourteen men in the class of 1947, with four others from earlier classes, taking their society name from a passage in John Milton's *Paradise Lost*. "The Gate," their charter recited, was "to represent Yale University which is the gateway to the attainment of wisdom for which we shall strive throughout our lives; and the Sword to represent devotion to the principles we shall seek to forward." Reflecting their experience and convictions as veterans, the founders pledged their succeeding members, in future not to exceed fifteen, would "not be selected from any one field of activity or social class, but shall reflect every phase of life in our University and in our Country." The society would "strive to promote everywhere, through the word, thought, and deed of its members, a devotion to the ideal of wisdom, moral fortitude, tolerance, and the international sincerity so fundamental to a world at peace."[37]

James Ketchum, a senior in the class, first approached Yale president Charles Seymour with the notion for a new society, which would be Yale's seventh, and Seymour (a Bonesman) agreed to personally approach the "Ancient Six" about adding another society. The existing groups resisted fiercely, but Seymour still advised Ketchum to proceed. Sword and Gate then petitioned the Undergraduate Activities Council to be allowed to go on campus and offer elections with the abovegrounds. The society was warned that, because of its obscurity, attracting members would be very difficult, and that it might do better to copy Elihu's tactics in 1904, announcing as a non-secret organization and waiting until after Tap Day to choose members. Then, when they were better known, they might petition the council again. Sword and Gate chose to remain underground, and in 1949, tapped Horace Taft, son of Ohio Senator Robert Taft, after the young man on Tap Day declined an election to Keys, his heart's desire, on his Bonesman father's direction, but in the end was passed over by Bones. Later members include Henry Luce Jr., son of the *Time* magazine founder; novelist John Knowles; and the former NBC president Brandon Tartikoff.[38]

Spade and Grave, the "society of 1864," had of course been a known secret society at its founding that year in the mid-nineteenth-century controversy with Bones over the *Lit.*, and was revived in 1951 by John Curtis Perry (later professor of history at Tufts and founder of the Institute for Global Maritime Studies) and his roommate Ronald Mitchell, aided by Robert Dresser, all class of 1952 and residents of Berkeley College. Perry was inspired by that society's history as told by Lyman Bagg in *Four Years at Yale*. Six of their first eleven members were from Berkeley, who to make up their fifteen added four men who were actually juniors chosen three or four months before April 1952's Tap Day (providing continuity into 1953), including Edwin Meese III, later President Reagan's attorney general. Their delegation in 1959 included Dick Celeste, Rhodes scholar and then successively U.S. congressman, governor of Ohio, director of the Peace Corps, and ambassador to India.[39]

The undergrounds had been formed, according to another column written by members of two of them in 1957, after World War II, "either spontaneously or from within an above-ground society," and thereby made the benefits of the senior society institution available to more people, while their "anonymity was a protest against certain abuses which the public nature of the established societies had brought about." A *News* column by another underground member the following year stated more simply, without citing a year, or a group name: "The first under-ground society was conceived by a group of men who felt that the number of then existing societies was insufficient and that qualified students were denied the opportunity of this unusual experience because of the simple fact of numbers." The undergounds' practices of withholding the names of members and refusing to acknowledge a society name and a continuous existence simply removed from discussion both the reputation of the society as a whole and the public attention on its membership. There were, it was said, virtually no alumni controls or rigid demands of tradition, and ritual was reduced "to a moderate (often negligible) expression of group identity and continuity."

The authors warned that "most below-grounds expect a commitment on or before Tap Day," and so were not to be considered as second-best alternatives to the established societies. Their actual workings were too varied for fair generalization: some, it was admitted, were similar to the abovegrounds, but others let each delegation choose exactly what it wanted to do at each meeting. "This may vary from a deeply personal and autobiographical approach to objective intellectual discussions, either oriented toward one field of interest or on different subjects according to the nature of the membership." Some were completely social, and others, like their landed brethren, had faculty advisors and even invited valued strangers, not in the underground's membership, to lead discussions. The question of whether such groups were planning "on going above-ground" was a misunderstanding of their fundamental purpose, to incorporate the senior society system's most beneficial aspects while omitting its abuses.[40]

A member of an underground in the class of 1960 has written that he was cautioned on joining that its "existence, name and membership were secret," and directed to dress, according to his invitation, in "dark suit, white shirt, black tie, and dark shoes." Meeting like their tomb-housed brethren twice weekly on Thursdays and Sundays, these men enjoyed once-weekly meals prepared and served by a chef in training for the Culinary Institute of America, then located in New Haven. This club's composition was not unlike the larger class of 1960: one athlete, one fraternity member, a married man, and a number of legacies and graduates of prestigious prep and day schools, but also a black, a Jew, and a number of academic achievers, two men who were raised in Europe and one in Asia, three students committed to pursuing international careers, and three "serious Protestants," one of whom became a Rhodes scholar and had turned down aboveground society offers on principle—the aggregate performing the classic Yale senior society function of introducing "classmates with academic and religious interests I rarely encountered otherwise."[41]

MANUSCRIPT AND ST. ELMO'S

Still, one "underground" had become "landed," as the letter to the *News* from Manuscript's current club proclaimed in 1955. It was founded by a member of the class of 1953, Gilbert Colgate, namesake of his grandfather, a member of Keys in 1883, later president of the family's toothpaste company. Two other Colgates had been in Keys, and his uncle in the class of 1924 had made Wolf's Head, but young Gilbert flunked out of English as a sophomore and lost his hockey team membership in consequence, all of which put paid to his dream of future membership in the existing aboveground societies. He gathered classmates who thought a new society was a fine idea, but they favored one that avoided athletes and political operators in favor of the nation's future novelists, dramatists, journalists, essayists, producers, directors, stage managers, or theatrical, film, or television personalities.

It openly proclaimed this creative/artistic focus, and its name came from the code booksellers used to price books on the flyleaf, where the ten letters of "manuscript" are each assigned a number from 1 to 10 (so, "NS" is $35). Two rooms at 96 College Street were rented above the tobacconist Owl Shop, across from the rooms of another underground, Sword and Gate; on Thursday night, members of the respective societies would pass each other silently. Since another founder lived in Saybrook College, beneath its Wrexham Tower, modeled on the church where Elihu Yale is buried in Wales, the society incorporated as Wrexham Foundation for legal and financial purposes as an educational institution under the laws of Connecticut, documented with tax exempt status by John Ecklund, then a graduate Bonesman at New Haven's leading law firm Wiggin and Dana, and later the treasurer of Yale.

The founding group was split roughly between those who felt they had no chance of election and wanted their own proper senior society, and others more interested in socializing over art, music, and theater. Their program, consequently, was a weekly one of talks or papers on such topics, held on the aboveground society schedule of Thursday nights, each member being responsible for two presentations during the year, and Sunday nights, where faculty fellow Imbre Buffum, a young associate professor of French, began the Manuscript tradition of dining with fine wines. When they decided the group was worth perpetuating, but without announcing their presence, Manuscript's representatives joined the election ceremony in Branford Court for the class of 1954, the club having worked out their list in advance.

In this replication, they had done something, they believed, which was in effect expressing their disdain for the senior societies by the contrary (but very Yale-ish) act of founding one themselves. The graduate membership itself had a tap committee, helping to elect incoming delegations by consensus of the current membership, alumni, and the corporate board, with introductory cocktail parties organized to assess prospects. In 1956, the foundation underwrote a scholarship in the humanities for "a senior who shall be judged to have written the best senior essay in the field of humanities," given in memory of Wallace Notestein, Sterling Professor of History at Yale and another Manuscript faculty fellow, and ther society later created the Quincy Porter Prize in the arts.[42]

Members of Manuscript's earliest delegations included Matthew Bruccoli (a cofounder in 1953), bibliographer of F. Scott Fitzgerald and biographer of that writer and of John O'Hara; Ted Morgan (class of 1954), Pulitzer Prize–winning author and journalist; David Calleo (1955), coauthor of *Inside Eli* and intellectual historian at Johns Hopkins; Henry Geldzahler (1957), Metropolitan Museum curator of American Art and New York City commissioner of culture, whose adult best friends were Andy Warhol and David Hockney; and Richard Rhodes (1959), Pulitzer Prize–winning novelist and historian. Its members in the nineteen-sixties included U.S. Senator H. John Heinz III (1960); David Gergen (1963), author and advisor to four American presidents; and Richard Brodhead (1968), president of Duke University. In the 1980s, its members included Cheryl Henson (1984), puppeteer and president of the Jim Henson Foundation, actress Jodie Foster (1985), screenwriter of the *Skulls* movie trilogy John Pogue (1987), and CNN news anchor Anderson Cooper (1989). Its honorary members from the Yale faculty have included artist Josef Albers, literary critic Cleanth Brooks, and political science professor Robert Dahl.

The society began looking for a different and bigger home in 1955. Unable to secure a residence at 344 Elm, they bought a house at 232 Dwight Street, but in due course sold that property after 344 became available again, and was purchased for all the society's available cash, borrowing through demand notes from members, and a mortgage. In 1961, a capital fund drive was launched when the decision was made to knock down that house and commission a "real" (although in Yale terms unconventional) tomb. For two years, the undergraduate delegations met in various residential college fellows' suites, particularly professor of French Imbrie Buffum's "flat" in Silliman College, or at the houses of honorary members in town.

The result, completed in 1963 on the 344 Elm Street site by Yale associate professor of Architectural Design King-lui Wu, was mid-twentieth-century modern but designed, in his words, "for privacy, not secrecy." Appearing from the outside to have only one street level, the exterior walls of four-inch by four-inch by sixteen-inch concrete blocks with a marble aggregate conceal, beyond an entrance hall which also serves as a gallery for painting and sculpture, multilevel subterranean floors with music room and library, and an interior courtyard, which enclosed a reflecting pool (with goldfish), permitting large areas of opaque glass to bring light and air deep into the building. The floors are of Italian marble, bluestone, and walnut blocks, with cabinetry and furniture and Moroccan rugs manufactured to the architect's specifications. Wu also designed many of the furnishings, and Albers designed the white brickwork intaglio mural which seems to float on the building's wall facing Elm Street.[43]

In his novel *Joe College* (2002), in a passage describing the Halloween party for which Manuscript had become well known, author Tom Perrotta wrote that, "Architecturally speaking, Manuscript was an anomaly at Yale. It had no pretensions to medieval grandeur or even garden-variety academic charm—no ivy climbing, weathered stone walls, no moat, turret, or slate roof. It was a low-slung, unapologetically suburban structure—just a ranch house, really—with a restaurant-quality kitchen, off-white wall-to-wall carpeting, and sliding glass doors that communicated onto a small patio. . . . No one I'd grown up with had lived in a house like this, a rambling, sparsely furnished pleasure palace made up almost entirely of denlike communal spaces."[44]

Manuscript's badge is triangular, with a circle at the bottom containing the letters MS; across the triangle curls a voluted, scroll-like design holding a shield with sun, sunflowers, and the superscribed letters. It is said that the former symbols suggest the platonic relationship between specifics and essences, in this instance intellectual qualities, according to conventions in use since the Renaissance. Manuscript in time even had an analog to Bones' Deer Island, a villa named Casa Fangati on the Italian island of Elba purchased in 1970 by David Calleo, its corporate parent's president, then the head of Johns Hopkins's European Studies progam, where recent Manuscript members enjoyed summer jobs and internships.[45]

In this same decade, an old Sheff fraternity finally followed Berzelius and Book and Snake into the ranks of the recognized senior societies. St. Elmo had been founded in 1889 as an unincorporated association within the Delta Phi fraternity, populated by members from the sophomore, junior and senior classes; its original clubhouse, at 111 Grove Street, was built in 1895. In 1912, a new clubhouse was constructed next door at 109 Grove Street, a structure designed by Kenneth M. Murchison which resembled a three-storied Elizabethan manor house. The Omicron chapter of Delta Phi severed its ties with the national fraternity in 1925, becoming an independent organization. While the founding of the college system in the 1930s caused the other Sheffield organizations to sell their buildings to the university, St. Elmo's did not and pressed on, incorporating itself as the Rhinelander Trust Association, and then reincorporating in 1964 as St. Elmo Incorporated. Yale did finally buy their hall (now known as Rosenfeld Hall, and used as annex housing for Timothy Dwight College) in 1962, but leased space back to the society.

Two years later, St. Elmo elected to become a secret society in the traditional sense, declaring a founding in 1962 and claiming a place in the 1964 yearbook's listing of senior societies and their members. Noted in their number for that class was John David Ashcroft, son of an evangelical preacher who boycotted Yale's social scene of alcohol and sex, and quarterback of Branford College's football team in its victory over Harvard's Elliott House in the intermural championship game played the fall afternoon in 1963 when President Kennedy was assassinated. Ashcroft was later governor of and then U.S. senator from Missouri, and President George W. Bush's first attorney general. When the university refused to renew the society's lease in its old hall, it moved to a building at 35 Lynwood Place, becoming "landed" like its fellow abovegrounds. Later members in its first decade as a senior society included federal judge Barrington Parker Jr. (1965) and all-pro NFL running back Calvin Hill (1969).[46]

EXTRACURRICULAR PROFICIENCY

While the Stoverian phrase "working for Yale" was no longer employed, the intensity of extracurricular activity had not significantly waned in the four decades since that novel's publication. Faculty and administrators, it was reported in 1958, often complained, "that campus life is too distressingly faithful a reproduction of the intense competition of American business life." There was, however, a new edge, the awareness of the prep school/high school division, 61 percent to 39 percent in Calvin Trillin's freshman class in 1953, in which, "High-school boys from the provinces may have felt ignorant of some things that the Eastern boarding-school people took for granted . . . but most of us, I think, got the feeling that a lot of the rich Eastern people were at Yale because of some entitlement of family or class or money and that we were there because, in ways that were perhaps not immediately apparent, we somehow deserved to be."

The residential college system, now two decades old, had broadened the range of choice, but the old verities obtained: the purpose of Yale College was the training of men of force and character. Through discipline and competition, in class and out, the system taught regularity, cooperation, hard but fair play, honesty, loyalty, and high moral purpose, to the end that the culture of the larger society might be perpetuated and leaders produced capable of understanding each other and their inheritance.[47] The residential colleges offered students new ways of expressing themselves and developing their powers. They permitted a social life for many undergraduates for whom that element was previously either prohibitively expensive or partially inhibited.

The mere fact of eating together produced a social homogeneity that was thoroughly lacking in the day of the eating clubs scattered throughout local catering establishments. In any given year, nearly two thousand upperclassmen were now taking part in intramural college sports, an increase from 10 percent in 1932 to 55 percent in 1953. Perhaps as many shared in other forms of activity within their colleges, serving on councils or committees, editing newspapers, writing for magazines, acting in dramatic productions, engaging in intramural debates, and running or just meeting with special interest clubs. One out of every three students not only carried a bursary job requiring from ten to fourteen hours a week, but seemed also to be able to take part in the extracurricular life of Yale, while still maintaining an academic rank in the upper brackets of his class.[48]

To the credit of the extracurricular activities, it could fairly be said that they strove for quality, and, if not always achieved, it was not for lack of effort. The identification of quality with recognition was and is in principle a reassuring feature of varied extracurricular programs, and it remained the basis of Yale's reputation as "Mother of Men," especially proficient ones. The man who gained the recognition of his classmates through a task will be exposed almost ex officio to new honors. "He may be first elected to his College Council, or as an officer of his class," wrote the associate dean of Yale College in 1953. "The Board of Deacons may take notice of him and the budget drive will profit by his services. And then for Senior Year he will likely be chosen for one, if not two societies."[49]

Yalies of this era had been assured by the Freshman Office that they had been admitted partly because that had the potential ability to lead, and the ideal of leadership gained force from the fact that Yale was, on the undergraduate level, a very cohesive body. The ten colleges, while providing previously unparalleled opportunities to know more men in more classes, were still secondary for most of these men to the numerous organizations and clubs and societies that were run on a university level. Another contemporary perspective on this enormous effort, often voiced by prior observers, was pronounced by a faculty member. "Yale is not only in and of America, it is close to New York. The young-men-on-the-make keep a weather eye to the sou'west. For one thing, they want jobs, and the mushroom growth of extra-curricular Yale is in part due to this purely practical urge; for another, there is pleasure and excitement in imitating metropolitan methods."[50]

Analyses of senior society membership retained fascination for the campus. The News ran a comparison after Tap Day in 1955 of the election classes from 1953 to 1956 and detected shifts in composition of the respective memberships. While 71 percent of the members were in fraternities in 1953, the number had dropped to 54 percent for the incoming class, in every society, although Bones and Wolf's Head were still two-thirds fraternity members. The decline in preparatory school graduates was more moderate, from 75 percent to 67 percent, although, without counting the twelve preppies in Manuscript, the number would have been lower.

In extracurricular activities, the pattern was less clear, although Wolf's Head remained largely composed of athletes, and Manuscript was, as befitted its purpose, "crowded with the literati."

Beyond these two outliers, the societies were "surprisingly uniform" in each choosing between three and five varsity athletes. The *News* board could claim eleven members in the 1956 society delegations, up from seven, and the radio station WYBC had five, having had none in 1953; the humor magazine the *Record* had three representatives, two below their 1953 figure. The calculus in the end did not identify "any given organization as the sure back door to tombdom." One constant was geographic allocation: roughly 36 percent of the society members came from within a fifty-mile radius of New York City. Of the one hundred five new society members, forty were known for scholarship, which was a percentage "not greatly out of line with the general University cross section." In sum, it was conceded, the societies were seen to "be evolving toward more solid grounds for selection than simply fraternity membership or 'wheeldom.'"[51]

President Griswold was closely following the same trends: his papers contain, for the class of 1957 elected in the spring of 1956, an eight-page analysis of the characteristics of every new member of the now seven societies, detailing their three-year averages, their secondary school type ("Prep." or "High"), academic majors, athletics (football, baseball, hockey, soccer, lacrosse, rugby, crew, tennis, track, swimming, fencing, and golf), activities (publications, with editorial office, fraternities, and "other," including the board of deacons, singing groups, junior prom committee membership, the Elizabethan Club and language clubs, or college bursary aideships); scholarship status; and "honors and awards" (academic honors, membership in the Aurelian or Torch honor societies, and all-Ivy or all-American sports honors).

Accumulated, these figures revealed that just over half were above the middle of the class in scholarship; almost three-quarters were prep school products; of the one-quarter membership from high schools, Elihu was the highest, with six, while Book and Snake took only two.

Fraternities claimed 63 percent of the membership, with the societies known for intellect or culture, Elihu and Manuscript, at the low end (six and two men, respectively), while the others ranged from nine to as many as thirteen (Bones, Berzelius, and Book and Snake). Fully 35 percent were on financial aid; only fourteen of the 105 were in the top 10 percent of their class in marks.[52]

Among the seniors so analyzed, and seemingly so "old Yale," were a number of men who in the decade to come were instrumental in effecting a sea change in Yale's admissions policies. In addition to individuals previously mentioned (Keys' Calvin Trillin, the *News* chairman and a future Yale Corporation member, and Manuscript's Henry Geldzahler, with no campus organization offices), these harbingers of change were Bones' R. Inslee "Inky" Clark, the Intra-Fraternity Council president, to become Yale's controversial dean of admissions under president Kingman Brewster, and Vernon Loucks, later CEO of health care giant Baxter International and Corporation member; Berzelius's Charlie O'Hearn, secretary of the charities drive, to become Brewster's assistant for alumni relations; and Wolf's Head's Henry S. "Sam" Chauncey, hockey manager and soon another Brewster assistant, who went on to become dean of admissions and university secretary.

President Griswold conducted an extensive correspondence at the time with Robert B. Fiske, the new president of Wolf's Head's corporate board (whose son of the same name, from the class of 1952, was to be the United States attorney for the Southern District of New York and then the first Whitewater special prosecutor). Griswold mailed Fiske a copy of *Inside Eli* to show the prevailing attitudes of "this community towards the several societies mentioned," including their own. In turn, Fiske sent Griswold the text of the remarks he made to his society's members in November 1956. In them, he recalled to his audience John Andrews's 1934 book on the founding of Wolf's Head, and the 1873 pamphlet the *Iconoclast*, which typified the scorn in which Wolf's Head's predecessors were held.

Fiske's speech acknowledged that "our senior societies are criticized as dull, stupid, frivolous, undemocratic." Dull and stupid were criteria too amorphous to refute, but the societies were no more undemocratic than life itself, he argued, and frivolity could be defended as a necessary response to the intellectual pressures of modern university life—but the gravity and vigor of the club's debates on important topics were hardly frivolous. Finally, "the opportunity which these societies provide for intimate companionship with fourteen diverse souls and the friendships engendered in such associations are one of the strengths of a loyal and happy Yale alumni body."

Pressed by Griswold to urge the undergraduate members in new directions, Fiske wrote them about perhaps inviting non-alumni among the faculty and administration to speak in the hall, and to reconsider their seriousness of purpose. The collegians replied that the twenty to twenty-five Sundays on which they hosted guest speakers were well filled, not only with some faculty, but with outstanding alumni, whom they continued to prefer to hear. Furthermore, while faculty opinion condemned the fraternities, the writers had experienced no such criticism with regard to the senior societies. Upon reviewing this response, Griswold, noting the societies' nature to resist change, believed them to be "all caught up in a secular trend in which the status quo is being rapidly eroded, and will ultimately leave them isolated and bankrupt if they do not understand the trend and move with it."

The president told Fiske that he had recently had this same discussion with University Chaplain Sidney Lovett, whom many undergraduates consulted when considering membership in the societies, and although Lovett was in his day (class of 1913) a member of Bones, he rendered advice "fairly and impartially." "Sid too was of the opinion that the spurious pamphlet I sent you some time ago came very close to taping the reputation of the several senior societies in the eyes and minds of the undergraduate public today. He confirmed my impression that Keys now stood at the very top in public esteem, with Berzelius and Elihu rising in the firmament and Bones and Wolf's Head declining; and that the main factor in this was the number of high-stand men in these societies— particularly in Keys."[53] (The 1957 Keys delegation claimed three men in

Phi Beta Kappa, one of them being Dennis "Denny" Hansen, winner of the Francis Gordon Brown Prize for outstanding junior and a Rhodes scholar, whose graduation was covered in *Life* magazine.[54])

In a later letter to Fiske, Griswold declared that he did not "particularly enjoy the role of Jeremiah" and of course saw nothing "wrong in recognizing talent and ability and outstanding character." It was "the failure to do so, out of a misunderstanding of the true meaning of democracy, that has got our educational system into so much trouble. Indeed it is precisely because I feel the senior societies fail to recognize such talent, ability, and character in such large measure that I am critical of them. They also fail, because of their extreme secretiveness, to reveal to the Yale public their true purposes and standards of selection." It was, this time from a product of the senior society system and the chief of the university which birthed it, the classic criticism: the value of the societies, in rewarding effort and excellence, was undermined when those standards were not consistently honored at elections, and the shields of privacy which protected the programs of education of these men within their tombs offended the larger campus community.

By decade's end, in 1959, even the *Yale Daily News* editorial page, on sober reflection and notwithstanding the annual controversies of past years, found several values in the system's continuation. "In the first place almost every important officeholder in the Yale administration belongs to or participates in some senior society. The President of the University, the Provost, the Secretary, and the Chaplain, and almost all the deans are active members. . . . There are also a large number of faculty men who participate in society programs. For this reason the societies are not only a fruitful meeting-ground for undergraduates and faculty, but they are also a subtle integrating force in a very self-conscious community."

To the credit side of the ledger, they "create more alumni loyalty than any other single institution at Yale, and they create more of this loyalty than exists at most American colleges." It could be concluded that the societies exercised "less evil pressure than they once did," although, on the debit side, some were "stuck in the past," some proved "to be a waste of time for members," while still others fostered snobbery; some juniors were "hurt by no knock on their door," and the groups were "a little too closely connected with the success ethic of Yale." Yet on balance, "kept in their proper perspective, senior societies can be a Good Thing."[55]

Apparently persuaded of that maxim and accepting election on Tap Day the next week were: to Book and Snake, Leslie Aspin Jr., chief student aide in Trumbull College, future Rhodes scholar, later chair of Congress's Armed Services Committee, and secretary of defense under President Clinton, and Porter Goss, congressman and then CIA director; to Wolf's Head, Lewis Lehrman, to be successively the president of Rite Aid, New York State gubernatorial candidate, and founder of the Gilder Lehrman Institute of American History; to Skull and Bones, David George Ball, creator at the Department of Labor of the 401(k) retirement account program, and David Holbrook, later president of the insurance behemoth Marsh & McLennan Companies; to Manuscript, Henry J. Heinz III, future United States senator from Pennsylvania; and to Scroll and Key, Angelo Bartlett Giamatti, who was to succeed Kingman Brewster as president of Yale and thereafter to serve as commissioner of Major League Baseball.

SPOOKS AND SPIES

The identification of graduates of Yale's senior societies ("spooks") with the clandestine intelligence services of the United States (the "spooks" of the Central Intelligence Agency) seems to have begun in this decade. In its early days, the CIA stood out even among Establishment institutions as hiring only through an informal network, on the theory that spies had to be absolutely trustworthy—hence, certified and nonethnic gentlemen—and financially incorruptible—hence, preferably rich. Furthermore, the overlap of prominent officers and directors of America's spies with membership in secret college clubs seemed to the public to be a natural career progression for those practiced in keeping, or discovering, secrets. That two society graduates have been directors of the agency—George H. W. Bush (Bones, 1949) and Porter Goss (Book and Snake, 1960, recruited to the CIA while a junior there through a political science professor who was a faculty advisor to the senior society, and appointed the agency's head forty-five years later by President Bush)—adds mightily to the impression.[56]

The first such agency in the twentieth century was referred to simply as "U-1," born in 1915 when President Woodrow Wilson determined that the State Department should take a more active role in intelligence matters. Secretary of State Robert Lansing entrusted the development of the new intelligence bureau to a person at one remove, a new counselor in the Department of State, Frank L. Polk, a Keysman in the Yale class of 1894 and a distant kinsman of President James K. Polk. Initially advising the government on issues arising from America's neutral status in World War I, Polk soon found himself coordinating the activities of those agencies that gathered intelligence data abroad; he also established liaison with the British and French embassies in counterintelligence matters, and oversaw the work of domestic intelligence services, such as the Bureau of Information, founded in 1908 and later known as the FBI.

The intelligence effort intensified when America entered the war in April 1917, and Gordon Auchincloss (Yale 1908, Keys) was appointed assistant counselor to help Polk coordinate secret activities. Auchincloss had the additional link to the intelligence community in being married to the daughter of Colonel Edward M. House, close personal advisor to his fellow Princeton alumnus Woodrow Wilson, and Auchincloss was to serve as chief secretary to the Inter-Allied War Conference for his father-in-law. Polk also continued intelligence work at war's end, setting up the "American Black Chamber," a unit charged with the responsibility of breaking the codes of foreign powers to read secret messages to their ambassadors in Washington, a program closed down in 1929 by incoming Secretary of State Henry Stimson, with the probably apocryphal words, "Gentlemen do not read each other's mail," a distinction dropped when the mail was Hitler's. Polk established the "foreign-intelligence section" within the State Department, which would continue in peacetime the clandestine activities his office had conducted during the war. By 1919, Congress had agreed to create for him the special post of undersecretary of state, the initiative that gave rise to the designation "U-1" for the department's intelligence unit, which was dissolved only in 1927.[57]

Frank Polk went on to become acting secretary of state from December 1918 to July 1920, and was the commissioner plenipotentiary of the United States to the peace conference at Versailles after Wilson's departure. Afterward, he became a founding partner of the New York law firm now known as Davis, Polk, & Wardwell and managed John W. Davis's presidential bid in 1924 (his partner Wardwell was Keys 1895). However, no particular public connection seems to have been made between his Yale senior society background and his subsequent work in the clandestine world. That connection, for graduates of Yale in the twentieth century, was to be a product of World War II and the Cold War that followed.

Authors on the topic commonly suggest that CIA personnel tend to be from the Ivy League, or more specifically from Harvard, Princeton, and Yale, and some argue that the rise of specific individuals within the intelligence hierarchy may be attributed to their being from one of these institutions. Certainly most of the people who initially made up the Research and Analysis branch of the OSS were academics from Ivy League schools, with Harvard and Yale contributing the largest number of recruits. This emphasis on the eastern academic establishment accurately reflected the condition of American higher learning in the humanities and the social sciences in the late 1930s, when northeastern academia dominated American higher education.[58]

Yale's identification with spies and spying goes back, of course, to Nathan Hale of the class of 1773, whose statue—with a British noose around his neck as he only regrets that he has but one life to lose for his country—stands not only in front of Connecticut Hall on the Old Campus in New Haven, but in front of the Central Intelligence Agency's headquarters in Langley, Virginia, now named after George H. W. Bush, who headed the agency before becoming president. No other American university, it appears, has sent so many of its graduates into the profession of intelligence gathering. Remote outposts in Africa and Asia in the Second World War saw both American members of the Office of Strategic Services (OSS) and British intelligence officers conclude festive occasions by linking arms and singing "The Whiffenpoof Song," based on Kipling's poem "Gentlemen-Rankers," with words distinctly appropriate to the art of spying, the anthem for those who thought of themselves as, "the legions of the lost ones . . . the cohort of the damned . . . 'til an alien turf enfolds us/and we die, and none can tell them where we died."[59]

The OSS and its relation to academe was later to be characterized by McGeorge Bundy as "a remarkable institution, half cops and robbers, half faculty meeting." Its founder, General William "Wild Bill" Donovan, wrote to President Roosevelt on November 18, 1944, declaring the need for a peacetime "Central Intelligence Service" which "will procure intelligence both by overt and covert methods and will at the same time provide intelligence guidance, determine national intelligence objectives, and correlate the intelligence material collected by all government agencies," with authority to "conduct subversive operations abroad," but "no police or law enforcement functions, either at home or abroad."

The OSS was dismantled in September 1945 by President Truman, but the system that replaced it had many connections to personnel who were graduate members of the Yale senior societies. Wilmarth Lewis (Keys 1918) had served from 1941 as chief of the Central Information Division of the Research and Analysis branch of the OSS, to establish a central registry of intelligence data based on the filing system he had developed for cataloguing the papers of Horace Walpole. He was recommended for the job by Librarian of Congress Archibald MacLeish (Bones 1915), who had been working with Donovan.[60] Robert Lovett (Bones 1917) chaired the government committee for President Truman tasked with advising the federal government on the postwar organization of American intelligence activities. The National Security Act of 1947 created the Central Intelligence Agency, and in 1951, Trubee Davison (Bones 1917) became its first director of personnel.

From Yale's class of 1943 alone, at least forty-two men entered intelligence work, largely in the OSS, and many remained on after the war to form the core of the new CIA. Moreover, when in 1948 the National Security Council authorized a study on intelligence coordination, Norman Holmes Pearson, a Yale professor with considerable OSS experience, recommended that each university have on its staff informal talent spotters who would forward the names of likely agents to the CIA. Each university should designate a faculty member to act as advisor to students considering careers in intelligence, and the CIA would maintain up-to-date lists of students with unusual talents or skills that might someday be useful to the agency.[61]

While it has been maintained that Princeton is the Ivy League campus with the best claim to ties to the CIA, because of Princetonians Woodrow Wilson and the brothers John Foster and Allen Dulles, only the last of whom was an OSS/CIA officer, a Yale historian in 1984 declared that Yale had influenced the agency more than any other university.[62] "The laying on of hands, quietly and effectively, in the college and in the classroom, at the master's tea and in the seminar, over a cup at Mory's and during a break in crew practice," had become quite accepted by the 1950s as a way of service to the nation.

Bolstered by their prominence within the residential college system, the college masters were known as contact points, usually conduits rather than recruiters, but the colleges' fellows and associate fellows, such as Davenport's Dean Acheson and Archibald MacLeish, Keys and Bones respectively, were also in positions of high government service. Other faculty and administrators were involved, among them Professor Wallace Notestein, later patron of Manuscript, and the chief Yale recruiter for the CIA in its early years, the crew coach "Skip" Waltz, the most highly compensated crew coach in the country, being paid an equal annual salary by the CIA. It was rumored that the senior societies were recruiting grounds as well, because it was apparent, as the leading historian of the intertwinings of Yale and the clandestine services has tartly observed, that their members "deeply believed in the wisdom of their own choices (and perhaps at times in the wonder of it) and were convinced they served Yale in ways that the beneficiaries of their noblesse oblige might never fully understand."

Charles Seymour (Bones 1910) had virtually validated such contacts while university president: his daughter had worked for the OSS in Switzerland and Germany, and he was on close terms with her boss, Allen Dulles, head of the CIA after 1953. Through his successor President Griswold, Seymour had Dulles meet in the Corporation Room at Woodbridge Hall with a large group of students interested in a career with the CIA. It must be remembered that this was an era of what has been called "sentimental imperialism," when Americans generally, upper middle-class American men broadly, and the Yale community specifically, thought of themselves as having a mission to the world: while enjoying the blessings of liberty, they felt themselves able to reshape the world to their benefit and, not incidentally, to their country's.[63]

At the highest international political level there were rapid and massive changes from the dynamic alliances of the Second World War into its successor the Cold War, and a response was required. It is hard, after the Cold War's conclusion with the Soviet Union's collapse in the 1980s, to remember how frightening the world looked in the early 1950s: Pentagon planners had actually picked a day—July 1, 1952—for the Soviet invasion of Western Europe. In the late 1940s and early 1950s, entering the CIA was a respectable, even honorable, thing for a sensitive young liberal to do. During the Korean War, the CIA also offered the singular advantage of being one of the few government agencies where liberals and leftists could work without fear of the shadow of Senator Joe McCarthy.[64]

Among those recruited to the CIA in these years were Tracy Barnes, a cousin of John Hay Whitney and Keysman graduating in 1933 who had worked for Allen Dulles's OSS team in Switzerland, joining the agency in 1950, leading the Guatemalan government's overthrow in 1952, then serving as CIA station chief in Germany and ending his clandestine

career in 1966, after being sidelined for five years following the failure of
the Bay of Pigs operation in Cuba in 1961. Another was a wartime (1943)
graduate of Keys and promoter of world federalism, Cord Meyer Jr., joining
in 1950, serving as second in charge of all espionage and clandestine operations, and ending as head of its International Organizations Division and
London station chief. Also recruited by the agency were one prewar and
two recent graduate members of Bones, known for very different traits
in later decades: Washington lawyer William Bundy (1939), later to be
the long-time editor of *Foreign Affairs* magazine; conservative journalist
William F. Buckley (1950), posted to Mexico; and, with his fluency in
Russian, liberal Yale University Chaplain William Sloane Coffin (entering
Yale with advanced standing as a junior and graduating in 1949).[65]

On the other hand, the three Yalies most famously identified with
the CIA were *not* members of any senior society while Yale undergraduates. These were Yale English Professor Norman Holmes Pearson
(class of 1932), the leader of U.S. counterespionage efforts in Western
Europe for the OSS and not an original CIA officer but a counselor at
its birth; James Jesus Angleton (1941), recruited by Pearson and chief
of the agency's counterintelligence staff from 1954 to 1975, who was
like so many others fooled by Cambridge spy Kim Philby; and Richard
Bissell (1932, turning down Bones), who as the CIA's deputy director/
Plans was the father of the U-2 spy plane and the controller of the Bay
of Pigs invasion, called by old CIA hands the second most powerful man
in government.[66] And whatever malign influence Yale secret society
antecedents had on America's spy culture, never was there anything like
the scandal of the University of Cambridge spies coming out of that
university's elite society, the Apostles, where of the thirty-one members
of elected between 1927 and 1939, fifteen were communists or otherwise
Marxist, including Guy Burgess and Anthony Blunt.[67]

Nevertheless, the association between the CIA and the Yale secret
societies has been burnished by writers of spy novels and makers of
motion pictures almost since the agency's birth. In Aaron Latham's 1977
novel *Orchids for Mother*, the thinly veiled story of James Jesus Angleton

employing in its title his CIA nickname, the protagonist says, "Langley's New Haven all over again right down to Nathan Hale . . . Secret society'd be closer, like Skull and Bones." "There are a lot of Bonesmen around, aren't there?," asks his young recruit from New Haven. Indeed, the master spy replies, "Oh, Langley's a regular haunted house."[68]

The master of the Cold War spy novel, John le Carré, had earlier added his imprimatur to the theme in his 1959 novel, *The Russia House.* "'Yale has these secret societies, you see, Harry,' Bob was explaining to me. 'Why, the place is shot through with them. If you've heard of Skull and Bones, Scroll and Key, you've still only heard the tip of the iceberg. And these societies, they emphasize the team. Harvard now—why, Harvard goes all the other way and puts its money on individual brilliance. So the Agency, when it's fishing to recruit in those waters, has a way of picking its team players from Yale and its high flyers from Harvard. I won't go so far as to say that every Harvard man is a prima donna or every Yale man gives blind obedience to the cause. But that's the broad tradition.'"[69]

Still others writing spy novels have continued to emphasize the theme, for satire or celebration, even as the Cold War wound down. Charles McCarry, whose author's biography notes that he was during the Cold War an intelligence officer operating under deep cover in Europe, Africa, and Asia, in his series of Paul Christopher novels about the CIA, writes of one admirable figure from the prior generation's OSS, Christopher's uncle Elliott Hubbard, whose wife ends overlong jovial male conversation at dinner parties by crying "Bones," at which his male guests would get up and leave the room and "the others, repeating a mysterious ritual they did not understand, would follow"; and of a second, laughable one, Waddy Jessup, about to be captured in occupied Burma and fearing execution by the Japanese, who asks his batman to shout the same word as a diversion when he flees mounted on an elephant, leaving his companion behind.[70]

The ever-provocative William F. Buckley Jr., Bones 1950 and CIA 1951, gave the identification a new boost with his series of Blackford Oakes spy thrillers: in the first of the ten-novel series, *Saving the Queen,* set in 1952, the hero in an employment interview is told, by way of warning, that "a copy of all Ivy League 1951 yearbooks is in Soviet hands, and a record is being entered on names, faces, dates of birth . . . all of them." Oakes not only shares with his creator these two career distinctions of membership in a senior society and in the CIA, but the twenty-six-year-old, newly fledged agent also manages in this first outing to bed the young British queen.[71]

The legend received its most sophisticated burnishing in 2006 with Robert De Niro's production and direction of Eric Roth's screenplay *The Good Shepherd*, called by the *New York Post* "the *Godfather* of spy films." The story relates the transformation of the OSS into the CIA, told through the life from 1939 to 1961 of one Edward Wilson, portrayed by Matt Damon as an admixture of Angleton, with his code name "Mother," and Bissell, running the Bay of Pigs invasion. The movie begins with Wilson's being tapped for Bones by a senior named John Russell (echoing the Russell Trust Association) after coming off the stage in a Yale Dramat staging of Gilbert & Sullivan, and features— soundtracked with choruses of "The Whiffenpoof song"—not one but two scenes of initiation into the society, the first for Wilson (including, in the screenwriter's telling, naked mud-wrestling and confession of a deep personal secret while lying naked in a sarcophagus), and the second years later for his son, who also joins the agency. There follow, over the years of the story, three reunion dinners at Deer Island, the society's rustic island retreat in the St. Lawrence River.

De Niro himself plays General William Sullivan, the Bill Donovan figure, who at Deer Island recruits Wilson for the OSS for the coming war, and Michael Gambon portrays Edmund's English literature professor, who has characteristics of the poetry-teaching spymaster Norman Holmes Pearson. Emphasizing the class and family ties, the narrative doubles back on itself, revealing by group photos in the imagined Bones hall that Wilson's father had been a society member, later a United States senator. John Russell's sister, played by Angelina Jolie, seduces Wilson on Deer Island's moonlit banks, and later they marry. At this same reunion retreat he meets an older graduate, "President of the Bones class of 1912," who becomes the first director of the CIA later in the film, only to be succeeded by John Russell.[72] While it is not known what the CIA thought of the film, the Yale senior society and its university, given their centrality to the drama, should in fairness perhaps have received licensing fees.

In his memoirs, Richard Bissell probably got it right. "There has been speculation in recent years," he wrote, "about the friendships established at schools like Groton [which he attended with Tracy Barnes] and Yale and their impact on organizations like the Central Intelligence Agency. I think there *was* an Ivy league establishment in the sense of a body of men who had similar backgrounds and knew one another well, and the existence of that group had a good deal of influence on public affairs. . . . If positions were available in various public institutions and members of the establishment were invited to fill them, I think it was more because these men knew one another than because of a deliberate policy of selecting only from a particular social group."[73] This nuanced view does not exclude Yale senior society members, but it does not see fit to mention it, either.

THE DECADE TURNS

In the fifties, a curious and contradictory time, it has been written the students at Yale were "intense yet never individualistic, their skepticism deep but muffled, their pursuit of the traditional forms of success and reward ardent but without zest." The patterns and attitudes established by the returning veterans in the postwar 1940s were continued, but not impeded or driven forward with fervor. Not until the end of the succeeding decade would the fifties' disenchantment with established goals become active disengagement from them; when "the fifties' desire for something more coherent and purposeful" metamorphosed into "the sixties' battlecry of Illegal, Immoral, Unjust." Fifteen years after Prosser Gifford, a Keysman of 1951 returning to Yale for graduate study after a Rhodes scholarship, wrote in the *Yale Daily News* seventy-five anniversary memorial volume in 1953 that the senior societies were "out-of-date" and "anti-democratic," the slogans in replacement would be, for the societies, Yale social life, and many other institutions, "irrelevant" and "elitist."[74]

The mild public teasing continued as the decade turned: the Yale Film Society ran an advertisement in the *News* on Tap Day in 1960, announcing "Tapping," in order "to enhance its prestige as well as a feeling of superficial camaraderie among its members," and the group was to be known as "Reel and Can." The newspaper's postelection editorial propounded the more balanced view of the previous several years, allowing that "the senior society experience can be a rewarding one for many undergraduates," but deploring the societies' "disintegrating force" on the college class, the pain felt by those not chosen, and the distractions provoked by the pre-tapping period, now beginning as early as February, ending in "lying, groveling, and overemphasis" on themselves in the two weeks preceding elections. Abolishing the societies, or doing away with one-day elections, were not solutions, so juniors needed to approach them even "without losing the sense of perspective," since neither joining, nor choosing which society to join, were life-shaping events.[75]

For the seekers and the sought, that was not an obvious conclusion. A Yale University Press–published study in 1958 by the staff of the Division of Student Mental Hygiene at the university's Department of University Health, titled *Psychosocial Problems of College Men*, concluded that "Election to a society is the highest honor a student can receive from his fellow undergraduates."[76]

In the elections for 1960, Bones and Book and Snake both wanted 1961's football captain, Paul Bursiek. The latter sent senior back Lee Mallory to the candidate's college room; the Bones messenger was 233-pound Mike Pyle, who was to go from New Haven to professional football with the Chicago Bears. When the clock struck eight, they both banged furiously on the door, elbowing each other for position. When it opened, Pyle plowed through and into Mallory, sending him hurtling against a wall. When Bursiek accepted the Book and Snake offer, Pyle "tore out of the room in a rage and trumpeted down the stairs like a mad elephant."[77] Moving Tap Day indoors did not still the passions which the event aroused.

CHAPTER THIRTEEN

BLACKS, WOMEN, AND MAY DAY
(1963–1970)

"By keeping in step with the male,
We proceed at the pace of a snail,"
Said the Dean of Admissions,
"Let's shift our positions
And get some fast women at Yale."
    —President A. Whitney Griswold, 1956[1]

The tumultuous "Sixties" have long been distinguished by historians from the full decade of the 1960s, which at the start largely resembled the late 1950s. A precise dividing line is elusive, but the change came somewhere between the assassination of President Kennedy—on the Friday before the Yale-Harvard football game was to occur in New Haven in November 1963—and the shift thereafter from relatively peaceful civil rights demonstrations to Black Power at home, accompanied abroad by the traumatic escalation of the Vietnam War, sweeping collegians into the military draft calls. The arc is exemplified by the successive presentations of the junior prizewinner of the Ten Eyck speaking contest in spring 1966, about his marching at Selma the year before, who

609

then won the DeForest Prize as a senior in 1967 with a speech calling for a negotiated end to the Vietnam War.

Then came the expansion of identity politics: African Americans and women in particular, but also Latinos, Asian Americans, and even homosexuals, constituting social demographics which had once avoided attention but now began to explore and celebrate their distinctiveness and to demand the respect which was due. References to "the Sixties," as the era receded, assumed less the character of a particular set of years than a set of connotations associated with the latter part of the decade into the early 1970s, carrying through the resignation of President Richard Nixon in 1974—an era marked by social, cultural, and political excesses[2] which were to engulf and transform the senior societies, and nearly or completely to extinguish a few.

Yale College, even as the decade began, was still demographically largely uniform: 1,033 entered in 1956 with the class of 1960, of whom 940 were to graduate. They were regionally less diverse than succeeding classes, with over four-fifths coming from east of the Mississippi, and only 1.5 percent from abroad. Diversity, for the admissions office then, was a matter of geography and socioeconomic background. The concept did not really embrace today's categories of religion, social class (among that year's intake were a Pillsbury, a Heinz, a du Pont, and the wonderfully named Merrill Lynch Magowan), ethnicity (no native-born Latinos, and only a handful with Asian ancestry), sexual orientation (no gays who were out of the closet), or—with women not yet admitted to Yale College—gender. In 1960, Yale still led all colleges in the number of its undergraduates whose families were listed in the *Social Register:* Harvard, Yale, and Princeton together accounted for 45 percent, with Yale's the largest share at 21 percent.

As diversity categories, religious and racial backgrounds were indeed to be avoided, since to do otherwise would constitute illegal discrimination. Roughly 10 percent of the freshmen were Roman Catholic, with about the same number of Jews, when, in the 1960 federal census, Catholics comprised 23 percent of the population, and Jews only 3 percent.

Many of those arrived in New Haven as legacies from elite schools, such as Yale's future president Angelo Bartlett Giamatti, named after both his paternal grandfather, Angelo, who came through Ellis Island in 1900, and his mother's father, Bartlett, who went from Andover to Harvard in the same year. Of the five blacks in the class, only three of whom graduated in 1960, none were to be elected to a fraternity or an aboveground senior society.[3]

The blackballing of the African American football player Raleigh Davenport by a southern member of the DKE fraternity in accordance with its national rules was, for the time, unsurprising evidence of the college's, not to mention the country's, lingering prejudices in 1959. Nevertheless, as vice chairman of the Undergraduate Board of Deacons, and chosen for the honorary society Torch (founded in 1916 to recognize ten juniors for merit and achievement, irrespective of society or fraternity affiliation), Davenport was thereafter elected to the revived underground senior society Spade and Grave, showing that those prejudices were receding.[4]

Still, in a college class ten times the size of the class in which the first senior society was founded in 1832, both groups comprised largely of America's elites, there were social strains in the overclass which were more subtle, the 1960 class's historian has written, "between those on their way up and those on their way down; between those with more money than privileged pasts, and vice versa; between those whose families were prominent New Yorkers, and those equally prominent but in parts of the hinterland, like Minneapolis, Savannah, or Chicago's North Shore." Of the Jewish students, fully a third were legacies, with most coming from prep schools, just over a quarter from private day schools, and slightly under a quarter from public high schools, including eleven from New Haven and five from New York City, but not a single Jew from a high school in Boston, Philadelphia, Chicago, or Baltimore.

Although there were class officers and committees, Yale had no significant student government, as the Senior Advisory Board was appointed by the administration. Prestige continued to flow to extracurricular activities, particularly varsity athletics, singing groups, fraternities, and aboveground senior societies. Fraternities had the allegiance of relatively few, compared to America's state universities, or to Princeton and its eating clubs: Yale's nine non-residential frats were joined by well under half the class. Of those brothers, four-fifths came from private schools, and less than one-fifth received scholarship aid from Yale. Two fraternities were closing down as the class of 1960 graduated, the latest victims, a quarter century on, of the success of the residential college system, and there was a fierce debate about whether they provided anything to the collegians that was not available elsewhere.[5]

The senior societies, on the other hand, while in the abovegrounds including only about 10 percent of the graduating class, continued to thrive with a notoriety and power far outweighing their numbers. The pronouncement of *The Pyschosocial Position of the College Man* that the societies were the summum bonum of the undergraduate experience probably overemphasized their importance in such a large class and overlooked substantial differences among the societies. Skull and Bones and Book and Snake sought leaders in athletics, campus publications, and other traditional activities, while Elihu and Manuscript elected men with undergraduate fame in the arts, religion, and student politics. As in the late 1950s, however, the junior-officered *Yale Daily News* now annually pronounced senior societies to be not especially objectionable, or even beneficial. Yale administrators, many of them society graduate members, criticized fraternities but—other than Chaplain Coffin—considered the societies almost beyond reproach, both because of their importance to generally recognized campus leaders, and because their practices remained generally private, unlike the fraternity festivities on most weekends.[6]

A NEW UNIVERSITY PRESIDENT AND NEW ADMISSIONS POLICIES

The untimely death of Whitney Griswold from cancer in 1963 meant a change of leadership for the university. Kingman Brewster, the Griswold administration's provost since July 1961, was the only administration officer who was both a close personal friend and had real administrative power and responsibility. Yale Corporation members Wilmarth Lewis and Edwin Blair, having sponsored Griswold's election and backed him in the 1950s, when he was a reformer battling traditionalism, had fallen out with their protégé when he moved toward modernization after 1960. They now did their best to prevent Griswold's own protégé Brewster from becoming the new president of Yale for the same reason, although the provost was the leading candidate, with tremendous support from the faculty, the youngest members of the Yale Corporation, and the undergraduates.

Blair's hesitations seem to have centered on Brewster's rejection of Blair's society Bones and other senior societies as an undergraduate (another Corporation member voting on his election, Harold "Doc" Howe II, had sought to tap him twenty-three years before, in 1940), and a sense that Brewster would somehow further change the Yale that Blair of the class of 1924 knew and loved. Lewis, with his strong bias toward the humanities and Yale's libraries, museums, and galleries, overtly complained that Brewster (a legal scholar) was not a humanist and lacked a PhD. His main grievance, however, was the provost's failure to promote S. Dillon Ripley, the head of the Peabody Museum—and a Keys alumnus, like Lewis—to a full professorship, because of Lewis's proprietary interest in the Peabody and "because his affection for other Keys men [was] always bright." In the end, the first vote of the Corporation on the final candidates on October 11, 1963, was in favor of Brewster 13–2, with Blair and Lewis opposed, and then the two senior fellows changed their votes to effect a unanimous election.[7]

Brewster, who famously said off the record that he did not become president of Yale, "to preside over a prep school on Long Island Sound," promptly recruited or promoted some young dynamos—all, perhaps to Blair's relief, with traditional senior society backgrounds from recent classes. These included, to rationalize and improve both Yale's operations and its student body quality: from management consultant Arthur P. Little, the 28-year-old Howard Phelan (Bones 1958) as director of

DAVID ALAN RICHARDS

management operations and university development; from Inland Steel; Phelan's football teammate and captain, the 29-year-old John "Jack" Embersits (also Bones), as the university's business manager; the 30-year-old Henry "Sam" Chauncey (Wolf's Head 1957, in the delegation which threatened to quit over the blocked election of a Jewish candidate), as Brewster's personal assistant; and most significantly, two years into the new administration, Chauncey's classmate and public school graduate R. Inslee "Inky" Clark (Bones 1957), raised from dean of Trumbull College to director of admissions, who in the words of his conservative critic and elder fellow Bonesman Bill Buckley took out his "democratic leveling guns" to decimate alumni sons and prep school graduates.[8]

Clark's predecessor Arthur Howe, who had become dean of admissions under Griswold in 1954, had already begun Yale's move from a class of "well-rounded men" to a "well-rounded class." Yale was receiving four times as many applications as in the 1950s as it had in the 1930s, when it rejected approximately one-fifth of its candidates. Now it was turning down three-fifths and expanding the percentage of those at the top of the academic ability scale. Still, selectivity was based not on academic meritocracy, but on demonstrated leadership: "Far and away the most important factor in any boy's chances of admission is what we considered his personal promise," Howe proclaimed, as selecting for characteristics of leadership potential was widely understood to be Yale's special mission. Howe also recognized that Yale needed to admit approximately 60 percent of its freshmen from the richest 3 to 5 percent of families so that they could fully pay tuition, room and board fees, and personal expenses, which would allow the university to offer some financial aid to the other 40 percent, in particular to middle-class applicants.

While his suggestion in 1956 that Yale admit women to the college was not well received, Howe did recruit to his staff the liberally minded Clark, the public school–educated son whose father had not attended college, and began to develop liaisons with alumni recruiting groups and to broaden recruitment in the public secondary schools, which in the early fifties Griswold, a prep school product, had attacked as the "rotten

614

pilings" of the American educational system, where liberal education in his view was subordinated to vocational education and life-adjustment courses.[9]

Griswold did not condone the kind of covert discrimination which had been practiced against Jews and other minorities at Yale since the 1920s, but neither was he interested in taking the initiative to root out continuing injustices, holding preferences and understandings, so ingrained as to be unconscious, that characterized most of the well-intentioned members of the American upper class before the sea change in sensitivities of the later 1960s. During Griswold's first five years in office, the Bronx High School of Science sent only seven graduates to the freshman classes of 1954 to 1958, while the Phillips Andover Academy, although nowhere near as academically selective, sent some 275. The largest feeder schools of that era (Andover, Exeter, Lawrenceville, Hotchkiss, and St. Paul's) each accounted for only one of the class of 1957's sixty-four members of Phi Beta Kappa, and other traditional feeder schools such as Groton, Hill, Kent, St. Mark's, St. George's, and Taft contributed none.[10]

When the student body was characterized as "diverse" early in this era, the notion was primarily one of geography. The proportion of students from New England and New York had decreased from 60 percent in Kingman Brewster's class of 1941, to 50 percent in the class of 1954, to 35 percent in the class of 1967, while the percentage of students from west of the Mississippi more than tripled over the same period—the vast majority of them, of course, being the products of public high schools. And the applicants from these schools, without the old admissions advantages of legacy histories or of seasoned private-school counselors, were measured by what has been characterized as a "subjective" version of meritocracy which "attempts to judge fairly between candidates, but based on personal judgments of quality, character and ability rather than numerical measures alone [SAT scores and class marks]." Brewster told an alumni convocation in 1966 that Yale was "making a conscious effort to be sure of the fact that we are a national institution whose ambition is nothing less than to try to frame a leadership for the nation in the years ahead."[11] If the senior societies had traditionally offered elections as a reward for proven campus leadership, they were now choosing from twelve hundred men all initially *admitted* to Yale as potential leaders of one sort or another.

Since many of the public high schoolers at Yale, still less than half of the incoming classes, were what 1957's Calvin Trillin called "high school heroes of one sort or another," representing more national versions of the old Yale image of organizational and athletic success, their need to meet more stringent academic and personal standards for admission also resulted in their achieving disproportionate distinction in every area of college life during the later 1950s, a trend which accelerated in the 1960s.[12]

A comparison of the freshmen in the Yale classes of 1952 and 1970, matriculating in 1948 (1,178 entering) with 1966 (a roughly similar 1,021), demonstrates the dramatic difference. Although school presidents or student council heads were only 5 percent of those entering Yale in 1948, in 1966 they were 22 percent of the class. So too with athletes and editors: varsity letter holders constituted 21 percent of the class in 1948, and 39 percent in 1966 (with varsity captains 3 percent in 1948, and 10 percent in 1966). Editors of school yearbooks or newspapers comprised 3 percent of freshmen in 1948, while in 1966 they were 39 percent.[13]

Put another way, the rate of improvement in matriculating leaders for the 1966 cohort over 1948 was an enlargement of approximately 400 percent in class presidents or leaders, a 900 percent jump in student editors, a 200 percent leap in varsity letters, and a 300 percent growth in the number of sports captains, so the distance between the two classes was greatest for editors and least for varsity letters. In comparison to Griswold and Howe, there occurred under Brewster and Clark spectacular progress in Yale's ability to recognize and reward leadership promise. Average combined SAT scores did go up significantly during those 18 years from approximately 1,200 in 1948 to roughly 1,400 in 1966, but the relative rate of academic improvement was moderate in comparison with the college's new record in matriculating leaders.[14]

This shift in the examplars of campus leadership was at first distinctly not reflected in the composition of the senior societies, purportedly comprised of those (re-proven) leaders. In 1953 before Tap Day of that year, a *Yale Daily News* analysis reported that approximately 75 percent of all society members for the previous two years (1951 and 1952) came from prep schools, of whom 15 percent came from Andover and 8 percent from Hotchkiss. For the class of 1956, the prep school component had dropped to 67 percent, a decline that would have been more dramatic had not the new aboveground Manuscript tapped twelve preppies in its first public election year, but the percentage was still at 70 percent for the class of 1957.[15]

The societies were thus seriously lagging in reflecting the changing composition of Yale College. The class of 1955, entering in 1951, had 413 students or 44 percent from public schools, and 653 or 56 percent from private schools. The number of high schoolers had increased at least 10 percent in each decade (1935, 21 percent; 1945, 30 percent; 1955, 44 percent, then creeping up by about one percent per annum during the Howe years of directing freshman admissions from 1954 to 1964). Yet the mix of private and public high school graduates in the abovegrounds at the middle and end of the fifties was still closer to the mix in the Yale class of 1935 than to anything else. Moreover, Yale also been lapped by its rivals in the Big Three in regard to admitting boys from public schools: not until the class of 1967, matriculating in 1963, was a Yale College class to contain more high school graduates than those from prep and day schools, a level of parity reached by Harvard in the 1940s and even by Princeton as early as 1955.[16]

Ten years after the 70 percent level of private school students' membership record in the abovegrounds of the class of 1957, the proportions had more than reversed, as the striving products of the public high schools succeeded markedly in undergraduate competition. In the graduating class of 1967, among the last to be admitted under the Howe admissions policies, Bones and Keys each contained a dozen American-born seniors, and three members born abroad (one, the Jewish captain of the Rugby Club, later chosen to be a South African Rhodes scholar). Fully three-quarters of the domestic dozen in each society were graduates of public high schools.

Of course, traditions of legacies, both for Yale and its senior societies, still held considerable sway: in college admissions, by written policy, "the father's whole record of service to both Yale and to American society" counted. Under this policy, the grandson and son of prominent Yale graduates of the classes of 1917 and 1948, respectively, was admitted in 1964, although scholastically he was halfway down his Andover class, when Yale took in 47 percent of legacy applicants, against only 27 percent for nonlegacy applicants. In his junior year George W. Bush, by then the president of both the Delta Kappa Epsilon fraternity and the college's Inter-Fraternity Council, was tapped for the Bones delegation of 1968, although not, as legend has it, by his father returned to campus.[17]

More representative of the future was Bush's own delegation's election, from the class of 1969, of Stephen Schwarzman, a Jewish graduate of the Abingdon, Pennsylvania, high school, the manager of the Yale College student agencies (laundry, etc.), and founder and chair of the Ballet Society of Davenport College, who as CEO of the Blackstone Group was in 2015 to give Yale its second largest gift ever, $150 million for the transformation of the former freshman Commons into the Schwarzman Cultural Center.

The Clark admissions wind swept remarkable changes into the Yale student body. The new dean of admissions' first class, the class of 1970, arriving on campus in the fall of 1966, was comprised of 58 percent public high school students, a jump from 52 percent the prior year, drawing on more such schools (478), and even more private schools (196), representing an increase in the number of students from Catholic and Jewish parochial schools. The class of 1970 entered with the highest Scholastic Aptitude Test scores in Yale's history, with half the incoming freshman scoring in the top one percent nationally, marks higher even than those of Harvard's incoming class, also a first for New Haven vs. Cambridge. There were more minorities than ever before of every kind: Jews, when by 1967 the number of Jewish freshmen exceeded 20 percent, and has averaged 25 percent in the last several decades; Catholics, on which it was said Yale had once maintained a 13 percent admissions ceiling; Italian Americans; and African Americans, for whose review Clark had purposely hired a black man for the admissions committee.

With an influx of scientists, the class also contained, due to Brewster's implemented preferences, an unprecedented number of artists, musicians, and actors. The most meritocratic aspect of the new admissions policies were the minimal consideration given to the traditional privileges of money, with a new "needs blind" admissions policy, removing financial need information from the applicants' packets in May 1967; or to family legacy, declining below Harvard's and Princeton's intake rate to about 14 percent from 1967 to 1972, for the classes of 1971 to 1976; or to Yale relationships with traditional "feeder" schools—the reduced Yale admission rate at St. Paul's School was covered in the *New York Times* in 1967.[18]

Four years into President Brewster's term, in a major statement on Yale's admissions policy published in the university's alumni magazine, he clearly enunciated his belief that selective universities like his own incurred a responsibility to maintain the American dream of equal opportunity for all. "There are relatively few institutions whose education does conspicuously offer a special career advantage, and they must be convincingly open to free, competitive admission based on merit. . . . If the Yale privilege, and the springboard to a headstart which it offers, were to be rationed by inheritance," Brewster warned, "if it were to be auctioned in return for financial support, if it were to be conditioned by racial or social or economic preference, we would by that measure be dealing a very serious blow to the 'opportunity sense' that is the greatest heritage and the greatest promise of this country."[19]

Even before this statement, the response of many alumni to its sentiments was communicated directly to Clark, in front of Brewster, through the university's governing body. In the first year of his admissions tenure, Clark was summoned to report on his changes in policy directly to the Yale Corporation, whose fourteen members were solidly white, male, and Protestant, with no Jews, no Catholics, and only two public high school graduates. One trustee who had grimaced during the presentation finally burst out: "Let me get down to basics: You're admitting an entirely different class than we're used to. You're admitting them for a different purpose than training leaders."

Clark responded mildly that in a changing nation, leaders might well come from nontraditional cohorts, including public high school graduates, Jews, blacks and other minorities, and even women. Shot back his interlocutor, "You're talking about Jews and public school graduates as leaders. Look around you at this table. These are America's leaders. There are no Jews here. There are no public school graduates here." The speaker's minor mistake in his last remark does not lessen his larger point, that those in power at this table—including New York City mayor John Lindsay and Pennsylvania governor William Scranton, both liberal Republicans and Episcopalian boarding school graduates, either of whom might possibly be the next president of the United States—had always recruited replacements in their own racial, religious, and economic images. Their collective unwillingness to trust others unlike them with that power finally reflected a desire to exclude.[20]

Nevertheless, under Brewster's leadership, Yale was doing exactly what sociologist E. Digby Baltzell, the popularizer of the term WASP (White Anglo-Saxon Protestant), had envisioned in his 1964 classic, *The Protestant Establishment: Aristocracy and Class in America*: "In a free society, while the establishment will always be dominated by upper-class members, it also must be constantly rejuvenated by new members of the elite who are in the process of acquiring upper-class status." The forceful and decided adjustment of the guidelines for acceptance represented "a systematic policy of aristocratic assimilation, as caste on the campus has steadily retreated before the modern admissions policies which stress individual accomplishment rather than family background."[21]

"THE NEGRO AT YALE"

An editorial so titled appeared in the *Yale Daily News* for April 8, 1959, triggered by an article published by Raleigh Davenport in the campus publication *Criterion*. In "Segregation, North and South," Davenport, whose rejection by DKE was placed at the door of the national fraternities' "anti-Negro practices," wrote that "Finding legally sanctioned discrimination in fraternities is disillusioning to a Negro at Yale." Bringing the point home to his classmates, he noted that "It is difficult for the Negro to sincerely internalize the spirit of the Yale 'blue' when he is cheered on the basketball court or in the Yale Bowl and rejected as a possible member in fraternity houses." Alluding to current events at Little Rock, the *News* editorialist warned his readers that they "do not need to march in Washington to be aware of the Negro problem in voting booths and schools. It is right here on York Street."[22]

Minority recruitment of blacks began under President Griswold, largely because of the efforts of dean of admissions Arthur Howe, whose family line included abolitionists, one of whom helped to found what became Hampton University. As Griswold's provost, Brewster attended President Kennedy's meeting in Washington with leaders of elite universities, urging them to recruit minorities, and returned to establish a program that would step up that recruitment at Yale. This began with a Carnegie Foundation grant for a Yale summer high school, intended to prepare promising black high schoolers for possible admission to Yale or other elite colleges. At Howe's advent in 1954, there were one or two blacks per class, and he used his connections with black schools and colleges to recruit, the numbers creeping up slowly.

In 1963, the newly installed President Brewster made "Inky" Clark the new dean of admissions, and by 1969, Yale had managed to enroll fully twenty-six black undergraduates. By 1975, 86 freshman blacks came to New Haven, and the average between 1975 and 1997 was ninety-one per year, or approximately 7 percent of each undergraduate class. Brewster, whose university was one of the first to award an honorary degree to the Rev. Dr. Martin Luther King, to the dismay of older alumni, was known to say "Yale wants to . . . turn out the black leaders of the future. The Martin Luther Kings." However improbable that tomorrow's Kings would find Yale's gothic colleges necessarily entrancing, the college can boast of Dallas Cowboys football great Calvin Hill (class of 1970), former Baltimore mayor and thereafter Hampton University president Kurt Schmoke (1971), and Harvard's Professor Henry Louis Gates Jr. (1973) as alumni of whom any institution would be proud.[23]

Only four blacks had graduated from an American college by 1830.[24] African Americans who attended and graduated from Yale College from the first, in 1857, until the 1950 graduating class of Levi Jackson, which included three blacks, were a rare and privileged group, overwhelmingly from the upper class of their generally disadvantaged, slave-descended stratum. They were usually in at least the third generation of literacy, the sons of ministers, teachers, and engineers, with some 30 percent having already graduated from other, mostly black, colleges. They often became professionals, doctors or teachers or lawyers.

Only thirty-one African Americans graduated from Yale through 1924, nine coming from New Haven high schools,[25] demonstrating the truth of W.E.B. Dubois's observation in 1910 in "The College-Bred Negro" that "Yale has never tried to attract Negroes, and, on the other hand, has never felt justified in refusing admittance to those who came qualified to enter." Admissions dean Corwin, who shared the patent antisemitism common to this era, stated flatly that "there has never been any negro question here, nor has the necessity been felt for adopting a policy of determining our acceptance of negroes."[26] Most of these pre–World War II classes contained only one African American—although there were three in 1904, two in 1905 and again in 1931, and four in 1906 and once more among the veterans of 1947—so their critical mass never exceeded 1.3 percent of a class.

The black graduates before 1924 did not isolate themselves from their white classmates, and even those who participated in all-black social groups were active in campuswide organizations: three had white roommates, two were active members of Linonia, one won the Ten Eyck prize, one was the treasurer of the Freshman Union, and two contributed to the *Yale Courant* and the *Lit.*[27] Still, as William Pickens of 1904, junior class winner of the Ten Eyck prize, was to warn his successors, "Not a single presumption will lie in his favor, neither as to scholarship, nor as to character."[28] Entering Yale as a junior after graduating from Talledega College, which had Yale-educated professors, and eligible by his marks for election to Phi Beta Kappa, Pickens was almost blocked there by a proposed membership rule change requiring four years of attendance in New Haven.[29]

By virtue of their customary route of admission, then, African Americans would not have been either graduates of New England preparatory schools, which were the primary source of the Yale student body, or thereafter, entering as juniors, members of any underclass fraternities, which in the nineteenth and early twentieth centuries paved the way to senior society elections at the close of those blacks' year of entry. When this social disability is added to the statistical difficulty of their infinitesimal numbers—if being tapped had been a lottery rather than a social choice, Pickens and every white classmate in a class of over three hundred had only a one in six chance of random selection to the forty-five senior society places—the absence of any African Americans in senior societies until 1949 is largely if not completely explained, as the classes grew in that year to 1,178, constituting (with only ninety elected) a one in thirteen chance for each man randomly selected. From 1924 to 1966, seventy-seven black students graduated from Yale College, their numbers never totaling more than 7/10ths of one percent of the total number of Yale graduates in their respective years. The great majority of this group graduated after World War II, with only seven blacks receiving Yale degrees from 1924 up to the signing of the armistice.[30]

In 1945, the Yale College students voted overwhelmingly in favor—87 percent for, 5 percent against, 8 percent with no opinion—of allocation of Yale Budget Drive charitable funds to finance university scholarships specifically for African Americans, at a time when all other

Yale College scholarships were granted without regard to race or creed. The university officially announced in 1948 that "Negroes are admitted on academic merit and entitled to all benefits of the university, whether this includes scholarships, other financial aid, or participation in athletics and extra-curricular activities."[31] But in an era of open admissions, the extreme paucity of black undergraduates was because of a shortage of applicants, and as academic standards rose, the lack was explained by a shortage of *qualified* applicants. Not until the Griswold/Brewster/Howe efforts, made manifest through Inky Clark's five-year admissions office tenure, did the number of blacks admitted begin to increase significantly: tripling from the 0.44 percent average achieved in 1957–1963 to 1.3 percent in 1967, then 2.4 percent in 1969, 4 percent in 1972, and 6 percent in 1973. Over three hundred black men and forty-five black women graduated from Yale College from 1966 to 1974.[32]

Lacking any commitment to racial diversity, Yale until the Brewster era had also lacked the commitment required to identify, recruit, admit, support, and graduate large numbers of blacks. Furthermore, the university's image as a white, wealthy, elitist, and stuffily traditional school had tended to discourage many blacks from applying to a college where they would be outnumbered 199 to one, and where there was no black professor who was permanent faculty until 1966.[33] Those African Americans that did apply and attend in the 1950s and early '60s were largely from prep schools such as Exeter, Andover, Northfield–Mt. Herman, Hotchkiss, New York's Horace Mann, and New Haven's Hopkins, schools which were traditionally Yale "feeders" with known and reliably consistent grading systems. Even then, these men felt marginalized, as evidenced by Raleigh Davenport, due to the conscious and unconscious attitudes of Yale's undergraduates, faculty, and administration.[34]

With the growth of campus interest in New Haven in civil rights activities in the South, in the early 1960s undergraduate attitudes began to change. Dr. Martin Luther King spoke at Woolsey Hall in 1959 at the invitation of David Ball (to be tapped for Bones that spring), and again at Battell Chapel in 1962. Yale chaplain Coffin, to the discomfiture of many alumni, participated in the Freedom Rides. Sixty-seven Elis abandoned classes in October 1963 to work for the Mississippi Freedom Ballot, including *News* chairman and future United States senator and vice-presidential candidate Joseph Lieberman '64, taking with him two fellow members of Elihu. The trio was literally chased out of the Mississippi Delta, leaving the day after another Yale student had been shot and wounded in Jackson. (Notably, none of Yale's black undergraduates went south to work in Mississippi, despite pleas from their white liberal classmates.)[35]

Their alma mater's approval of such pioneering civil rights efforts manifested itself in the granting of an honorary degree to Dr. King by Yale at the graduation of the class of 1964. African American applications to Yale had risen from about thirty in 1960 (ten were admitted) to 755 a decade later, an increase achieved without significant pressure from the federal government, the courts, or the local or national black populations. An emerging black consciousness, related to their increasing numbers, led to the founding of an informal group for African American students in the fall of 1964, which by 1965 was calling itself the Yale Discussion Group on Negro Affairs.[36]

A significant partner in the Brewster administration's educational effort, and like the more controversial Coffin an old Bonesman, was McGeorge Bundy, by then president of the Ford Foundation, described the tides of change thusly: "Black demand, white awareness, riots in the cities, and the death of Martin Luther King" were all contributing factors, but "the deeper and more durable cause was the growing conviction that there was a fundamental contradiction between an asserted opposition to racism and the maintenance, by whatever process of selection, of essentially all-white colleges and professional schools." In this reading, the fundamental desegregation of Yale occurred mainly because the Brewster administration believed Yale had not convincingly demonstrated its commitment to the principle of equal opportunity, and moved to remedy this failing.[37]

Yale's traditional self-image as a "democratic" community revolved around the idea of equal opportunity, although the college had been quite comfortable with elites, selective societies, and unequal outcomes. A new conception of Yale's obligations to leadership had emerged after the Second World War, the idea that Yale had an obligation to provide direct *institutional* leadership for society's betterment. In this effort President Brewster had the university community wind at his back (excluding a significant portion of the alumni), with a less parochial faculty and a student body increasingly unwilling to stand aside from national social issues. In the words of Brewster's biographer: "As the ability to play a leadership role in America had been extended to nonclericals, non-Anglo-Saxons, non-Protestants, non-Easterners, and the nonwealthy, and as that extension had been embodied in Yale's widening notion of diversity, so Yale should now increase its notion of diversity to include the nonwhite. If Yale failed to keep pace with society by failing to include a more representative cull of society's future leaders, Yale's importance to society would correspondingly decline."[38] This was a logic the senior societies also saw and followed.

For their 1961 delegation, with only four blacks in the class of 1,060 (comprising roughly one-third of one percent), Elihu elected the African American Joseph Chester Glass III to a system which, with ninety members in the six abovegrounds, included a bit less than 10 percent of that class. In the class of 1965, Skull and Bones elected Orde Coombs, from the Caribbean island of St. Vincent, who served as the secretary of Dwight Hall and the only black member of the Senior Advisory Board. Coombes's classmate Barrington Parker Jr., by then a black federal circuit court judge, said to a national magazine, "Skull and Bones wanted to tap campus leaders, and Orde was a big man on campus."[39]

The following year, both Berzelius and St. Elmo's elected African Americans, and there were two American blacks and one Nigerian elected for 1967 to Scroll and Key, Elihu, and Skull and Bones respectively, from a class containing twelve American blacks (1.16 percent) and six from Africa. Bones' Nigerian member that year, Bernard Ikechukwu Afoeju, was the president of the Union of African Students in New Haven. Keys' choice was Allard Allston Jr., a South Carolina high school graduate serving successively as vice president, secretary, and moderator of the Negro Affairs organization, soon renamed the Black Student Alliance at Yale (BSAY), an eighty-member group sponsoring its first issue-oriented conference that spring and claiming approximately 90 percent of all Yale black students. Notably, one of his new clubmates in Keys was Whit Griswold Jr., Hotchkiss and St. Mark's, and son of the late Yale president.

In the class of 1968, containing fourteen American blacks and four Africans, Keys elected one from each demographic, and Elihu, Manu-script, and St. Elmo's each chose one African American, while Bones elected to George W. Bush's delegation a West Indian soccer star, Roy Austin, later that president's ambassador to Trinidad and Tobago. For the 1969 class, with twenty-three American blacks (2.18 percent of the class), five were tapped, for Bones, Elihu (two), and St. Elmo's (two). And for 1970—a class with thirty-five African Americans, comprising 3.43 percent of their full number of 1,021 men and (now) women, with another eight black classmates from abroad—Bones tapped a Ghanaian, Wolf's Head an American and a Nigerian, Keys two American blacks, Elihu two, St. Elmo's two (in a delegation including Prescott Bush III), and Berzelius and Book and Snake one each. With only 105 seniors in the seven recognized ("aboveground") societies, these eleven blacks constituted 10.5 percent of their aggregate delegations, which was a remarkable two and one-half times their demographic percentage (4.2 percent) in the class of 1,021.[40]

Given the election of Raleigh Davenport to the underground Spade and Grave in 1960, followed by the election there of a Jamaican for 1966 and an American black for the 1969 delegation, a few more black collegians were almost certainly elected to the other undergrounds in these same years, making the true percentage of African American elections to senior societies even higher. (Indeed, it was a black undergraduate, Roderick Mobley of the class of 1999, who was to refound Spade and Grave in the twenty-first century after its demise and second disappear-ance in the turmoil of 1970.)[41] It is no small irony that, in the classification of Yale undergraduates by ethnic and religious types and American regions of origin, such relative demographic "overrepresentation" in the senior societies had not been evidenced since the 1830s and 1840s, in the recruitment by Bones and Keys of Southerners from slave-owning families for their debating skills and dash.

TAPPING STRATEGIES AND PROGRAMS

Of course, the senior societies of the nineteen-sixties (or Wolf's Head in 1957 seeking to elect Larry Bensky) were not insisting on taking Jews or blacks into their ranks; rather, they were insisting on their rights, indeed their sense of human dignity, to take in their old friends from school or new friends on campus who happened to be black or Jewish in origin.

Yet within a Yale College dramatically diversified by the admission of non-WASPS and non-preppies, the senior societies themselves no longer loomed so large in the undergraduate consciousness. As Bart Giamatti observed of this era in his history of Scroll and Key, "What a freshman in 1914 had heard of societies from his preparatory school masters, and a freshman in 1944 might hear from one of his numerous classmates whose relatives had attended Yale, a freshman in 1974, more likely than not from a public high school, with no previous Yale ties, would not hear at all. *That ingrained consciousness of societies, that shared sense of what they meant, disrupted in the forties, seemingly reasserted in the fifties, disappeared like smoke in the late sixties.* Indeed, the last time all the senior societies printed the results of their tap of new members in the *Yale Daily News* was April 28, 1967. All senior societies had to adapt to the new circumstances more extensively, and faster . . . than at any time in their history."[42]

Adaptation began by making sure the juniors knew exactly what the procedures for election were, and when they would begin and conclude. Skull and Bones published a major announcement in the *News* in April 1963, confirming the society's belief "that the ten-day period prior to Tap Day ought to be used to inform the junior without pressure of the alternatives available to him," and "negotiations between its members and juniors concerning elections are incompatible" with the society's here-pronounced objectives of non-interference with the academic life of the community and unpressured junior decision-making. Thus, prior to the second of May's Tap Day, "an alumnus of Skull and Bones will notify some, but not all, of the prospective members that an election would be offered," but no commitment was required; additionally, some offers "will be made on Tap Day with no prior notification" (thus saving face for both sides if candidates rebuffed the society and the seniors had to go further down their list of prospects). "At no time," the statement concluded, "will an undergraduate or graduate member of Skull and Bones discuss elections with a junior."[43] To even the scales, in a system of electing in the rooms, when other societies often required pre-tap pledges, mighty Bones no longer wished to lose men who in prior decades were kept in complete ignorance of their chances.

All societies, according to the *News* report of the 1963 Tap Day, were "supposedly pretapping," and the entire ceremony ("dull, dull, dull") was finished in twelve minutes. The address 493 College Street was "election central," where representatives of the now eight aboveg-rounds kept track of commitments made by their preferred juniors as they were registered on six blackboards (Scroll and Key sharing with Manuscript, and Elihu with Berzelius). The *Yale Daily News* reporter snarked: "'It's sort of what they have instead of God,' said Hemingway."[44]

With their tongues only partly in their cheeks, the authors of a profile of the senior society system published in a class book of this decade wrote that "if the society had had a good year, this is what the 'ideal' group would consist of: a football captain; a Chairman of the *Yale Daily News*; a conspicuous radical; a Whiffenpoof; a swimming captain; a notorious drunk with a 94 average; a film-maker; a political columnist; a Chairman of the *Lit.*; a foreigner; a ladies' man with two motorcycles; an ex-service man; a negro, if there are enough to go around; [and] a guy nobody else in the group had ever heard of, ever."[45]

No one senior society would be likely to have exactly such a complexion of membership, but the description is evocative of the diversity that was now actively sought by most if not all societies. There had been a marked shift from a similarly specific description recorded in W. E. Decrow's *Yale and "The City of Elms, . . ."* regarding the membership of Skull and Bones in 1882, eighty-six years before: "As a rule, of the fifteen members chosen, two are editors of the *Yale Literary Magazine*, one or two are chosen from each of the three great athletic interests— base-ball, football, and boating—one from the staff of each of the Yale newspapers, one or more for high scholarship, and so on, the intention being, apparently, to secure representative men from all the leading student interests in class."[46]

Unsought was continued harassment. Three seniors the next year, members of two underground societies, broke into five of the abovegrounds, taking insignia, memorabilia, and tap information; they were caught by three members of Bones who surprised them in that society's tomb. The Yale administration, noting that the society halls were private property and thus not within the province of the campus police, left the remedy to the respective invaded societies, which apparently chose not to press charges once materials returned and property damage ($1,500 at Wolf's Head) was repaid.[47]

The same year the *News* reported that the dean's office was continuing its policy, which had never been publicly announced, of inviting the societies to obtain academic and extracurricular records (although not College Board scores) of the junior class. Said Dean Georges May, "The records certainly serve a useful purpose. If societies are trying to elect members on the basis of intellectual ability, I feel we ought to provide them." The dean noted that students might request that their records be withheld, but said that no one had ever made such a request. Historically, it appears, the societies had been issued an invitation to review the sanitized cumulative record cards and take notes. Underground societies were eligible, too, so long as they identified themselves and could be recognized as members of a registered underground society, and about half accepted the invitation. Associate professor of Philosophy Richard Bernstein wrote a letter to the *News* editor to complain about the abuse of privacy (when students could not have known of the opt-out procedure), but he was angrier that the college administration was cooperating with the senior society system rather than allowing "these anachronistic societies with their invidious and pervasive influences [to] wither away."[48]

The larger community's attitude was evidenced by the campus newspaper feature prior to the May 1964 Tap Day, titled "The Agony, The Ecstasy: 1964 Spooks Speak: Tap Day Revisited, Secrecy Reexamined." Six prominent seniors from as many senior societies were interviewed, the majority suggesting, "that the reward of prestige is invariably a powerful, if irrational attraction to membership," although several stressed that "personal" reasons were "the final factors in their decision." Members of Manuscript and Elihu proved willing to discuss "almost any feature of their societies' programs," while the Bonesmen, Rhodes scholar Thomas Rowe and basketball captain Rick Kaminsky, declined to disclose any detail of that society's rituals, although they insisted on the value of the experience, in which Rowe said "masks fall and barriers disappear," and which "may have the longest and deepest influence on me" of anything he had ever done.[49]

Alongside the report of these interviews was a sidebar graph of membership characteristic statistics for seven of the abovegrounds for the classes from 1959 to 1963, accompanied by editorial summary. Major differences among them were revealed by the numbers. Berzelius was found to be "fairly diverse" (albeit only by the standards of the time): three-quarters membership from the Northeast, over two-thirds in fraternities, and less than 20 percent "scholars." Book and Snake had "very few" scholars, but an 85 percent membership in fraternities, and over two-thirds from private schools. Elihu, reflecting Yale's changing demographics, with 40 percent of its members from public high schools, had the highest percentage of those with scholarly distinction, and nearly equal numbers of fraternity and non-fraternity members.

Manuscript, the outlier consciously seeking creative types in the arts, was the only society with over half its membership from public high schools, and barely trailed Elihu (17 to 20) in members with scholarly distinction. The two oldest societies reflected the priorities of Old Yale. Keys, with a high percentage of athletes, derived two-thirds of its delegations from the Northeast, and four-fifths of its men were prep school graduates. Bones similarly took three-quarters of its successive memberships for these years from the Northeast, with 70 percent being in fraternities, and at least 50—and more usually 60 to 70—percent athletes, but, the compiler noted, with "an average of two or three conspicuously high successful scholars" each year amid the jocks.[50]

The *News* report of elections for 1964 confirmed that, with extensive pre-tapping during the prior week, the night was marked with little tension or anxiety. "Impeccably-dressed" seniors march from their tombs between 7:00 and 7:30 P.M. to their meeting places in the colleges, while alumni were stationed within the clearing office, and each tapping senior positioned outside the room of a junior who was to be tapped. One possible drama was avoided: football captain H. Abbott Lawrence, accepting an offer from Book and Snake which had sent two men to his room, explained later that one of his tappers was protection for the other, since Bones had considered sending its alumnus, Chicago Bears center Mike Pyle, to his room: "I told them not to, and they didn't." At 10:00 P.M., the society members, new and old, retreated to Fraternity Row for postelection parties.[51]

The following year's (1965's) Tap Day newspaper report served only to confirm the new pattern, forced into place by reforms patiently extracted from the societies by Dean DeVane the decade before. The return to the rooms, where juniors could not see who else was being elected to which societies, brought with it a vastly expanded series of time-limited pre-tap negotiations, conducted over lunch or dinner with senior society members who expressed interest in "examining" them. They had indeed "expanded to the point where one is rarely tapped by a society he has not had previous contact with."[52]

For the successful and/or fortunate, the attention could be over-whelming: a number of juniors were made election offers by as many as six undergrounds, and faced a countless series of meal "appointments" and an uninterrupted deluge of telephone calls. If asked, Berzelius, Elihu, and Manuscript disclosed their first fifteen. Bones was known to approach its choices through an alumnus, although the offerees were invited to consult with current members on their own initiative, and rumors flew thick and fast: university secretary Howard Weaver, assistant director of admissions Charles McCarthy, and other Bones alumni were said to have made twenty-one offers, for fifteen openings, with five commitments by the close of the ten-day "official" pre-tap interval, and in 1966, some candidates alleged the receipt of midnight telephone calls from the offices of Henry Luce (Bones) and John Lindsay (Keys).[53]

Many of these approaches by distinguished alumni were successful; others were not. Chaplain William Sloane Coffin, who had his own post-graduation issues with the society system, approached *Yale Daily News* chairman Joe Lieberman '64 on behalf of Bones, and Lieberman's thoughtful written response is preserved in the Coffin papers. He had considered the offer, he wrote, for the prestige and because he might effect reform from within. But Coffin's refusal to explain the society's program as one which could not be explained, and the candidate's dis-satisfaction with the changes effected in Bones to date which "were not enough," compelled him to choose to Elihu instead, "because I was fully informed of their program and liked it, and was especially excited by the group of people they tapped" (he had their names in advance), and "of course, the [Elihu] building even has windows." The Elihu windows have always-drawn interior blinds, and Bones still tapped Lieberman anyway, and was declined.[54]

Another *News* officer, vice chairman Jacques Leslie, approached by director of athletics Delaney Kiphuth three years later, was told he would be offered a tap on election night unless he specifically reported back that he did not wish to join. Writing about it thirty-three years later in a magazine article aptly titled "Smirk from the Past," Leslie revealed that he decided not to bother with a response although he was leaning toward Elihu. Told by a fellow student who was a freelance photographer that the *New York Times* was planning a story on that year's election, he advised him of the probable Bones/Elihu confrontation expected at Leslie's Branford College door. The front page of the second section of the next day's *Times* featured an action shot of the Bones elector's striking Leslie's shoulder while blocking his rival with his hip: "Skull was first," the caption concluded, "but he chose Elihu." Below was a second photograph, showing Olympic swimming champion Donald Schollander being tapped for Bones, the caption concluding "He accepted membership."[55] Unmentioned in the article was the election of the then-obscure George W. Bush.

The truncated tapping process still attracted crowds: onlookers gathered on the streets to watch the society members parade silently in double file from their tombs, in the hour before tapping, breaking off to enter the residential colleges where their prospects were waiting; even there, spectators gathered on the stairs. When the Harkness Tower bells rang promptly at eight p.m., dormitory doors opened and seniors burst in, demanding acceptance to election. The *News* reported that "an estimated 10 to 20 undergrounds which keep their membership and meeting places secret, will induct juniors at the same time" on election day. The remaining incongruity from earlier decades was the seniors' formal dress, in suits of dark browns, grays, and blues, while all around them were their candidates in shirtsleeves, sweaters, and soiled sport coats.[56]

By 1966, the social and psychological pressures on the juniors in the pre-tap week caused Keys to join Bones in announcing in the *News* that no requirement of a commitment to accept election was required after the initial contact, and that elections to some not so notified would be offered on election day. Manuscript and Book and Snake each announced that they would notify only some juniors of proposed elections, while Manuscript's announcement also promised that tappees would be "given a full and frank description of purposes and activities of the society." In a first formal appearance in the campus newspaper for an underground,

Mace and Chain called on its fellow societies to "respect the intelligence and integrity of the juniors and . . . offer them a full opportunity for discussion of the society experience," promising "an open presentation of the program of their society," while following Dean May's rules for the abovegrounds in not offering election until the official dean-proscribed pre-tap week.[57]

Particularly poignant is the recollection of his experiences that year by a gay man in the class of 1967, Paul Monette, in his autobiography, which won the 1992 National Book Award for nonfiction and was published three years before his AIDS-related death in 1995 at age fifty. Monette was the editor of his residential college's newspaper and its literary magazine, as well as the college literary magazine *The Criterion* and director of the Yale Arts Festival. Because the societies "all wanted a token artist or two, my role as poet/impresario put me on the short list," courted by four of the eight abovegrounds, "swept up and taken to lunch by the captain of the hockey team and the editor of the *Yale Lit.*"

In the end, like Joe Lieberman, Monette went with Elihu, which "had the reputation of being the most diverse and the least preppie of the Societies, politically correct before its time. Where the others reluctantly tapped a token Jew, girding themselves for the country-club fights to come, Elihu chose four Jews to be my brothers, and a Cuban and an African American to boot. *Quel* melting pot. More to the point, they chose three queers as well, though that would never be spoken aloud, even within the sanctum walls. . . . And I accepted without question that the main agenda for senior year would be my becoming brothers in blood with the fourteen members of my delegation. . . . Thursday would be our tribal night come autumn, when each of us would be required to present an autobiography to our fourteen brothers. . . . [But] I already knew I would lie when I told my story."[58]

This was to change: in 1975, Skull and Bones openly embraced the new diversity and celebrated its leadership pattern when it tapped Miles Watson, the president of the Gay Activists Alliance, and a member of the Keys crowd of 1988 was to remember that by his year, it had become "almost traditional" to elect two gays annually. The Bones club of 2011, it was reported, included two gay students, one bisexual, and one transgender.[59]

By 1967, in addition to the seven abovegrounds and as many or more undergrounds, there had been formed with some of the Seven Sisters colleges at least six coed societies, most open to both juniors and seniors. Gathering in hotels halfway between Yale and the schools in question, two met with Vassar girls (they were known as "Vaya" and "Vale"), three with women from Smith, and one with Mt. Holyoke, most taking five girls and five boys, two-thirds of the canonical number of fifteen. The members were not allowed to date, and their activities were bounded by strictly imposed intellectual limits. Writing of these groups' more traditional rivals, one campus newspaper editorialist mused sarcastically: "What a small tribute it is to Yale—unique in having spawned secret societies—that so many students think it necessary to go behind locked doors, with 14 other arbitrarily chosen students, many of whom they've never met before, to establish something truly valuable in the way of human relations."[60]

To the contrary, it was a large tribute, even if a leap of faith, to an arcane (and, given the intense labor which went into identifying those chosen for election, hardly arbitrary) social system which their Yale College forbears had found rewarding for going on 140 years. Kingman Brewster was quoted in a front-page story on the secret societies in the *Wall Street Journal* in 1968, saying, "There are so many of them now, including some whose existence is dubious or hard to confirm, that the bright line between in-group and out-group is fuzzy." About one in four Yale seniors now belonged to a senior society of some sort.[61]

Their "secret" programs, at least for the abovegrounds and many of the undergrounds, were now reasonably well known. "Autobiographies" or "Personal Histories" were an integral part of most, although Scroll and Key and Manuscript were said to have departed from this pattern and delivered talks on chosen topics, claiming that as much might be gleaned thereby about a member's personality. Still, the confessional history remained a serious and central component of the society experience, whether delivered according to ancient rumor in Bones while lying in a coffin, or around a large table in the main meeting room at Elihu, or in a circle of easy chairs at Wolf's Head.

"An Auto," declared the 1968 *Class Book*, "is simply this: on one evening during the year, a member has *his* night. For those not inclined to introspection, it is often an entirely new and frightening experience: the obligation to look into oneself, attempt to organize coherent self-description, and express it lucidly. Seeing at last one purpose for the vaunted secrecy, the member feels timidly free to disclose feelings and emotions with the assurance that the 'family privacy' of the institution will prevail." Secrets shared and weaknesses made vulnerable, the article's authors concluded, tended to pull a group together, even if only as a starting point for deeper friendship. (In his famous New Journalism essay of 1976, "The 'ME' Decade," Tom Wolfe [a Yale PhD but not an undergraduate there] argued that another result of what he called these "lemon sessions" within the Yale senior societies was a new level of self-involvement and narcissism: "No matter how dreary the soap opera, the star was *Me*."[62])

Guest speakers had become more frequent, too: the undergrounds, with little institutional rigidity, freely made use of the talent and diversity represented in the Yale faculty, while the abovegrounds continued to require that all guests be alumni, and then—other than Bones, Keys, and Wolf's Head—loosened that stricture by composing a list of "honorary alumni." In another variation on the "Auto," Berzelius had each member write a separate letter to each of his fourteen "brothers," telling him of the writer's feelings toward him. The less-structured undergrounds practiced acting and playwriting, and listened to recorded concerts, or even devoted an entire night to dirty jokes. Despite the still largely ignorant junior's pledging at the outset to spend two evenings a week for the whole academic year, doing who really knew what with some who were necessarily strangers, the dropout rate remained remarkably low, especially in the ritual-bound abovegrounds, although the undergrounds also lost a few brothers every year.[63]

This sudden loyalty was not, according to Professor Chris Argyris, the head of Yale's Industrial Administration department (an alumnus of Elihu and a popular speaker with almost all the undergrounds), merely the result of a new member's having a vested interest in maintaining the prestige of his society and thus persuading himself that the experience was worth the effort. "Of course there is an inevitable amount of rationalization and egoistic self-deception in the seniors' new-found enthusiasm. But this is overlooking the very real personal benefits which many seniors receive from their society experience." Because the societies gave their members a unique opportunity to build a society and culture all their own, Argyris maintained, "with many of their own rules and particular behavioral patterns, students respond to such an opportunity with a great deal of excitement."

To the admiring jibe that Yale societies had been practicing group psychotherapy for 135 years when it had been in vogue in the Western world for only the prior four decades, Argyris maintained that "you can't think in terms of therapeutic effects with the degree of efficiency of current psychological group therapy. Yet, on the other hand, many undergo marked changes—we may, in a very broad sense, even call them therapeutic changes—because of their society experience. Of course, others merely have their behavioral and personality patterns reinforced." Furthermore, the abovegrounds' emphasis on rigid and secretive ritual, the professor believed (echoing Goethe's insights of almost two centuries before), "also is linked to a general desire to have a deep commitment to something wholly outside oneself," and the continued growth and success of the Yale senior society system reflected "a general search among younger people to escape a compartmentalized and de-personalized world and to find and develop more profound relationships with their peers." Argyris also dismissed the notion that the lack of women at Yale made the men channel their energies into the societies: "I don't think the homosexual impulse is at all primary, and certainly was and is not conscious."

Commenting at the same time, David Riesman, famed author of *The Lonely Crowd* and Harvard professor of Social Relations, saw more functionally, and not incorrectly, "an achievement orientation and competitiveness at Yale" which tended to perpetuate the ultimate manifestations of achievement, here the senior society. "Yale has always seemed more competitive than Harvard. . . . This kind of achievement orientation is only in recent decades entering Harvard, which was always in a sense . . . Georgian rather than Masonic."[64]

Also to be noted is that the society members' alumni bonds with the Alma Mater had not frayed. The aboveground societies now contributed about $30,000 a year for scholarship funds, when tuition with room and board was roughly $3,000, and an analysis of gifts revealed that 90 percent of the members of the three oldest societies, Bones, Keys, and Wolf's Head, gave to the alumni fund, while the overall rate for Yale graduates was only about 50 percent. This was in the pattern of the munificent gifts of Sterling and Harkness: "They [the more recent donors] did so," a society alumnus reflected to the *Wall Street Journal*, "because they loved Yale all the more for having been members of the societies."[65]

CONVULSIONS IN THE GREATER WORLD

The unsettling of the settled ways of Yale College, never an isolated community, was exacerbated and accelerated by national events and trends: the election of the young, liberal John F. Kennedy, the Cuban missile crisis, then the president's assassination, the rise of Goldwater conservatism, the first student lunch counter sit-ins to protest Southern segregation, the construction of the Berlin wall, the flowering of rock'n'roll, and the development of the birth control pill. In these very years, the lawsuit that established the right of privacy forming the basis for the Supreme Court's *Roe v. Wade* decision legalizing abortion had its origin in New Haven. Both the conservative Young Americans for Freedom, backing Goldwater, and the Northern Student Movement, the northern counterpart to the Student Nonviolent Coordinating Committee (SNCC), were formed at Yale or in close association with the university within months of the matriculation of the class of 1964, both—despite disparate goals—a part of grassroots youth movements combining activism and ideology with hostility to ruling elites.

The Yale Political Union, long considered a proving ground for future public figures, saw the establishment of a Progressive Party as well as a Party of the Right, joining established Conservative and Liberal caucuses. Outside the Political Union arose the Yale Socialists, the Yale Student Peace Union, the George Orwell Society (for Marxist socialists), and the libertarian Calliopean Society (named after Yale's third literary society, which had disappeared in the 1850s). While university chaplain Coffin was pressing students into dangerous service in Mississippi, William F. Buckley Jr. and Goldwater were calling students to rise against creeping collectivism at home and communist tyranny abroad.[66]

President Griswold in 1958 had maintained that a Yale education was not intended simply to advance "self-expression," but to prepare her graduates for "responsible membership in society after graduation." In a 1963 open letter to Yale alumni addressing the civil rights movement, *News* chairman Joe Lieberman, citing Griswold, evidenced the absorption of this message in declaring that "We envision Yale as a training ground for a democratic elite." When Yale College under Brewster turned more explicitly to admitting an intellectual meritocracy at a time when the desired future looked very different to increasingly antagonistic communities within the alumni and the nation, debate and conflict were guaranteed to ensue about the socio-economic characteristics of the leaders Yale purported to educate, as well as among the vastly more diverse applicants who were accepted.

Precisely when this occurred cannot be confined to one year—the titles of the many available histories of "pivotal years" include 1964, 1965, and 1968, and the same themes of upheaval are detailed in recent books by graduates of two Yale classes of the decade—*On the Cusp: The Yale College Class of 1960 and a World on the Verge of Change*, and *Class Divide: Yale '64 and the Conflicted Legacy of the Sixties*—but the widening separation of the seams of the old consensus was visible throughout the decade's back end.[67]

The Free Speech Movement which roiled the Berkeley campus of the University of California in the autumn of 1964 is identified by most commentators as the ground zero of the explosion that permanently disturbed the stability of American universities. As pollster Daniel Yankelovich put it, "The campus upheavals of the sixties gave us the first premonitory sign that the [tectonic] plates of American culture, after decades of stability, had begun to shift."[68] Berkeley's troubles in the West were followed, sometimes more violently, by Harvard, Cornell (the newspaper photograph of rifle-carrying blacks leaving the Cornell Student Union won that year's Pulitzer Prize), and Columbia in the East in 1968,[69] and two years later at Yale on May Day 1970 in demonstrations surrounding the trial of Black Panther Bobby Seale, and then the following week, most tragically, with the National Guard's killing of students at Kent State in Ohio.

It was of course Vietnam, called by one journalist "the San Andreas fault in the hearts and minds of Americans," which most fundamentally challenged presumptions that had informed the Cold War thinking of the 1950s that had done so much to define American attitudes and experiences in the years following the Second World War. It ran like a pestilence through American society, impeaching the "system" and its leadership in the eyes of a generation, largely shattering the conventional faith in the decency of American purposes.[70] For some, the war was combat, for others journalism, for others active, even violent, protest, and for most it was avoidance—but none escaped what one member of the class of 1964 at his twenty-fifth reunion called "the scars of our interaction with history in the Indochinese peninsula."[71]

Three members of Elihu had gone off to Mississippi in the fall of 1963. Four members of Skull and Bones after their graduation in 1966 all enlisted: John Kerry (future Senator, presidential candidate, and secretary of state), Frederick Smith (later the founder of Federal Express), David Thorne (to be President Obama's ambassador to Italy), and Richard Pershing (grandson of "Black Jack" Pershing, America's senior military commander in the First World War). Before leaving, Kerry had written his

Class Day speech in the quiet of the Bones tomb, calling for a restricted U.S. role in Vietnam, and also about the duty to serve. On February 17, 1968, Second Lieutenant Dick Pershing, who had last seen his clubmates at the November 1967 Yale-Harvard football game, perished near Hung Nuhn in Vietnam.[72]

For that quartet and its class, military enlistment was an acceptable postgraduate choice. (The first open forum on the Vietnam War at Yale, in 1965, saw Chaplain Coffin in a minority, criticizing Joe Lieberman for supporting the war.) As the casualties mounted and the nation soured on the execution of the war, its conduct became increasingly contested across the country's campuses, along with much else that followed in the name of national defense. Many who joined the services during those years of combat, like Kerry on his return home in testimony before the Congress, joined those who did not in challenging the hegemony of Cold War presumptions that still held sway among their elders. Others, like Dick Cheney, in and out of Yale College twice while briefly a member of the class of 1964, sought student deferments or, like the class of 1968's George W. Bush, alternative service in National Guard units. Following the establishment of a lottery to induct draftees with low lottery numbers, no names from the class of 1970 were to appear on Woolsey Hall's memorial to Yale's Vietnam dead.

The war strain was so great that at the June 1969 graduation, William McIlwaine Thompson, the class secretary, was permitted to be the first speaker at a university commencement since 1894 (other than President Kennedy, for whom an exception had been made in 1962); Thompson, a Nixon voter in 1968, told the graduates, faculty members, and parents that "frustration and despair" because of the Vietnam war had overwhelmed his class. Over time, the disagreements over race and that war, when joined by the contemporaneous cause and conflict of women's liberation in the succeeding decades, birthed what Patrick Buchanan called the "culture war" at the 1992 Republican National Convention.

One historian has concluded that these disagreements have now become so rooted in different ways of "apprehending reality, of ordering experience, [and] of making moral judgments," that they have under-girded both the institutionalization and the politicization of two funda-mentally different cultural systems.[73] The senior societies had, of course, nothing directly to do with these larger developments, but at their dif-ficult birth and through their growth in the 1960s, in the disdain for all forms of authority which necessarily accompanied the many and varied targets of protest, the prestige and cohesion of these venerable organiza-tions were sorely tested, and some were to go under.

THE ADMISSION OF WOMEN

On Yale's Commencement Day in 1773, Nathan Hale argued the affirmative in a debate on the question, "Whether the Education of Daughters be not without just reason more neglected than that of our Sons." He won the debate, but not the point. Roughly a century later, Daniel Coit Gilman helped persuade Augustus Sweet to establish a School of Fine Arts at Yale, with the donor's express wish and condi-tion of his gift that women be admitted (the first two, and thus the first two women students at Yale, were daughters of Bones alumnus Professor Benjamin Silliman Jr., Alice and Susan Silliman, entering in 1869). Another full century on, compared to the decades-long patterns of fitful admission into Yale College of the sorts of undergraduates who were not Caucasian males of Protestant stock, the eventual inclusion of women was relatively swift. Although the institution was in many respects a different place in 1960 than it had been before World War II, as far as women were concerned little had changed since 1934, when the university secretary is said to have harrumphed to the wife of a law student, "Young woman, we tolerate women at Yale, but we don't encourage them."[74] In time, bringing women into Yale College would transform gender relations at the institution and contribute to reducing the barriers to professional careers for women in the society at large.

By 1960, it has been estimated that women comprised 36 percent of American undergraduate students.[75] They were a significant presence at that level in most of the other schools of the Ivy League, whether through "full" coeducation (Cornell, admitting limited numbers since 1872) or "coordinate" coeducation (at Harvard, with separately administered Radcliffe College, whose students attended classes and socialized with Harvard males, and Brown with Pembroke College, since separate but unequal was the conventional wisdom on the sexes at Harvard, Yale, and Princeton until the late 1960s). Yet culturally and symbolically, Yale and other prestigious all-male institutions and traditions, from Rhodes scholarships to White House stag dinners, seemed to define leadership and excellence in male terms. As a *New York Post* columnist crudely put it, "[w]hat makes a dumb broad smart all of a sudden? They don't even let broads in a joint like Yale."[76]

Even before admissions dean Howe in 1956 broached the notion of all-female residential colleges, in the Oxbridge manner of separate colleges for women, proposals to coeducate Yale College had been discussed, since the 1910s, but as Yale professor Thomas Bergin noted, "such suggestions had never been taken seriously by either the great majority of the alumni, the Corporation, or the undergraduates themselves."[77] Howe had stated the obvious: the all-male college was "outmoded," both positively harmful, since the separation of academic and social life was no longer the American social norm, and—to Yale's detriment—clearly less appealing to the current generation of intellectually gifted male students that the college sought to attract (especially high school graduates, long educated with girls, who found Yale's single-sex arrangement bizarre). Some prospects began to decline admission in New Haven for rival institutions which were coeducational, and the Yalies' "weekend exodus" in search of female companionship at the Seven Sisters colleges and in New York City disrupted the residential colleges' founding purpose of fostering community.

The strong countervailing concern was that women would not occupy the positions of responsibility and authority in American society that the graduates of Yale, "Mother of Men" in its school anthem, had occupied and should continue to occupy. Even Yale's psychiatrist-in-chief,

Dr. Robert L. Arnstein, argued that something would be lost if women came to Yale: a rare, hard-to-define ability to form close male friendships, which would ultimately detract from campus life and the educational process. Furthermore, the fear persisted that if Yale College educated fewer males, its contribution to the American establishment would inevitably decline, and thus over time and inevitably so too would the school's prestige and influence.

An allied fear among alumni with Yale family histories was that reducing the number of men admitted (no one thought an expansion of the college's undergraduate population would occur any way but incrementally) meant, in a zero-sum game, that many fewer slots for their sons. The *News* warned that coeducation would "come down the chimney, like a plague," and Griswold moved quickly to calm the alumni waters roiled by Howe's proposal in 1956 by stating flatly for their magazine that "We are far from convinced that it [coeducation] would be the right course of action. There is not the remotest possibility of its taking place in time in the forseeable future."[78]

That future accelerated quickly under his successor Brewster, and a more liberally minded Yale Corporation and student body that pushed him. The Griswold-appointed Committee on the Freshman Year in its 1962 report had held that "We think Yale has a national duty, as well as a duty to itself, to provide the rigorous training for women that we supply for men." This opinion was ahead of undergraduate sentiment: a poll the next year of the 1963 freshmen in the class of 1967 confirmed opposition to coeducation by a ratio of three to one, with their giving much the same reasons as those of the alumni: tradition, custom, preservation of the Yale image, and a belief that women were not men's equals. This attitude changed in short order: by May 1966, four out of five undergraduates polled said they would favor some sort of undergraduate education for women at Yale if adequate financial backing were available.[79] Certainly part of the explanation was the increasing fraction (from 1963, a majority) of each incoming class which came from the coeducational public high schools.

Brewster responded by reopening the question of establishing a coordinate women's college in New Haven, and in December 1966, Yale and Vassar College agreed to conduct a joint study to investigate the possibilities of some form of joinder of their institutions (in 1966, only 5 percent of all male undergraduates were in all-male institutions like Yale and Princeton, and they were just two of eighteen all-male and thirty-five all-female colleges to plan coeducation or coordinate affiliation between 1966 and 1968[80]). When Vassar jilted Yale in November 1967—presumably having nothing to do with an earlier football game halftime formation by the Yale Marching Band showing a "Y" proceeding slowly into a "V"—Brewster chose to press on with direct admissions.

On November 4, 1968, a student-sponsored "Co-Education Week" brought to New Haven seven hundred women from twenty-two Northeastern colleges to spend six days at Yale in two three-day shifts. (The *Yale Daily News* featured a formal announcement, placed by a member of Elihu, that Skull and Bones, "in cooperation with the New Haven Garden Club," would that week hold "an open house for all Yale's co-eds" and gave instructions on how to find its tomb.) The Yale Corporation voted to admit women to Yale College on a full coeducational basis in the fall of 1969. Brewster was said to have promised alumni that Yale was committed to producing "1000 male leaders a year," so that the number of men would not be reduced, but five hundred women would be admitted, half first-year students in the class of 1973, and half sophomore and junior class transferees.

Thousands of applications came in, including one from a thirteen-student Radcliffe dormitory applying for admission as a unit. In September 1969, 588 women undergraduates enrolled, including from 2,850 applications, 230 fresh(wo)men, meaning only one in fourteen applicants was admitted, compared with admission of one man for ever 7.5 applicants. Three-quarters of them were from public high schools, comprising 18.3 percent of the class of 1973, of whom 18.3 percent were Yale daughters, as against 12.5 percent of the 1,029 men. Of the 358 women transferees, 203 enrolled as juniors in the class of 1971, and 155 as sophomores in the class of 1972, 44 of the aggregate being alumni daughters. Six in the class of 1971's intake and ten in 1972's were black women.

The Seven Sisters colleges, close to Yale in social composition and geography, provided more than their share. Of the transferring females, fully 124 were from just three of them, Smith, Vassar, and Wellesley. The number of coeds at Yale was to rise incrementally, to 1,500, once new housing became available, and the women's admissions quota was dropped forever in December 1972. The talent of the first five hundred which Yale selected was so high that they were to be dubbed "the Super-women," and their gender was to earn consistently higher grades than men at Yale until the ratio of applications to acceptances for the two sexes began to level out.[81]

As noted in a *New York Times Magazine* article on the admission of the first classes of coeds, which the author, a member of the class of 1970, said, "on paper were the female versions of Nietzsche's *Ubermensch*," their male counterparts were pondering one question. Where everything was so masculine—the entire residential college system, the social clubs, and the weekend dating system were all predicated on Yale's being an all-male institution, as were the absence of bathtubs, the four-inch thick dormi-tory doors designed for the male hand, and the lack of a gynecologist in the student health department—just how were the women going to change the college?

One high school senior from Minneapolis told the *Wall Street Journal* that she "would be willing to forego baths for four years to gain her ambition in life: membership in Skull and Bones." But it was a serious question, said the *Times* piece: "What about Mory's, the Whiffenpoof haunt, or secret societies like Elihu, Book and Snake, or Skull and Bones? Will the tombs open for women?" These questions paralleled those asked in a *Yale Daily News* article published the February before they arrived: "Will Mory's go coed? Will the girls be admitted to the senior societies? (That is, if anybody cares whether anybody is ever admitted to a senior society)."[82]

Two women graduate students arriving at Yale the year before the admission of females to Yale College, Janet Lever and Pepper Schwartz, took the school "as a laboratory" to examine the sudden intrusion of females in the 1969-70 academic season, looking at "one year in the life of an institution, one year of great change, compromise and discussion" in their 1971 book, *Women at Yale: Liberating a College Campus.* Shocked at finding their own admission to Mory's where they felt like "intruders," could only occur on "ladies' night . . . open to us only as dates and wives," they were even more perturbed by the "mausoleum-like" tombs of the senior societies, although they acknowledged their role and power.

"The 'tombs,' they wrote, "as the societies are called have traditionally marked the apex of achievement—an encouragement to begin making a success of one's life from the freshman year on. Besides their prestige value, they offer a chance to become friends with the people 'most likely to succeed.' And they introduce the ambitious student to successful, often famous society alumni. . . . While many students reject the elitism that is inherent in the societies, an important minority regard the societies as part of their journey toward 'making it.' In that sense, they do give a 'tone' to the campus."[83] From their sociologist/feminist perspective, the authors lamented that there were "no major changes" in any of the abovegrounds during the implementation of Clark's new policies and before coeducation, while contradictorily then noting that "they are composed of an elite of achievers who run the gamut of nationality, race, religion, and political affiliation."

They quoted a member of the Students for a Democratic Society (SDS) who defended his membership in St. Elmo's, "and many 'hip' looking people would tell us about the benefits of their society." They cited a member of Bones whom they had known before he was tapped, when he made light of the secret societies, but was now "quite serious about his organization and quite committed" to his fellow members. "While we have seen this same kind of allegiance among fraternity men, we have never seen it in someone who would certainly be anti-establishment and anti-fraternity on almost any campus we could imagine. Perhaps the elitism of the society of fifteen, as opposed to the quasi-elitism of a fraternity of eighty, made the difference." But given the senior society ethos, "these men were literally hand-picked as 'leaders of leaders,'" and the "institutional directive is to join the inner circle of those who succeed."[84]

Lever and Schwartz clearly and correctly recognized that the philosophy of leaders and leadership cadres was a continuing theme of Yale life, and this gave the senior societies a special kind of validity, since they were "societies of merit, not inheritance," and as such fit well into a competitive, democratic system. Yet if the men of Yale were still achievers, still leaders, "it was to be expected that the Yale women would also fit into this category, and this brought up a very serious question: "How would the new 'chosen' mesh with the old? How would traditional female role assignment, i.e., subordinate and unchallenging womanhood, mesh with the Yale woman's inheritance of the Yale ethos, to succeed and, especially, to *lead*? Obviously, changes and compromises would be essential if Yale were truly to incorporate a new kind of Yalie into her code. A revision of traditional roles would take place—or a serf population would be created. No one really knew which way it would go."[85]

The only illustrations in *Women at Yale* were a number of cartoons by Gary Trudeau, class of 1970 and Keys, from his *Yale Daily News* comic strip *Bull Tales*, later famous as the nationally syndicated *Doonesbury*. The first reproduced is of his title character, sitting in his dorm room on election day (here quoting the internal monologue word balloon) "in a new J. Press suit, waiting the nod from a prestigious society which he will flatly turn down in his protest against elitism!" At 6:30 P.M., late in the Tap Day afternoon, Mike Doonesbury opens his door to a frazzled-looking, dress-suited senior gripping a walkie-talkie, who says "Skull and Bones, accept or reject, Goddamit." In the final panel, Doonesbury looks directly at the reader and thinks, "My only regret is that I am not on the john right now." Only *News* readers would know that his character was recalling the legend of Kingman Brewster, declining a Bones tap from his locked toilet stall in 1941.[86]

During the November 1968 Co-Education Week, some of the senior societies (Lever and Schwartz's book says there were then about twenty, above and below ground) had sponsored open houses, although most held their luncheons in nearby halls, thereby preventing the exposure of their private meeting rooms.[87] When would women, the newest but last caste, be admitted to the tombs? Professor Argyris, for one, had no concerns about that prospect for the system. "At Yale, the coed societies [with the Seven Sisters schools] undergo the same kind of experience as the all-male ones. In my view, in fact, they have a richer experience." He concluded (opining in 1968) that if Yale were to go coed—estimating, wrongly in the event, that it would take another five years—"this will not undermine the society impulse per se; but there will be greater pressure to co-educate the societies." His interlocutors, recent Yale graduates of the all-male class of 1967, were not so sure: "It's a pretty safe bet to say that twenty-five years from now, black-suited seniors will be seen marching but in lock-step at some such dire hour as midnight, as ferociously serious as ever. Whether an occasional skirt will come swishing out of the dark and heavy portals is interesting to ponder."[88]

MAY DAY AND THE LONG FALL FROM GRACE

The imminence of the arrival of women, which made men's senior societies seem suddenly old-fashioned, and the on-campus controversies over the great issues of war and race roiling the nation, making the societies seem trivial, resulted by the spring of 1969 in a partial collapse of undergraduate respect for the traditional verities of the entire system. "Can it possibly be true," a Yale professor wrote in to the Yale Daily News, "that those who would save Biafra, help the Hill [New Haven's blackest, poorest neighborhood], reorganize the curriculum, resist the draft, stop the war, feed the migrant fruitpickers, get rid of neckties in the dining halls and parietal hours [limiting women's presence in the dormitories], bring in coeds and enshrine Che [Guevara]—that they would also like to join a secret society?"[89]

The strains had been building for some time. Fewer and fewer collegians had previous Yale and/or senior society affiliations. To take Scroll and Key as an example: only three members of the 1967 crowd had previous Yale and senior society ties. In the late 1930s, the number of Keysmen with Yale ancestors was 64 percent, dropping to 51 percent in the 1940s, then to 48 percent in the 1950s, and to 35 percent in the 1960s. Even fewer knew about their society from having forebears in it, on average only 8 percent, or less than two in each fifteen of the 1960s, whereas in the late '30s it had been 20 percent, then 18 percent in the postwar '40s, and even in the '50s, twice as many at 16 percent.

While fewer students came into the societies with preconceptions, also fewer were those in some sense automatically attached to the past, or feeling any obligation to perpetuate it in a form their fathers and brothers had preserved. New members, showing the strain in the college and in their personal harmonics, also felt less inclination to remain if they were not happy: in each of the portraits of the Keys crowds from 1967 to 1972, fewer than fifteen members are shown, although full delegations had been tapped originally. The 1970 delegation, one of whose members was an SDS leader and later remembered by its own society as "the group that almost sank Keys," had two dropouts in its first month, never met in their usual sanctum, kept many rituals only loosely, invited outsiders to visit (although not to meetings), and fought hard with the alumni to admit women.

The club for 1971 which they elected was initiated the week after the tumultuous May Day weekend and addressed by the patrician World War II veterans John Lindsay '44 and Avery Rockefeller '49. Comprised of seven whites, four blacks, and three Hispanics, it was similarly fractured, the diversity so great that bonding was hard to achieve, and the full fifteen never met together. Keys was hardly alone in the continuing disarray: a member of its 1972 delegation, interviewed for membership at Berzelius and Book and Snake in the spring of 1971, found that at the former they watched Berzelius's color television on Sunday nights, and that few members of Book and Snake troubled any longer to attend the regular dinners.[90]

Yale College's social changes had been vertiginous. When the class of 1970 arrived in 1966, they had short hair, ties and jackets were mandatory in the dining halls (and had been since 1952), and if a woman was found in a student room after parietal hours, the penalty was expulsion. By their senior year, hair was often shoulder length, tie-dyed T-shirts might be worn to meals, and not only were the parietal rules gone, but a coeducational Yale even had coed dormitories.[91] Moreover, the whole notion of the value of leadership was at issue, in a new era that now elevated communal values over the hierarchical ones that had formed the core of the senior society system since its inception. When Calvin Trillin returned to Yale in 1970 to write about changes there, he "asked a group of seniors whether they had anyone in their class who was going to be President. After a puzzled silence, one young man said, 'President of what?'"[92]

On April 28, 1967, the *Yale Daily News* printed the spring's election results for all the abovegrounds. This was the last time it was ever to happen. The following spring, some members of the junior class held a meeting a week before Tap Day to protest the "intentional secrecy and rigidity of the societies," with one student declaring, with casual disregard for the concept of private property, let alone the traditions of private clubs: "There is an elitist quality to the present society structure which perturbs many people. We are also concerned that societies use their time and funds for constructive projects in the community." The *News* editorialist concurred: "The closed attitude which most of the societies maintain tinges Yale with parochialism and anachronism." The day after this editorial appeared, society elections were published on page four, but Bones, Keys, Wolf's Head, and Manuscript did not announce theirs.[93]

In the spring of 1969, the senior society system came under the most sustained assault since the class vote in 1883 calling on the Yale administration to abolish the system. One *News* columnist, titling his piece "'Tis Pity She's a Whore," analogized the senior societies to a prostitute, and Yale to a pimp for tolerating the whore's continual appeal to the seduced customers, the undergraduates. By the week before Tap Day, urged on by another *News* opinion writer, firebrand Tim Bates, who favored choosing participants in societies by lottery, more than 275 members of the class of 1970 had signed a pledge not to accept election or, alternatively, not to enter the society buildings unless and until alumni trustees effected a number of specific reforms.

The petitioners' formal demands included that the incoming delegations have the right to establish their own house rules (by which was meant being able to bring in a friend or a date); that they be allowed to make the tombs available "to a wider segment of the Yale community" having "a legitimate need for the facilities of the societies," such as undergrounds, or an art exhibit; and that they be "informed about and consulted on financial affairs in order to make those funds available to a wider segment of the Yale community." These were felt to be the "minimum innovation necessary if the societies wish to remain in tune with other changes taking place at Yale, and if they wish to remain relevant to the students they purport to serve." More alarmingly, the pledge's sponsors claimed that an equal number of students refused to sign, preferring the radical position that the societies should simply disband, pushing the aggregate numbers of society opponents up to nearly half the class. Even within the societies there were such rumblings: a member of the 1971 Bones delegation, Wilbur Johnson, teaching in New Haven's ghetto the summer after being tapped, asked to make use of some of his society tomb's rooms for classroom space and was denied.

Two other *News* editors pushed back, calling Bates's stance "presumptuous and sanctimonious" and concluding that the "attempt to fit society decisions to a recklessly egalitarian new-liberal dogma falls flat." To the *News* reporter whose article on the juniors' petition challenge was titled "Societies Face Sea of No Faces," representatives of the societies themselves stated that while they believed they would complete their full delegations, they had found it much more difficult during pre-tap to get advance, affirmative promises to join. Several of the undergrounds admitted to being hard-pressed to fill their quotas of fifteen, and even Spade and Grave, described in the story as "the oldest, most prestigious, and wealthiest of the undergrounds," found itself with only nine members by year's end. Meanwhile, the coed undergrounds with Vassar, Mt. Holyoke, and Smith declared their existence was threatened by next year's influx of coeds.[94]

The graduate boards of the landed senior societies were understandably not prepared to consider sharing their real estate and overestimated wealth with the invitees of neophyte members or outside groups, and their current delegations pushed through the traditional elections, all in due course achieving their canonical fifteens. Yet the pressure for "reforms" could not and was not completely resisted, as reviewed in a *News* article published the following fall. While a study of seven of the eight abovegrounds found that the changes effected were more symbolic than substantive, with more fundamental reforms blocked by "alumni, member conservatism, and by the societies' inability to define their relation to the community," and by the lack of undergraduate financial control (only in Elihu did the seniors share that board power).

Five—Book and Snake, Bones, Manuscript, Elihu, and St. Elmo's— were now said to "seem" to have the authority to set their own "house rules," meaning admission of non-members to their halls when meetings were not in progress. Berzelius and Wolf's Head could not revise such rules without the approval of their alumni, then unforthcoming, but Berzelius members could now bring their friends into their tomb. Elihu, the most liberal of them all, was said to be in the process of developing a program "aimed generally towards the community," without providing details. All shied away, in this fall of 1969, from the larger question of coeducation, believing it too soon in the academic year to think about.[95]

A Manuscript subcommittee composed half of current undergraduates and half graduate members proposed in early 1970 that the delegation be enlarged to about 30, including juniors, and that the society drop out of the tapping system, allowing prospective members to meet at the society before committing. By later that spring, the Manuscript delegation of 1969–70 had became unruly and disrespectful of the society experience, inviting strangers into the house, alienating faculty advisors, ignoring their membership bills, and preferring to eat pizza and smoke dope in the basement rather than dine with their elders upstairs. The society's trustees met to discuss actually disbanding the society, while establishing an ad hoc committee to consider further reforms. These, which were provisionally approved, including broadening the Thursday night meetings to include women, underclassmen, and graduate students, while reserving Sunday nights for the year's delegation and all honorary and graduate members.[96]

Into this fraught atmosphere for one particular senior society, and overwhelming others who had been attempting to complete their contingents before elections on April 24, 1970, swept the Yale-wide crisis afterward known as May Day. The date, the first weekend in May, had traditionally been College Weekend, devoted to plays, picnics, and drinking contests.

A murder in New Haven had led to the indictment of the national leader of the Black Panthers, Bobby Seale, for a trial to be held right next to the Yale campus. The Black Panthers, the Yippies, and other groups called for a massive rally on the New Haven Green on the first of May and a shutdown of the university, and rumors promised violence across the campus and city. The peril seemed real: up at Harvard on April 15, an SDS rally protesting the Panther trial, involving three thousand marchers, resulted in the hospitalization of 214 people and $100,000 in property damage when Harvard closed its gates to the participants. Posters went up in Cambridge thereafter, reading: "Come to New Haven for a Burning on May Day."

Storefronts in New Haven were boarded over, and before thousands gathered on the Green that weekend, Yippie Abbie Hoffman and local Panther Doug Miranda both called for Yale to be burned down; ultimately, there were two fires in the Law School, and a bomb went off in Ingalls Rink. In anticipation of chaos, the undergraduates decided to strike and shut down classes, which the faculty itself voted might be suspended. Suspicion arose that President Nixon, who hours before May Day announced the invasion of neutral Cambodia (his speech closing with the claim that "Here in the United States, great universities are being systematically destroyed"), and Vice President Agnew (who attacked Brewster's patriotism for saying publicly that he was "skeptical of the ability of black revolutionaries to

achieve a fair trial anywhere in the United States") both wanted one particular university to explode in violence in order to fan hostility toward
academia among the majority of Americans.

As it happened, tragedy was averted, despite the presence of tanks
on the roads leading into New Haven and four battalions of National
Guardsmen who had received gas grenades, ammunition, and the
word that they would not be prosecuted "if you shoot someone while
performing a duty for the State of Connecticut." Reversing the Harvard
example, Yale chose to open its residential college gates to the 15,000
protesters for shelter, children's day care, food (granola, brown rice,
salad, and fruit punch), and more speeches and "workshops" in the
courtyards. This followed a two-and-a-half-hour rally on the Green
damning and blasting Brewster, whom Yippie Jerry Rubin persisted
in calling "Kingston Brewer," and, of course, the police. As urged by
and privately agreed with the university administration in advance, the
speakers had otherwise counseled calm, and the crowd was with them.
Thirty-seven people were arrested, but only one was a Yale student, and
he was soon released.[97]

Classes at Yale resumed on May 4. Later that afternoon, National
Guardsmen at Kent State University in Ohio, armed with the same orders
and weaponry as their brethren in New Haven, shot into an unarmed
crowd of student protesters. Crosby, Stills & Nash were to sing of the
victims, "*four dead in Ohio*," not naming the ten wounded there. Yale
had literally dodged several bullets.

The senior societies could not deflect or otherwise control the events
of May Day—indeed, this year they were ignored, there being *no* cov-
erage of or commentary on the senior societies in the student newspaper
in the run-up to the weekend—but May Day certainly upended them.
Because of the strike and its attendant turmoil, there was no Tap Day.
Instead, each society moved independently in late April and early May
to select new members as best they could amid the campus unrest.

Of course, the clear and present danger was the prospect of violence
to persons and property, on the prevention of which the societies'

black members in particular—now to be found in virtually all of the
abovegrounds—were focusing their leadership skills, while Doug Miranda
cried, "the Panther and the Bulldog gonna move together!" Senior Glenn
de Chabert '70, the former head of the Black Student Alliance at Yale,
which included almost all of the college's 250 black students, was a
member of Wolf's Head and of the Yale Strike Coordinating Committee
formed by the black undergraduates, caught between self-serving pseudo-
revolutionaries and an unjust system. He worked with that committee's
chair, sophomore William Farley '72; the juniors Ralph Dawson '71,
moderator of the BSAY, and his classmate and the class's secretary,
Kurt Schmoke, who both were to follow de Chabert into Wolf's Head
(Schmoke declining a Bones tap in an antiestablishment gesture); and
freshman Henry Louis Gates Jr. '73 (to be tapped for Book and Snake),
among others. The group had become so alarmed at the escalating threats
of violence that they attempted to force the black female members of
the BSAY to seek protection during the weekend rally within the strong
stone walls of the Scroll and Key tomb, much against the women's wishes.
In the end, after May Day, Miranda was to castigate the BSAY for "jivin'
and half-steppin'" and failing to follow the Panthers' lead.[98]

Not at all foreseen, but resulting almost as swiftly because of May
Day and the social currents which underlay it, was the partial collapse
of the senior society system itself, in the effective extinguishment that
spring of some of its exemplars.

The venerable underground Spade and Grave, using a new rented
house because their previous one had burned down, found that members
began to lose interest in the group in the winter of 1969, although seven
men for the 1970 delegation were successfully tapped. Given little guidance by their departing graduate members and left to their own devices,
they became increasingly vocal about how the society system had to be
changed. Their year started with a retreat to the house of one member's
parents in New Hampshire, where they gave their autobiographies,
but cohesion did not follow, and by January 1970 they felt the end was
nearing. The atmosphere was reflected in that year's *Yale Banner*, chaired

by one of their members, Jeremy Travis: it was now in two volumes, between colorful "super-graphic" covers, full of informal photographs of bearded, side-burned, and mustachioed undergraduates. By the spring of 1970, while dealing with the larger questions of militant blacks and the expanding Vietnam War, the membership had little or no inclination for internal Yale matters like electing a delegation of successors.[99]

Another underground, Mace and Chain, similarly disappeared. Even Scroll and Key was roiled with the iconoclastic spirit of its 1970 crowd—who insisted that their group photograph not be taken in their tomb, but outside before a split-rail fence in a Woodstock-like field, with the men garbed in paramilitary shirts and shorts—and heard calls from graduates seriously debating closing the place down. Calvin Trillin that year met Carlos Stoddard, class of 1926, chairman in his day of the *News*, and then serving as executive secretary of the Yale University Council. "He told me, shaking his head in sadness and puzzlement, that the seniors in Keys were quite a different sort of crowd than we had been [in Trillin's class of 1957]. 'You know what they told me?,' he said. 'They told me that the Keys garden is elitist.' 'The Keys garden is supposed to be elitist, Mr. Stoddard,' I said, trying to cheer him up."[100]

The disruptions at Manuscript far exceeded those at Keys. Shortly before the traumatic events of the long May Day weekend, one of the members of Manuscript's ad hoc committee decided to issue fifty invitations to various members of the Yale community, calling on them all to become members, and even held a cocktail party in the house to welcome them. Thereafter, seniors in the current delegation actually tapped twenty-five men, indicating that they planned a different sort of society. They compounded the offense to their elders by offering up their building to the visiting protesters for lodging and meetings over May Day. The society's horrified trustees reacted swiftly, repudiating all election offers, terminating the year's program for the class of 1970, and changing the locks at their hall. It was a real possibility that this, the seventh landed senior society, would never again reopen its newly locked doors.[101]

CHAPTER FOURTEEN

THE INTEGRATION OF WOMEN
AND DECLINE OF ELITES
(1971–1991)

The radical changes that Yale went through in the late 1960s brought
an end to the defined role of societies as respected campus icons and
drove them into the nebulous limbo that continues today. When bombs
are exploding in the Whale [Ingalls Rink], Black Panthers are stirring
up passions on the Green, and o my! I have classes with women!, the
propriety of two free meals a week with fourteen relics of the past was
doubted by many undergraduates.

—Yale campus tabloid *Rumpus*, April 1997[1]

FEMALES ON BOARD

The prevailing characterizations or perceptions of the women who
entered Yale in the fall of 1969 were variously of superwomen,
pioneers, "geisha girls," potential wives, or confessional mothers, but
not seen as individuals or campus leaders or scholars. Two angry coeds
complained in the *News* in 1972 that they felt "no Yale man is under the

pressure a woman here feels to 'be all things to all people'—including the roles of Mother Earth figure, sex counselor, friend—and general Superwomen."[2]

While the question of their membership in the senior societies seemed initially to be deferrable, should that significant policy decision be made by their male membership and respective graduate boards, the women still faced the same question that had bedeviled prior minorities in Yale College: how would so few in a visible caste produce recognized, peer-elected leaders? Nor was legacy status any particular driver. Because of the gender quota, alumni daughters had about half the probability of being admitted to Yale College as alumni sons. To the classes of 1973–1976, Yale admitted the following numbers of women legacy applicants: 50 of 269; 46 of 235; 49 of 196; and 74 of 210. In those classes, 42, 37, 34, and 47 women matriculated, respectively.

The number of coeds was to increase incrementally, once new housing became available, but the admissions quota on women was only dropped forever in December 1972. By 1979, women comprised almost 45 percent of Yale College, yet not until fall 2010 were females to constitute more than half the Yale undergraduate population.[3] Fully half of the Yale senior society abovegrounds were to be slow in bringing women into their delegations' memberships, and not until 1991, over two decades after their first year of admission, were females to be invited as fully fledged members to cross the iron-doored threshold of the last, and oldest, of the aboveground tombs to welcome them.

Harvard College did not exhibit a different standard at the apex of its social system: up in Cambridge, despite the incorporation of the Radcliffe women into Harvard classes and many shared extracurricular activities, women were simply not admitted to the eight exclusive male final clubs. Having an undergraduate membership of around 40 apiece, they admitted as members only 3 percent of that university's 6,600 undergraduates. In 1984, considering these organizations to be "private," and after they uniformly refused to admit women, Harvard severed ties by cutting off A.D., Fly, Delphic, Spee, Owl, Phoenix-SK, and Fox from the university steam system, and decreed that with the exception of athletic teams and choral groups, no single-gender organizations could advertise events or meet on campus. The failure of Owl to include women caused Senator Ted Kennedy to resign in 2006, and Massachusetts governor Deval Patrick was criticized on the same grounds for his membership in Fly.[4]

Carving out their own social space on campus, Harvard women founded five women's clubs between 1991 (by which date coeds had been permitted to join all but one of the Yale abovegrounds) and 2008, beginning with Bee and followed by the Isis, Pleiade, the Sabliere Society, and La Vie, accounting in their aggregate number about 5 percent of eligible female undergraduates. Males left out of Harvard's final clubs themselves joined fraternities, rather than founding new final clubs, or some analog of Yale's underground senior societies, or of its underground coed societies with the Seven Sisters colleges. Not until the fall of 2015 did one of the Harvard men's final clubs offer to elect women.[5]

In their first years in New Haven, the new Yale women believed that their proportional distribution among the twelve residential colleges was at their personal cost, even though giving the men the experience of living in a coeducational environment. Two female members of the class of 1973 called on the university to end the discriminatory admissions quota which limited their intake: "Until Yale recognizes that women as well as men may be 'leaders' (responsible contributors to society), no woman can have equal status at Yale." An undergraduate petition calling "upon Yale University to end sex discrimination in all aspects of university life," supported by a "strong affirmative action program," attracted 1,793 signatures and was presented to President Brewster and representatives from the U.S. Department of Health, Education and Welfare during the department's special visit to New Haven on April 16, 1971.[6]

Where it counted most, in securing leadership positions in Yale College's traditional student publications and organizations, the women's extracurricular climb was very slow. In 1978, a woman was elected president of the Political Union, and another became editor in chief of the *Yale Daily News* in 1979, with a second in 1988. In 1989, the first woman was elected president of the Yale College Council; in 1995, women were both the union's president and speaker; and only in 1997 was the second woman elected to the YCC presidency. The college's males who discouraged or directed women away from positions of leadership and responsibility had no hatred or dislike of women. Rather, the idea of women as leaders was, in the first two decades of coeducation, simply a function of the same sort of callousness which in essence underlay the barriers that handicapped people found across the country until the 1970s.[7] So, if women were to be taken into the senior societies, it could not be on the old metric of leadership of a major campus organization.

The societies were initially perplexed at the prospect of coeds. Even the alumni board of a professedly liberal society like Manuscript, knowing that some change was inevitable, had decided before the females were to arrive in the September 1969 that, although a majority of its trustees had no objection to women as undergraduate members, it was more "prudent to wait to assess the sentiments of undergraduate members whose actual experience with coeducation will make them better judges of its effects on an undergraduate group." The chair of Manuscript's tap committee that year joked that the society could choose to revise the procedure whereby new members were physically tapped. "We could one-up Bones and other cross-town rivals in acquiring a female member by simply blowing in her ear. 'She would follow us anywhere,' he reasoned."[8]

The tapping procedure for the next incoming delegation of Manuscript was indeed revolutionary, but not in any way that might have been foreseen when the tap chair made his quip. The boarding up of the Manuscript house to its undergraduate members just before May Day in 1970 meant that there was no delegation elected for the class of 1971, while the society's trustees struggled with the question of whether to call it quits after eighteen successful years or to reconstitute the society on some new basis. Douglas Crowley, a graduate member of the class of 1963 now back on campus, was approached with this dilemma in September 1970 by Ian Siggins, a fellow Manuscript board member and then the Episcopal chaplain of the university.

Siggins advised Crowley that the senior seminar of History, the Arts, and Letters ("HAL") had a remarkably pleasant and able group of ten, all of whom were not then in any society. HAL, a now-discontinued major, was then an intense two-year program of interdisciplinary studies focusing on European intellectual and cultural history (its detractors sometimes called it "Cocktail Party 101," while its supporters saw value in its cross-fertilization of music and art with history and philosophy). Additionally, HAL's faculty included leading professors involved with Manuscript in this era, including Cleanth Brooks, Beekman Cannon, and Eugene Waith, so in some sense the stars were favorably aligned for the otherwise startling proposition that the entire HAL contingent, although smaller than fifteen, be made the compact core of a 1971 delegation for Manuscript.

Two other Yale senior societies had admitted women to membership by this date: Book and Snake and the ever-liberal Elihu, in the chaos of May Day when there was no Tap Day, had each quietly elected five coeds, who had been among the 250 admitted to Yale as juniors and transferees from other institutions in 1969. This revolutionary event in senior society history was not reported at the time in the campus newspaper or elsewhere. Among those women admitted to the sophomore class in 1969, there were now three women in HAL in the class of 1971, who welcomed the opportunity to join Manuscript. The addition over the early part of the academic year of like-minded recruits from other humanistic disciplines, including women from the class of 1972 who joined early, enabled a roughly equal representation of men and women in the full delegation. In later years, Manuscript was to call this group the "Renaissance Class," representing the rebirth of Manuscript from a temporary grave. It was a remarkable group for Yale College as well, even if the odds toward success were stacked by its preexisting intellectual excellence: the delegation produced a Clare Fellow, a Henry Fellow, a Marshall Fellow, a Woodrow Wilson Fellow, and a Rotary Fellow.[9]

The key feature for the saga of the senior societies, of course, was that women were now, by the spring of 1971, members of three of their number, albeit with a significant gender imbalance, but nonetheless holding meetings with the men. Yet other impediments to social and political equality of the sexes in New Haven were still solidly in place. What President Brewster affectionately called the "barbaric mixer," where women were bused in from the Seven Sisters campuses to Yale's residential colleges for mixing with the men at weekend dances, did not end with the admission of Yale's own coeds. This weekend system, where the males had time-controlled interactions with non-Yale women, or away from New Haven at the mixers held on the Seven Sisters campuses, did not suddenly cease as the center of campus social life. Mixers were still deemed necessary because of the eight-to-one ratio of men to women on campus; conversely, many Yale men might conclude that to date a local coed was to take on at least seven other rivals.

Upperclassmen in their old social grooves were especially perpetuators of this model and practiced an "incest taboo" against dating women in their residential colleges. Of roughly 1,000 women then admitted, only 31 of those dancing to the music of B. B. King at the 1970 prom were from Yale. Coeducation, in other words, commenced with a separation of social/romantic life and "everyday" life, with men and women developing friendships or brother-sister relationships more than romantic relationships, which still tended to be confined to the weekend.[10] Nor, in a senior society system which often used its graduates in the administration and faculty for recruitment, did the coeds have mentors or role models. Yale University employed only two tenured and three female professors in 1971, while only 7 percent of the assistant professors were women, no associate professors were women, and of course, none had been Yale undergraduates who had experienced senior societies as members.[11]

Again, despite Yale's emphasis on athletics, a fundamental part of the college's established center of social interaction since the late nineteenth century, none of the programs of varsity sports, club sports, or residential college intramural sports had been adapted for women upon their arrival at Yale. This lack of opportunity was not designed maliciously, but was instead part of a greater—and national—social disregard for the place of women in athletics, to be changed dramatically by developments in the judicial case law and federal regulations resulting from the passage of Title IX of the United States Education Amendments of 1972. This law was itself an extension of the Civil Rights Act of 1964, which stated in part that "No person in the United States shall, on the basis of sex, be excluded from participation in, be denied the benefits of, or be subjected to discrimination under any education program or activity receiving federal financial assistance."

Yale's initial pace in developing a women's athletic program was consistent with the Governing Board of Athletics' report that determined "which sports are 'safe'" for females. Following the 1973 appointment of a woman director of recreational and instructional programs, thirteen women's sports subsequently were granted "varsity" status: tennis, field hockey, squash, basketball, crew, fencing, gymnastics, swimming, lacrosse, volleyball, cross-country, track and field, and softball. Yale's only undefeated athletic team in the year of graduation of the freshwomen who arrived in 1969 was the women's tennis team; the next year, the Yale women's basketball team won its first victory in Ivy League competition by beating Radcliffe 42–27. National news was made when, in the Yale physical education director's office some twenty varsity women crew members, protesting unequal locker rooms and shower facilities, bared their breasts, inscribed "Title IX." Increased funding for women's varsity sports followed, so that by 1986 they were competitive within their division.[12]

Initially, too, the most prestigious social organizations barred them. President Brewster charged his special assistant Sam Chauncey not only with handling the administrative aspects of coeducation on campus, but with bringing private institutions identified with Yale into the new social order. Obedient to this direction, Chauncey demanded that the Yale Club of New York City, not at all controlled by the university, admit women to membership on the same basis as all the male Yale degree holders, on the threatened but legally baseless penalty of being denied the use of the

Yale name (the New York Yale Club admitted women in 1969, but not until 1974 were they permitted access to all areas of the club other than the swimming pool, where nude bathing had been the prior regime).

For another example, Mory's, the famed Yale drinking establishment and unofficial Whiffenpoof headquarters, only admitted female members in 1974, after several lawsuits and the loss of its liquor license.[13] And when Chauncey went with the same request on special mission to the corporate board of his old senior society Wolf's Head, the trustees, citing what they styled his fundamental misunderstanding of the society's ethos, summarily expelled him from membership in a closed board meeting held in an upstairs private dining room at Mory's—and then had the group's lunch tab billed to Chauncey's house account.[14]

More typical of the oldest abovegrounds was the initial reaction of Scroll and Key. As soon as women were known in 1968 to be admitted to Yale College, much passionate talk ensued about admitting them to the society during each succeeding election season. The pressure to admit was to mount as other, less venerable societies took them in. The first argument was that Keys ought to reflect the composition of Yale College (not that in some ways it ever had), and the second, that coeds' absence gave a objection to those who had no other quarrel with the place.

The Kingsley Trust Association membership was solicited in 1970 for its opinion of coeducation: while 42 responses from Keysmen applauded the idea of inclusion, 125 expressed significant reservations, and the split was not always on generational lines (although a majority of respondents from the classes prior to 1951 signaled opposition by a ratio of four to one, while younger classes split approximately evenly). A graduate committee concluded in 1973 that no single graduation year's delegation should have the authority to determine so significant a change, "until such time as it is clear that coeducation is plainly the desire of the Kingsley Trust Association."

Not until the winter of 1975 was another committee of this aboveground's graduates appointed to make a recommendation, which again concluded that the society should remain all-male. In 1977, the football quarterback resigned from Keys because its alumni would not even let him make a pro-coeducation plea to their convocation. A third committee, reporting in 1982, imposed a moratorium for five years until induction of the class of 1988 (in which year a coed was to scrawl "Phallocentrism is boring" across their hall's steps). The trustees, pushed along by graduate member and former Yale president Bart Giamatti, formally recognized that their society had drifted more and more from the center of campus respect, as verified by their election results, where too often the reason had been their stance on women. They resolved to admit them, without a vote of the full graduate membership, beginning with the class of 1990 after a year of preparation. This decision was announced in the *New York Times* before graduate members received their formal notice letter, which, the newspaper said ruefully, was equivalent "to discovering you had marital troubles by coming home to an empty house." The six women to whom Keys offered election, including one African American, the co-moderator of the BSAY, all accepted. The delegation of 1991 was to elect a woman to its highest office.[15]

The same sort of internal debates contemporaneously roiled Skull and Bones and Wolf's Head, comprising with Keys the three oldest in the system, all of which had chosen not to admit women for decades after coeducation was introduced. They were pressed annually to the contrary by their successive delegations, starting with the Bones club of 1971's attempt to tap two women. A delegation of current members and recent graduates drove to New York City, "in someone's microbus, you know," one of them recalled, "marijuana smoke billowing out the windows," to meet an alumni gathering who fed them cocktails and dinner at a French restaurant on the Upper East Side. The establishment's representatives there told their New Haven visitors that the club did not belong to fifteen Yale seniors with dilated pupils. The outraged alumni thwarting that particular attempt (over the contrary opinion of former Yale admissions director Inky Clark) included McGeorge Bundy, George W. Bush's uncle and investment banker Jonathan Bush, and public relations legend John "Tex" McCrary. They threatened, if the undergraduates persisted, to shut down the tomb for a year and choose the next delegation themselves[16] (as Manuscript's trustees had indeed done the year before, for different reasons).

Similar rebuffs in the public perpetuation of all-male cultural institutions in a now-coeducational establishment that was Yale College led many women to question whether "Yale really had a genuine commitment to educate us [women], or whether we had simply been brought into the student body because it was thought that the future white male Yale leaders would need to know how to act with women and blacks."[17] Even demographic equality was slow in coming: it was not until 1974, five years after initial coeducation, that the Yale admissions department was to adopt a policy of sex-blind admissions[18] (although Harvard did not do the same with Radcliffe women until two years after that).

Nevertheless, despite all these institutional and attitudinal obstacles, a few more women gained membership in the aboveground senior societies simply because they were present. "With girls around," one society member from the late 1950s was to observe pithily but correctly, "you couldn't do any of that stuff with a straight face."[19] In the wake of the membership reforms in Elihu and Manuscript, the two old Sheff societies Book and Snake and Berzelius in the spring of 1971 each elected five females to their respective delegations for the class of 1972.[20] At that date, from the Yale feminist viewpoint, progress ground to a halt, and the all-male holdouts among the abovegrounds, Bones and Keys and Wolf's Head, were to be publicly pilloried for their stance for the next two decades. But, truth to tell, the three most ancient societies had an even larger challenge in maintaining a place of respect within Yale College.

Combined with the presence of women on the campus, which upended the fundamentals of all preexisting male undergraduate hierarchies and their vaunted—but increasingly disrespected—status, was a genderless disdain for "elitism." This was in the air from the late 1960s, making "leadership" less potent as a precondition for society membership (and that had never been true for all societies, or even all the slots in any of them). The attitude to which the cries of "elitism" gave voice ultimately transcended all questions of racism or sexism. Rather, the feeling was one of compulsive egalitarianism, opposed per se to any system that, for whatever reason, in whatever fashion, rewarded one individual over another.

Yale history professor Gaddis Smith was to remember: "The climate of the sixties was one that looked down on distinction, elites, and special privilege. The societies experienced a withdrawal from self-congratulatory publicity, because there was embarrassment over that. There was some discussion that the societies were in their last years because they were too out of touch with the new cultural climate."[21] Campus publication editorial boards seemed to agree. The last *Yale Daily News* listing of society elections had appeared in the spring of 1967; the last lists to appear in the class yearbook were in 1969 and 1970, and for the 1971 yearbook, Keys, Wolf's Head, and Berzelius had to take out a paid advertisement to appear. A *News* columnist was to maintain that senior society members were "no more different or more talented or even more likable than any random sampling of 15 Yalies."[22]

Even the societies' storied rosters of national leaders in politics and business now worked against them. The issue of the "old boy network" was critical to the debate over the all-male groups. They smacked, said a member of the Yale Women's Center, of the old Yale adage "Put a few white men in a room and let them run the world." A coordinator of the Undergraduate Women's Caucus wrote in a letter to the *News* that, since joining an all-male society was thought to bring "job opportunities after graduation" and "business and political networking later on," it was "ridiculous to maintain that the secret societies' exclusion of women is an apolitical and morally neutral act." Responses of the societies' graduate members to the effect that the delegations were stratified horizontally by class year with only intermittent contacts with alumni from the preceding or following years (unlike a fraternity), and that it was deemed bad form to list a secret society on a resumé, were summarily dismissed by the critics.[23]

The presidency of George H. W. Bush, and the pre- and postelection fascination of the media with his undergraduate membership in

Skull and Bones, did not help. When Bush and Mikhail Gorbachev were conducting a summit in 1989, a satirist's column in the *New York Times* had the American president offering the reformist Russian leader aid in joining the International Monetary Fund and the World Bank:

"Gorbachev: Do not think me ungrateful, but actually, I was hoping to join the real insiders' club —Skull and Bones.

"Bush: I don't know, Gorby. It's not the ethnic thing, but if I can't get Maggie [Thacher] in . . . these guys are real conservative."[24]

The *Yale Daily News* front-page article for the spring 1971 elections, authored by a woman and announcing the sudden but substantial admission of females to the societies in the second year of rising women seniors in the college, was titled "Women Enrich Tombs." It celebrated the fact that "four senior societies and one fraternity-secret society have enlarged their spirit of brotherhood to include brothers and sisters. They are Book and Snake, Manuscript, Berzelius, Elihu, and St. Anthony Hall." The just-initiated women of the class of 1972 quoted in the piece cited various reasons for joining, including the pioneer spirit, curiosity, and iconoclasm: one in Book and Snake said, "I joined for the same reason I came to Yale," and another in a second, unidentified aboveground said she "hoped to break as many all-male traditions as possible."

But many more named the desire to end the social isolation they felt as a significant gender minority in a large, predominantly male institution. These women considered themselves "well accepted by their spooks" and praised the benefits gained from membership as a major justification for accepting their invitations to join. They felt that both genders had made natural and acceptable accommodations to the new intimacy, although they noted small changes in the men's behavior around women. Most remarkably, the *News* article noted that "these upperclass women have found more easily in an exclusive organization what they could not find 'naturally' in the Yale community." As incoming sophomore class transfer students, they had had more difficulty establishing themselves socially than had the women in the class behind them with twice their numbers. Against all expectations, the senior societies, or at least a substantial component of the larger system, had performed their traditional task of integration of the college's newest caste. Coeducation's "widespread implications," the article concluded, "have affected and changed one seemingly inviolate institution—the secret society system."

On the societies' side, the male members were said to have recognized the need to make women members for "both humanistic and economic reasons": diversity was traditionally a goal of membership, and financial pressures increased the incentive. Although the ratio of the sexes within the canonical number of fifteen members continued to present problems, the quick and dramatic alteration in membership policy had redeemed the system, assuring it of a continued existence. The changeover from brotherhood to "brother and sisterhood" was most painful, not within the new, mixed-gender delegations, but on the alumni side. St. Anthony's, the "fraternity-secret society," was threatened with possible exclusion by its national headquarters if it accepted women, but survived the challenge and even compelled change in the organization's national constitution.[25] And the graduate boards of those more conservative societies, choosing not to permit the admission of women within the first year that junior class women were available for election as rising seniors, were to continue their formal and increasingly marginalized opposition for decades.

The "hypocrisies" of senior society members swimming in the newly egalitarian sea of Yale College continued to be called out. Shortly following the spring 1971 article on "enrichment" of the tombs by women appeared a News column titled "Unspooking Tombs." This turned out to be the last piece to be published on societies in this academic year, which ended with a strike by custodial and maintenance workers that in fifty days caused more violence and vandalism than had occurred during the May Day upheaval of the prior spring. All the themes of the social(ist) reform petitioners of the 1969 juniors were sounded again by the columnist. "How can one black militant, a leading spokesman of last spring's Mayday activities, choose to be among the current members of one of the most exclusive senior societies, a society which still doesn't have any women in it? How can one of the organizers of the charity drive for New Haven justify belonging to a society whose building sits unoccupied for most of the day, while thousands of New Haven residents live crowded together in cramped apartment buildings? How can one of Pierson's most outspoken defenders of the community last spring now be a member of a society that does nothing for the community?"[26]

The criticism was not completely fair. Back when the "community" was perceived as just Yale College, Wolf's Head on its fortieth anniversary in the 1920s had funded three undergraduate scholarships, and other societies had similar histories of gifting college-wide scholarships or undergraduate prizes in their members' names. The society always most generous of all to Yale had long been Scroll and Key, and in this new era of an enlarged "community," the Keys delegation of 1970 had made two loans, one to the radio station WYBC and a second to the *Yale Record*, the first loans made outside the membership of the society, because they wished to open out toward the broader community, in this case to other worthy college organizations.

The same year the Keys board approved grants to the Yale Charities Drive and to the Calvin Hill Daycare Center, followed in 1971 by grants to the Student Community Housing Corp., to Afro-American, Inc., and to the Hill Daycare Center again, with yet more community organization grants made in 1972. In 1976, the Kingsley Trust Association was to present the Yale Corporation with a gift of $100,000 to initiate the John Hay Whitney Professorship in Yale College.[27] This society's generosity to the university itself and to non-member student prizewinners, commencing in the late nineteenth century with establishment of the John Addison Porter and Ten Eyck prizes, was unparalleled and, prior to the Whitney professorship gift, largely unknown.

In the election season of 1972, the societies were to run the gamut in their responses to the continuing barrage of criticism. On the one end was Elihu, which published a letter declaring its current delegation (the very first of any society to include women) saw "no purpose in secrecy and therefore intend to be completely open and honest regarding our activities, procedures, and election criteria." They maintained "a house, not a tomb . . . which is open to members (undergraduate, graduate, and faculty), their guests, and the invited public." "Education," broadly understood "to mean the intellectual and the personal, the formal and the informal," was their programmatic theme: "basically, it is up to each year's group to design their own educational experience." In the hopes of a diverse incoming delegation, they openly invited any member of the junior class interested in their society "to call 436-1328 in the evenings and leave a message for the chairman."[28] This senior society's demystification was complete.

On the spectrum's other end was Skull and Bones, which continued its own tradition, constant for the decades from 1963 through the 1980s, of publishing a letter in the campus newspaper detailing the dates before which no junior would be contacted about election, and after which in the week preceding Tap Day some juniors would be notified of an election offer, to be supplemented by additional offers on Tap Day itself. No other senior society, aboveground or underground, made any public announcement of policy or program. The week thereafter, three days before the date of elections, an unsigned notice appeared in the *News* declaring that "Societies Elections" would take place in student rooms at eight o'clock. On Tap Day itself, the campus newspaper ran the list of those elected as new Whiffenpoofs, but there was no mention then or thereafter of the senior societies.

THE END OF "LINE-TAPPING"

In 1977 a classmate of George W. Bush's from the class of 1968, Ron Rosenbaum, published a magazine article titled "The Last Secrets of Skull and Bones," which has been called "the locus classicus of all Bonesology" (an honorific bestowed in apparent ignorance of George Frazier's *Esquire* piece of 1955, which was both longer and more accurate about Yale's oldest senior society). The volume of *Esquire* magazine for 1977 containing Rosenbaum's piece had by the early 1980s been so often worn and mutilated by readers that it had to be put into the preservation section of the university library, although photocopies were kept available at the reference desk, which were themselves then pilfered; the New Haven public library copy of that year's bound volume also disappeared.[29]

Rosenbaum took fierce joy in relating and "exposing" the society's traditions, but his true, elegiac theme was that Skull and Bones was in decline, possibly terminally. Its offers of election were increasingly rebuffed, and its formerly secret rituals—thanks partly to articles like Frazier's and Rosenbaum's—increasingly known. Manuscript, by the mid-eighties, was virtually open to the public except for one dinner a week, and St. Elmo's, Berzelius, and Book and Snake became known for inviting guests to themed parties. Except for the three oldest of the senior societies, membership was not taken as seriously as in the past, and each year, some members quit, a practice virtually unheard of in the most of the 1960s and before, and many seniors were increasingly casual about attending meetings.[30]

The larger problem was simply that elitism, on which the secret societies' prestige and exclusivity had been grounded for almost one hundred fifty years since Skull and Bones's founding, was now dishonored and derided by the current undergraduates. A *Yale Daily News Magazine* article in 1974 heralded the change: "The myth that the societies set out to tap the top 15 WASPs in the class is no longer correct." A Bones alumnus was quoted there as saying that "The homogeneity of the senior society has been replaced by a respect for individuality. The idea of bringing in campus leaders has disappeared. It doesn't matter any more that the candidate's the captain of the football team. If the guy's an asshole, we don't want him."

Although the college newspaper still ran articles on the societies in April during election season, the pieces' titles and tone became increasingly dismissive. Many if not most students seemed hardly aware of them, and one student was quoted in 1980 as saying, "I know absolutely nothing about them. I mean, they don't do anything, do they?" A column from

1982 complained that "Any education they provide is tangential to their basic purpose [alleged to be exclusivity] . . . in order to set their members apart." No mention whatsoever was made of their historic tradition of honoring campus organization leaders by election. The *New York Times* article published that year on Tap Day found that "many students seemed more interested in the impending deadline for senior essays and the assignment of dormitory rooms for next year."[31]

When the national wire services reported in the late winter of 1991 that Bones might elect women, the *Yale Daily News* did not even run a follow-up story. That society, the paper's (female) managing editor told the *Boston Globe*, is "not a burning issue. It's an elitist thing, and elitism isn't in anymore."[32] No better evidence might be found than the fact that the first campus newspaper treatment on the prospect of women finally entering Yale's oldest senior society was in the *News'* April Fool's Day issue, titled "Bonesmen Vote to Tap Animals." This reported that the society "decided to admit members regardless of kingdom, phylum, class, order, family, genus or species. Rumored to be among this year's tappees are animals, wild and house-broken, fictional characters, and folks who have never even heard of Yale . . . President Bush '48's dog Millie is on the Bones short-list for tap night April 18."[33] Even Bull and Stones in its day a century before had not been so scathing in its disrespect.

At the end of the century, another major magazine study discerned a very different theme in the membership of the senior societies, fore-shadowed in its title: "Tomb of Their Own: What's Really Wrong with Skull and Bones," an article for the *New Republic* by Franklin Foer. "To put it crudely, Yale's secret societies—once ground zero of the Eastern establishment—are now high temples of political correctness, the ulti-mate in Ivy League politics," in a year when the Bones delegation had "more women than men and as many African Americans as WASPS." Back in the day, he noted, the societies were proudly, even offensively elitist, having a purpose of shaping the characters of leaders who would in turn shape the world," a "kind of noblesse oblige" that modern students found "deeply embarrassing."

The increasing derision of societies turned on its head the charge of elitism which had caused them to be largely shunned or even extinguished after Mayday, and they altered to save themselves. "Beginning in the late '70s," Foer wrote, "they swung open their doors to women, gays, and minorities—people anxious to join, if only to proclaim victory over the racist patriarchy. And, once the societies were filled with people of color, white liberals had fewer qualms about joining." Approaching the new century, the senior societies were flourishing again, Skull and Bones having virtually no turndowns in the previous five years. Wolf's Head and Berzelius, he reported, regularly then had more African Americans than whites; the current Bones club was comprised of "three African-Americans, four students of East Asian descent, two Jews, and a Latino, the balance being white"; and all groups dividing their elections more or less equally between men and women.

Foer's fundamental complaint was that the diversification of the societies had been effected in a strange way. The logical path would have been simply to honor the hallowed rhetorical commitment to demonstrated leadership or other proven or perceived merit, namely seeking out Yale's highest-achieving students of all races and backgrounds. This had clearly happened with the influx of talented blacks in the late 1960s, but was harder with the coeds who until the mid-1990s were too few in number and generally excluded from campus leadership positions, other than athletic captaincies of women's varsity teams. "But the rush to diversify [thereafter] wasn't an effort to finally live out the 'best and brightest' creed," Foer lamented, "it was an escape from that creed, an effort to deny that groups like Skull and Bones represented an elite at all—because, if they did, then no one could rationalize joining."

In consequence, the dominant criterion for membership became identity: not what you had done (newly denigrated as "line-tapping," as in the "line" of football captains or of *Yale Daily News* chairs), but what you were. Elections degenerated into an elaborate quota system in which outgoing members jostled to make sure they had successors who looked like them. A Korean American student in Wolf's Head threw a tantrum, breaking into tears and storming out of the meeting when his delegation proposed choosing a student of another Asian American extraction; this provoked an argument by a Chicano clubmate who said he felt strongly that a Chicano perspective should always be represented, which could not be done by a Puerto Rican or Salvadoran. "If you're head of the Korean American Students at Yale or the Black Student Alliance or the Yale Lesbian, Gay, Bisexual, and Transgender Cooperative," Foer wrote, "you're a solid bet for Bones. At Wolf's Head, the presidents of certain African American and Latino fraternities are usually shoo-ins. But, if you're a black student who heads the campus anti-abortion group or a lesbian physics major who's never attended an anti-homophobia rally, you don't stand a chance."[34]

The old standbys, the head of the Political Union or the *News* chairman, were rarely tapped by the top societies, being seen as unseemly climbers. The result was predictable, virtually a repetition of what had occurred in the founding of Wolf's Head over a century before: those excluded in 1997, starting with the passed-over *Yale Daily News* chairman and the untapped woman president of the Yale College Council, formed a new senior society, called "Hack and Tool," meeting in the Athenaeum Room of Saybrook College.[35]

WOMEN INTO BONES AND WOLF'S HEAD

For the senior societies which remained all male, nothing in applicable law required the admission of women. Prohibiting sex discrimination in private clubs was not a matter of federal law, like the Civil Rights Act of 1964, but of tests under Connecticut state law. Bones and Wolf's Head met those tests, which distinguished private clubs (exempt from most anti-discrimination laws) from public meeting places (which are not), in having "generally selective" membership, "formalized procedures" for becoming a member, and no services provided to non-members in furtherance of trade or business.[36]

Nevertheless, graduate committees of Skull and Bones had considered coeducation within the society in 1971 and again in 1986, and both times these committees were unanimously against any such change. The outside world continued to mock. The *Boston Globe* columnist George Frazier, recollecting in a 1973 column about the Yale-Harvard game a Bones legend which he had written about in his 1955 *Esquire* piece, teased: "The presence of puellae in the student body [at Yale] isn't exceptional, for these days they're ubiquitous. But who would have thought that there'd come a time when they'd be in secret societies, a circumstance that might give Bones some temptation to proselytize, since wrestling in the nude is wrestling in the nude, and where does it say anything about a member's sex?"[37]

Reenergized by the admission of women into Scroll and Key (and St. Anthony's Hall now had a female majority), leaving only Wolf's Head and Skull and Bones as the last all-male abovegrounds (and the only two Bonesmen on the Yale Corporation were now outnumbered by five female trustees), the newly initiated Bones delegation for 1990–91 in the spring of their junior year again pressed their society's corporate board and graduates revisiting the tomb to reconsider the perennially deferred issue of coeducation. In the fall, they doubled down, advising the board that they were considering tapping women in the following spring's elections. In measured response, believing it time to conclude the matter decisively, the Russell Trust Association organized a series of six meetings in February 1991, to be held in New Haven, New York, Boston, Chicago, Los Angeles, and Washington, D.C., to involve in the discussion as many graduate members as possible before the organization's midwinter graduate meeting in New Haven in late February, preceding a definitive vote at the board's meeting the first week of April (and thus before the next annual elections).

Wolf's Head, too, was under public pressure: Benno Schmidt Jr., Wolf's Head alumnus of the class of 1964 and president of Yale since 1986, had publicly announced that he would not attend society functions until it admitted women. Wolf's Head had voted on coeducation in 1976, and the votes were overwhelmingly against, approximately 700 to 12; Yale administrator George Vaill, from the Wolf's Head delegation of 1935, observed that coed societies had had problems with rules against dating when members became attracted to one another. Another alumnus threatened to "raze the building" before permitting the reform.[38]

This seemed irrelevant to most students. An article appearing in the *New York Times* in 1979 titled "Ivy League Women Face Social Barriers" reported that the previous few years had seen men "chosen by the more prestigious all-male [Yale senior society] groups turning down membership in favor of a coeducational" one, and quoted a female member of Berzelius, which was coed: "The all-male clubs are seen by a lot of people as snobby, over-the-hill places, and the activist women on campus aren't oriented to anything as traditional as that."[39] In the spring of 1984, posters appeared across the campus featuring the symbols of Keys, Bones and Wolf's Head, and saying, "DON'T FOOL YOURSELF DON'T JOIN The members of these societies are not the 'best men' of Yale. They want us to think they are. These men are either too spineless to say no to being 'chosen,' or they wholeheartedly endorse continuing a patriarchal power structure."

Another poster appeared in 1990, after Scroll and Keys' admission of women, reading: "JUNIOR MEN: DON'T SELL OUT. TURN DOWN SKULL AND BONES AND WOLF'S HEAD."[40] When the story of the Bones board's deliberations ran on the Associated Press wire, it included a quotation from Sara Romelyn, a Yale senior and project coordinator for the Yale Women's Center, who said that the fact that clubs like Bones and Wolf's Head were still seen as "icons of the Yale experience" sent "a strong message that Yale women are still not 100 percent welcome."[41]

Prior to the April 1991 meeting, the RTA board, under the new leadership of Muhammad Saleh (born in Palestine and a member of the 1968 Bones delegation with George W. Bush), met frequently with the undergraduates and heard the results of the regional gatherings, to all of which the current club had sent representatives to argue their case. The trustees decided to submit any final decision to the membership at large as a recommendation, while requesting the graduate members to vote ratification of the board decision (not the path that Scroll and Key had taken two years before in effecting the admission of women by board vote only, without graduate ratification). This, a significant modification of the prior proposal for resolution, which foresaw only a board vote, meant that there would be no final decision before the next day of elections.

In a six-page, single-spaced letter from the undergraduate club addressed to "Most Worthy Alumni," meant to be private but—sent out in 850 copies—soon quoted extensively in national newspapers like the *New York Times*, the *Washington Post*, and the *Wall Street Journal*, as well as in the campus newspaper, the board was accused of having been "coerced [by the political pressure of some graduates] out of a leadership role it had promised to fulfill." The letter damned as unworkable a board resolution which proposed forming a twenty-member club composed of ten men and ten women, who would eat together and debate at their Thursday meetings, but would break into separate gender groups on Sundays to share their autobiographies and emotional (sexual) histories.[42]

The 1991 club's seniors then decided to act unilaterally, without asking for further prior permission, and tapped seven women, refusing to release that number (although it soon leaked) or their names to the now fully attentive national press. They had argued strenuously with their trustees, maintaining that the failure to coeducate was losing "the best and the brightest" who were women (now 45 percent of the student body), as well as some of the preferred male candidates who felt that they could learn more from a coeducational society; that their group was an object of campus ridicule and as a result deemed both discriminatory and bigoted; and that the self-education which beyond debates had become the core of the society's program, copied thereafter by virtually all their rivals as a senior society's main program, could not be fulfilled in an all-male club to nearly the same degree as it might in a coed one.

The graduate collective, these seniors concluded, was too remote from the dramatically changed undergraduate demographics and "clearly not ready to make the decision [for women] itself, because it does not realize how urgent it is that it be made." Likening their quest to the civil rights movement, they declared: "We have taken what we see to be the only rational course of action in the face of a fundamental change in the society at large, in Yale itself, and, as a result, in the role that Skull and Bones must play in the Yale community if it is to survive and remain true to its ideals."[43]

The society board's reaction was swift, eerily like Manuscript's in election season some twenty-one years before, then virtually obscured in the chaos of May Day. The *Washington Post* described the trustees' choice "to crush the rebellion with a speed unseen since the Soviet tanks rolled into Prague in 1968." Over the weekend after elections, the locks on the Bones tomb were changed, closing admission to all except by appointment, and all undergraduate activities were suspended for one year. No further elections were to be offered to the class of 1992, but the board pledged to the larger membership to continue meanwhile to seek a resolution of the controversy through collective best judgment and formal ratification of any settled recommendation.[44]

The *Washington Post* contacted but failed to elicit hometown comment on the confrontation from President George W. Bush, Senators John Kerry and John Chaffee, and journalist Bill Buckley. The otherwise conservative Senator David Boren, described by the newspaper as "one of the many Bonesmen in Congress" and a member of the Yale Corporation, did respond: "The decision of this year's club to accept women members should be respected and accepted. After there has been more time for reflection by all those concerned, I hope that the newly elected class will be allowed to fully use the facilities." The *Post* story, which featured a picture of the deserted, locked tomb, also made clear that the 1991 club's contention that they were losing candidates because of the single-sex policy was indeed true. The piece quoted the senior editor of the *New Republic*, Jacob Weisberg of the class of 1986, then an intern at that magazine, who told the reporter that Senator Kerry had telephoned him at his intern's office to relay an offer of election: he replied that he declined to join a club that excluded women.[45]

The national media response, led by the august *New York Times*, was immediate and predictable: "High Noon on High Street: A Fight for the Soul of Skull and Bones" was the title of an editorial, which observed: "The alumni are fighting a losing battle. Women have been attending Yale for more than 20 years, and the existence of an all-male institution in this determinedly coeducational society is plainly an uncomfortable anachronism, if not an affront." The same day *Times* columnist Anna Quindlen quoted approvingly from the electing club's letter to the alumni, and concluded: "These are guys I'd share a tomb with happily. Give them back their keys, and let the bonding begin."[46]

The seniors were defiant, declaring to the *Boston Globe* that "the group will definitely continue to exist even if we are not able to get back in the building." (Their housing problem was soon solved by the Manuscript delegation's agreement to allow them to use that society's hall.)[47] They said further that "leading civil rights members in the nation" and "key figures in the Yale Law School" had offered to help them in a lawsuit against the board. They were also counting on alumni proponents of their position, like Senator Boren, to eventually win the day.[48] On campus, the overwhelming majority of students were supporting the seniors (although maintaining "it's about time") and slamming the RTA board. The other all-male society, Wolf's Head, did not issue a comment, nor did its alumnus President Schmidt.

The current controversy, now generating threats of lawsuits and fracturing both Bones and its vaunted secrecy, revived the perennial arguments, now in their second century, about all senior societies and the privileges of exclusion associated with them. A junior who had declined a Keys tap told the *Times* that "Basically, it comes down to whether you'd rather be one of the excluded, or one who excludes," and a member of Manuscript noted that "Secret societies have a base of privilege for members, including a neat building, decent food, and a network of alumni. Why should some people get it and not others?" A senior, and former editor in chief of the *Yale Daily News*, reflected: "I don't sense that Bones' decision to go coed is a great victory for feminists or women. I don't see what is gained by having a club that discriminates against all Yale students, instead of just Yale men."[49]

Within Skull and Bones, the disrupted dialogue resumed between the outcasts of the current club and the beleaguered trustees, and by April 21, a mutual decision was reached that there would be no further discussions by either side with the press or other outsiders. The board pledged to make a decision before the middle of June, and submit that to the membership for ratification, with the poll result to be announced before August 1. Then, a transition committee would be appointed to implement the final decision as ratified by the members.

With both official and clandestine sources stifling themselves, the press continued to celebrate the organizational disaster and query the hidden reasons. A columnist in the *Boston Globe*, "To get to 'the crux' of the matter . . . asked a Yale colleague what the big fuss over women was all about. There must be some secret male bonding rituals," she wrote, "like peeing in the punch bowl or gatoring on the floor or shooting beers. But his answer was, basically, sex. 'Obviously, at that age, sex would have to be under discussion, and I suspect that is why Bones is so reluctant to take women,' said my friend, whose grandfather was a Bonesman." (This sexual squeamishness was not exclusive to Bones graduate members: women in the first Keys delegation to include them were discomfited to hear in an address from their distinguished alumnus, society historian, and professor of English Maynard Mack, that they were "sovereign states" and, as such, entreated not to "form alliances."[50])

Nor was the concern for "gender privacy" exclusively a male preoccupation. Mrs. June Bingham, whose first husband had been a member of the class of 1936, wrote to the *New York Times* after the story appeared on the Bones club lockout. After identifying herself as "widow of a member of Skull and Bones, wife of a member of Berzelius, mother of a member of Scroll and Key, stepmother and mother-in-law of two more Bonesmen," and praising Bones for inventing, "100 years ahead of our encounter groups, a structure that elicits precious intimacy between 15 participants," she too advocated separation of the sexes, "when the time came for talk about the tender issues that American men so rarely seem able to share with one another."[51]

Although the *Boston Globe* reporter's story was at least the third published account to describe the RTA board's proposal to split an enlarged club membership into separate single-sex groups for "the sharing of emotional and life histories," it was the first to recognize plainly that the preservation of female modesty was animating a board whose eight members were not unanimously for change and had graduated at Yale from three (class of 1988) to fifty-two (class of 1939) years before. Only four of this RTA board's members had experienced Yale College coeducation as undergraduates. Furthermore, they seemed largely tone-deaf to the fact that their "separate but equal" proposal unwittingly revived a concept discredited decades before in the civil rights era of the 1960s as a subtler form of discrimination. Yet the fundamental difference was patent, as a Bones alumnus maintained to a reporter, "There's a much greater difference between a man and a woman than between a Wasp and a Jew."[52]

It was argued by the opponents of coeducation in the society that this "reform" was *not* inevitable, despite the sea change in Yale College demographics: there were still five men-only singing groups, and three now for women alone, and in a revival of their fortunes, about a dozen men's fraternities, and now five sororities. An article in the *Yale Alumni Magazine* for summer 1987, almost two decades after coeducation's inception, had reported that there was little current objection on campus to single-sex endeavors. Sixteen athletic teams for men and sixteen for women even exemplified the college administration's own recognition of the validity and viability of student organizations separation by gender. Yale president Benno Schmidt, despite his no-attendance stance with regard to his own all-male senior society Wolf's Head, had announced that his administration would take no action to compel any society to change, and the college dean confirmed that there was a place on campus for single-sex groups.

To the current Bones club that had publicly expressed discomfort with the society's diminished status on campus, in their long, self-justifying letter which reached some newspapers before it had reached all the alumni who were its addressees, the graduate contras responded that if women were to be admitted, by-laws designating "members of the Junior Class" as prospective candidates and not amended since 1961 (well before undergraduate coeducation in New Haven) should be changed in a deliberative manner by all members of the organization. Furthermore, they argued, a fact not appreciated by the current club was that the society's membership had survived prior periods of scorn, envy, and misunderstanding, and a bout of "political correctness" was not something to which a group with markedly internal goals should succumb, so long as fifteen strong male candidates still existed in the junior class.

Nor, if the 1991 "shadow club" was finally repudiated, was election of a new delegation by a graduate electorate unprecedented. It had happened in Bones itself in 1946, choosing the members of a club when the predecessor club had been effectively extinguished by the accelerated academic year at the end of World War II. It had happened at Manuscript in 1970 during May Day. And it had happened at Elihu just a few years before, in April 1983, when one of their delegations tried to turn their house into a "people's shelter," and the seniors were themselves ejected from occupancy with suspension of elections, publicly announced by the Elihu board in the *Yale Daily News*.[53] Opponents wishing to block coeducation in Bones even had preliminary discussions that the "illegal club," caught up in this maelstrom, might be given advice and financial aid for a few years should they choose to begin a senior society of their own, until their own alumni might assume that burden.

The Russell Trust Association board scrambled to contain the damage. At a meeting in May, following the April lockout, the board recommended 6 to 2 that the society's all-male tradition be ended, a decision to be reviewed by a national membership ballot, conducted by an independent accounting firm, to ratify or reject that vote, in a tally at the end of July. Proponents of both sides of "the Issue," with the RTA board represented by former Yale chaplain Sidney Lovett (1950), and the rebellious seniors by Austan Goolsbee (1991), later President Obama's first chief economic advisor, agreed to stop discussing the coeducation issue in public. More than 86 percent of the membership, identified by the *Washington Post* as "the Boodle," cast ballots, and the Reverend Lovett confirmed to the press that the vote was 368 to 320 for women's admission.[54]

The board's Transition Committee moved to mollify those angered by this result, while recommending that the shadow club be confirmed as members. These individuals, six women among them, included the president of the Yale Dramat, the co-moderator of the BSAY, the captain of the football team, the president of the Yale Political Union, the unit commander for her Army ROTC corps and top columnist for the *News*, and the incoming captain of the Yale women's lacrosse team.

This report of the general replication of the society's traditional success in electing campus leaders did not pacify the all-male tradition diehards. William F. Buckley and other society alumni promptly filed a lawsuit against the RTA board, seeking an injunction to nullify the alumni vote, arguing that the by-laws did not clearly permit the admission of women, and to order a convention of Bones members to resolve the issue of coeducation. The board agreed to obey the injunction, and the current seniors of the shadow club were balked of their expected initiation. Buckley from the class of 1950 found an ally in Jay Fetner of the class of 1961, who launched a petition drive to oust the current society board, accompanied by a ten-page memo arguing that confidentiality would not last, and that "date-rape . . . lies in our medium-term future."[55]

In due course, the lawsuit was stalled to permit a special meeting of members on October 24, 1991, to vote on three points at issue: the amendment of the corporate by-laws, to either add the words "male" and "female" before the phrase "members of Yale College" in defining eligibility for election, or to merely add the word "male;" to elect those tapped by the club of 1991 as members of 1991–92, or to negate their election; and to continue the current board, or to compel them to resign. The diehards lost on all three counts.[56]

This left Wolf's Head, the third to be founded of the old Yale Academic College senior societies in 1883, the last aboveground to be all male, having held four votes on coeducation since 1977. Two months after Bones, on December 12, 1991, that society too voted to admit women, changing their original constitutional characterization as all male, with more than 80 percent of its members approving the change.[57]

So, over two decades after being admitted to the formerly all-male college in 1969, women became the last caste to enter Yale's competitive democracy of senior societies, following the public high school graduates, then Jews, African Americans, and gay men. Compared to the previous battles about the merits and fairness of the system, the storming of this last social barrier was the most vociferously contested within and publicly debated without of all the controversies over all the preceding years. The fierce demand for this final diversity made by the male undergraduates in Keys, Bones, and Wolf's Head, the three senior societies which had epitomized the famous system for its first century, encountered the grim opposition of their respective alumni members for twenty years precisely *because* these alumni had the most invested in the prestige and age of their respective organizations and had difficulty imagining a different future.

In truth, only the measurable decline of that prestige, and the increasing irrelevance of what they most treasured about their own undergraduate careers, persuaded them to change their minds and hearts. Once again, as it had so often in its tumultuous history over 160 years, the system evolved to save itself.

EPILOGUE

Do you want to be successful?
Form a club!
Are your chances quite distressful?
Form a club!

Never mind the common friendships
That no politician has!
Seek the really righteous rounders
And the athletes of the class!
And you'll get your heart's desiring—
And the rest will get the raz!
Form a club!

—"Song at which all good News Editors Shudder,"
Stephen Vincent Benét and J. F. Carter, 1917[1]

Yale College in 2017 is a very different place from the college of 1832 when the senior society system was birthed, but perhaps not so different from the college of a century before where Stephen Vincent Benét and his roommate could poke fun at the Yalies' propensity to form new organizations when old ones were, for any reason, deemed insufficient.

Over four-tenths of the undergraduate population today consists of minority students, and the Yale dean of admissions makes an Asian recruiting trip to Mumbai, Delhi, Singapore, Hong Kong, Shanghai, and Beijing.[2] As of fall 2014, Yale College's student body was 49 percent of minority descent, including 11 percent black, 12 percent Hispanic, 23 percent Asian, and 3 percent Native American. Today, white American males comprise only just over a quarter of Yale's undergraduates. The profile of the class that will graduate in 2019 is markedly different since the millennium. Chosen from over 30,000 applicants, the 1,364 enrolled freshmen and women came from forty-nine states, the District of Columbia, and Puerto Rico, and sixty other countries; approximately one-seventh were first generation college students, two-thirds received financial assistance, and only just over a tenth of them had any legacy affiliation. Fully six-tenths hailed from public schools, only four-tenths were white, and the male /female ratio was 51 to 49.[3]

The composition of the senior societies' membership today reflects this change, but more surprising to their decades of detractors would be their sheer numbers: there are at least forty-seven, their names noted in an annual *Yale Daily News* announcement signed by all of them. This sets forth the dates of that year's Tap Week and Tap Night; the ground rules for election offers (only within Tap Week, no "exploding" offers which expire, and no acceptance to be binding until Tap Night begins); the dates when interviews may begin (now starting in February); and, as required by the Connecticut Hazing Law, a mutual pledge that all acts of hazing are understood to be strictly forbidden.[4]

As the result of an initiative by a former Yale College Council president, seven new societies were created for the class of 2016 (some, like Ring and Candle, revived from decades before and funded by their alumni), to make the society system even more inclusive,[5] with the result that more than half the seniors in Yale College are now in senior societies, still secret as to membership and, for most, meeting place. The proliferation of societies has led to less reverence for the system overall, but when the junior class council of 2015 invited the class's members by email to opt out of the election process, only twelve of some thirteen hundred juniors decided against participating in the process.[6]

In 1982, Timothy Dwight College master Thomas Bergin of the class of 1925 recalled a conversation that he had had with his contemporary, Bonesman and *Time* magazine founder Henry Luce of the class of 1920. What was the point, Luce inquired of Bergin, of the underground secret societies that had appeared on campus after World War II? "I replied," Bergin wrote, "that the undergraduates recognized the desirability of the intimate association offered by the traditional senior secret societies, but many felt that they were too blatantly 'prestigious.' Luce responded, 'What the hell is wrong with prestige?' His was, I think, the authentic voice of old Yale."[7]

In a college which since Kingman Brewster's presidency in the 1960s explicitly sought to admit "leaders" in all fields of endeavor, the undergraduates in the new Yale elevated diversity over prestige, and the private exchanges of trust and revelations (Bergin's "desirability of the intimate association") over public promotion for demonstrated campus leadership. Leadership was still rewarded by the societies—the Bones clubs of 2013 and 2015, for example, included Rhodes scholars, both women, one a varsity track star and the other the managing editor of the *News*. But that personal talent had not, for decades now, been the best indicator of probable membership.

After the century's turn, the mystique of the senior societies intermittently continued to fascinate the non-Yale world, from the sphere of low culture to that of high politics. This broad spectrum ran from the release of the *Skulls* film trilogy of thrillers[8] through the 2004 presidential contest, which matched against one another two Bonesmen, George W. Bush (class of 1968) and John Kerry (1966), from an organization with only eight hundred living members (one contemporaneous commentary in the *New York Times*, recalling a legend of its rituals, was titled "Nude Wrestling? Good Practice for Politics").[9]

When founded in the first half of the nineteenth century, the Yale secret societies had no external purpose, but only the internal one of self-education: the founders of Skull and Bones created a program to teach themselves extemporaneous speech, unavailable in the standard curriculum of the day, and those of Berzelius to learn European science that they were not being taught by their scientific school professors. These societies' successors and imitators for a half century invented variations on such formal programs. Nevertheless, the sheer intimacy of groups of fifteen and the two long evenings each week they were together led, within a few decades thereafter, into sessions of personal revelation and examination, the primary thematic program of most of them today.[10] This marks their primary difference from Harvard's final clubs and Princeton's eating clubs, as well as more prosaic and quotidian college organizations like fraternities and sororities.

Their critics in the second half of the nineteenth century and the first half of the twentieth were right to criticize them for exclusivity—how could it be otherwise when they took in, until modern times, much less than a quarter of the undergraduates?—and for the demonstrated arrogance and perceived rudeness that often followed in exclusivity's wake. But it is historically demonstrable that striving for society membership through competing for campus organization leadership positions produced for the growing republic, over time, literally hundreds of national leaders in politics, business, academia, medicine, and literature.

It is also well founded that the electing seniors within the societies, as well as those passed over, worried about the charge of exclusivity, and balancing it with their own sense of electoral fairness and student-mandated standards of achievement, blended ambition with democracy. They tapped for their exclusive groups social castes barred from entry into the uppermost reaches of American society, long before their elders in the Yale administration—and similarly in the United States—elevated Jews, blacks, gays, and women to similar positions of prominence, whether on the campus or in the nation.

Their vociferous critics were unmindful of this largely hidden history (a woman *News* columnist in 1985 imagined that "if someone gained access to the annual pictures of the three all-male societies, up until the last few years the members would probably all look alike—with a few token Jewish-looking men scattered here and there if one were lucky,"[11] when Jews and blacks had been elected in mounting numbers for half a century). Their detractors in the post-1960s hammered the societies for their small membership, their private tombs, their accumulated wealth, and their refusal to admit guests, demanding the fulfillment of purposes of social service, philanthropy, and public entertainment to which the societies never aspired, and which none of them had ever promised to anyone.

It is no wonder that the senior societies largely withdrew, where they could, from campus notice, except for the undisguisable presence of their provoking, windowless tombs, and the announcement of their annual elections. Their respective "secrets" of internal names and hidden rituals are now largely known or otherwise discoverable, for those that care to inquire across the public records of the last 180 years, but the interior life of the annual delegations, the intangibles in which they truly traffic, in privacy as well as secrecy, are still familiar only to their initiates, and living this life is clearly seen as desirable in the Yale College of today.

ACKNOWLEDGMENTS

A lthough this book is the made up from an extensive and intensive review of published or printed material detailing the history of Yale College's senior secret societies, histories written by their members, their detractors, and outsiders, and the text's revelations are perhaps more of the existence of those obscure or even forgotten sources than of "secrets" never before exposed, the quest to find them required the frequent ministrations of the staff of the Manuscripts and Archives division of the Yale University Library, for which the author is very grateful. Supplementing that help were Christine Kaisman and Debbie Nugent of the Yale Club of New York library. I also wish to thank my assistant, Ellen Gonzalez, who remained patient while resolving my struggles with computer technology and its wonders. John Silbersack of the Trident Media Group bravely took on the literary agency assignment for a completed manuscript, and offered useful editorial guidance. Thanks, too, to Claiborne Hancock of Pegasus Books for his enthusiasm and careful editing.

My substantial debts to prior historians of Yale College and its societies, and of American university education generally, are apparent from the Selected Bibliography which follows.

I also received the generous cooperation of the corporate officers of several of the trust associations which are the corporate parents of the senior societies herein described, but given the book's subject matter and the sensitivities of their societies' membership, the names of those individuals must remain an unrevealed secret. I can only hope the final product (unreviewed by any of them before publication) is no betrayal of their trust in my treatment of the materials so provided.

Assistance which can be openly acknowledged has come from several friends and colleagues, including Professor Charles Hill, Henry "Sam" Chauncey Jr., Geoffrey Neigher, Ravi D. Goel, F. Michael Kail, Thomas Gottshall, Patrick Pinnell, Paul Goldberger, Coit Liles, Michael Gates Gill, Kathrin Day Lassila, E. Ward Smith, Edward McDermott, William L. Clements Library director Kevin Graffagnino (University of Michigan), Houghton Library director Tom Hyry (Harvard University), and Beinecke Rare Book and Manuscript Curator of Modern Books and Manuscripts Timothy Young (Yale University).

The poems of Stephen Vincent Benét which have been excerpted here are quoted with the kind permission of the writer's son, Thomas Benét.

A "director's cut" of the text of this book in word-searchable format, including a chapter on the impact of senior society membership on the reconstruction of the Yale Corporation in the 1860s through the "Young Yale" movement, and treatment of the necessity for and incorporation of the parent "trust associations" for the societies and other material that did not survive the editing process but may be of interest to those wishing to know more (or even just whether their ancestors were named as being members of these groups), may be found in Yale's Manuscripts & Archives.

SELECTED BIBLIOGRAPHY

Abramson, Rudy. *Spanning the Century: The Life of W. Averell Harriman 1891–1986.* New York: William Morrow, Inc., 1992.

Acheson, David C. *Acheson Country: A Memoir.* New York: W. W. Norton, 1993.

Acheson, Dean. *Among Friends: Personal Letters of Dean Acheson.* New York: Dodd, Mead, 1980.

———. *Present at the Creation.* New York: W. W. Norton 1996.

Adler, Jerry. "God, Men and Bonding at Yale." *Newsweek,* April 28, 1991.

Aiken, E. E. *The Senior Society System.* New Haven, Conn.: Tuttle, Morehouse & Taylor, 1852.

Allmendinger, David F., Jr. *Paupers and Scholars: The Transformation of Student Life in Nineteenth Century New England.* New York: St. Martin's, 1975.

Allyn, Avery. *A Ritual of Freemasonry Illustrated by Numerous Engravings to Which Is Added a Key to the Phi Beta Kappa. With Notes and Remarks.* Boston, Mass.: John Marsh and Co., 1831.

Amory, Cleveland. *The Proper Bostonians.* New York: E. P. Dutton, 1947.

Andrews, John William. *History of the Founding of Wolf's Head.* Lancaster, Pa.: Lancaster Press, 1934.

Andrews, Mary Raymond Shipman. "The Courage of the Commonplace." *Scribner's Magazine,* July 1911.

Atkinson, Brooks, ed. *The Complete Essays and Other Writings of Ralph Waldo Emerson.* New York: Modern Library, 1950.

Axtell, James. *The Making of Princeton University: From Woodrow Wilson to the Present.* Princeton, N.J., and Oxford, England: Princeton University Press, 2006.

Bagg, Lyman Hotchkiss. *Four Years at Yale by a Graduate of '69.* New Haven, Conn.: Charles C. Chatfield & Co., 1871.

Baird, William Raimond. *American College Fraternities.* Fifth Edition. New York: published by the author, 1898.

Baker, Carlos. *Ernest Hemingway: A Life Story.* New York: Scribner's, 1969.

———, ed. *Ernest Hemingway: Selected Letters, 1917–1961.* New York: Scribner's, 1981.

Baker, Paul D. *Richard Morris Hunt.* Cambridge, Mass.: MIT Press, 1980.

Baldwin, Ebenezer. *Annals of Yale College.* New Haven, Conn.: B. & W. Noyes, 1834; second ed., 1838.

Ball, David. *A Marked Heart*. Bloomington, Ind.: iUniverse, 2012.

Baltzell, E. Digby. *The Protestant Establishment: Aristocracy & Caste in America*. New York: Random House, 1964.

Barron, James. "Male Fortress Falls at Yale: Bonesmen to Admit Women." *New York Times*, July 25, 1991.

Barrows, Chester L. *William M. Evarts: Lawyer, Diplomat, Statesman*. Chapel Hill: University of North Carolina Press, 1941.

Bartlett, Edwin Griffin. "A History of Delta Kappa Epsilon." *DKE Quarterly*, Vol. 1, No. 2, April 1883.

Bascomb, John. *Secret Societies in College*. Pittsfield, Mass.: Berkshire County Eagle, 1868.

Bass, Paul, and Douglas W. Rae. *Murder in the Model City: The Black Panthers, Yale, and the Redemption of a Killer*. New York: Basic Books, 2006.

Beers, Henry A. *The Ways of Yale in the Consulship of Plancus*. New York: Henry Holt, 1895.

Belden, Ezekiel Porter. *Sketches of Yale College with Numerous Anecdotes and Embellished with More Than Thirty Engravings*. New York: Saxton and Miles, 1843.

Bell, Millicent. *Marquand: An American Life*. Boston, Mass.: Little, Brown, 1979.

Bemis, Samuel Flagg. *John Quincy Adams and the Union*. New York: Alfred A. Knopf, 1956.

Benét, Stephen Vincent. *The Beginning of Wisdom*. New York: Henry Holt, 1921.

———. "Poem Written for the Hundredth Anniversary of the Kingsley Trust Association." Read June 9, 1942. Manuscripts and Archives, Yale University.

———. "The Songs of Dear Old Yale," 1917, Stephen Vincent Benét Papers, Yale Colleciton of American Literature, Beinecke Rare Book and Manuscript Library, Yale University.

Bergin, Thomas. *The Game*. New Haven, Conn.: Yale University Press, 1984.

———. "My Native Country." In *My Harvard, My Yale*, edited by Diana Dubois. New York: Random House, 1982.

———. *Yale's Residential Colleges in the First Fifty Years*. New Haven, Conn.: Yale University Press, 1983.

Betsky, Aaron. *James Gamble Rogers and the Architecure of Pragmatism*. Cambridge, Mass.: MIT Press, 1994.

Bird, Kai. *The Color of Truth: McGeorge Bundy and William Bundy: Brothers in Arms: A Biography*. New York, Simon & Schuster, 1998.

Birmingham, Stephen. *The Later John Marquand*. New York: Lippincott, 1972.

Bissell, Richard M., Jr. *Reflections of a Cold Warrior: From Yalta to the Bay of Pigs*. New Haven, Conn.: Yale University Press, 1996.

Bledstein, Burton J. *The Culture of Professionalism: The Middle Class and the Development of Higher Education in America*. New York: W. W. Norton, 1976.

Bond, Horace Man. *Black American Scholars*. Detroit, Mich.: Balamp, 1972.

Borders, William. "Bones and Keys Rattle in the Night at Yale," *New York Times*, April 29, 1967.

Branch, Taylor. *Pillar of Fire: America in the King Years 1963–65*. New York: Simon & Schuster, 1998.

SELECTED BIBLIOGRAPHY

Brinkley, Alan. *The Publisher: Henry Luce and His American Century.* New York: Alfred A. Knopf, 2010.

Bristed, Charles Astor. *Five Years in an English University.* G. P. Putnam & Sons: New York, 1852.

Brock, H. L. "College Ways in America." *New York Times Magazine,* May 28, 1933.

Brown, Buster. "Skull and Bones: It's Not Just for White Dudes Anymore." *Atlantic,* February 25, 2013.

Bruccoli, Matthew. *An Artist Is His Own Fault: John O'Hara on Writers and Writing.* Carbondale: Southern Illinois University Press, 1977.

———, ed. *The O'Hara Concern: A Biography of John O'Hara.* New York: Random House, 1975.

———, ed. *Selected Letters of John O'Hara.* New York: Random House, 1978.

———. *Some Sort of Epic Grandeur.* New York and London: Harcourt Brace Jovanovich, 1981.

Buck, Polly Stone. *We Minded the Store: Yale Life & Letters During World War II.* New Haven, Conn.: self-published, 1975.

Bullard, Allan B. *The Education of Black Folk.* New York: Harper and Row, 1973.

Bundy, McGeorge. "For the Defense." *Yale Literary Magazine,* February 1939.

———. "The Issue Before the Court." *Atlantic,* 240:5, November 1977.

Bush, Barbara. *Barbara Bush: A Memoir.* New York: Scribner's, 1994.

Bush, George W. *A Charge to Keep.* New York: William Morrow, Inc., 1999.

———. *41: A Portrait of My Father.* New York: Crown, 2014.

Calleo, David P. and Henry S. F. Cooper. *Inside Eli: or How to Get on at Yale.* New Haven: privately printed, 1957.

Camp, Walter. *Jack Hall at Yale: A Football Story.* New York and London: D. Appleton, 1909.

———. "Yale Athletics, A Review of Its History." *Illustrated American,* April 19, 1890.

Canby, Harry Seidel. *Alma Mater: The Gothic Age of the American College.* New York: Farrar & Rinehart, 1936.

———. *American Memoir.* Boston, Mass.: Houghton Mifflin, 1947.

Carnes, Mark C. *Secret Ritual and Manhood in Victorian America.* New Haven, Conn., and London: Yale University Press, 1989.

Caro, Robert. *The Power Broker: Robert Moses and the Fall of New York.* New York: Alfred P. Knopf, 1974.

Carrott, Richard G. *The Egyptian Revival: Its Sources, Monuments and Meaning (1808–1858).* Berkeley: University of California Press, 1968.

Cash, Wilbur J. *The Mind of the South.* New York: Vintage, 1991.

Catalogue 2003. N.p., Russell Trust Association, 2003.

Catalogue of Members: Yale Chapter of Phi Beta Kappa Alpha of Connecticut. New Haven, Conn.: Price, Lee and Adkins, 1905.

Catalogue of the Alpha Delta Phi. New York: published by the Executive Council, 1899.

Catalogue of the Calliopean Society, Yale College, 1839. New Haven, Conn.: printed by B. L. Hamlen, 1839.

Catalogue of the Delta Kappa Epsilon Fraternity, Aldice G. Warren, ed. New York: Published by the ΔKE Council, Press of John C. Winston, 1910.

Catalogue of the Graduate Members of the Linonian Society of Yale College During One Hundred Years, From Its Foundation in September, 1753. New Haven, Conn.: published by the Society, 1853.

[The Twelfth General] Catalogue of the Psi Upsilon Fraternity. N.p.: Executive Council of the Psi Upsilon Fraternity, May 1917.

Catalogue of the Society of Brothers in Unity, Yale College, Founded A.D. 1768. New Haven, Conn.: published by the Society, 1854.

Chamberlain, Daniel. "The Value of Literary Societies in American Education." *University Quarterly*, Vol. 3, April 1861.

Chamberlain, Joshua L., ed. *Universities and Their Sons: Yale University Its History, Influence, Equipment and Characteristics.* Boston, Mass.: R. Herndon, 1900.

Chase, James. *Acheson: The Secretary of State Who Created the American World.* New York: Simon & Schuster, 1998.

Chauncey, Henry "Sam," Jr., John T. Hill, and Thomas Strong. *May Day at Yale, 1970 Recollections of the Trial of Bobby Seale and the Black Panthers.* Westport, Conn.: Prospecta Press, 2015.

Childs, Richard S. "The Elks in Our Midst." *Harkness Hoot*, April–May 1931.

Chittenden, Russell H. *History of the Sheffield Scientific School of Yale University 1846–1922* Vol. 1. New Haven, Conn.: Yale University Press, 1928.

Coffin, William Sloane, Jr. *Once to Every Man.* New York: Atheneum, 1977.

Cohane, Timothy. *The Yale Football Story.* New York: G. P. Putnam's Sons, 1951.

"College Ingenuity." *Yale Literary Magazine*, Vol XXIV, No. 4, February 1864.

Colt, George Henry. *Brothers.* New York: Scribner's, 2012.

Concerning Elihu. New Haven, Conn.: Elihu Club, 1952.

Constitution of Alpha Delta Phi.

Constitution of Delta Kappa Epsilon.

"Constitution of the Elihu Club." June 1912. Manuscripts and Archives, Yale University.

Cooper, H.S.F., and Thomas C. Wallace, eds. Stephen Parks, producer. *Manuscript (1953–2002).* New Haven, Conn.: Wrexham Foundation, 2002.

Cooper, Jacob. *William Preston Johnston: A Character Sketch.* New Haven, Conn.: prepared for the Class of 1852 in Yale University, 1878.

Corson, William R. *The Armies of Ignorance: The Rise of the American Intelligence Empire.* New York: Dial Press, 1977.

Courtney, Steve. *Joseph Hopkins Twichell: The Life and Times of Mark Twain's Closest Friend.* Athens: University of Georgia Press, 2008.

Coxe, Macgrane. *Chancellor Kent at Yale 1771–1781: A Paper Written for the Yale Law School.* New York: privately printed, 1909.

Crapo, William W., "Linonia and the Brothers," *Yale Literary Magazine*, February 1886.

Crawford, Albert Beecher, ed. *Football Y Men 1872–1929.* New Haven, Conn.: Yale University Press, 1962.

SELECTED BIBLIOGRAPHY

————. *Phi Beta Kappa Men of Yale 1788—1959*. New Haven, Conn.: Yale University Press, 1968.

Cross, Wilbur L. *Connecticut Yankee: An Autobiography*, New Haven, Conn.: Yale University Press, 1943.

C.S.P. 1842–1989 C.C.J. New Haven, Conn.: Kingsley Trust Association, 1990.

Cummins, Anastasia. "Women at Yale: The Social Process of Coeducation at Yale College." Senior prize essay, June 2015. Manuscripts and Archives, Yale University.

Davis, Kenneth F. *F.D.R.: The Beckoning of Destiny 1882–1928*. New York: G. P. Putnam's Sons, 1972.

Davis, Lanny J., and G. Barry Golson. "Secret Societies." *Yale Banner*, 1968.

Deacon, Richard. *The Cambridge Apostles*. London: Robert Royce Limited, 1985.

Decrow, W. E. *Yale and "The City of Elms, . . ."* Third Edition. Boston, Mass.: W. E. Decrow, 1885.

Deming, Clarence. *Yale Yesterdays*. New Haven, Conn.: Yale University Press, 1915.

Dempsey, Rachel. "Real Elis Inspired Fictional 'Shepherd.'" *Yale Daily News*, January 18, 2007.

Depew, Chauncey M. *My Memories of Eighty Years*. New York: Scribner's, 1922.

de Tocqueville, Alexis. *Democracy in America*. New York: Knopf, 1945.

Dexter, Franklin Bowditch. *Documentary History of Yale University 1701–1745*, New York: Arno Press & New York Times, 1969.

————. *The Literary Diary of Ezra Stiles*. New York: Scribner's, 1901.

————. *A Selection from the Miscellaneous Historical Papers of Fifty Years*. New Haven, Conn.: privately printed, 1918.

Diamond, Sigmund. *Compromised Campus: The Collaboration of Universities with the Intelligence Community, 1945–1955*. Oxford, England: Oxford University Press, 1992.

Donaldson, Scott. *Archibald MacLeish: An American Life*. Boston, Mass., New York, and London: Houghton Mifflin, 1992.

————. *By Force of Will: The Life and Art of Ernest Hemingway*. New York: Viking Press, 1977.

Donnelly, Honoria Murphy, with Richard N. Billings. *Sara & Gerald: Villa America and After*. New York: Times Books, 1982.

Dubois, Diana, ed. *My Harvard, My Yale*. New York: Random House, 1982.

Duffy, Herbert S. *William Howard Taft*. New York: Milton, Balch, 1930.

Duke, Alex. *Importing Oxbridge: English Residential Colleges and American Universities*. New Haven, Conn., and London: Yale University Press, 1996.

Dumenil, Lynn. *Freemasonry and American Culture 1880–1930*. Princeton, N.J.: Princeton University Press, 1984.

Duyckinck, Whitehead C. *Incidents of Our College Live Gleaned from Memorabilia and Diaries*. New Haven, Conn.: 1900.

————. *Student Life at Yale Sixty Years Ago, 1861–1865, A Reminiscence*. Plainfield, N.J.: prepared for the class meeting, 1925.

Dwight, Timothy. *Memories of Yale Life and Men 1845–1899*. New York: Dodd, Mead, 1903.

————. *What a Yale Student Ought to Be: The Introductory Lecture of the ΦBK Course for 1886–'87.* New Haven, Conn.: Yale University, 1887.

Earle, Walter K. *Mr. Shearman and Mr. Sterling and How They Grew.* New York: Yale University Press, 1963.

Eliot, Ellsworth, Jr. *Yale in the Civil War.* New Haven, Conn.: Yale University Press, 1932.

Elson, Robert T. *Time Inc. The Intimate History of a Publishing Enterprise 1923–41.* New York: Atheneum, 1968.

Emerson, Ralph Waldo. *Essays: First Series.* Boston, Mass.: James Monroe & Co., 1836.

————. *Nature.* Boston, Mass.: James Monroe & Co., 1847.

————. *Nature: Addresses and Lectures.* Boston, Mass.: James Monroe & Co., 1847.

Emerson, William Waldo, and Waldo Emerson Forbes. *The Journals of Ralph Waldo Emerson.* Boston Mass.: Houghton Mifflin, 1903–1904.

The Fall of Skull and Bones Compiled from the Minutes of the 76th Regular Meeting of the Order of File and Claw 9.29.76. New Haven, Conn.: published by the Order, 1876.

Farr, Finis. *O'Hara: A Biography.* Boston, Mass.: Little, Brown, 1973.

Faulkner, William. "Turnabout," in *Collected Short Stories of William Faulkner.* New York: Vintage International, 1995.

Fenton, Charles A. *Selected Letters of Stephen Vincent Benét.* New Haven, Conn.: Yale University Press, 1960.

————. "Social Solemnity," in *Seventy Five, infra.*

————. *Stephen Vincent Benét: The Life and Times of an American Man of Letters, 1898–1943.* New Haven, Conn.: Yale University Press, 1958.

Fitzgerald, F. Scott. *The Beautiful and the Damned.* New York: Harper, 2013.

————. *The Great Gatsby.* New York: Scribner's, 1924/2004.

————. *Tender is the Night.* New York: Scribner's, 1933/2003.

————. *This Side of Paradise.* New York: Alfred A. Knopf, 1996.

Flanagan, Caitlin. "The Dark Power of Fraternities." *Atlantic,* March 2004.

Flexner, Simon, and James Thomas Flexner. *William Henry Welch and the Heroic Age of American Medicine.* New York: Viking, 1941.

Foer, Franklin. "Tomb of Their Own: What's Really Wrong with Skull and Bones." *New Republic,* April 17 and 24, 2000.

Forster, E. M. *Howard's End.* London: Edward Arnold, 1910.

Fournier, George T., and James K. Mcauley, "The Men's Final Clubs," *Harvard Crimson,* October 5, 2010.

"Forerunners of Tap Day." *Yale Alumni Weekly,* May 20, 1910.

Fox, Lyttleton. "One Foot in the Grave and One in the Tomb," *Town & Country,* February 1940.

Franklin, Fabian. *The Life of Daniel Coit Gilman.* New York: Dodd, Mead, 1910.

Fraser, Ray. *Westward by Rail: The New Route to the East.* New York: Longman's, Green & Co., 1870.

Frazier, George. "The Bones Boys." *Boston Globe,* April 9, 1964.

————. "Yale's Secret Societies." *Esquire,* September 1955.

Freedman, Samuel G. "'Tap Day': Fading Bit of Old Yale," *New York Times*, April 16, 1982.

French, Robert Dudley, compiler. *The Memorial Quadrangle: A Book about Yale*. New Haven, Conn.: Yale University Press, 1929.

Friend, Craig Thompson and Lori Glover, eds. *Southern Manhood: Perspectives in Masculinity in the Early National South*. Athens and London: University of Georgia Press, 2001.

Fulon, John H., and Elizabeth H. Thomson. *Benjamin Silliman 1770–1864: Pathfinder in American Science*. New York: Henry Schuman, 1947.

"Fun in College Societies," *Denver Tribune-Republican*, April 25, 1886.

Gabriel, Ralph Henry. *Religion and Learning at Yale: The Church of Christ in the College and University, 1757–1957*. New Haven, Conn.: Yale University Press, 1958.

Garver, John Anson. *John William Sterling, Class of 1864, Yale College*. New Haven, Conn.: Yale University Press, 1929.

Gavit, John Palmer. "Social Barriers and 'Hush Dope' at Yale." *New York Post*, May 15, 1922.

Geiger, Roger, ed. *The American College in the Nineteenth Century*. Nashville, Tenn.: Vanderbilt University Press, 2000.

Geismar, Pamela, Eva Hart Rice, and Joan O'Meara Winant. *Fresh Women: Reflections on Co-Education and Life after Yale 1969/1989/2009*. New Haven, Conn.: Pamela Geismar Print, 2010.

Giamatti, A. Bartlett. *A History of Scroll and Key 1942–1972*. New Haven, Conn.: published by the Society, 1978.

Gill, Brendan. *States of Grace: Eight Plays by Phillip Barry*. New York: Harcourt Brace Jovanovich, 1975.

———. *Here at the New Yorker*. New York: Random House, 1975.

Gillette, Howard, Jr. *Class Divide: Yale '64 and the Conflicted Legacy of the Sixties*. Ithaca, N.Y., and London: Cornell University Press, 2015.

Gilman, Daniel Coit. *The Launching of a University and Other Papers*. New York: Dodd, Mead, 1906.

Gist, Noel P., "Secret Societies: A Cultural Study of Fraternalism in the United States." *The University of Missouri Studies*, Vol. XV, No. 4, October 1, 1940.

Gitlin, Jay, and Baisie Gitlin. *Mory's: A Brief History*. New Haven, Conn.: Mory's Preservation, Inc., 2014.

Glover, Lori. "Let Us Manufacture Men: Educating Elite Boys in the Early National South," in Thompson & Glover, eds., *Southern Manhood: Perspectives in Masculinity in the Early National South*. Athens and London: University of Georgia Press, 2001.

Goethe, Johan Wolfgang von. *Wilhelm Meister's Apprenticeship*, trans. Thomas Carlyle. New York: Collier Books, 1962.

Goldberger, Paul. "Romantic Pragmatism: The Works of James Gamble Rogers at Yale University." Senior honors essay, May 1, 1972. Haas Arts Library Special Collections, Yale University.

Goldstein, Gordon M. *Lessons in Disaster: McGeorge Bundy and the Path to War in Vietnam.* New York: Henry Holt, 2008.

Goldstein, Warren. *William Sloane Coffin Jr.: A Holy Impatience.* New Haven, Conn.: Yale University Press, 2004.

Goodwin, Doris Kearns. *The Bully Pulpit: Theodore Roosevelt, William Howard Taft, and the Golden Age of Journalism.* New York: Simon & Schuster, 2013.

Gordon, Gideon. "Yale Senior Societies: History," April 25, 1951; "Why There's a Tap Day," April 30, 1951; "Societies: Who's Been Tapped," May 2, 1951, *Yale Daily News.*

"A Graduate of the Seventies." "Discussion of 'Tap Day.' Some History Recalled in Answer to the Leader in the June 'Lit.'" *Yale Alumni Weekly,* June 24, 1905.

Green, Fitzhugh. *George Bush: An Intimate Portrait.* New York: Hippocrene, 1989.

Griffin, Peter. *Less Than a Treason: Hemingway in Paris.* New York and Oxford, England: Oxford University Press, 1990.

Griguere, Joy. *"The dead shall be raised": The Egyptian Revival and 19th Century American Commemorative Culture.* PhD, University of Maine, 2009.

Griswold, A. Whitney. *In the University Tradition.* New Haven, Conn.: Yale University Press, 1957.

Grover, Stephen. "Secret Groups Thrive at Yale while Interest in Fraternities Lags." *Wall Street Journal,* December 11, 1968.

Guo, Jerry. "Inside Yale's Secret Societies." *Connecticut Journal,* May 29, 2008.

Gurney, Stephen S., and Jonas Zdanys, eds. *True Fellowship in All Its Glory.* New Haven, Conn.: Kingsley Trust Association, 1992.

Hadley, Arthur Twining. *Universities and Their Sons: Yale University.* Boston, Mass.: R. Herndon, 1900.

———. "University Progress" (speech to Buffalo Yale Club dinner). *Yale Alumni Weekly,* March 6, 1914.

Hadley, Morris. *Arthur Twining Hadley.* New Haven, Conn.: Yale University Press, 1948.

Hale, Edward Everett. "A Fossil from the Tertiary." *Atlantic,* July 1879.

Hall, B. H. *A Collection of College Words and Customs.* Cambridge, Mass.: John Bartlett, 1856.

Hall, G. Stanley. *Youth.* New York: D. Appleton, 1906.

Hall, Peter. "'Noah Porter Writ Large.' Reflections on the Modernization of American Higher Education," in Roger Geiger, ed., *The American College in the Nineteenth Century.* Nashville, Tenn.: Vanderbilt University Press, 2000.

———. *The Organization of American Culture, 1700–1900: Private Institutions, Elites, and the Origins of American Nationality.* New York: New York University Press, 1982.

Halliday, Carl. *A History of Southern Literature.* New York: Neale, 1906.

Hallock, R. E. "The Last Man Tapped." *Gunter's Magazine,* September 1906.

Harding, Thomas S. *College Literary Societies: Their Contributions to Higher Education in the United States 1815–1876.* New York: Pageant Press, 1971.

Harrison, Mrs. Burton [Constance Carrie]. *Recollections Grave and Gay.* New York: Scribner's, 1911.

Hastings, William T. *Phi Beta Kappa as a Secret Society With Its Relations to Freemasonry and Antimasonry.* Washington, D.C.: United Chapters of Phi Beta Kappa, 1965.

SELECTED BIBLIOGRAPHY

Hatfield, J. H. *Fortunate Son: George W. Bush and the Making of an American President.* New York: St. Martin's, 1999.

Havemeyer, Loomis. *"Go to Your Room": A Story of Undergraduate Societies and Fraternities at Yale.* New Haven, Conn.: Yale University Press, 1960.

———. *The History of the Book and Snake Society and the Cloister Club, 1863–1945.* New Haven, Conn.: Yale University Press, 1955.

———. *The Story of Undergraduate Yale in the Second World War.* New Haven, Conn.: Yale University Press, 1960.

———. *Yale's Extracurricular & Social Organizations 1780–1960.* New Haven, Conn.: Yale University Press, 1961.

Hemingway, Ernest. *The Fifth Column: Four Stories of the Spanish Civil War.* New York: Scribner's, 1932.

———. *A Moveable Feast.* New York: Scribner's, 1964.

———. *To Have and to Have Not.* New York: Scribner's, 1937.

Hemingway, Marcelline. *At the Hemingways: A Family Portrait.* Boston, Mass.: Little, Brown, 1962.

Herman, Thomas. "The Inscrutable King of Yale," 1968. Manuscripts and Archives, Yale University.

———. "Lots of Girls Applying to Yale but Learning Is Not Always Reason." *Wall Street Journal,* January 2, 1969.

Hersey, John. *Letter to the Alumni.* New York: Alfred A. Knopf, 1970.

Herskowitz, Mickey. *Duty, Honor, Country: The Life and Legacy of Prescott Bush.* Nashville, Tenn.: Rutledge Hill Press, 2003.

Herzstein, Robert E. *Henry R. Luce: A Political Portrait of the Man Who Created the American Century.* New York: Scribner's, 1994.

Higgs, Robert J. "Yale and the Heroic Ideal, *Götterdammerung* and Palingenesis, 1865–1914," in *Manliness and Morality,* ed. J. A. Mangan and James Walvin. New York: St. Martin's, 1987.

Hiller, Stephen. "How Black Students Arrived at Yale." *Yale Daily News,* September 25, 1973.

Hirsch, Mark. *William C. Whitney, Modern Warwick.* New York: Dodd, Mead, 1948.

Historical Register of Yale University 1701–1937. New Haven, Conn.: Yale University Press, 1939.

Hobbs, Jeff. *The Short and Tragic Life of Robert Peace: A Brilliant Young Man Who Left Newark for the Ivy League.* New York: Scribner's, 2014.

Hocmuth, Marie and Richard Murphy. "Rhetoric and Elocutionary Training in Nineteenth Century Colleges," in Karl M. Wallace, ed., *History of Speech Education in America.* New York: Appleton-Century-Crofts, 1954.

Hodgson, Godfrey. *The Colonel: The Life and Wars of Henry Stimson 1867–1950.* New York: Alfred A. Knopf, 1990.

Hofstadter, Richard, and Wilson Smith. *American Higher Education, A Documentary History.* Chicago, Ill.: University of Chicago Press, 1968.

Holahan, David. "The Bad News Bones." *Hartford Courant,* May 29, 1988.

Holbrook, Richard. *Boys and Men: A Story of Life at Yale.* New York: Scribner's, 1909.

Holden, Reuben. *Yale: A Pictorial History.* New Haven, Conn.: Yale University Press, 1967.

Holt, Henry. *Garrulities of an Octogenerian Editor.* Boston, Mass., and New York: Houghton Mifflin, 1923.

Holzman, Michael. *James Jesus Angleton: The CIA, and the Craft of Counterintelligence.* Amherst: University of Massachusetts Press, 2008.

Hooker, Arthur. *The Founding of Elihu.* New Haven, Conn.: 2012.

Horowitz, Daniel. *On the Cusp: The Yale College Class of 1960 and a World on the Verge of Change.* Amherst and Boston: University of Massacusetts Press, 2015.

Horowitz, Helen Lefkowitz. *Campus Life: Undergraduate Culture from the End of the Eighteenth Century to the Present.* New York: Knopf, 1987.

Howland, Henry E. "Undergraduate Life at Yale." *Scribner's,* Vol. XXII, No. 1, July 1897.

Hughes, Nathaniel, Jr. *Yale's Confederates: A Biographical Dictionary.* Chattanooga: University of Tennessee Press, 2008.

Hughes, Rupert. "Secret Societies at Yale." *Munsey's,* June 1894.

Huizinga, Johan. *Homo Ludens: A Study of the Play-Element in Culture.* London, Boston, Mass., and Henley-on-Thames, England: Routledge & Kegan Paul, 1955.

Huntington, Samuel. *A History of the Class of 1863.* New Haven, Conn.: Tuttle, Morehouse & Taylor, 1905.

Hurd, Richard. *A History of Yale Athletics: 1840–1888, Giving Every Contest with Harvard, Princeton, Pennsylvania, Columbia, Wesleyan, and Others in Rowing, Foot Ball, Base Ball, Track Athletics, Tennis.* New Haven, Conn.: privately printed, 1888.

———. "The Yale Stroke." *Outing,* Vol. XV, December 1889.

Hyde, Miles G. *The One Time Wooden Spoon at Yale.* New York: Albert A. Ochs, 1899.

Hynes, Samuel. *The Unsubstantial Air: American Flyers in the First World War.* New York: Farrar Straus & Giroux, 2014.

Iconoclast. New Haven, Conn., October 13, 1873.

Isaacson, Walter. "My Heritage Is Part of Who I Am." *Time,* August 7, 2000.

Isaacson, Walter, and Evan Thomas. *The Wise Men: Six Friends and the World They Made: Acheson, Bohlen, Harriman, Kennan, Lovett, McCloy.* New York: Simon & Schuster, 1986.

Jacob, Margaret C. *Living the Enlightenment: Freemasonry and Politics in Eighteenth-Century Europe.* New York and Oxford, England: Oxford University Press, 1991.

Jaes, Theodore. "Ivy League Clubs." *Town & Country,* August 1973.

Jaffe, Irma B. *Trumbull: Portrait Artist of the American Revolution.* Boston, Mass.: New York Graphic Society, 1975.

Jeffrey-Jones, Rhodri. *Cloak and Dollar: A History of American Secret Intelligence.* New Haven, Conn.: Yale University Press, 2002.

Jenks, A. E. "Social Life at Yale." *Lippincott's,* Vol. 40, 1888.

Johnson, Carl Sanfred. *Fraternities in Our Colleges.* New York: Intrafraternity Foundation, 1972.

Johnson, Owen. "The Social Usurpation of Colleges, Part II—Harvard." *Collier's,* Vol. XLIX, No. 10, 25 May 1912.

————. "The Social Usurpation of Colleges, Part III – Yale." *Collier's,* Vol. XLIX, No. 12, June 8, 1912.

————. *Stover at Yale.* New York: Frederick A. Stokes, 1912.

Johnston, W. C. "The Literary Societies of Yale College." *University Quarterly,* Vol. 1, January 1860.

Judis, John B. *William F. Buckley, Jr.: Patron Saint of the Conservatives.* New York: Simon and Schuster, 1988.

Kabaservice, Geoffrey. *The Guardians: Kingman Brewster, His Circle, and the Rise of the Liberal Establishment.* New York, Henry Holt, 2004.

————. "Kingman Brewster and the Rise and Fall of the Progressive Establishment." PhD dissertation, March 1999. Film D11240, Manuscripts and Archives, Yale University.

Kahn, E. H., Jr. *Jock: The Life and Times of John Hay Whitney.* Garden City, N.Y.: Doubleday, 1981.

Kahrl, William K. "Yet time and change shall not prevail To break the friendships formed at . . . " *New Journal,* Vol. 2, No. 6, February 9, 1969.

Kant, Immanuel. "An Answer to the Question: What Is Enlightenment," in Pauline Kleingeld, ed., *Toward Perpetual Peace and Other Writings on Politics, Peace, and History.* New Haven, Conn.: Yale University Press, 2006.

Karabel, Jerome. *The Chosen: The Hidden History of Admission and Exclusion at Harvard, Yale, and Princeton.* Boston, Mass., and New York: Houghton Mifflin, 2005.

Karl, Frederic. *William Faulkner American Writer: A Biography.* New York: Weidenfeld and Nicolson, 1989.

Kelley, Brooks Mather. *Yale: A History.* New Haven, Conn., and London: Yale University Press, 1974.

Kellogg, H. L. *College Secret Societies: Their Customs, Character, and the Efforts for Their Suppression.* Chicago, Ill.: Ezra A. Cook, 1874.

Kett, Joseph F. *Rites of Passage: Adolescence in America 1790 to the Present.* New York: Basic Books, 1977.

Kimball, Robert, ed. *Cole: A Biographical Essay by Brendan Gill.* Woodstock, N.Y., and New York: Overlook Press, 2004.

King, Nicholas. *George Bush: A Biography.* New York: Dodd, Mead, 1980.

Kingsley, William L. *Yale College: A Sketch of Its History,* 2 vols. New York: Henry Holt, 1879.

Kinkaid, Katherine. *How an Ivy League College Decides Admissions.* New York: W. W. Norton, 1961.

Kluger, Jeffrey. *The Sibling Effect: What the Bonds Among Sisters and Brothers Reveal about Us.* New York; Riverhead Books, 2011.

Knowles, John. "The Yale Man." *Holiday,* May 1953.

Kristof, Nicholas D. "Ally of an Older Generation amid the Tumult of the 60's." *New York Times,* June 18, 2000.

Krotzer, Henry W. "Stones of Yale, II," *Yale Alumni Magazine,* January–February 1949.

Lamoreaux, David. "*Stover at Yale* and the Gridiron Metaphor." *The Journal of Popular Culture,* Vol. XI, Fall 1977.

Lane, William Coolidge. *Catalogue of the Harvard Chapter*. Cambridge, Mass.: 1912.

———. "The Telltale, 1721." *Publications of the Colonial Society of Massachusetts, Transactions*, XII (January 1909).

Lassila, Kathrin Day, and Mark Alden Branch. "Whose Skull and Bones?" *Yale Alumni Magazine*, May–June 2006.

Latham, Aaron. *Orchids for Mother*. Boston, Mass.: Little, Brown, 1971.

Lathrop, W. W. "College Secret Societies." *University Quarterly*, Vol. 3, April 1861.

Lear, Jonathan. "How Yale Selected Her First Coeds," *New York Times Magazine*, April 13, 1969.

Le Bot, André. *Scott Fitzgerald, a Biography*. Trans. William Byron. New York: Doubleday, 1983.

Le Carré, John. *The Russia House*. London: Hodder & Stoughton, 1989.

Lemann, Nicholas. *The Big Test: The Secret History of the American Meritocracy*. New York: Farrar Straus and Giroux, 1999.

Leslie, Jacques. "Smirk from the Past." *Salon*, March 1, 2000.

Lever, Janet, and Pepper Schwartz. *Women at Yale: Liberating a College Campus*. Indianapolis, Ind.: Bobbs-Merrill, 1971.

Levine, David O. *The American College and the Culture of Aspiration, 1915–1940*. Ithaca, N.Y., and London: Cornell University Press, 1986.

Levy, Paul. *Moore: G. E. Moore and the Cambridge Apostles*. New York: Holt, Rinehart & Winston, 1979.

Lewis, Harry Sinclair. "Unknown Undergraduates." *Yale Literary Magazine*, June 1906.

Lewis, Wilmarth S. *One Man's Education*. New York: Alfred A. Knopf, 1967.

Linonia Society. *Constitution and By-laws of the Linonian Society, of Yale College*. New Haven, Conn.: Morehouse & Taylor, 1859.

Lipson, Dorothy. *Freemasonry in Federalist Connecticut*. Princeton, N.J.: Princeton University Press, 1977.

Livermore, Charles F. "The First Harvard-Yale Boat Race," *Harvard Graduates' Magazine*, II, December 1889.

Loftus, John, and Mark Aarons. *The Secret War against the Jews: How Western Espionage Betrayed the Jewish People*. New York: St. Martin's, 1984.

Lubenow, W. C. *The Cambridge Apostles, 1820–1914: Liberalism, Imagination and Friendship in British Intellectual and Professional Life*. Cambridge, England: Cambridge University Press, 1998.

Lyman, Chester. "Origins of the Yale Lit." *Yale Literary Magazine*, February 1886.

Mack, Maynard. *A History of Scroll and Key 1842–1942*. New Haven, Conn., 1942/1978 (published by the Society).

MacLeish, Archibald. "New-Yale." *Fortune*, Vol. IX, No. 3, March 1934.

MacShane, Frank. *The Life of John O'Hara*. New York: E. P. Dutton, 1980.

Mangin, J.A., and James Walvin, eds. *Manliness and Morality: Middle-Class Masculinity in Britain and America, 1800–1849*. Manchester, England: University of Manchester Press, 1987.

Mangold, Tom. *James Jesus Angleton: The CIA's Master Spy Hunter.* New York and London: Simon and Schuster, 1991.

Marquand, John P. *H. M. Pulham, Esq.* Boston, Mass.: Little, Brown, 1941.

———. *The Late George Apley: A Novel in the Form of a Memoir.* Boston, Mass.: Little, Brown, 1937.

Martin, Edward S. "Undergraduate Life at Harvard." *Scribner's,* Vol. XXI, No. 5, May 1897.

McBride, Mary Gorton. *Randall Lee Gibson of Louisiana: Confederate General and New South Reformer.* Baton Rouge: Louisiana State University Press, 1997.

McBrien, William. *Cole Porter: A Biography.* New York: Alfred A. Knopf, 1998.

McCosh, James. "Discipline in American Colleges." *North American Review,* May–June 1878.

McLachlan, James. *"The Choice of Hercules,* American Student Societies in the Early Nineteenth Century," in Lawrence Stone, ed., *The University in Society Vol. II Europe, Scotland and the United States from the 16th to the 20th Century.* Princeton, N.J.: Princeton University Press, 1974.

McWilliams, Wilson Carey. *The Idea of Fraternity in America.* Berkeley, Los Angeles and London: University of California Press, 1973.

Meacham, Jon. *Destiny and Power: The American Odyssey of George Herbert Walker Bush.* New York: Random House, 2015.

Mellon, Paul. with John Baskett. *Reflections in a Silver Spoon.* New York: William Morrow, 1992.

Member, A. "Senior Societies and the Lord Jehovah." *Harkness Hoot,* May 1933.

Mendell, Clarence W. "Social System in the College." *Fifty Years of Yale News: A Symposium on Yale Development to Commemorate the Fiftieth Anniversary of the Yale Daily News.* New Haven, Conn.: Yale Daily News, 1928.

Mendenhall, Thomas. *The Harvard–Yale Boat Race 1852–1924 and The Coming of Sport to the American College.* Mystic, Conn.: Mystic Seaport Museum, 1993.

Meyer, D. H. *The Instructed Conscience: The Shaping of the American National Ethic.* Philadelphia: University of Pennsylvania Press, 1972.

Meyers, Jeffrey. *Hemingway: A Biography.* New York: Harper & Row, 1985.

Millegan, Kris, editor. *Fleshing Out Skull & Bones: Investigations into America's Most Powerful Senior Society.* Waterville, Ore.: Trine Daily, 2003.

Milne, David. *America's Rasputin: Walt Rostow and the Vietnam War.* New York: Hill & Wang, 2008.

Minnigerode, Meade. *The Big Year: A College Story.* New York and London: G. P. Putnam's Sons, 1921.

Minutaglio, Bill. *First Son: George W. Bush and the Bush Family Dynasty.* New York: Times Books, 1999.

Mitchell, John. *Reminiscences of Scenes and Characters in College: By a Graduate of Yale, of the Class of 1821.* New Haven, Conn.: A. H. Maltby, 1847.

Monette, Paul. *Becoming a Man: Half a Life Story.* New York, San Diego, and London: Harcourt Brace Jovanovich, 1992.

Moore, Paul, Jr. *Presences: A Bishop's Life in the City.* New York: Farrar Straus and Giroux, 1997.

———. "A Touch of Laughter," in *My Harvard, My Yale,* ed. by Diana Dubois. New York: Random House, 1982.

Morison, Elting E. *The Letters of Theodore Roosevelt,* Volume VII. Cambridge, Mass.: Harvard University Press, 1954.

———. *Turmoil and Tradition: A Study of the Life and Times of Henry L. Stimson.* Boston, Mass.: Houghton Mifflin, 1960.

Morison, Samuel Eliot. *Three Centuries of Harvard.* Cambridge, Mass.: Harvard University Press, 1936.

Moseley, Laura Hadley, ed. *Diary 1843–1852 of James Hadley, Professor of Greek in Yale College, 1845–1872.* New Haven, Conn.; Yale University Press, 1951.

Nelson, Fred A. "A History of Admissions at Yale College, 1701 to 1966." January 1966. Kingman Brewster papers, Manuscripts and Archives, Yale University.

Nettleton, George Henry. "American Universities and Colleges. I—Yale University." *Frank Leslie's Popular Monthly,* Vol. XLII, No. 5, November 1896.

———. *The Book of the Yale Pageant 1716–1916–21 October 1916.* New Haven, Conn.: Yale University Press, 1916.

———. "On Realities." *Yale Literary Magazine,* February 1896.

———, ed. *Yale in the World War.* 2 vols. New Haven, Conn.: Yale University Press, 1926.

Norton, Charles Eliot, Arthur T. Hadley, William M. Sloane, and Brander Matthews. *Four American Universities.* New York: Harper & Brothers, 1895.

Oder, Norman. "Senior Societies: Changes Came Slowly Despite Some Criticism." *Yale Daily News,* April 13, 1982.

———. "Senior Societies: Coeducation Brought Change; Importance Now Downplayed." *Yale Daily News,* April 13, 1982.

———. "Senior Societies over the Years: A Long History of Influence at Yale." *Yale Daily News,* April 12, 1982.

O'Gorman, James F. *Henry Austin: In Every Variety of Style.* Middletown, Conn.: Weslyan University Press, 2010.

O'Hara, John. *Appointment in Samarra.* New York: Random House, 1934/1994.

———. *BUtterfield 8.* New York: Penguin, 1935.

———. *A Rage to Live.* New York: Random House, 1945.

Oldenberg, Don. "Bush, Kerry Share Tippy-Top Secret." *Washington Post,* April 4, 2004.

Oren, Dan A. *Joining the Club: A History of Jews and Yale.* New Haven, Conn., and London: Yale University Press, 1985.

Osterweis, Rollin. *Romanticism and Nationalism in the Old South.* Baton Rouge: Lousiana University Press, 1971.

———. *Three Centuries of New Haven, 1638–1938.* New Haven, Conn.: Yale University Press, 1953.

Paine, Ralph D. *College Years.* New York: Scribner's, 1909.

———. *The First Yale Unit: A Story of Naval Aviation, 1916–1919.* Two vols. Cambridge, Mass.: Riverside Press, 1925.

Pak, Susie J. *Gentlemen Bankers: The World of J. P. Morgan.* Cambridge, England, and London: Harvard University Press, 2013.

Parmet, Herbert. *George Bush: The Life of a Lone Star Yankee.* New York: Scribner, 1977.

Patterson, James T. *Mr. Republican: A Biography of Robert A. Taft.* Boston, Mass.: Houghton Mifflin, 1972.

Patton, Cornelius Howard, and Walter Taylor Field. *Eight O'Clock Chapel: A Study of New England College Life in the Eighties.* Boston, Mass., and New York: Houghton Mifflin, 1927.

Perkins, N. C. "Secret Societies among Us." *Yale Literary Magazine,* December 1856.

Perrotta, Tom. *Joe College.* New York: St. Martin's, 2000.

Peterfreund, Diana. *Secret Society Girl.* New York: Delacorte, 2006.

Pfister, Joel. *The Yale Indian: The Education of Henry Roe Cloud.* Durham, N.C., and London: Duke University Press, 2009.

Phelps, William Lyon. *Autobiography with Letters.* Oxford, England: Oxford University Press, 1939.

Phillips, Kevin. *American Dynasty: Aristocracy, Fortune, and the Politics of Deceit in the House of Bush.* New York: Viking, 2004.

Pickens, William. *Bursting Bonds.* Boston, Mass.: Jordan and Moore, 1927.

———. "Southern Negro in Northern University." *Voices of the Negro,* Vol. II, No. 3, 1905.

Pierson, George Wilson. *The Education of American Leaders Comparative Contributions of U.S. Colleges and Universities.* New York: Praeger, 1969.

———. *Yale: The University College 1921–1937.* New Haven, Conn.: Yale University Press, 1955.

———. *A Yale Book of Numbers: Historical Statistics of the College and University, 1701–1976.* New Haven, Conn.: Yale University Press, 1983.

———. *Yale College: An Educational History 1871–1921.* New Haven, Conn.: Yale University Press, 1952.

Pinnell, Patrick L. *Yale University: An Architectural Tour.* Second Edition. The Campus Guide. New York: Princeton Architectural Press, 1999/2013.

Piper, P. F. "College Fraternities." *Cosmopolitan,* Vol. XXII, No. 6, April 1897.

Plimpton, George A. "The Yale Secret Societies." *Harvard Lampoon,* Vol. CXXVIII, No. 3, November 18, 1949.

Porter, John Addison. "College Fraternities." *Century,* Vol. XXXVI, September 1888.

———. *Sketches of Yale Life.* Washington, D.C.: Arlington, 1886.

———. "The Society System of Yale College." *New Englander,* Vol. CLXXX, May 1884.

Porter, Noah. *The American Colleges and the American Public.* New Haven, Conn.: Charles C. Chatfield, 1870.

———. *In Memoriam: Joseph Earl Sheffield, A Commemorative Discourse.* New Haven, Conn.: 1882.

Potter, David. *Debating in the Colonial Chartered Colleges: A Historical Survey, 1642–1900.* New York: Teachers' College, Columbia University, 1944.

Preston, Andrew. *The War Council: McGeorge Bundy, the NSC, and Vietnam.* Cambridge, Mass: Harvard University Press, 2006.

Pringle, Henry F. *The Life and Times of William Howard Taft.* 2 vols. New York: Farrar & Rinehart, 1949.

———. "Young Men on the Make." *Harper's,* January 1929.

Rader, Benjamin G. *American Sports from the Age of Folk Games to the Age of Spectators.* Englewood Cliffs, N.J.: Prentice-Hall, 1983.

Reidy, Chris. "Bastion of Bones." *Boston Globe,* March 4, 1991.

Reminiscences of Scenes and Characters in College: By a Graduate of Yale of the Class of 1821. New Haven, Conn.: A. H. Maltby, 1847.

Report of the Committee on Numbers and Scholarship, Yale College, April 1903. Manuscripts and Archives, Yale University.

Rhodes, Richard. "Shell Games." In *My Harvard, My Yale,* edited by Diana Dubois. New York: Random House, 1982.

Richards, David Alan. "Kipling and the Rhodes Scholars." *Kipling Journal,* March 2012.

———. *The Making of the Corporation 1969.* Manuscripts and Archives, Yale University.

Richards, Jeffrey. "'Passing the Love of Women': Manly Love and Victorian Society," in J. A. Mangan and James Walvin, eds., *Manliness and Morality: Middle-Class Masculinity in Britain and America, 1800–1849.* Manchester, England: University of Manchester Press, 1987.

Robbins, Alexandra. "George W., Knight of Eulogia." *Atlantic,* May 2000.

———. *Secrets of the Tomb: Skull and Bones, The Ivy League, and the Hidden Paths to Power.* New York: Little, Brown, 2002.

Roberts, J. M. *The Mythology of the Secret Societies.* London: Watkins, 2008.

Rogers, James Gamble. "James Gamble Rogers—Yale Architect." Senior honors essay, April 30, 1968. Manuscripts and Archives, Yale University.

Rosenbaum, Ron. "The Last Secrets of Skull and Bones: An Elegy for Mumbo-Jumbo." *Esquire,* September 1977.

———. *The Secret Parts of Fortune: Three Decades of Intense Investigations and Edgy Enthusiasms.* New York: Random House, 2000.

Rossano, Geoffrey, ed. *The Price of Honor: The World War One Letters of Naval Aviator Kenneth MacLeish.* Annapolis, Md.: Naval Institute Press, 1991.

Roth, Eric. *The Good Shepherd Screenplay and Commentary.* New York: Newmarket, 2006.

Rudoph, Frederick. *The American College and University: A History.* New York: Vintage, 1962.

———. *Mark Hopkins and the Log: Williams College, 1836–1872.* New Haven, Conn.: Yale University Press, 1956.

———. "Neglect of Students as a Historical Tradition," in *The College and the Student.* ed. Lawrence E. Dennis and Joseph F. Kauffman. Washington, D.C.: American Council on Education, 1966.

Rusk, Ralph, ed. *The Letters of Ralph Waldo Emerson,* Vol. 1. New York: Columbia University Press, 1939.

Santayana, George. "A Glimpse of Yale." *Harvard Monthly,* Vol. XV, No. 3, December 1892.

Schiff, Judith. "How the Secret Societies Got That Way." *Yale Alumni Magazine,* September/October 2004.

———. "To Freedom's Fallen." *Yale Alumni Magazine,* March 1997.

———. "When the Shooting Stopped." *Yale Alumni Magazine,* September 1995.

———. "When Yale Schooled for War." *Yale Alumni Magazine*, December 2002.

Schiffrin, André. *A Political Education: Coming of Age in Paris and New York*. Hoboken, N.J.: Melville Home Publishing, 2007.

Schuyler, Montgomery. "The Architecture of American Colleges II—Yale." *The Architectural Record*, Vol. XXVI, December 1909.

———. "Works of the Late Richard M. Hunt." *The Architectural Record*, Vol. V, July 1895–June 1896.

Schwab, J. L. "The Yale College Curriculum, 1701–1901." *Educational Review*, Vol. XXII, June 1901.

Schwartz, Charles. *Cole Porter: A Biography*. New York: Dial, 1977.

Scully, Vincent, Catherine Lynn, Eric Vogt, and Paul Goldberger. *Yale in New Haven: Architecture & Urbanism*. New Haven, Conn.: Yale University Press, 2004.

Sears, J. B. *Philanthropy in the Shaping of Higher Education*. Washington, D.C.: 1922.

"Secret Societies." *Yale Literary Magazine*, April 1864.

"Secret Societies among Us." *Yale Literary Magazine*, December 1865.

"Secret Societies at Yale." *Harper's*, February 7, 1874.

"Secret Societies of Yale College." *New York Herald*, May 22, 1893.

"Secret Society Elections at Yale." *Frank Leslie's Weekly*, June 8, 1893.

Selden, William K. *Club Life at Princeton: An Historical Account of the Eating Clubs at Princeton University*. Princeton, N.J.: Princeton Prospect Foundation, 1994.

Semple, Robert B., Jr. "High Noon on High Street." *New York Times*, April 17, 1991.

Senex, Eli. "Wooden Spoon Memories." *Yale Alumni Weekly*, May 27, 1908.

"Senior Societies." *Yale Literary Magazine*, November 1868.

"Senior Societies and the Lord Jehovah." *Harkness Hoot*, May 1933.

The Seventh Book of Genesis, Otherwise Known as the Gospel Accrding to Schrolleankee, February, 1874. New Haven, Conn.: Methodist Book Concern, 1874.

Seventy-Five: A Story of a Generation in Transition. New Haven, Conn.: Yale Daily News, 1953.

Shand-Tucci, Douglas. *Harvard University*. Princeton, N.J.: Princeton University Press, 2001.

Sharfstein, Daniel J. *The Invisible Line: A Secret History of Race in America*. New York: Penguin, 2009.

Shaw, Arthur Martin. *William Preston Johnston: A Transitional Figure of the Confederacy*. Baton Rouge: Louisiana State University Press, 1943.

Sheldon, Henry D. *The History and Pedagogy of American Student Societies*. New York: D. Appleton, 1901.

———. *Student Life and Customs*. New York: D. Appleton, 1901.

Sherman, George. [MS] *Diary, Yale College, Class of 1839*. Manuscripts and Archives, Yale University.

Sherwood, John. "Reminiscences of '39 at Yale." *University Magazine*, Vol. III, No. 11, November 1890.

Shipton, Clifford. "Ye Mystery of Ye Ages Solved, or How Placing Worked at Colonial Harvard & Yale." *Harvard Alumni Bulletin* 57, 1954–55.

Silliman, Benjamin. *Address Delivered before the Association of the Alumni of Yale College in New Haven, August 17, 1842.* New Haven, Conn.: B. L. Hamlen, 1842.

Simmel, Georg. *The Sociology of Georg Simmel*, trans. Karl H. Wolff. Glencoe, Ill: Free Press, 1950.

———. "The Sociology of Secrecy and Secret Societies," trans. Albion W. Small. *American Journal of Sociology*, XI, January 1906.

Singer, Mark. "La Cabeza de Villa." *New Yorker*, November 27, 1989.

"Skull & Bones." *Time*, May 20, 1940.

Slosson, Edwin E. *Great American Universities.* New York: Macmillan, 1910.

Smallwood, M. L. *A Historical Study of Examination and Grading Systems in Early American Unviersities.* Cambridge, Mass.: Harvard University Press, 1935.

Smith, Bradley F. *The Shadow Warriors: O.S.S. and the Origins of the C.I.A.* New York: Basic Books, 1983.

Smith, Richard Norton. *The Harvard Century: The Making of a University to a Nation.* New York: Simon and Schuster, 1986.

Smith, Ronald A. *Sports and Feedom: The Rise of Big-Time College Athletics.* New York and Oxford, England: Oxford University Press, 1988.

Smith, Sally Bedell. *Reflected Glory: The Life of Pamela Churchill Harriman.* New York: Simon & Schuster, 1976.

Smyth, Nathan A. "The Democratic Idea in College Life." *Yale Literary Magazine*, April 1896.

Soares, Joseph. *The Power of Privilege: Yale and America's Elite Colleges.* Stanford, Calif.: Stanford University Press, 2007.

The Songs of Yale. New Haven, Conn.: Thomas W. Pease, 1860.

Specter, Michael. "Skull and Bones at Yale: First No Women, Now No Club." *Washington Post*, April 16, 1991.

Starr, Harris E. *William Graham Sumner.* New York: Henry Holt, 1925.

Steinbreder, John. *The History of the Yale Club of New York City.* New York: Legendary LLC, 2014.

Steiner, Bernard C. *The History of Education in Connecticut.* Washington, D.C.: Government Printing Office, 1893.

Stern, Michael. *Yale's Hidden Treasures: Mystery of the Gothic Stone Carvings.* United States: Carvingswithclass, 2012.

Stevens, Albert C. *The Cyclopedia of Fraternities: A Compilation of Existing Authentic Information and the Results of Original Investigation as to the Origin, Derivation, Founders, Development, Aims, Emblems, Character and Personnel of More Than Six Hundred Secret Societies in the United States.* New York: E. B. Treat, 1907.

Stewart, Donald Ogden. *By a Stroke of Luck! An Autobiography.* New York: Paddington, 1975.

———. "The Higher Learning in America II—Yale." *Smart Set*, December 1921.

Stimson, Henry L., and McGeorge Bundy. *On Active Service in Peace and War.* 2 vols. New York: Harper & Brothers, 1948.

Stocking, Walter. "Presentation Week at Yale." *Hartford Press*, June 26, 1866.

Stokes, Anson Phelps. *Memorials of Eminent Yale Men: A Bibliographical Study of Student Life and University Influences during the Eighteenth and Nineteenth Centuries.* 2 volumes. New Haven, Conn.: Yale University Press, 1914.

Strong, Leah. *Joseph Hopkins Twichell: Mark Twain's Friend and Pastor.* Athens: University of Georgia Press, 1966.

Sturtevant, Julian Morson, Jr. *Julian M. Sturtevant: An Autobiography.* New York: Fleming H. Revell, 1896.

Suitable Quarters: Elihu Celebrates the 100th Anniversary of Its Landmark House on New Haven Green. New Haven, Conn.: Elihu Club, 2012.

Sulloway, Frank J. *Born to Rebel: Birth Order, Family Dynamics, and Creative Lives.* New York: Pantheon, 1996.

Sumner, William Graham. "The Ways and Means for Our Colleges." *Nation,* Vol. XI, September 8, 1870.

Sutton, Antony C. *America's Secret Establishment: An Introduction to the Order of Skull & Bones.* N.p.: Trine Day, 2002.

Swanberg, W. A. *Luce and His Empire.* New York: Scribner's, 1972.

———. *Whitney Father, Whitney Heiress.* New York: Scribner's, 1980.

Sweezy, Paul M., and Leo Huberman, eds. *F. O. Matthiessen (1902–1950): A Collective Portrait.* New York: Henry Schumn, 1950.

Synnott, Marcia G. "The Admission and Assimilation of Minority Students at Harvard, Yale, and Princeton, 1900–1950. *History of Education Quarterly,* Fall 1979.

———. *The Half-Opened Door: Discrimination and Admissions at Harvard, Yale, and Princeton, 1900–1970.* Westport, Conn.: Greenwood, 1970.

———. *Student Diversity at The Big Three: Changes at Harvard, Yale and Princeton Since the 1920s.* New Brunswick, N.J., and London: Transaction, 2013.

Syrett, Nicholas. *The Company He Keeps: A History of White College Fraternities.* Chapel Hill: University of North Carolina Press, 2009.

Taft, Helen Herron. *Recollections of Full Years.* New York: Dodd, Mead, 1914.

Taft, John. *Mayday at Yale: A Case Study in Student Radicalism.* Boulder, Co.: Westview Press, 1976.

Taft, William Howard. "President Taft's Speech." *Yale Alumni Weekly,* March 26, 1909.

———. "Some Recollections of My Days at Yale." *Fifty Years of Yale News: A Symposium on Yale Development to Commemorate the Fiftieth Anniversary of the Yale Daily News.* New Haven, Conn.: Yale Daily News, 1928.

Tanenhaus, Sam. "William F. Buckley: The founder," *Yale Alumni Magazine,* May/June 2008.

Taylor, William. *Cavalier and Yankee: The Old South and the American National Character.* New York: George Brazilier, 1961.

Thomas, Evan. *The Very Best Men: Four Who Dared: The Early Years of the CIA.* New York: Touchstone, 1995.

Thompson, Henry C. M. *In the Early Eighties and since with Yale '83.* Boston, Mass.: privately printed by subscription, 1933.

Thwing, Charles F. "College Men First Among Successful Citizens." *Forum,* June 15, 1893.

———. *A History of Higher Education in America.* New York: D. Appleton, 1906.

Tiger, Lionel. *Men in Groups.* New York: Random House, 1969.

Tilton, Eleanor M. *Letters of Ralph Waldo Emerson.* New York: Columbia University Press, 1995.

Tompkins, Calvin. *Living Well Is the Best Revenge.* New York: Viking, 1971.

Tracy, Charles. *Yale College: Sketches from Memory.* New York: Yale Alumni Association of New York, 1874.

Trillin, Calvin. *Remembering Denny.* New York, Farrar Straus & Giroux, 1993.

Trotman, Philip. *The History of the Berzelius Society: A Publication to Commemorate the 150th Anniversary of the Society.* New Haven, Conn.: Colony Foundation, 1999.

Vaill, Amanda. *Everybody Was So Young: Gerald and Sara Murphy: A Lost Generation Love Story.* Boston, Mass., and New York: Houghton Mifflin, 1998.

———. *Hotel Florida: Truth, Love and Death in the Spanish Civil War.* New York: Farrar Straus & Giroux, 2014.

Velsey, Donald, and John Leinenweber. *A History of Spade and Grave: The Society of 1864–1914*, N.p.: Andrew Morehouse Trust Association, Inc., 2014.

Vesey, Lawrence R. *The Emergence of the American University.* Chicago, Ill., and London: University of Chicago Press, 1965.

von Bothmer, Bernard. *Framing the Sixties: The Use and Abuse of a Decade from Ronald Reagan to George W. Bush.* Amherst: University of Massachusetts Press, 2010.

Voorhees, Oscar M. *The History of Phi Beta Kappa.* New York: Crown, 1945.

Walker, Charles R., ed. *The Collected Poems of H. Phelps Putnam.* New York: Farrar Straus & Giroux, 1971.

Wallace, Karl, ed.; *History of Speech Education in America: Background Studies.* New York: Appleton-Century-Crofts, 1954.

Wallace, Thomas, ed., H.S.F. Cooper, assoc. ed., Stephen Parks, production. *Reflections on Manuscript 1953–2012.* New Haven, Conn.: Manuscript Society, 2012.

Wallace, William N. *Yale's Ironmen: A Story of Football & Lives in the Decade of the Depression & Beyond.* New York, Lincoln, Neb., Shanghai: iUniverse, Inc., 2005.

Ward, Geoffrey, and Ken Burns. *The Roosevelts: An Intimate History.* New York: Knopf, 2014.

Warner, Robert Austin. *New Haven Negroes: A Social History.* New York: Arno Press and New York Times, 1969.

Warren, Aldice G. "History of Delta Kappa Epsilon." Records, Gerald R. Ford Memorial Library, Delta Kappa Epsilon International Fraternity Headquarters, Ann Arbor, Mich.

Wecter, Dixon. *The Saga of American Society: A Record of Social Aspiration 1607–1937.* New York: Scribner's, 1937.

Wedge, Bryant M., M.D., ed. *Psychosocial Problems of College Men.* New Haven, Conn.: Yale University Press, 1958.

"The Week: 'Tap Day' and Its Place at Yale." *Yale Alumni Weekly,* May 29, 1907.

Welch, Lewis Shelden, and Walter Camp. *Yale: Her Campus, Class-Rooms, and Athletics.* Boston, Mass.: L. Page, 1899.

SELECTED BIBLIOGRAPHY

Wertenbaker, Thomas J. *Princeton, 1746–1896.* Princeton, N.J.: Princeton University Press, 1946.

White, Andrew Dickson. *Autobiography of Andrew Dickson White.* 2 vols. New York: Century, 1922.

———. "Yale in '53." *Yale Literary Magazine,* February 1886.

Whitehead, John, *The Separation of College and State: Columbia, Dartmouth, Harvard, and Yale, 1776–1876.* New Haven, Conn.: Yale University Press, 1973.

Whiton, James. "The First Intercollegiate Regatta." *Outlook,* Vol. 18, No. 5, June 1901.

Wilgoren, Jodi Lynne. "Black & Blue: Yale Volunteers in the Civil Rights Movement, 1963–65." Senior Essay in History, April 13, 1992. Manuscripts and Archives, Yale University.

Wilner, Isaiah. *The Man Time Forgot: A Tale of Genius, Betrayal, and the Creation of Time Magazine.* New York: HarperCollins, 2006.

Wilson, Edmund. "Harvard, Princeton, and Yale." *Forum,* September 1923.

———. "Profiles: A Prelude—II Landscape, Characters, and Conversations from the Earlier Years of My Life." *New Yorker,* May 6, 1967.

Winks, Robin W. *Cloak & Gown 1939–1961: Scholars in the Secret War.* New York: William Morrow, 1987.

Winnick, R. H. ed. *Letters of Archibald MacLeish 1907–1982.* Boston, Mass.: Houghton Mifflin, 1983.

Winterer, Caroline. *The Culture of Classicism: Ancient Greece and Rome in American Intellectual Life, 1780–1910.* Baltimore, Md.: Johns Hopkins University Press, 2002.

Wolfe, Tom. "The 'ME' Decade." *New York,* August 23, 1976.

Wolff, Geoffrey. *The Art of Burning Bridges: A Life of John O'Hara.* New York: Alfred A. Knopf, 2003.

Wood, John Seymour. *College Days, or Harry's Career at Yale.* New York: Outing, 1894.

———. *Yale Yarns: Sketches of Life at Yale University.* New York: G. P. Putnam & Sons, 1895.

Woodward, Bob, and Walter Pincus: "Bush Opened Up to Secret Yale Society: Turning Points in a Life Build on Alliances." *Washington Post,* August 7, 1988.

———. "George Bush, Man and Politician." Washington Post, August 11, 1988.

Wooley, Knight. *In Retrospect—A Very Personal Memoir.* N.p.: Privately printed, 1975.

Wooster, James Willet. *Edward Stephen Harkness 1874–1940.* New York: William E. Rudge, Printer, 1949.

Wortman, Marc. *The Millionaires' Unit: The Aristocratic Flyboys Who Fought the Great War and Invented American Airpower.* New York: Public Affairs, 2006.

Wyatt, David. "The Last Spring at Yale." *Virginia Quarterly Review,* Spring 1977.

"Yale College." *Scribner's,* Vol. XI, No. 6, April 1876.

"Yale Secret Societies." *Boston Globe,* July 3, 1873.

Yankelovich, Daniel. *New Rules: Searching for Self-Fulfillment in a World Turned Upside Down.* New York: Random House, 1981.

Young, Jesse Allen. "A Century of Blacks at Yale, 1874–1974." Scholar of the House Paper, 1974. Manuscripts and Archives, Yale University.

ENDNOTES

INTRODUCTION

1 Sheldon, Henry Davidson, *The History and Pedagogy of American Student Societies* (New York: D. Appleton, 1901), p. 175.

2 McLachlan, James, "The *Choice of Hercules*, American Student Societies in the Early Nineteenth Century," in Lawrence Stone, ed., *The University in Society Volume II Europe, Scotland and the United States from the 16th to the 20th Century* (Princeton, N.J.: Princeton University Press, 1974), p. 459.

CHAPTER ONE: BONDING IN SECRET

1 Roberts, J. M., *The Mythology of Secret Societies* (London: Watkins, 2008), pp. 25–27.

2 Gist, Noel P., "Secret Societies: A Cultural Study of Fraternalism in the United States," *The University of Missouri Studies*, Vol. XV, No. 4 (October 1, 1940), p. 20.

3 Huizinga, Johan, *Homo Ludens: A Study of the Play-Element in Culture* (London, Boston, Mass., and Henley-on-Thames, England: Routledge & Kegan Paul, 1955), pp. 4–19.

4 McWilliams, Wilson Carey, *The Idea of Fraternity in America* (Berkeley, Los Angeles, and London: University of California Press, 1973), pp. 22–23.

5 Simmel, Georg, "The Sociology of Secrecy and Secret Societies," trans. Albion W. Small, *American Journal of Sociology*, XI (January 1906), pp. 444–452, 464; Goethe, Johan Wolfgang von, *Wilhelm Meister's Apprenticeship*, translated by Thomas Carlyle (New York: Collier, 1962; 1968), pp. 490–491.

6 Gist, *op. cit.*, p. 9; Roberts, *op. cit.*, pp. 32–33.

7 Dumenil, Lynn, *Freemasonry and American Culture 1880–1930* (Princeton, N.J.: Princeton University Press, 1984), p. 4; Roberts, *op. cit.*, pp. 34–36, 47; Lipson, Dorothy, *Freemasonry in Federalist Connecticut* (Princeton, N.J.: Princeton University Press, 1977), pp. 17–25; on the London lodges and the 1659 oath, Jacob, Margaret C., *Living the Enlightenment: Freemasonry and Politics in Eighteenth-Century Europe* (New York and Oxford, England: Oxford University Press, 1991), pp. 87–88.

8 Allen, Devere, "Substitutes for Brotherhood," *World Tomorrow*, Vol. VII (1924), p. 74; Lipson, *op. cit.*, p. 1. In an essay in the *Decennial Record of the Class of 1896, Yale College* (New York: DeVinne Press, 1907, p. 13), Henry Selden Johnston wrote: "A comment on the American people has been frequently made that they are inordinately given to forming a multiplicity of secret orders and associations. Certainly in colleges this propensity has developed to a high degree, and Yale has indulged in due proportion."

9   Rothblatt, Sheldon, *The Modern University and its Discontents: The Fate of Newman's Legacies in Britain and America* (Cambridge, England: Cambridge University Press, 1997), pp. 106–178; Rothblatt, "The Student Sub-culture and Examination System in Early 19th Century Oxbridge," *The University in Society*, ed. Lawrence Stone, 2 vols. (Princeton, N.J.: Princeton University Press, 1974), Vol. 1, pp. 252–256.

10   Lubenow, W. C., *The Cambridge Apostles, 1820–1914: Liberalism, Imagination and Friendship in British Intellectual and Professional Life* (Cambridge, England: Cambridge University Press, 1998), pp. 28–29; Kant, Immanuel, "An Answer to the Question: What is Enlightenment?" in Kleingeld, Pauline, ed., *Toward Perpetual Peace and Other Writings on Politics, Peace, and History* (New Haven, Conn.: Yale University Press, 2006), p. 17 (the Latin phrase is found in Horace's *Epistles*, 1.2.40, and was a recognized motto in Enlightenment circles).

11   McWilliams, *op. cit.*, pp. 170–171.

12   On the Moral Society, Gabriel, Ralph Henry, *Religion and Learning at Yale: The Church of Christ in the College and University, 1757–1957* (New Haven, Conn.: Yale University Press, 1958), pp. 72–77; on Harvard's Spy Club, Lane, William Coolidge, "The Telltale, 1721," *Publications of the Colonial Society of Massachusetts, Transactions*, XII (January 1909), pp. 225–228.

13   "first effective agency," Rudolph, Frederick, *The American College and University: A History* (New York: Vintage, 1962), p. 137; Adams quoted in Morison, Samuel Eliot, *Three Centuries of Harvard 1636–1936* (Cambridge, Mass.: Harvard University Press, 1936), p. 61; vita activa, McLachlan, James, "The Choice of Hercules, American Student Societies in the Early Nineteenth Century, in Stone, *op. cit.*, p. 483.

14   McLachlan, *op. cit.*, pp. 486–487. *The Yale Illustrated Horoscope* for May 1889 was still writing of the senior society men as "Yale's choice *literatti*" [*sic*].

15   On Crotonia, or perhaps Critonia, *Supplement to the Ninth Record of the Class of 1852* (Montelier, Vt.: Argus and Patriot Press, 1900), p. 23; on Linonia and Brothers in Unity, Elliot, Henry B., "The Two Oldest College Societies," *College Courant*, January 27 and February 10, 1872; Harding, Thomas S., *College Literary Societies Their Contributions to Higher Education in the United States 1815–1876* (New York: Pageant Press International Corp., 1971), p. 35.

16   Sheldon, Henry D., *Student Life and Customs* (New York: D. Appleton, 1901), pp. 89–95, 125–129; Rudolph, *op. cit.*, pp. 141–144; de Tocqueville, Alexis, *Democracy in America* (New York: Knopf, 1945), vol. 1, p. 303; Bledstein, Burton J., *The Culture of Professionalism: The Middle Class and the Development of Higher Education in America* (New York: W. W. Norton, 1976), p. 198.

17   Craigie, William and James Hurlburt, *A Dictionary of American English on Historical Principles* (Chicago, Ill.: 1938), IV, p. 2065; Clay, Henry, "The American System" (1832), *Works*, ed. Calvin Colton (New York, 1904), VIII, p. 464; Howe, Daniel Walker, *Making the American Self: Jonathan Edwards to Abraham Lincoln* (Cambridge, Mass.: Harvard University Press, 1978), pp. 136–137.

18   Chamberlain, Daniel, "The Value of Literary Societies in American Education," *University Quarterly*, Vol. 3, April 1861, pp. 356, 359.

19   Lubenow, *op. cit.*, p. 35.

20   Gist, *op. cit.*, p. 80. "A simple promise is not enough; the obligation ordinarily states the conditions of secrecy: the candidate must not write, print, or impart verbally

any of the secrets related to passwords, ritual or other secret features. These are the supreme taboos of secret fraternalism." *Ibid.*, p. 93.

21 Jacob, *op. cit.*, pp. 153–154.

22 Linonia Society, *Constitution and By-laws of the Linonian Society, of Yale College* (New Haven, Conn.: Morehouse & Taylor, 1859), p. 3, Article I, Section II; "hundred boys," Garrison, Lloyd M., "Social Life at American Colleges," *Outlook*, vol. L (1894), p. 257; "intellectual free-trade territory," Richards, Jeffrey, "'Passing the Love of Women': Manly Love and Victorian Society," in Mangan, J. A. and James Walvin, eds., *Manliness and Morality: Middle-Class Masculinity in Britain and America, 1800–1849* (Manchester, England: University of Manchester Press, 1987), pp. 95–98.

23 Lubenow, *op. cit.*, p. 25; Lewis, C. S., *The Four Loves* (New York: Harcourt, Brace, 1960), pp. 87–127; McWilliams, *op. cit.*, pp. 28–29, 59.

24 Rudolph, Frederick, *Mark Hopkins and the Log: Williams College, 1836–1872* (New Haven, Conn.: Yale University Press, 1956), p. 104.

25 Dwight, Timothy, *Memories of Yale Life and Men* (New York: Dodd, Mead, 1903), pp. 69–70.

26 Lubenow, *op. cit.*, pp. 25–26; *Reminiscences of Scenes and Characters in College: By a Graduate of Yale of the Class of 1821* (New Haven, Conn.: A Maltby, 1847, p. 25, and to the same effect is Professor Benjamin Silliman, in *Address Delivered Before the Association of the Alumni in Yale College in New Haven, August 17, 1842* (New Haven, Conn.: B. L. Hamlen, 1842), p. 12, who also added that "not a few" of the departures were "from the operations of the rules of discipline, which show no favor to the indolent, negligent, apathetic or vicious youth." In college and fraternity catalogues, death has always been denoted by an asterisk. Baird, William R., *American College Fraternities*, Fifth Edition (New York: published by the author, 1898), p. 21.

27 Forster, E.M. *Howards End*, Chapter 22 (London: Edwin Arnold, 1910): "Only connect! That was the whole of her sermon. Only connect the prose and the passion, and both will be exalted, and human love will be seen at its height."

28 Lubenow, *op. cit.*, p. 27; Levy, Paul, *Moore: G. E. Moore and the Cambridge Apostles* (New York: Holt, Rinehart & Winston, 1979), pp. 65–66; Deacon, Richard, *The Cambridge Apostles* (London: Robert Royce Limited, 1985), pp. viii–ix, 2–3.

29 Lubenow, *op. cit.*, pp. 30–31, 42–43; Deacon, *op. cit.*, pp. 6–7.

30 Printed in McAlister, Edith F. B., *Sir Donald MacAlister of Tarbert* (London: Macmillan, 1953), pp. 127–128. The Apostles were also fortified by generations of family ties (the way Yale senior societies sometimes developed over the college generations) among the Quaker family "intellectual aristocracy" of the Darwin-Wedgewood-Reverat-Stephen clans: see the discussion and genealogical charts in Levy, *op. cit.*, pp. 19–25. The Apostles did not elect a female member until 1970.

31 Rudolph, Frederick, *Mark Hopkins, op. cit.*, p. 105; Winterer, Caroline, *The Culture of Classicism: Ancient Greece and Rome in American Intellectual Life, 1780–1910* (Baltimore: Johns Hopkins University Press, 2002), pp. 62–66, 81–83. On Chi Delta Theta, *Yale Literary Magazine*, February 1884, p. 150, and *Yale News*, March 16, 1887.

32 Founder Charles Clark Young's account in *A Record of the Members of the Kappa Alpha Fraternity* (New York: A. H. Kellogg, 1892), pp. 7–8.

33 Syrett, Nicholas, *The Company He Keeps: A History of White College Fraternities* (Chapel Hill: University of North Carolina Press, 2009), pp. 29–31; Simmel,

Sociology, op. cit., pp. 330–376, 347–348; Kett, Joseph E., *Rites of Passage: Adolescence in America, 1790 to the Present* (New York: Basic Books, 1977), pp. 29–31, 42.

34 On Phi Beta Kappa, Johnson, Clyde Sanfred, *Fraternities in Our Colleges* (New York: National Interfraternity Foundation, 1972), p. 12; Porter, Noah, *The American Colleges and the American Public* (New Haven, Conn.: C. Chatfield & Co., 1879), p. 200.

35 *The Laws of Yale College* (New Haven, Conn.: Baldwin & Treadway, 1832), p. 3.

36 Rudolph, *op. cit.*, p. 104.

37 "two elements," Sheldon, *Student Life, op. cit.*, pp. 187–188; "general resemblance," Piper, P. F., "College Fraternities," *Cosmopolitan*, Vol. XXII, No. 6, April 1897, p. 646; "Secret Societies at Yale," *Harper's*, February 7, 1874, pp. 125–126.

38 Syrett, *op. cit.*, p. 38.

39 *Ibid.*, p. 38. "This rivalry has become traditional, and where these fraternities meet a life-long contest for supremacy exists." Piper, *op. cit.*, pp. 642–643.

40 *Kappa Alpha Record* (Clinton, Mass.: Colonial Press, 1941), p. 101.

41 Constitution of Alpha Delta Phi, Section 6, Article II, Alpha Delta Phi Records, Manuscripts and Archives, Yale University; Constitution of the Delta Kappa Epsilon Fraternity, article III, section 1, Delta Kappa Epsilon Records, vol. 3 (1888–1958, Constitution), University of North Carolina.

42 Rudolph, *op. cit.*, p. 101; Voorhees, Oscar M., *The History of Phi Beta Kappa* (New York: Crown, 1945), pp. 128–129, 182–183 (the original Union application for a chapter is at Yale); Syrett, *op. cit.*, pp. 13 and 310–311, note 2.

43 "middle-class equivalent," Kett, *op. cit.*, p. 260; Syrett, *op. cit.*, pp. 14–15.

44 Jonathan Pearson diary, entries for December 3, 1832, and December 11, 1833, Union College; Hislop, Codman, *Eliphlet Nott* (Middletown, Conn.: Wesleyan University Press, 1971), pp. 389–390.

45 Flanagan, Caitlin, "The Dark Power of Fraternities," *Atlantic*, March 2014, pp. 72–91; Syrett, *op. cit., passim.*

46 All quotations from Johnson, *Fraternities, op. cit.*, p. 19–20.

CHAPTER TWO: THE SECRETS OF PHI BETA KAPPA

1. Initiation ritual described in Voorhees, *op. cit.*, p. 9; "Yale Phi Beta Kappa: Alpha of Connecticut Chapter History," http://pbk.yalecollege.yale.edu/information/alpha-connecticut-chapter-history, accessed February 27, 2014; letter of William Short, second President of Phi Beta Kappa at William and Mary, to Edward Everett, July 8, 1831 (the "Short Letter"), reprinted in Hastings, William T., *Phi Beta Kappa as a Secret Society with Its Relations to Freemasonry and Antimasonry* (Washington, D.C.: United Chapters of Phi Beta Kappa, 1965), p. 84.

2. Current, Richard Nelson, *Phi Beta Kappa in American Life: The First Two Hundred Years* (New York: Oxford University Press, 1990), p. 8.

3. Tyler, Lyon G., "Brief Personal Sketches," *The William and Mary College Quarterly*, April 1896, pp. 245–254; Voorhees, *op. cit.*, pp. 105–106.

4. Porter, John Addison, "College Fraternities," *Century*, Vol. XXXVI, May 1884, p. 750.

5. The records of the mother chapter from 1776 to 1781 are preserved at William and Mary, were originally published in the *William and Mary Quarterly* for April 1896, and are reprinted in Hastings, *op. cit.*, at pp. 52–82 ("Hastings Minutes").

6. Hale, Edward Everett, "A Fossil From the Tertiary," *Atlantic*, July 1879.

7. Hastings Minutes, p. 71.

8. Short Letter, p. 84.

9. Hastings, *op. cit.*, pp. 4–5, correcting Voorhees, *op. cit.*, pp. 10–11; Current, *op. cit.*, pp. 10–11.

10. Short Letter, p. 84.

11. Hastings Minutes, p. 74.

12. Voorhees, *op. cit.*, pp. 20–22.

13. Form of Charter Party in Manuscripts and Archives, Yale University, p. 2, reproduced in facsimile in Voorhees following p. 116. The "Form of Initiation" in the Yale chapter records, even after the deletion of the phrase which made the oath one to "the Supreme Being," required the initiate to "promise that you will be true and faithful to the Society . . . and will preserve honorably the secrets of the same." Manuscripts and Archives, Yale University.

14. Crawford, Albert Beecher, *Phi Beta Kappa Men of Yale 1789–1959*, New Haven, Conn.: Yale University Press, 1968), p. 15.

15. Voorhees, *op. cit.*, p. 27.

16. Crawford, *op. cit.*, pp. 10–11; Voorhees, *op. cit.*, p. 34

17. Voorhees, *ibid.*, p. 183.

18. Hastings Minutes, pp. 80–81.

19. Hale, *op. cit.*, p. 24.

20. Voorhees, *op. cit.*, p. 38.

21. *Ibid.*, pp. 3–4.

22. Voorhees, *op. cit.*, p. 357.

23. Hale, *op. cit.*, p. 3.

24. Transcribed in Voorhees, *op. cit.*, pp. 31–32, from an untitled manuscript written by Jonathan Leavitt, Yale Class of 1785, in the Yale Alpha records now in Manuscripts and Archives, Yale University, RU 58, Box 4, Folder 238, there catalogued as "Constitution," and again in Box 4, Folder 240, there supplied the title "The Origin and Progress of the ΦBK Society," the title used by Hastings in his reprinting of (only) the first few pages as Appendix III to his history at pp. 86–89. The second theft, in June 1787, which required the picking of three locks, is described by Leavitt at p. 3 of his manuscript, quoted by Voohees at his p. 32. The "small trunk" containing the society's seal and letters were delivered in 1837 to William H. Russell, class of 1833 and secretary of the Alpha of Connecticut that year, tutor in Yale College in 1835–36, and primary founder of Skull and Bones in 1832. On the second theft and eventual restoration, see Voorhees, *op. cit.*, p. 32; Crawford, *op. cit.*, p. 17.

25. Manuscripts and Archives, Yale University, quoted in Hastings, op.cit., p. 13. Interestingly for a letter of that date, Nash called the Dartmouth chapter's antagonists "*Antis.*"

26. Lane, William Coolidge, *Catalogue of the Harvard Chapter* (Cambridge, Mass.: Phi Beta Kappa, 1912), p. 121.

27. *Ibid.*, p. 120.

28. As summarized in Hastings, *op. cit.*, p. 44; Bemis, Samuel Flagg, *John Quincy Adams and the Union* (New York: Alfred A. Knopf, 1956), p. 77, and on Morgan's murder, pp. 276–277; Dumenil, *op. cit.*, pp. 5–7; Lipson, *op. cit.*, pp. 3, 269–282; Holt, Michael F., "The Antimasonic and Know Nothing Parties," in Schlesinger, Arthur

M., Jr., *History of U.S. Political Parties* (New York: Chelsea House, 1973), vol. 1, pp. 575–592.

29. On the "sign" and the "grip," see Lewis, A. N., ed., *Supplement to the Ninth Record of the Yale Class of 1852* (Montpelier, Vt.: Argus and Patriot Press, 1900), p. 24. The mysterious Allyn is most fully described in Hastings, *op. cit.*, Appendix VI, pp. 96–104. On his not being a member of Phi Beta Kappa, see Voorhees, *op. cit.*, pp. 184–185.

30. Allyn, Avery, *A Ritual of Freemasonry, Illustrated by Numerous Engravings; With Notes and Remarks, to which is added a Key to the Phi Beta Kappa* (Boston, Mass.: L. Fitzgerald, 1831), pp. 296–297. Allyn published an earlier edition, in New York, with no reference to Phi Beta Kappa, in 1828, with publisher William Gowan.

31. *Ibid.*, pp. 296–297. The Bavarian Illuminati were an Enlightenment-era secret society founded on May 1, 1776, by the Jesuit-taught Adam Weishaupt, who was the first lay professor of canon law at the University of Ingolstadt in Upper Bavaria. In his reply to the Antimasons in *The Genius of Masonry* (1828), Dartmouth PBK member Samuel Knapp had praised Phi Beta Kappa by saying it was a branch of the Illuminati, brought by Jefferson. Current, *op. cit.*, pp. 54–55. On the Illuminati, whose founder had tried to join a Masonic lodge in 1774 but found the fees too high and the secrets already too well known, see Roberts, *op. cit.*, pp. 133–144. The purported connection of Skull and Bones with the Illuminati is also cited in: Robbins, Alexandra, *Secrets of the Tomb: Skull and Bones, The Ivy League, and the Hidden Paths of Power* (New York: Little Brown, 2002), pp. 82–83; Sutton, Antony C., *America's Secret Establishment: An Introduction to the Order of Skull & Bones* (n.p.: Trine Day, 2002), pp. 77–80; Rosenbaum, Ron, *The Secret Parts of Fortune: Three Decades of Intense Investigations and Edgy Enthusiasms* (New York: Random House, 2000), pp. 160–162; and in *New York* magazine for November 25, 2013, p. 35. No true connection between the Illuminati and Phi Beta Kappa has been traced by the PBK society's historians Voorhees and Hastings, and the improbability of the connection is well expressed in his *Cyclopedia of Fraternities* (New York: E. B. Treat, 1907) by Albert Stevens, at p. 345: "The Illuminati was founded in 1776, and it is hardly likely that a few boys at the College of William and Mary in Virginia, in those days of extremely infrequent letter-writing and trans-Atlantic voyages, were inspired in their formation of a Greek-letter society by the illustrious foreigner whose name is linked to an order which for a short time was grafted upon Freemasonry and then disappeared forever."

32. Allyn, *op. cit.*, pp. 297–299 Allyn's limitation of "one third" of the class being elected may be a silent reference to the rule at Yale, enacted in the revision of the constitution in 1787, to limit election to "not more than one third of a class." According to computations by Voorhees, *op. cit.* at p. 56, the figures for Phi Beta Kappa membership as a percentage of the class in these decades are Yale, 36%; Harvard, 31%; and Dartmouth, 33% (although Crawford, *op. cit.* at p. 13, gives cogent reasons why these figures are probably mildly inflated due to deaths or dropouts of members after election but before graduation).

33. *Reminiscences, op. cit.*, p. 106.

34. Lane, *op. cit.*, p. 152.

35. Voorhees, *op. cit.*, pp. 188–191; Hastings, *op. cit.*, pp. 48–50; Current, *op. cit.*, pp. 55–57.

36. Lane, *op. cit.*, p. 152.

37. Allyn, *op. cit.*, second edition, New York, 1831, p. 259.

38. Before the publication of the Boston edition of Allyn's book, Edward Everett, in addition to Chancellor Kent, had been invited to be orator at the Yale chapter's anniversary meeting for 1831, in September 1830, and when Kent accepted for the 1831 meeting, Everett agreed to speak at the anniversary in 1832. Letters from Everett to Alpha of Connecticut corresponding secretary A. N. Skinner, September 14, 1830 and October 9, 1830, Manuscripts and Archives, Yale University.

39. Quoted in Coxe, Macgrane, *Chancellor Kent at Yale 1771–1781: A Paper Written for the Yale Law School* (New York: privately printed, 1909), p. 30.

40. Tracy, Charles, *Yale College: Sketches from Memory*, (New York: Yale Alumni Association of New York, 1874), reprinted in the *New-York Evening Post* for January, 12–13, 1874. The secrecy "taken back" was with respect to the election of new members, since those rejected, "ought never to know the manner in which their claioms have been discussed." Current, *op. cit.*, p. 57.

41. In the inside margin of the minute book, the secretary has written of the motion which was passed in an asterisked addition: "The original words were these: Voted that the injunction of secrecy in regard to the constitution, laws & proceedings of this Alpha of this Phi Beta Kappa be dissolved, & that the same be no longer regarded as obligatory upon it, present members, or imposed upon those who may be hereafter admitted." Minutes of Alpha Chapter of Phi Beta Kappa, Manuscripts and Archives, Yale University, September 13, 1831 ("Alpha of Connecticut Minutes").

42. Alpha of Connecticut Minutes, February 27, 1832, June 7, 1832, and June 11, 1832. The minutes do not record names of candidates who were not chosen, nor explain why there were two sets of elections for the Class of 1833. The source of the oft-cited tale that Skull and Bones was founded in some occasion of "disappointment" over Phi Beta Kappa elections this year is Lyman Bagg's *Four Years at Yale (By a Graduate of '69)* (New Haven, Conn.: Charles C. Chatfield, 1871), p. 146, since repeated in many journalistic and book accounts which followed (e.g. George Plimpton in his *Harvard Lampoon* article of November 11, 1949, "The Yale Secret Societies," p. 11, and even in the most recent history of Phi Beta Kappa [1990], Current, *op. cit.*, p. 62).

43. Something similar—elimination of secrecy for Phi Beta Kappa, followed by student dissatisfaction leading to the formation of a new group—happened far from New Haven and roughly at the same time as Bones was founded. The "History" in *The Twelfth General Catalogue of the Psi Upsilon* (n.p.: Executive Council of the Psi Upsilon Fraternity, 1917), records (at pp. xvi–xvii) that "With both its mystery and its social motive gone, Phi Beta Kappa had lost its charm and its attractiveness to the undergraduate mind, and the students saw that new societies to be organized by them must be founded upon entirely different ideals," and so on November 24, 1833, the Psi Upsilon Fraternity was founded at Union College in Schenectady, New York, by members of the classes of 1836 (three being members of Phi Beta Kappa) and 1837, beginning as a secret society.

44. *Catalogue of Members Yale Chapter of Phi Beta Kappa Alpha of Connecticut* (New Haven, Conn.: The Price, Lee and Adkins, 1905), pp. 95–97 for class of 1833.

45. Bagg, *op. cit.*, p. 178 (at an earlier date than Bagg's history, in a newspaper article by William Stocking, class of 1865, "Presentation Week at Yale," *Hartford Courant*, June 26, 1866, the senior societies are styled "the greater *quindecimviri*").

CHAPTER THREE: THE FOUNDING OF SCULL AND BONE

1. Bagg, *op. cit.* at p. 146, seems to have been the first to suggest in print that Bones was founded for that reason: "Some injustice in the conferring of Phi Beta Kappa elections seems to have led to its establishment, and apparently it was for some time regarded throughout college as a sort of burlesque convivial club." Elections for the class of 1833 resulted in a number of new members, thirty-four, that exceeded the Phi Beta Kappa constitutional limit of a third of the college class's size, which would have been thirty-one; holding two elections suggests that a second intake round was required to soothe hurt feelings, resulting in the plentiful number. However, for six Brothers of Phi Beta Kappa (made up of initiates from *both* votes) to then found a new group in protest, as the core of the first fourteen-member club of Skull and Bones, *without* giving up membership in the old organization while Russell served as senior undergraduate officer, makes no social or political sense.

2. Morison, Elting E., *Turmoil and Tradition: A Study of the Life and Times of Henry L. Stimson* (Boston, Mass.: Houghton Mifflin, 1960), p. 33.

3. Kingsbury, Frederick D. (class of 1846), "Early Memories of New Haven," *Yale Alumni Weekly*, May 27, 1910, pp. 892–894; Dexter, Franklin B., "Historical Sketch," paper read December 7, 1913, in Witherspoon, Alexander M., *The Club: The Story of Its First One Hundred Twenty-Five Years 1838–1963* (New Haven, Conn.: printed for members of the club, 1964), pp. 8–9.

4. Class division names, *The Laws of Yale College*, 1832, p. 11; the "class" and Dwight's opinion, Mendenhall, Thomas, *The Harvard–Yale Boat Race 1852–1945 and the Coming of Sport to the American College* (Mystic, Conn.: Mystic Seaport Museum, 1993), p. 9; Porter, *American Colleges, op. cit.*, pp. 191–192; Horowitz, Helen Lefkowitz, *Campus Life: Undergraduate Cultures from the End of the Eighteenth Century to the Present* (New York: Knopf, 1987), p. 38; "applause," Sheldon, *Student Life, op. cit.*, p. 123.

5. Deming, Clarence, *Yale Yesterdays* (New Haven, Conn.: Yale University Press, 1915), p. 14; *Third Record on the Class of 1833 in Yale College* (New Haven, Conn.: 1870), p. 7.

6. "judgment of men," Sheldon, *Student Life, op. cit.*, p. 124, quoting practically verbatim from, and citing Martin, Edward S., "Undergraduate Life at Harvard," *Scribner's Magazine*, May 1897, pp. 534–535, but attributing the activity to all colleges of this era; "relative rank," Porter, Noah, "Additional Notices-Instructions and Discipline," in Kingsley, William, *Yale College: A Sketch of Its History*, 2 vols. (New York: Henry Holt, 1879), pp. 504–505.

7. On admission age, *The Laws of Yale College*, 1832, p. 3. The demographic calculations are made from the statistical summary, identifying the place of birth of 101 members of the class of 1833 (not all of whom graduated), in *Third Record of the Class of 1833 in Yale College* (New Haven, Conn., 1870), pp. 132–133. On New Haven vs. Boston, Allmendinger, David F. Jr., *Paupers and Scholars: The Transformation of Student Life in Nineteenth Century New England* (New York: St. Martin's, 1975), p. 25; Martin, Edward S., "Undergraduate Life at Harvard," *Scribner's Magazine*, May, 1897, p. 533.

ENDNOTES

8. Hall, Peter, *The Organization of American Culture, 1700–1900: Private Institutions, Elites, and the Origins of American Nationality* (New York: New York University Press, 1982), pp. 162, 311.

9. Sturtevant, Julian Morson, Jr., ed. *Julian M. Sturtevant: An Autobiography* (New York: Fleming H. Revell, 1896), pp. 79–80.

10. Dexter, "On Some Social Distinctions at Yale and Harvard before the Revolution," *A Selection, op. cit.,* pp. 203–22; "farmers, store-keepers," Shipton, Clifford K., "Ye Mystery of Ye Ages Solved, or How Placing Worked at Colonial Harvard & Yale," *Harvard Alumni Bulletin* 57 (1954–55): 258–263; "appraisals," Kelley, *op. cit.,* pp. 75–78.

11. Avery quoted in "Yale College One Hundred Years Ago," *Hours at Home,* February 1870, p. 333.

12. Mendenhall, *op. cit.,* p. 6.

13. Horowitz, *op. cit.,* p. 28.

14. Sheldon, *op. cit.,* pp. 132–133; half-holiday, *Yale News,* March 1, 1887.

15. Steiner, Bernard C., *The History of Education in Connecticut* (Washington, D.C.: Government Printing Office, 1893), pp. 154–155, 189; "Yale College," *Scribner's Monthly,* April 1876, p. 776; Allmendinger, *op. cit.,* p. 87; Leonard, Lewis Alexander, *Life of Alphonso Taft* (New York: Hawke Publishing, 1920), pp. 33–34.

16. McLachan in Stone, *op. cit.,* p. 466.

17. Meyer, D. H., *The Instructed Conscience: The Shaping of the American National Ethic* (Philadelphia: University of Pennsylvania Press, 1972), p. 68; McBride, Mary Gorton, *Randall Lee Gibson* (Baton Rouge: Louisiana State University Press, 1997), pp. 39–40; "The Yale Report of 1828," reprinted in Hofstadter and Wilson, *American Higher Education: A Documentary History* (Chicago, Ill.: University of Chicago Press, 1961), pp. 278 *et seq.* It is said that Yale with this report was "far more influential than provincial Harvard where Unitarianism and the absence of a missionary impulse were encouraging a climate of self-satisfied isolation." Rudolph, *op. cit.,* p. 151.

18. Morison, Samuel Eliot, *op. cit.,* p. 260; Sturtevant, *op. cit.,* pp. 84–85, 90–91.

19. Hocmuth, Marie, and Richard Murphy, "Rhetoric and Elocutionary Training in Nineteenth Century Colleges," in Wallace, Karl, ed., *History of Speech Education in America* (New York: Appleton-Century-Crofts, 1954), p. 156; *Records of the Yale Corporation,* October 23, 1776, Manuscripts and Archives, Yale University.

20. Kelley, Brooks Mather, *Yale: A History* (New Haven, Conn.: Yale University Press, 1974), p. 158; Potter, David, *Debating in the Colonial Chartered Colleges: A Historical Survey 1642–1900* (New York: Teacher's College, Columbia University, 1942), pp. 82–83. For Emerson on and to his brother, Charles Chauncy Emerson, July 15, 1828, see Rusk, Ralph, ed., *The Letters of Ralph Waldo Emerson* (New York: Columbia University Press, 1939), vol. 1, pp. 238–240.

21. "Eloquence and Eloquent Men," *New-England Magazine,* II (February, 1832), pp. 93–100.

22. debaters in a section, Dexter, Franklin B., *A Selection from the Miscellaneous Historical Papers of Fifty Years* (New Haven, Conn.: Privately printed, 1918), pp. 386–387; Schwab, J. L., "The Yale College Curriculum, 1701–1901" *Educational Review,* Vol. XXII, June 1901, p. 4.

23. Dexter, Franklin B., editor, *The Literary Diary of Ezra Stiles* (New York: Scribner's, 1901), vol. III, p. 30; Yale Report, p. 11; *Catalogue of the Officers and Students of Yale College, November 1822.*

24. Aaron Dutton, in "A dissertation of the manner of rendering the exercises of the Linonian Society pleasing and useful" (Orations and Dissertations of the Linonian Society, 1772–1802, pp. 39–40, Manuscripts and Archives, Yale University), puts it thusly: "Extempore disputation requires as much study as written composition, & perhaps more. . . . [But] very many, who dispute extempore, pay little or no attention to the question, till they come into the society, & depend principally upon the arguments & observations, which the occasion shall suggest." On business sessions, Porman, George B., "Rhetorical Practice in Colonial America," in Wallace, Karl, *op. cit.*, p. 77.

25. On the programming of the "debates" at Linonia and Brothers, Harding, *op. cit.*, p. 47, and Beers, H. A., *The Ways of Yale in the Consulship of Plancus* (New York: Henry Holt, 1895), pp. 7–8, 144–145; on the Philagorian, see Constitution and Records of the Philagorian Society 1828–1830, Manuscripts and Archives, Yale University, and Stokes, *op. cit.*, on Porter, vol. 1, pp. 330–331.

26. *College Courant*, June 25, 1870, p. 434; Allmendinger, *op. cit.*, p. 87; Baldwin, Ebenezer, *Annals of Yale College* (New Haven, Conn.: B. & W. Noyes, 1834), pp. 229–230; Mendenhall, *op. cit.*, pp. 7–8; Deming, *op. cit.*, pp. 8–14; on Silliman, Mack, *op. cit.*, p. 24.

27. No sports, Sherwood, John, "Reminiscences of '39 at Yale," *University Magazine*, Vol. III, No. 11, November 1890, p. 26; Warren, *op. cit.*, p. 5; and Kelley, *op. cit.*, p. 213; Chamberlain, Daniel, *op. cit.*, p. 355; "rank in honor with valedictorian," Elliott, Ellsworth, Jr., *Yale in the Civil War* (New Haven, Conn.: Yale University Press, 1932), p. 61.

28. Hall, Peter, *Organization*, *op. cit.*, pp. 172–173, 175.

29. Baldwin, *op. cit.*, pp. 234–235; Johnston, W. C., "The Literary Societies of Yale College," *University Quarterly*, Vol. 1, January 1860, pp. 116, 118. In Professor Edward Coe's essay on "The Literary Societies" in Kingsley, *op. cit.*, vol. 1, at p. 328, he writes: "Both were secret, so far as the names of their officers and the details of their transactions were concerned. Long after they had become distinctively 'open societies,' the ancient pledge still exacted the promise to be 'true to the secrets,' and this promise was for many years required even of candidates before whom the character and advantages of each [of Linonia and of Brothers] were displayed, to aid them in their decision."

30. Mack, *op. cit.* pp. 5–6. This information was derived by computing the number of Bones names in the lists of honors-holders by Kingsley, *op. cit.*, Vol. 1, pp. 360, 365, 502–504, as supplemented by the unpublished minute books and published registers of Phi Beta Kappa, the programs of commencement and the Junior Exhibition, *Catalogue of the Graduate Members of the Linonian Society of Yale College During One Hundred Years, From Its Foundation in September, 1753* (New Haven, Conn.: published by the society, 1853), and *Catalogue of the Society of Brothers in Unity, Yale College, Founded A.D. 1768* (New Haven, Conn.: published by the society, 1854), in Manuscripts and Archives, Yale University.

31. Johnson, Owen, "The Social Usurpation of Our Colleges III—Yale," *Collier's*, June 8, 1912, p. 13.

32. "no office," Johnston, *op. cit.*, p. 124; *Yale News*, March 5, 1878.

33. "Where Officers Were Trained for the Union Army," *New Haven Register Magazine*, October 15, 1961; *Record of the Class of 1833*, pp. 87, 130.

34. *Catalogue 2003* (n.p.: The Russell Trust Association, 2003), pp. 417–418.

35. Taft, William Howard, "President Taft's Speech," *Yale Alumni Weekly*, March 26, 1909, p. 662.

36. Wood, George Ingersoll, "Reminiscences Pertaining to the Origin of the Club," June 11, 1885, Manuscripts and Archives, Yale University Library (emphasis in original manuscript).

37. Crapo, William L., "Linonia and the Brothers." *Yale Literary Magazine*, February 1886, p. 199.

38. Bristed, Charles Astor, *Five Years in an English University* (G. P. Putnam: New York, 1852, pp. 100–101.

39. Sheldon, *op. cit.*, pp. 136–138; Bristed, *op. cit.*, pp. 467–471.

40. Kingsley, *op. cit.*, pp. 315–320; Andrews, John William, *History of the Founding of Wolf's Head* (Lancaster, Penn.: Lancaster Press, 1934), p. 19.

41. The only agenda item for the Yale faculty meeting of November 13, 1832, was the voted decision that "Robertson of the senior class be suspended for the remainder of the term, having been the leader in his class . . . in shouting, groaning, and various outrageous and detestable noises in front of the [Commons] Hall." Faculty Records, 1817–1850, Yale College, p. 118, 13 November 1832, Manuscripts and Archives, Yale University.

42. Bristed's *Five Years in an English University* devotes several pages to the Apostles, contrasting them favorably with Yale societies: "These men did not make any parade of mystery, or aim at notoriety by any device to attract attention; they did not have special chambers for meeting, with skeletons in the corner, and assemble in them with the secrecy of conspirators; nor did they wear breastpins with initials of bad Greek sentences, or other symbolic nonsense on them, as our young [American] Collegians do." Bristed, *op. cit.*, pp. 166–168.

43. Sturtevant, *op. cit.*, p. 102, writing of Yale in 1826 on the "top fifteens" chosen by the Yale faculty; "hierarchical," Horowitz, Helen, *op. cit.*, p. 13.

44. *Third Record of the Class of 1833*, pp. 132–133 on place of birth, and pp. 133–136 on roommates for four years of college course; members of Phi Beta Kappa for that class given in *Catalogue of Members Yale Chapter, op. cit.*, pp. 95–97.

45. Tutors, Bagg, *op. cit.*, p. 116. The *Yale News* for March 11, 1878, in criticizing the Bones society condemned the behavior of such graduates: "how the younger tutors cling to their old customs, boarding together and endeavoring to be as *exclusive* as possible."

46. Dwight, *op. cit.*, pp. 222–223.

47. On Waite and Evarts, *Yale Courant*, June 19, 1875. On Evarts and William Howard Taft, see Taft, Helen Herron, *Recollections of Full Years* (New York: Dodd, Mead, 1914), pp. 25–26.

48. *Third Record of the Class of 1833*, pp. 75–77; Robbins, *op. cit.*, skull plate following p. 88.

49. The plate is reproduced as the frontispiece to Hastings, *op. cit.*

50. Porter, *American Colleges, op. cit.*, pp. 168–169.

51. Belden, Ezekiel Porter, *Sketches of Yale College with Numerous Anecdotes, and Embellished with More Than Thirty Engravings. By a Member of That Institution* (New York: Saxton & Miles, 1843), pp. 127–128.

52. Bagg, *op. cit.*, p. 153; *The Fall of Skull and Bones* Compiled from the Minutes of the 76th Regular Meeting of the Order of the File and Claw (New Haven, Conn.: Published by the Order, 1876), p. 6.

53. Wood, op. cit; Hoskowitz, Mickey, *Duty, Honor, Country* (Nashville, Tenn.: Rutledge Hill, 2003), pp. 31–32.

54. Bagg, *op. cit.*, p. 182; on the imitators, Kellogg, H. L., *College Secret Societies: Their Customs, Character, and the Efforts for their Suppression* (Chicago, Ill.: Ezra A. Cook: 1874), p. 8. *Time* magazine, in its May 31, 1926 issue, published its own list of Yale senior society imitators: "At the University of Virginia there is the famed Raven, dedicated to the dark memory of Edgar Allen Poe. At Colgate there are weird Skull and Scroll, and Gorgon's Head. University of California has its Skull and Key and its Golden Bear. Other famed senior societies: Owl and Serpent (Chicago), Iron Cross (Wisconsin), Skull and Snakes (Leland Stanford), Iron Wedge (Minnesota), Quill and Dagger (Cornell), Innocents (Nebraska), Mystical Seven and Skull and Serpent (Wesleyan)."

55. Johnson, Samuel, *A Dictionary of the English Language, Eighth Edition* (London: 1799), vol. II, not paginated (Webster's marked copy of this Johnson edition is in the Rare Book Division, New York Public Library); Webster, Noah, *An American Dictionary of the English Language* (Springfield, Mass.: George and Charles Merriam, 1850), pp. 994, 1038.

56. Bagg, *op. cit.*, pp. 454–456; Kingsley, *op. cit.*, Vol. 1, p. 309.

57. See "Genealogical Chart of General, Greek-Letter, College Fraternities in the United States," Stevens, *op. cit.*, p. 330.

58. Kingsley, *op. cit.*, Vol. 1, p. 358.

59. *Yale Banner*, dated issues as named, Manuscripts and Archives, Yale University.

60. *History of the Class of 1834 in Yale College* (New Haven, Conn.: Tuttle, Morehouse & Taylor, Printers, 1875), p. 15.

61. Syrett, *op. cit.*, pp. 98–99.

62. The original Alpha of Williamsburg medal is shown next to the Alpha of Connecticut medal in the illustrations in Voorhees, *op. cit.*, following p. 116. The Chi Delta Theta badge is described in Belden, *op. cit.*, p. 127.

63. Bagg, *op. cit.*, pp. 144–145. Belden of the class of 1844 in his *Sketches of Yale College, op. cit.*, pp. 127–128, writes that "the symbols of the badge are unknown; they are probably not so death-like as the badge itself. . . . The badge is worn as a square, gold, breast-pin." A drawing of the square Bones badge, surrounded on all four sides with a narrow border of (acanthus?) leaves, is to be found in an illustration of all the junior and senior society badges in the *Yale Banner* for October 8, 1847. By that date, the Bones badges were gold. *The Yale Courant* for October 24, 1866, contains an interview with an unnamed Bones member of the class of 1838, describing "a pin that was worn at the time which consisted of a plain gold plate with a Skull and Cross Bones engraved upon it. This pin was imitated by a rival Society, being the same in shape but different in engraving."

64. Bagg, *op. cit.*, 143; *Yale Courant*, November 15, 1873, p. 104; Peterfreund, Diana, *Secret Society Girl* (New York; Delacorte Press, 2006), p. 151. Yale's badge fetish was merely part of a national phenomenon, as evidenced by an article from a Kenyon College contributor: "No one who has ever been associated with a College, can have failed to notice the self-consequential air which Freshmen assume, when they exhibit for the first time their newly-donned Secret Society badges." Lathrop, W. W., "College Secret Societies," *University Quarterly*, vol. 3, April 1861, p. 277. On fraternity badges generally, see Syrett, *op. cit.*, p. 98, and Slosson, Edward, *Great American Universities* (New York: Macmillan, 1910), p. 337.

65. Roberts, *op. cit.*, pp. 27–42; Mack, *op. cit.*, pp. 41–42.

66. Hughes, Rupert, "Secret Societies at Yale," *Munsey's,* June 1894. *Horoscope* for May 1883 (p. 4) described a Bones prospect as "practicing talking with a match in his mouth while undressing in order to prepare for the 'Crab,'" and noted of another that "the 'Crab' will look well on his nightdress."

67. Plimpton, *op. cit.*, p. 93.

68. Sweezy, Paul M. and Leo Huberman, eds., *F. O. Matthiessen (1902–1950): A Collective Portrait* (New York: Henry Schuman, 1950), pp. ix–x.

69. Frazier, George, "Yale's Secret Societies," *Esquire*, September 1955, p. 106. However, according to Sweezy, *op. cit.*, p. 91, Matthiessen left his Bones pin in his hotel room.

70. Elliot, *op. cit.*, pp. 24, 42; *Catalogue of Psi Upsilon Fraternity* (n.p.: Executive Council of the Ps Upsilon Fraternity, 1917), p. 88. In July 1918, a Major Denig wrote to the widow of 2nd Lieut. John Williams Overton, Bones 1913, who had asked that "a certain pin" be sent to his mother if he got hit during the battle at Soissons, and his badge was found on his body and returned as requested.

71. "William Henry Vanderbilt," *Yale News*, May 24, 1892, and *Yale Alumni Weekly*, May 24, 1892; "Skip Gould and Vanderbilt," *New York Herald*, May 24, 1901; Vanderbilt, Arthur, II, *Fortune's Children: The Fall of the House of Vanderbilt* (London: Michael Joseph, 1989), p. 202. On Vanderbilt's badge, see Mack, *op. cit.*, p. 220, citing the *New York World* for May 25 and 27, 1892, and *New York Herald*, May 28, 1892; on Vanderbilt Hall, see Pinnell, Patrick, *The Campus Guide Yale University Second Edition* (New York: Princeton Architectural Press, 2013), pp. 40–41. Comparative dormitory room costs, *Yale University v. Town of New Haven*, 43 L.R.A. 190 (1899), 71 Conn. 316, 42 A. 87, p. 93.

72. Printed catalogues for Phi Beta Kappa commenced in 1806 at Harvard and Dartmouth, producing the first Greek-letter fraternity catalogues to be printed in the United States, while Yale used manuscript rolls from the beginning through 1808, Voorhees, pp. 51, 101–104.

73. Bagg, *op. cit.*, p. 150–151.

74. *Ibid.*, pp. 146–147, 151.

75. *Idem.*, p. 154.

76. Gist, *op. cit.*, p. 70.

77. Bagg, *op. cit.*, pp. 150, 152; Plimpton, *op. cit.*, p. 93. See also Robbins, *op. cit.*, p. 128 on "Skull and Bones Time." Although rarely noticed, the pendulum on the tall case-clock in the second floor main lounge at the Yale Club in New York City is engraved with the legend "S.B.T."

78. Robbins, *op. cit.*, p. 129; Bagg, *op. cit.*, p. 153, while acknowledging the nomenclature, cannot bring himself to write the actual words. The word "Patriarch" is the signature to a letter from the society to the *Yale News* of March 26, 1878, and the author writes of himself as among "the few who were blessed with the Eulogian mysteries."

79. E.g., "Eulogians" in *Yale Review*, March 1857, p. 89; Catholic *Encyclopedia*, www.catholic.org/encyclopedia/view.php?id=4418, accessed May 29, 2013. (New York: Robert Appleton, 1913). *Yale News* for May 24, 1878, in reporting on elections, writes of a man accepting "the Eulogian pledge."

80. The Greek *barberoi* is regularly translated as "foreigners." Thucydides, *History of the Peloponnesian War* (New York: Penguin, 1972), translated by Rex Warner, p. 37, n.

3. "Barbarian" was an onomatopoeic rendering of what sounded to the Greek ear as their inane babbling ("bar bar"), and "barbarian" was taken up in due course by the Romans to identify those savage unfortunates who resided outside their empire and did not speak Latin. Cannadine, David, *The Undivided Past: Humanity Beyond Our Differences* (New York: Knopf, 2013), p. 221.

81. *The Laws of Yale College*, 1832, *op. cit.*, p. 3; "tenacious attachment," Winterer, *op. cit.*, p. 62; Osterweis, Rollin G., *Romanticism and Nationalism in the Old South* (Baton Rouge: Louisiana University Press, 1971), pp. 27–28.

82. On Greece and New Haven, Osterweis, Rollin G., *Three Centuries of New Haven* (New Haven, Conn.: Yale University Press, 1953), pp. 233, 268, 459, 463; on *Graeca Majora* and Yale, Winterer, *op. cit.*, pp. 32–35; "chef d'oeuvre," Woolsey, T. D., "Address Commemorative of Chauncey Allen Goodrich," quoted in Hocmuth and Murphy, *op. cit.*, p. 163. On the statue, Steiner, *op. cit.*, p. 167.

83. Robbins, *op. cit.*, p. 130, quoting with translation but without citation to Bagg, *op. cit.*, p. 151.

84. Pierson, George Wilson, *Yale: The University College 1921–1937* (New Haven, Conn.: Yale University Press, 1955), pp. 315–321.

85. Bagg, *op. cit.*, p. 153; Robbins, *op. cit.*, pp. 90, 125–127; Brinkley, Alan, *The Publisher: Henry Luce and His American Century* (New York: Alfred A. Knopf, 2010), p. 73. On McGeorge Bundy's Bones name, Preston, Andrew, *The War Council: McGeorge Bundy, the NSC, and Vietnam* (Cambridge, Mass.: Harvard University Press, 2006), p. 2, and Goldstein, Gordon M., *Lessons in Disaster: McGeorge Bundy and the Path to War in Vietnam* (New York: Henry Holt, 2008), p. 9; on George W. Bush, Smith, Jean Edward, *Bush* (New York: Simon & Schuster, 2016), p. 15. William F. Buckley Jr., knight errant of conservatism, chose "Cheevy," after Edward Arlington Robinson's "Miniver Cheevy," whose deluded hero pines for the age of chivalry and regrets that he was born too late. Tanenhaus, Sam, "William F. Buckley: the founder," *Yale Alumni Magazine*, May/June 2008.

86. Belden, *op. cit.*, pp. 128–130.

87. Deming, *op. cit.*, p. 92, reprinted from *Yale Alumni Weekly*, May 10, 1910.

88. A Graduate of the Seventies, "Discussion of 'Tap Day'," *Yale Alumni Weekly*, June 24, 1905, p. 759; "Forerunners of Tap Day," *Yale Alumni Weekly*, May 20, 1910, p. 867.

89. Mack, *op. cit.*, pp. 183, 251.

90. *Ibid.*, pp. 1, 12, for 1842, for the Bones election that precipitated Scroll and Key; Bagg, *op. cit.*, pp. 147–148, for 1869; "Forerunners of Tap Day," *op. cit.*

91. *Historical Register of Yale University 1701–1937* (New Haven, Conn.: Yale University Press, 1939), p. 13; *The Songs of Yale* (New Haven, Conn.: Thomas W. Pease, 1860), pp. vi–viii; Belden, *op. cit.*, p. 131; Kelley, *op. cit.*, pp. 221–222.

92. Kelley, *op. cit.*, p. 221; Moseley, Laura Hadley, ed., *Diary 1843–1852 of James Hadley* (New Haven, Conn.: Yale University Press, 1951), p. x. On Taft's "store clothes," Matthiessen, "Alphonso Taft, Class of 1833: Lawyer and Statesman," in French, Robert Dudley, *The Memorial Quadrangle* (New Haven, Conn.: Yale University Press, 1929), p. 307.

93. The Townsend Prizes were founded by Yale Law professor Isaac H. Townsend (Yale 1822) with a gift of $1,000, the income to be distributed annually in five premiums of $12 each to seniors preparing the "best specimens of English composition." The DeForest Prize was endowed by a wealthy New Havener for a gold medal worth

$100, "to be given annually to the scholar of the Senior Class who shall write and pronounce and English Oration in the best manner, the President and Professors being the judges." In 1853, "[t]o save two separate trials, one for the Townsend Premiums, and one for the DeForest Medal, six instead of five Townsend prizes are awarded, and then the six pronounce their orations in the Chapel, when the 'DeForest' is given by the vote of the Faculty." *University Quarterly*, Vol. 3, January 1861, pp. 208–209; *Yale News*, May 5, 1887.

94. Yale is the first college in the United States at which there is evidence of a real marking system (President Ezra Stiles ranked students by four Latin characterizations in 1782), but Yale did not have grades until 1813, setting a scale of 1 to 4 (4.0 on a decimal system, or later 400 points), a system never used at Harvard, as described in Smallwood, M. L., *An Historical Study of Examinations and Grading Systems in Early American Universities* (Cambridge, Mass.: Harvard University Press, 1935), pp. 42–43, 45–47, On the "biennial," Chamberlain, Joshua L., *Universities and Their Sons* (Boston, Mass.: R. Herndon Company, 1900), section on Yale by C. H. Smith, p. 89. On the 2.50 benchmark, "The Junior Appointments," *Yale News*, January 13, 1888. On the "2 average" and "rustication," Smallwood, *op. cit.*, p. 47, citing Belden, *op. cit.*

95. Depew, Chauncey M., *My Memories of Eighty Years* (New York: Scribner's, 1922), p. 5.

96. Identification of the number of valedictorians and salutatorians is made through comparing Bones club membership to the lists for the same years in Kingsley, *op. cit.*, Vol. 1, p. 502. On the ancient honors of valedictorian and salutatorian, which ended with the commencement exercises of 1894, see Deming, *op. cit.*, pp. 80–84. On the academic sibling rivalry in the Taft family, see Goodwin, Doris Kearns, *The Bully Pulpit: Theodore Roosevelt, William Howard Taft, and the Golden Age of Journalism* (New York: Simon & Schuster, 2013), p. 27.

97. *New Haven Evening Register*, May 31, 1878. *Horoscope* for April 1884 (p. 1) noted that "Bones has a passion for valedictorians," and in discussing the prospects for election, often identified probable valedictorians at the end of their junior year. Rudolph, *op. cit.*, p. 289, notes that "by the turn of the century at Yale the valedictorian could count on *not* being elected to a senior society," attributing the phenomenon to the fact that "what mattered for so many young men was not the course of study but the environment of friendships, social development, fraternity houses, good sportsmanship, athletic teams . . . In all of this the classroom was not very important."

98. "The Townsend and DeForest Prize," *Yale News*, May 5, 1887. For Townsend Prize winners, Kingsley, *op. cit.*, p. 360; Scroll and Key had twenty-four winners in the same period. Poem in *Yale Review*, March 1857, pp. 90–91. "Jack" and "Gill" have not been identified, but Bonesmen took three of the five Townsends that year.

99. Kingsley, *op. cit.*, Vol. 1, pp. 420 ff., and Vol. II, pp. 54–175.

100. On the distinction of "philosophical oration" appointments, Mack, *op. cit.*, p. 6. Bones members also made up 49 of the 102 Townsend Prize winners (as against 13 for Scroll and Key). After its founding, Keys had more Class Orators and Class Poets than Bones, however, in the classes from 1842 through 1853 (six to Bones' four). In the same run of years, Keys had three DeForest Prize winners, including the first. In his autobiography *Connecticut Yankee* (New Haven, Conn.: Yale University Press, 1943), at p. 76, Wilbur Cross of the class of 1885, later Sterling Professor of English, dean of the Yale Graduate School, and governor of Connecticut, after

whom that state's parkway is named, was to boast that he had won "the DeForest Gold Medal against five competitors, all of whom were members of Yale's oldest senior society."

101. Huntington, Samuel, *A History of the Class of 1863* (New Haven, Conn.: Tuttle, Morehouse & Taylor Co., 1905, p. 191; Hirsch, Mark, *William C. Whitney, Modern Warwick* (New York: Dodd Mead & Company, 1948), pp. 15, 17–18.

102. Dwight, *op. cit.*, p. 30; Kelley, *op. cit.*, p. 174. The eight ranking distinctions for the Junior Exhibition were, in descending order: philosophical orations, high orations, orations, dissertations, first disputes, second disputes, first colloquies, and second colloquies (see the list in *The Yale Courant* for January 6, 1866, p. 19).

103. Mack, *op. cit.* pp. 41–45, and, at 212, quoting I. S. Peet, class of 1845. On the thrice-a-year elections of officers in Linonia and in Brothers, Harding, *op. cit.*, pp. 40–41; no member could be elected twice to the same office.

104. "Skull and Bones," *Time*, May 20, 1940.

105. Hall, *Organization, op. cit.*, p. 312.

106. Sharfstein, Daniel J., *The Invisible Line: A Secret History of Race in America* (New York: Penguin, 2001), p. 58, quoting George W. Smalley; "Randall Gibson," *DKE Quarterly* 11 (1893), pp. 26–27.

107. *Catalogue of the Calliopean Society, Yale College, 1839* (New Haven, Conn.: Printed by B. L. Hamlen, 1839), pp. 3–4; on Whig and Clio geographic proclivities, Wertenbaker, Thomas J., *Princeton, 1746–1896* (Princeton, N.J.: Princeton University Press, 1946), p. 206.

108. Kelley, *op. cit.*, p. 222; Kingsley, *op. cit.*, Vol. 1, p. 320; Bagg, *op. cit.*, pp. 221–223.

109. Pierson, *op. cit.*, p. 64; on Southern defensiveness, see Taylor, William, *Cavalier and Yankee: The Old South and the American National Character* (New York: George Brazilier, 1961), pp. 96 ff.

110. Glover, Lori, "Let Us Manufacture Men: Educating Elite Boys in the Early National South," in Thomson & Glover, eds., *Southern Manhood: Perspectives in Masculinity in the Early National South* (Athens and London: The University of Georgia Press, 2001), pp. 36–37; Sturtevant, *op. cit.*, p. 100; Horowitz, Helen, *op. cit.*, p. 28; on housing, Allmendinger, *op. cit.*, pp. 88–89, also noting that 58% of the student body roomed in town in the 1850s.

111. Sherwood, *op. cit.*, p. 26. On slovenly scholars and his own sartorial pride, Kentuckian and Bonesman (1852) William Preston Johnston, quoted in Shaw, Arthur Marvin, *William Preston Johnston: A Transitional Figure of the Confederacy* (Baton Rouge: Louisiana State University Press, 1943), p. 41.

112. On "honor," Ayers, Edwin L., in Wilson & Ferris, *Encyclopedia of Southern Culture* (Chapel Hill: University of North Carolia Press, 1989), p. 1483; "tetchy," Cash, Wilbur J., *The Mind of the South* (1941; rpt., New York, Vintage, 1991), p. 171; "character," Bledstein, *op. cit.*, p. 34.

113. Sturtevant, *op. cit.*, p. 99; Sherwood, *op. cit.*, p. 25. For evidence that there were conflicts even at Southern colleges where planters' sons confronted rules invented in New England and largely maintained by New England–trained clergy, see Horowitz, Helen, *op. cit.*, p. 28.

114. *Catalogue of the Calliopean Society, op. cit., passim*; on Taylor and Johnston, Hughes, Nathaniel Jr., *Yale's Confederates: A Biographical Dictionary* (Chattanooga: University of Tennessee Press, 2008), pp. 112–113, 205–206, and Shaw, *op. cit.*, p. 36.

115. Osterweis, *Romanticism, op. cit.*, pp. 94–95. Andrew Dickson White was to remember, in his college career of 1849–1852, hearing "the greatest political questions sounding in our ears; Webster, Calhoun and Clay making their final speeches." White, "Yale in '53," *Yale Literary* magazine, February 1886, p. 217.

116. Quoted in Sharfstein, *op. cit.*, p. 65. Gibson, the younger brother of Randall Lee Gibson (elected Class Orator for 1853), was a second president of Linonia, and won prizes for debate and declamation.

117. Osterweis, *Romanticism, op. cit.*, p. 128; Halliday, Carl, *A History of Southern Literature* (New York: Neale Publishing, 1906, pp. 130–134, 138–140).

118. Belden, *op. cit.*, p. 128.

119. Yale graduates' numbers in service and death, Thwing, Charles F., *A History of Education in America* (New York: D. Appleton and Company, 1906), p. 367, and William Maxwell Evarts's speech in *College Courant*, February 5, 1870, p. 79. Jeff Davis Legion census in Hughes, *op. cit.*, pp. xvi, 41–42, 143.

120. Harrison, Burton N., "The Capture of Jefferson Davis," *Century*, vol. 27, 1, November 1883, pp. 130–145. Harrison entered Yale from the University of Mississippi as a sophomore, and became president of Linonia, editor of the *Lit.*, and Class Orator. For biographical sketches of Harrison, Perkins, and the other noted Yale Confederates, see Hughes, *op. cit.* and Davis, William C., *"A Government of Our Own": the Making of the Confederacy* (New York: Free Press, 1994). William Preston Johnston, then president of Tulane in New Orleans, was to serve as chair of the committee in charge of funeral services for Jefferson Davis in 1889; the prosecutor at Davis's trial for impeachment in 1867 was William Maxwell Evarts, another Bonesman.

121. *Biographical and Historical Record of the Class of 1853 in Yale College, For the Fifty Years from the Admission of the Class to College* (New Haven, Conn.: 1881), pp. 43–44.

122. On the number of generals, see Stokes, *op. cit.*, Vol. II, pp. 294–295, who names twenty-five graduates and non-graduates as Union Army generals (omitting William Seward Pierson, Bones 1836, and Joseph Cook Jackson, Bones 1857), and six (including a law school graduate) as Confederate Army generals (omitting Henry R. Jackson, Elisha Paxton, and William Preston), which is apparently the source for Kelley, *op. cit.*, p. 198, and that census for the Confederates is expanded and corrected by Hughes, *op. cit.*, p. xviii. Of the 237 names of graduates in Hughes's *Yale's Confederates* from the class of 1833 onward, 29 are Bonesmen from the classes of 1835 through 1859.

123. Hughes, *op. cit.*, pp. 16, 83, 113, 177; Lewis, *op. cit.*, p. 107, on the returns of Johnston and Gibson; quotation from Gibson in Ellsworth, *op. cit.*, p. 66. Gibson's classmate Andrew Dickson White, running into him in New York City the week before the Yale commencement, persuaded Gibson to attend. The class secretary then sought Professor Thomas Thacher's permission (he managed the alumni meetings) to have Gibson speak, "pointing out the public interests involved and urging that there was a chance that might be good fruit at the South as well as at the North," and Thacher "took the point in a moment." *The Class of 'Fifty-Three in Yale College, A Supplementary History* (New Haven, Conn.: Tuttle, Morehouse & Taylor, 1894), p. 32; Sharfstein, *op. cit.*, pp. 148–150.

124. Johnson, Owen, *Stover at Yale* (New York: Frederick A. Stokes, 1912), p. 265. Cecil Rhodes had the same idea in creating the Rhodes scholarship program, to bring

college-age Americans and British Empire colonists to Oxford University for "great advantage for them in giving breadth to their view for their instruction in life and manners . . . ," as he wrote in his will. See Richards, David Alan, "Kipling and the Rhodes Scholars," *Kipling Journal*, March 2012, pp. 22–3, 27.

125. Mack, *op. cit.*, p. 212.
126. Faculty Records, 1817–1850, Yale College, p. 128, December 25, 1833, Manuscripts and Archives, Yale University.
127. Faculty Records, 1817–1850, Yale College, 3, 5, August 9, 1842, Manuscripts and Archives, Yale University; *Laws of Yale College, 1832, op. cit.*, p. 32.
128. Bagg, *op. cit.*, pp. 152–154.
129. Robbins, *op. cit.*, p. 2 illustration.
130. Diary of George Sherman, Yale College class of 1839, Manuscripts & Archives, Yale University.
131. On debate format, Robbins, *op. cit.*, pp. 133–135; "Cider-mill," *Reminiscences of Scenes and Characters, op. cit.*, p. 105. From the first club of 1833 through the club of 1848, Bones tapped fifteen presidents of Linonia, and twenty-eight presidents of Brothers, according to the respective societies' catalogues, where the presidents but no other officers are noted.
132. On Taft, *Yale Alumni Magazine*, March/April 2013, p. 37; on Bush and Kerry, anecdote from Professor Charles Hill, the teacher of the new course, to the author. While teaching at Yale, Taft would frequently visit the Bones tomb. Wooley, Knight (Bones, 1917), *In Retrospect—A very personal memoir* (privately printed: 1975), p. 2.
133. "Skull & Bones Skull to Be Auctioned," *Huffington Post*, March 18, 2010.
134. Crapo, *op. cit.*, pp. 199–200.
135. Robbins, *op. cit.*, pp. 133–134.
136. Bagg, *op. cit.*, pp. 152–153; Duplex Family Geneology, http://nytompki.org/Genie/duplex/duplex-register/d2.htm (Second Generation, No. 7, wife Vashti Duplex Creed); "Yale Celebrates 150th Anniversary of First African American Graduate," http://news.yale.edu/2007/5/30/Yale-celebrates-150th-anniversary-first-african-american-graduate, accessed May 16, 2014.
137. Bagg, *op. cit.*, p. 146.
138. Baird, William R., *American College Fraternities* (New York: 1898), pp. 202-204. From these parent chapters at Union and Hamilton, the Greek-letter fraternity was introduced into most of the colleges of New England and New York by 1840. In the twentieth century, Yale's Psi Upsilon chapter renounced its national affiliation and became the Fence Club.
139. Bartlett, Edward Griffin, *DKE Quarterly*, Vol. 1, No. 2, April 1883, p. 84.
140. Bagg, *op. cit.*, pp. 152–153; "decidedly literary," Baird, *op. cit.*, p. 35. The assertion of Robbins, *op. cit.*, p. 84, that the original Bones club of 1833 "tapped the majority of its members from the junior society Alpha Delta Phi" is wrong, as Alpha Delta Phi was not started at Yale until 1836.

CHAPTER FOUR: THE "OPPOSITION" OF SCROLL AND KEY
1. Pierson, *Yale Book of Numbers, op. cit.*, p. 50.
2. The list is in the Bones Scrapbooks in the Scroll and Key tomb, Mack, *op. cit.*, p. 201.
3. Stevens letter, July 14, 1841, Henry Stevens Papers, Special Collections, University of Vermont Libraries.

4. *Catalogue of the Alpha Delta Phi, op. cit.*, pp. 83, 87–91; *The Twelfth General Catalogue of the Psi Upslion Fraternity, op. cit.*, pp. 67–68.

5. Mack, *op. cit.*, p. 8. The formation of Scroll and Key was *not* an instance of what sociologists call "schismatic differentiation," where fraternal orders "have been torn by internal dissensions which have culminated in the complete secession of disgruntled and dissatisfied elements." Gist, *op. cit.*, p. 46. Kingsley and his mates did not secede, but rather chose to form their own group, without ever having been members of the Scull and Bone. There are real parallels to schismatic differentiation, nonetheless. "These schismatic or secessionist orders bear much the same relation to the parent organizations as religious sects do to the older bodies from which they have separated. In general the secessionists have tended to take over most of the characteristic features of the original order, frequently even preserving the name with slight modifications. So far as the functional and structural patterns are concerned, the societies remain the same." *Ibid.*

6. Stevens letter, August 6, 1842, Henry Stevens Papers, Special Collections, University of Vermont Libraries.

7. Mack, *op. cit.*, pp. 11–12.

8. *Ibid.*, pp. 12–13.

9. *Idem.*, pp. 1, 197.

10. *Record of the Class of 1843, Yale College* (New York: John F. Trow, 1859), pp. 96–97.

11. Mack gives no date for the William Kingsley memoir (now in the Keys tomb), but says it was taken as dictation by his daughter Mrs. Henry Farnam in his "latter years." Mack, *op. cit.*, p. 202.

12. Sulloway, Frank J., *Born to Rebel: Birth Order, Family Dynamics and Creative Lives* (New York: Pantheon, 1996), p. 351 and *passim*; Kluger, Jeffrey, *The Sibling Effect: What the Bonds Among Brothers and Sisters Reveal About Us* (New York: Riverhead, 2011), pp. 71–73. See also Colt, George Henry, *Brothers* (New York: Scribner's, 2012), chapter two, "Good Brother, Bad Brother: Edwin and John Wilkes Booth," pp. 24–82, examining the title pair and a litany of "brothers so different that it seems impossible they could have the same parents": Armand and François–Marie Arouet (Voltaire), Maximilien and Augustin Robespierre, Gansevoort and Herman Melville, and Jimmy and Billy Carter.

13. Mack, *op. cit.*, pp. 4, 5, 200.

14. Porter, Noah, *Joseph Earl Sheffield, A Commemorative Discourse* (New Haven, Conn.: 1882), pp. 18–20.

15. Mack, pp. 1–2, 13, 24–25.

16. *Ibid.*, pp. 13, 25, 204.

17. *Idem.*, pp. 13, 25–28, 204–205, 207. The society beneath a cut of their symbol printed in a local newspaper gave public thanks "to the Fire Department and the citizens of New Haven for their prompt and energetic exertions at the late fire in Street's Building" on December 26, 1842.

18. Bagg, *op. cit.*, pp. 155–156, 164.

19. Mack, *op. cit.*, p. 199.

20. Bagg, *op. cit.*, p. 155; *Rumpus*, April 1997. The motif of the right hand below was also in use on the badge of Phi Beta Kappa, although that hand pointed to the stars in the upper left corner.

21. Mack, *op. cit.*, pp. 3, 199–200.

22. Hall, B. H., *A Collection of College Words and Customs* (Cambridge, Mass.: John Bartlett, 1856), p. 296.
23. "Pinomania," *College Courant*, July 17, 1869, p. 49.
24. Mack, *op. cit.*, p. 14.
25. "The American Scholar," *Nature: Addresses and Lectures* (Boston, Mass.: James Monroe, 1849), pp. 110–111; *Nature* (Boston, Mass.: James Monroe, 1836), pp. 24–25; "Over-soul," *Essays: First Series* (Boston, Mass.: James Monroe, 1847), pp. 252–253.
26. White, Andrew Dickson, *The Autobiography of Andrew Dickson White*, 2 vols. (New York: Century Company, 1905), I, p. 29; on Emerson's appreciation of New Haven, Tilton, Eleanor M., *Letters of Ralph Waldo Emerson* (New York: Columbia University Press, 1995), Vol. X, 1870–1881, p. 92. Sharfstein, *op. cit.*, p. 56.
27. Bledstein, *op. cit.*, p. 259.
28. *Ibid.*, pp. 206–207.
29. *The Journals of Ralph Waldo Emerson*, ed. William Waldo Emerson and Waldo Emerson Forbes, 10 vols. (Boston, Mass.: Houghton Mifflin, 1903–04), Vol. 9, p. 41.
30. Mack, *op. cit.*, pp. 14–15, 19.
31. *Ibid.*, pp. 29–30, 43.
32. Kingsley, *op. cit.*, pp. 310–311; Kelley, *op. cit.*, pp. 222–223.
33. *College Courant*, November 27, 1869, p. 320.
34. Bagg, *op. cit.*, p. 156.
35. Moseley, *op. cit.*, p. 176; *Yale Review*, March 1857, pp. 88–89.
36. Bagg, *op. cit.*, pp. 148, 156–157.
37. Mack, *op. cit.*, pp. 238–239.
38. "Who Wants to Be in Yale's Scroll and Key? Or the Latest Prank Attempt Gone Awkward," April 16, 2009, www.ivygateblog.com/2009/yales-scroll-key-and-the-latest-prank-attempt-gone-awkward#more_5606, accessed May 28, 2013; *C.S.P 1842–1989*, p. 6. Bones tomb intruders in 1876 in their pamphlet, *The Fall of Skull and Bones, op. cit.*, pp. 4–5, reported finding a copy of the 1868 catalogue of Scroll and Key: "From the catalogue we learn that the President and Secretary of Scroll and Key are known 'inside' as CHILO and EUMENES, and that, as in Bones, each member had a nickname given him. Some of these are handed down from class to class, and of these Glaucus, Prasagatus and Arbaces appear to be the favorites." A letter from a Keysman signed Arbaces is in the *Yale News* for March 19, 1879, and the issue for May 22, 1878 reports the return to campus to help settle an election dispute by "Eumenes, '73, and Chilo, '67."
39. Giamatti, A. Bartlett, *A History of Scroll and Key 1942–1972* (New Haven, Conn.: published by the society, 1978), p. 3; Bagg, *op. cit.*, p. 157.
40. Deming, *op. cit.*, pp. 92–93; Mack, *op. cit.*, pp. 183, 251.
41. Bagg, *op. cit.*, pp. 162–163.
42. Mack, *op. cit.*, p. 206.
43. Bagg., *op. cit.*, pp. 501–503; Pearce, John Irving, "Breaking Up the Bully System," *Yale Scientific Monthly*, Vol. XVIII, October 1911, pp. 43–46; Kingsley, *op. cit.*, vol. 2, pp. 462–477. It has been argued that the word was not, "as some suppose, of vulgar, or bovine derivations, but a corruption of the proud Greek word Βουλη, a . . . patriarch." *Yale Record*, January 14, 1874, p. 203.
44. Bagg, *op. cit.*, p. 503.

45. The Robinson song ("Air: Jeremiah") is quoted in Robbins, *op. cit.*, p. 148.

46. Bagg, *op. cit.*, p. 153; Robbins, *op. cit.*, pp. 92, 143. Peterfreund's 2002 novel *Secret Society Girl* adds to the list of the treasures in "Rose and Grave," her book's stand-in for Bones, both a Shakespeare folio and Cold War nuclear codes, *op. cit.*, p. 133.

47. Bagg, pp. 221–223; Kelley, *op. cit.*, p. 222.

48. Osterweis, *Three Centuries, op. cit.*, p. 266.

49. Robbins, *op. cit.*, p. 83. It was described well before Robbins's 2002 book, in 1876 in the pamphlet of *The Order of the File and Claw, op. cit.*, p. 5.

50. Bagg, *op. cit.*, pp. 478–479.

51. Mack, *op. cit.*, pp. 157–158.

52. *Ibid.*, p. 211.

53. The data on the Bones clubs and Keys crowds of 1844 and 1845 are compiled from the respective societies' *Catalogues* and the previously cited *Catalogues* of Alpha Delta Phi and Psi Upsilon.

54. Havemeyer, Loomis, *"Go to Your Room."* (New Haven, Conn.: Yale University, 1960), p. 10.

55. *Yale Banger* (New Haven, Conn.: 1845), Manuscripts and Archives, Yale University.

56. Bagg, *op. cit.*, p. 160.

57. Mack, *op. cit.*, p. 207; Bagg, *op. cit.*, p. 161.

58. Havemeyer, *"Go to Your Room,"* p. 53, says of Sword and Crown only, "we have little information about it," and Bagg, *op. cit.*, p. 173, spends only two sentences on it, noting that it had fifteen members in 1843, and describing its badge.

59. Belden, *op. cit.*, p. 131. An attempt may have been made in 1867 to revive Sword and Crown: the *Yale Courant* for March 20, 1867, ran a letter from a correspondent about a friend claiming to have seen at an engraver's in New York City, "a die which he was told was being made for some fellows at Yale. . . . He thought it was a 'crown' combined with either a 'sword' or a 'torch.'" The letter protested the thought of a fourth senior society ("there are not enough good men in a class for more than two") and apparently nothing came of the effort.

60. Mack, *op. cit.*, p. 210.

61. Belden, *op. cit.*, pp. 130–131, reproducing the Dart and Star cut.

62. *The New Haven Morning Courier* for August 15, 1844, contains the advertisement; *Yale Banger, op. cit.*, p. 4.

63. Havemeyer, *"Go to Your Room,"* p. 53. In his 1903 memoir, *Memories of Yale Life and Men, op. cit.*, p. 67, President Timothy Dwight was to note the creation (actually, the revival) of Star and Dart in his senior year of 1849, but wrote that "it passed away I scarcely know how."

64. Quoted in Mack, *op. cit.*, p. 207.

65. *Ibid.*, pp. 31–37, 207, 210.

66. Dwight, *op. cit.*, pp. 56–57.

67. Hall, *op. cit.*, pp. 172–173.

68. Class statistics, Pierson, *Yale Book of Numbers, op. cit.*, pp. 4–6; Cooper, Jacob, *William Preston Johnston: A Character Sketch* (New Haven, Conn.: prepared for the class of 1852, 1878), pp. 9–10.

69. White, *op. cit.*, pp. 67–68; McBride, *op. cit.*, pp. 38–39; *College Courant*, July 14, 1872; on Gibson's black ancestor, Sharfstein, *op. cit.*, pp. 20–21, 192–196. At Cornell, White's first official faculty member, and his first professor of physics, first dean of

the law school, second professor of Latin, and first chair of American history (at any U.S. college) were all members of Bones.

70. White, *op. cit.*, p. 67.

71. John Englehardt's letter is contained in Hofstadter and Smith, *op. cit.*, I, pp. 466–467. On Yale and the rifles, see Kelley, *op. cit.* p. 219.

72. Pierson, *Yale Book of Numbers, op. cit.*, p. 60; Kelley, *op. cit.*, p. 296.

73. Mack, *op. cit.*, p. 44.

CHAPTER FIVE: THE MAKING OF TOMBS, TEAMS, AND GIFTS

1. As Keys historian Mack writes (*op. cit.*, p. 60), "the Bones structure suggested a kind of permanence to outsiders that no other society could ignore." This was true of the American fraternity system generally: "The building of [the Delta Kappa Epsilon log cabin lodge at Kenyon College in Gambier, Ohio, in 1855] was a great impetus to the owning of society homesteads. Before this the various chapters [of American fraternities] had been accustomed to rendezvous stealthily in college garrets, at village hostels, or anywhere that circumstances and pursuing faculties made most convenient. But when the assurance was once gained that the fraternities might own their own premises and make them permanent abiding-places, the whole system became straightway established on a lasting foundation." Porter, John Addison, "College Fraternities," *op. cit.*, p. 753.

2. Seutonius, *Lives of the Twelve Caesars* (London: George Bell & Sons, 1893), p. 91.

3. Holden, Reuben, *Yale: a Pictorial History* (New Haven, Conn.: Yale University Press, 1967), unpaginated, Buildings of Yale: 1717–1850 (map), and illustration nos. 28, 30, 38, 40, 42, 44, 48.

4. Pinnell, *op. cit.*, p. 53; the conjoined Latin mottoes, quoted in Bagg, *op. cit.*, p. 152, have been translated idiomatically.

5. Bagg, *op. cit.*, p. 145; Decrow, W. E., *Yale and "The City of Elms, . . ."* (Boston, Mass.: W. E. Decrow), 1885; Griguere, Joy, *"The dead shall be raised": The Egyptian Revival and 19th century American commemorative culture* (PhD, University of Maine, 2009), p. 126.

6. Peterfreund, *op. cit.*, pp. 64, 135.

7. Robbins, *op. cit.*, p. 25; Howland, *op. cit.*, p. 22.

8. Bagg, *op. cit.*, p. 170; Robbins, *op. cit.*, p. 67.

9. Peterfreund, *op. cit.*, p. 39: "It [not walking in front of the society's tomb] was an unwritten rule on campus: the college equivalent of refusing to walk in front of a haunted house in our childhood neighborhoods."

10. Howland, *op. cit.* p. 22.

11. Pinnell, *op. cit.*, pp. 25–27, 52–54, 131; Holden, *op. cit.*, pp. with plates 45 through 48 and Chronological List of Buildings. The construction contract for the "Convention Hall at New Haven" specified Davis as the architect, and is signed by John Sheldon Beach (class of 1839) and Henry Baldwin Harrison (1846) for the society, and Atwater Treat as contractor: now digitized, Russell Trust Association, Inc., Yale University, Manuscripts and Archives, Yale University Library ("Treat Contract"). In 1860, the Kappa Kappa Kappa society at Dartmouth erected a hall in Hanover, New Hampshire, on College Street, which much resembled the original block of the Bones tomb. Meacham, Scott, *Halls, Tombs and Houses: Student Society Architecture at Dartmouth*, http://www.dartmo.com/halls/hallscontent4.html. text accompanying

notes 91–92, accessed May 21, 2015: "The original designers of these structures wished to have them declare their purpose distinctly and to proclaim to everyone in unmistakable terms that they were intended to veil something from the vulgar gaze; and not only from the vulgar gaze, but the gaze of every one except of an exclusive and selected few, who alone were to be permitted to the threshold."

12. Commission des Sciences et Arts d' Égypt, *Description de l'Egypte, ou Recueil des observations et des recherches qui ont été faiteseny Egypte pendant l'expédition de l'armée française, publié par les ordres de Sa Majesté l'empereur Napoleon le Grand*, 9 volumes text, 11 volumes plates, and an atlas (Paris, 1809–1828); Denon, Dominique Vincent, *Voyage dans la Basse et la Haute Egypte pendant les campagnes du general Bonaparte*, 3 volumes (Paris: P. Didot l'aîné, 1802). Austin based his design of the Grove Street cemetery gate on a mixture of the temples of Esna and Ashmunien (Hermopolis Magna), drawing on one plate from Denon's *Voyage* and one from the *Description*: Carrott, Richard G., *The Egyptian Revival: Its Sources, Monuments and Meaning (1808–1858)* (Berkeley: University of California Press, 1968), p. 205 and plates 69, 70, and 71.

13. Carrott, *op. cit.*, pp. 50–51, 59, 138, 163, 193; Bunker Hill monument and the graves of the presidents, Giguere, *op. cit.*, pp. 158–161, and O'Gorman, James, *Henry Austin: In Every Variety of Architectural Style* (Middletown, Conn.: Wesleyan Press, 2010), pp. 117–120; Emerson in Atkinson, Brooks, ed., *The Complete Essays and Other Writings of Ralph Waldo Emerson* (New York: Modern Library, 1950), p. 61.

14. Denon, *op. cit.*, plates 12 (figure 3) (plate 66 in Carrott, *op. cit.*), 33, 39.

15. Pinnell, *op. cit.*, p. 158, on Town and Davis; Jaffe, Irma B., *Trumbull: Portrait Artist of the American Revolution* (Boston, Mass.: New York Graphic Society, 1975), pp. 128–129, with reproduction of Town and Davis's *Pinacotheca for Colonel Trumbull's Picture Gallery*, Benjamin Franklin Collection, Yale University.

16. On the gift of, use, and repurposing of the Trumbull Gallery, see Steiner, *op. cit.*, pp. 155–156; Sizer, Theodore, "The Trumbull Gallery," *Yale Alumni Weekly*, November 4, 1932, pp. 166–168; Fulton, John H., and Elizabeth H. Thomson, *Benjamin Silliman 1779–1864 Pathfinder in American Science* (New York: Henry Schuman, 1947), pp. 164–172; Pinnell, *op. cit.*, pp. 53–54.

17. William Crapo to Robert Bliss, November 21, 1851, ALS, Bliss Collection, Manuscripts and Archives, Yale University. *Vir* is Latin for *man*. Dexter, *op. cit.*, p. 304: "The undergraduates felt that he [Thacher] sympathized with them more actively and fully than any of his associates, and the graduates look to him as their closest and most direct bond of connection with the College."

18. Treat Contract, *op. cit.*

19. *The Fall of Skull and Bones, op. cit.*, pp. 1–6.

20. "Fun in College Societies," *Denver Tribune-Republican*, April 25, 1886.

21. Warren, Aldice G., "History of Delta Kappa Epsilon," Records, Gerald R. Ford Memorial Library, Delta Kappa Epsilon International Fraternity Headquarters, Ann Arbor, Mich., p. 95; Dwight, Hawes, and Hayward, *Catalogue of the Delta Kappa Epsilon Fraternity* (New York: published by the ΔKE Council, 1910), p. 76.

22. Dwight, Hawes, and Hayward, *op. cit.*, p. 76; Decrow, *op. cit.*, pp. 35–35. Holt, Henry, *Garrulities of an Octogenarian Editor* (Boston, Mass., and New York: Houghton Mifflin, 1923), p. 43: "I advanced the money for one of the junior 'tombs' (halls without windows) and [had] written for its associates a blood-curdling oath of secrecy." In Alice Dunley's engraving *Secret Society Buildings in New Haven*, appearing

in *Harper's Weekly* for February 7, 1874, the DKE windowless hall is shown with those of Bones, Keys, and Psi Upsilon. The Alpha chapter of Delta Kappa Epsilon at Kenyon College claims the honor of building, occupying, and owning the first hall of a college fraternity in the United States, but this was a log cabin out in a wooded ravine, the twenty by forty foot structure being ten feet high, chinked and plastered with mud and clay mortar, fitted with double-shuttered window, and its walls and roof sound-deadened with sawdust and charcoal. Warren *Catalogue*, *op. cit.*, pp. 92–95, and Porter, "College Fraternities," *op. cit.*, p. 753, with a line illustration. It was built in 1855, the year before the Bones tomb, and is long perished.

23. Stewart, Donald Ogden, *By a Stroke of Luck! An Autobiography* (New York: Paddington Press, 1975), p. 63.

24. Scully, *op. cit.*, p. 119; Figure 98 in the Scully volume reproduces the front elevation described, now in the Library of Congress Prints and Photographs AIA/AAF Collections, Call Number Unprocessed in PN 13 CN 2010:100.

25. *College Courant*, November 27, 1869, p. 329, and December 4, 1869, p. 335, and January 15, 1870, p. 31; Mack, *op. cit.*, pp. 60–65, 227; Bagg, *op. cit.*, p. 158; Pinnell, *op. cit.*, pp. 152–153.

26. Bagg, *op. cit.*, p. 158.

27. "Fun in College Societies," *op. cit.*; *The American Architect and Building News*, November 25, 1876; Mack, *op. cit.*, pp. 65, 229.

28. Pinnell, *op. cit.*, p. 153.

29. Baker, Paul D., *Richard Morris Hunt* (Cambridge, Mass.: MIT Press, 1980), pp. 186–189 on the Yale campus buildings, and *passim*.

30. Schuyler, Montgomery, "Works of the Late Richard M. Hunt," *Architectural Record*, vol. V., July 1895–July 1896, p. 112; Baker, *op. cit.*, p. 191; Schuyler, Montgomery, "The Architecture of American Colleges: Yale," *Architectural Record*, vol. XXVI, December 1909, p. 416. The message to Rodman is described in the *Yale News*, May 3, 1878; "tea chest," *Yale News*, May 22, 1878, June 7, 1878. The Keys hall is styled the "Sacred Zebra"in the *Horoscope*, May 23, 1881, p. 4.

31. Depew, *op. cit.*, p. 7.

32. *The Laws of Yale-College* (New Haven, Conn.: T. & S. Green, 1774), p. 11; Deming, *op. cit.*, p. 188.

33. Smith, Ronald A., *Sports and Freedom: The Rise of Big-Time College Athletics* (New York and Oxford, England: Oxford University Press, 1988, pp. 3–4, 26–29; Kelley, *op. cit.*, pp. 214–215; Mendenhall, *op. cit.*, pp. 2–3, 11.

34. *Yale Literary Magazine*, July 1851, p. 367.

35. Mendenhall, *op. cit.*, pp. 15–20; Thwing, *op. cit.*, p. 385; Whiton, James, "The First Intercollegiate Regatta," *Outlook*, vol. 18, no. 5 (June 1901), pp. 286–289; Hurd, R. M., "The Yale Stroke," *Outing* XV (December 1889), pp. 230–231; Livermore, Charles F., "The First Harvard-Yale Boat Race," *Harvard Graduates' Magazine* II (December 1893), p. 226; Smith, *op. cit.*, pp. 33–34.

36. Holt, *op. cit.*, p. 185: "In those days, the partiality of Yale for high-sounding names was noticeable: Harvard was content with a 'club' [instead of the Yale Alumni 'Association,' later the Yale Club of New York]. Similarly, [Harvard] was content with a 'yard,' while Yale had a 'campus,' and Harvard had a 'boat club,' while Yale had a 'Navy.'"

37. *Catalogue of Psi Upsilon Fraternity, op. cit.*, pp. 82–83, 86, 88, 89; census of commodores, Bagg, *op. cit.*, p. 423;1879 tap results and the crew, *Yale News*, May 23, 1879.

38. Hurd, Richard, *A History of Yale Athletics: 1840–1888* (New Haven, Conn.: privately printed, 1888), p. 84; Wood, John Seymour, *College Days, or Harry's Career at Yale* (New York: Outing Company, 1894), p. 82; Deming, *op. cit.*, pp. 195–198; Bagg, *op. cit.*, p. 314; Bushnell, Samuel, "Baseball," in Kingsley, *op. cit.*, Vol. 2, pp. 365–375; Kelley, *op. cit.*, pp. 299–300; Wood also writes (at p. 164) of the Yale-Harvard baseball game: "The rivalry of the two great universities seems to be bred in the bone—inherited from our fathers who fought on the lakes of New Hampshire and Massachusetts for aquatic supremacy. Old rows never forgiven, old sores never healed, bled afresh on these occasions."

39. Wood, *op. cit.*, p. 262.

40. *Iconoclast*, vol. I, no. 1 (all published), October 1, 1873, pp. 5–6 (emphasis supplied). In his 1873 commencement day speech to the alumni, William Maxwell Evarts said of the senior societies, including his own of Bones: "They are a curse to the college, interfering . . . with the selection of university crews and ball clubs and they have much to do with the disgraceful series of defeats which have attended Yale for several years." *Yale News*, February 8, 1878, reprinting his speech from the *Hartford Courant*, June 26, 1873. On the Yale-Harvard baseball series, Kelley, *op. cit.*, p. 300. On Carter's curve ball, *Yale News*, January 31, 1878; on Stagg's streak, Patton and Field, *op. cit.*, p. 279. The presidents of the University Base Ball Club are given in *Yale Pot-Pourri*, Vol. XXII, 1887, p. 196. The captains of the baseball teams are given in Hurd, *op. cit.*, pp. 104–106.

41. Hurd, *op. cit.*, p. 53; Thwing, *op. cit.*, p. 386; Deming, *op. cit.*, pp. 208–213; Kelley, *op. cit.*, p. 213.

42. Bergin, Thomas, *The Game* (New Haven, Conn.: Yale University Press, 1984), pp. 3–4, 8–9; Patton and Field, *op. cit.*, p. 284; Smith, *op. cit.*, p. 73; Hurd, *History, op. cit.*, pp. 80–82.

43. Gabriel, *op. cit.*, pp. 146–147; Bagg, *op. cit.*, p. 304; Kelley, *op. cit.*, pp. 227–228, 298.

44. In the Latin: "Pereat tristitia, Pereat osores, Quivis antiburschius, Atque irrisores." Gabriel, *op. cit.*, p. 147; Bagg, *op. cit.*, p. 302; Parker, Horatio William, "Music at Yale," in Nettleton, G. H., ed., *The Book of the Yale Pageant* (New Haven, Conn.: Yale University Press, 1916), pp. 225–226.

45. Gabriel, *op. cit.*, p. 147–148; Kelley, *op. cit.*, p. 228.

46. Robbins, *op. cit.*, pp. 57–58; Bagg, *op. cit.*, p. 302. *College Courant* for 24 June 1868 recorded its aggravation at society members showing displeasure and leaving the room "if a neutral should happened to whistle or sing the air" of their societies.

47. Mack, *op. cit.*, pp. 55–56, 225. Skull and Bones had a new marching anthem, "I shall be his Dad," in the late 1860s. *College Courant*, June 24, 1868.

48. Bagg, *op. cit.*, pp. 659–665.

49. *Ibid.*, pp. 128, 134–136, 405–408; "more craved," Deming, *op. cit.*, pp. 85–87; New York *Tribune*, June 15, 1859; "History of Yale's Prom," *New Haven Evening Register*, January 11, 1897; Senex, Eli, "Wooden Spoon Memories," *Yale Alumni Weekly*, May 27, 1908; Hyde, Miles G., *The One Time Wooden Spoon at Yale* (New York: Albert A. Ochs,1899), *passim*, with a plate of the badge, p. 9.

50. Bagg, *op. cit.*, pp. 421–422; Deming, *op. cit.*, pp. 89–90; Kelley, *op. cit.*, p. 221; "Origin of the Promenade," *Yale News*, February 1, 1887.

51. Bagg, *op. cit.*, p. 614. "Many prefer the Wooden Spoon to any other college honor or prize, because it comes directly from their classmates, and hence, perhaps, the Faculty disapprove of it, considering it as a damper to ambition and college distinctions." Hall, B. H., *op. cit.*, p. 313.

52. *Ibid.*, p. 423; names of the winners are set forth in Hyde, *op. cit.*, pp. 33–34, with Bones winners in the years 1852, 1861–1865, 1868–1869, and 1871, and Keysmen for 1855–1859 and 1866.

53. Flexner, Simon, and James Thomas Flexner, *William Henry Welch and the Heroic Age of American Medicine* (New York: Viking, 1941), p. 175.

54. *Gallinipper*, vol. ?, no. ! [*sic*], November 9, 1853.

55. "Secret Societies among Us," *Yale Literary Magazine*, December 1865, pp. 85–90.

56. *Yale Review*, Vol. 1, No. 1, February 1857, pp. 14–15.

57. *Gallinipper*, Vol. VII, No. 1, 1858.

58. Mack, *op. cit.*, p. 153.

59. Olof Page, class of 1865, quoted by Mack, *op. cit.*, p. 153.

60. Faculty Records, July 15, 1859 and September 14, 1859.

61. Bagg, *op. cit.*, p. 151.

62. Linonia and Brothers, Harding, *op. cit.*, p. 38; Mack, *op. cit.*, pp. 46–47, 214–215.

63. Courtney, Steve, *Joseph Hopkins Twichell: The Life and Times of Mark Twain's Closest Friend* (Athens and London: University of Georgia Press, 2008), pp. 2–4, 39–49, 129–130; Strong, Leah, *Joseph Hopkins Twichell: Mark Twain's Friend and Pastor* (Athens: University of Georgia Press, 1966), pp. 12–16, 162; *Mark Twain's Letters Volume 2 1867–1868* (Berkeley: University of California Press, 1990, p. 281.

64. Mack, *op. cit.*, pp. 47, 215.

65. *Ibid.*, pp. 54, 224.

66. *Idem.*, pp. 47–50, 221–223, describing an initiation of 1848 (including Gothic arches, and dark-robed priests but for one in white sable) through quotation from Keys records for July 4, 1848; the Latin language "Form of Initiation into C.S.P." adopted by the class of 1849 is also set forth.

67. *The College Experience of Ichabod Academicus Illustrated by William T. Peters, and dedicated to their brother collegians by the editors, H.F.P. and G.M.* (n.p: s.n., New Haven, Conn., 1850), p. 6.

68. Flexner and Flexner, *op. cit.*, p. 45.

69. Mack, *op. cit.*, pp. 54, 224. In John Wood's 1894 novel *College Days*, set in the mid-1870s, Harry's Uncle Dick is "out all night at his senior society 'spread'" and needs to recoup with two bottles of soda water and a lemon because he feels "like a 'biled owl,' as Artemus Ward says" (*op. cit.*, p. 35).

70. Bagg, *op. cit.*, p. 150.

71. *Ibid.*, pp. 149–150. See also the description of Bull and Stones' harassment of the Bones initiation and the Keys tap in June 1871, *College Courant*, June 17, 1871, p. 294.

72. Kellogg, *op. cit.*, p. 45.

73. *College Courant*, June 10, 1871, p. 274; *Yale Courant*, May 23, 1874.

74. Mack, *op. cit.*, p. 183; *College Courant*, July 3, 1869, p. 16.

75. Bagg, *op. cit.*, p. 148.

76. *Ibid.*, p. 149; "Presentation Week at Yale," *Hartford Courant*, June 26,1866; *College Courant*, July 3, 1869, p. 16. The Keys crowd of 1872 was similarly packed and forecast: *College Courant*, June 10, 1871, p. 274, and June 17, 1871, p. 294. The

midnight election announcement is found in Duyckinck, W. C., *Incidents of Our College Life Gleaned from Memorabilia and Diaries* (New Haven, Conn.: June 26, 1900).

77. Harrison, *op. cit.*, p. 271; William Howard Taft to Helen Herron Taft, July 6, 1885, William Howard Taft Papers, Library of Congress; "pillow talk," Moore, Paul [Wolf's Head], *Presences: A Bishop's Life in the City* (New York: Farrar Straus & Giroux, 1997), p. 49; generally, Robbins, *op. cit.*, pp. 154–157.

78. Morison, Elting, *op. cit.*, pp. 34–35.

79. Robbins, *op. cit.*, pp. 135–138; *Harkness Hoot*, May 1933, p. 6; "therapy groups," Isaacson, Walter and Evan Thomas, *The Wise Men: Six Friends and the World They Made* (New York: Simon & Schuster, 1986), p. 81.

80. Mack, *op. cit.*, pp. 90–91.

81. *Ibid.*, pp. 106–107.

82. The Kingsley Trust Association's December 1871 letter of gift for the Porter Prize, Manuscripts and Archives, Yale University; "Porter Prize" http://www/yale.edu/secretary/prizes/porter.

83. Steiner, *op. cit.*, p. 228; Mack, *op. cit.*, p. 76; *Yale Illustrated Horoscope*, May 1889, p. 4. The Ten Eyck evolved as a contest out of the Junior Exhibition by way of the Townsend Prizes, featuring eight competitors with no set subjects (Phelps, William Lyon, writing of the class of 1887 in his *Autobiography with Letters* (Oxford, England: Oxford University Press, 1939), p. 151, also notes that "the winner was usually elected to a Senior Secret Society;" the prize thus became the award for the best oration in the junior class, a warmup for the senior year's DeForest Prize. The author cannot forbear to note that he won the Ten Eyck Prize in 1966 and the DeForest Prize in 1967.

84. *New York Times*, July 10, 1918; *C.S.P. Catalogue, op. cit.*, p. 511.

85. Garver, John Anson, *John William Sterling, Class of 1864, Yale College* (New Haven, Conn.: Yale University Press under the direction of the Trustees of the Estate of John W. Sterling, 1929), pp. 4, 16, 26, and 105 ("His indebtedness to his senior society is expressed in his will . . . but, in later years, he never attended one of its formal meetings"); Earle, Walter K., *Mr. Shearman and Mr. Sterling and How They Grew* (New Haven, Conn.: Yale University Press [commissioned by Shearman & Sterling], 1963), pp. 51–52, 63, 185; MacLeish, Archibald, "New-Yale," *Fortune*, vol. IX, no. 3, pp. 70–71.

86. "$15,000,000 Sterling Bequest to Yale," *New York Times*, July 17, 1918; "The Sterling Bequest," *Yale Alumni Weekly*, August 23, 1918, calling the gift the "greatest in the history of American universities" and the estate "one of the largest ever amassed by a man pursuing strictly a professional career."

87. Robbins, *op. cit.*, p. 5. In Ron Rosenbaum's article, "The Last Secrets of Skull and Bones," *Esquire*, September 1977, p. 165, the number is $15,000; in Peterfreund's 2002 novel *Secret Society Girl*, the figure is an inflation-adjusted $20,000, *op. cit.*, p. 132.

88. Garver, *op. cit.*, pp. 110–111, 113; on Rogers's Bones election decline, *Horoscope*, April 1889, p. 1.

89. On the Adams and Johnson gifts, see *Yale Alumni Magazine*, November/December 2013, pp, 20–21. On the Schwarzman gift, see *New York Times*, May 12, 2015, p. C1.

90. Pinnell, *passim*.

91. Bagg, *op. cit.*, p. 164. In the newspapers of the time, the "Diggers" was a name given to an Indian tribe located in the Rocky Mountains.

92. "Best literary men." Bagg, *op. cit.*, p. 440; "most successful," Mott, F. L., *A History of American Magazines*, 5 vols. (Cambridge, Mass.: Belknap Press, 1930–1968), vol. 2 (1850–1865), p. 95; "favorite . . . vehicle," Kelley, *op. cit.*, p. 226; "Coalitions," *Yale Review*, February 1857, p. 24; generally, Bagg, *op. cit.*, pp. 425–443, and Kingsley, *op. cit.*, Vol. I, 338–351.

93. Bagg, *op. cit.*, pp. 426–427, 441.

94. *Catalogue of the Psi Upsilon Fraternity*, *op. cit.*, p. 87.

95. *Yale Literary Magazine*, December 1856, pp. 86–89.

96. "Collegial Ingenuity," *Yale Literary Magazine*, February 1864, Vol. XXIV, No. 4, second issue, pp. 125–128. Bagg published a history of the controversy in his book of two years later, *op. cit.*, pp. 165–166, where he added the "worm" characterization. "Toadying and bullying" in Duyckinck, Whitehead C., *Student Life at Yale Sixty Years Ago, 1861–1865: A Reminiscence* (Plainfield, N.J.: prepared for the class meeting, 1925), p. 8.

97. On the Linonian Society background of the quarrel, see Mack, *op. cit.*, pp. 154, 245, and Velsey, Donald, and John Leinenweber, *A History of Spade and Grave: The Society of 1864-2014* (N.p.: Andrew Morehouse Trust Association, Inc., 2014), pp. 3–4.

98. The story of the class meeting and the seizure of the offending issues, thus "mismanaging the sacred trust confided to them [the Bones editors] by time-honored usages of Old Yale," is given in the second issue of the February 1864 issue of the *Lit.* edited by the new board, at pp. 165–166. "It is enough to say that by it [the suppression] the members of that Society exhibited a degree of arrogance which forced upon the college world the alternative either of entire submission or energetic resistance. It would have been an insult to Yale manhood to doubt for an instant under what circumstances would be the decision, especially after the full vindication which the independence of the 'Lit. Editors' received from the class of 1864." Duyckinck, *op. cit.*, p. 9.

99. "Secret Societies," *Yale Literary Magazine*, April 1864, pp. 235–238.

100. Bagg, *op. cit.*, p. 166; Velsey and Leibenweber, *op. cit.*, pp. 16–17; badge, Andrews, *op. cit.*, p. 161.

101. "Senior Societies," *Yale Literary Magazine*, November 1868. The full quotation is "Mors sceptrum ligonibus aequat," from which the verb has been deleted. The S.L.M. cut appears in the *Yale Banner* for October 3, 1868.

102. Bagg, *op. cit.*, pp. 168–169; *College Courant*, July 3, 1869, p. 16; January 29, 1870, p. 66; and December 1869, p. 367.

103. Yeg2 S121, Manuscripts and Archives, Yale University.

104. The Diggers lived on in literature: John Seymour Wood's *College Days*, describing the Yale College of the mid-1870s, uses "Spade and Grave" as a stand-in for Bones and "Book and Lock" as a substitute for Keys (*op. cit.* pp. 25, 58, 372, 396). And in Peterfreund's 2002 novel *Secret Society Girl*, the colloquial name she uses for the member of her mythical senior society Rose & Grave, also a stand-in for Skull and Bones, is "Diggers," *op. cit.*, p. 44.

105. "Fun In College Societies," *op. cit.* The text of the *Yale Literary Chronicle* of 1873 also describes this episode.

106. "Presentation Week at Yale," *op. cit.*

107. Bagg, *op. cit.*, pp. 171–172; *New Haven Evening Register*, November 11, 1872: "The following members of the Senior Class received elections to 'Bull and Stone' last Saturday night: L. B. Almy, H. E. Benton, A. B. Boardman, E. H. Buckinham, J.

A. Clemmer, C. Dewing, J. W. Gott, F. C. Goode, D. W. Huntington, H. Meyer, H. E. Sadler, F. J. Shephard, W. C. Stewart, S. N. White, F. H. Wright. Rumor says this society has been in existence over a quarter of a century, and numbers among its alumni some of Yale's most illustrious graduates. Only once before in the history of its existence was it deemed expedient to appear with pins. That was in 1870."

108. *Yale Literary Chronicle*, p. 17.
109. Bagg, *op. cit.*, p. 173. Both the *Yale Index*, vol. 1, no. 1, dated June 30, 1869 (Presentation Day), and the *Pot-Pourri* for 1868–69 (at p. 30), in printing the senior society memberships lists both the members of S.L.M. for 1869 and of E.T.L., the latter's fifteen being: Charles Bullis, Henry Burnham, Andrew J. Copp, John C. Grant, Edward Hedges, Dennis McQuillen, Henry Missimer, Edward C. Seward, Thomas W. Swan, John M. Thayer, Stanley P. Warren, Edward P. Wilder, and Francke S. Williams.
110. Bagg, *op. cit.*, pp. 172–173; Mack, *op. cit.*, pp. 156–157. *Yale Lit.* (for November 1868) reported that Bull and Stones was "an avowed imitation of the two reputable societies . . . generally understood to be a sort of burlesque of them, and to have no intention of perpetuating itself." *Yale Banner* for October 3, 1868, includes the delegation names for that year (the class of 1869) and the cut of the coffin lid.
111. Bagg, *op. cit.*, pp. 171–172.

CHAPTER SIX: PROVOCATIONS OF POPPYCOCK, AND TAP DAY'S INVENTION
1. Bascom, John, *Things Learned By Living* (New York: G. P. Putnam, 1913, pp. 7, 46; "Bascom, John 1827–1911," *Dictionary of Wisconsin History*, http://www.wwisconsinhistory.org (keyword=Bascom).
2. Rudolph, *Mark Hopkins, op. cit.*, pp. 110–111.
3. Bascom, John, *Secret Societies in College* (Pittsfield, Mass.: Berkshire County Eagle, 1868), pp. 5–6, 8–10, 13–16.
4. Slosson, *Great American Universities* (New York: Macmillan, 1910), p. 103.
5. Selden, William K., *Club Life at Princeton: An Historical Account of the Eating Clubs at Princeton University* (Princeton, N.J.: Princeton Prospect Foundation, 1994), pp. 2–4.
6. Axtell, James, *The Making of Princeton University: From Woodrow Wilson to the Present* (Princeton, N.J.: Princeton University Press, 2006), pp. 291, 15, and generally, pp. 291–309. Shortly before his death, even Cottage Club alumnus F. Scott Fitzgerald (class of 1917) pronounced his malediction on "a lousy cruel system," whose "ragged squabble of club elections with its scars of snobbishness and adolescent heartbreak" he would gladly abolish. Turnbull, Andrew, ed., *The Letters of F. Scott Fitzgerald* (New York and London: Scribner's, 1964), p. 445 (November 13, 1939).
7. Selden, pp. 7–10, and *passim*; Wilson, Edmund, "Profiles: A Prelude II, Landscapes, Characters, and Conversations from the Earlier Years of My Life," *New Yorker*, May 6, 1967; "religious frenzy," Axtell, *op. cit.*, p. 309. Wilson proposed to curb the eating clubs by adopting a "Quadrangle Plan" of residential colleges, but the notion was defeated, perceived by alumni as a threat to submerge or eliminate their clubs, and he soon thereafter left Princeton. Karabel, Jerome, *The Chosen* (New York: Houghton Mifflin, 2005), pp. 64–70. Only one Princeton president was ever an eating club member (Robert Goheen, class of 1936, president in 1957–1972).
8. Sheldon, *History and Pedagogy, op. cit.*, pp. 167–169; Morison, Samuel Eliot, *op. cit.*, p. 424; on the Hasty Pudding constitution, Harding, *op. cit.*, p. 44, and the Institute of

1770, *Catalogue of the Officers and Members of the Institute of 1770, of Harvard University* (Cambridge, Mass.: Welch, Bigelow, 1868), p. 27 (emphasis in original).

9. Bagg, *op. cit.*, pp. 112–115; Johnson, Owen, "The Social Usurpation of Our Colleges: II—Harvard, *Collier's*, Vol. XLIX No. 10, May 25, 1912, p. 13.

10. Sheldon, *op. cit.*, pp. 170–171; "most aristocratic," Morison, *op. cit.*, pp. 181–182; Porc and PBK, Current, *op. cit.*, p. 61; "The Porc," *Time*, February 26, 1940; "notice of Harvard," Fraser, Rae W., *Westward by Rail: The New Route to the East* (New York: Longmans, Green., 1870), pp. 254–255; "club formula," Hughes, Tom, "The Harvard Societies," *College Courant*, April 8, 1871, p. 159; adornment, Wecter, Dixon, *The Saga of American Society: A Record of Social Aspiration 1607–1937* (New York: Scribner's, 1937), pp. 276–278. On the secrecy of Hasty Pudding and Porcellian, "The Harvard Clubs," *Yale Record*, March 18, 1874, pp. 311–312.

11. Wecter, *op. cit.*, pp. 278–279; Morison, *op. cit.*, p. 424: "Between 1875 and 1890, these [underclass or waiting clubs] were mainly chapters of national fraternities; but the Harvard chapters found their obligations to brethren from other colleges onerous, surrendering their charters, and becoming local clubs."

12. Shand-Tucci, Douglass, *Harvard University* (Princeton, N.J.: Princeton University Press, 2001), p. 101.

13. Fournier, George T., and James K. Mcauley, "The Men's Final Clubs," *Harvard Crimson*, October 5, 2010.

14. *Ibid.*; on the Fly fireplace and FDR, Shand-Tucci, *op. cit.*, p. 101. Franklin Roosevelt's failure to be asked to join Porcellian constituted "the bitterest moment in [his] life up till then," in the words of a relative, and it gave him "an inferiority complex" in his wife Eleanor's view. Davis, Kenneth F., *F.D.R.: The Beckoning of Destiny 1882–1928* (New York: G. P. Putnam, 1972), pp. 154–155; Ward, Geoffrey, and Ken Burns, *The Roosevelts: An Intimate History* (New York: Alfred A. Knopf, 2014), pp. 89–90. Two of Theodore's sons and three of Franklin's became Porcellian members, but more conservative members of the Roosevelt family attribute FDR's turn toward socialism to this rejection.

15. "The man," Johnson, Owen, "The Social Usurpation of Colleges, Part II—Harvard," *Collier's*, May 25, 1912, p. 14; "taboos" and "stroke," Amory, Cleveland, *The Proper Bostonians* (New York: E. P. Dutton, 1947), pp. 299–304.

16. Amory, *op. cit.*, p. 304; Morison, *op. cit.*, p. 425, also tells the Kaiser Wilhelm story, and Ward and Burns, *op. cit.*, p. 133, note that President Roosevelt, his son-in-law, and thirty-eight other members of Porcellian slipped into a private dining room at the White House for the club's ceremonial, traditional toast to the groom, while cousin Franklin stood outside with the other guests.

17. Morison, *op. cit.*, p. 425, records: "From 1878, when the A.D. purchased a house of its own, every final club has shaken down its graduates for a house, each new one surpassing the last in size and luxurious appointments." On Whitney, Beschloss, Michael, "From White Knight to Thief," *New York Times*, September 14, 2014.

18. Martin, Edward S., "Undergraduate Life at Harvard," *Scribner's*, vol. XXI, February, 1897, p. 543.

19. Morison, *op. cit.*, p. 42; Sheldon, *History and Pedegogy, op. cit.*, pp. 168–169.

20. Robbins, *op. cit.*, pp. 124–125.

21. Pierson, *Yale Book of Numbers, op. cit.*, pp. 5–6.

22. R.R.J. '76, "Yale's Senior Society System," *Yale Critic*, June 20, 1882, p. 5.

ENDNOTES

23. Wood, *op. cit.*, p. 25; Bones legacies, *New-York Evening Post*, February 5, 1884.
24. *Catalogue of the Delta Kappa Epsilon Fraternity, op. cit.*, p. 113.
25. Holt, *op. cit.*, pp. 33, 35, 39, 41–45, 81–82, 94. The new tomb, given the reunion's date of 1902, was almost certainly that of Book and Snake at the corner of Grove and High Streets, constructed in 1901. The "ground glass" windows in the Bones tomb were in the rear extension built in 1883.
26. Kellogg, *op. cit.*, pp. 79–80.
27. As quoted in Barrows, Chester L., *William M. Evarts: Lawyer, Diplomat, Statesman* (Chapel Hill: University of North Carolina Press, 1941), p. 8.
28. Lyman, Chester, "Origins of the Yale Lit.," *Yale Literary Magazine*, February 1886, pp. 181–191; Kingsley, *op. cit.*, vol. 1, p. 351; Stokes, *op. cit.*, vol. II, p. 269; "The Yale Literary Magazine," *Yale News*, December 15, 1886.
29. Lyman, *op. cit.*, pp. 186–187; Barrows, *op. cit.*, pp. 11–12; *Record of the Class of 1837 of Yale University* (Springfield, Mass.: Weaver, Shipman, 1887), pp. 13–17. Many Yale classes have adopted the adjective "famous" as descriptive of their character, but the class of 1837, out of one hundred four graduates—including a man whom many historians think should have been president (Tilden), a chief justice (Waite), a secretary of state (Evarts), an attorney general and minister to England (Pierrepont), and a member of the National Academy of Sciences (Silliman)—seems to have had their self-interested judgment confirmed. Stokes, *op. cit.*, vol. II, p. 268.
30. Kellogg, *op. cit.*, p. 41, for "radical testimonies"; "Yale Secret Societies," *Boston Globe*, July 2, 1873, for "holy horror."
31. *Hartford Courant*, June 26, 1873.
32. Sheldon, *op. cit.*, pp. 133–135; Harding, *op. cit.*, pp. 157, 262; Kelley, *op. cit.*, pp. 222–223; Potter, *op. cit.*, p. 89; Johnston, *op. cit.*, pp. 117–120, 126. As more comprehensively stated by Rudolph, *op. cit.*, pp. 145–146, for which description at Yale the phrase "senior societies" may be substituted for his "fraternities": "The literary societies [at all colleges] declined not so much because the fraternities robbed them of their purpose but because the fraternities created a higher level of loyalty and intruded new political complications into literary-society elections. They also declined as the colleges themselves took over some of their old purposes: built up broader collections of books, opened the libraries more than once a week, introduced respectable study in English literature, discovered history as a field of study, [and] expanded the sciences," citing, *inter alia*, Kingsley, *op. cit.*, vol. 1, p. 320–323.
33. On the demise of the two literary societies, see Mack, *op. cit.*, pp. 174–175; "joint committee," Harding, *op. cit.*, p. 263; "decline in attendance." Potter, *op. cit.*, pp. 89, 92; "one evening," Chamberlain, Daniel, *op. cit.*, p. 351; "blow and gas," *College Courant*, April 2, 1869; "post hoc," *College Courant*, April 29, 1871; "printing press," *College Courant*, February 10, 1872.
34. Steiner, *op. cit.*, p. 166; Thacher in Kellogg, *op. cit.*, p. 79.
35. Quoted in Stokes, *op. cit.*, Vol. II, p. 270.
36. Freeman, Harrison B., "Letters: The First Yale Crew Flag," *Yale Alumni Weekly*, February 9, 1912, p. 516.
37. Mendenhall, *op. cit.*, p. 23.
38. Freeman, *op. cit.*, p. 516.
39. Bagg, (signing as "A Graduate of '69'"), *Yale Courant*, letter, December 6, 1873; Mack, *op. cit.*, pp. 158–160, 246.

40. *Yale Courant*, December 6, 1873.
41. "negatively mysterious," Andrews, *op. cit.*, p. 24; 1858 quote, unsourced in Hodgson, *op. cit.*, p. 36; Hodgson, Geoffrey, *The Colonel: The Life and Wars of Henry Stimson* (New York: Alfred A. Knopf, 1990), p. 36; *Yale Courant*, October 10 and 24, 1866; *Yale Courant*, March 23, 1878; class size in Pierson, *Yale Book of Numbers*, p. 7.
42. Bagg, *op. cit.*, pp. 147, 169; *College Courant*, June 24, 1868, on the contrasting pin wear among classes, and on night dress display; *Yale News*, March 11, 1878, damning "puerile practices as wearing their pins on their night shirts." E. E. Aiken's article is in the *Yale Critic*, April 14, 1882.
43. *The American Heritage Dictionary of the English Language*, Fifth Edition (Boston, Mass., and New York: Houghton Mifflin Harcourt, 2011), p. 1371; http://www.merriam .webster/co/dictionary/poppycock, accessed February 27, 2014.
44. Mack, *op. cit.*, p. 162.
45. *The Galaxy: An Illustrated Magazine of Entertaining Reading*, New York, March 1871, p. 474, cited by Robert Ingersoll in a public address in New Haven as reported in the *Yale News* for March 5, 1878.
46. *Yale Literary Chronicle*, 1873, p. 31.
47. *College Courant*, June 24, 1868. Andrews, *op. cit.*, p. 28, saying the story might be apocryphal, cites a Buffalo, New York, newpaper report of 1890 relating that a Bonesman was lying ill in his room, missing the Thursday night meeting. Clubmates making an appearance sat in one-hour shifts by the sickbed, while completely ignoring the man's roommate. After the second visitation, the roommate, bolting the door, informed the next arrival that no deaf-mutes need apply.
48. *College Courant*, June 24, 1868.
49. *Yale Literary Chronicle*, pp. 4, 19, citing the *College Courant* letter.
50. An official notice was sent out by Skull and Bones: "You are especially cautioned against certain members of Yale College, who are wearing a badge almost the exact fac-simile of our own, *and trying to pass themselves off for what they are not.*" Mack, *op. cit.*, p. 248.
51. Mack, *op. cit.*, pp. 167, 248.
52. Lewis, Wilmarth S., *One Man's Education* (New York: Alfred A. Knopf, 1967), p. 94.
53. banner, *Yale Courant*, January 3, 1874; pantomine, *Yale Courant*, January 31, 1874, p. 206.
54. *Yale Literary Chronicle*, 1873, pp. 15–16.
55. *Yale News*, June 7, 1878; *Yale Courant*, October 24,1866. *Iconoclast* of 1873 noted (at p. 5) that "a Bones man is not at liberty to speak of his society or pin in the presence of other human beings, and . . . if reference is made to them he feels deeply wounded and insulted."
56. *College Courant*, June 24, 1868.
57. Mack, *op. cit.*, p. 3.
58. *Yale News*, May 28, 1878; May 29, 1878.
59. "College Journals," *Yale Record*, May 26, 1876, p. 392.
60. Bagg, *op. cit.*, pp. 32, 454–456.
61. *College Courant*, October 29, 1870, p. 283.
62. Bagg, *op. cit.*, pp. 461–467.
63. "History of The Banner," *Yale News*, December 7, 1886.
64. *Statistics of Yale '77*, p. 4; *Iconoclast*, p. 1.

65. *Iconoclast*, pp. 2–6.

66. *Yale Literary Chronicle*, pp. 1, 2, 10, 11, 12, 15.

67. Mack, *op. cit.*, pp. 220–221. *Yale Naughty-Gal All-Man-Ax for 1875*, *op. cit.*, p. 7, says *Seventh Book* was, "written by a sophomore in revenge for having some of his *memorabilia* appropriated by one of the college societies," which was probably Keys, and the Latin motto on that pamphlet's front wrapper begins: "Dum mens grata mane nomen landesquae Seventy-Six."

68. *The Seventh Book of Genesis* (New Haven, Conn.: Methodist Book Concern, 1874), pp. 5–6, 9–10, 15–16.

69. Whittemore, Arthur D., "The Coming Society," *Yale Literary Magazine*, January 1874, pp. [159]–165.

70. *Yale News*, March 11, 1878. While the satire seems mild, at least one senior society member, John Addison Porter 1878, son of one of the founders of Keys, was to write: "During this year [1878] a daily anti–Senior Society newspaper was started and vigorously conducted so as to thwart the society men in every way." Porter, "The Society System of Yale College," *New Englander*, CLXXX, May 1884, p. 377.

71. Law, William H., "The Birth of 'The *Yale News*'," Manuscripts and Archives, Yale University. Law was not wrong about the wire-pulling politics: see Duffy, Herbert S., *William Howard Taft* (New York: Mitton, Balch, 1930), pp. 5–6.

72. "Yale" [William McMurtie Speer] letter to the editor, *Nation*, November 15, 1883.

73. *Nation*, November 22, 1883.

74. *Yale Courant*, November 7, 1866.

75. Mack, *op. cit.*, p. 245, citing Keys scrapbooks for 1867.

76. *Seventh Book of Genesis*, *op. cit.*, pp. 10–13; *Yale Courant*, January 3, 1874; Mack, *op. cit.*, pp. 220–221.

77. *Yale Courant*, May 23, 1874, pp. 348–349.

78. *The Fall of Skull and Bones*, *op. cit.*, p. 7; Andrews, *op. cit.*, p. 43, is probably correct in concluding that "'File and Claw' [was] obviously another manifestation of the chameleon, 'Bull and Stones.'"

79. *Skull and Bones*, Yale Archives Yeg.2 R9 1, p. 1.

80. *The Harvard Advocate*, February 2, 1877, pp. 109–110; *The Princetonian*, February 8, 1877, its very first issue; *New Haven Evening Register*, March 2, 1877.

81. *Seventh Book of Genesis*, *op. cit.*, pp. 14–15; *Yale Courant*, January 17, 1874; Plimpton, *op. cit.*, p. 70.

82. Andrews, *op. cit.*, p. 55.

83. *New Haven Evening Register*, November 11, 1872, listing L. B. Almy, H. E. Benton, A. H. Boardman, E. H. Buckingham, J. A. Clemmer, C. Daring, J. W. Gott, F. C. Goode, D. W. Huntington, H. Meyer, H. E. Sadler, F. J. Shephard, W. C. Stewart, S. N. White, and F. H. Wright.

84. *Yale Naughty-Gal All-man-ax for 1875*, p. 9.

85. *Yale News*, p. 7.

86. Mack, *op. cit.*, pp. 161, 247; *New Haven Daily Palladium*, June 18, 1878.

87. *Yale News*, June 17, 1878; see also the newspaper reports in the *New Haven Evening Register*, June 15, 1878; and the *New Haven Daily Palladium*, June 17, 1878. *Yale News* and *Evening Register* reports are both reprinted in Millegan, *op. cit.*, pp. 477-483.

88. *Yale News*, June 12, 1878; Millegan, *op. cit.*, p. 482.

89. Mack, *op. cit.*, pp. 157, 162; Andrews, *op. cit.*, p. 54; *Yale News*, June 18, 1878.

90. *Yale Year Book*, vol. 1, no. 1, p. 3, the cut and names repeated in *Supplement to the Yale News*, vol. X, no. 10, June 13, 1878; *Yale News*, June 17, 1878, on McDonald's and Wilcox's (otherwise anonymous) editorship of the *Year Book*.

91. "private caucus," Aiken, E. E., "The Secret Society System. IV," *Yale Critic*, June 2, 1882, as expanded, after the semicolon, in his book of the same title (New Haven, Conn.: Tuttle, Morehouse & Taylor, 1882), p. 59. Exclusion of Bonesmen may have occurred earlier: "Some years ago the 'Bones' men put on such airs as to greatly incense their neutral classmates. It resulted in open rupture. 'Bones' men were ostracized in class elections." "Fun in College Societies," *op. cit.*

92. *Yale Courant*, May 23, 1874.

93. Hadley, Arthur, to George Greuner, July 29, 1925, Arthur Hadley Family Papers, Manuscripts and Archives, Yale University ("Hadley Letter").

94. *Yale Courant*, May 22, 1875.

95. Hadley Letter, *op. cit.*

96. *Yale Courant*, May 29, 1875.

97. *Yale Courant*, May 27, 1876, p. 328. The society's legal title was "The Livingston Trust Association."

98. *Yale Courant*, May 29, 1875.

99. Barricaded entry, "Drift of 'Tap Day' Talk," *New-York Evening Post*, May 10, 1913, reprinted in *Yale News* for May 15, 1913, as "A Real History of Tap Day."

100. Hadley Letter, *op. cit.* This book's account of how Tap Day began corrects that given in Pierson, *Yale College 1921–1937, op. cit.*, p. 137

101. "Old Time Society Elections," *Yale Alumni Weekly*, May 23, 1913, reporting that "It is said that the Class of '78, when Juniors, were the first to break up the situation by coming down from their rooms to the stone steps of their entries—Durfee steps for the most part, as the Juniors were quartered there at the time," but the other sources alongside Hadley suggest that it was rather the class of 1877 when juniors presented themselves for the first time on the dormitory steps. *Horoscope* of May 1883 (p. 1), describes "juniors [who] have had their new spring suits padded on the right shoulder in anticipation," and the first appearance of the phrase "Go to your room" appears in *Illustrated Horoscope* for May 1887 (p. 7), and again in May 1889 (p. 3): "the precipitate '*g't'y'room*' is hissed into his willing ear." *Yale News* for May 24, 1878, says that one candidate "retired to his room, heard the prescribed formula, 'I offer you election to the so-called Skull and Bones Society,' and promptly accepted." *Horoscope* of May 1888 writes of a candidate, "padding his shoulder for the heavy hand of a Bones man," and *Yale Illustrated Horoscope* for May 1889 (pp. 1, 3) writes of "shoulders [being] spanked" and "slapped." A *New York Times* article on the expansion of the Bones tomb in 1903, "Change in Skull and Bones," September 13, 1903, similarly dates this change: "Till about 1875 the members of the societies were elected by announcements in their college rooms. Since then the practice of giving elections on the campus at the annual 'tap day,' each person elected being slapped between the shoulders, has been followed."

102. *Yale Alumni Weekly*, May 27, 1903; construction, Pinnell, *op. cit.*, pp. 28–31; fence, Welch and Camp, *op. cit.*, p. 33.

103. "Society Elections. Seniors," *Yale Courant*, May 27, 1876, p. 327.

104. *Yale News*, May 23, 1878, May 23, 1879; *Yale Illustrated Horoscope*, May 1888, p. 3.

105. *Yale Courant*, May 26, 1876.

106. "muzzling," Andrews, *op. cit.*, p. 42; election of anti-society crusaders, Porter, "Senior Society System," *op. cit.*, p. 390.

107. Wood, *College Days, op. cit.*, p. 145; Havemeyer, *Go to Your Room, op. cit.*, pp. 12–14; Bagg, *op. cit.*, pp. 94, 106.

108. Reported in *Yale News*, November 4, 1881.

109. *Yale Courant*, November 15, 1873.

110. McCosh, James, "Discipline in American Colleges," *North American Review*, May–June 1878, p. 433.

111. *Yale Courant*, May 29, 1875, p. 349. The faculty resolution of June 2, 1875, is reprinted in the *Courant* for June 5, 1875, proclaiming that no "secret society [shall] hereafter be formed or exist in the Sophomore class." The song verse is from Wood, *College Days, op. cit.*, p. 136. *Yale Index* which appeared in June 1875 draped the sophomore society lists in funereal black.

112. Goodwin, *op. cit.*, p. 30. Taft's father Alphonso wrote William's younger brothers that he "doubt[ed] that such popularity is consistent with high scholarship," but William protested to his mother: "If a man has to be isolated from his class in order to take a high stand I don't want a high stand. The presidency of Delta Kap takes none of my time except so much as I spend on Saturday night which I should use anyhow. There's got to be some relaxation." Pringle, Henry E., *The Life and Times of William Howard Taft* (New York: Farrar & Rinehart, 1939), vol. 1, p. 35; William Howard Taft to Louise Torrey Taft, November 4, 1874, William Howard Taft Papers, Library of Congress.

113. Andrews, *op. cit.*, pp. 49–51; Sheldon, *op. cit.*, pp. 172–174; initiation details, Patton and Field, *op. cit.*, p. 239.

114. Havemeyer, *op. cit.*, p. 8; *Yale News*, November 17, 1880.

115. Porter, *op. cit.*, p. 195, first printed in the *New Englander* for July 1870 and reprinted in New Haven in *College Courant* for July 17, 1869, p. 40.

116. Rudolph, *The American College, op. cit.*, pp. 148–149.

117. Wood, *College Days, op. cit.*, pp. 281–282; Aiken, Edwin, "The Secret Society System. V," *Yale Critic*, 20 June 1882, p. 2.

CHAPTER SEVEN: THE SOLUTION OF WOLF'S HEAD

1. Andrews, *op. cit.*, p. 56.

2. *Yale Critic*, March 24, 1882, the phrase "free, democratic Yale" being changed in the book version to "in the name of freedom," Aiken, *op. cit.*, p. 9.

3. Aiken, *op. cit.*, pp. 25, 35–37, 46, 53, 57, 61–66. The inherent tension in grading senior society member student performance was mentioned in a newspaper article a decade before: "It is also asserted that preference is shown to them, particularly the members of Skull and Bones, in the studies of the course, and in the examinations by such of the faculty as were members of that organization. That this has ever been intentionally done, I emphatically disbelieve . . . [but] true or not true [such suggestions]—current among the undergraduates, hurt the morale of the college, and tend to destroy the democratic spirit synonymous with Yale. "Yale Senior Societies," *Boston Globe*, July 3, 1873.

4. Porter, John Addison, "Society System," *op. cit.*

5. *New Haven Courier*, November 19, 1883; *Nation*, November 15, 1883.

6. *Yale Literary Magazine*, February 1884, pp. 194–195; *Yale News*, February 4, 1884; "Yale's Latest Tumult," *New-York Evening Post*, February 4, 1884; "Bones and Keys

on Top," *New Haven Morning News*, February 2, 1884; "Lively Times at Yale," *New York Times*, February 2, 1884. Down in New Jersey, *Princetonian* had opined that "the bare defeat of that movement . . . is probably the sounding of the death knell of the secret societies at Yale," February 8, 1884.

7. "Yale's Latest Tumult," *New-York Evening Post*, February 4, 1884; Andrews, *op. cit.*, p. 65.

8. "Yale's Latest Tumult," *op. cit.*

9. *New Haven Daily Palladium*, July 31, 1883.

10. *New Haven Morning News*, February 2, 1884; Andrews, *op. cit.*, pp. 6–8.

11. Andrews, *op. cit.*, pp. 68–69.

12. *Ibid.*, pp. 206, 236.

13. *Idem.*, p. 200.

14. Kelley, *op. cit.*, p. 216; the chapter "Eating Clubs" in Beers, *op. cit.*, pp. 100–132. On the Moriarty's menu, Thompson, Henry C. M., *op. cit.*, p. 121, and Gitlin, Jay, and Baisie Bales Gitlin, *Mory's A Brief History* (Mory's Preservation, Inc.: New Haven, 2014), p. 10.

15. Thompson, *op. cit.*, pp. 7, 17, 75, 96, and 166; Andrews, *op. cit.*, p. 195.

16. Andrews, *op. cit.*, pp. 195, 208, 212–213. Bowen considered his eating club, "to be a unique one, for it consisted for the most part of pre-eminent names," apparently an oblique reference to the Bones and Keys members as well as his future clubmates in Wolf's Head.

17. Andrews, *op. cit.*, p. 209.

18. *Ibid.*, p. 297.

19. Pinnell, *op. cit.*, pp. 28–30, 62, 106.

20. Steiner, *op. cit.*, p. 181; Andrews, *op. cit.*, pp. 197, 201: "The private seats were then a drug on the market. One day a student was found to be buying them up at 25 cents a seat. The mystification was intense until his study was visited. There the seats were hanging on the wall. Within each seat was framed a portrait of a member of the faculty."

21. The *Yale Courant*, May 29, 1875, p. 341, writing of onlookers, "commenting on the Bones in the severest terms for leaving out a most worthy man who deserved an election if any one ever did;" May 27, 1876, pp. 322–323, 327. In his *New Englander* essay, Porter defines "suping" as "currying favor with society men," Porter, *op. cit.*, p. 392.

22. *Horoscope*, May [15], 1883.

23. Andrews, *op. cit.*, p. 74.

24. *Ibid.*, pp. 78–79.

25. *Idem.*, pp. 80–84.

26. Patton and Field, *Eight O'Clock Chapel: A Study of New England College Life in the Eighties* (Boston, Mass., and New York: Houghton Mifflin, 1927), p. 115; "Funeral of E. J. Phelps," *New York Times*, March 12, 1909.

27. Andrews, *op. cit.*, p. 84; *Historical Register of Yale University 1701–1937* (New Haven, Conn.: Yale University Press, 1939), p. 540.

28. Andrews, *op. cit.*, pp. 90–91.

29. *Ibid.*, pp. 95–103.

30. *Idem.*, pp. 103–105.

31. *Critic and Good Literature*, March 8, 1884, pp. 109–110.

32. *Critic and Good Literature*, March 22, 1884, p. 137.

ENDNOTES

33. "J. Addison Porter, Dead," *New York Times*, December 18, 1900.

34. Porter, *op. cit.*, pp. 377–393; *Yale News*, March 15, 1878, p. 1. It has been asserted about Porter's article and others appearing in the 1880s and 1890s "laying bare the *sanctum sanctorum* of secret societies, fraternity life, and team sports on campus," that "Articles on Skull and Bones or Hasty Pudding were not meant for alumni, who knew as much as they needed or wanted to know about the collegiate subculture, nor were they describing new developments, for most of the organizations had flourished for decades. Rather, they were aimed at parents who were nongraduates but who were beginning to entertain thoughts of a college education for their children." Kett, *op. cit.*, pp. 184–185.

35. Roth, Leland M., *The Architecture of McKim, Mead & White 1870–1920: A Building List* (New York: Garland, 1978), p. 120.

36. Pinnell, *op. cit.*, pp. 165–166, 174; "Without a Name," *New Haven Palladium*, July 11, 1884. The architectural plans for the "Phelps Association Hall" are in the McKim, Mead & White Architectural Record Collections, PR 42, Department of Prints, Photographs, and Architectural Collections, Rolled Drawings N51 00-284, 4-inch and 2-inch tubes, The New-York Historical Society.

37. Andrews, *op. cit.*, pp. 108–115. According to Havemeyer, *Go to Your Room, op. cit.*, p. 61, "the Egyptian symbol represents the Nile River which is life while the wolf's head means death," and "no member is allowed to wear his pin outside their hall."

38. *Horoscope*, April 1884, pp. 1–2.

39. Andrews, *op. cit.*, pp. 116–117; "diamonds," "Secret Societies of Yale College," *New York Herald*, May 22, 1893; *Horoscope*, May 1885, p. 3.

40. *The New York World*, June 19, 1884.

41. Andrews, *op. cit.*, pp. 119–121.

42. *Yale News*, March 4; March 30, 1885.

43. Welch and Camp, *op. cit.*, p. 107.

44. *Catalogues* of Psi Upsilon and Delta Kappa Epsilon, *op. cit.*

45. Andrews, *op. cit.*, pp. 159–162.

46. *Ibid.*, p. 169.

47. *New Haven Journal and Courier*, January 19, 1886.

48. *New Haven Register*, January 24, 1886.

49. *Idem.* (no other report of Depew's speech has been located); "Chauncey Mitchell Depew, B.A. 1856," *Yale University Obituary Record of Graduates Deceased During The Year Ending July 1, 1928, Number 87* (New Haven, Conn.: published by the University, 1928), pp. 4–8.

50. *Horoscope*, May 1886, p. 2; *Horoscope* (2), May 1886; *Yale Illustrated Horoscope*, May 1887, p. 1.

51. *Horoscope*, May 1886, p. 2; *Illustrated Horoscope*, May 1887, pp. 2–3, 7.

52. Andrews, *op. cit.*, pp. 173–174.

53. *Ibid.*, pp. 178–182.

54. Mack, *op. cit.*, pp. 248–249, quoting a letter dated July 6, 1940 from George E. Eliot, Keys 1886.

55. *Yale Illustrated Horoscope*, May 1888. In its May 1889 issue, the publication returned to this point: "The 'Crab' has recently been taken from its prominent place on the necktie and put in a less conspicuous postion on the vest," commending the change and criticizing Keys for not making it.

56. Mack, *op. cit.*, p. 248; Hughes, *op. cit.*, in Millegan, *op. cit.*, p. 570.
57. Unidentified newspaper quoted in Andrews, *op. cit.*, p. 186; "C. Wyllys Betts Prize," *Yale News*, January 23, 1892.
58. Packard, Lewis R., "The Phi Beta Kappa Society," in Kingsley, *op. cit.*, vol. 1, p. 327.
59. Bagg, *op. cit.*, pp. 228, 231.
60. "Revival of Phi Beta Kappa—Prospects of the Society," *Yale News*, March 10, 1884; "Phi Beta Kappa," *Yale Literary Magazine*, March 1884, pp. 230–231.
61. Voorhees, *op. cit.*, p. 256.
62. *Yale News*, March 10, 1884.
63. *Yale News*, May 1, 1884.
64. *New-York Evening Post*, March 24, 1884.
65. *Yale Literary Magazine*, February 1884, p. 187.

CHAPTER EIGHT: THE THREAT TO YALE DEMOCRACY

1. Wood, John Seymour, *Yale Yarns: Sketches of Life at Yale University* (New York: G. P. Putnam, 1895), p. 22.
2. Pierson, *Yale Book of Numbers*, *op. cit.*, pp. 4–6, 69–70, 81. A census in the *Yale News* for October 22, 1886, showed students from thirty-eight states and territories and eight foreign countries (China, England, Hawaii, India, Japan, Saxony, Mexico, and Turkey) in the college (both Academical and Sheffield parts).
3. Pierson, *ibid.*, p. 85; on age, *New-York Evening Post*, June 16, 1886.
4. Santayana, George, "A Glimpse of Yale," *Harvard Monthly* XV (1892), pp. 92–93, reprinted in *George Santayana's America: Essays on Literature and Culture*, ed. James Ballowe (Urbana: University of Illinois Press, 1967). On Santayana's visit and article, "the most perceptive study of Yale ever penned by a stranger," Pierson, *Yale College 1871–1921, op. cit.*, pp. 5–9, 579.
5. Slosson, *op. cit.*, p. 70; Boston ditty quoted in Amory, *op. cit.*, p. 14; Yale limerick quoted in Astrachan, Anthony, "Class Notes," Dubois, Diana, ed., *My Harvard, My Yale* (New York: Random House, 1982); p. 214; Corbin, John, *Which College for the Boy? Leading Types in American Education* (Boston, Mass.: Houghton Mifflin, 1908), p. 18; Wilson, Edmund, "Harvard, Princeton, and Yale," *Forum*, September 1923, 70, p. 1874.
6. Bagg, *op. cit.*, p. 521. In *Stover at Yale*, Le Baron tells Stover about "the right crowd" who run things: "Money won't land a man in it, and there'll be some in it who work their way through college." Johnson, *op. cit.*, p. 27.
7. "valets," Slosson, *op. cit.*, p. 70; Jenkins, A. E., *Lippincott's*, vol. 40, 1887–1888, p. 293; see also Johnson, Owen, "The Social Usurpation of Our Colleges III—Yale," *Collier's*, June 8, 1912, p. 23, on prior disfavor to rich students' keeping of horses, and then automobiles.
8. Dwight, Timothy, *What A Yale Student Ought To Be* (New Haven, Conn.: Yale University, 1887), pp. 16–17.
9. Hadley, "University Progress," *Yale Alumni Weekly*, March 6, 1914, p. 642; Santayana, *op. cit.*, p. 94.
10. Gilman, Daniel Coit, *The Launching of a University and Other Papers* (New York: Dodd, Mead, 1906), p. 191.
11. Slosson, *op. cit.*, p. 66.
12. Lewis, Harry S[inclair]., "Unknown Undergraduates," *Yale Literary Magazine*, June 1906, pp. 335–338.

ENDNOTES

13. "equality of opportunity," Pierson, George Wilson, *Yale College 1871–1921* (New Haven, Conn.: Yale University Press, 1953), p. 42, and "'Stover At Yale'—An Explanation," *Yale Alumni Weekly*, March 29, 1912; Hadley, Arthur T., in Norton, Charles Eliot, Arthur T. Hadley, William M. Sloane, and Brander Matthews, *Four American Universities* (New York: Harper & Brothers, 1895), p. 83; Camp, Walter, "Senior Society Elections at Yale," pp. 74–79; "'Tap Day' at Yale," *New York Tribune*, May 18, 1901.

14. *Yale 1883: The Book of the Class Compiled after the Quartercentury Reunion* (printed for the class: 1910), p. 51.

15. Franklin, *op. cit.*, p. 10; Johnson, *op. cit.*, p. 246; Wendell, Barrett, *Harvard Monthly*, December 1901, 33, p. 101; "Yale Facing the Biggest Crisis in Its History," *New York Times*, April 6, 1913; man of action, DeVane, Clyde, "The College in a National University," in *Seventy-Five: A Study of a Generation in Transition* (New Haven, Conn.: Yale Daily News, 1953), p. 6.

16. Syrett, *op. cit.*, p. 137; Stimson quoted, Hodges, *op. cit.*, p. 37; Stimson, Henry, and McGeorge Bundy, *On Active Service in Peace and War* (New York: Harper & Brothers, 1948), p. xv.

17. Arnold, George A., "American Yale," *Yale Literary Magazine*, June 1902, pp. 337–338.

18. Berman, Pemberton, "The Spirit of Boyishness," *Yale Literary Magazine*, May 1902, pp. 291–292; Farrand, "Summa Cum Laude," quoted in *Yale News*, March 17, 1910; "Yale College," *Scribner's*, *op. cit.*, p. 594; Pierson, *op. cit.*, pp. 117–120, on Hadley, and p. 269.

19. Lord, Franklin A., "Scholarship," *Yale Literary Magazine*, April 1897, p. 29; Slosson, *op. cit.*, p. 47; Ehrich quoted in Oren, Dan A., *Joining the Club: A History of Jews and Yale* (New Haven, Conn., and London: Yale University Press, 1985), pp. 12–13. Ehrich's conclusion is odd: Bones tapped both the valedictorian and salutatorian for the class of 1868, and the valedictorian for Ehrich's class of 1869, along with eight other members of Phi Beta Kappa, including three men whose high stand was sufficient for them to be named tutors after they graduated.

20. Oviatt, Edwin S., "On Shams," *Yale Literary Magazine*, January 1896, p. 134; Report of the Committee on Numbers and Scholarship, Yale College, April 1903 (the "Fisher Report"), Yale College Committee Records, Manuscripts and Archives, Yale University, p. 131, discussed and excerpted in Pierson, *Yale College, op. cit.*, pp. 238–242; "intellectual attainments," *Yale Alumni Weekly* May 31, 1905; Parmalee, Maurice, "Yale and the Academic Ideal," *Yale Courant*, December 1906, p. 129; *Yale Courant* statistics cited and discussed in Slosson, *op. cit.*, pp. 67–68; Harvard finals clubs elections and Phi Beta Kappa, Johnson, Owen, "The Social Usurpation of Our Colleges II—Harvard," *Collier's*, May 25, 1912, p. 14; Hadley quoted in *New York Times*, June 23, 1915.

21. "Yale system," Nettleton, George Henry, "On Realities," *Yale Literary Magazine*, February 1896, p. 178 (Nettleton had been tapped for Keys, class of 1896, and later became chair of Yale's English Department and then dean of Yale College); Johnson, *Stover, op. cit.*, p. 16.

22. Canby, Henry Seidel, *Alma Mater: The Gothic Age of the American College* (New York: Farrar and Rinehart, 1936), pp. 130–131; "History of Music at Yale," *Yale News*, April 18, 1891. The Glee and Banjo Clubs toured the country with concerts. *Yale News*, April 15, 1882.

23. Fisher Report, *op. cit.*, p. 131; Paine, Ralph, *College Years* (New York: Scribner's, 1909), p. 242; Canby, *op. cit.*, p. 71; Johnson, *op. cit.*, p. 321.

24. Holbrook, Richard, *Boys and Men: A Story of Life at Yale* (New York: Scribner's, 1900), pp. 59–60; Rudolph, *American Colleges, op. cit.*, pp. 148–149; Rudolph, *Mark Hopkins, op. cit.*, p. 116; *New York Tribune*, May 30, 1892.

25. Thwing, Charles, "College Men First Among Successful Citizens," *Forum* 15 (June 1893), p. 500; Santayana, *op. cit.*, p. 95; "Prominent Yale Graduates," *Yale News*, December 6, 1887; "Yale Men in Congress," *Yale News*, 1891; on Theodore Roosevelt, Wilmarth Lewis, *op. cit.*, pp. 94–95.

26. "literary college," Bledstein, *op. cit.*, p. 239; Slosson, *op. cit.*, p. 59. This notion persisted for at least the next century: one character in *The Paragon*, John Knowles's novel of 1971 about the Yale of 1953 (New York: Random House, p. 16), says to a classmate: "You've got to understand that Yale is Wall Street and the State Department and all that, Yale is, well, Yale is American success, much more so than Harvard, Harvard is too idiosyncratic, and much more so than Princeton, Princeton is too casual, too Southern-oriented."

27. "Secret Societies at Yale," *Harper's*, February 7, 1874, pp. 125–126; Hughes, Robert, "Secret Societies at Yale," *Munsey's*, June 1894, reprinted in Millegan, *op. cit.*, p. 571; Sheldon, *Student Life, op. cit.*, pp. 176–177; Nettleton, George Henry, "American Universities and Colleges. I—Yale University," *Frank Leslie's Popular Monthly*, November 1896, p. 499; magazine short stories include R. E. Hallock's "The Last Man Tapped, a Tale of the New Haven Campus," *Gunter's Magazine*, September 1906, and Mary Raymond Shipman Andrews's "The Courage of the Commonplace," *Scribner's*, July 1911; "Happy Yale Juniors. Selected for Election to Skull and Bones and Scroll and Keys," *New York Times*, May 28, 1886; "Members of the Wolf Head," June 2, 1886. *New York Tribune* also published election results with commentary, e.g. "Yale Senior Elections," May 28, 1892, as did the Hartford *Times*, e.g., May 27, 1892.

28. Horowitz, Helen, *op. cit.*, p. 12; Rudolph, *Mark Hopkins, op. cit.*, p. 116; Slosson, *op. cit.*, pp. 59–60; Geiger, Roger, ed., *The American College in the Nineteenth Century* (Nashville, Tenn.: Vanderbilt University Press, 2000), pp. 14–15.

29. Beers, Henry, *The Ways of Yale in the Consulship of Plancus* (New York: Henry Holt, 1895), p. 10.

30. "Dwight Hall," *Yale News*, September 1, 1886; "History of Dwight Hall," *Yale News*, December 20, 1886; Welch and Camp, *op. cit.*, p. 52; Slosson, *op. cit.*, p. 58; Gabriel, *op. cit.*, pp. 189–191; Arnold, *op. cit.*, p. 338; "Dwight Hall ring," Pierson, *Yale College, op. cit.*, p. 13; "Bones tunnel," *Horoscope*, April 1889, p. 1, and *Yale Illustrated Horoscope*, [May] 1891, p. 2; Goodrich refusal, "Yale Senior Societies," *New York Tribune*, June 7, 1896 In *Stover at Yale, op. cit.*, p. 205, a character opines about the "Bones list," "You've got to include the pitcher of the nine and the president of Dwight Hall, haven't you?"

31. Slosson, *op. cit.*, p. 59.

32. Welch and Camp, *op. cit.*, pp. 62–64; Patton and Field, *op. cit.*, pp. 220–223; "happy communion," Pierson, *op. cit.*, p. 14; "Pope," Fish and Runk, eds., *Horoscope*, [May] 1892, p. 1; "Student Handbook," *Yale News*, September 27, 1887.

33. Smith, Ronald, *op. cit.*, pp. 73, 84–87; "muckers," Kelley, *op. cit.*, p. 302; on Camp's contributions, see Marshall, John S., "Walter Camp and His Gridiron Game," *American Heritage* XII (October 1961), pp. 50–55, 77–81.

34. "athletic field purchase," Steiner, *op. cit.*, pp. 218–219; "friction," Presbrey, Frank, ed., *Athletics at Princeton* (New York: Frank Presbey, 1901), p. 56.

ENDNOTES

35. Camp, Walter, "Yale Athletics, A Review of Its History," *Illustrated American* (April 19, 1890), p. 27.

36. Smith, *op. cit.*, pp. 122, 148; "Rah! Rah! Rah! Yale!," *Yale News*, July 1, 1887. Poem by B. A. Gould Jr., Harvard '91, in *Echoes of the Harvard-Yale Football Game of 1890 Being A Collection of Ephemeral But Entertaining Expressions of Rejoicings of the Hour* (Cambridge, Mass.: Charles H. Thurston, December 1890).

37. Welch and Camp, *op. cit.*, p. 453; Canby, *op. cit.*, p. 26.

38. Rader, Benjamin G., *American Sports from the Age of Folk Games to the Age of Spectators* (Englewood Cliffs, N.J.: Prentice-Hall, 1983), pp. 20–26.

39. *Yale News*, April 10; May 9; and May 18, 1888; the volume's full title is *A History of Yale Athletics 1840–1888 Giving Every Contest with Harvard, Princeton, Pennsylvania, Columbia, Wesleyan, and Others in Rowing, Foot Ball, Base Ball, Track Athletics, Tennis.*

40. 1905 statistics, Robbins, *op. cit.*, pp. 69–70; "Standing of the Athletic Men in '90, '91, and '92," *Yale News*, January 23, 1891; "Standing of the Editors of the College Papers," *Yale News*, January 30, 1891.

41. Figures taken from Fisher Report, *op. cit.*, p. 129, with regard to junior prom chairmen, class deacons, and *Lit.* editors, and otherwise compiled from society and fraternity catalogues and issues of *Horoscope*. In Meade Minnigerode's novel about his class of 1910, *The Big Year: A College Story* (New York and London: G. P. Putnam, 1921), p. 215, a character says: "I don't see why you should go [be tapped for] anything, Benson, just because you're president of the Glee Club—unless Keys needs you to sing tenor over there on Thursday nights!"

42. Welch and Camp, *op. cit.*, p. 98; *Horoscope*, May 1898, pp. 5–6. On the Ten Eyck, see "According to Tradition," *Yale Alumni Weekly*, April 23, 1902.

43. Holbrook, Richard, *op. cit.*, p. 37; Welch and Camp, *op. cit.*, p. 98; Fisher Report, *op. cit.*, p. 129; "Yale Society Elections," *New-York Evening Post*, May 24, 1900.

44. Holbrook, *op. cit.*, p. 54.

45. Canby, *American Memoir, op. cit.*, pp. 152, 156, 166–167, 169.

46. *Yale '97 Class Book*, p. 42; Wooster, James Willet, *Edward Stephen Harkness 1874–1940* (New York: William E. Rudge, 1949), pp. 26, 28–29; Pierson, *Yale: The University College 1921–1937, op. cit.*, pp. 213–215; Kelley, *op. cit.*, p. 91; Betsky, Aaron, *James Gamble Rogers and the Architecture of Pragmatism* (Cambridge, Mass.: MIT Press, 1994), pp. 4–5, 55–61, 104, 140, 153, 155.

47. Pinnell, *op. cit.*, pp. 56–57.

48. Howland, *op. cit.*, pp. 21–22.

49. *Statistics of Yale, '74*, pp. 20–21. Smyth, Nathan Ayer, "The Democratic Idea in College Life," *Yale Literary Magazine*, April 1896, pp. 272–276; *Yale Horoscope*, May 1891, pp. 5–9.

50. "Yale Societies Doomed," *New York Times*, December 8, 1900; Havemeyer, *op. cit.*, pp. 16–19; Pierson, *Yale College, op. cit.*, pp. 234–237; *Horoscope*, May 1901, p. 10; Horoscope, [May] 1901, p. 6. For years afterwards, one member from each of Scroll and Key and Skull and Bones were appointed as members of the defuct sophomore society Eta Phi, "so that things would be handed down in perpetuity in case they should ever be revived," as Henry Luce, the 1920 Bones appointee, wrote his parents. Brinkley, *op. cit.*, p. 74.

51. Nettleton, George Henry, "On Realities," *Yale Literary Magazine*, February 1896, p. 179.

52. *New York Times*, May 29, 1893; Welch, Flexner and Flexner, *op. cit.*, p. 45; Nettleton, "American Universities and Colleges," *op. cit.*, p. 500.

53. *Yale Illustrated Horoscope*, May 1888, pp. 1–2, 4, 6.

54. *Horoscope*, April 1899, p. 5.

55. *Frank Leslie's Illustrated Weekly*, May 29. 1907, p. 823.

56. Flexner and Flexner, *op. cit.*, pp. 174–175.

57. *Horoscope*, May 1885, p. 2.

58. *Yale Literary Magazine*, June 1885, p. 379–380; June 1887, p. 389; June 1888, p. 430; June 1889, pp. 432–433; June 1896, pp. 408–409; June 1899, p. 448; June 1890, p. 439; June 1900, p. 426; June 1903, p. 342; "Yale Announcements," *New York Times*, May 24, 1889; *Yale Alumni Weekly*, May 30, 1906.

59. "Yale Society Elections," *New-York Evening Post*, May 24, 1901; "Tap Day at Yale," *New York Times*, May 24, 1901; "Intense Feeling At Yale," *New York Tribune*, May 24, 1901; "Yale Men Slurred by Senior Societies," *New York Herald*, May 24, 1901; "Skip Gould and Vanderbilt," *New Haven Register*, May 24, 1901; "Stop at Captain Gould," *New Haven Daily Palladium*, May 24, 1901; *Yale Alumni Weekly*, May 29, 1901.

60. "Tap Day Surprises Many," *New Haven Palladium*, May 22, 1903; "Yale Tap Day Exercises," *New Haven Journal and Courier*, May 26, 1905; "Several Surprises at Yale's 'Tap Day' Exercises," *New York* [*Times* or *Herald* or *Tribune*], May 23, 1903; *Yale Alumni Weekly*, May 27, 1903; "Yale's Brightest Man a Farmer," *New York World*, June 14, 1904. Pierce received his MA degree at Yale in 1905, and a PhD in 1908; a member of the faculty there from 1906, he became associate professor of English in 1926, but advanced no further in the faculty, and committed suicide in 1935 after several years of ill health (a path eerily similar to that of Keysman Denny Hansen, discussed in chapter 12 below).

61. *Ibid.*, *New York World*.

62. "No Society For Shevlin," *New Haven Evening Register*, May 26, 1905.

63. "so-called surprises," *Yale Alumni Weekly*, May 28, 1902.

64. *Horoscope*, [May] 1892, p. 3.

65. *The Yale Illustrated Horoscope*, [May] 1891, p. 4; Minnegerode, *op. cit.*, p. 217; "It Is Touch and Go at Yale," New York Sun, May 27, 1894.

66. May 1891 *Illustrated Horoscope*, p. 2; *Yale Alumni Weekly*, 29 May 1907, p. 823.

67. Wilson, *op. cit.*, p. 1876; *Frank Leslie's Illustrated Weekly Newspaper*, 8 June 1893.

68. *History of the Class of Eighteen Hundred Ninety-Nine, Yale College* (New Haven, Conn.: 1919), p. 18.

69. "As To Tap Day," *Yale Alumni Weekly*, 27 May 1903. Another, longer letter, relating the same history and almost certainly from the same correspondent, "A Graduate of the Seventies," titled "Discussion of 'Tap Day,'" appeared in the *Yale Alumni Weekly* for June 24, 1905, p. 759.

70. Gavit, John Palmer, "Social Barriers and 'Hush Dope' at Yale," *New York Post*, May 15, 1922; Stewart, *op. cit.*, p. 60.

71. "little mingling," "Yale's Happy Forty-Five," *New-York Evening Post*, May 20, 1911; "no athletic training," "It Is Touch and Go at Yale," *New York Sun*, May 27, 1894; Depew, "Hadley Elected President of Yale," *New Haven Daily Palladium*, May 26, 1899; building vantage points, "The Yale Senior Societies," *New Haven Journal and Courier*, May 27, 1898; crowd composition, "Yale's Tap Day Guerdons," *New-York*

Evening Post, May 20, 1910; poem, Hooker, *Achievements of the Class of 1902, Yale College, from Birth to the Year 1912* (1913), p. 106.

72. "annual meeting" and policeman's gossip, "Yale's Tap Day Tremors," *New-York Evening Post*, May 19, 1911; Dwight Hall balcony audience, "Tap-Day Surprises Many," *New Haven Daily Palladium*, May 22, 1903; "Tap Day on Yale Campus," *New York Sun*, May 26, 1905; automobiles and Durfee and Farnam windows, *Yale Alumni Weekly*, May 29, 1907, p. 828; "Mory's" and "lined with hacks" and the tappers' campus entry points, Minnigerode, *op. cit.*, pp. 222, 224; "Secret Societies of Yale College," *New York Herald*, May 22, 1893; "heathenish rite," "It Is a Weird Ceremony That Takes Candidates into Yale's Secret Societies," *New York Herald*, Conn. section, May 27, 1906; separate gate entries, "'Go to Your Room, Sir!' Tap Day Same on Yale Campus," *New York Herald*, May 24, 1905; "gallery . . . mothers," *Yale Alumni Weekly*, May 31, 1905; Pass of Thermopylae, Kelley, *op. cit.*, p. 307; Welch and Camp, *op. cit.*, pp. 99–10.

73. "young Hercules," "'Taps' Given to 45 Yale Juniors," *Hartford Courant*, May 24, 1907, and also "Lucky Yale Men," *New Haven Daily Palladium*, May 28, 1897; "melancholy visage," "Yale Senior Societies," *New York Tribune*, June 7, 1896; black suites and derbies, Pierson, *Yale College 1921–1937, op. cit.*, p. 137; last Wolf's Head elector, *New Haven Daily Palladium*, May 27, 1898; MacLeish, *New Haven Journal-Courier*, May 21, 1915; "up a tree," "Yale's Happy Forty-Five," *New-York Evening Post*, May 20, 1911; high vantage points, *Yale Alumni Weekly*, June 1, 1904; fifteen minutes, "Wait for Chapel Chimes at Five," *New Haven Courier*, May 28, 1908; Wolf's Head precipitate tap, *New Haven Daily Palladium*, May 28, 1909; pace, *Yale Alumni Weekly*, May 30, 1906, p. 771; "halfway across," "Yale Tap Day Brings out Many Campus Callers," *New Haven Evening Register*, May 25, 1906; "Yale's Juniors Slapped," *New Haven Evening Register*, May 28, 1897; Robinson second tap, "Surprises at Yale Tap Day," *New Haven Journal and Courier*, May 20, 1910, and "Tap Day Is Held at Yale," *New Haven Daily Palladium*, May 20, 1910.

74. "cheers," "The Secret Society System at Yale," *The Kappa Alpha Journal*, vol. VIII, no. 9, June 1891, p. 507; fainting, Johnson, *op. cit.*, p. 208, and in Clarke, "Senior Society Elections," *New Haven Journal and Courier*, June 26, 1899; "cry," *New York Sun, op. cit.*; Wolf's Head precipitate tap, *New Haven Palladium*, May 28, 1909; on Hoyt, *New York Herald*, May 24, 1895; circle of singers, *Yale Alumni Weekly*, May 29, 1907, p. 828, and June 12, 1907, p. 876; "boarding house," *New Haven Daily Palladium*, May 26, 1899.

75. "first touched," *New York Sun, op. cit.*; "honor man" and "last man chosen," "Tap Day on Campus," *New Haven Journal and Courier*, May 27, 1898; Hallock, R. E., "The Last Man Tapped," *Gunter's Magazine*, September 1906, p. 166; "Tap Day Quiet at Yale," *Daily Princetonian*, May 16, 1913; Camp, Walter, *Jack Hall at Yale: A Football Story* (New York and London: D. Appleton, 1909), p. 163.

76. "Few Tap Day Surprises," *New Haven Journal and Courier*, May 27, 1905; "dope sheets," "Dray Passed by at Yale Tap Day," *New Haven Evening Register*, May 27, 1907, and "Yale's Tap Day Tremors," *New-York Evening Post*, May 19, 1911; Kirkpatrick, *Daily Princetonian*, May 20, 1910; Rosey's dope sheet, Stewart, *op. cit.*, p. 60, and Oren, *op. cit.*, p. 337. On the Rosenberg patriarch's trick of writing a society candidate's name and sealing it in an envelope before elections, see Havemeyer, Loomis, *Out of Yale's Past* (New Haven, n.d.), pp. 84–86. In Rosey's obituary notice

in the college newspaper, it was said that he was an honorary member of all six senior societies. *Yale Daily News*, May 5, 1951.

77. *New York Sun, op. cit.*; Minnigerode, *op. cit.*, pp. 207–208, 211–212; *Buffalo Courier*, [Sept. or Oct.] 1892, cited by Mack, *op. cit.*, n. 99, p. 250; "Skull and Bones Has Chimney Fire," *New Haven Journal-Courier*, November 29, 1909. The "burly naked arm shoot[ing] forth to clutch and drag in the proselytes" is reported once more in *Time* for May 31, 1926, and described again in Travis Ingraham's 1931 novel, *Young Gentlemen, Rise* (New York: Farrar & Rinehart, 1930, p. 28): "Down out of nowhere like an axe descending fell a gigantic white arm, culminating in a large hand which fastened about the neck of the neophyte, yanked him within."

78. "Secret Society System at Yale," *op. cit.*, pp. 505–506; *Buffalo Courier, op. cit.*; trial testimony, "Yale Senior Societies," *New York Tribune*, June 7, 1896; "Has Taps Sounded for Tap Day?," *New York Evening Telegraph*, March 30, 1913, reporting that Wolf's Head also marched two by two with a left foot heavy stomp; Vaill, Noah, *Stover in Bones* (n. p.: privately printed, 1913), pp. 42–43.

79. Porter's essay reprinted in Kimball, Robert, ed., *Cole: A Biographical Essay by Brendan Gill* (Woodstock, N.Y. and New York: Overlook Press, 2004), p. 21; Walker, Charles R., ed., *The Collected Poems of H. Phelps Putnam* (New York: Farrar Strauss & Giroux, 1971), p. 14, third of six numbered sonnets. The second stanza of the sonnet VI contains another hidden society reference: *"Then say that we were bells cast into flesh, /And every wind that rustled in our blood/Stirred in our skulls clear poignant chimes and fresh/And poured them out a brilliant dreamful flood."* (p. 17).

80. *New York Tribune*, June 7, 1896; *New Haven Courant*, September 19, 1895; undershirt, Stewart, *op. cit.* p. 73.

81. Mack, *op. cit.*, pp. 92–93; "Scroll and Key," *New York World*, May 25, 1892; "Scroll and Key Society," *New York Tribune*, May 31, 1892; Twichell sermon, Twichell Papers, Beinecke Rare Book & Manuscript Library, Yale.

82. A. D. White to F. Burton Harrison, May 15, 1895.

83. Hitler's silverware in Wolf's Head, Singer, Mark, "Our Far-Flung Correspondents: La Cabeza De Villa," *New Yorker*, November 27, 1989, p. 111, and Rosenbaum, Ron, "The Last Secrets of Skull and Bones: An Elegy for Mumbo-Jumbo," *Esquire*, September 1977, reprinted in Rosenbaum's *The Secret Parts of Fortune* (New York: Random House, 2000), p. 139, saying the utensils are in Scroll and Key; Minnigerode, *op. cit.*, p. 205; doorway ornamentation, "In Shadow of Skull and Bones," *New-York Evening Post*, May 4, 1912; *Time*, May 31, 1926; Pringle, Henry, "Young Men on the Make," *Harper's*, January 1929, p. 153; autobiography coffin and its nonexistence, and Bones whore and her nonexistence, Holahan, David, "The Bad News Bones," *Hartford Courant*, May 29, 1988; sanctification of objects in tombs, Vaill, Noah, *Stover in Bones* (n. p.: privately published, May 15, 1913), p. 42. Before being incorporated into his novel, Minnigerode published the Tap Day chapter "Hush Stuff" in *Collier's* for February 26, 1921, where it was illustrated by Raymond Moreau Crosby, Keys 1898.

84. Robert Taft tap, "Few Surprises at Tap Day," *New Haven Evening Register*, May 8, 1909. Robert Taft affected some indifference, writing his mother before Tap Day in May 1909: "There is great excitement thorugh our class especially. Some people take it terribly seriously, but I can't feel that it really decides very much." Patterson, James, *Mr. Republican: A Biography of Robert Taft* (Boston, Mass.: Houghton Mifflin,

1972), p. 38. The William Howard Taft nucleus of fellow Bonesmen in federal service was to be rivaled again thirty years later in the administrations of Franklin Roosevelt, when Secretary of War Henry Stimson called on Allan Klots (1909, special assistant to the secretary of state), Harvey Bundy (1909, assistant secretary of state and then special assistant to the secretary of war), and George Harrison (1910, special consultant to the secretary of war), while serving with Archibald MacLeish (1915, assistant secretary of state), Robert Lovett (1918, assistant secretary of war for air), and Averell Harriman (1913, ambassador to the U.S.S.R.), making a tiny clique of wealthy Republicans serving a Democratic president. Hodgson, *op. cit.*, pp. 246–247.

85. "Secret Society System at Yale," *op. cit.*, p. 506; basement wall lists, Johnson, *op. cit.*, pp. 287, 344, and *New York Sun*, "Tap Day on Yale Campus," May 26, 1905; bets, *New York Sun*, *op. cit.*; Harriman wagers, "'Taps' on Rubber Coats," *New York Tribune*, May 17, 1912.

86. *New York Sun*, *op. cit.*; *Horoscope*, May 1886, p. 1, noted that those tapped would miss chapel as "the effects of initiation last night might last for several days," and *Yale Illustrated Horoscope* for May 1891 wrote of "the privilege of partaking of the dilute lemonade and corn starch ice cream which Bones supplies its chosen men"; Benét, Stephen Vincent, *The Beginning of Wisdom* (New York: Henry Holt, 1921), pp. 104–105; Wilson, *op. cit.*, p. 1875. Wilson also discussed the Yale senior society system in his memoirs in *New Yorker* for May 6, 1967, pp. 98–100: "I felt a certain respect for the importance given at Yale to intellectual achievement. Scholarship counted as well as athletics, and the editor of the *Yale News* and the editor of the *Yale Lit.* were ex officio tapped from Bones. At Princeton [c. 1912–1916], you had no incentive to excel in any such pursuit."

87. Fisher Report, *op. cit.*, pp. 3, 62, 132; "Yale's Juniors Slapped," *New Haven Evening Register*, May 28, 1897; "Yale's Tap Day Elections. Nephew of Secretary Taft Fails to Get into Any Senior Society," *New York Times*, May 25, 1906.

88. Hooker, *op. cit.*, pp. 3–5, 9, 11; "New Yale Senior Club," *New York Times*, March 21, 1903; "Wealthy Yale Men Form 'Open' Club," *New York Herald*, March 21, 1903; *Yale Alumni Weekly*, March 18, 1903; "On March 20th the Elihu Club announced its existence publicly," *Yale College Class Book 1903* (New Haven, Conn.: June 1903), p. 182; *Yale Literary Magazine*, June 1903, p. 344; "elections by mail," and varying numbers of members, Minnigerode, *op. cit.*, pp. 207–208; *Horoscope*, May 1903; *Suitable Quarters: Elihu Celebrates The 100th Anniversary of Its Landmark Home on New Haven Green*, pp. 1–2, 5.

89. Brown, Elizabeth Mills, *New Haven, A Guide to Architecture and Urban Design* (New Haven: Yale University Press, 1976), p. 64; Federal Writers Project, *Connecticut: A Guide to its Roads, Lore, and People* (Boston, Mass.: Houghton Mifflin Company, 1938), p. 235; Pinnell, *op. cit.*, pp. 108–109; *Suitable Quarters, op. cit.*, p. 5.

90. Pfister, Joel, *The Yale Indian: The Education of Henry Roe Cloud* (Durham, N.C.: Duke University Press, 2009), pp. 2, 15, 46–47, 50, 58–63, 68–69, 73. Henry Roe Cloud's personal Elihu Club delegation photograph is to be found in the Ravi D. Goel Collection of Henry Roe Cloud, Manuscripts and Archives, Yale University. In 1907 for the class of 1908, eight days after Tap Day, Elihu elected fourteen men, including the president of the dramatic association, the treasurer of Dwight Hall, the track team captain, the Apollo Glee Club leader, and the tennis team captain, so it

was fulfilling the function of recognizing leaders in all walks of campus life omitted by the three senior societies. *Yale Alumni Weekly*, June 15, 1907, p. 852. Notably, a Chinese American, Bartlett Golden Yung, son of Yung Wing, LL.D. 1854 (and DKE member), and Mary Louise Kellogg, was elected to Wolf's Head in 1902; born in Hartford, Conn., he went to Shanghai to work from 1912 onward.

CHAPTER NINE: THE CONFUSIONS OF STOVER AND DISRUPTIONS OF WAR

1. Johnson, *op. cit.*, p. 342.
2. Schiff, Judith, introduction to Johnson, Owen, *Stover at Yale* (New Haven, Conn.: The Yale Bookstore, 1997), p. vi.
3. Quoted in DelBanco, Andrew, "Colleges: An Endangered Species," *New York Review of Books*, March 10, 2005. Fitzgerald's biographer says that at Princeton, Fitzgerald "planned to succeed according to the guidelines set forth in Owen Johnson's *Stover at Yale*." Bruccoli, Matthew, *Some Sort of Epic Grandeur* (New York and London: Harcourt Brace Jovanovich, 1981), p. 43.
4. *Yale Alumni Weekly*, May 3, 1912; Halberstam, Michael J., "Stover at the Barricades," *American Scholar*, vol. 38, No. 3, Summer, 1969, p. 470.
5. Morison, Elting E., ed., *The Letters of Theodore Roosevelt* (Cambridge, Mass.: Harvard University Press, 1954), vol. VII, 433–434.
6. Lamoreaux, David, "*Stover At Yale* and the Gridiron Metaphor," *Journal of Popular Culture*, vol. XI, Fall 1977, pp. 331, 333; "novel with a purpose," Johnson, quoted in *Current Literature*, July 1912, p. 95.
7. Lewis, Sinclair, "Owen Johnson Himself," *Book News Monthly*, May 1912, p. 625; Lamoreaux, *op. cit.*, p. 341 n. 19.
8. Johnson, *op. cit.*, pp. 13, 29, 79, 210, 265–266, 273, 276, 288, 330, 332, 342, 385–386.
9. Higgs, Robert J., "Yale and the heroic ideal, *Götterdämerung* and palingenisis, 1865–1914," in Mangin, J. A., and James Walvin, *Manliness and Morality: Middle-Class Masculinity in Britain and America 1800–1940* (Manchester, England: Manchester University Press, 1987), p. 170.
10. See generally, on republic civil individualism and liberal individualism, Robert B. Bellah, Richard Madsen, William M. Sullivan, Ann Swidler, and Steven M. Tipton, *Habits of the Heart: Individualism and Commitment in American Life* (New York: Collier, 1968).
11. Mack, *op. cit.*, p. 179. A substantial excerpt was reprinted in *Yale Alumni Weekly* itself, April 5, 1912, and the book itself was reviewed there in the issue of May 3, 1912, identifying it as "a philippic directed against certain tendencies and facts at present-day American universities in general, and Yale in particular . . . " while an editorial of May 17, 1912, complained that "the human nature in Yale's Campus institutions has been translated into sinister influences, their immense and long proven power for good ignored."
12. *New York Times*, March 25, 1912, and March 31, 1912.
13. Johnson, Owen, "The Social Usurpation of Our Colleges II—Harvard," *Collier's*, May 25, 1912, p. 14. The other articles in the series appeared on May 18 and on June 8, 5, and 22.
14. Johnson, Owen, "The Social Usurpation of Our Colleges III—Yale," *Collier's*, June 8, 1912, pp. 12–13, 23–25.
15. Mack, *op. cit.*, pp. 180–181.

16. Johnson, "III—Yale," *op. cit.*, p. 25; Johnson, *Stover, op. cit.*, p. 335.

17. "1912 Vindicates Social System," *Yale News*, May 9, 1912; "45 Juniors 'Tapped' in the Rain," *New York Herald*, May 17, 1912.

18. "Society Men Locked Out," *New Haven Journal-Courier*, May 24, 1912; "Yale Gates Glued Shut on Society Men," *New York Times*, May 24, 1912.

19. Harriman estate, Smith, Sally Bedell, *Reflected Glory: The Life of Pamela Churchill Harriman* (New York: Simon & Schuster, 1976), p. 82, and Abramson, Rudy, *Spanning the Century: The Life of Averell Harriman, 1891–1986* (New York: William Morrow, 1992, p. 91; Harriman on Porcellian, Isaacson and Thomas, *op. cit.*, p. 82. On the decades-long interplay of the Harriman family and Skull and Bones, see Robbins, *op. cit.*, pp. 164–166.

20. Stewart, Donald, "The Higher Learning in America II—Yale," *Smart Set*, December 1921, pp. 52–53.

21. Durfee baseball games, Marlin, Jane, "Yale: Her Fads and Fancies," *Paterson Magazine*, February 1898, p. 192; rain gear, *New York Tribune*, May 17, 1912; Harriman letter, Abramson, *op. cit.*, p. 107.

22. "Authors Have A Say," *New York Tribune*, May 17, 1912; "Owen Johnson Attacks His Critics," *New York Times*, May 19, 1912.

23. Pierson, *Yale College, op. cit.*, p. 256.

24. Tomkins, Calvin, *Living Well Is the Best Revenge* (New York: Viking, 1971), p. 14.

25. Vaill, Amanda, *Everybody Was So Young: Gerald and Sara Murphy—A Lost Generation Love Story* (Boston, Mass., and New York: Houghton Mifflin Co., 1998), pp. 1–2. 31–33. 34–36. 45–46; Vaill, Amanda, *Hotel Florida: Truth, Love and Death in the Spanish Civil War* (New York: Farrar Straus & Giroux, 2014), p. 115.

26. Donnelley, Honoria Murphy, with Richard N. Billings, *Sara & Gerald: Villa America and After* (New York: Times Books, 1982), pp. 9, 127–128.

27. Schwartz, Charles, *Cole Porter: A Biography* (New York: Dial Press, 1977), pp. 22–24, 26, 30, 33, 255, 262, and 273; Kimball, Robert, "Cole Porter, College Man," *Yale Alumni Magazine*, November 1992, pp. 39–43; "Football Song Writing: Cole Porter, Latest Yale Composer of Big Game Choruses, Looks to New Hits 'Bull Dog' and 'Eli' to Cheer Team to Victory Next Week," *New Haven Register*, November 13, 1911; McBrien, William, *Cole Porter: A Biography* (New York: Alfred A. Knopf, 1998), pp. 28, 31, 42–43, 389 (quoting Porter's *"Oh, its awfully hard to concentrate at Yale . . . For the extra curriculum/Makes the gay life at Yale."*); Porter's Keys anthems and Murphy on Porter quoted in Kimball, *op. cit.*, pp. 9–10, 14, and Brendan Gill's introductory biographical essay, pp. x–xi. *Saturday Chronicle* for May 11, 1912, reported: "Cole Porter, leader of the Musical Clubs, might get Bones or he might get Keys, but nobody seems certain that he will get anything."

28. Johnson, *op. cit.*, p. 6. In his introductory biographical essay to Kimball's *Cole (op. cit.*, p. xi), Bonesman Brendan Gill writes that "one cannot help wondering what the handsome burly athletes of the Porter era, with their suspicion of cleverness, their pursuit of the manly, their strenuous Christianity, thought of the exquisite pagan hedonist in their midst. Well, it appears that they liked him very much." In Donald Ogden Stewart's 1921 magazine article [endnote 20 above], *op. cit.*, p. 61, he was to observe about his spring 1915 election: "The present system is the unplanned result of many years' slow growth in which the interest of Yale have always been the prime consideration; the indications are that the societies

themselves are already applying the corrective to the present ill in the shifting of their standards for 'successful' men."

29. "Unique Yale Tap Day Situation," *New Haven Journal-Courier*, March 14, 1913; "150 for Yale Reforms," *New York Times*, April 14, 1913; "Yale Sophomores Line Up," another front-page story, *New York Times*, April 15, 1913; first petitions, "Has Taps Sounded for Tap Day?," *New York Morning Telegraph*, March 30, 1913; Webb, Eugene, "The Sophomores and the Senior Societies," *Yale Courant*, April 1913; "Mending Yale Societies," *New-York Evening Post*, April 16, 1913; *Daily Princetonian*, April 18, 1913.

30. Bangs, F. H., and C. Bennitt, L. F. Carr, W. P. Campbell, W. W. Crocker, T. B. Denègre, E. B. Harrison, H. A. Pumpelly, J. D. Robb, and H. G. Woodruff, untitled pamphlet, quoted in full in *Yale Alumni Weekly*, April 18, 1913, p. 776, with a reprinting of the editorial of the *Yale News* on this statement, and reprinted in full in the *New-York Evening Post*, April 16, 1913.

31. *Eavesdropper*, Vol. 2, No. 1, January 19, 1914, p. 2.

32. Wolf's Head, "Has Taps Been Sounded for Tap Day?," *New York Morning Telegraph*, March 30, 1913; "322," April 26, 1913, Manuscripts and Archives, Yale University.

33. "Yale Tap Day to Be Quiet and Queer," *New York Herald*, May 11, 1913.

34. "Yale's Society Revolt," *New York Times*, May 1, 1913; "'Tap Day' at Yale," editorial, *New York Times*, May 17, 1913.

35. Wolf's Head, "Tap Day on Thursday," *New Haven Saturday Chronicle*, May 11, 1912; "Yale Tap Day Said to Be So Quiet and Queer," *New Haven Journal*, May 14, 1913; "Tap Day Interest Intense," *New York Times*, May 15, 1913.

36. "Man In Tree Features Tap Day Ceremony at Yale," *New Haven Journal & Courier*, May 16, 1913; "Jones Is Pleased over Yale Tap Day, " *New Haven Register*, May 16, 1913; "Yale's Tap Day Is Marked by Levity," *New Haven Journal*, May 16, 1913; "Seniors' Gibes End Tap Day's Gravity," *New York Times*, May 16, 1913; "The 1913 Tap Day," *Yale Alumni Weekly*, May 23, 1913.

37. "Minutes of Junior Meeting on Wednesday night, January 23, 1914 . . . In Osborn Hall;" "Yale's Senior Societies," *New-York Evening Post*, February 18, 1914; "Unique Yale Tap Day Situation," *New Haven Journal-Courier*, March 13, 1914; "This Is Tap Day at Yale," *New York Times*, May 14, 1914; "not a woman," "Honor 45 Juniors in Yale's Annual Tap Day Rites," *New York Herald*, May 15, 1914; Berkeley Oval, Pinnell, *op. cit.*, p. 104.

38. "The Class List," *Yale News*, April 18, 1914; "The Societies and the Juniors," *Yale Alumni Weekly*, April 24, 1914, also quoting the *News*; "Junior Class List," *Yale News*, April 29, 1914; "Yale Tap Day Will Not Be on Campus," *Brooklyn Eagle*, May 3, 1914; "Yale Bides New Tap Day," *New-York Evening Post*, May 14, 1914; "Big Interest in Tap Day Today," *New Haven Journal-Courier*, May 14, 1914.

39. MacLeish, Donaldson, *op. cit.*, p. 57; MacLeish on David Acheson, Winnick, R. H., *Letters of Archibald MacLeish 1907–1982* (Boston, Mass.: Houghton Mifflin, 1983), p. 47; "Denatured Tap Day Comes to Yale," *New York Times*, May 15, 1914; "Tap Day Reformer Is 'Untapped'," *New York Herald*, May 15, 1914; "Tap Day Makes History," *New-York Evening Post*, May 15, 1914; "Stick Close to List of Juniors," *New Haven Journal-Courier*, May 15, 1914; "Yale Leaders in Tap Day Reform Get Coveted Taps," *New York World*, May 15, 1914; fired as crew coach, Isaacson and Thomas, *op. cit.*, p. 85; Truman, Acheson, and Harriman, Abramson, *op. cit.*, p. 440.

40. Jones announcement, *Yale News*, May 8, 1915; "Skull and Bones Twice Rejected," *New Haven Journal-Courier*, May 21, 1915; "Yale's Great Oak Sees 'Tap Day' Again," *New York Times*, May 21, 1915; "Tap Day Back on Campus at Yale," *New York Herald*, May 21, 1915.

41. "'Tap Day' At Yale," *New York Times*, May 19, 1916; "One Rejection Marks Tap Day," *New Haven Journal-Courier*, May 19, 1916, also noting that George Mosher Murray rejected Bones for Wolf's Head, a first; "A Yale Tradition Shattered," *New York Times*, May 20, 1916; "One Rejection Marks Tap Day," *New Haven Journal*, May 20, 1916.

42. Hugh Bayne to Morris Hadley, September 27, 1915, Hadley Family Papers, Manuscripts and Archives, Yale University.

43. Pierson, *Yale College, 1871–1921, op. cit.*, pp. 435–437, 444–474; Kelley, *op. cit.*, pp. 348–355; "The Yale Spirit of Defense," *Yale Alumni Weekly*, October 20, 1916; Jones speech, *Yale Alumni Weekly*, May 4, 1917; "Yale in the War—An Epitome," *Yale Alumni Weekly*, November 23, 1917; "A Militarized Yale," *Yale Alumni Weekly*, October 11, 1918; Stokes, "Yale's Contribution to the War," *Yale Graphic*, March 20, 1919; ambulance service, Flint, Joseph Marshall, "The Yale Mobile Hospital Unit," in Nettleton, G. H., editor, *Yale in the World War Part One* (New Haven, Conn.: Yale University Press, 1926), pp. 437–440, and Donaldson, Scott, *Archibald MacLeish: An American Life* (Boston, Mass., New York, and London: Houghton Mifflin, 1992), pp. 87–89.

44. "Yale Dinner at Fort Sill," *Yale Alumni Weekly*, April 26, 1918; Wortman, Mark, *The Millionaire's Unit: The Aristocratic Flyboys Who Fought the Great War and Invented American Air Power* (New York: Public Affairs, 2006), pp. 137–138; Robbins, *op. cit.*, pp. 144–146; Green, Fitzhugh, *George Bush: An Intimate Portrait* (New York: Hippocrene, 1989), p. 50; prior removal of remains and on purchase vs. grave desecration, Loftus, John, and Mark Aarons, *The Secret War against the Jews* (New York: St. Martin's, 1984), p. 592 n. 32; Rosenbaum, "I Stole the Head of Prescott Bush: More Skull and Bones Tales," *New York Observer*, July 17, 2000; Herskowitz, Mickey, *Duty, Honor, Country: The Life and Legacy of Prescott Bush* (New York: Thomas Nelson, 2003), pp. 38–39, doubting the accusation in Prescott Bush's only biography; *Yale Daily News*, October 14, 1988, quoting the director of the Fort Sill Museum to the effect that there was no evidence that Geronimo's skull was ever removed from the grave contained within the museum's site, and that an iron door does not exist on Geronimo's grave; "complex and contradictory mores," Lassila, Kathrin Day, and Mark Alden Branch, "Whose Skull and Bones?," *Yale Alumni Magazine*, May–June 2006.

45. Wilson, *Yale Alumni Weekly*, April 20, 1917; Pierson, *op. cit.*, pp. 445, 464, 470; "'For Country' Part of Famous Yale Pledge," *New Haven Register*, April 22, 1917; *Yale Alumni Weekly*, January 26, 1917 and October 5, 1917; Reed, E. B., "The Yale of Today," *Yale Alumni Weekly*, November 23, 1917.

46. Archibald MacLeish poem first published in April 1919 *Lyric*; Wortman, *op. cit.*, pp. xiv–xv, 5–12, 28–34; "Twelve Men with Wings," *Time*, September 8, 1941; Davison, F. T., "The First Yale Naval Aviation Unit" in Nettleton, *op. cit.*, pp. 443–447, and Schieffelin, John Jay, "The Second Yale Unit," in Nettleton, pp. 449–453; *Yale News*, November 14, 1916, naming the members of the unit in reprinting an article by Rear Admiral Robert E. Peary; *Yale Alumni Weekly*, October 20, 1916, and January 26; March 30; and May 4, 1917; Hynes, Samuel, *The Unsubstantial Air:*

American Flyers in the First World War (New York: Farrar Straus & Giroux, 2014), pp. 26–29; "The Millionaire's Unit," http://www.millionairesunit.org/index .php?option=com-content=view&id=23&Itemid=36, accessed August 28, 2014. On Lovett federal appointments, Issacson and Thomas, *op. cit.*, p. 21; Lovett and Faulkner, Hodgson, *op. cit.*, p. 245; "Turn About," *Saturday Evening Post*, March 5, 1932, p. 6, where the Lovett character (named Bogard in the story), is described thusly: "He was past twenty-five; looking at him, one thought, not Phi Beta Kappa, exactly, but Skull and Bones, perhaps, or possibly a Rhodes scholarship." Coincidentally, the actor Gary Cooper, who played the (Bonesman) Lovett character in *Today We Live*, was also to play Joe Chapin, the unlucky hero and Bonesman in the film version of John O'Hara's *Ten North Frederick* (1955).

47. "Yale Seniors Tapped," *New York Times*, April 20, 1917; "Charlie Taft Honored on Yale's Tap Day," *New York Tribune*, April 20, 1917; *Yale News*, April 23, 1917; "Only Thirty-Four Tapped on Yale Campus," *New Haven Journal-Courier*, April 20, 1917; "Yale Will Revive Tap Day This Year," *New York Times*, May 4, 1919. On Lewis, see Lewis's memoirs, *op. cit.*, pp. 87–88, and Winks, Robin, *Cloak and Gown: Scholars in the Secret War 1939–1961* (New York: William Morrow, 1987), pp. 96–102. On Barry, see Gill, Brendan, introduction to *States of Grace: Eight Plays by Philip Barry* (New York: Harcourt Brace Jovanovich, 1975), pp. 20–22, 47.

48. "Tap Day at Yale Finds Honored Ones in Training Camp." *New York Herald*, April 20, 1917; "brutal business," Donaldson, *op. cit.*, p. 58, also noting Archie's delight when his son Bill was elected to membership thirty-two years later; MacLeish letter of September 30, 1917, Rossano, Geoffrey, *The Price of Honor: The World War One Letters of Naval Aviator Kenneth MacLeish* (Annapolis, Md.: Naval Institute Press, 1991), pp. 16–17, 27; Wortman, *op. cit.*, p., 99–103; Hynes, *op. cit.*, pp. 254–256; Robbins, *op. cit.*, pp. 108–109; *New York Times*, April 20, 1917; Lovett on K. MacLeish, Winnick, *op. cit.*, pp. 54–55; Nettleton, *op. cit.*, vol. I, pp. 284–287; Paine, Ralph D., *The First Yale Unit: A Story of Naval Aviation 1916–1919* (Cambridge, Mass.: Riverside Press, 1925), vol. I, pp. vii–viii, 88–89, 159–168, and vol. II, pp. 321–325, 350–373.

49. private train, Lewis, *op. cit.*, p. 121. The reference to a Bones initiation in the headquarters of the Navy's Northern Bombing Group, in Robbins, *op. cit.*, p. 109, is unsourced (although apparently from Isaacson and Thomas, *op. cit.*, p. 93) and incorrect: Lovett was initiated before he was ordered to France in August 1917 (Wortman, *op. cit.*, p. 123), as proven by the photograph of his Bones delegation (the first and last time all the men were to be together in New Haven) reproduced in Issacson and Thomas at p. 65.

50. Keys, Lewis, *op. cit.*, p. 121; Elihu, *Suitable Quarters*, *op. cit.*

51. Jones, *Yale Alumni Weekly*, May 4, 1917; McCormick, *Yale Alumni Weekly*, May 23, 1919; Schieffelin, *op. cit.*, pp. 449–453; Paine, *op. cit.*, vol. I, pp. 289–293.

52. *Yale News*, May 21, 1918; *Yale Alumni Weekly*, April 26, 1918

53. *New York Times*, May 4, 1919; Wortman, *op. cit.*, pp. 136–137; Isaacson and Thomas, *op. cit.*, p. 93; Lassila and Wortman, *op. cit.* Depew became after graduation Assistant to the federal district attorney for Western New York, William ("Wild Bill") Donovan, later to head the Office of Strategic Services in WWII, but Depew's political career was cut short when he died in 1924.

ENDNOTES

54. "American Ace a Bones Man," *New York Times*, May 16, 1919; *Yale News*, May 16, 1919; Wortman, *op. cit.*, p. 267; Paine, *op. cit.*, Vol. II, pp. 267–292; *Yale Alumni Weekly*, May 23, 1919.

55. Schiff, Judith, "To Freedom's Fallen," *Yale Alumni Magazine*, March 1997, p. 88.

CHAPTER TEN: DIVISIONS OF CASTE AND EXPANSION OF THE SYSTEM

1. Baltzell, E. Digby, *The Protestant Establishment: Aristocracy and Caste in America* (New York: Random House, 1964), p. 110.

2. *Yale Daily News*, January 1, 1926.

3. Oren, *op. cit.*, pp. 22, 66, 337 n. 3, 338 n. 18; Karabel, *op. cit.*, p. 200; "Dormitories and Democracy," *Yale Alumni Weekly*, December 6, 1905.

4. Synnott, Martha G., *The Half-Opened Door: Discrimination and Admissions at Harvard, Yale, and Princeton, 1900–1930* (Westport, Conn.: Greenwood Press, 1979), pp. 127, 129, 155.

5. Oren, *op. cit.*, p. 19.

6. Jewish enrollment, Synnott, Marcia C., "The Admission and Assimilation of Minority Students at Harvard, Yale, and Princeton, 1910–1950," *History of Education Quarterly*, vol. 19, no. 3, Fall 1979, p. 290; Baltzell, *op. cit.*, p. 130; Jones quoted in Oren, *op. cit.*, p. 43.

7. Caro, Robert, *The Power Broker: Robert Moses and the Fall of New York* (New York: Alfred A. Knopf, 1974), pp. 1–2, 38–47; Synnott, *The Half-Opened Door, op. cit.*, pp.145–146; individual vs. team sports, Hall, G. Stanley, *Youth* (New York: D. Appleton, 1906), pp. 84–8, and Lamoreaux, *op. cit.* pp. 337–338.

8. Oren, *op. cit.*, pp. 35, 339 n. 31.

9. Sauna, Marianne Rachel, "'Going Greek': A Social History of Jewish College Fraternities, 1895–1945," PhD diss., Columbia University, 1994, pp. 19–21, 54–56; Oren, *op. cit.*, pp. 25–26; Synnott, *The Half-Opened Door, op. cit.*, pp. 168–169. By 1918, there were three Jewish social clubs or fraternities at Yale, and six at Harvard. Synnott, "Admission and Assimilation," *op. cit.*, p. 293.

10. Baltzell, *op. cit.*, p. 210; Hapgood, Norman, "Jews and College Life," *Harper's Weekly*, January 15, 1916, p. 53; Oren, *op. cit.*, pp. 320–321; Synott, *op. cit.*, pp. 139–143, 152: "Almost three-fourths, or 307, of the 420 Jewish students in the classes of 1911 through 1925 had prepared in the local high schools [of New Haven, Hartford, and Bridgeport]"; Rostow, Eugene, "The Jew's Position," *Harkness Hoot*, November 23, 1931; on Rostow, Oren, *op. cit.*, pp. 88–89, and Bissell, Richard M., Jr., *Reflections of a Cold Warrior: From Yalta to the Bay of Pigs* (New Haven, Conn.: Yale University Press, 1996), p. 9, and Milne, David, *America's Rasputin: Walt Rostow and the Vietnam War* (New York: Hill & Wang, 2008), pp. 16–24.

11. *Minutes of the Twenty-Sixth General Meeting of the Elihu Club, New Haven, Conn., Nov. 18, 1911*, p. 3.

12. Synnott, *The Half-Opened Door, op. cit.*, pp. 131–132; Oren, *op. cit.*, pp. 70–71, 343 n. 7, 348 n. 19. Yale did not have a Catholic chapel for students until 1938. There is hardly any scholarship on how elite, private colleges and universities discriminated against Catholics, according to Horowitz, Daniel, *On the Cusp: The Yale College Class of 1960 and a World on the Verge of Change* (Amherst and Boston, Mass.: University of Massachusetts Press, 2015), p. 65.

13. Synnott, *The Half-Opened Door, op. cit.*, pp. 130–132; Janish, Herbert, "Catholicism and Culture: The American Experience of Thomas Lawrason Riggs, 1888–1943,"

Catholic Historical Review 68, July 1982, pp. 451–468. Synnott does chart a decline in the Catholic members of the senior societies from 1912 to the class of 1927, from 8 to 3 (see Table 5.1, p. 132). O'Hara letter quoted in Wolff, Geoffrey, *The Art of Burning Bridges: A Life of John O'Hara* (New York: Alfred A. Knopf, 2003), p. 46.

14. Warner, Robert Austin, *New Haven Negroes: A Social History* (New York: Arno Press and *New York Times*, 1969), pp. 175–176, 246–247, 249 n, 31, 254; Synnott, *op. cit.*, p. 133; Pickens, William, *Bursting Bonds* (Boston, Mass.: The Jordan and Moore Press, enlarged edition, 1923), chapter 6 and pp. 127 and 131. Harvard College's first black graduate was Richard T. Green of the class of 1870 (Yale's first was Richard Henry Green of the class of 1856, and its third after Boucher was John Wesley Manning, 1881), and the first black Harvard undergraduate elected to Phi Beta Kappa was William Monroe Trotter of the class of 1895.

15. Thirty blacks, seven blacks, Association of Yale Alumni estimates in Kabaservice, Geoffrey, "Kingman Brewster and the Rise and Fall of the Progressive Establishment," PhD thesis, Yale University, 1999, pp. 35–351, and class of 1916, p. 96; www.yale.edu.alpha.zeta_chapter.htm, and en.wikipedia.org/wiki/Alpha_Phi_Alpha, each accessed November 12, 2014.

16. Bullard, Allan B., *The Education of Black Folk* (New York: Harper and Row, 1973), p. 53.

17. Synott, *op. cit.*, p. 134; Oren, *op. cit.*, pp. 71–72.

18. Up at Harvard, President Charles W. Eliot commented that "in a few cases . . . negroes were taken into athletic organizations on account of their remarkable athletic merit," but that he "never heard of negroes being admitted to fraternities or clubs at Harvard." Synott, "Admission and Assimilation," *op. cit.*, p. 293.

19. Carnegie Foundation figures, Pierson, *Yale the University College, op. cit.*, p. 662 n. 9; Pierson, *Yale Book of Numbers*, p. 94 on society memberships, *1929 Yale College Classbook*, and Oren, *op. cit.*, p. 183.

20. Synott, "Admission and Assimilation," *op. cit.*, p. 291; Wallace, William, *Yale's Ironmen: A Story of Football & Lives in the Decade of the Depression and Beyond* (New York: Universe, 2005), p. 6.

21. Bergin, Thomas, on his "caste-ridden Yale of the twenties," in "My Native Country," in Dubois, *op. cit.*, pp. 162–163.

22. Benét, Stephen Vincent, "The Songs of Dear Old Yale," Stephen Vincent Benét Papers, Yale Collection of American Literature, Beinecke Rare Book & Manuscript Library, Yale University.

23. alumni sons increase, Kelley, *op. cit.*, p. 406; Benét, *op. cit.*, pp. 63–64; public vs. private schools, Noyes, Edward S., "Selecting Him," *Seventy-Five, op. cit.*, pp. 32–37.

24. Pak, Susie J., *Gentlemen Bankers: The World of J. P. Morgan* (Cambridge, Mass.: Harvard University Press, 2013), pp. 144–145, 158, and works cited at 304–305 and 312. President Eliot at Harvard maintained that discrimination by individuals did not matter as long as "the university, like the state, leaves its members free to do their own social sorting." It was enough that "all students in Harvard University—as students—are treated by the University precisely alike without regard to class, caste, or race." Synott, "Admissions and Assimilation," *op. cit.*, p. 293.

25. Oren, *op. cit.*, p. 89. A graduate of the class of 1979, Oren spoke about his book at a date when four of the senior societies had admitted woman, and all had admitted blacks and Jews: "Much progress has been made in making Yale a more democratic institution," adding that "the societies had been monitors rather than initiators of

ENDNOTES

exclusionist trends. The role of societies has not been an insidious role but a realistic one." *Yale Daily News*, November 4, 1988.

26. Pierson, *op. cit.*, pp. 3–15, (Angell and the senior societies) 76; Kelley, *op. cit.*, pp. 369–371; on Hutchins and Angell, see Dzuback, Mary Ann, *Robert Maynard Hutchins: Portrait of an Educator* (Chicago, Ill.: University of Chicago Press, 1991), pp. 30, 32–33, 36–39. The senior society component of membership among the Alumni Fellows and Successor Trustees is substantial: according to a statistical study made in 1969, providing a census of the two categories since 1905 (marking the election of Bonesman Payson Merrill as the first lay Successor Trustee), 80 percent of the Alumni Fellows and 69 percent of the Successor Trustees, or 76 percent of all members of the Yale Corporation from 1905 to 1969, were members of the senior societies, ranking exactly in the order of the founding of those societies or incorporation from Sheff into the system (38 from Bones, 17 from Keys, 5 from Wolf's Head, 4 from Elihu, 2 from Berzelius, 1 from Book and Snake, and 3 from St. Anthony Hall). Richards, David Alan, *The Making of the Corporation 1969*, Appendix III, Manuscripts and Archives, Yale University.

27. Pierson, *Yale The University College, op. cit.*, pp. 24, 145, 455, 487–492, 515–517.

28. *Yale Alumni Weekly*, November 21 and December 5, 1919; Elihu badge announcement to its members and graduates, May 1920.

29. Swanberg, W. A., *Luce and His Empire* (New York: Scribner's, 1972), p. 41; Herzstein, Robert E., *Henry R. Luce: A Political Portrait of the Man Who Created the American Century* (New York: Scribner's, 1994), pp. 38–41; Brinkley, *op. cit.*, pp. 55–70; Wilner, Isaiah, *The Man Time Forgot: A Tale of Genius, Betrayal, and the Creation of Time Magazine* (New York: HarperCollins, 2006), pp. 47–50, 54, 58.

30. "Yale Will Revive Tap Day This Year," *New York Times*, May 4, 1919; Brinkley, *op. cit.*, p. 72. Luce once described the society as "a religion," and described it to his parents as "the most exclusive society in the world." Elson, Robert T., *Time, Inc.: The Intimate History of a Publishing Enterprise 1923–1941* (New York: Athenaeum, 1968), pp. 44–45; Brinkley, p. 74. Many years later, in his troubled marriage to Clare Boothe Luce, he blamed his impotence with her partly on her disregard for his senior society membership. Morris, Sylvia Jukes, *Price of Fame: The Honorable Clare Boothe Luce* (New York: Random House, 2014), pp. 192–193.

31. Wilner, *op. cit.*, pp. 3, 59, 65; Swanberg, *op. cit.*, p. 49.

32. Wilner, *op. cit.*, pp. 92–93. Remarkably, *Time*'s rival *Newsweek* also began with a Bones pedigree: Averell Harriman in 1933 founded a publication called *Today* which he merged with another magazine in 1937 to become *Newsweek*. Abramson, *op. cit.*, pp. 250–252.

33. *Yale News*, May 16 and 17, 1919; Robbins, *op. cit.*, p. 110.

34. *A Twenty-Five Year Record: Class of 1919, Yale College* (New Haven, Conn., 1946), [3]; "The Tapiad" excerpt quoted here is the chorus to the text printed in Fenton, Charles A., *Stephen Vincent Benét: The Life and Times of an American Man of Letters, 1898–1943* (New Haven, Conn.: Yale University Press), p. 63.

35. Letter to Shreve C. Badger, July 1918, in Fenton, Charles, ed., *Selected Letters of Stephen Vincent Benét* (New Haven, Conn.: Yale University Press, 1960), pp. 15–18.

36. Benét, *op. cit.*, p. 104. It is said that the 1927–28 *Lit.* board of editors refused to elect a chairman until after Tap Day, so as to defy Skull and Bones. Pierson, *Yale: The University College, op. cit.*, pp. 289–290.

37. Gavit, John Palmer, "Social Barriers and 'Hush Dope' at Yale," *New York Post*, May 19, 1922.

38. *New York Times, New York Herald*, and *New York Tribune*, May 19, 1922. Spock was later to write that his election, "seemed proof that I'd become an acceptable fellow at last, or at least had learned to act like one." Spock, Benjamin, "The Mother's Boy and the New Coach," in Dubois, *op. cit.*, p. 154.

39. *New York Times*, May 9, 1926; Kahn, E. H., Jr., *Jock: The Life and Times of John Hay Whitney* (Garden City, N.Y.: Doubleday, 1981), pp. xiii, 2, 10, 15, 57. The first John Hay Whitney Professorship in the Humanities, established in 1977 with $750,000 raised by Scroll and Key through its membership and Whitney's many friends, was held by Bart Giamatti, Keysman and later Yale's nineteenth president. Kahn, p. 306.

40. *New York Herald Tribune*, May 18, 1928; Mellon, Paul, *Reflections in a Silver Spoon* (New York: William Morrow, Inc., 1992), pp. 114–117; Kahn, *op. cit.*, p. 299.

41. *Yale Alumni Weekly*, June 7, 1929, and reported in the *New York Times* for the same date.

42. Kahn, *op. cit.*, p. 57.

43. Pringle, Henry F., "Young Men on the Make," *Harper's Monthly*, January 1929, pp. 150–151; "A Magazine Writer on Yale's Social System," *Yale Alumni Weekly*, January 18, 1929. Pringle was considerably more respectful of the society experience a decade later in his biography of Taft: "He was tapped for Skull and Bones, an honor by no means due to the fact that his father was one of its founders or to the prominence at Yale of the Taft name. The senior society pays the tribute of election not merely to athletes or college intellectuals. It seeks men of outstanding personality and great force in undergraduate life and Taft was such. Throughout his life the memory of Skull and Bones was precious. He was certain that it represented the very best among all the excellent phases of Yale life. He returned to its meetings when he could." Pringle, Henry F., *The Life and Times of William Howard Taft* (New York: Farrar & Rinehart, Inc., 1939), vol. 1, p. 40.

44. *New York Times*, May 17, 1929; May 16 and 18, 1930.

45. Hobson, *Yale Daily News*, April 10, 1931; *New York Herald Tribune*, May 14, 1931.

46. Pierson, *Yale The University College, op. cit.*, pp. 290–293; *Nation*, 6 May 1931; Schiff, Judith Ann, "The Hoot Heard 'Round the World," *Yale Alumni Magazine*, March/April 2006.

47. Childs, Richard S., "Elks in Our Midst," *Harkness Hoot*, April/May 1931.

48. *New York Herald Tribune* and *New York Times*, May 15, 1931; *New York Times*, May 22, 1931; on the Bissell refusal to Bones, Thomas, Evan, *The Very Best Men: Four Who Dared: The Early Years of the CIA* (New York: Touchstone, 1995), p. 92, quoting from Bissell's then unpublished "Memoirs," and Bissell, *op. cit.*, pp. 9–10; Kabaservice, PhD thesis, *op. cit.*, p. 119; on Bissell's stated reason, Bird, Kai, *The Color of Truth: McGeorge Bundy and William Bundy: Brothers in Arms* (New York: Simon & Schuster, 1998), p. 59. Childs may have come under family pressure to allow his election: his grandfather and father were both Keysmen.

49. *New York Times*, May 9 and 12, 1933; *New York Herald Tribune*, May 12, 1933; *Yale Alumni Weekly*, May 26, 1933; May 18, 1935 "furtively," *Yale Alumni Weekly*, May 19, 1933.

50. Brock, H. L., "College Ways in America," *New York Times Magazine*, May 28, 1933.

51. *Yale News*, May 7, 1934 (the editorial is unsigned, but the chair of the *News* that year was Lyman Spitzer Jr., who was elected to Bones the following week); *Yale Record*, May 1934; *New York Times*, May 7, 1934.

52. *Yale Alumni Weekly*, May 18, 1934, p. 646; *New York Times*, May 13, 1934; *New York Herald Tribune*, May 11, 1934.

53. The *Hoot's* demise, Pierson, *The University College, op. cit.*, pp. 308, 613–614 n. 33; poem, *Harkness Hoot*, May 1934.

54. Rogers, James Gamble III, "James Gamble Rogers—Yale Architect," Senior Honors Essay, April 30, 1968, Manuscripts & Archives, Yale University, pp. 1–2, 6–11, 15–17, 42, and (on the Wolf's Head tomb) 62; Goldberger, Paul, "Romantic Pragmatism: The Work of James Gamble Rogers at Yale University," Senior Honors Essay, May 1, 1972, Haas Arts Library Special Collections, Yale University, pp. 56, 58; Cleveland, Reginald, "Mr. Harkness's Gifts Cover a Wide Field," *New York Times*, January 19, 1930, sec. IX, p. 5; Rogers, James Gamble, "The Future of Yale College," typescript dated March 27, 1928, p. 1, Commonwealth Fund Archives, Rockefeller Archives Center, Poncantico Hills, N.Y., and in Angell MSS, Yale; Betsky, *op. cit.*, pp. 32, 108 (the Rogers double room floor plan), 113–114, 119–120, 140–143, 153, 161, 251 n. 10; Pierson, *Yale the University College, op. cit.*, pp. 212–220, 238, 248; Kelley, *op. cit.*, pp. 372–376; Duke, Alex, *Importing Oxbridge: English Residential Colleges and American Universities* (New Haven, Conn., and London: Yale University Press, 1996), pp. 91–124; on Harvard, Smith, Richard Norton, *The Harvard Century: The Making of a University to a Nation* (Cambridge, Mass. and London: Harvard University Press, 1986), pp. 94–95, 351 n. 29; on Professor Tinker, MacLeish, "New-Yale," *op. cit.*, p. 74. The Wolf's Head hall commission and design are not discussed in *Bertram Grosvenor Goodhue* by Richard Oliver (New York: The Architectural History Foundation/MIT Press, 1983), except to be noted in the List of Buildings and Projects, p. 288. On this tomb's amenities, see the description in Muenzen, Paul, "Voices from the tombs speak," *Yale Daily News*, April 17, 1988.

55. wall carvings, Stern, Michael, *Yale's Hidden Treasures: Mystery of the Gothic Stone Carvings* (United States: Carvingswithclass, 2012), pp. 7, 97–98, and Betsky, *Ibid.*, pp. 143, 153, 155; Fox, Lyttleton, "One Foot in the Grave and One in the Tomb," *Town & Country*, February, 1940, p. 43. In the legend to the map of the Yale campus in MacLeish's "New-Yale" article in March 1934's *Fortune*, at p. 79, it reads in pertinent part, "To the left of Pierson [College] like a huddle of disconsolate sheep are the doomed junior fraternities with the new Wolf's Head senior society tomb (Mr. Harkness is a member) looming largest."

56. "separate countries," Havemeyer, *Go to Your Room, op. cit.*, pp. 73–74; Chittenden, Russell, E., *History of the Sheffield Scientific School of Yale University 1846–1922* (New Haven, Conn.: Yale University Press, 1928), vol. two, p. 493; Slosson, *op. cit.*, p. 52; Fitzgerald, F. Scott, "May Day," *Smart Set*, July 1920, reprinted in Bruccoli, ed., *The Short Stories of F. Scott Fitzgerald, A New Collection* (New York: Scribner's, 1989), p. 121. Sheff graduation numbers, *The '93S. Class Book* (New Haven, Conn., June 1893), p. 129.

57. Hadley, in Norton, *op. cit.*, p. 60; *Universities and Their Sons, Yale University* (Boston, Mass.: R. Herndon Company, 1900), pp. 248–249.

58. Moore, John D., "Around the Campus," *Yale Alumni Weekly*, May 5, 1933; *Yale Alumni Weekly*, May 12, 1933.

59. *Yale Alumni Weekly*, May 26, 1934.
60. "Newcomers Among Senior Societies," *Yale Alumni Weekly*, May 26, 1933; Chittenden, *op. cit.*, vol. two, p. 494; Trotman, Philip, *The History of the Berzelius Society* (New Haven, Conn.: Colony Foundation, 1991), pp. 12–15, 19–21, 24–53; Havemeyer, *Go to Your Room*, *op. cit.*, pp. 75–76; Berzelius report to graduates on college plan impact, February 10, 1933; 1934 election results in Berzelius News Letter, May 17, 1934; request for candidate evaluation, B.T.A. Council letter, February 15, 1935; Berzelius Alumni Advisory Campaign Committee letter, November 16, 1936; Berzelius News Letter, May 28, 1937. Angell was the fourth Yale president to be an honorary member of Berzelius: Theodore Dwight Woolsey was so elected in 1865, Timothy Dwight in 1886, and Arthur Hadley in 1899. Photographs of the interior of the Berzelius tomb, taken from the society's website, were published in *Rumpus* in November 1999.
61. Chittenden, *op. cit.*, pp. 494–495; Trotman, *op. cit.*, p. 29.
62. "Newcomers," *op. cit.*; Havemeyer, Loomis, *The History of the Book and Snake Society and The Cloister Club 1863–1955* (privately printed: New Haven, Conn. 1956), pp. 20–21.
63. Havemeyer, *op. cit.*, pp. 23–24, 30, 33, 41, 52–54, 57, 59, 68, 74–79.
64. St. Anthony's, Havemeyer, *"Go to Your Room," op. cit.*, p. 106 Fox, *op. cit.*, p. 78. The interior of the Book & Snake tomb is described extensively with floor plans in the campus tabloid *Rumpus* for September 1997, in Moussach, Jane W., "They Let Us In. What Were They Thinking?"
65. "Senior Societies and the Lord Jehovah," *Harkness Hoot*, May 1933, pp. 63–64.
66. *Bulletin of the Phelps Association*, Number 18, December 1936.
67. *New York Herald Tribune*, May 10, 1935; *New York Times*, May 10, 1935, and May 8, 1936.
68. Donkey's Head, *Yale Alumni Weekly*, May 21, 1937. Donkey's Head was founded by members of the class of 1940, including Marshall Green, who said "the sole purpose . . . was to disparage the secret societies. At one event, fourteen of us dressed up all in black and carried a coffin around. This was clearly not Bill [Bundy]'s cup of tea, but Robert French, the master of Jonathan Edwards, thought it terribly funny." Interview with and reported in Bird, *op. cit.*, p. 61.
69. Elections, *New York Times* and *New York Herald Tribune*, May 8, 1936, May 14, 1937, May 13, 1938, and May 12, 1939; wave of rebellion, Fox, *op. cit.*, p. 81.
70. Fox, *op. cit.*, p. 81.
71. Oren, *op. cit.*, pp. 87–88; *New York Times*, May 14, 1937. The second Jew to be tapped by Skull and Bones was Thomas Guinzburg, 1950, and the third was Benjamin Zucker, 1960, the grandson of an Orthodox rabbi.
72. Hallock, "The Last Man Tapped," *Gunter's Magazine*, September 1906; Andrews, Mary Raymond Shipman, "The Courage of the Commonplace," *Scribner's*, July 1911; Minnigerode, Meade, "Hush Stuff," *Collier's*, February 26, 1921; cartoon, Hokinson, Helen E., *New Yorker*, May 12, 1934, p. 24.
73. Marquand, John P., *The Late George Apley: A Novel in the Form of a Memoir* (Boston, Mass.: Little, Brown, 1937), quotations (Thomas Apley to son George) at p. 73, and pp. 71, 79, 80. The "Club" is identified as Porcellian in Birmingham, Stephen, *The Later John Marquand* (Hagerstown, Md.: Lippincott, 1972), pp. 30–31. Marquand, Harvard 1915, was never asked to join any social club there at all, passed over by

Hasty Pudding and all the final clubs; his high school background shut him out of this exclusive club world, and because Yale honored him first with an honorary degree (1950 to Harvard's 1953), he gave all his literary manuscripts to Yale. Bell, Millicent, *Marquand: An American Life* (Boston, Mass.: Little, Brown, 1979), p. 75. In Marquand's later satirical novel with a Harvard man as the protagonist, *H. M. Pulham, Esquire* (Boston, Mass.: Little, Brown, 1941, at p. 208), the author all but switches alma maters: "We walked up and down the platform at New Haven and talked about Yale and wondered why we were always prejudiced against it. You had to admit that they dressed better there than at Harvard. They had a better social sense and a better sense of reality. Bill said if he had a boy, though God knew he did not want to get married and tied up with a family, that he would send him to Yale if he had to earn his living afterwards. 'Harry,' he said, 'you should have gone to Yale.'" *Yale Daily News* announced the gift of the book's manuscript on its front page, May 6, 1941.

74. "Perquisites," Gill, Brendan, introduction to *States of Grace, op. cit.*, pp. 11–19; Farr, Finis, *O'Hara: A Biography* (Boston, Mass.: Little, Brown, 1973), pp. 76–77.

75. Karl, Frederick, *William Faulkner: American Writer: A Biography* (New York: Grove Press, 1989), pp. 82, 94, 96–97, 110–111, 407, 1047; Blotner, Joseph, *Faulkner* (New York: 1984), pp. 190–191; on Stone, *History of the Class of 1914 Yale College*, pp. 319–320; Faulkner, William, "Turnabout," *Collected Stories of William Faulkner* (New York: Vintage International, 1995), pp. 411–413, 415, 425, 435, 565, 598. George Frazier, the *Boston Globe* columnist who was to write an insightful article entitle "Yale Secret Societies" of *Esquire* magazine in September 1955, and often discussed them in his newspaper column thereafter, usually just prior to the Yale-Harvard football game, wrote on 23 November 1974: "I rather doubt if Ol' Doc Hemingstein and Bill the Faulk were writing today they would use Bones as a symbol of augustness."

76. Bruccoli, *op. cit.*, pp. 43, 138, 204, 337, 341, 385, 442; Stewart, "The Higher Learning in America," *op. cit.* The first article in the *Smart Set* series, subtitled "I—Princeton University," was by John Peale Bishop, Fitzgerald's clubmate and a poet and novelist, an assistant editor of *Vanity Fair* when Stewart arrived, also to live in Paris, becoming in 1924 the best friend there of MacLeish. Donaldson, *op. cit.*, p. 132; Stewart, *By A Stroke of Luck!, op. cit.*, pp. 44–45. Stein to Hemingway, Hemingway, Ernest, *A Moveable Feast* (New York: Scribner's, 1964), p. 29. On Fitzgerald and MacLeish, Donaldson, *op. cit.*, pp. 152, 159, 178. Hemingway to Fitzgerald on the distortion of the Murphys, May 28, 1934, Baker, Carlos, ed., *Ernest Hemingway Selected Letters* (New York: Scribner's, 1981), p. 407.

77. Fitzgerald, F. Scott, *This Side of Paradise* (New York: Alfred A. Knopf, 1996), pp. 56–57. (Edmund Wilson, in his memoirs in *New Yorker* [May 6, 1967] credits Fitzgerald with inventing this jape for a Triangle production.) Earlier in the book (p. 37), Fitzgerald wrote that Amory had decided to attend Princeton, although "Yale had a romance and glamor . . . and [his prep school's] men who had been 'tapped for Skull and Bones,' but Princeton drew him most, with its atmosphere of bright colors and its alluring reputation as the pleasantest country club in America." He described his eating club Cottage as "an impressive mélange of brilliant adventurers and well-dressed philanderers" (p. 44), although in the end he deplored the system (see endnote six in Chapter Six).

78. Fitzgerald, F. Scott, "The Popular Girl," *Saturday Evening Post*, February 11, 1922 (Part I); Fitzgerald, "Basil and Cleopatra," *Saturday Evening Post*, April 27, 1929; Fitzgerald, *The Beautiful and the Damned* (New York: Harper Press, 2013 ed.), pp. 341–342.

79. Fitzgerald, F. Scott, *The Great Gatsby* (New York: Scribner, 1924/2004 ed.), pp. 3, 4. 6. 7; Skull bookplate reproduced in Churchwell, Sarah, *Careless People: Murder, Mayhem and the Invention of the Great Gatsby* (London: Virago, 2013), pp. 331–332; "100 Best Novels" (http://www.modernlibrary,com/top-100/100-best-novels), Modern Library, retrieved January 11, 2015. In the Baz Luhrmann film version of *The Great Gatsby* (2013), Nick Carraway calls Tom Buchanan "Boaz," the Bones internal name for the football captain, and Tom in turn calls Nick "Shakespeare," thereby implying that they were in Bones together. http://www.publicbookshelf.com/fiction/great-gatsby/younger-vulnerable-8

80. Fitzgerald, F. Scott, *Tender Is the Night* (New York: Scribner, 1933/2003 ed.), pp. 88–89, 115, 117, 158. In Nelson Aldrich's *Old Money: The Mythology of America's Upper Class* (New York: Alfred A. Knopf, 1988), at p. 46, he writes: "In the 1920s and 1930s, this double image of club life reflected the felt helplessness of the observer to *get in*. The 'social' novelists of the day—Fitzgerald, Marquand, and O'Hara—returned again and again to the snob's agony of belongingness. . . . Fitzgerald was proud to be friends, as he thought, with the Gerald Murphys and with Tommy Hitchcock. . . . Scott Fitzgerald and Tommy Hitchcock might be friends, but there was no way, even if he had gone to Harvard, that Scott Fitzgerald could belong to the Porcellian Club. To belong to the Porcellian Club, it was not enough—it still isn't—that one be friends with a member. One has to have been friends with him always, and in that elusive past perfect tense of the verb *to be* the socially ambitious read their sad fate."

81. Schiff, Judith Ann, "Yale's First Student," *Yale Alumni Magazine*, May/June 2004; Sanford, Marcelline Hemingway, *At the Hemingways: A Family Portrait* (Boston, Mass.: Little, Brown, 1962), p. 19.

82. Le Vot, André, *F. Scott Fitzgerald, A Biography*, trans. William Byron (New York: Doubleday, 1983), p. 220; Hemingway, *A Movable Feast, op. cit.*, p. 185; Meyers, Jeffrey, *Hemingway: A Biography* (New York: Harper & Row, 1985), pp. 72, 148–150, 170.

83. Vaill, *Hotel Florida, op. cit.*, pp. 39, 63, 65 (on MacLeish), 254–255; Hemingway, Ernest, *To Have and to Have Not* (New York: Scribner's, 1937, p. 239, and at p. 240, about the patent medicine which is the basis for the millionaire's fortune: "Grateful users from all over the world keep writing in discovering new uses and old users are as loyal to it as Harold Tompkins, the fiancé, is to Skull and Bones or [British Prime Minister] Stanley Baldwin to Harrow." "Frances" in the first quotation was Frances Coates, a high school classmate of Hemingway's who spurned his suit and married another classmate, John "Jack" Grace, who did not attend Yale and thus was not a Bonesman: see Elder, Robert K., "To Have and To Have Not," *The Paris Review: The Daily*, May 4, 2017.

84. Hemingway, Ernest, *The Fifth Column and Four Stories of the Spanish Civil War* (New York: Scribner's, 1938/1969), pp. 62–63. There is no evidence that Gellhorn ever aborted a wedding with a Bonesman (her long affair with Frenchman Bertrand de Jouvenal ended shortly before her meeting Hemingway, whose third wife she became in 1940). See Moorehead, Caroline, *Martha Gellhorn: A Life* (London: Chatto & Windus, 2003), *passim*.

85. Vaill, *Hotel Florida, op. cit.*, pp. 96–97, 119, 200–207, 315; Baker, Carlos, *Ernest Hemingway, A Life Story* (New York: Scribner's, 1969), pp. 313–314; Meyers, *op. cit.*, p. 302; Griffin, Peter, *Less Than a Treason: Hemingway in Paris* (New York and Oxford, England: Oxford University Press, 1990), p. 124. Hemingway had a habit of unleashing attacks on Donald Ogden Stewart (a model for Bill Gordon in *The Sun Also Rises*), John Dos Passos, and Archibald MacLeish "so harsh and extreme as to end all possibilities of continuing friendship." Baker, *op. cit.*, p. 379.

86. Meyers, *op. cit.*, pp. 71, 282; Donaldson, *op. cit.*, p. 50; Griffin, *op. cit.*, pp. 149, 171.

87. "class," Bruccoli, Matthew, *The O'Hara Concern: A Biography of John O'Hara* (New York: Random House, 1975), pp. 21–22. 28–29; on Phelps's columns, MacShane, Frank, *The Life of John O'Hara* (New York: E. P. Dutton, 1980), p. 11; Wolff, Geoffrey, *The Art of Burning Bridges: A Life of John O'Hara* (New York: Alfred A. Knopf, 2003), pp. 48–49, 53; on Owen Johnson, O'Hara, John, foreword to the Modern Library 1994 edition of *Appointment in Samarra* (New York: Random House, 1934/1994), p. vii.

88. Wolff, *op. cit.*, pp. 70–71; Bruccoli, *op. cit.*, p. 42.

89. MacShane, *op. cit.*, pp. 43, 117; Bruccoli, *op. cit.*, pp. 60–62; O'Hara to John Hersey, May 26, 1965, in Bruccoli, Matthew, ed., *Selected Letters of John O'Hara* (New York: Random House, 1978), p. 475.

90. Bruccoli, *op. cit.*, p. 164; Wolff, *op. cit.*, pp. 50, 120; MacShane, *op. cit.*, p. 177; Farr, *op. cit.*, p. 77. According to Brendan Gill (*Here at the New Yorker*, New York: Random House, 1975, p. 117), "It seemed . . . that there wasn't anything he didn't know about college and prep-school matters, down to the chants of the youngest schoolboy at Lawrenceville. It was, for example, a Bones custom never to speak of the secret society itself but to speak of its in terms of its location in New Haven; one said, 'How are things on High Street?' O'Hara knew that, though he didn't tell me he knew it; he revealed it indirectly many years later, when he was anxiously awaiting word of his election to the Century Club. Happening to encounter his neighbor in Princeton, Frederick B. Adams, who is both a Bones man and a Centurion, O'Hara said, 'Tell me, Fred—how are things on Forty-Third Street? [the location of the Century]."

91. O'Hara, John, *BUtterfield 8* (New York: Penguin, 1935), pp. 45–46, 51–52.

92. O'Hara, John, *A Rage To Live* (New York: Random House, 1949), pp. 76–77, 129, 329.

93. Gill, Brendan, *States of Grace, op. cit.*, pp. 18–19.

94. O'Hara, John, "Writing—What's in It for Me?," in *"An Artist Is His Own Fault": John O'Hara on Writers and Writing*, ed. Matthew J. Bruccoli (Carbondale: Southern Illinois University Press, 1977), pp. 70–71; Wolff, *op. cit.*, pp. 288–289, 300; MacShane, *op. cit.*, pp. 151, 196–197; Bruccoli, *op. cit.*, pp. 183, 283. When Yale president Kingman Brewster was asked why Yale had not offered the writer an honorary degree, Brewster replied "Because he wanted it too much." Brendan Gill (see endnote 90) concludes (at p. 19): "Acrimoniously at odds with the world, though the world could not be sure why, he was the last person likely to be tapped for Bones. He would have stood waiting in vain on Tap Day, and afterward he would have found reason to believe that unknown enemies had ruthlessly conspired to deprive him of the honor he so richly deserved. But there would have been no enemy, no conspiracy; there would have been only his nature."

95. O'Hara to Moses, August 1959, Bruccoli, *Selected Letters, op. cit.*, pp. 299–300. O'Hara touched for the last time on the Yale senior societies in *10 North Frederick*,

for which he won the National Book Award in 1955, in which the protagonist Joe Chapin is a member of Wolf's Head, whose son drops out of Yale so as not to be passed over by the same senior society. O'Hara, John, *Ten North Frederick* (New York: Penguin, 2014), pp. 50–51, 129, 212, 235, 399. Another novel of these decades which mentions the societies is Travis Ingraham's *Young Gentlemen, Rise* (New York: Farrar & Rinehart, 1930), about the Yale class of 1928, citing Bones (pp. 88–89) and Keys (p. 150).

CHAPTER ELEVEN: WORLD WAR AGAIN, AND OTHER CASTES BROKEN

1. Marquand, *op. cit.*, p. 19. Magazine articles about Yale (e.g., *Time* and *Newsweek* for June 11, 1951) customarily named Sinclair Lewis, Philip Barry, Thornton Wilder, Walter Millis, and Stephen Vincent Benét as Yale's constellation of writers.
2. Kelley, *op. cit.*, pp. 386–387; "maturity," Pierson, *Yale College 1921–1937, op. cit.*, p. 376.
3. Pierson, *ibid.*, pp. 432–444.
4. 1916 vs. 1941, Kabaservice, *Kingman Brewster, op. cit.*, pp. 94–97; W.B., letter to the editor, *Yale Daily News*, March 6, 1940, p. 4.
5. "Senior Societies," *Yale Daily News*, May 2, 1938.
6. Bundy, McGeorge, "Visions & Revisions: The Senior Societies, I," *Yale Daily News*, May 6, 1938; column award, Bird, *op. cit.*, pp. 27, 60.
7. Morris, Richard L., Jr., "Visions & Revisions: II. The Senior Societies," *Yale Daily News*, May 9, 1938.
8. Bundy, McGeorge, "Visions & Revisions: The Senior Societies, III," *Yale Daily News*, May 11, 1938.
9. "Senior Society Elections," *Yale Daily News*, May 12, 1939.
10. Bundy, McGeorge, "For the Defense," *Yale Literary Magazine*, February 1939, pp. 7–8.
11. Bird, *op. cit.*, pp. 60–61. Bill Bundy recalled: "It was a very intense experience. It stretched you. You had to think for yourself and you learned a lot about human beings and the different qualities of men. It became a lot of fun. It was an important part of my life." Mac felt the same way: "It was and is an important part of my life. It does focus around the intense experience of learning to trust your colleagues. In our case, it was fifteen white, Anglo–Saxon Protestants. Even today we meet irregularly as a group and individually. It is a remarkable institution." *Ibid.*, pp. 61–62. On mother Bundy's pressure, Kabaservice, *The Guardians, op. cit.*, p. 69.
12. Goldstein, *op. cit.*, p. 8.
13. *Time*, May 20, 1940; speech extract from 1941's Walton Dowdell Thomas, shortly to be tapped for Bones.
14. Robbins, *op. cit.*, p. 109.
15. *Yale Daily News*, May 11, 1940.
16. Jackson, William E., "Cabbages and Kings: Now It Can Be Told," *Yale Daily News*, May 18, 1939.
17. "Skull and Bones," *Time*, May 20, 1940, pp. 59–60; "act of heroism," Lemann, Nicholas, *The Big Test: The Secret History of the American Meritocracy* (New York: Farrar Straus & Giroux, 1999), p. 148. One memoir says that Brewster's *News* office door was locked and broken down by his Bones tapper. Astrachan, Anthony, "Class Notes," in DuBois, *op. cit.*, p. 215. George Frazier in his *Boston Globe* column for April 9, 1964, celebrating Kingman Brewster's inauguration as Yale's first president

in living memory not to be a senior society member, relates an oft-repeated story that Brewster was "finally located in a basement bathroom, where, without even rising, he shook his head to indicated that he declined the honor." The Brewster bathroom refusal story was retailed again in *Wall Street Journal* on December 11, 1968. In the *Time* cover article on Brewster dated June 23, 1967, his rejection of Bones is mentioned twice. On the true story, Harold ("Doc") Howe's aborted tap attempt, Kabaservice, *The Guardians, op. cit.*, p. 69, citing a personal interview with Howe.

18. Brewser, Kingman Jr., "Introduction," *Stover at Yale* (New York: Collier, 1968), p. vi.

19. Kingman Brewster, Jr. to Clarence W. Mendell, March 15, 1962, MSS 572 11–1, "Provost—Personal, Brewster—3, Manuscripts and Archives, Yale University. To student journalist R. Thomas Herman, Brewster said in 1968: "It was simply that I didn't want to spend two nights a week behind closed windows for purposes which were not prescribed in advance. . . . Furthermore, I was having a great social life and couldn't see losing two more nights a week." Herman, R. Thomas, "The Inscrutable King of Yale," p. 23, Manuscripts and Archives, Yale University. On Jackson's sister, Kabaservice, *The Guardians, op. cit.*, p. 69.

20. Kabaservice, *The Guardians, op. cit.*, p. 69; Kabaservice, "Kingman Brewster," *op. cit.*, p. 227, from interview with Mary Griswold.

21. *Yale Daily News*, April 14 and May 8, 1941.

22. Andrews, *op. cit.*, p. 14.

23. The Phelps Association, Bulletin No. 22, December 1940, pp. 1–3.

24. Buck, Polly Stone, *We Minded the Store: Yale Life & Letters during World War II* (New Haven, Conn.: self-published, 1975), pp. 1–6, 20, 26–27, 34–35, 42–43, 49–50; Kelley, *op. cit.*, pp. 396–402; Havemeyer, Loomis, *The Story of Undergraduate Yale in the Second World War* (New Haven, Conn.: Yale University, 1960), pp. 13, 16–17. 19, 23–24, 38–39, 56, 74; *The Nineteen Forty-Three Yale Banner*, pp. 27–47; *The Nineteen Forty Four Class Book*, pp. 20–27; Schiff, Judith Ann, "When Yale Schooled for War," *Yale Alumni Magazine*, December 2002, p. 88.

25. Kinglsey Trust centennial notices and Benét poem collected in the Arnold G. Dana Scrapbook Collection, titled *Yale Old and New*, Manuscripts and Archives, Yale University.

26. *Yale Daily News*, December 3 and 4, 1942; "minority groups," Schaap, Dick, "Lux et Veritas," *New York Herald Tribune*, June 7, 1965.

27. Giamatti, *op. cit.*, p. 4.

28. Coffin was to remember: "Quirky, mawkish, sophomoric, whatever you want to call it, I can only say that in 1949, even for a pretty skeptical guy like me, it worked. It worked for the whole group." Quoted in Oldenberg, Don, "Tippy-Top Secret, Yale's Bush and Kerry Share Patrician Past of Skull and Bones," *Washington Post*, April 4, 2004.

29. Schiff, Judith Ann, "Old Yale: When the Shooting Stopped," *Yale Alumni Magazine*, Summer 1995, p. 112.

30. Buck, *op. cit.*, pp. 165–172; *Yale Daily News*, September 12, 1946.

31. Fenton, Charles, "Social Solemnity," *Seventy-Five, op. cit.*, pp. 43–44.

32. Parmet, Herbert, *George Bush: The Life of a Lone Star Yankee* (New York: Scribner, 1997), pp. 20–25; Phillips, Kevin, *American Dynasty: Aristocracy, Fortune, and the*

Politics of Deceit in the House of Bush (New York: Viking, 2004), pp. 20–25. Phillips (at pp. 42 and 200) asserts that George H. W. Bush "depended on his father's help to arrange an underage and unqualified entrance into the naval air program [because he could not satisfy the normal flight-school entry requirement of two years of college]" which "might have been quite manageable with a telephone call from Prescott Bush to one of three fellow Yale Skull and Bones men (the secretary of war, the assistant secretary of war for air, or the assistant secretary of the navy for air)," but no other Bush biographer supports this hypothesis.

33. Parmet, *op. cit.*, pp. 36–59; Phillips, *op. cit.*, p. 26; on AUV, Green, Fitzhugh, *George Bush: An Intimate Portrait* (New York: Hippocrene Books, 1989), p. 49. The Andover yearbook for 1942, GHWB's graduation year, shows more activities for him than anyone else in the class of over two hundred boys. King, Nicholas, *George Bush: A Biography* (New York: Dodd, Mead, 1980) pp. 16, 20–21.

34. On veterans' maturity, diversity, and Negro scholarships, *1948 Yale Class Book* (New Haven, Conn.: 1948), pp. 37–38, 40, 42–43; on G.I. Bill grant, Cohane, Tim, *The Yale Football Story* (New York: G. Putnam, 1951), p. 374; on football team names, Bergin, Thomas, *The Game* (New Haven, Conn.: Yale University Press, 1984), p. 324; King, Nicholas, George Bush: A Biography (New York: Dodd, Mead, 1980), pp. 38–40; *1949 Class Book*, p. 57.

35. Phillips, *op. cit.*, p. 42; baseball stadium seat, Bush, George W., *41: A Portrait of My Father* (New York: Crown, 2014), p. 72; Bush, Barbara, *Barbara Bush: A Memoir* (New York: Scribner's, 1994), pp. 26–29; Green, *op. cit.*, pp. 48–49; on Chafee, Rubin, Alissa, "Senate Centrist John H. Chafee Is Dead at 77," *Los Angeles Times*, October 26, 1999.

36. Loftus and Aarons, *op. cit.*, pp. 362 and 592, citing confidential interviews with Skull and Bones members, and Shapiro, Bruce, "Bush Ape 'Just Elitist,'" *New Haven Independent*, November 3, 1988.

37. Pincus, Walter, and Bob Woodward, "Bush Opened Up to Secret Yale Society; Turning Points in a Life Build on Alliances," *Washington Post*, August 7, 1988, and "George Bush: Man and Politician," *Washington Post*, August 11, 1988; Berke, Richard L., "Million-Dollar Team Keeping Bush Campaign in the Money," *New York Times*, May 23, 1988. Woodward, as a member of Book and Snake in the class of 1965, would have absorbed much lore about Bones long before becoming the famous investigative reporter at the *Post*, and it was speculated that Woodward's sources for Deep Throat (before Woodward himself publicly identified his source as Mark Felt) might have been Bonesmen Ray Price and Richard Moore, high Nixon aides. Rosenbaum, *The Secret Parts, op. cit.*, p. 162.

38. Green, *op. cit.*, pp. 52–53; Minutaglio, Bill, *First Son: George W. Bush and the Bush Family Dynasty* (New York: Times Books), pp. 24–25; Bearak, Barry, "His Great Gift, to Blend In: Team Player Bush: A Yearning to Serve," *Los Angeles Times*, November 22, 1987. George H. W. Bush was to name one of his sons Neil Mallon Bush.

39. Letter dated March 10, 1949 from undergraduate members of Scroll and Key to society alumni; *Yale Daily News*, April 12 and 25, and May 12, 1949.

40. "Yale Men," *Ebony*, July 1950; Cohen, Leonard, "The Sports Parade," *New York Post Home News*, November 28, 1948; Williams, Joe, "Jackson's to Be Tapped for Fabulous Bones," *New York World-Telegram*, May 11, 1949. Scroll and Key debated

offering Jackson a tap, and did, but the first black man would not join that society until the class of 1967, when the children of all the classes of 1948 and 1949 were in college. Giamatti, *op. cit.*, p. 4. Jackson's biography and election to the captaincy are in Cohan, *op. cit.*, pp. 333–334. The first Italian American Yale football captain was Joseph Fortunato (1954), tapped for Bones. Bergin, *op. cit.*, pp. 190, 274, 364.

41. *1949 Yale Class Book*, p. [33].

42. *New York Times, New York Herald Tribune, New Haven Journal-Courier, New Haven Register*, May 13, 1949; pre-tap pledge, Oren, *op. cit.*, p. 162, and Plimpton, *op. cit.*, p. 69; later Jackson comment, Meers, Erik, "Integration Remembered," *New Journal* 25, 1991–1993, February 5, 1993, p. 24. *New York Times* also featured the election of the "Ebony Express" as team captain on its front page, "Yale Elects First Negro Captain as Jackson Heads Football Team," November 23, 1948, noting that Harvard had appointed an African American as varsity football manager.

43. Fenton, *Seventy-Five, op. cit.*, pp. 43–44.

44. Green, Yale's 103rd captain and third leading ballcarrier by his day, was the son of a carloader for the Texas & Pacific Railroad. Bergin, *op. cit.*, pp. 274–275.

45. Baltzell, *op. cit.*, p. 279, without further citation, a quotation repeated many times in magazine journalism on the society system. A better example of Jackson's wit was his reaction to Yale football coach Herbert Hickman's characterization of his not too sturdy line as "the seven dwarfs," to which Jackson's response was, "I guess that makes me Snow White." Bergin, *op. cit.*, pp. 197–198.

46. Oren, *op. cit.*, p. 162; Judis, John B., *William F. Buckley, Jr.: Patron Saint of the Conservatives* (New York: Simon and Schuster, 1988, pp. 58–59). Buckey's post-graduation bestseller, *God and Man at Yale* (1951), saying that neither Catholics and Jews had "social prestige of any sort" at Yale and attacking his alma mater as offering undergraduates a godless and collectivist education, brought on a forceful reaction which "should undermine the confidence of those who believe in a unified conspiratcy of men from Skull and Bones," earning the public, printed wrath of Reuben Holden (Bones 1940), McGeorge Bundy (1939), Frank Ashburn (1925), and the Rev. Henry Sloane Coffin (1897), who said Buckley's Catholicism "distorted" his outlook and he "should have attended Fordham or some similar institution." Horowitz, Daniel, *op. cit.*, pp. 54–55. His book's dustjacket identified Buckley's society membership, and the author had some misgivings about mentioning it—"nothing more than snob appeal"—but saw it clinched what his publisher desired to emphasize, that this was an attack on the citadel mounted from within. Tanenhaus, *op. cit.*

47. Weber, Bruce, "Thomas Guinzburg, Paris Review Co-Founder, Dies at 84," *New York Times*, September 10, 2010. Guinzburg and Buckley were the two leading contenders for chairmanship of the *Yale Daily News*, but Guinzburg was more interest in getting out the news rather than writing editorials, and so took the managing editorship by agreement with Buckley. Judis, *op. cit.*, p. 54.

48. Oren, *op. cit.*, p. 163; Oder, Norman, "Senior Societies," *Yale Daily News*, April 13, 1982; "Survey: Senior Society Elections, May 1955, A. Whitney Griswold papers, Manuscripts and Archives, Yale University.

49. Campus policeman John J. Gill to Dean Richard C. Carroll, November 19, 1949. In a letter from Plimpton to George Frazier quoted extensively in Frazier's magazine article, "The Yale Secret Societies," *Esquire*, September 1955, p. 116, Plimpton

gives more, sometimes slightly different, and, given the official police report's text, incorrect details (in his retelling, presumably as reported to him by Loeb, Loeb went to the tomb with the search party and demanded the building be searched, to see for himself how much of the article was accurate, but the police demurred, "as nervous about the power of Bones apparently as the aspiring undergraduate"). In April 2000, three thousand copies of the campus tabloid *Rumpus* for that month, with a four-page insert of Skull and Bones, identifying its current members, were redistributed to residential college basements and recycling bins, and Bones was accused of the mischief in the next month's issue.

50. *1950 Class Book*, p. 47.

CHAPTER TWELVE: REFORMS, REVELATIONS, AND RIVALS UNDERGROUND

1. *Yale Daily News*, May 5, 1950.

2. *Harvard Crimson*, November 23, 1950.

3. "Smith Explores Inner Sanctum of Bonesmen, Reveals Tense Tapping, Portentous Tombs," *Current*, vol. X, no. X, 6 December 1951.

4. Halberstam, Michael J., George Abrams, and Ronald P. Kriss, "Yale: High Society Yale Dances to Senior Society Tune, but Minority Refuses to Get in Step," *Harvard Crimson*, November 2, 1952.

5. Knowles, John, "The Yale Man," *Holiday*, May 1953. *Yale Daily News* ran a front-page piece on Knowles's article on April 17, 1953. Knowles was tapped by an underground senior society, Sword and Gate.

6. Frazier, George, "Yale's Secret Societies," *Esquire*, September 1955, pp. 106–116. In his 1955 article, the reporter-detective with the divorcees is not identified, but in his column for January 24, 1962, Frazier admitted that this was his own research methodology. His final such column drawing on his knowledge of Yale secret societies appeared before the Harvard-Yale game of 1973 on November 23.

7. Poore, Charles, "We Must Be Pacemakers in a Free World," *New York Times Magazine*, February 28, 1950.

8. Acheson, David C., *Acheson Country: A Memoir* (New York: W. W. Norton, 1993), pp. 202–204; Chase, James, *Acheson: The Secretary of State Who Created the American World* (New York: Simon and Schuster, 1998), p. 370. Dean Acheson's own rendition of the Corporation election story does not mention the Hutchins feint with his fellow Keysman Lewis, and describes Edwin Foster Blair, class of 1924 and Bones, as "manager" of the Griswold candidacy: Acheson, Dean, *Present At the Creation* (New York: W. W. Norton, 1996), pp. 371–373. Classifying the voting Corporation members by senior society, six were Bonesmen, four from Keys, two members of Wolf's Head, and one from Elihu (thirteen senior society graduates in all), with only three neutrals as fellow board members.

9. *Time*, June 11, 1951; Kabaservice, "Kingman Brewster," *op. cit.*, pp. 227–228; Horowitz, David, *op. cit.*, p. 47. In *Remembering Denny*, Calvin Trillin writes of his senior year, 1957, that "'Shoe' meant more to us than 'white shoe.' It could indicate a background of boarding schools and trust funds—something like what 'preppy' came to mean a decade later, although without the scorn that term carried with it. It could mean dress or behavior that reflected such a background, even if the person involved came from entirely different circumstances. . . . It could also mean something approaching cool or suave. . . . Apparently, the brown shoe people were the bright student council presidents

from white middle-class high schools who had been selected by Yale to be buffed up a bit and sent out into the world, prepared to prove their high-school classmates right in voting them the most likely to succeed. Black shoe people were beyond the pale." He also mentions the theory "that the phrases derived from similar classifications that were used in the Navy during the Second World War to distinguish among ship's officers and naval pilots and those young ensigns and lieutenants who wore their white shoes to the dress-uniform functions that were a regular part of your wear if you were attached to the admiral's staff." Trillin, *op. cit.*, pp. 31–32.

10. *Newsweek*, June 11, 1951.
11. Griswold, A. Whitney, *In the University Tradition* (New Haven, Conn.: Yale University Press, 1957), p. 75; 1946 faculty rank, *Seventy-Five, op. cit.*, p. 66.
12. Strong, Dennis, letter to *Yale Daily News*, April 25, 1950; Moses, Dick, "On the Whole," *Yale Daily News*, April 26, 1950, referencing the Strong letter.
13. *Yale Daily News*, May 12, 1950.
14. *Yale Daily News*, April 30 and May 4, 1951.
15. Milton Devane tap, with Levi Jackson and Fenno Heath, *Yale Daily News*, May 13, 1949; *Yale Daily News*, April 25 and 28, 1952. The statistical analysis cited by Weinberg was in Gideon Gordon's article "Societies: Who's Been Tapped" in the May 2, 1951 *News*.
16. *Yale Daily News*, May 5 and 9, 1952.
17. "Olds Plan" details, *Yale Daily News*, May 5, 1952, and editorial on June 12, 1953, and Griswold interview on January 14, 1953. The "DeVane Plan," originally styled the "Olds Plan," was finally printed in full on May 6, 1953 in *Yale Daily News*.
18. Letter to Dean DeVane, January 1, 1953; *Yale Daily News*, March 26, 1953.
19. Letter to the Class of 1954 by Hamilton D. Harper and Philip M. Glover, March 9, 1953, generously excerpted on May 2, 1953 in the *Yale Daily News*.
20. Letter from Carlos F. ("Toddy") Stoddard Jr., on behalf of the Special Committee of the Kingsley Trust Association, March 13, 1953.
21. Letter from Donald F. Keefe to the Representatives of the Senior Societies, March 23, 1953, and enclosure; letter from O'Keefe to the Graduate Representatives of the Senior Societies, April 15, 1953. The plan had been submitted to the Yale College Dean under cover letter dated April 9, 1953, signed by fifteen members of the class of 1953 assembled from the six abovegrounds.
22. "Yale University Abolishes Tap Day Ritual; Ceremony Called Humiliating to Rejected," *New York Times*, March 27, 1953.
23. *Yale Daily News*, April 8, April 16, and May 6, 1953; *Time*, May 3, 1953.
24. *Yale Daily News*, May 4, 1953.
25. *Yale Daily News*, May 6, 1953.
26. Trillin, *op. cit.*, p. 93; *New York Times*, April 30, 1954.
27. *Yale Daily News*, April 27, 28, and 29 and May 9 and 14, 1955. The biographical sessions of Wolf's Head are described in Muenzen, Paul, "Voices from the Tombs Speak," *Yale Daily News*, April 17, 1985, and by a member as events "when the bonding takes place."
28. Devane and Fenton articles, *Yale Daily News*, April 24 and 25, 1956. A similar series of educational articles was run in 1958: see *Yale Daily News*, April 28, 1958, by Scott Sullivan '58; April 29, 1958, by Thomas K. Swing '58; and on April 29, 1958, by the anonymous member of an underground.

29. *Yale Daily News*, April 28, 1956, p. 8; on Trillin, informally interviewed by William Horowitz '29 before following his path from Kansas City back east a quarter of a century later, "as [Horowitz] frequently did for Jewish boys considering going from the Paris of the Midwest to the City of Elms," see Horowitz, David, *op. cit.* p. 51.

30. Oren, *op. cit.*, pp. 162–163. During Chauncey's student days at Groton (where he was a scholarship student, as at Yale), that prep school admitted students whom he understood were its first-ever Jew and first-ever black man. Lemann, *op. cit.*, p. 141. Lehrman was a German Jew whose family had come to America in the middle of the nineteenth century. Raised as a Jew and, after marrying an Episcopalian and converting to Catholicism, Lehrman was a graduate of the Hill School, and a Yale a member of the Fence Club, while serving as undergraduate director of the Yale Summer Camp for Underprivileged Children. Horowitz, David, *op. cit.*, pp. 229–230.

31. *Yale Daily News*, April 17, 1957; Trillin, who himself did not read *Stover* until decades later, *op. cit.*, pp. 34–36, 92.

32. *Yale Daily News*, April 18 and 29, and May 1, 1957. Schiffrin, described by Trillin *op. cit.*, p. 36, as "the son of intellectuals who had fled France in 1941," was born in Paris, and became the managing director of publishing at Pantheon Books. His anti-society piece in the *News*, "If You Have the Time," was cowritten with Michael Cooke, an Afro Carribean who was Class Day Poet, Scholar of the House, and All-American in soccer, and may well, according to Horowitz, *op. cit.*, p. 261 n. 24, have had multiple offers from aboveground senior societies, but perhaps he discouraged them in the pre-tapping period; Cooke later became a tenured Yale professor of English and master of Berkeley College. Professor Weiss (son of immigrants, high school dropout, City College BA, Harvard PhD, joining the faculty of Yale College as its only Jewish full professor, whose son Jonny was a member of the class of 1960, Horowitz, *op. cit.*, p. 65) had been attacking the senior society system since 1951, with a speech to the Aurelian Honor Society which was reprinted in the *Yale Daily News* and the *Yale Literary Magazine*. *Yale Daily News*, April 17, 1951, and *Yale Literary Magazine*, May 1951, p. 3, with that magazine's editors finding that "despite his statement to the contrary, Mr. Weiss is virtually advocating the abolition of the societies. . . "

33. Schiffrin, André, *A Political Education: Coming of Age in Paris and New York* (Hoboken, N.J.: Melville House, 2007), pp. 127–128. He received a full scholarship on the recommendation of Paul Mellon, and as a senior he won the Snow Prize, given to the man "who has done the most for Yale" (pp. 122, 140).

34. *Yale Daily News*, April 30, 1957. Manuscript's first published membership list appeared on May 3, 1957, in the *Yale Daily News*, and the strongest advocate for the society coming above ground was David Calleo '55, who was then president of the Yale Political Union and who served thereafter for decades as the society's corporate president. Wallace, Thomas, ed. *Reflections on Manuscript 1953–2012* (New Haven, Conn.: 2012), pp. 18–19.

35. Calleo, David P., and Henry S. F. Cooper, *Inside Eli or How to Get on at Yale* (New Haven, Conn.: privately printed, 1957), pp. 5–7. *Yale Daily News*, April 18, 1957, hailed the publication approvingly as "an irreverent and scurrilous critic of Yale mores if ever there was one." Trillin, *op. cit.*, p. 31, discusses the authors and the pamphlet, "written in a tone that may have reflected some exposure to the works of Evelyn Waugh."

36. *Yale Daily News*, May 5, 1955.

37. The Charter of the Sword and Gate Society; *Sword & Gate Society Undergraduate Handbook*. The name is taken from Milton's passage in Book XII, lines 633–649, on the expulsion of Adam and Eve by "the brandisht sword of God" through "th' Eastern Gate." Sword and Gate's tomb is at 18 Linwood Street, and its corporate parent is the Hale Foundation.

38. Havemeyer, *"Go to Your Room,"* *op. cit.*, p. 71; on Taft, Plimpton, *op. cit.*, p. 95.

39. Velsey and Leinenweber, *op. cit.*, pp. 47–52; *Yale Daily News*, April 16, 1957.

40. *Yale Daily News*, April 16, 1957, and April 30, 1958. Daniel Horowitz in his history of the class of 1960 writes, "When I had to present my autobiography to my underground senior society at Yale [Spade & Grave], I focused on how I looked at the world as both an insider and an outsider . . ." Horowitz, *op. cit.*, p. 33.

41. Horowitz, *ibid.*, pp. 154–155, on Spade and Grave.

42. Cooper, H. S. F. Jr., Thomas C. Wallace, eds.: Stephen Parks, producer, *Manuscript (1953–2002)* (New Haven, Conn.: Wrexham Foundation, 2002), *passim*.

43. *Ibid.*, pp. 71–73, 79–84; Wallace, ed, *Reflections on Manuscript*, *op. cit.*, pp. 47 and 74–78; "Ingenious Use of a Narrow Site," *Architectural Record*, November 1965; "King-liu Wu: Noted Architect and Popular Instructor," *Yale Bulletin & Calendar*, Vol. 31, No. 1, August 30, 2002.

44. Perrotta, Tom, *Joe College* (New York: St. Martin's, 2000), p. 109, in his novel's setting year of 1982.

45. Havemeyer, *"Go to Your Room,"* *op. cit.*, pp. 70–71; Guo, Jerry, "Connecticut Journal: Inside Yale's Secret Societies," http:www.gadling.com/2008/05/29. connecticut-journal-inside-yales-secret-societies).Gadling.com, retrieved July 9, 2015; on Elba, Wallace, ed., *Reflections on Manuscript*, *op. cit.*, pp. 48–49, 53–55.

46. Guo, *ibid.* On Ashcroft, Gillette, Howard, Jr., *Class Divide: Yale '64 and the Conflicted Legacy of the Sixties* (Ithaca, N.Y., and London: Cornell University Press, 2015), pp. 9 and 232 n. 35. The players in the 1963 Harvard-Yale freshman soccer game were not told of the assassination until the match finished, and this may well have been true of Ashcroft's and other contests. Monette, Paul, *Becoming A Man: Half a Life Story* (New York: Harcourt Brace Jovanvioch, 1992), p. 107.

47. Trillin, *op. cit.*, p. 112; Wedge, Bryant M., MD, ed., *Psychosocial Problems of College Men* (New Haven, Conn.: Yale University Press, 1958), p. 12; Trillin, *op. cit.*, p. 41; "Imitation or Reformation?" *Yale Daily News*, April 16, 1957.

48. DeVane, Clyde, "The College in a National University," in *Seventy-Five*, *op. cit.*, p. 3; Pierson, G. W., "The Yale Approach," Seventy-Five, *op. cit.*, p. 19; "Bursary System at Yale," *Yale Daily News*, April 29, 1959.

49. Fenton, Charles, "Social Solemnity," in *Seventy-Five*, *op. cit.*, p. 44; Carroll, Richard, "Extra-Curricular Proficiency," *Seventy-Five*, *op. cit.*, p. 45.

50. Carroll, *ibid.* pp. 45–46. See also Sewall, Richard B., "An Educator Evaluates," *Seventy-Five*, *op. cit.*, p. 58. Sewall, in his fall 1953 address to the matriculation assembly of the class of 1957, referred without enthusiasm to a view of Yale as "a stepping-stone to what we Americans fondly call 'success'—success in general terms, what *Time* magazine had in mind a few months ago when it said, 'As every Yale man knows, Yale is more than a great university; it is also a school for success.'" Quoted in Trillin, *op. cit.*, p. 50.

51. "Society Breakdowns," *Yale Daily News*, May 12, 1955.

52. Records of A. Whitney Griswold, Manuscripts & Archives, Yale University.

53. *Ibid.*, Fiske to Griswold, November 12, 1956; Fiske speech, dated November 13, 1956; Griswold to Fiske, November 17, 1956; Michel Leisure '57 to Fiske, December 21, 1956; Griswold to Fisk, January 14, 1957; Griswold to Fiske, November 22, 1957.

54. "A Farewell to Bright College Years," *Life*, June 24, 1957; Trillin, *op. cit.*, pp. 29–30. When *Life* was considering running the feature, the man overseeing the University News Bureau was Carlos Stoddard, Keys 1926 and former *Yale Daily News* chair, who as a matter of fairness and diplomacy sent to the magazine not only Hansen's name, but that of a man from Bones as well, Steve Ackerman. Trillin, *op. cit.*, pp. 83–84.

55. "The Time Has Come," *Yale Daily News*, May 4, 1959.

56. On Goss, Horowitz, *op. cit.*, pp. 231–232. The use of "spook" by both the CIA and the societies is noted in Rosenbaum, Ron, "An Elegy for Mumbo-Jumbo" in *Esquire*, September 1977 (p. 85), and the CIA connection is considered (pp. 148–149).

57. Jeffreys-Jones, Rhodri, *Cloak and Dollar: A History of American Secret Intelligence* (New Haven, Conn.: Yale Unversity Press, 2002), pp. 60–63, 67–68, 70; on Stimson, Hodgson, *op. cit.*, p. 203.

58. Smith, Bradley F., *The Shadow Warriors: O.S.S. and the Origins of the C.I.A.* (New York: Basic Books, 1983), pp. 360–362.

59. Winks, *op. cit.*, pp. 15–16, and p. 485 n. 1. On Hale, and making the point that it was not his spying skills which distinguished his service, but rather his volunteering for what could not be commanded because of the stigma against spying, see Corson, William R., *The Armies of Ignorance: The Rise of the American Intelligence Empire* (New York: Dial Press, 1977), pp. 488–491.

60. Winks, *op. cit.*, pp. 97–101; Lewis, *op. cit.*, pp. 334–366; Kahrl, William L., "Yet time and change shall not prevail To break the friendships formed at . . . ," *New Journal*, vol. 2, no. 6, 9 February 1964.

61. Winks, *op. cit.*, p. 35, on class of 1943; on Pearson, Diamond, Sigmund, *Compromised Campus: The Collaboration of Universities with the Intelligence Community, 1945–1955* (Oxford, England: Oxford University Press, 1992), p. 53. Robbins, *op. cit.*, p. 187, lists a number of Bonesmen with CIA connections.

62. On Princeton, Hersh, Burton, *The Old Boys: The American Elite and the Origins of the CIA* (New York: Scribner's, 1992), p. 4; on Yale, Professor Gaddis Smith in 1984, quoted in Blow, Rich, "The Secret Link," *New Journal*, vol. 16, no. 6, April 20, 1984.

63. "laying on of hands," Winks, *op. cit.*, p. 35; on Walz, Notestein, the residential college system and senior societies as recruitment pools, and "sentimental imperialism," Winks, *op. cit.*, pp. 36–40, 51–56, 59, 119.

64. Thomas, Evan, *The Very Best Men: Four Who Dared: The Early Years of the CIA* (New York: Touchstone, 1995), p. 12; Kahrl, *op. cit.*

65. On Barnes's CIA career (and Keys), Thomas, *op. cit.*, pp. 74–86, 334–338, 366; on Cord Meyer Jr.'s CIA career, Hendrickson, Paul, "Behind the Scenes of a CIA Life: Cord Meyer's Trek from One-World Crusader to CIA Official," *Washington Post*, February 7, 1978, and Winks, *op. cit.*, pp. 443–444; on William Bundy's CIA career, Bird, *op. cit.*, pp. 156–181; on Buckley's CIA career, Diamond, *op. cit.*, pp. 172–177, 328–329 n. 21, and Judis, *op. cit.*, pp. 89–93; on Coffin's, Goldstein, Warren, *William*

Sloane Coffin Jr.: A Holy Impatience (New Haven, Conn.: Yale University Press, 2004), pp. 71–78, and Coffin, William Sloane Jr., *Once to Every Man, a Memoir* (New York: Atheneum, 1977), pp. 86–94.

66. On Angleton, see Mangold, Tom, *Cold Warrior: James Jesus Angleton: The CIA's Master Spy Hunter* (New York: Simon & Schuster, 1991), pp. 31–37, and Holzman, Michael, *James Jesus Angleton: The CIA, and the Craft of Counterintelligence* (Amherst: University of Massachusetts Press, 2008), pp. x–xi, 50, and 321,who credits Angleton's skills in parsing ambiguity to his training in the New Criticism at Yale under Professor Maynard Mack (Keys 1932 and the society's first historian). Angleton's mentor, Yale professor and OSS veteran Norman Holmes Pearson, is credited with the suggestion of developing "a cadre, one eventually including thousands of academics, who could 'tap' young people for the secret intelligence services, as if for acceptance by Skull and Bones." Holzman, *op. cit.*, p. 251. On Pearson, see Winks, pp. 247–321. On Bissell, see text accompanying endnote 48 in Chapter Ten, and Thomas, *op. cit., passim.*

67. Holzman, *op. cit.*, pp. 100–101; no scandal, Sinclair, Andrew, "Recruiting the right stuff," [London] *Sunday Times*, January 17, 1988, reviewing Winks's book.

68. Latham, Aaron, *Orchids for Mother* (Boston, Mass.: Little, Brown, 1971), p. 298, and see also pp. 12, 16 for more Yale/Hale text.

69. Le Carré, John, *Russia House* (New York: Alfred A. Knopf, 1989), p. 291. Le Carré did something similar on Skull and Bones in *The Night Manager* (London: Penguin, 2013), p. 354: "The Prescotts were old Yale people, of course, and a couple of them had Agency connections—how could they not have?—and there was even a rumor, which Ed Prescott had never even specifically defined, that he was in same way related to old Prescott Bush, George Bush's father."

70. McCarry, Charles, *The Last Supper* (London and New York: Duckworth Overlook, 1983/2010), pp. 52, 99–101, 180 (see also, in the Duckworth editions: *Second Sights* [1974/2009], pp. 88, 318; *The Better Angels* [1979/2003], p. 68.

71. Buckley, William F., Jr., *Saving the Queen* (New York: Doubleday, 1976), pp. 13, 35, 44, and 192-193. The Buckley series titles are *Saving the Queen; Stained Glass; Who's On First; Marco Polo, If You Can; The Story of Heni Tod; See You Later, Alligator; High Jinx; Mongoose, R.I.P.; Tucker's Last Stand; A Very Private Plot;* and *Last Call for Blackford Oakes.*

72. Sarris, Andrew, "At the Movies," *New York Observer*, December 26, 2006; Roth, Eric, *The Good Shepherd: The Shooting Script* (New York: Newmarket Press, 2006), pp. 11–14, 16–17, 29–34, 105–106, 116–117, 123–125; on the non–New Haven shooting locations, Dempsey, Rachel, "Real Elis Inspired 'Shepherd'." *Yale Daily News*, January 18, 2007.

73. Bissell, *op. cit.*, p. 7.

74. Giamatti, *op. cit.*, pp. 25–26; Gifford, Prosser, "A Student Evaluates," in *Seventy-Five*, *op. cit.*, p. 55.

75. *Yale Daily News*, May 5 and 6, 1960.

76. Wedge, *op. cit.*, p. 11.

77. Frazier, George, "The Bones Boys," *Boston Herald*, April 9, 1964. The Pyle/Mallory dustup was recollected in the opening paragraphs of a *Wall Street Journal* front-page article by Stephen Grover on Yale senior societies, "Secret Groups Thrive At Yale While Interest In Fraternities Lags," December 11, 1968.

CHAPTER THIRTEEN: BLACKS, WOMEN, AND MAY DAY

1. Quoted in Holden, Reuben A., *Profiles and Portraits of Yale University Presidents* (Freeport, Me.: Bond-Wheelwright, 1968), p. 136.

2. von Bothmer, Bernard, *Framing the Sixties: The Use and Abuse of a Decade from Ronald Reagan to George W. Bush* (Amherst: University of Masachusetts Press, 2010), p. 2, calling them the "long 1960s" or the "bad 1960s."

3. Horowitz, David, *op. cit.*, pp. xvii, 2, 9, 16–17; Arthur Howe, "Dean Howe Replies," *Yale Daily News*, November 2, 1962; *Social Register* percentages, *Yale Daily News*, November 23, 1963.

4. Horowitz, *op. cit.*, pp. 13, 91; on Torch, Havemeyer, *"Go to Your Room," op. cit.*, p. 89. Ironically, it had been the Yale chapter of DKE which had admitted the Chinese student Yung Wing, class of 1854, who is said to have been the only person of color to be initiated into a college fraternity in the antebellum period. By the 1920s, a number of fraternities had amended their constitutions to include regulations barring all but white Christian men. Syrett, *op. cit.*, pp. 217, 253–254, 260.

5. Lamb, William Pollack, Jr., "Senior Year," *Class Book 1960*, p. 34; Horowitz, *op. cit.*, pp. 10–11, 56.

6. Wedge, *op. cit.*, pp. 10–14.

7. Kabaservice, "Kingman Brewster," *op. cit.*, pp. 239–253; on Howe's failed tap, Kabaservice, *The Guardians, op. cit.*, p. 69; Winks, *op. cit.*, pp. 97–98.

8. "Long Island Sound," Kabaservice, "Kingman Brewster," *op. cit.*, p. 335; Herman, *op. cit.*, p. 19. As stated by Franklin Foer in "What's Really Wrong with Skull and Bones: Tomb of Their Own," *New Republic*, April 17 and 24, 2000: "In fact, it was men from the secret societies, like Yale administrators R. Inslee Clark, William Sloane Coffin, and Sam Chauncey, who ended the dominance of their kind, the boarding-school elite."

9. Kinkaid, Katherine, *How an Ivy League College Decides Admissions* (New York: W. W. Norton, 1961), pp. 7, 25–28, and *passim*; Griswold, *Report to the Alumni, 1952–53* (New Haven, Conn.: Yale University, 1953), p. 3; Kabaservice, "Kingman Brewster," *op. cit.*, p. 301; Soares, Joseph, *The Power of Privilege: Yale and America's Elite Colleges* (Stanford, Calif.: Stanford University Press, 2007), pp. 36–38, 41, 51, 54–56, 66–71; on Clark, Lemann, *op. cit.*, p. 149.

10. Kabaservice, "Kingman Brewster," *op. cit.*, p. 309.

11. *Ibid.*, pp. 218, 304, 306; Brewster quoted in Soares, *op. cit.*, p. 82.

12. *Idem*, pp. 305–306. President Brewster in answering a letter from an alumnus about leaders with stronger character than brains wrote: "[W]hile the academic threshold is higher than ever, we have more extracurricular achievers in [the class of] 1970 than we did in 1967; far more in the class of '67 than in 1952. So the canard that we have shifted to 'brains only' myopia is not borne out by the record." Letter to Bayard Walker dated June 26, 1967, Kingman Brewster Papers, Manuscripts and Archives, Yale University.

13. "Alumni Board Comparision of Classes of 1952 and 1970," Kingman Brewster Papers, Manuscripts and Archives, Yale University.

14. Soares, *op. cit.*, pp. 87–88; Pierson, George, *Yale Book of Numbers, op. cit.*, pp. 101–102.

15. *Yale Daily News*, May 4, 1954 and May 12, 1955; 1956 membership chart, A. Whitney Griswold Papers, *op. cit.*

16. All data on class composition derives from *Seventy-Five*, *op. cit.*, p. 33, as summarized in Giamatti, *op. cit.*, p. 22.

17. Statistics for Bones and Keys delegations of 1967 compiled from the *Yale 1967 Class Book*; on Bush admission, Karabel, *op. cit.*, pp. 344–345, and Minutaglio, *op. cit.*, pp. 58–75. The percentage of legacies in Bush's class was 19.6 percent, and his verbal SAT score put him in the bottom 10 percent of his class, although he ranked 114th out of 238 at Andover. Kinsley, Michael, "How Affirmative Action Helped George W. Bush," *Time*, January 2003, p. 70. On his tap, see *New York Times*, July 29, 2000; Minutaglio, *op. cit.*, pp. 104–105; and Kristof, Nicholas D., "Ally of an Older Generation amid the Tumult of the 60's," *New York Times*, June 19, 2000. George W. Bush's daughter Barbara Bush (class of 2004) was elected to the underground Sage and Chalice. *New York Times*, May 23, 2004. After moving into the White House, Bush nominated or appointed at least ten Bonesmen to significant administration positions, among them the head of the Securities and Exchange Commission, William Donaldson '53; general counsel of the Office of Homeland Security, Edward McNally '79; ambassador to Poland, Victor Ashe '67; Bush's clubmate, assistant attorney general and then ambassador to Australia, Robert McCallum '68; his clubmate, ambassador to Trinidad and Tobago, Roy Austin '68; and his clubmate, acting director of the National Institute of Mental Health, Dr. Rex Cowdry '68.

18. Kabaservice, "Kingman Brewster," *op. cit.*, pp. 322–326; Oren, *op. cit.*, pp. 208–211; on legacies, Soares, *op. cit.*, pp. 85–87 and Table 4.2; Borders, William, "Ivy's Admissions Irk Prep Schools," *New York Times*, April 30, 1967.

19. Brewster, Kingman, Jr., "Admission to Yale: Objectives and Myths," *Yale Alumni Magazine*, October 30, 1966, pp. 31–32. The admissions cap on Catholics in the early 1950s was alleged by the Catholic chaplain of that era. Lemann, *op. cit.*, p. 142.

20. Karabel, *op. cit.*, p. 272; Oren, *op. cit.*, p. 391 n. 27; meeting notes, Women's Advisory Council, February 1969, Manuscripts & Archives, Yale University. Corporation records are sealed for seventy-five years after the resignation of the Yale president in office at the time, meaning that evidence—if it exists—of the attack on Clark would not come to light until 2052, and the only source is Kabaservice's oral history project of 1993. Soares, *op. cit.*, pp. 78–79.

21. Baltzell, *op. cit.*, pp. 8, 341. "WASP" was first used in print not by Baltzell, but by Erdman B. Padmore, Yale sociologist, in the January 1962 issue of the *American Journal of Sociology*.

22. *Yale Daily News*, April 8, 1959; on national fraternity policies and Yale, Kabaservice, "Kingman Brewster," *op. cit.*, p. 367.

23. *Yale Daily News*, September 21, 1955 and May 29, 1963; Kabaservice, "Kingman Brewster," *op. cit.*, p. 321.

24. Bond, Horace Mann, *Black American Scholars* (Detroit, Mich.: Balamp Publishing, 1972), p. 14.

25. Young, Jesse Allen, "A Century of Blacks at Yale, 1874–1974," Scholar of the House Paper, Manuscripts and Archives, Yale University, p. 7 and Appendix 5, pp. 57–59.

26. *Ibid.*, pp. 22–26; Dubois, W.E.B., *The Atlanta University Publications* (New York: Arno Press, 1968), p. 10; Corwin quoted in Oren, *op. cit.*, p. 72.

27. Young, *op. cit.*, pp. 15–16.

28. Pickens, William, "Southern Negro in Northern University," *Voices of the Negro*, vol. II, no. 3, 1905, p. 324.

29. Hiller, Stephen, "How Black Students Arrived at Yale," *Yale Daily News*, September 25, 1973.

30. Young, *op. cit.*, p. 32.

31. "Yale Men," *Ebony*, 5:9, January 1950, p. 20; Synnott, *op. cit.*, p. 174.

32. Kabaservice, *op. cit.*, pp. 352–353, (1957–1963 figures) 355; Young, *op. cit.*, pp. 42, 49.

33. Kabaservice, *ibid.*, pp. 354, 357–358, 366; *Yale Daily News*, April 2, 1966.

34. Kabaservice, *idem.*, p. 357.

35. Ball, David George, *A Marked Heart* (Bloomington, Ind.: iUniverse, 2012), pp. 62–69, 74; Coffin, *op. cit.*, pp. 82–125; Wilgoren, Jodi Lynne, "Black & Blue: Yale Volunteers in the Civil Rights Movement, 1963–65," senior essay in History, Yale College, April 13, 1992, pp. 15–16, Manuscripts and Archives, Yale University; Gillette, *op. cit.*, pp. 26–28; Sack, Kevin, "Trip South in '63 Gave Lieberman a Footnote, and Hold, in History," *New York Times*, September 26, 2000; Branch, Taylor, *Pillar of Fire: America in the King Years 1963–65* (New York: Simon & Schuster, 1998), pp. 156–159.

36. Kabaservice, *op. cit.*, pp. 349, 350, 368–369.

37. Bundy, McGeorge, "The Issue before the Court," *Atlantic*, 240:5, November 1977, p. 42.

38. Kabaservice, *op. cit.*, p. 375.

39. Brown, Buster, "Skull & Bones: It's Not Just for White Dudes Anymore," *Atlantic*, February 25, 2013.

40. These figures were computed by comparison of the lists of black undergraduates for the classes of 1960 through 1970 contained in Young, *op. cit.*, pp. 60–62, and also in Kabaservice, "Kingman Brewster," *op. cit.*, Appendix N, pp. 694–698, with the names of those elected to the seven aboveground senior societies in the annual classbooks from 1960 to 1970. In Stephen Grover's 1968 *Wall Street Journal* article "Secret Groups Thrive at Yale While Interest in Fraternities Lags," December 11, 1968, a "recent graduate" is quoted as saying, "with some irony," that "There's hardly a Negro who doesn't get an offer to join a society. Everyone thinks that a Negro is going to add something special to these secret society meetings." On Roy Austin's greater satisfaction with his 1968 Bones delegation than with his class's treatment of him, Holahan, David, "The Bad News Bones," *Hartford Courant*, May 29, 1988. By way of contrast, a magazine article on the Ivy League clubs, published in 1973, reported about the Harvard final clubs that "except as servants or occasional guests, blacks have never set foot in half the clubs. Perhaps ten or fifteen belong to the other half, and most of those are in Fly Club, where they comprise nearly fifty percent of the membership." Jaes, Theodore, Jr., "Ivy League Clubs," *Town & Country*, August 1973.

41. Velsey and Leinenweber, *op. cit.*, pp. 85–87.

42. Giamatti, *op. cit.*, p. 2, emphasis supplied.

43. *Yale Daily News*, April 19, 1963.

44. *Yale Daily News*, May 3, 1963.

45. Davis, Lanny, and Barry Golson, "Senior Societies," *1968 Class Book* (New Haven, Conn.: 1968), p. 238 (Davis '67 was chairman of the *Yale Daily News* and a member of Spade and Grave, and his classmate Golson a member of Wolf's Head).

46. Decrow, *op. cit.*, p. 33.

47. *Yale Daily News*, April 28, 1964.

48. *Yale Daily News*, May 1 and 6, 1964.

49. *Yale Daily News*, May 6, 1964.

50. *Yale Daily News*, May 6, 1964.

51. *Yale Daily News*, May 8, 1964.

52. *Yale Daily News*, April 29, 1965.

53. *Yale Daily News*, May 7, 1964, and April 28, 1966. For the 1967 election for the class of 1968, Bones' fifteen most wanted juniors were called to a meeting one evening at the admissions office and informed of their selection by athletic director Delany Kiphuth and others. *Yale Daily News*, April 27, 1967.

54. Dated April 25, 1963, William Sloane Coffin Jr. Papers, Manuscripts and Archives, Yale University Library. Tellingly, on the chaplain's conflicted view in 1963, Lieberman wrote: "I must thank you for the honesty of your offer to me including the expression of doubt concerning the existence of Societies at Yale. Because of my deep admiration for you, I left your office totally confused and quite depressed over the confusion your presence in the name of Skull and Bones brought to me." In his letter, Lieberman is sure that Thomas Rowe, a future Rhodes scholar, would join him in Elihu, but Rowe went to Bones. On the Bones tap, Baum, Geraldine, "Moderating and Moralizing, Lieberman Toils in the Center for the Record," *Los Angeles Times*, October 20, 2000.

55. Leslie, Jacques, "Smirk from the Past," *Salon*, March 1, 2000; Borders, William, "Bones and Keys Rattle in the Night at Yale," *New York Times*, April 29, 1967.

56. *Yale Daily News*, April 30, 1965.

57. *Yale Daily News*, April 12 and 20, 1966.

58. Monette, Paul, *Becoming a Man: Half a Life Story* (New York, San Diego, Calif., and London: Harcourt Brace Jovanovich, 1992), pp. 134–135.

59. Robbins, *op. cit.*, p. 137, reports that many Bones seniors came out as gay in the early seventies; on Keys, Guernsey and Zdanys, *op. cit.*, pp. 79–80; on the Bones club of 2011, Brown, *op. cit.*

60. Davis and Golson, *op. cit.*, p. 251; *Yale Daily News*, April 27, 1967.

61. Grover, *op. cit.*

62. Davis and Golson, *op. cit.*, pp. 241–242; Robbins, *op. cit.*, p. 198; Wolfe, Tom, "The 'ME' Decade," *New York*, August 23, 1976, pp. 32–33. Keys' program of "optionals" also sometimes included "autobiographical show and tell": Guernsey and Zdanys, *op. cit.*, p. 97.

63. Davis and Golson, *ibid.*, pp. 242–243, 247.

64. *Ibid.*, pp. 248–249.

65. Grover, *op. cit.*

66. Gillette, Howard, Jr., *Class Divide: Yale '64 and the Conflicted Legacy of the Sixties* (Ithaca, N.Y., and London: Cornell University Press, 2015), p. xvii and pp. 1–32, *passim*; Yale's experience was not singular: see Klatch, Rebecca, *A Generation Divided: The New Left, the New Right, and the 1960s* (Berkeley: University of California Press, 1999), *passim*.

67. Griswold, A. Whitney, "A Proposal for Strengthening the Residential College System in Yale University," 1958, A. Whitney Griswold Papers, Manuscripts and Archives, Yale University; Margolis, Jon, *The Last Innocent Year: America in 1964— The Beginning of the "Sixties"* (New York: William Morrow, 1999); Patterson, James T., *The Eve of Destruction: How 1965 Transformed America* (New York: Basic Books, 2012); Kaiser, Charles, *1968 In America: Music, Politics, Chaos, Counterculture, and the*

Shaping of a Generation (New York: Weidenfeld & Nicolson, 1988); Horowitz, *op. cit.*; Gillette, *op. cit.*

68. Yankelovich, Daniel, *New Rules: Searching for Self-Fulfillment in a World Turned Upside Down* (New York: Random House, 1981), p. 175.

69. The President's Commission on *Campus Unrest*, Campus Unrest (Washington, D.C.: 1970), *passim*.

70. MacPherson, Myra, *Long Time Passing: Vietnam and the Haunted Generation* (New York: Doubleday, 1984), p. 11; Stern, Lawrence, "America in Anguish, 1965 to 1973," in *A Short History of the Vietnam War*, ed. Allen Reed Millett (Bloomington: Indiana University Press, 1978), p. 3.

71. Drennen, Bill, "Miscarriage: Reflections on a War," in Robert G. Kaiser and Jethro Lieberman, eds., *Later Life: The 25th Reunion Classbook; The Class of 1964* (New Haven, Conn.: Yale University, 1989), p. 504. See also Reston, James, "New Haven: God and War at Yale," *New York Times*, April 26, 1967.

72. Kerry was to organize a 25th anniversary remembrance of Pershing's death for their Bones club at Arlington National Cemetery. "Keepers of the Crypt," *Baltimore Sun*, March 23, 2004, quoting Kerry's 1968 letter to his parents expressing his anguish at Pershing's death.

73. Yale graduation, *New York Times*, June 10, 1969; Hunter, James Davison, *Culture Wars: The Struggle to Define America* (New York: Basic Books, 1991), pp. 34. 42.

74. Schiff, Judith, "The first female students at Yale," *Yale Alumni* Magazine, September/October 2009; Kabaservice, "Kingman Brewster," *op. cit.*, p. 416. Only one faculty member, Yale historian George Pierson, voted against coeducation.

75. Coit, Nancy, *The Grounding of Modern Feminism* (New Haven, Conn.: Yale University Press, 1987), p. 219.

76. Quoted in Remnick, David, "American Hunger," *New Yorker*, October 12, 1998, p. 64.

77. On Howe, Soares, *op. cit.*, p. 103; Bergin, Thomas, *Yale's Residential Colleges in the First Fifty Years* (New Haven, Conn.: Yale University Press, 1983), p. 100; *New York Times*, September 29 and 30, 1956.

78. "Women at Yale Proposed by Dean of Admissions Howe," *Yale Daily News*, September 28, 1956; Arnstein, Dr. Robert, "Letter to Coeducation Forum," *Yale Daily News*, April 27, 1966; Kabaservice, "Kingman Brewster," *op. cit.*, p. 421.

79. Doob, Leonard, et al., *The Education of First Year Students in Yale College* (New Haven, Conn.: Yale University, 1962), p. 13; *Gate '67*, Vol. 1, No. 2, March 1964, pp. 10–13; *Yale Daily News*, May 18, 1966.

80. Kabaservice, "Kingman Brewster," *op. cit.*, p. 446; Lever, Janet and Pepper Schwartz, *Women at Yale: Liberating a College Campus* (Indianapolis, Ind.: Bobbs-Merrill, 1971), p. 5; "The Co-Education White Paper: Everything You Need to Know," *Yale Daily News*, November 7, 1968; Borders, William, "Yale Going Coed Next September," *New York Times*, November 15, 1968.

81. Kabaservice, *ibid.*, pp. 472–473; Co-Education Week, *New York Times*, November 5, 1968; admission of women, *New York Times*, November 15, 1968; applications, *New York Times*, November 24 and December 8, 1968; *New York Times*, April 14, 1970.

82. Lear, "How Yale Selected Her First Coeds," *New York Times Magazine*, April 13, 1969; Herman, R. Thomas, "Lots of Girls Applying to Yale but Learning Is Not Always Reason," *Wall Street Journal*, January 2, 1969; Linden, Tom, "Girls, Girls, Girls," *Yale Daily News*, February 14, 1969.

83. Lever and Schwartz, *op. cit.*, pp. 14–15.

84. *Ibid.*, pp. 24–26.

85. *Idem.*, pp. 27–28.

86. *Idem.*, p. 25, originally appearing in *Yale Daily News* on April 25, 1969. According to *Newsweek*, October 15, 1990, p. 64, Trudeau was tapped by Bones but "chose membership in the rival Scroll and Key, which puts his Bonesman-bashing strips in a different context. This is exactly the kind of secret score-settling that so annoys members of the Bush family." See *Doonesbury* strips for June 27 through July 2, 1988, and, in the month preceding the first President Bush's inauguration, December 17 and 19–31, 1988, and February 5, 1990. On young George's anger at Trudeau, see Meacham, John, *Destiny and Power: The American Odyssey of George Herbert Walker Bush* (New York: Random House, 2015), p. 290.

87. Lever and Schwartz, *op. cit.*, pp. 15, 32.

88. Davis and Golson, *op. cit.*, pp. 252–253.

89. Mintz, Professor Sidney, *Yale Daily News*, March 31, 1969.

90. Giamatti, *op. cit.*, pp. 5–7, 32–34; Gurnsey and Zdanys, *op. cit.*, pp. 1–2, 11–12, 22–23.

91. Guerney and Zdanys, *op. cit.*, p. 1.

92. Trillin, *op. cit.*, p. 6.

93. *Yale Daily News*, April 23, 24, 26, and 27, 1968.

94. *Yale Daily News*, March 11, March 12, April 4, April 21, and April 24, 1969. On Wilbur Johnson's classroom proposal, Holahan, *op. cit.*, and Robbins, *op. cit.*, p. 199. The notion that the senior societies' facilities or underlying land might be reclaimed for social centers for the university had been voiced in the spring of 1968 by Yale planner Edward Barnes: "Someday we hope secret societies will die out, and we can use their land and buildings for social centers." *Ibid.*, April 4, 1969.

95. *Yale Daily News*, October 18, 1969.

96. Cooper and Wallace, *op. cit.*, pp. 24–25, 28, 90, 93–95.

97. Bass, Paul, and Douglas W. Rae, *Murder in the Model City: The Black Panthers, Yale, and the Redemption of a Killer* (New York: Basic Books, 2006), pp. 118–163; Chauncey, Henry "Sam," Jr., John T. Hill, Thomas Strong, *May Day at Yale, 1970 Recollections of the Trial of Bobby Seale and the Black Panthers* (Westport, Conn.: Prospecta Press, 2015), *passim*; Taft, John, *Mayday at Yale: A Case Study in Student Radicalism* (Boulder, Colo.: Westview Press, 1976), *passim*; Kabaservice, "Kingman Brewster," *op. cit.*, pp. 516–528, 537–538; Hersey, John, *Letter to the Alumni* (New York: Alfred A. Knopf, 1970), pp. 13–27, 56–57, 61–62, 77; Guernsey and Zdanys, *op. cit.*, pp. 8–11; Wyatt, David, "The Last Spring at Yale," *Virginia Quarterly Review*, Spring 1977, pp. 347–354.

98. No Tap Day, Gurnsey and Zdanys, *op. cit.*, p. 11, describing a clandestine rendezvous with one candidate beside the Old Campus statute of President Woolsey; protecting black coeds, Gates, Henry Louis, Jr., introduction to Chauncey, Hill & Strong, *op. cit.*, pp. 7–8; Schmoke and Bones, *Baltimore Sun*, March 23, 2004. The black American in Keys that year was Ronald Matchett; besides Keys and Wolf's Head, there were also black members in the 1969–70 delegations of Bones, Berzelius, Book & Snake, Elihu, and St. Elmo's (or, all but Manuscript).

99. Velsey and Leinenweber, *op. cit.*, pp. 66–70.

100. Giamatti, *op. cit.*, pp. 6, 34; Trillin, *op. cit.*, pp. 82–83. Not until the portrait of the first Keys crowd to include women, taken in 1990, were the members all to be again

attired in formal black. Guernsey & Zdanys, *op. cit.*, p. 99. Mace and Chain was revived and acquired a property in 2006. Niarchos and Zapana, "Yale's secret social fabric," *Yale Daily News*, December 5, 2008.

101. Cooper and Wallace, *op. cit.*, pp. 25, 90–91, 94–95; Wallace, *Reflections on Manuscript, op. cit.*, pp. 50–52.

CHAPTER FOURTEEN: THE INTERGRATION OF WOMEN AND DECLINE OF ELITES

1. Sklar, David, "All the Things They Didn't Want You to Know," *Rumpus*, April 1997.

2. Cummins, Anastasia, "Women at Yale: The Social Process of Coeducation at Yale College," senior prize essay, 2015, http://elischolar.library.yale.edu/mssa_yale_history, pp. 29–31; Coffin, Harriet, "Women of Yale," *New York Times*, July 15, 1971; Kaplay, Cathy, and Gay Miller, "'Superwomen' or 'Babes'?" *Yale Daily News*, April 19, 1972.

3. Synnott, Martha Graham, *Student Diversity at the Big Three: Changes at Harvard, Yale, and Princeton since the 1970s* (New Brunswick, N.J., and London: Transaction Publishers, 2013), p. 31 and Table 3.2, p. 151.

4. *Ibid.*, p. 13; *Yale Daily News*, November 27 and December 13, 1984, March 8, 1988; on Kennedy withdrawal, *Harvard Crimson*, January 17, 2006; on Patrick withdrawal, *Boston Globe*, August 3, 2006.

5. Synnott, *op. cit.*, pp. 132–133; Mcauley, James, "The Men's Final Clubs," *Harvard Crimson*, October 5, 2010; Mcauley, James, "The Women's Final Clubs," The *Harvard Crimson*, October 7, 2010; Seely and Birdgood, "With an Invitation, a Gender Barrier at Harvard Falls," *New York Times*, September 12, 2015.

6. "Undergraduate Women at Yale" [1971], in envelope "Sex Discrimination at Yale," Kingman Brewster Papers, Manuscripts and Archives.

7. Women student leaders, Hoffman, Emily, and Elisabeth Polon, eds., *Reflections on Coeducation: A Critical History of Women at Yale* (New Haven, Conn.: n.p., 2010), *passim*; *New York Times*, October 7, 1979; Oren, *op. cit.*, p. 292. The phenomenon persists: since 2000, only two women have been elected to the presidency of the Yale College Council, the last in 2007. *Yale Daily News*, September 11, 2015. In 1983, the first woman Alumni Fellow, a 1977 graduate, was elected to the Yale Corporation. In 1987 the criterion of "high manhood" was removed from the qualifications for the Francis Gordon Brown Memorial Prize, and it was awarded to a woman.

8. Cooper and Wallace, *op. cit.*, pp. 88–89.

9. *Ibid.*, pp. 25–29, 95, 98–99, 101. According to its undergraduate handbook, the underground Sword and Gate elected two women the next year to its delegation of 1972.

10. Cummins, *op. cit.*, pp. 32–34; *New York Times*, April 14, 1970.

11. Pierson, George, "Faculty," in *A Yale Book of Numbers, op. cit.*

12. Synnott, *Student Diversity, op. cit.*, pp. 144–145; *New York Times*, June 3, 1973.

13. Steinbreder, John, *The History of the Yale Club of New York City* (New York: Legendary Publishing, 2014), pp. 103–106; Gitlin and Gitlin, op. cit, pp. 30–32; Synnott, *Student Diversity, op. cit.*, p. 145.

14. Interview with Sam Chauncey, September 21, 2014.

15. Giamatti, *op. cit.*, pp. 43, 45–46, and 57 n. 10; *Yale Daily News*, March 9, 1988; Daniels, Lee, "Another Club at Yale Admits Women," *New York Times*, March 9, 1988; Gurnsey and Zdanys, *op. cit.*, pp. i, 68–69, 78–81, 85–86, 92, 106.

16. Holahan, *op. cit.*

17. Brown, *op. cit.*

18. Wagner, Barbara, "Living through Coeducation," in Geismar, Pamela, Eve Hart Rice, and Joan O'Meara Winant, *Fresh Women: Reflections on Coeducation and Life after Yale* (United States: Pamela Geismar, 2010), p. 25.

19. Trillin, *op. cit.*, p. 93.

20. Berzelius's official history (Trotman, *op. cit.*, pp. 48, 77) twice mentions the date of election of its first coed delegation, but gives no further detail. Elihu's brief history *Suitable Quarters, op. cit.*, notes that society was the first to elect women in 1970, but gives no detail of date or deliberations.

21. Quoted in Robbins, *op. cit.*, p. 71. See, by way of example, Pablo Cruise's column "Tap, tap, the beat goes on" in *Yale Daily News*, April 18, 1979.

22. "Secret societies: tricks or treats?," *Yale Daily News*, April 22, 1980.

23. Barnes, Patricia, "Mystery of Yale Secret Societies Draws Students," *New Haven Register*, April 19, 1985.

24. Aaron, David, "If the Summit Were Bugged," *New York Times*, December 9, 1989.

25. Orrick, Phyllis, "Women Enrich Tombs," *Yale Daily News*, April 23, 1971.

26. Alexander, Lawrence, "Unspooking Tombs," *Yale Daily News*, April 28, 1971.

27. Giamatti, *op. cit.*, pp. 42, 44.

28. *Yale Daily News*, April 19, 1972.

29. "locus classicus," Foer, *op. cit.*, about Frazier's "Yale Secret Societies," *op. cit.*; mutilated *Esquire* copies, Muezen, Paul, "Voices from the Tombs Speak," *Yale Daily News*, April 27, 1985.

30. Oder, Norman, "Senior Societies: Coeducation Brought Change; Importance Now Downplayed," *Yale Daily News*, April 14, 1982.

31. Kakutani, Michiko, "Things that Go Tap in the Night," *Yale Daily News Magazine*, April 17, 1974 (echoed in Lavery, Brian, "Behind the Walls of Yale's Secret Societies," *Yale Herald*, Summer 1997: "[S]ome senior society members question whether their constituency reflects a forced diversity that changes the character and intended nature of the secret society itself. 'All societies want to be diverse in terms of race, gender, and sexual orientation. There's a *de facto* quota system,' a former Book and Snake member said"; Freedman, Samuel, "'Tap Day' Fading Bit of Old Yale," *New York Times*, April 16, 1982.

32. Reidy, Chris, "Bastion of Bones," *Boston Globe*, March 4, 1991.

33. *Yale Daily News*, April 1, 1991.

34. Foer, *op. cit.*; Robbins, *op. cit.*, p. 149, writing in 2002: "Rather than reward merit, the societies now often lean toward rewarding ethnicity, which turns the groups into overtly poitically correct hyperventilators and the candidates into token quota taps."

35. "No Tomb. No Name. No Life." *Rumpus*, October 1998; Foer, *op. cit.* Unlisted in the 2015 *Yale Daily News* announcement of all the societies on election procedures, Hack and Tool seems to have perished.

36. Rosen, Jeff, "Welcome the, Uh, Bonesmen of Penzance," *Yale Daily News*, April 19, 1991.

37. Frazier, George, "Goodnight, Poor Yale,' *Boston Globe*, November 21, 1973.

38. According to the recollection of Sam Chauncey, recounted in *Yale Daily News*, April 14, 1982; "raze the building," Rosenbaum, *op. cit.*, p. 89.

39. Bennetts, Leslie, "Ivy League Women Face Social Barriers," *New York Times*, April 6, 1979.

40. *Yale Daily News*, April 7, 17, and 24, 1972; Holahan, *op. cit.*

41. Rosenthal, Larry, "Shh! Secretive Skull & Bones at Yale May Let Women in," *New Haven Register*, February 21, 1991.

42. Rosenthal, Larry, "Secret Club at Yale May Allow Women," *Philadelphia Inquirer*, February 22, 1991.

43. "Secret Yale Club Admits Women, Alumni Angry," *New York Times*, April 15, 1991; "Yale Club Accepts Women; Alumni Are Outraged," *New York Times*, April 19, 1991; "Yale Skull & Bones Society Elects Women amid Furor," *Wall Street Journal*, April 15, 1991; Coyle, Pamela, "Old-Timers Shut Down Skull & Bones," *New Haven Register*, April 15, 1991; Parry, Ellan, and Jodi Wilgoren, "Alumni Lock Tomb after Bones Taps Women," *Yale Daily News*, April 15, 1991; Specter, Michael, "Skull and Bones at Yale: First No Women, Now No Club," *Washington Post*, April 16, 1991; "Women in the Crypt? Old Bonesmen Say No," *New York Times*, April 18, 1991; Bernard, Anne, "Rattled Bones," *Boston Globe*, April 16, 1991; Von Drehle, Dave, "Yale's Skull and Bones Club Stirs a Tempest in a Tomb," *Miami Herald*, April 20, 1991.

44. *Ibid.*, all ten newspaper articles.

45. Specter, *op. cit.*

46. [Semple, Robert B., Jr.] *New York Times*, April 18, 1991; Quindlen, Anna, "Skullduggery," *New York Times*, April 18, 1991.

47. Wallace, *op. cit.*, p. 25; *Yale Daily News*, April 10 and 25, 1991. It has been reported that Manuscript's price for the loan of their hall was the right to hold a yearly party in the Bones tomb once it reopened, and Bones reneged. *Rumpus*, April 2001.

48. *Boston Globe*, April 16, 1991.

49. *New York Times*, April 18, 1991.

50. English, Bella, "'Skull' Club Has Rocks in Its Head," *Boston Globe*, April 22, 1991; on Mack's speech, Guernsey and Zdanys, *op. cit.*, pp. 93–96. The Bones board members were not wrong about the inherent awkwardness of a mixed group delivering "emotional" (i.e., sexual) histories: Kakutani, *op. cit.*, quoting a member of Book & Snake, which had admitted six women for that year: "It's really quite a feat if you can get all the women to talk about their sexual experiences. It's a taboo subject at Yale."

51. *New York Times*, April 25, 1991. Mrs. Bingham was the widow of Congressman Jonathan Brewster Bingham, class of 1936, and the mother of Timothy Bingham, class of 1967.

52. Barnes, Patricia G., "Mystery of Yale Secret Societies Draws Students," *New Haven Register*, April 19, 1985.

53. Freedman, Samuel, "Tap Day: Fading Bit of Old Yale," *New York Times*, April 18, 1982.

54. "Secret Society Moves to Admit Women," *Washington Post*, June 11, 1991; "Skull & Bones Votes to Admit Women," *Washington Post*, September 25, 1991; "Skull & Bones Votes to Admit Women," *Yale Daily News*, September 4, 1991; "Skull and Spare Ribs," *Economist*, November 2, 1991.

55. *Yale Daily News*, September 6 and 9, 1991; Thomas, Dana, *New York Times*, September 6, 1991; "Yale Society Wins Delay on Women," *Washington Post*, September 7, 1991. The Buckley lawsuit plaintiffs included Fetner and members of the classes of 1938, 1939, 1940, 1941, and 1959, including three past presidents of RTA. Precisely the same fear of sexual mischief was raised by the president of Porcellian Club's alumni group when Harvard University announced that from 2017, members of single-sex clubs would be barred from holding leadership positions

on campus: "Forcing single-gender organizations to accept members of the opposite sex could potentially increase, not decrease, the potential for sexual misconduct." Saul, Stephanie, "Rules May Force Elite Harvard Clubs to Abandon Longtime All-Male Status," *New York Times*, May 7, 2016.

56. Hevesi, Dennis, "Shh! Yale's Skull and Bones Admits Women," *New York Times*, October 26, 1991.

57. "Yale's Wolf's Head Admits Women, " *Deseret News*, December 19, 1991.

EPILOGUE

1. Quoted in Pierson, *Yale College, op. cit.*, pp. 366–367.

2. *Yale Daily News*, October 16, 2015.

3. Cole, David, "The Trouble at Yale," *New York Review of Books*, January 14, 2016; Yale Factsheet (2014–2015), Facts and Statistics, February 4, 2015; Press Release, Office of Undergraduate Admissions, October 2015.

4. *Yale Daily News*, March 25, 2014.

5. "Seven New Senior Societies Established," *Yale Daily News*, October 8, 2015; Lasilla, Kathrin, "Reform of the Senior Societies," *Yale Alumni Magazine*, May/June 2015.

6. "less reverence," "Yale's Secret Social Fabric," *Yale Daily News*, December 5, 2008; opt-out, *Yale Daily News*, February 17 and March 3, 2015; "Society Opt-in Offered Again," *Yale Daily News*, February 29, 2016.

7. Dubois, *op. cit.*, pp. 165–166.

8. On *The Skulls*, see Noah, Timothy, "The Skulls Is No Brotherhood of the Bell," *Slate Archives*, March 28, 2000; *Daily Princetonian*, April 6, 2000. Other films of these years included, as well as *The Good Shepherd* (2006) discussed in Chapter 12, *Indiana Jones and the Kingdom of the Crystal Skull* (2008), which featured a shot of the Bones tomb being run toward by a motorcycle, and Elihu member and director Alan Hruska's 2009 film *Reunion*, which explored a mythical reunion of fellow society members some twenty-three years after graduation, loosely inspired by a gathering of Hruska's own 1955 Elihu delegation. The television series *Gossip Girl* featured a character, Chuck, who tries to infiltrate what he calls "the crème de la crème of senior societies," Skull and Bones.

9. Busmiller, Elizabeth, *New York Times*, February 2, 2004.

10. Noting that there are now over forty senior societies, Mark Branch ("Open Secrets," *Yale Alumni Magazine*, July/August 2014, p. 37) reports: "[T]he new societies are built on the same template as the old: 14 to 16 seniors, chosen with diversity of experience in mind, meet every Thursday and Saturday, deliver lengthy and intimate 'biographies' of themselves to their fellow members (these days, a biography might last up to five or six hours and include old home videos and PowerPoint presentations)." In Jeff Hobbs's 2014 biography *The Short and Tragic Life of Robert Peace, op. cit.*, Hobbes tells of the life history presentation in his and Peace's senior year in Elihu, where Peace told a four-hour version, including his father's conviction for murder, about which none of the club members had known.

11. Rony, Dorothy, "Why I Refused to Join a Senior Society," *Yale Daily News*, January 15, 1985. Not all *News* writers were so ignorant: J. Kirby Simon noted that same year that "In fact, the societies have historically made a far greater commitment to the recognition of merit than have corresponding institutions at other schools." "Joining a 'Society' Is a Personal Choice," *Yale Daily News*, April 19, 1985.

INDEX

INDEX

INDEX